The Making of the Mosaic

A History of Canadian Immigration Policy

SECOND EDITION

In this second edition of *The Making of the Mosaic*, Ninette Kelley and Michael Trebilcock have extensively revised and updated their examination of the ideas, interests, institutions, and rhetoric that have shaped Canada's immigration history. Beginning their study in the pre-Confederation period, the authors interpret major events in the evolution of Canadian immigration policy, including the massive deportations of immigrants during the First World War and Depression as well as the establishment of the Japanese-Canadian internment camps during the Second World War. Additional chapters provide perspective on immigration in a post-9/11 world, where security concerns and a demand for temporary foreign workers play a significant role in immigration policy reform.

Widely recognized as one of the most comprehensive and authoritative works on the subject, *The Making of the Mosaic* clarifies the attitudes underlying each phase and juncture of immigration history, and in this new edition provides vital perspective on the central issues of immigration policy that continue to confront us today.

NINETTE KELLEY works for the United Nations High Commissioner for Refugees (UNHCR).

MICHAEL TREBILCOCK is a professor in the Faculty of Law at the University of Toronto.

D0143931

The Making
of the Mosaic

A History of
Canadian Immigration Policy

SECOND EDITION

Ninette Kelley and Michael Trebilcock

UNIVERSITY OF TORONTO PRESS
Toronto   Buffalo   London

© University of Toronto Press Incorporated 2010
 Toronto   Buffalo   London
 www.utppublishing.com
 Printed in Canada

ISBN 978-0-8020-9536-7

First edition 1998
Reprinted 2000

Printed on acid-free, 100% recycled paper with vegetable-based inks

---

Library and Archives Canada Cataloguing in Publication

Kelley, Ninette
The making of the mosaic: a history of Canadian immigration policy/Ninette
Kelley and Michael Trebilcock. – 2nd ed.

Includes bibliographical references and index.
ISBN 978-0-8020-9536-7

1. Canada – Emigration and immigration – Government policy – History.
I. Trebilcock, Michael J., 1941–   II. Title.

JV7233.K44 2010   325.71'09   C2010-901238-0

University of Toronto Press acknowledges the financial assistance to its publishing program of the Canada Council for the Arts and the Ontario Arts Council.

University of Toronto Press acknowledges the financial support for its publishing
activities of the Government of Canada through the Canada Book Fund.

Contents

Acknowledgments

With respect to the first edition, over the many years that we worked on this book, we were blessed with talented and committed research and editorial assistance from: Audrey Macklin, Katherine Welsh, Aaron Bloomenthal, Brinley Evans, Jonathan Daniels, Ari Slicker, Tim Brown, Kathy Kehoe, Susan Lewthwaite, and Jenna Wilson, to all of whom we are greatly indebted. We are also indebted to anonymous reviewers for the University of Toronto Press for helpful comments on earlier drafts; to Howard Adelman, Constance Backhouse, David Beatty, Barbara Jackman, Frank Marrocco, Craig Brown, Irene Dicaire, John Frecker, Tom Clark, and legal staff of the Immigration and Refugee Board for comments on portions of the manuscript; to Gerry Hallowell of the Press for sage advice; to Beverly Beetham Endersby, editor to the Press, for meticulous attention to the manuscript; to our secretaries, Margot Hall, Chris Black, and Lynn Lavallee, for their skilful and patient typing and retyping of, and endless corrections to, the manuscript; and to our spouses and families for accepting impositions and offering tolerance and support well beyond the bounds of reason or affection.

With respect to the second edition, we are grateful for the committed research and editorial assistance from Adam Beatty; we are also indebted to those who provided helpful comments on drafts: Krista Daley, Erin Kelley, Richard Kurland, Nancy Goodman, Gladys MacPherson and Peter Showler; and to our secretary, Wynanda Hofstee for her skilful and patient coordination of corrections and edits. We are solely responsible for all remaining errors and omissions.

The views expressed in this book are our own and do not necessarily reflect the views of the institutions with which we have been associated.

The Making of the Mosaic

A History of Canadian Immigration Policy

Introduction: Ideas, Interests, Institutions, and Issues Shaping Canadian Immigration Policy

The Project

This book addresses a question that, throughout history, has confronted all individuals and groups who have chosen to live in a state of civil society with one another, and who view social, political, and economic relationships as integral to their self-definition. How does one define and justify the conditions for community membership? In the context of the modern nation state, this question directs our attention primarily to our immigration policies – that is, who may become citizens and who must remain strangers – for nations imply boundaries, and at some point boundaries imply closure. Contemporary public debates, in Canada, the United States, Western Europe, and elsewhere, focusing on the central features of domestic immigration policies, reflect the deep conflicts that immigration issues have always provoked.

While our examination of this issue focuses on Canada, it is nevertheless set against a backdrop of global migration trends. There are currently 192 million people, including 16 million refugees, living outside their place of birth,[1] more than twice as many as were estimated in 1975. Today, approximately one out of every thirty-five persons in the world is a migrant.[2] While this global number has increased substantially over time, the rate of increase has remained remarkably consistent. For example, between 1965 and 1990 the annual growth rate in migration was was approximately 2.1 per cent as compared to its present rate of 2.9 per cent.

The distribution of migrants, however, has shifted dramatically. In 2000, migrants made up 10 per cent of the population of seventy countries as compared to just forty-eight countries thirty years earlier. Moreover, from

1980 to 2000, the number of migrants living in the developed world more than doubled, from 48 million to 110 million, as compared to a more modest increase from 52 million to 65 million in the developing world. Currently some 60 per cent of the world's migrants live in the developed world and account for more than two-thirds of the population growth in some regions. For example, from 1980–2000 immigration accounted for 89 per cent of population growth in Europe and approximately 75 per cent of population growth in North America.[3]

It is trite to observe that Canada is a country of immigrants, as is indeed the case for most of the countries of the so-called New World. However, this does not imply and has never implied that entry into our community is open to all. Indeed, central features of the social, political, and economic history of Canada have informed debates about what the terms of our immigration policy should be. It is equally trite to predict that immigration issues will be at the heart of future debates about what it means to be a Canadian and to be a member of the Canadian community.

In spite of the often central place of immigration in domestic law and policy, only in relatively recent years have philosophers, economists, sociologists, political scientists, lawyers, and other scholars begun to give serious attention to developing theoretical paradigms for analysing immigration policy and to testing the implications of those paradigms in rigorous empirical ways. However, this book is neither systematically theoretical nor systematically empirical. Its perspective is essentially historical. Moreover, its main focus is the history of immigration policy, not the social or cultural histories of various immigrant groups who have settled in Canada.[4] Although the focus is primarily the history of post-Confederation Canadian immigration policy, it is impossible to understand the evolution of that policy from 1867 onwards without some perspective on the inheritances from prior periods: hence this study begins with a brief chapter on the pre-Confederation history of Canadian immigration policy.

The approach taken in this book is to describe and interpret the major epochs or episodes in the evolution of Canadian immigration policy with a view to uncovering the ideas or values, the interests, and the issues that engaged public debates, as well as examining the institutions through which these ideas, interests, and issues were mediated in each of these periods.

In this book, the story of Canadian immigration policy is told from the perspective of the major participants involved in the different stages in the policy's evolution. We have tried to avoid the temptation to be judgmental about their moral characteristics from the comfortable vantage point or supposedly enhanced sensibilities of the contemporary social and intellectual milieu. However, a reflective re-examination of our collective past reveals a set of core normative and ethical values that have been fundamental in the making of the Canadian mosaic and, when rendered explicit, provide perspective on the central issues of immigration policy that confront us today and will do so in the future.

Because this project is primarily historical, it does not attempt to deduce a set of ideal immigration policies from *a priori* analysis of first principles (philosophic, sociological, or economic). However, in the next two sections of this chapter we present a brief review of the central and enduring ideas and interests at stake and their relationship to the institutions involved in immigration policy generally as a basis for examining the critical and changing contours of Canadian immigration policy summarized in the third section of this chapter. The latter provides the reader with a general road map of the historical journey pursued in detail in later chapters, briefly tracing how ideas, interests, and institutions interacted in relation to specific issues in the evolution of Canadian immigration policy.

The Ideas[5]

In an oft-cited observation, John Maynard Keynes once remarked that, 'soon or late, it is ideas, not vested interests, which are dangerous for good or evil.'[6]

At the heart of debates over immigration policy, in all Western democracies, including Canada, now and in the past, lie two core ideas or values (we use these terms interchangeably) that stand, to some irreducible degree, in opposition to each other: liberty and community. Theories of liberty and community present themselves with almost endless variations, but, for the purposes of this book, the essence of the two ideas, in the context of immigration policy, can be fairly readily captured.

All theories of liberty, as Joseph Carens points out, 'begin with some kind of assumption about the equal moral worth of individuals. In one way or another, all treat the individual as prior to the community. Such foundations provide little basis for drawing fundamental distinctions between citizens and aliens who seek to become citizens.'[7] Carens goes on to review three contemporary approaches to liberal theory: libertarianism, social contractarianism, and utilitarianism.

From a libertarian perspective, propounded by scholars such as Robert Nozick,[8] individual property rights play a central role. In a state of nature, individuals have rights to acquire and use property and to alienate it voluntarily. The existence of the state is justified only to the extent that it is required to protect property rights and facilitate their voluntary transfer. In this view, if citizens choose to enter into contracts of employment with aliens, or to sell them land, homes, or businesses, and if aliens wish to move to Canada, they should be free to do so, provided that, in doing so, they do not violate the rights of anyone by imposing involuntary burdens on others. The rights of both citizens and aliens would be violated were externally imposed constraints applied to such transactions.

From a social contractarian perspective, as exemplified prominently in the writings of John Rawls,[9] an ideal social constitution would be constructed behind a veil of ignorance, where individuals know nothing about their own personal situations, such as class, race, sex, natural talents, religious beliefs, or individual goals, values, and talents. The purpose of the veil of ignorance is to nullify the effect of specific circumstances which put individuals at odds, because natural and social contingencies are arbitrary from a moral point of view and therefore are factors which ought not to influence the choice of principles of justice. Rawls argues that people in this original position would choose two principles. The first principle would guarantee equal liberty to all. The second would permit social and economic inequalities only so long as they were to the advantage of the least well-off (the 'difference' principle) and attached to positions open to all under fair conditions of equal opportunity. People in this original position would give priority to the first principle, forbidding a reduction of basic liberties for the sake of economic gains.

Applied to immigration, as Carens points out, specific contingencies that may set people at odds are whether one is a citizen of a rich nation or of a poor nation, and whether one is already a citizen of a particular state or one is an alien who wishes to become a citizen. A fair procedure for choosing principles of justice, applying the social contractarian view, therefore excludes knowledge of these circumstances. Rather than a national view of the original position, a global view should be taken ('the universal brotherhood of man'). Behind this global veil of ignorance, and considering possible restrictions on freedom, the perspective of those who would be most disadvantaged by the restrictions – in this case, the perspective of the alien who wants to emigrate – should be adopted. Very few restrictions on immigration can be morally justified, save those which, according to the Rawlsian view, are required for the sake of the liberty of all, such as maintaining public order and security. To cite a metaphor used by Carens, it does no one any good to take so many people into a lifeboat that it is swamped and everyone drowns.[10] But short of a reasonable, as opposed to a hypothetical, expectation of this prospect, largely unconstrained immigration would seem to be implied by Rawls's social contract theory.[11]

From a utilitarian perspective, the utilities or disutilities experienced by both citizens and aliens would be entered in the utilitarian calculus. Some citizens would gain from being able to enter into employment or other contractual relationships with prospective immigrants. Others, such as consumers, might benefit from access to cheaper goods, services, or labour. Scale effects in the private and public sectors that derive from a larger population base might benefit citizens generally. Moreover, dependency effects might benefit local taxpayers if immigrants were over-represented in the wage-earning age category relative to existing citizens, contributing more in taxes than the costs entailed in providing them with social services. In contrast, some citizens could lose if they were displaced from their jobs or if their wages were depressed through the additional competition that immigrants may bring to labour markets. Other costs might include higher housing prices, congestion externalities of various kinds, and a negative dependency effect in the case of young, old, infirm, or unemployed immigrants who take more in social benefits than they contribute in taxes.

These costs and benefits accruing to citizens would have to be measured against the costs and benefits accruing to immigrants by being permitted entry. In most cases, one assumes that for them the benefits substantially outweigh the costs, otherwise immigrants would presumably not have chosen to resettle in another land. Moreover, to the extent that many immigrants will have made the wrenching decision to resettle because of economic privation or religious, ethnic, or political oppression or persecution in their homelands, the gains to them from being permitted to join a new and more congenial community could be very substantial. Thus, from a utilitarian perspective, which perhaps may provide more scope for restrictions on immigration than either the libertarian or the social contractarian perspective, relatively open borders would, in general, still be dictated.

In opposition to these liberal values stand the core values of community. Here, it is asserted, in the context of immigration policy, that controlling which strangers may enter is a powerful expression of a nation's identity and autonomy. Sovereignty entails the unlimited power of a nation, like that of a free individual, to decide whether, under what conditions, and with what effect it will consent to enter into a relationship with a stranger.[12]

A prominent articulator of this view is Michael Walzer.[13] In justifying this view, he draws analogies among neighbourhoods, clubs, and families.

While it is true that, in the case of neighbourhoods, people are free, in general, to enter and exit as they please, he argues that, in so far as nations may be analogized to neighbourhoods, permitting unconstrained entry by aliens in any numbers from anywhere in the world would destroy the concept of neighbourhood. He argues that it is only the nationalization of welfare (or the nationalization of culture and politics) that opens the neighbourhood communities to whomever chooses to come in. Neighbourhoods can be open only if countries are, at least potentially, closed. Only if the state makes a selection among would-be members, and guarantees the loyalty, security, and welfare of the individuals it selects, can local communities take shape as 'different' associations determined solely by personal preference and market capacity.

Walzer claims that if states ever became large neighbourhoods, it is likely that neighbourhoods would become little states. Their members would organize to defend the local politics and culture against strangers. Historically, it is claimed, neighbourhoods have turned into closed or parochial communities whenever the state has been open. Thus, Walzer rejects the analogy of states as neighbourhoods and instead analogizes states to clubs and families, where members are free to determine the conditions of membership. Walzer concludes that:

> The distribution of membership is not pervasively subject to the constraints of justice. Across a considerable range of the decisions that are made, states are simply free to take in strangers (or not) – much as they are free, leaving aside the claims of the needy, to share their wealth with foreign friends, to honor the achievements of foreign artists, scholars, and scientists, to choose their trading partners, and to enter into collective security arrangements with foreign states. But the right to choose an admissions policy is more basic than any of these, for it is not merely a matter of acting in the world, exercising sovereignty, and pursuing national interests. At stake here is the shape of the community that acts in the world, exercises sovereignty, and so on. Admission and exclusion are at the core of communal independence. They suggest the deepest meaning of self-determination. Without them, there could not be *communities of character,* historically stable, ongoing associations of men and women with some special commitment to one another and some special sense of their common life.[14]

Unlike liberal theories, which imply no or few limitations on entry, Walzer's theory, at least without further qualification, appears to permit almost any limitations on entry that a state should choose to impose. Two controversial features of his theory are the notion that political sovereignty is a near-absolute value – a view increasingly challenged by the evolution of international human rights norms – and the notion that the only communities of character are those that reflect ethnic, religious, cultural, or ideological commonalities[15] – a view that many liberals would challenge on the grounds that common commitments to liberal civic institutions and mutual tolerance of intermediate subcommunities of interest can sustain communities of character. In any event, these two core ideas, liberty and community, clearly frame the major issues that must be confronted in the design of any country's immigration policies.

The Interests

An austere Public Choice perspective on the policy-making process asserts that, just as the functioning of private markets is widely assumed to be dominated by material self-interest, so should the political process be conceived of as an implicit 'market' where the relevant actors – voters and special interest groups (demanders), politicians, bureaucrats, regulators (suppliers), and the media (intermediaries) – tend to be motivated by material self-interest. For their part, politicians will adopt a policy not because it is thought likely to promote the broader public interest or some objective social-welfare function but because it will maximize political support.[16]

In any political community, the ideas of liberty and community are typically articulated by interest groups in the political process. Some interest groups will have a reasonably well-defined material self-interest in relation to the issues in question. Other interest groups will include community, church, and public interest groups with no direct self-interest in relation to the issue but a commitment in principle to particular ideas or values.

In decisions concerning the conditions of entry for immigrants, the rhetoric of public debate may often disguise the true interests and ideas at play. For example, it will often be strategic for an interest group to disguise its self-interest under the rubric of a broader normative idea in order to engage the support of other members of the political community who may share the idea but not the interest. Similarly, those who espouse particular ideas that are unappealing to other members of the community may disguise those ideas (e.g., racist values) under the rubric of other values (e.g., cultural homogeneity) that are more appealing to a broader segment of the community. Thus, an understanding of the real ideas and interests at play in each epoch requires a careful interpretation of the rhetoric of public discourse. The material interests likely to be most directly engaged by immigration policy include the following groups.

Business groups, in general, are likely to favour a permissive immigration policy, in part as a way of relieving shortages or bottlenecks in the supply of skilled or unskilled labour, and in part because an increase in the supply of either kind of labour is likely to have the tendency to depress local wage levels. In addition, a growing population base is likely to increase aggregate demand for goods and services, and thus enhance the prosperity of the business sector. On the other hand, to the extent that some immigrants, particularly of the entrepreneurial or professional classes, may become a potential source of competition to local businesses or professionals, there may be less enthusiasm in some business quarters for an open immigration policy.

Labour groups are likely to favour an immigration policy biased towards family reunification, and perhaps admission of entrepreneurs with capital, and against the admission of skilled and unskilled labour in sectors where admitted workers are likely to be competing for jobs and wages with indigenous workers. Thus, the admission of workers would tend to be favoured only in instances where they are willing to perform jobs that the indigenous workforce is unable or unwilling to perform.

Ethnic groups comprising previous immigrants are likely to support an open immigration policy, especially one that stresses family reunification and that favours preferential access for individuals of similar ethnic, cultural, religious, or political backgrounds, especially during times when their countries of origin are experiencing political or economic stress. Previous decisions on admission policies may thus create a form of path dependency in terms of future policies.

While they are an amorphous class, taxpayers in general are likely to favour an immigration policy that imposes the fewest demands on the public purse. Such a policy is likely to entail a preference for immigrants who will be productive members of the community and contribute more, in the way of taxes, than the costs they impose on the community in terms of increased educational, health, unemployment, public housing, law enforcement, and social welfare expenditures. This preference would suggest a bias towards admitting skilled workers whose services are likely to be in high demand and entrepreneurs with capital, and less enthusiasm for admitting unskilled workers, relatives of other citizens (particularly very young, old, or infirm relatives), and many refugees.

While ideas and interests are clearly important determinants of public-policy outcomes, they must be mediated through institutions in order to be translated into public policy. Much contemporary literature, especially in the political sciences, emphasizes the importance of the choice and design of state institutions as an independent variable in determining policy outcomes (the so-called new institutionalism).[17]

In a Canadian context, Michael Atkinson[18] argues that the organization and character of political institutions play a critical role in determining policy outcomes in Canada. However, the study of political institutions cannot take place in isolation from the study of ideas and interests. Institutions do not suddenly appear fully formed: they have to be invented. Clearly the organization and character of institutions reflect both competing social forces that struggle to embed their interests in these institutions and ideas about appropriate arrangements for governance. However, once institutions are adopted, they tend to exert an independent influence on what interests and ideas in particular policy domains are given effect to or marginalized in subsequent public-policy decisions. According to Carolyn Hughes Tuohy,[19] for some 'new institutionalists,' state institutions assume a privileged role in the explanation of policy outputs. They represent a 'crystallization' of the effects of economic factors, ideas, and interests, and they constitute the primary vehicle through which these factors are brought to bear on policy; but they also generate ideas and interests through a process of institutional evolution over time.[20]

In the context of the evolution of immigration policy, this book attempts to be sensitive both to the interaction of ideas and interests that shaped the institutions of public policy making in this area, and also to how these institutions in turn shaped the ideas and interests that were articulated in the public policies governing immigration.

The Issues: A Historical Reprise

In the course of the journey chronicled in this book, our hope is to deduce from Canadian historical experience an understanding of the ideas, interests, and institutions that have been influential over time in shaping the evolution of Canadian immigration policy. In this context, how and why did our perceptions of ourselves as a community change over time, and what shifts in the configuration of ideas or interests best explain these changes? How has our contemporary communal self-definition been shaped by the lessons of history? As Canadians continue to grapple with immigration issues in the future, what do the lessons of history suggest that we might aspire to become? These are the questions addressed throughout this book. However, in order to provide the reader with a brief orientation to the evolution of Canadian immigration described in detail in succeeding chapters, we offer the following brief sketch of the central issues at stake in each of the major periods.

In the period prior to the British conquest of Quebec in 1760, both the French and the British colonies in North America were little more than trading posts that were treated as minor pawns by the Imperial powers engaged in larger and recurrent dynastic European conflicts. This situation changed dramatically with the arrival of the Loyalists in the last years of the eighteenth century, following the American War of Independence, and again in the middle years of the nineteenth century, with the huge 'pauper' immigration from Britain (especially Ireland). From about the middle of the seventeenth century through to the abrogation of the Imperial Preferences in the middle of the nineteenth century, mercantilist theories of economic development played a significant role in both British and French Imperial views as to the role of their colonies. For the Imperial powers, the colonies were valuable to the extent that they were sources of cheap and reliable staples, thus reducing the need of the Imperial powers to use specie in purchasing these products from their rivals. The colonies also provided a modest market for goods from the home country.

By the mid-nineteenth century, mercantilist theories were gradually discredited, and, with the advent of colonial self-government and British free-trade philosophy, this rationale for the colonial relationship disappeared. Furthermore, after the end of the Napoleonic Wars in 1815, increases in birth rates and the rate of family formation, together with the effect of the Industrial Revolution, led to a huge surplus of workers; as a result, Britain began to see the colonies as a major outlet for potentially politically disruptive and socially costly excess labour. The material interests of various British economic groups – rural landlords, trade unions, shipping companies – tended in the same direction, towards increased emigration. At the same time, colonial landowners and businesses saw profit arising from the influx of land-hungry immigrants and cheap, unskilled labour. Continuing apprehensions about American expansionist ambitions also influenced attitudes of the colonial elite with respect to levels and sources of immigration and patterns of settlement that they promoted, and indeed provided an important impetus for Confederation.

Following Confederation, immigration policy was regarded as one of the cornerstones upon which the new nation would develop. For Canada to survive as an independent, prosperous nation, economic growth was essential and, in turn, was dependent upon a larger population and an expanding market. Since immigrants were needed to promote economic expansion both by their labour and by their consumption, for the first three decades following Confederation there were few obstacles in the way of their admission to Canada. The relatively open posture towards immigrants throughout this period has led some to characterize the immigration policy of the day as being informed by liberal values. Yet this open posture is best seen as a central feature of the National Policy, as a way to ensure the consolidation of the Dominion through the settlement of the West and the development of an industrial base in central Canada, and as a policy that advanced the economic interests of those who stood to gain from such development. Railway promoters, land developers, mine operators, and manufacturers all benefited from an expanding population and an abundant labour supply. In fact, neither immigration policy nor other federal policies at the time were premised on economic or philosophical liberalism. While liberal values were often referred to as a rationale for the open immigration posture of the period, they were not pursued rigorously, as evidenced by the heavy state support for many of the major economic ventures of the day, most notably railway construction (through subsidies) and manufacturing (through protectionism). Liberal values were also largely absent in the treatment of immigrants and others similarly marginalized. Immigrants, while relatively free to enter Canada, were viewed as a cheap source of labour rendered cheaper by the utilization of contract labour schemes which left immigrant workers largely captive employees, many with severely limited rights of citizenship.

During the first thirty years following Confederation, the most prominent voices in debates over immigration were those of employers, trade unions, and nationalists (or nativists). Employers consistently called for an open policy and an aggressive promotional campaign, while trade unions demanded the reverse. Organized labour bitterly protested against assisted immigration, contract labour schemes, and the massive importation of Asian labourers, all of which were alleged to depress local wages, displace indigenous workers, and undermine strikes. Anglo-Canadian nationalists also supported union demands for immigration restrictions, but for different reasons. Their concern was principally with the development of a homogeneous society based on British values, traditions, and institutions. Anglo-Canadian nationalists pressed for an immigration policy that was selective and that promoted British immigrants over all others. Their demands were sharply at variance with those of French Canadians, who were concerned that the linguistic and cultural balance that existed at the time of Confederation not be upset. Amid these competing concerns and values, economic interests held paramountcy within the government, not only for the first thirty years after Confederation, but throughout most of the next half-century as well.

The massive population growth and economic prosperity that had eluded the nation in the first three decades following Confederation finally became a reality at the turn of the century. Between 1896 and 1914, more than 3 million people emigrated to Canada (many from central and southern Europe), and dramatic growth was experienced in agricultural, manufacturing, and service industries. Cities mushroomed across the country, and the population of the prairies increased by close to 1 million in the first decade of the century. Immigration was central to these transformations, and immigration policy became an intense source of controversy among an expanding array of groups and individuals. The traditional participants continued to be involved in this discourse, each expounding the positions that had been carved out over previous decades. Employers applauded the government for its aggressive promotion of immigration and resisted any attempts to restrict the importation of immigrant workers. Trade unions continued to demand the reverse, while nationalists argued for a more selective admissions policy. New participants also emerged in immigration debates. Law-enforcement officials blamed the increased crime statistics on the admission of those who did not share the values and traditions of their host society and who transplanted their violent ways to the Canadian community. Churches and social service providers, whose charitable efforts were stretched well beyond their capacity and who were daunted by the magnitude of the problems within the ever-expanding urban ethnic ghettos, called for an immigration policy that was cognizant of the ills and tensions that were endemic to the overcrowded, ethnically diverse city slums. Many physicians and sociologists, influenced by the emerging popularity of eugenics theory, cautioned against the admission of those whose inferiority would be genetically transmitted to future generations.

Amid this growing controversy surrounding immigration policy, both the Liberal and the Conservative governments of the day paid greater heed to economic interests than to non-material values. Economic progress was the overriding objective and, to the extent that an expansive immigration policy was needed to ensure a steady and malleable supply of workers, it would continue to be pursued. As a concession to those who argued for more restrictive policies, however, the government amended the Immigration Act in 1906 and 1910 to provide for greater selectivity in the admissions process in order to weed out undesirable immigrants. To enable the government to respond flexibly to economic conditions at any given time, Cabinet was given enhanced powers to exclude any class of immigrant where it deemed such exclusion to be in the best interests of the country. The implementation of Cabinet directives rested with the minister of the Interior, who administered policy with enormous discretion that was often delegated to departmental officials beyond the purview of judicial or parliamentary scrutiny. Most significantly, restrictive regulations on the admission of Chinese (head taxes), East Indians (continuous journey requirements), and Japanese (a voluntary emigration quota) drastically reduced the volume of Asian immigration, reflecting nativist sentiments.

Between 1915 and 1930, little changed in either the focus of immigration policy or the manner in which it was implemented. The First World War led to a dramatic decline in immigrant admissions, which were slow to rise in the years following the conflict because of the economic uncertainties prevalent in the immediate postwar years. With respect to the treatment of immigrants within Canada, the incarceration of close to 9,000 individuals of enemy-alien birth during the war illustrated how easily the rights of immigrants could be circumscribed, even in the absence of credible or compelling cause. The strengthened deportation provisions of 1919, which were used to remove from Canada labour and political activists, further underscored this point, as did the virtual exclusion of all Asian immigrants to Canada in the 1920s and the persistent discrimination that Asians endured within Canadian society as a whole.

The exclusion of Asian immigrants did not signify a decline in the influence of economic interests, who had traditionally argued against any such controls. By the time the Asian exclusionary laws and regulations were adopted, there was no longer a pressing demand for their labour. The Empire Settlement Agreement, the Railroad Agreement, and the permit system ensured that the labour requirements of the country's leading economic concerns would be met with British and European workers. And, while communitarian ideas were influential in the exclusion of Asian immigrants, they were unsuccessful in their demands for greater selectivity in the admission of European workers. The doors to Canada were not narrowed until 1929, with the onset of the Great Depression.

The 1930s mark a period in Canadian history when economic interests and other values largely converged. Throughout this period there was general support for the government's restrictive immigration policies. The country was so ravaged by the economic depression that few questioned the wisdom of tight immigration controls. One area which did attract controversy, however, was deportation policy, and here the debate did not necessarily proceed along traditional lines. The massive deportation of indigent immigrants with fewer than five years' residence was a subject of intense concern primarily within municipalities, which were responsible for public relief. Some municipal officials saw deportation as an effective way of reducing demands on their overtaxed welfare budgets. Other officials regarded this as a cruel and inhumane policy and refused to use the deportation provisions of the Immigration Act in such a manner. Co-operative Commonwealth Federation (CCF) members of Parliament also protested against the deportation of thousands of immigrants whose only failing was being unemployed in a jobless environment. Perhaps because deportations were carried out expeditiously and generally at some remove from the public eye, the large numbers of deportees did not cause concern among the public at large. It is also probably true that most people were simply too preoccupied with their own troubles to worry about foreigners whose continued presence meant more demands on shrinking public funds.

While the deportation of the indigent was not the subject of significant public controversy, the removal of labour activists was a notably contentious issue. In this case the government pursued a course of action encouraged by employer interests who wanted to see the country rid of foreign radicals and labour activists. Fear of communism was initially used as a rallying cry to win public support for a policy that would not tolerate foreign influences disrupting worksites with union drives and calls for worker solidarity. Many political leaders, judges, law enforcement officers, and members of the country's established press supported Prime Minister Bennett's resolve to root out communism with the 'iron heel of ruthlessness.' Yet the government's strong-arm tactics eventually backfired, not only censured by left-of-centre politicians and associations but also criticized by leading intellectuals and the mainstream liberal press. The decade closed with a new Liberal government under Mackenzie King easing up on political deportations, contrary to the interests of many employers, but in line with the sentiment of many Liberal party supporters.

The Second World War years demonstrated the injustice that the immigration policy of the day could produce. The forced relocation of close to the entire Canadian population of Japanese descent, the confiscation of their property, and the attempt to deport most to Japan following the war left one of the bitterest legacies of this period. The exclusion of Jewish refugees in the face of mass extermination abroad was another. The fact that both policies were widely supported reflected less the influence of one group of interests over another than general ideological, cultural, and racial values held by the Canadian population at large. These values were, to some extent, reinforced by economic concerns over the competitive impact of the Japanese in various industries, the opportunity to acquire confiscated assets from the Japanese at depressed prices, and the potential competition that Jewish immigrants might pose in various industries; but these concerns were secondary to racially and culturally motivated values.

After the war, growing public recognition that a large part of the rationale for the war had been to contest the grotesque implications of claims of racial superiority made by the Nazi regime led to a progressive re-evaluation of discriminatory Canadian immigration policies, first in the context of a willingness to accept a significant number of displaced persons in refugee camps and elsewhere in Western Europe, many of whom were Jewish. Community, church, and ethnic organizations were influential in promoting more humane refugee policies. However, Canada was slower to respond to this challenge than were many other countries, and racist and ideological values continued to influence Canadian immigration policy in the immediate postwar period. This area of influence was reflected in the clear order of preference for admitting immigrants from various source countries (with a high priority assigned to immigrants of British origins, and very restrictive policies applied to Asians, Africans, and West Indians), in a greater willingness to accept refugees from oppressive left-wing rather than right-wing regimes, and in the application of national security considerations in the admission of refugees and other immigrants where real or perceived Communist sympathies often operated as a disqualification. However, the long-standing conflict between employer and labour interests sharply narrowed during this period, with growing acceptance of the fact that, at least in the booming postwar economy, immigrants tended to contribute to, rather than hamper, further economic growth and job creation. Nevertheless, conflict between employers and organized labour interests continued over issues such as contract labour and assisted-passage schemes for skilled and unskilled workers, which organized-labour interests viewed as detrimental to local working conditions. By and large, again, the opinion of employer interests tended to have more influence with government on these issues.

Through the 1960s and 1970s, the values supporting the case for a racially non-discriminatory immigration policy tended to become more firmly entrenched and widely held, as did those favouring a relatively generous family reunification policy. Beginning in the early 1960s, independent immigrants had generally been selected overseas on economic criteria designed to screen them on the basis of their capacity for self-sustainability, economic contributions, and compatibility with domestic labour market needs, rather than country of origin. The tentative economic consensus among conflicting interests as to the case for a relatively open immigration policy also tended to become more robust during this period. There was also a growing consensus that immigrants were entitled to some due-process protections, in the sense that conditions governing their entry and expulsion should be explicitly articulated and transparent, and that deportation decisions by immigration officials should be subject to challenge before a neutral tribunal. Public debates provoked by the issuance of government White and Green Papers on immigration policy tended to shift the focus of policy making from the executive to the legislative forum, culminating in the passage of a new Immigration Act in 1976, with wide political and public support. A significant new set of political influences continued to emerge, with ethnic, religious, and community organizations playing a major and apparently influential role in political and public debates over future immigration policy, and generally supporting more liberal immigration policies. In this period, salient values and material interests were not viewed, at least by politically active interests, as presenting sharp conflicts. Another set of influences, to which it is difficult to ascribe precise weight but which were nevertheless clearly of increasing significance, comprised external considerations: Canada, much influenced by its minister of External Affairs, and later prime minister, Lester Pearson, had staked out for itself a prominent, middle-power, honest-broker role both in the increasingly multi-racial British Commonwealth and in larger international fora, such as the United Nations, with a growing developing-country membership and increasing endorsement of international human rights regimes that the United Nations promoted. The credibility of this role would clearly have been seriously compromised by the maintenance of explicitly discriminatory immigration policies. By the early 1970s, Canadian immigration policy had become markedly more liberal – politically, economically, and legally – than in any previous period of its history.

In the late 1970s and throughout the 1980s, the apparent consensus over both values and economic interests that had emerged in the 1960s and early 1970s was severely tested by the government's responses to what was perceived as a major refugee crisis. Since the end of the Second World War, most refugees had been selected overseas and sponsored by

Canadian relatives or church and community organizations, or by the federal government on the basis of economic criteria. Beginning in the late 1970s, the dramatic increase in refugees claiming sanctuary at the Canadian border and from within Canada, mostly from non-traditional source countries, was widely perceived simultaneously as threatening to overwhelm the administrative machinery for making admissibility determinations and as threatening Canada's control of its borders and its ability to select independent immigrants on the basis of potential economic contributions.

While the government ultimately prevailed in enacting new legislation to control the refugee influx, the intense political and public debates provoked by its responses – particularly among the non-governmental organization (NGO) community, comprising principally ethnic, religious, and community organizations who mostly viewed the government's initiatives as repressive and inhumane – now further underscored the political saliency of this constituency. Another striking feature of immigration policy in this period was the continuing economic consensus favouring a relatively open door policy, supported by both major employer and organized-labour interests and most federal political parties, despite severe recessions in the early 1980s and early 1990s.

During the most recent period in Canadian immigration policy (1995–2008), annual immigration levels remained relatively robust, with 240,000 persons on average immigrating to Canada each year – one of the highest immigration rates in the industrialized world. These years, however, saw a somewhat surprising reversal of the moves towards greater transparency and accountability that had characterized immigration policy since the introduction of the 1976 Immigration Act. Beginning in the late 1990s the ability of the immigration system to attract those whom the country most required from an economic perspective, and to protect those who were legitimately in need of international protection, was increasingly questioned. A number of factors contributed to the growing doubt.

Among them were studies which pointed to the fact that immigrants were faring less well economically than they had in previous periods and that they were experiencing integration difficulties stemming in part from language barriers as well as the non-recognition of their foreign credentials. In addition, immigration processing times were expanding, leading business interests to argue that the system simply was not able to respond to labour-market needs in an efficient and effective manner. These claims were supported by reports from the auditor general pointing to growing backlogs, overworked immigration officers, vague assessment criteria, and inconsistent decision making, all of which limited the country's ability to maximize the economic and social benefits of immigration. The refugee system, too, was subject to growing criticism, which became especially vocal in 1999 with the arrival off the west coast of Canada of four un-authorized boats carrying hundreds of Chinese migrants, many of whom subsequently made asylum requests. Claims from some quarters in the United States and Canada that the country's immigration laws and bor-ders were far too porous to safeguard security resonated most forcefully following the terrorist attacks on the World Trade Center and the Pentagon in 2001. Although none of the attackers were foreigners who had passed through Canada, the fear unleashed by those attacks provoked a much harder look at Canadian immigration policy and a greater willingness on the part of the authorities, the public, and the courts to relax safeguards of individual liberty in favour of enhanced security.

The Immigration and Refugee Protection Act in 2002 was informed by security concerns, although not entirely shaped by them, since the legisla-tion was drafted long before the 9/11 attacks. Compared to the legislation it replaced, the new act was striking in its lack of detail, with large areas of immigration policy left to executive discretion by way of regulation. In this key respect, it resembled much earlier acts that characterized the first half of the twentieth century. Unlike those acts, however, the 2002 legislation did not exclude on the basis of race and did reiterate the broad purposes to which the act was dedicated, including social, demographic, and eco-nomic objectives, the facilitation of family reunification, and the protec-tion of refugees.

The regulations passed under this new act further refined the selection of economic immigrants, with greater emphasis placed on education and skills and considerable discretion left to immigration officers to deter-mine the potential of an applicant to adapt in Canada. They also consider-ably expanded the scope for admitting temporary workers, a change much applauded by business interests while of concern to labour unions and rights advocates, who were critical of the lack of protections afforded such workers and the risk of their being abused. In regard to family reunifica-tion, the act and regulations broadened the concept of family in sig-nificant ways while tightening requirements for and, in effect, restricting those who were eligible to sponsor. The refugee determination system was changed to restrict access, so that a wider range of individuals were not eligible to seek Canada's protection. Deportation provisions were broadened, as was the authority of the executive to deny admission to certain persons or order their removal on security grounds. The limited due-process guarantees afforded to challenges of these decisions in court were the subject of considerable litigation throughout the period.

The period ended as it began: in controversy. This time the focus of attention was on the use of executive discretion, occasioned by the announcement of the minister of Citizenship and Immigration that in future the minister would issue guidelines to immigration officers as to the type of immigration applications to be given priority in processing. Business and commercial interests applauded the announcement, on the understanding that priority would be given to economic immigrants, including foreign workers, in demand within their industries. Other groups were sharply critical, fearing that the new guidelines would inject a greater degree of arbitrariness into the immigration system, further expanding non-transparent executive decision making and unfairly placing family members and persons seeking to immigrate on humanitarian and compassionate grounds at the end of the queue.

It would not be appropriate to close this brief reprise of the history of Canadian immigration policy without noting continuing and tragic legacies of early settlement in Canada. First, the settlement process devastated Canada's First Nations, whose traditional ways of life were radically and irreversibly disrupted by violence, European diseases, and alcohol, and by the avarice and insensitivity of land developers, both public and private, who, through one stratagem or another, expropriated most of their lands and largely remitted the Native people to an impoverished way of life, often on remote reserves. Finding ways to redress or mitigate the gross injustices perpetrated on these people by subsequent settlers remains a challenge that Canada continues to grapple with today. Second, the legacy of bitterness initiated by the British conquest of Quebec in 1760 has entailed for many French Canadians the perception that immigration has often been an Anglophone plot to overwhelm their distinctive language and culture with numbers. Thus, while immigration policy towards strangers at our gates has been dramatically transformed, the core of Canada's problem in reaching some understanding of itself as a community relates much more to relations among strangers *within* our gates: the three founding 'races,' or three solitudes – where the sources of Canada's future challenges lie deeply embedded in the history of immigration policy recounted in this book. In this crucial respect, we remain prisoners of our past.

CHAPTER TWO

From Wilderness to Nationhood, 1497–1867: 'The Land God Gave to Cain'[1]

In this chapter, the populating of Canada is traced from the time of first European contact (1497) to Confederation (1867) – a period of almost 400 years. For our purposes this period can appropriately be divided into three subperiods. The first subperiod, extending from the initial significant European contact to the conquest by Britain of New France (1497–1760), is dominated by European-based imperial and dynastic rivalries between Britain and France, punctuated by intermittent wars in which each country's colonial possessions in British North America were minor pawns in the larger European conflicts. The Conquest effectively marked the end of France's North American aspirations, although it left behind a sizeable French-speaking population in what was to become modern-day Quebec, and a much smaller one in Acadia (principally modern-day Nova Scotia and New Brunswick).

The second subperiod (1783–1812) is dominated by a large influx of Loyalist refugees and American land-seekers following the American War of Independence. This wave of immigrants, which ended with the War of 1812 between Canada and the United States, gave Canada its first major body of settlers of British descent, and directly led to the creation of two new colonies: New Brunswick and Upper Canada (present-day Ontario).

The third subperiod begins after the War of 1812 but, in terms of immigration patterns, really dates from the beginning of the 1830s and runs to about 1850. During this time Canada experienced a massive influx of immigrants from Britain, induced to leave primarily by generally depressed economic conditions and displacement from farming pursuits and skilled occupations as a result of new agricultural practices, famine, and technological change. Many of these immigrants – the overwhelming majority of them Irish – arrived in Canada destitute, and realistically aspired less to becoming landed settlers than to being artisans and labourers in the rapidly growing cities of central Canada.

According to the first census after Confederation, in 1871 (by which time British Columbia and Prince Edward Island had joined Confederation, Rupert's Land had been transferred by Britain to Canada, and the province of Manitoba had been created),[2] of the total population of Canada (including British Columbia) of about 3.6 million people, 32 per cent were of French extraction, 24 per cent Irish, 20 per cent English, 26 per cent Scottish, and a further 6 per cent German. The remaining 2 per cent of Canada's population included some 30,000 Dutch people, 21,500 blacks, and 23,000 Native people. These figures ought to be accepted with some caution. In particular, simply because the census takers did not make the time or the effort to travel to more distant native communities, the number of Native people may have been substantially larger than the official figure – probably closer to 100,000. As well, some ethnic groups such as the Chinese are not listed in the census, although there were Chinese immigrants in Canada before 1867.

In spite of the mass immigration in the decades before Confederation, in one sense Canada could not accurately be portrayed at Confederation as a nation of immigrants. In 1867, 79 per cent of the population had been born in Canada. Moreover, the proportion of immigrants varied greatly from province to province. For example, more than one in three residents of what is now Ontario were immigrants, compared with one in twelve in what is now Quebec.

Over the almost 400 years prior to Confederation, substantial influxes of immigrants occurred in only two quite limited periods: from 1783 to 1812, with the arrival of the Loyalist and American settlers; and from 1830 to 1850, with the predominantly Irish immigrant influx – in effect, fewer than 50 years out of almost 400. Immigrants to the British North American colonies, both in these two spans of time and over the period as a whole, were overwhelmingly of British origin. French immigration, even during the French regime in New France from 1608 to 1760, amounted to a mere handful of settlers (10,000), and thereafter was almost non-existent.

Certain values and interests, both in the home country and in the receiving colonies, increasingly shaped the patterns of, and policies towards, immigration. Until late in the eighteenth century, the colonies in Canada were of little more than minor strategic interest to British and French Imperial powers. Following the Conquest in 1760, British assimilationist plans to dilute the French presence in New France through British immigration were largely unsuccessful, at least until the coming of the

Loyalists. However, from about the middle of the seventeenth century through to the abrogation of the Imperial Preferences in the middle of the nineteenth century, mercantilist theories of economic development also played a significant role in shaping Imperial views as to the value of the colonies to both Britain and France. As suppliers of cheap and reliable staples, including fish, fur, wheat, and timber, the colonies offset in some measure the need of the Imperial powers to use specie in purchasing these commodities from actual or potential Imperial rivals. In return, the colonies provided a modest outlet for manufactured or processed goods from the home country. With the progressive discrediting of mercantilist theories over the latter part of the eighteenth century and the first part of the nineteenth century, culminating in Britain's repeal of Imperial Preferences in the 1840s, this rationale for the colonial relationship disappeared, and it was not fortuitous that the adoption of a philosophy of free trade by Britain in the 1840s was accompanied by the granting of a substantial measure of self-government to the colonies, followed shortly thereafter by Confederation.

Until the end of the Napoleonic Wars in 1815, the British government discouraged emigration, in part because of the country's military needs, and in part in order to avoid the loss of tenants for agricultural landlords, or workers for the burgeoning factory sector created by the Industrial Revolution. However, after the end of the Napoleonic Wars, a combination of factors produced a huge surplus of workers, including a dramatic increase in birth rates and the rate of family formation, changes in agricultural practices from tillage to pasturage, the effect of technological change on the demand for labour in the industrial sector, and the effect of the Poor Laws, so that the colonies now began to be seen as a major outlet for potentially politically disruptive and socially costly surplus labour. The growth in demand for both wheat and timber, commodities whose production was more labour-intensive relative to the fishing and fur trades, along with vast expanses of underdeveloped land, provided the colonies with the capacity to absorb productively much of this surplus labour.

These values, of course, were often conjoined with the material interests of various economic groups which stood to benefit from a substantial increase in immigration: landlords in Scotland and Ireland seeking to clear their estates of excess tenantry; parishes seeking to reduce the burden of the Poor Law Relief rates; trade unions seeking to reduce the pressure of surplus labour on wages; shipping companies and their assorted agents who stood to profit greatly from a new source of business; and, in the colonies, landowners, developers, jobbers, and speculators who stood to benefit from the influx of masses of land-hungry immigrants seeking a new source of economic independence, and, later in the period, farmers, and mining, manufacturing, railway, and other enterprises, seeking cheap sources of mostly unskilled labour. In addition, in the period from the American War of Independence to Confederation, ongoing apprehensions about expansionist threats from American interests (the 'Manifest Destiny') significantly influenced attitudes among the colonial elite towards desirable levels and sources of immigration, and settlement priorities.

Only in the last twenty years before Confederation, after the termination of the Imperial Preferences and the granting of self-government, did anything suggestive of the outlines of a coherent development strategy for the colonies emerge among the colonial leadership. This entailed developing internal and continental markets through appropriate transportation networks; pushing westward into the prairies and beyond in developing the next agricultural frontier; and, through a combination of policies such as tariffs, urban infrastructure development, and transportation links, promoting some significant measure of industrialization and a more diversified economy.

The Beginnings of European Settlement: From Contact to Conquest, 1497–1760

As Olive Patricia Dickason remarks,

> Canada, it used to be said by non-Indians with more or less conviction, is a country of much geography and little history. The ethnocentricity of that position at first puzzled, and even confused, Amerindians, but it has lately begun to anger them. How could such a thing be said, much less believed, when their people had been living here for thousands of years. As they see it, Canada has 55 founding nations rather than just the two that have been officially acknowledged ... History, for its part, has been described as a document-bound discipline. If something was not written, preferably in an official document, it was not historical. Thus were pre-literate societies excluded from history and labelled pre-historic, or perhaps proto-historic ... In other words, Canada's history began with the arrival of Europeans.[3]

The issue of who Canada's first immigrants were and when they arrived is unsettled. It is indisputable that the Aboriginal peoples were here thousands of years before any Europeans. Many Native tribes have elaborate traditions that start with the belief that humanity had its beginnings here in Canada.[4] Thus, many Native people would reject the notion that they should be characterized as immigrants. By contrast, archaeologists believe that North American Indians originated in Asia, probably Siberia, and came over the land bridge that connected Asia and North America during the Ice Age, thousands of years ago. Scientific opinion is divided as to when the migration occurred, with estimates ranging from 13,000 to 100,000 years ago. However, by about 11,000 years ago, Native people were inhabiting the length and breadth of the Americas, with the greatest concentration being along the Pacific coast of the two continents.[5] About 10,000 years ago, according to scientists, the Ice Age ended. The run-off from the melting glaciers caused the sea level to rise, which in turn caused the land bridge to Asia to be submerged. For almost 10,000 years, the Americas' population rose through natural increase only. At the time of the first European contact with North America, that of the Norse in A.D. 1000, the Native population of North America north of Mexico may have been as large as 10 million. About 500,000 Native people were living in the territory of present-day Canada, with the principal population concentrations being on the Northwest Coast and in what is today Southern Ontario.[6]

While Viking explorers from Iceland and Greenland made occasional contact with people on the East Coast of North America as early as A.D. 1000, the first Western European explorers stumbled onto North America at the end of the fifteenth century while searching for the Northwest Passage to the 'Indies,' as China and India were collectively known. They were primarily motivated by an economic factor: the enormous cost of transporting spices, necessary for the preservation of meat, overland from the Indies. After 1500, there was intense competition among the Spanish, Portuguese, Dutch, English, and French for control of the New World.[7] However, it was only the French and British who would compete for control of present-day Canada. The other European nations were more interested in land to the south.

On 24 June 1497, John Cabot, an Italian explorer operating under letters patent granted by Henry VII of Great Britain, became the first European to reach Canada, when he discovered the Grand Banks off Newfoundland and formally claimed the island for England. During the next century, Canada's first industry was founded as English, Spanish, Portuguese, and French fishermen regularly visited on a seasonal basis to compete to harvest the cod, known as the 'beef of the sea.' By the late 1570s, England, France, Spain, and Portugal were sending some 400 vessels and 12,000 men a year to the cod and whale fisheries.[8] British

sovereignty over Newfoundland was not clearly established until the beginning of the eighteenth century, and, during the seventeenth century,
small French and British settlements were established there.

Shortly after Cabot's 'discovery,' the French established a presence in
British North America. On 24 July 1534, the French explorer Jacques
Cartier, at the entrance to Gaspé Harbour on the Gulf of St Lawrence,
erected a large wooden cross and claimed the newly discovered territory
for the King of France, Francis I. On his second voyage the following year,
Cartier journeyed up the St Lawrence River, visited Quebec, and went on
to Montreal. Five years later, Cartier returned to New France as part of a
larger expedition and established a small settlement near Quebec City,
which did not survive the first disastrous winter. This unsuccessful initial
effort at colonization, the outbreak of war with Spain, and subsequent
internal conflict in France between Huguenot and Catholic deflected
French attention from further efforts at colonization in North America
for most of the sixteenth century, leaving New France largely to seasonal
fishermen and fur traders. The extent of the lack of interest in the
American discoveries is exemplified by the fact that none of seven reprint-
ings of a world-geography reference book in French between 1539 and
1558 mentioned the New World.[9] British interest was equally tenuous. It
took more than a century after Cabot discovered Newfoundland in 1497,
and nearly seventy-five years after Cartier sailed up the St Lawrence in
1535, for a permanent European presence to be established in Canada.[10]

THE DEVELOPMENT OF CANADA (QUEBEC)

At the close of the sixteenth century, France revived an interest in its
colonization efforts in North America. In 1603, Pierre de Monts, a
Calvinist supporter of Henry IV, was granted a fur-trading monopoly over
New France, then conceived of as comprising modern-day Quebec and
most of the Maritimes, although boundaries were not clearly established.
In return, he was obliged to settle sixty colonists there each year, and to
establish missions among the Native peoples.[11] He recruited Samuel de
Champlain to lead the first colonizing mission. Champlain journeyed up
the St Lawrence River in 1603 and returned the following year to winter
on an island on the present-day boundary between Maine and New
Brunswick, and again in 1605 and 1606 to winter at Port-Royal in the Bay
of Fundy. This location proved ineffective as an obstacle to interlopers
engaged in fur trading near the mouth of the St Lawrence,[12] and in 1608
the settlement was mostly relocated to Quebec City, where Champlain

built a 'habitation' which became the first permanent French settlement. However, with colonization efforts largely dependent on the seasonal fur-trading and fishing industries, a large-scale permanent settlement was not a priority of the French regime. During the winter of 1620–1, no more than sixty colonists lived at Quebec, and for the first fifty years of its existence it was little more than a trading post.

Having obtained the support of Cardinal Richelieu, the leading member of Louis XIII's Royal Council from 1625 to 1642, Champlain finally convinced the French government to embark upon a policy of more aggressive colonization, reflecting the increasing influence of mercantilist theories of economic development. To this end, Cardinal Richelieu in 1627 established the Compagnie de la Nouvelle France (Company of New France, or the Compagnie des Cent-Associes, Company of 100 Associates), which, in return for title to all the lands claimed by France in North America and a monopoly on all commercial activities except fishing, undertook to settle 4,000 French Catholics in the territory between 1627 and 1643. The company's initial venture, in 1628, was to send to Quebec four ships containing 400 people and the materials and commodities required to clear land and establish a permanent settlement. However, England and France were once more at war in Europe in 1627, and in July 1628 the company's ships were captured off Gaspé by an English-Scottish armed expedition led by the Kirke brothers, which in July 1629 forced Champlain's outpost near Quebec City to surrender.[13] The colony was restored to France in 1632 under the Treaty of Saint-Germain-en-Laye, and Champlain returned to Quebec in 1633 to begin reconstruction of the colony. Although the fur trade prospered, the permanent settlement remained tiny in scale. When Champlain died in 1635, there were only 150 settlers on the St Lawrence. In 1645, facing financial failure, the Company of 100 Associates, while retaining its land rights, handed over its fur-trading monopoly to the Communaute des Habitants, a group of Canadien merchants, which agreed to assume the obligation of settling the colony. However, their efforts proved little more successful.

With some modifications, the French seigneurial system of land tenure was instituted along the banks of the St Lawrence River. Under this system, the local seigneur, or lord, received large land grants from the company and was a vassal to the King, with authority to distribute land in smaller plots to settler-tenants in return for dues. Actual occupancy was a condition for obtaining a plot of land. As of 1663, only ten of the seventy seigneuries granted had any settlers.[14] In 1663, the French Crown withdrew all privileges from the Company of 100 Associates and made New France a Crown colony. As of the time of the Royal takeover, about 3,000 settlers lived in what is now Quebec, nearly two-thirds of them in the Quebec City area. In contrast to Britain's minimal efforts to maintain a presence in Canada (mainly confined to Newfoundland), the new French administration embarked upon an aggressive policy of expansion. The Royal official in charge of New France was Jean-Baptiste Colbert, a member of the Great Council of State of Louis XIV, and the King's chief bureaucrat. Implementation of French administrative policy for the colony was placed in the hands of Jean Talon, the first intendant of the colony, who reorganized and centralized the colony's administration. The administrative structures so established largely remained unchanged for the entire century of French Royal control of New France. For nearly a hundred years, the colonists lived under a form of benevolent authoritarianism – there were no newspapers, no Parliament, no toleration of dissent, no religious pluralism (the Roman Catholic Church played a central role in education and social services), and no freehold land tenure.[15]

Colbert and Talon were committed to making the colony more self-supporting, in particular by developing more stable sources of revenue besides fur trading, such as lumbering, shipbuilding, mining, fishing, small scale manufacturing, and trade with the West Indies. In order to develop these activities, the settlement required capital, managerial talent, and skilled labour. Talon, early in his tenure, concluded an agreement with the Compagnie des Indes Occidentales (Company of the West Indies) to bring out a number of settlers to New France. More than 4,000 immigrants were sent to New France in the decade after 1666.[16]

However, in its 150 years as a French colony, no more than 10,000 immigrants came to Quebec. Of those who emigrated to Quebec, almost 4,000 were *engagés* committed under three-year contracts as indentured servants to established farmers or fur traders. Approximately 3,500 were soldiers released from military service. In the late 1660s, about 1,000 single women from orphanages and homes of charity ('filles du roi') were shipped out to redress the disproportionate number of females to males in the colony. Typically they chose a husband within two weeks of their arrival. Towards the end of the French regime, 1,000 prisoners (salt smugglers, for the most part) were sent to Canada. At most, 500 immigrants had come on their own. In the last sixty years of the French regime, no more than 4,000 immigrants came to Quebec. Almost all the settlers were French.[17] Notwithstanding the modest levels of immigration, the population of New France began to grow rapidly, almost exclusively as a result of a very high birth rate. The population grew from 3,000 in 1663 to 20,000 in 1712, and to 70,000 in 1760.[18] High birth rates were encouraged by financial bonuses for large families, incentives to marry young, and fines for fathers whose children grew older at home without marrying.[19] Over this period, emigration to all of Britain's North American colonies (mainly along the eastern seaboard of the United States) amounted to almost one million people, resulting in a total population as of 1760 of almost two million – a disproportion that high birth rates in New France could not remotely offset.[20]

Attempts were made early in the French regime to establish a more complete and compact settlement in Quebec, but most of the efforts towards economic diversification came to little, and, by the 1670s, with France increasingly preoccupied with European concerns, enthusiasm waned for investing further capital in Canada. The fur trade continued to dominate the commerce of the colony. France evolved what has been termed a 'river empire,' with long tentacles of influence stretching thousands of miles beyond the area of settlement. The colony's influence extended through the Great Lakes to the Prairie West, southward into the Mississippi and Ohio river basins, and all the way to the Gulf of Mexico.[21] The 1670s and 1680s saw the most dramatic territorial expansion of the fur trade that was to take place in the history of New France, and, in the thirty years of relative peace following the Treaty of Utrecht in 1713, the fur trade experienced a period of unprecedented growth and prosperity.[22] However, by 1700, agriculture had become a major economic activity in New France, with three out of four Canadien families involved in farming.

Over at least the first century of the French regime, relations with neighbouring Native tribes were central to the welfare of the colony.[23] The Native nations who lived north and south of the St. Lawrence were part of a trading network in which furs were exchanged for European trade goods.[24] Champlain, as early as 1609, developed a loose alliance with the Huron living in agricultural communities east of Georgian Bay, off Lake Huron, as well as the nomadic hunting tribes of Algonquins and Montagnais (often referred to collectively as Algonquians), who ranged as far northeast as the Gulf of St Lawrence and as far north as James Bay. The Huron offered the Algonquian tribes corn in return for furs, which they traded with the French. By the 1620s, the Huron supplied between one-half and two-thirds of the furs acquired by the French.[25] Champlain sought to cement relationships with the Huron by missionary activities, by sending, first, Recollet priests into their settlements beginning in 1615 and, then, Jesuits, beginning in 1627.[26] However, at the time of French-Indian contact at the beginning of the seventeenth century, the Huron and

Iroquois were at war. Champlain was persuaded in 1609 to join the
Algonquians and Huron in an attack on the Iroquois to the southwest.
The Iroquois Confederacy, or the League of Five Nations, as it was often
called, was established by the late fifteenth century and was based in what
is now upstate New York. With the arrival of the Europeans, economic motives – competition for the fur trade – were added to more traditional
reasons for tribal warfare. While the Huron had once outnumbered the
Iroquois, between 1635 and 1640 a series of smallpox epidemics, contracted from the French priests and fur traders who lived among the
Huron, reduced their numbers by perhaps as much as 70 per cent. In
1649, the Iroquois mounted a major attack on the Huron, which led eventually to the fall of Huronia. Shortly thereafter, French traders began
to replace the vanquished Huron middlemen in the fur trade. Armed
conflicts with the Iroquois continued intermittently throughout the
seventeenth century.[27] These disrupted the colony's economic base and
endangered French settlements, thus further deterring immigration from
France.[28] By 1693, the Five Nations were suffering heavy losses as a result
of war and disease, and could no longer maintain their dominance on the
north shore of Lake Ontario; in 1701, they made peace with the French
and thirteen Western tribes, thus marking the end of Iroquois resistance
to French expansion.[29]

   With the outbreak of the Seven Years' War in 1756, rival British and
French claims to control of North America reached a climax. Quebec was
taken in 1759 in the famous Battle of the Plains of Abraham, and Montreal
in 1760. After the Conquest, most of Quebec's 4,000-member military and
political elite sailed back to France. With the end of the Seven Years' War,
consummated in the Treaty of Paris of 1763, and the issuance of a Royal
Proclamation in the same year pertaining to New France, Britain hoped
that a large influx of English-speaking settlers would begin. The proclamation in effect announced a program of assimilation. Official status as the
state religion was to be withdrawn from the Roman Catholic Church.
French civil law was to be replaced with British legal institutions, and the
seigneurial system of land distribution was abandoned, as British soldiers
were to be encouraged to retire in the colony on land that would be
granted in freehold. As soon as a substantial number of these newcomers
were settled in Quebec, the governor was to call a general assembly of
their representatives to make laws consonant with those of England.[30]

   This strategy never materialized, in large part because the expected influx of British immigrants failed to materialize. The first British governor,
General James Murray, did not call an assembly, but governed with the

assistance of an appointed council consisting primarily of seigneurs and Roman Catholic clergy. His policies were followed by Sir Guy Carleton, who succeeded him in 1765. In 1769, Carleton recommended statutory recognition of Quebec's institutional and social life, as he understood it. At first, British officials resisted the proposal, but, with the threat of open rebellion developing in the colonies to the south, in 1774 the Quebec Act was passed by the British Parliament. The act retained French civil law, property rights arrangements, and marriage law; guaranteed the continuing status of the Roman Catholic Church; and abandoned the proposal to institute an elected assembly. The Quebec Act also restored the earlier boundaries of Quebec, to embrace the Ohio Valley and Great Lakes region. These boundaries had been severely truncated following the Conquest in an attempt to placate the Native tribes, who were resistant to further encroachments on their land by colonists, but settlers from the Thirteen Colonies to the south had continued to move into these regions, and they saw the Quebec Act as a deliberate attempt to thwart legitimate expansion.[31] The Quebec Act thus contributed to American hostility towards the British in the events which soon culminated in the American Revolution.

The legal, political, and religious components of the Quebec Act were included in order to placate French-Canadian interests in the absence of substantial non-French immigration following the Conquest. However, the revolution in the American colonies soon led to a large influx of American settlers – the Loyalists – to the Atlantic colonies and to Quebec. Those who settled in Quebec complained that their rights as British subjects were violated by the terms of the Quebec Act, and they agitated for constitutional change. The Quebec Act remained in force for less than twenty years.

THE DEVELOPMENT OF THE ATLANTIC REGION

While, early in the seventeenth century, Acadia loomed as large in French colonial thinking as did Canada on the St Lawrence, efforts to establish a viable permanent settlement in the area proved faltering. While the geographic extent of Acadia was subject to some ambiguity, it included present day Nova Scotia (including Cape Breton), New Brunswick, and Prince Edward Island (where Jacques Cartier had landed in 1534). The settlement established by Champlain at Port Royal on the Bay of Fundy was reestablished in 1610 by Jean de Biencourt de Poutrincourt, a French nobleman and former associate of de Mont's. Three years later, the settlement was sacked by an English freebooter, Samuel Argall, and little remained of the settlement until it was re-established in the 1630s. After France's claim to Acadia had been recognized by the Treaty of Saint Germain-en-Laye in 1632, a new governor of the settlement, Isaac de Razilly, was appointed. However, de Razilly died in 1635, provoking quarrels among two rival seigneurs over his succession that precluded any significant expansion of the settlement.[32] In 1654, the settlement was taken over by an invading English expedition, at which time its population was little more than 200.[33] While formal French occupation was restored in 1667 under the Treaty of Breda, France had largely abandoned any efforts at active promotion of the settlement. By 1670, Acadia had a population of about 400–500 and of about 900 by 1686. Population increases were largely accounted for by very high birth rates, not immigration.[34]

After war broke out in Europe in 1689, an invading force of New Englanders attacked Port Royal in 1690 and overpowered the French garrison. The New Englanders retained Acadia for seven years, until France regained the colony under the Treaty of Ryswick in 1697. With the outbreak of war in Europe in 1702, Acadia again became a target for seafaring raids from New England, which were successfully resisted until 1710, when a large expedition of New Englanders, supported by British military supplies, overran the settlement.

Under the Treaty of Utrecht of 1713, which ended yet one more episode of Franco-British European military conflict, France ceded finally to Britain all of its eastern-seaboard possessions, other than Île Royale (Cape Breton), Île St-Jean (Prince Edward Island), the islands of St Pierre and Miquelon (off the south coast of Newfoundland), and fishing rights on the north coast of Newfoundland. The treaty also recognized Britain's claim to the huge Hudson Bay drainage basin that had been granted by the British Crown to the Hudson's Bay Company in 1670. As of 1713, there were perhaps 2,500 Acadians living permanently in Nova Scotia, mostly in the fertile marshlands on the Bay of Fundy and along the eastern coast of present-day Nova Scotia.

Mostly farmers, the Acadians maintained good trading relations with the 3,000–6,000 Mi'kmaq living in the area, in part because the marshlands were of little interest to the Mi'kmaq, and with the New Englanders to the south, with whom they traded agricultural produce for manufactured or processed goods. While the Treaty of Utrecht specified that French inhabitants of Nova Scotia had one year to relocate to French territory or to remain as subjects of the British Crown, the colonial authorities were not enthusiastic about reinforcing the French presence in

Cape Breton, and most Acadians remained as the beneficiaries of unofficial acquiescence. By 1755, the Acadian population had grown rapidly to more than 13,000.[35] In the meantime, the French had developed Louisbourg on Île Royale (Cape Breton) into a major military and commercial entrepot. In 1716, Louisbourg comprised about 600 people, mainly displaced French fishermen from Placentia, Newfoundland. By the 1740s, it had become a major garrison, inhabited by some 2,600 people, including 600 soldiers.[36] The total French civilian population on Cape Breton had grown from 2,500 in 1720 to 4,000 in 1740, many of them involved in the fisheries. The maximum number of permanent European settlers in the Atlantic region between 1720 and 1740 never exceeded 15,000, and the indigenous population was not more than 4,000.[37]

War broke out again between Britain and France in 1744 (the War of the Austrian Succession), and an attack on Louisbourg by New Englanders in 1745 was successful. However, as a result of complicated Imperial machinations, Louisbourg was returned to France in exchange for Madras (India) in the Treaty of Aix-la-Chapelle in 1748, arousing the outrage of many New Englanders. In these conflicts, the Acadians in Nova Scotia, who claimed 'neutral' status and who persistently refused to swear an oath of allegiance to the British Crown if this would entail an obligation to take up arms against their fellow Frenchmen, were widely suspected of supporting the French (e.g., by providing food supplies). By the late 1740s, the British government had become committed to a policy of deliberate settlement of Nova Scotia, at public expense, through immigration (the first major commitment of this kind in British North America), in order to strengthen the British presence. Between 1749 and 1764 more than £600,000 was invested in establishing a non-French population in Nova Scotia through promises of land and ancillary forms of support. Settlers were recruited in Britain from among recently disbanded solders and sailors, and from among London's artisans. More than 2,500 people sailed from Britain in 1749, many of them from Ireland. In 1750–1, the British government promoted the immigration of about 1,500 foreign Protestants, chiefly Swiss, French Huguenots, and Germans, who were settled at Lunenburg.[38]

In 1755, Lieutenant-Governor Lawrence, following the renewal of undeclared war in North America between France and Britain (a year before the beginning of the Seven Years' War),[39] decided it was imperative to resolve the Acadian problem definitively through forced deportation.[40] Lawrence and his council decided that the Acadians should be dispersed among the several colonies on the continent through forced transshipment ('Le Grand Dérangement'). More than 3,000 Acadians were transported to southern British colonies in the United States, and their houses and barns burned to deprive those who escaped of shelter. As many as a third of the passengers died on many of the ships. Other Acadians escaped to Prince Edward Island and Cape Breton, or to uninhabited districts of the colony, mainly in present-day New Brunswick.[41] Others who had initially returned to France subsequently resettled in Louisiana.[42] Those Acadians who made their way to Prince Edward Island and Cape Breton gained only temporary respite. In 1758, another British expedition against Louisbourg forced its surrender, and another 6,000 Acadians were forcibly removed from their homes, more than 3,500 of them from Prince Edward Island, most of whom were sent back directly to France.[43]

In 1758, Lawrence published a proclamation throughout British North America, inviting settlers to claim unoccupied Acadian lands. About 7,000 New Englanders moved to Nova Scotia between 1760 and 1766, attracted by offers of free land, transportation, and initial material support. In 1764, after the British had won control of the northern colonies, the policy relating to the expulsion of Acadians was rescinded. Over the ensuing years, 3,000 Acadians returned to find that their farms had been taken over by English-speaking newcomers, mostly from New England. By 1800, Acadians in Nova Scotia numbered 4,000, in New Brunswick 3,800, and in Prince Edward Island 700. According to a census in 1767, Nova Scotia contained 6,930 Americans, 912 from England, 2,165 from Ireland, 173 Scots, 1,936 Germans, and 1,265 Acadians, apart from blacks and Native people.[44] Immigrants who came to Nova Scotia between 1767 and 1775 included some 2,000 settlers from Ulster, Northern Ireland; more than 750 from Yorkshire, England; and nearly 200 from Scotland. Thus, New Englanders comprised more than 50 per cent of Nova Scotia's population of 20,000 in 1776.[45] As of 1775, the population of Prince Edward Island was about 1,500, comprising immigrants from Scotland, Ireland, and England, but predominantly Scots. Both Prince Edward Island and Cape Breton were annexed to Nova Scotia after the Treaty of Paris in 1763. Prince Edward Island became a separate colony in 1769.

The settlement of Nova Scotia had a substantial effect on the Native population. Between 1715 and 1725, a series of violent incidents in Nova Scotia eventually escalated into a larger Indian war with New England, where Mi'kmaq, Malecite, and Abenaki fought together to resist further British incursions into their territory. A peace was reached in Boston in 1725, where the British promised not to interfere in Indian territory, and the Native peoples, in turn, acknowledged King George as the rightful possessor of the province. By 1749, the Indians were convinced that British concepts of land ownership and settlements were disastrous to their interests and declared war against the British. Colonial authorities, led by Governor Cornwallis, responded with a declared policy of extermination. Bounties for Indian scalps were offered, and the Mi'kmaq were hounded into French territory. By 1750, there were probably no more than a 1,000 Mi'kmaq living in Nova Scotia, and perhaps 2,000 Native people remaining in the entire Atlantic region.[46] A new peace treaty with the Mi'kmaq was concluded in 1761 by the colony of Nova Scotia, along the lines of the 1725 agreement. In 1762, the Nova Scotia government declared that it would maintain rights to Mi'kmaq land 'reserved or claimed by the Indians,' but these claims were not clearly agreed upon by both parties at the time and were not accepted by incoming settlers.[47]

Newfoundland had older but humbler beginnings than other colonies in Canada. In order to establish British sovereignty against competing claims by France, efforts were made early in the seventeenth century to establish permanent settlements in the colony, again through the medium of a trading monopoly. In this case, the London and Bristol (Newfoundland) Company, founded in 1610, was granted rights to the whole island by Britain. But farming proved infeasible on the rocky soil, and the difficulties of establishing year-round settlements daunting. Neither the Newfoundland Company nor its successors were successful, and, by 1680, there were only about 2,000 settlers, mostly of British origin, living in forty tiny settlements along the coast.[48] France continued to contest British claims to the island through the latter part of the seventeenth century and established some small settlements on the island. Most of the tiny British settlements were defenseless, and between 1696 and 1708 the French deported more than half the population to England.[49] Under the Treaty of Utrecht in 1713, the British finally gained formal possession of the entire island. Although at this time the French had nearly as many permanent residents as the British in Newfoundland, mainly clustered around Placentia, under the treaty the French agreed to evacuate their inhabitants and to abandon permanent residences and fortifications. The French fishermen were removed to Cape Breton, chiefly to Louisbourg. However, Britain made no attempt to treat Newfoundland as a formal colony, to encourage settlement, or to establish a year-round government. Thus the island developed independently of any government policy or supervision. The permanent population grew from 1,000 in 1720 to about 1,200 in 1744.[50] As of 1732, 90 per cent of the permanent population were English, but most of the new immigrants during the eighteenth century came from southern Ireland, induced to emigrate by famine and un-employment. Until late in the eighteenth century, Newfoundland was seen principally as a base for seasonal fishing activities and not as a perma-nent settlement. By the end of the century, the permanent population had grown to almost 19,000.

As in Nova Scotia, Newfoundland's original inhabitants, the Beothuk, suffered severely from the presence of settlers. By the mid-nineteenth century, with increasing numbers of fishermen on the Newfoundland coast, it became difficult for the Beothuk to gain access to their summer campsites and their traditional fishing sources. The pressure on them became more intense in the early 1700s, with European settlements in the northeast and the interior of Newfoundland engaged in the estab-lishment of salmon fisheries, fur trapping, and the spring seal hunt. The Beothuk continuously withdrew from contact with the Europeans, who occasionally hunted them for sport, but starvation and tuberculosis took a greater toll, and the tribe appears to have died out completely by the 1820s.[51]

Thus, by 1763, the 150–year conflict between France and Britain for Imperial domination of the northern colonies in North America had finally concluded, with formal British sovereignty established by the Treaty of Paris in the colony of Canada; in Nova Scotia, to which Prince Edward Island and Cape Breton were annexed; and in Newfoundland. However, the populations in these colonial outposts remained tiny, and were dwarfed by, and vulnerable to, pressures by inhabitants in Britain's Thirteen Colonies to the south, as events were quickly to demonstrate.

The First Refugee Movement: The Coming of the Loyalists, 1783–1812

THE LOYALIST INFLUX

In the mid-1770s, the territory that is now called Ontario was part of the province of Quebec. The Royal Proclamation of 1763 had reserved all of this land for Indians and had made commitments that it would not be set-tled on without band consent. The Quebec Act of 1774 had sought to establish an effective British presence in the region by restoring the pre-Conquest boundaries, but ostensibly with a view to more effective en-forcement of treaty obligations to the Native peoples. The only European settlement of any size was located on the outskirts of present-day Windsor, where French-Canadian farmers who supplied Fort Detroit had established farms.[52] Apart from this settlement, almost the entire western portion of the province of Quebec was one continuous forest. Not many more Indians than Europeans lived in the entire area at this time. In the words of Kenneth Norrie and Douglas Owram, 'It was the hinterland of a hinterland.'[53] Early in the French regime, perhaps 20,000 to 25,000 Huron and possibly even more Algonquians had lived in the region, but the Iroquois attacks in the 1640s and 1650s had destroyed their villages. For a time the Iroquois themselves established villages north of Lake Ontario, but, for reasons that are unclear, these settlements had disappeared well before the last half of the eighteenth century.

In Quebec, while the fur trade continued to prosper, and high natural birth rates had increased the population from 70,000 at the time of the Conquest to approximately 140,000 by the mid-1780s, little of the hoped for immigration had occurred, either from the New England states or from Britain itself. Meanwhile, Nova Scotia likewise had developed very little economically between the end of the Seven Years' War in 1763 and the beginning of the early 1780s.[54] But the course of British North America's history was about to change dramatically.

In April 1775, long-simmering tensions between the British Imperial authorities and local inhabitants in the thirteen American colonies to the south escalated into the War of Independence. American attempts to draw the colonies of Quebec and Nova Scotia into rebellion against the British failed, as did American assaults on Montreal and Quebec.[55] As the rebels gained the upper hand in the conflict with Britain in the south, and word of a preliminary peace settlement began to circulate, many Loyalists gathered in those ports still controlled by the British, particularly New York, seeking to migrate. Some emigrated to Britain and the Caribbean, but a substantial majority headed north. The Loyalist migration that got under way in 1783 furnished British North America with its first large influx of English-speaking settlers and constituted the first major refugee movement to British North America.[56] In all, a total of some 40,000 to 50,000 Loyalists moved north during the hostilities and immediately thereafter. About 15,000 settled in Nova Scotia, and another 15,000 in the St John River valley in what became New Brunswick in 1784; 750 on Prince Edward Island; 1,000 on Cape Breton; and about 10,000 in Quebec, mainly in the western part of the province (later Ontario). More than half of the total were civilian refugees, the remainder being officers and troops. A high proportion of the new settlers, especially those in the military, came from Scotland and Ireland, or were mercenaries from various

German principalities.[57] By 1784, it was becoming possible for Loyalists to return to the United States without fear of persecution, and many did.

Among the Loyalist immigrants were more than 3,000 blacks who had been promised freedom by the British authorities if they would desert the rebel side and serve in His Majesty's forces.[58] Most were transported to Nova Scotia. Despite the ostensible commitment to equal treatment, such equality was far from realized.[59] In 1791, about 1,200 of Nova Scotia's black Loyalists accepted the chance to emigrate to the West African colony of Sierra Leone. Apart from the free blacks, some 1,500 black slaves were brought to Canada by white Loyalists.[60] Indeed, slavery had existed in Canada since 1628, and in 1759 there were 3,600 slaves in New France: about 1,100 blacks and the balance 'Panis' (or Indians).[61] In 1796, a group of 568 Jamaican descendants of runaway black slaves (the Maroons) who had formed settlements in the hills in Jamaica, from which they periodically mounted raids on the sugar plantations, were deported by British authorities to Nova Scotia after an insurrection at Trelawny Town, but in 1800 most were deported again, also to Sierra Leone, out of concern by colonial authorities over the costs of maintaining them.[62]

In addition to the black Loyalist refugees, almost 5,000 Iroquois who had supported the British side in the conflict were ultimately settled in Upper Canada. The First Nations were virtually abandoned by their British allies in the rush to settle the war. Britain transferred to the Americans sovereignty over lands south of the Great Lakes and as far west as the Mississippi River, ignoring the fact that most of the land was claimed by Native peoples.[63] The Iroquois prevailed on Sir Frederick Haldimand, governor of Canada from 1778 to 1784, to grant new lands to them in an area north of Lakes Ontario and Erie. In 1783–4, the government purchased large tracts of land from the Mississauga (as the British called the Ojibwa) on the north shore of Lake Ontario and gave part of this territory along the Grand River Valley to the Iroquois. The Proclamation of 1763 recognized the Great Lakes area as Indian territory, and hence, in theory, the Indians had to agree to surrender the land to the Crown before settlement could proceed.

Governor Haldimand, in order to minimize tensions with the French population by providing farms for Loyalist soldiers and refugees in the western region of Quebec, in 1782 purchased a large area of land from the Mississauga on the west bank on the Niagara River, and in 1783 a further agreement was entered into, surrendering all lands bounded roughly by present-day Gananoque to the eastern end of the Bay of Quinte, in both cases for a nominal consideration. By the late 1780s, the British believed that they had obtained title to the entire Niagara Peninsula and the whole north shore of Lake Ontario, except for a large tract of land between the head of the lakes (i.e., present-day Hamilton) and Toronto. Between 1805 and 1818, the government successfully pressured the Mississauga to sell this last remaining tract. Between the 1790s and the 1820s, smallpox, tuberculosis, and measles had killed almost two-thirds of the Mississauga on the western end of the lake, and by 1798 white settlers had acquired large tracts of the Iroquois' original land on the Grand River.[64] After the Treaty of Paris of 1783, which marked the end of the American War of Independence, pressure from Loyalist settlers led to a major political re-organization of British North America. The first stage came in 1784, when a governor-generalship was established to administer Britain's remaining North American colonies.[65] In Quebec, where about 10,000 Loyalists had arrived during and after the War of Independence expecting to find familiar institutions, such as freehold land tenure, British laws, Protestant religious establishments, and representative government, these pressures were dealt with by the colonial authorities in two ways: first, beginning in 1784, by channeling most of the exodus of Loyalists from Lower to Upper Canada and organizing settlement land for them there, and, second, by providing more congenial institutions within Lower Canada. These two responses were reflected in the enactment by the British Parliament of the Constitutional Act of 1791, which divided Quebec into two provinces, Upper and Lower Canada. While, in Lower Canada, the population was still overwhelmingly French, British institutions of law and government were to be established for the benefit of the Loyalist immigrants.[66] According to John Finlay and Douglas Sprague, the Constitutional Act of 1791 provided 'a legal framework for blending the institutions of two official cultures in a single state.'[67] Initially this arrangement seemed to meet with the acquiescence of the French population, but this state of tranquility was not to endure for very long. Between 1805 and 1810, British and Canadian parties fought constantly over the issue of the destiny of Lower Canada. During the governorship of Sir James Craig, three elections to the Legislative Assembly were held within the first three years of his arrival, where the outcome was dominated by the Parti Canadien. In frustration, Craig rounded up the editors and chief contributors to *Le Canadien*, a French-Canadian political magazine, and twenty of the most ardent nationalists were jailed on charges of seditious libel.[68]

In the meantime, Montreal fur traders, at this time primarily Scottish and English merchants, adjusted to the geographic terms of settlement of the War of Independence and the loss of territory in the southwest by expanding their operations into the region north and west of Lake Superior. In the 1780s, Montreal traders merged in a syndicate called the North West Company. By 1800, the North West Company was acquiring more than four times as much fur as the Hudson's Bay Company and all other rivals. However, this portended increasing conflict with the Hudson's Bay Company in territory which it had previously regarded as its own. In 1810, the Earl of Selkirk, a Scottish philanthropist, had acquired a controlling interest in the Hudson's Bay Company, and in 1811 obtained from the company a grant of 116,000 square miles in the Red River valley, on the eastern shores of Lake Winnipeg, where he planned to establish a settlement of Scottish and Irish immigrants.[69] The North West Company strongly objected to Selkirk's grant, and in a loose alliance with the Metis (people with a mixed ancestry resulting from marriages between French fur traders and Indian women from tribes with whom they dealt) became involved in a series of armed conflicts with representatives of the Hudson's Bay Company and Lord Selkirk's settlers. Under pressure from the British Colonial Office to end the anarchic state of affairs, and in return for an exclusive monopoly on the fur trade in the region, the two companies agreed to merge in 1821, with the North West Company acquiring stock in the Hudson's Bay Company.

THE IMPACT ON UPPER CANADA

In Upper Canada, as of 1785 – two years after the end of the War of Independence – there were between 5,000 and 7,000 Loyalists. By 1791, the European population of Upper Canada was probably not much more than 12,000. However, the first lieutenant-governor of the colony, John Graves Simcoe, aggressively promoted the colony as a home not only for Loyalists, but also for Americans attracted more by cheap land than by loyalty to Britain. The initial influx of Loyalists received land grants and other forms of assistance, such as food, clothing, implements, building materials, and seed. In addition, Loyalist compensation claims for abandoned property often involved significant British payments.[70] In the case of the subsequent influx of American settlers, Crown land was available for sixpence an acre plus survey costs and an oath of allegiance at a time when settlers were moving into New York, and into the Ohio country, where land was selling, on average, for two dollars an acre.[71] The land granting system took two forms.[72] Simcoe allowed members of the executive and legislative councils to receive large grants of 3,000 to 5,000 acres of land, and their children could obtain an additional 1,200 acres each. A second system consisted of immigrants obtaining location tickets to 200 acres of land on the promise that they would develop it. Once these individuals had built their homes, fenced the land, and cleared the road allowance, they could gain title.

A stream of Americans continued to arrive until 1812, settling the north shore of Lakes Erie and Ontario. However, approximately 10 per cent of Upper Canada's early immigrants were of German ethnic origin. These immigrants arrived in a variety of ways. First, during the American War of Independence, some 12,000 German mercenaries hired by the British were stationed in Canada. About 2,400 were offered grants of land and decided to stay.[73] In addition, members of several pacifist religious sects, such as Quakers, Dunkards, and Mennonites, were attracted to Canada from the United States after Simcoe granted an exemption from military service to conscientious objectors. These sects tended to settle in cohesive, compact groups in Upper Canada, which became a magnet for further immigrants of German origin. By 1800, the population of Upper Canada had reached 50,000, and by 1815 had grown to 95,000. About 80 per cent were of U.S. origin, of whom 25 per cent were Loyalists.

THE IMPACT ON THE ATLANTIC REGION

Nova Scotia, as it then was, bore the brunt of the Loyalist immigration. In 1783, it still had barely 20,000 settlers, and now faced an influx of more than 30,000 Loyalist immigrants. The primary need was to find land on which to relocate the immigrants. However, the British authorities in the 1760s had provided free grants of millions of acres in lots of 20,000 to 150,000 acres to individuals and to companies residing or formed in England. In many cases, little or no effort was made to improve the land. From 1760 to 1773, almost 5.5 million acres, including much of the best land in Nova Scotia, was granted to associations and individuals on condition that they bring in settlers. However, once title had been granted, the settlement condition was almost impossible to enforce.[74] The local government successfully petitioned British authorities for permission to revest the lands in the Crown by a process of escheat for failure to meet the conditions of the initial grant, enabling the government to regain title quickly to 2.5 million acres of Nova Scotia. In the spring of 1783, the British government committed itself to providing a free grant of 100 acres for every Loyalist household head, with 50 more acres for each member of his family, and additional acres according to his seniority if he had held military rank. The government also committed itself to providing food rations for several years, and materials and tools to help the refugees shelter themselves and begin clearing their land.[75]

While 20,000 Loyalists were landing in peninsular Nova Scotia to create Shelburne and to transform many established communities such as Halifax, almost as many headed instead to continental Nova Scotia by travelling up the Bay of Fundy towards the St. John River. By the fall of 1783, some 14,000 Loyalists had arrived at the mouth of the St John and other landing sites along the Fundy shore. Discontented with their remoteness from Halifax, and the apparent lack of interest of the colonial authorities there, Loyalist spokesmen quickly began demanding that the region should become a colony in its own right, to which the British government assented in June 1784, thus creating the colony of New Brunswick.[76] After a belated and small migration of Loyalists to Cape Breton Island began in 1784, that island also became a colony in its own right. Prior to 1815, immigrants from the British Isles came chiefly from the Scottish Highlands and from Ireland. Most of the Scots were drawn to Nova Scotia, and many of the Irish to Newfoundland and New Brunswick. Between 1801 and 1803, more than 7,000 Scots sailed to British North America. Almost one-quarter landed in Prince Edward Island and more than half in Nova Scotia. Within seven or eight years, at least 1,500 more Scots reached Prince Edward Island, and others came to Cape Breton and eastern Nova Scotia. In one of the few early efforts at systematic colonization, the Earl of Selkirk also established a settlement of about 800 Scottish immigrants on Prince Edward Island in 1802.[77] As of 1800, about 100,000 people lived in the five Atlantic colonies.

The several hundred Loyalists who relocated on Prince Edward Island became victims of duplicity on the part of the land proprietors. From 1768 to 1772, almost the entire land area of Prince Edward Island – 1.4 million acres – was given away by the British government under a system that resembled in some respects the Quebec seigneurial system. The island was divided into long belts of land stretching from north to south, which were allocated by lot, until all sixty-seven townships of roughly 20,000 acres each had been granted to soldiers, politicians, and courtiers favoured by the British government. The new landlords were required to pay a small annual fee, or quitrent, for their lands, and promised to bring over settlers. To attract Loyalists to their land, the large land proprietors promised them grants of land with secure title, but, once the settlers had cleared their lands, erected buildings, and planted orchards, the proprietors denied written title deeds to those who wanted to become freeholders rather

than remain tenants. Many obtained no redress and left the island disaffected. Those who remained fought for seventy-five years for justice (the
'escheat movement'). Not until 1860 did the Land Commission recommend that free grants be made to those who could prove that their ancestors had been attracted to the island by the original promises made to the
Loyalists, and the matter was not resolved until 1873, in conjunction with
Prince Edward Island's entry into Confederation.[78]

The official British posture towards emigration during this period was
generally to discourage it. A combination of labour needs during the
Napoleonic Wars and a groundswell of concern over the loss of tenants
from the landlords of the Scottish Western Highlands and Ireland resulted in 1803 in the passage of the first British legislation regulating the
transport of immigrants across the Atlantic. Officially intended to improve
conditions on immigrant vessels by restricting how many passengers could
be carried and requiring a physician on each vessel, the Passenger Act of
1803[79] was primarily designed to raise the price of passage beyond the
reach of those seeking to leave.

THE CLOSING OF THE SOUTHERN BORDER: THE WAR OF 1812

In 1812, Britain found itself at war with the United States for the second
and final time. Andrew Jackson, then a general, and subsequently
president, announced the objective of the war as the conquest of all of
the British dominions on the continent of North America.[80] With seven
million Americans and only 700,000 residents in the British dominions,
British military forces committed to the Napoleonic War, intense political
tension and instability in Lower Canada, and concerns about the loyalties
of many of the American settlers in Upper Canada, prospects for the
Canadian colonies did not look promising. However, the American commitment to the war effort proved to be relatively weak, and hostilities
ended in a stalemate. Under the Treaty of Ghent of 1815, the pre-war
borders were restored. After the war, the British government reversed its
policy of encouraging migration from the United States by denying
Americans the right to buy Crown land if they had been in the colony for
less than seven years. This marked an important turning-point, after which
immigration was encouraged from Britain rather than from the United
States. The war intensified Upper Canadians' loyalty to the colony and
to Britain, and sparked anti-American feelings that continue today to
define a part of Canada's national identity.[81] Canadian apprehensions of
American aspirations to its 'Manifest Destiny'[82] continued to influence

immigration and settlement policy until Confederation, and indeed were a significant stimulus for Confederation.

'The Greatest Folk Movement of Modern Times':[83] Immigration to British North America, 1815–1867

The population of British North America of European origin grew from a little more than 250,000 in 1791 to 1.6 million in 1845, and to more than 3 million in 1871 (the year of the first census taken after Confederation). Between 1790 and 1845, probably more than 750,000 Britons settled in British North America. About one-half of the emigrants were Irish, one-third English and Welsh, and one-quarter Scottish. The first census in the Dominion of Canada (1871) reported 850,000 Irish, about one-quarter of the national population, concentrated principally in Ontario, New Brunswick, and Newfoundland. In the 1830s and 1840s, perhaps as many as 60 per cent of all immigrants were Irish.[84]

A combination of Old World poverty and New World opportunity had propelled the massive exodus of emigrants from Britain to British North America.[85] However, 'push' probably dominated 'pull' factors. In the latter part of the eighteenth and the first half of the nineteenth century, Britain experienced an enormous population increase. Following the end of the Napoleonic Wars in 1815, a general economic recession set in which exacerbated the problem of reabsorbing demobilized soldiers into civilian employment. In England, the Poor Laws created an army of unemployed on relief, imposing a crippling financial burden on the local parishes in raising Poor Law Relief rates. In Scotland, the practice of subdividing crofts on the marriage of the crofter's children reduced land holdings to divisions too small to support a family. In both Scotland and Ireland, a change in agricultural practice from tillage to pasturing led to the consolidation of many farm holdings, and the displacement of tenants and a reduction in employment for farm labourers. The Irish potato famine of 1847 created an army of paupers for whom emigration was the last best option. In addition, technological changes that occurred in the course of the Industrial Revolution had rendered redundant many spinners and weavers who practiced their trade by hand. The advent of steam power also rendered obsolete many workshops spread around the country in places where running water was plentiful.

While British officials in Canada were concerned about the potential threats to public health of large numbers of pauper immigrants, many of them nevertheless favoured immigration from the British Isles. They thought that a larger population, particularly in the vulnerable colonies of Upper and Lower Canada, would protect British territory from encroachment by the United States. As Lord Elgin, the governor general of Canada, wrote in 1848, 'Climate and contiguity point out Canada as the most natural resort for the surplus population of England and Ireland, and I am convinced that filling up the back settlements of the Province with resident agriculturalists furnishes the only possible chance of preventing Canada from becoming a State of the Union.'[86]

IMMIGRATION POLICIES IN THE SENDING COUNTRY

This combination of factors led the British government to re-evaluate fundamentally its attitude to emigration. In the decade or so after the end of the Napoleonic Wars and the War of 1812 in North America, limited attempts at systematic settlement schemes were undertaken by the British government.[87] In 1816, a number of British soldiers whose period of service expired while they were garrisoned in Canada were persuaded to take up land in settlements between the St. Lawrence and Ottawa Rivers. Each settler was given a plot of land according to rank, and rations for eight months. In 1820, the military colonists were joined by 167 families from Lanarkshire, who also received free land and rations, but by 1823 hardly a settler was still to be found on his original plot. In 1819–20, a similar scheme was undertaken, involving 3,000 unemployed Scottish weavers. In 1823, free passages and land were offered to 500 immigrants from the south of Ireland, under a scheme administered by Peter Robinson, the commissioner of Crown lands in Upper Canada, in the Bathurst area, and a subsequent, more ambitious scheme, also led by Robinson, in 1825 involved resettling more than 2,000 Irish immigrants near Peterborough. In all cases, within two or three years, very few settlers remained on their land. By the late 1820s, the British government had concluded that organized colonization efforts did not warrant the cost and largely abandoned them.

During the emigration fever of the 1830s and 1840s, the British government largely confined its efforts to desultory enforcement of the safety provisions of the Passenger Acts. Regulating transatlantic passage was mostly ineffectual both because the powerful transportation companies resisted it, and because landowners, anxious to rid themselves of surplus tenants and labourers, also resisted reforms which they feared would raise passage rates to prohibitive levels. Those regulations that were imposed tended to be easily circumvented, and so failed to reduce substantially the incidence of death on board ships and the incidence of disease introduced to the receiving country. In his report of 1839, Lord Durham wrote of the 'abominable' conditions of immigrant ships arriving in British North America and of the ways that captains evaded the regulations:

> I have been informed by a shipmaster that, on one occasion, he came up the St. Lawrence with upwards of thirty cases of [cholera] fever among the passengers, many of whom were in a state of delirium. Fearing that on his arrival in port he should get into trouble he quietly landed fourteen of the most violent of his poor wretches on the island of Orleans to shift for themselves. The harbour-master boarded him on his arrival, but he persuaded the other passengers who were not ill to come on deck and get into a fight in the noise and hubbub of which screams and cries of the sick never reached the ears of the officer who was glad to escape from the scene of the uproar. When night came on he landed the remainder with their luggage in the usual way.[88]

The British Parliament in 1834 amended the Poor Law Relief Act to permit parishes to raise money on the security of their Poor Law Relief rates in order to meet the expenses incurred in dispatching to the colonies poor people on the rolls. From 1836 to 1846, Poor Law commissioners provided assistance to 14,000 people in England and Wales to facilitate their emigration, and to a substantial number of Irish from 1847 onwards, many of them coming to Canada.[89] Landlords in both Ireland and Scotland also sometimes provided financial assistance with passages in order to rid themselves of tenants.[90]

Another source of financial assistance was the immigration funds of various trade unions. From 1844 to the early 1860s, many of the larger unions provided funds to assist in emigration for their members. The purpose of these expenditures was to clear particular trades of surplus workers, and so maintain wage levels, but it was quickly found that the money which could be allocated to this purpose had an insignificant impact on the problem of surplus labour, and after 1860 the expenditure of union monies for emigration funds was abandoned.[91] 'Friendly societies' also played a role in promoting emigration. A number of these societies focused their efforts on single women emigrants, including the London Female Emigration Society, formed in 1850; the British Ladies Emigration Society, formed in 1859; and the Female Middle Class Emigration Society, formed in 1861, which assisted with the cost of passage and also provided a staff of matrons to travel to the colonies with single female emigrants where ships were not already provided with stewardesses. Most single women were employed in the colonies as domestic servants, milliners, or seamstresses, with a smaller subset employed as nurses or as teachers in primary schools, in particular with the advent of common school policies in the colonies after 1850.[92] With the passage of the Factory Acts, beginning in 1815, overseers of poor children were no longer able to place them in factories and sought other avenues for ridding themselves of this burden. In many cases, workhouse children, as well as juveniles convicted of crimes, were forced to become unwilling emigrants, being placed with employers in the colonies as domestic servants or farmhands. In 1830, the Society for the Suppression of Juvenile Vagrancy was established with the object of promoting emigration among destitute children, and in 1848 the London Ragged Schools began sending out destitute children in large parties to the colonies.[93]

In 1828, the Colonial Office, in what was the first step towards developing an institutional structure for the processing of immigrants in the country of reception, appointed A.C. Buchanan as resident superintendent and agent for immigrants, stationed at Quebec.[94] In due course, he appointed a network of agents in other centres, reporting to, and receiving instructions from him, and carried out a wide range of duties, including receiving immigrants on landing, distributing landing money, clothing and feeding the indigent, hearing complaints, launching proceedings against shipmasters who violated laws, directing newcomers to places of employment, and transshipping newly arrived immigrants to their ultimate destinations. Initially, the cost of this operation was borne by the British government, but after 1854 the cost was assumed by the government of the colony of Canada. In 1834, the British government also began the practice of appointing domestic immigration agents at most of the major British ports of embarkation to monitor compliance with the Passenger Act, to advise emigrants on shipping and land arrangements, and to counteract the efforts of confidence men selling tickets on nonexistent ships, although the impact these agents had on the appalling conditions on most immigrant vessels appears to have been minimal.[95]

IMMIGRATION POLICIES IN THE RECEIVING COLONIES

Land Grants

After the enactment of the Constitutional Act of 1791, the land system began to take two forms. The first involved what were termed 'official settlers' – those granted lands without condition on account of service or position. The other class of settlers were the immigrants whose right to land came from their potential role in developing the colony and who acquired land, subject to certain conditions. With respect to the first class, as noted earlier, in Prince Edward Island and large parts of Nova Scotia, dating back to the 1760s, vast amounts of land had been granted to absentee proprietors by the Imperial government for services rendered, real or contrived. In both Upper and Lower Canada, after the Constitutional Act, the lieutenant-governor commonly rewarded members of his Executive and Legislative Councils or other major figures in the colonial administration with large land grants. In addition, under the Constitutional Act one-seventh of all land granted had to be set aside as Clergy Reserves to support the Church of England.

In Upper Canada, out of the 17 million acres surveyed in 1837, only about 1.5 million acres then remained ungranted. Of these millions of acres granted, less than one-tenth had actually been occupied, and much less reclaimed and cultivated. In Lower Canada, out of 6 million acres surveyed in the new townships, two-thirds were either granted or sold, but only one-twentieth of the land granted was occupied by settlers.[96] These policies of large grants to former military officers, officials, and political favourites, apart from providing great scope for political corruption and patronage, also had the effect of breaking up settlements or forcing them into more distant areas, where access to basic amenities was often extremely limited. These policies attracted increasing criticism. The intellectual genesis of much of the criticism derived from the writings of Edward Gibbon Wakefield, who, beginning in the early 1830s, argued against both lavish alienation of land in large grants to officials and free grants of land to individual settlers.[97] In his view, the appropriate way of establishing an efficient ratio of labour to land was to auction off land in economic units to the highest bidder. A free grant of land to a poor settler was often a liability instead of an asset. Wakefield claimed that experience showed the wisdom of settlers working for others until they could earn enough to purchase land outright. Such a method effected a gradual, not premature, conversion of labourers into landowners. Moreover, the proceeds from land sales, together with a tax that he proposed should be imposed on all land granted, should constitute an emigration fund to be devoted to financing the emigration of labourers. In 1830, the British colonial secretary sent a special commissioner to the British North American colonies, John Richards, to enquire into land policy. His report echoed many of the criticisms of Wakefield, and anticipated similar criticisms by Lord Durham in his famous report of 1839.[98] Thus, beginning in 1832, the practice of making large grants to officials and others either unconditionally or conditionally upon subdividing and settling the land became much less common, and the sale at auction, subject to an upset price, of individual farming units to individual settlers became much more the norm. Indeed, very few immigrants in the mass migrations of the 1830s and 1840s benefited from free land grants.[99]

Apart from official unconditional grants to officials, large grants were sometimes made to individual colonizers on condition that they settle subunits of the land. Lord Selkirk's efforts in Prince Edward Island and Red River have already been noted. In addition, he also set up a much less successful settlement at Baldoon, in Upper Canada, in 1804 that was ravaged during the War of 1812.[100] In Upper Canada, undoubtedly the leading colonizer in this category was Colonel Thomas Talbot.[101] In 1803, Talbot was given 5,000 acres outright by the government of Upper Canada, plus a commitment for an additional 200 acres for every settler to whom he surrendered a free grant of 50 acres. Thus, the only limit on the amount of land he could acquire was his ability to secure settlers who would be willing to accept his terms. Later, the Executive Council ruled that Talbot must surrender the free grant of 50 acres to the individual out of his personal grant of 5,000 acres, which would limit the government's obligation to a total of 20,000 acres. In each Talbot settlement, every male settler over sixteen years of age received a free grant of 50 acres on condition that he would, within three years, clear and sow 10 acres, build a habitable house, and open to traffic half the roadway in front of his lot. An additional 150 acres could be purchased for 12 shillings per acre. Talbot did not grant title to a lot until these settlement conditions had been met. This benevolent despotism led to the settlement of twenty-eight townships in Upper Canada by 1836, although by this time he was viewed by the government of Upper Canada as a government unto himself and was required to wind up his affairs and hand over to the Executive Council the management of the Talbot settlements.

A somewhat similar strategy was pursued by colonial administrations through the agency of land companies.[102] The best-known and most successful was the Canada Land Company, which was able to acquire over 2 million acres of the best land in the province of Upper Canada in the mid-1820s for some £348,000, to be paid in sixteen annual instalments. Lots, either improved or unimproved, were offered for sale to settlers either for cash or on an instalment plan. Similar, but more modest, land companies were formed in Lower Canada in 1825 (the British American

Land Company) and in New Brunswick in 1831 (the New Brunswick Land Company). However, like large grants to officials and former military officers those to land companies were superseded by a system of government auctions of agricultural lots to individual settlers.[103]

Restrictions on Immigration

As the wave of immigrants began to increase in the early 1830s, concerns developed in the colonies over both their numbers and their health status. In 1830, a temporary fever hospital was erected on the south bank of the St. Lawrence opposite Quebec, at Pointe-Levy, and in 1831 the Executive Council of Lower Canada established a second quarantine hospital at Grosse Île, in an attempt to contain an outbreak of cholera that had devastated the north of England the previous year. This was the first major Canadian public health measure. Facilities at Grosse Île were made permanent and enlarged following a major cholera epidemic that arrived with immigrants to Canada in 1832.[104]

In 1832, Lower Canada proposed a head tax on immigrants amounting to five shillings per adult, with the revenue being used in part to provide indigent people with passages to Upper Canada and in part to finance immigrant hospitals in Montreal and Quebec, and to assist Montreal immigration societies.[105] In 1842, New Brunswick adopted a law which levied a tax on new arrivals to assist indigent fellow travelers. This money was to be paid into the provincial treasury, while monies expended on giving relief could be obtained only by applying to the legislature. This latter body did not meet until the immigration season was over, so the money was collected for a purpose for which it could never be spent. After a massive influx of Irish immigrants in 1847, when more than 100,000 arrived in a single year, many destitute and diseased, a third of whom were to die within a year, the Canadian legislature both increased the head tax and adopted a sliding scale that varied the tax by month of arrival to encourage people to land in Canada during the summer months, when outdoor work was more plentiful. After 1856, when the Imperial government ceased funding the immigration agent in Quebec, expenses of this agency were met from this tax. Similarly, both Nova Scotia and New Brunswick, following the 1847 famine immigration, imposed a landing tax on all immigrants, ranging from ten shillings to twenty shillings per head, depending on time of arrival, and five shillings per capita if the ships bringing the immigrants were quarantined.[106]

Promotional Activities

For most of the period leading up to Confederation, colonial authorities were content to leave to shipowners and their agents, and 'return men,' the promotion of emigration to the colonies. However, as immigration tapered off sharply in the 1850s – in 1859 and 1860, it had fallen to little more than 6,000 a year – and as the exodus of immigrants to the United States from British North America continued, and indeed increased,[107] the colony of Canada embarked on a modest immigration promotional program. To this end, beginning in 1854 the province allocated a small sum of money to advertise its attractions in England and on the Continent, mainly through the publication of pamphlets distributed abroad by agents in the Department of Agriculture, which had responsibility for immigration. In 1859, an official was dispatched to England to open an office in Liverpool, and in the following year another official was sent to Germany, in both cases to promote the emigration of farmers or agricultural labourers. Demands for Canada to undertake more active efforts both to attract and to retain immigrants led to the appointment of three select committees of the Canadian legislature in 1859 and 1860 to examine the question.[108] This modest initial promotional program was progressively expanded, complementing efforts by the shipping companies, which engaged in aggressive promotional campaigns of their own. As these promotional campaigns assumed larger proportions, often distinguished visitors from Great Britain, Germany, and the United States were invited to Canada at government expense with a view to returning home as advocates and emissaries for the colonies. Often testimonials were solicited, subject to appropriate editing, from successful immigrants. The material was used abroad by government or shipping companies or agencies in public meetings, press stories, or advertising. How much effect any of these promotional efforts actually had on the numbers or types of immigrants is unclear.[109]

IMMIGRATION PATTERNS IN THE BRITISH
NORTH AMERICAN COLONIES

Over the period from 1815 to 1867, the population increase was most dramatic in Upper Canada, where the numbers rose from 95,000 in 1815 to 952,000 in 1851 (in that year for the first time surpassing the population of Quebec, or Lower Canada).[110] In the first three decades of the nineteenth century, the economic development of Upper Canada was centered on wheat, increasingly supplemented by the timber trade. By the end of the 1840s, Upper and Lower Canada were on the eve of a new era of significant industrialization, with the advent of the steam engine and the railways, where internal markets, both Canadian and American, came to be seen to be equally as important as, or more important than, transatlantic markets, and where the dynamic sectors of the economy would increasingly shift to the cities. In Lower Canada, as a result of extremely high birth rates (not immigration), the French population increased more than tenfold in the century after the Conquest, reaching 850,000 in 1861.[111] In the cities, there was a steady influx of anglophones, so that, by the early nineteenth century, 40 per cent of the population of Quebec City and 33 per cent of that of Montreal was anglophone.[112] As of 1861, 22 per cent of the total population of Lower Canada – 260,000 people – were not French Canadians (compared with about 500 English-speaking residents in the mid-1760s).[113]

Estimates suggest that, between 1815 and 1838, 22,000 immigrants from Scotland, 13,000 from Ireland, and 2,000 from England came to the colony of Nova Scotia. The large influx of Irish immigrants in the 1830s and 1840s largely passed Nova Scotia by. The population of Nova Scotia increased from 202,500 in 1838 to 338,000 in 1871.[114]

In New Brunswick, immigration lagged badly until 1800, but thereafter the colony attracted significant numbers of settlers until the 1850s. The driving force of its economy was timber, which was a highly volatile industry, depending very much on international markets. In the 1820s and 1830s, the stream of immigrants was steady, but in the 1840s the number increased dramatically. In 1842, 8,000 Irish emigrated to New Brunswick; in 1846, 9,000; and, in 1847, 17,000, with the numbers falling off quite sharply thereafter, in part as a result of diversions to the United States, Australia, and New Zealand, and in part as a result of head taxes on immigrants that the colonies had recently imposed. The population of New Brunswick increased from 154,000 in 1840 to 286,000 in 1871.[115]

Prince Edward Island had a population of 32,000 by 1833, and the permanent population of Newfoundland doubled between 1814 and 1830, to 40,000.[116] Newfoundland did not acquire formal status as a colony until 1824. Between 1845 and 1869, the population of Newfoundland increased to 146,000.[117] The population of Prince Edward Island increased to 80,900 in 1861, and to 94,000 in 1871. Between 1800 and 1871, the population of the whole Atlantic region had increased from approximately 100,000 to 900,000 people.[118]

In addition to the influx of blacks during the Loyalist migration to Nova Scotia, about 2,000 former slaves sought refuge in Canada during the War of 1812,[119] after British promises of a choice of military service or free transportation to a British possession in North America as an inducement for desertion. Another movement of blacks entered British North America between 1820 and 1860 via the famous 'Underground Railway,' which smuggled escaped slaves from the American South out of reach of American courts. Over this period, perhaps as many as 30,000 ex-slaves made their way to Canada. Most settled near the southern border of Upper Canada, where some innovative, although ultimately unsuccessful, forms of communal settlements were attempted, and a few joined the existing black population in Nova Scotia. A substantial number of the refugee slaves returned to the United States when the Emancipation Act of 1863 freed slaves after the U.S. Civil War,[120] although black settlers and settlements remained permanent features of Canadian society.

Gross immigration numbers or general population trends tend to obscure an important phenomenon: outmigration. Between 1815 and 1839, between a half and three-quarters of the number of immigrants to arrive in British North America emigrated from British North America to the United States. This was the beginning of a recurring trend throughout the nineteenth century. From the 1860s to the end of the century, in fact, more people would leave the country than enter it. The first serious outmigration occurred in the seigneurial districts of French Canada. There an agricultural crisis in the 1830s, combined with the failure of the Rebellions of 1837 and 1838, forced many to leave their Native province. The unavailability of productive land in the traditional seigneurial regions and the opening of textile mills in the cities of New England induced more than 40,000 people to leave the province for the United States in the 1830s. This figure increased to 90,000 in the 1840s, and to 190,000 in the 1850s. In Canada West (Ontario), most of the movement into the United States was into the agricultural districts of the American Midwest, a migration that was, to a small extent, arrested by the opening of Manitoba after 1870. In the 1860s, a major exodus from the Atlantic region began. By 1889, just under 100,000 Native Maritimers resided in the United States, chiefly in New England.[121]

In Douglas Owram's classic account of the settlement of the Canadian West, *Promise of Eden*,[122] he points out that, from as early as 1734, the region beyond the Great Lakes had been a hinterland for Canadian fur traders, first, under the French regime and, then, under Montreal-based Scottish merchants, whose activities were later organized under the aegis of the North West Company. However, until about 1815 the Canadian Northwest was seen solely as a fur-trade hinterland and enduring wilderness, and not as a settlement frontier.[123] The fur-trade network tended to focus on the subarctic areas of the region, and created a harsher and more northerly impression of the region, given that little of the fur-trading activity traversed what is now considered agricultural land in southern parts of the region.[124] This northern orientation was further emphasized by British fascination early in the nineteenth century with the search for the Northwest Passage.[125] The one exception to this image was the Selkirk colony, established on the banks of the Red River in 1811.

The Red River settlement was developed with an initial influx of about 300 Scottish and Irish settlers, supplemented shortly afterwards by smaller numbers of Swiss and French Canadians and, from within the region, by former officers and employees of the fur trade who had retired to the colony.[126] The settlement served the economic purpose of a supplier of food and provisions for the fur-trade posts throughout the interior. In 1822, there were almost 1,300 people in the Red River settlement; in 1856, 6,700; and, in 1871, almost 12,000.[127] By the mid-1820s, many of the early immigrants had left Red River for Upper Canada or the United States, and, as the remaining colonists died, the population became increasingly composed of Metis (who had originally seen the settlement as a threat), especially since there was no large European immigration from outside. Of Red River's total population in 1871, 5,754 were of French mixed-blood descent, and 4,083 of British mixed-blood origin. However, for most of this period, the Red River settlement was widely seen as an oasis in the wilderness that was able to survive because of unique climatic factors.

At the time when the Hudson's Bay Company absorbed the North West Company in 1821, the total number of men engaged in the fur trade in the area was 2,000 to 3,000,[128] and it is unlikely that there were ever more than 60,000 people, including Native people, living between the Rocky Mountains and Lake Superior at any time in the first half of the nineteenth century, most of whom led nomadic or semi-nomadic existences dictated by the season, the hunt, tribal wars, and trading activities.[129] A period of stability obtained in the region between 1821 and the 1840s, largely as a result of the absence of competition among fur traders. However, the economic position of the Hudson's Bay Company altered drastically in the 1840s. The American settlement frontier was drawing ever closer, and with it came an advance guard of fur traders determined to take over some of the business of the Hudson's Bay Company. Moreover, in 1849, in the famous Sayer trial, a Metis trader who was charged with illegally trafficking in furs and violating the Hudson's Bay Company's claimed monopoly on the fur trade was convicted, but the judge imposed no sentence, in effect providing a licence for the Metis and others to compete with the company.[130] More important, the company's role in the region was about to be overtaken by the agricultural frontier.

While the Metis and country-born population doubled in the Red River area every fifteen to twenty years, that of the Plains Indians seriously declined in the mid-nineteenth century. In 1837–8, a smallpox epidemic ravaged the Canadian Plains tribes and reduced the Assiniboine and Blackfoot populations by two-thirds. Other European diseases carried along the trade routes, such as scarlet fever, measles, influenza, whooping cough, and tuberculosis, took a heavy toll, as did the dissoluteness promoted by American whisky traders in the mid-1860s.[131] By the 1860s, the number of buffalo had begun to dwindle dramatically, and the Metis, who relied on annual buffalo hunts, faced a precarious future. By the 1850s, estimates suggest that only about 18,000 Plains Indians lived in the Northwest.

According to Owram, between 1856 and 1869 the image of the West was transformed in Canadian writings, and political and public discourse, from a semi-arctic wilderness to a fertile garden well adapted to agricultural pursuits. This newly discovered potential allowed the West to be seen as the means by which Canada would be lifted from colony to nation. In the late 1840s, some commentators advanced highly ambitious plans for the connection of the Atlantic and Pacific Oceans, in part driven by the idea of constructing a land route to Asia. Technological developments, in particular the building of the railway, made these proposals vaguely plausible and sparked interest in Imperial circles in Britain. One of the implications of these schemes for a transcontinental railway was that they involved, to some degree, the introduction of settlement into the region. On 14 September 1855, the Toronto *Globe* noted that the last wild land in the western peninsula of Canada West (formerly Upper Canada) had been sold. With this sale, Canadians were threatened with a new and possibly crucial factor – confinement.[132] A small group of expansionists, exemplified by people like George Brown, the editor of the Toronto *Globe,* and subsequently leader of the Reform Party in Canada West, began to promote the idea of western expansionism as the key to Canada's future economic and political development. In July 1857, an expedition formed under the auspices of the Canadian government and led by a University of Toronto professor of chemistry and geology, Henry Youle Hind, left Toronto for the Northwest. The British government also supported a private exploration party sponsored by the prestigious Royal Geographical Society and led by Captain John Palliser. Hind and Palliser, in reports on their explorations, divided the Prairie region into identifiable subregions which defied most of the traditional generalizations, and, by the early 1860s, it had become commonplace in Canada to view large parts of the region as being fertile and capable of sustaining a vast population.[133]

As agriculture assumed greater importance, expansionists began to appeal not only to those in the East who would benefit from annexation through trade, but to those who would go west to take up new farms. The farm, rather than the fur trade or Asia, was now seen as the primary source of development, and there would be a joint extension of settlement and commerce. In terms of external relations, western expansionism would permit the development of a British North American nation with enough power and population to withstand any hostile pressures from the south. By the late 1860s, the idea of expansion became an umbrella solution for all of Canada's problems.[134]

The Pacific coast was the last area of Canada to be settled. The northwestern coast of North America remained unexplored by Europeans until the 1770s. Initially, Spain, Russia, Britain, and the United States competed for control of the North Pacific coast. Eventually, the sector between Russian Alaska and Spanish California was disputed by only Britain and the United States, which in 1818 agreed to joint occupancy of the Oregon Territory. In 1846, the two countries consented to extend the international border along the 49th parallel from the Prairies to the Pacific, and to include Vancouver Island in British jurisdiction. While Captain James Cook, on behalf of the British government, had mapped the Northwest Coast in 1778 in yet one more search for the Northwest Passage, little organized settlement occurred until the middle of the next century.[135]

The agricultural attractions of the far West, especially the Willamette Valley, led to the beginning of American settlement in the late 1820s, with pioneers trekking overland from the mid-continent in covered wagons across the famous Oregon Trail. The first immigrants arrived in Victoria in the 1840s, and were mostly fur traders from the East. Mining began soon after, when coal deposits were found on the east coast of Vancouver Island. In 1848, Vancouver Island was formally established as a British colony and leased to the Hudson's Bay Company for ten years as custodian of British interests in the West. As of 1854, there were no more than 1,000 Europeans living in British Columbia, most of them near Victoria, on Vancouver Island.[136]

To that juncture, the fur trade had dominated the economic and political organization of the region. American maritime fur traders dominated the coastal trade from the mid-1790s until the mid-1820s, by which time the sea otter was virtually extinct as a result of overhunting. The coastal Indians initially functioned as middlemen and traded European goods to interior groups in return for furs. The entry around 1810 of Canadian fur traders from the East into the interior, however, took away much of the Indian middlemen's trade.[137] Native peoples had been living along the Pacific coast for thousands of years. It was estimated that nearly half of the total Indian population of Canada lived in British Columbia at the time of initial European contact in the late eighteenth century. At this time, there may have been more than 60,000 Native people along the coast of what is now British Columbia and in the Alaska Panhandle, and some 30,000 to 40,000 in the interior of British Columbia.[138]

The very modest rate of settlement on the West Coast changed dramatically in 1857 with the discovery of gold in the Fraser River, provoking a major gold rush, attracting thousands of men, mostly from California, including several thousand Chinese and several hundred blacks,[139] who made their way to the interior of British Columbia in the spring of 1858. Some 25,000 immigrants in total arrived in British Columbia in that year. In order to reaffirm its jurisdiction over the region, the British government rushed through Parliament legislation constituting mainland British Columbia a formal British colony on 2 August 1858, and took over direct administration of Vancouver Island from the Hudson's Bay Company. The administration of the two colonies was merged in 1866. By the late 1860s, some 12,000 non-Native people lived in British Columbia, including about 1,000 Chinese.[140]

In order to avoid conflict between Indians and settlers, James Douglas, who was the first governor of the colonies of Vancouver Island and British Columbia, beginning in 1851 purchased the Indians' land before settlement occurred. Between 1850 and 1854, he made fourteen treaties with groups living in areas where Europeans wanted to settle. He purchased in total roughly 380 square miles of land, or about 3 per cent of Vancouver Island, while allowing the Indians to select the land they wished to retain as reserves. When settlement on Vancouver Island grew in the late 1850s, Douglas continued to make efforts to purchase the Indians' lands and set aside reserves. Lack of funds made the process more difficult. The British Colonial Office refused to lend Vancouver Island money for Indian land payments and insisted that funds be raised locally. Thus, after 1859 Indians received no compensation for their lands. Indian reserves were set aside without acquiring title from the Indians to the land on which settlement was occurring.[141]

Conclusions

In reviewing the major features of the process of populating British North America over the almost four centuries between Cabot's discovery of Newfoundland and Confederation, several factors emerge. First, until the Royal takeover of New France in 1663, neither France nor Britain took seriously the challenge of establishing a significant settlement in British North America. Indeed, this remained true for Britain's northern colonies until the Conquest in 1760. Until this time, the French and British colonies in North America were little more than trading posts that were treated as minor pawns by the Imperial powers in recurrent European conflicts.

Second, while various domestic policies both in Britain and in the colonies can be identified that shaped patterns of immigration over the pre-Confederation period, the significance of purely adventitious events unrelated to domestic policies directly bearing on immigration should not be discounted, for example, which explorers sailing under which flags reached which parts of the British North American coastline first in the latter part of the fifteenth and early part of the sixteenth century; the Loyalist immigration influx as a by-product of the American War of Independence in the latter part of the eighteenth century; the closure of the border to American settlers and intensified efforts to attract British immigrants as a result of the War of 1812, which was itself in part a by-product of the European Napoleonic Wars; the potato famines in Ireland in the middle of the nineteenth century; and the impetus lent by the American Civil War to the faltering drive towards Confederation.

Third, the process of settlement had exacted one major set of casualties – Canada's first immigrants, the Native people – whose numbers had been ravaged by European diseases, whose traditional lifestyles had been radically disrupted by economic development, and who had been largely dispossessed of their lands by the relentless advance of the agricultural frontier, leaving them mostly marginalized on remote reserves, where they largely disappeared from the consciousness of most Canadians for most of the century following Confederation. The Imperial civil administration in North America was dominated by two ideas concerning Native Indians in the 1830s: that as a people they were disappearing, and that those who remained should either be removed to communities isolated from whites or else be assimilated, principally as farmers. During the 1830s, an extensive British parliamentary inquiry into the conditions of Aboriginal people throughout the Empire concluded that unregulated frontier expansion had been disastrous for Native people. In 1850 and 1851, two Land Acts were passed by the Canadian legislature, which made it an offence for private individuals to deal with Indians concerning their lands. The nature of Indian land tenure was not elaborated, so that it was unclear what Indian title actually meant. Under the Management of Indian Lands and Properties Act of 1860, Canada took over Indian administration from the Colonial Office, and the commissioner of Crown lands became chief superintendent of Indian affairs.[142] By the early twentieth century the entire Native population of Canada and the United States was less that one million, or ten per cent of the population at the time of initial European contact.[143]

Fourth, the conflicts between the two founding European immigrant races – French and British – dominate much of the history of the pre-Confederation period from the time of the Conquest onwards. The Conquest did not, as it did for the Acadians, lead to the expulsion of the French, but, rather, to the first assimilationist attempt in the form of the Royal Proclamation of 1763, which was predicated on a substantial influx of British immigrants but which, in its absence, failed to submerge the French population or to suppress its basic social, religious, and legal institutions. The Quebec Act of 1774 was a provisional and messy compromise that attempted to recognize some elements of the French reality, while seeking to accommodate British settlers and their institutions. The Constitutional Act of 1791, driven largely by the influx of Loyalists, by creating the two colonies of Upper and Lower Canada attempted to accommodate dual aspirations through a kind of 'separate but equal' strategy, but within Lower Canada the dominance of British migrants in the executive arm of government and in the commerce of the colony meant that the French population was anything but equal, and the extension to them of a popularly elected Legislative Assembly was increasingly seen as a largely empty charade. Following popular uprisings in both Lower and Upper Canada that were interpreted by British authorities as disturbing evidence of the prospect of a new independence movement in North America, the Act of Union of 1840, following Lord Durham's report, in which he stated, in a oft-quoted phrase, that he found 'two nations warring in the bosom of a single state,' was the second attempt at assimilation, this time by merging the two provinces together in a single province with two regions, Canada East and Canada West, on the assumption that British majoritarianism would over time subordinate the French. Instead, during the 1850s and early 1860s, political paralysis set in, as the formation of stable coalitions and governments proved impossible. And so yet another attempt at rapprochement was made, in the form of Confederation in 1867 (which comprised Quebec, Ontario, Nova Scotia, and New Brunswick but did not initially include Newfoundland, Prince Edward Island, the Prairies, or British Columbia), with federalism, on the one hand, providing a substantial measure of provincial autonomy, and bicameralism, on the other, providing equal representation in the Upper House by region, designed to ensure that the smaller provinces would not be overwhelmed by the larger provinces in federal decision making. The shape of Canadian Confederation was thus a direct product of the history of the populating of British North America.

Fifth, the impetus for Confederation was a defensive measure, in significant part driven by external factors, in particular long-standing apprehensions by Canadian colonists of American expansionist ambitions and the threat of absorption.

With Confederation, a major chapter in the history of British North America had come to an end. The beginnings of a geographically far-flung, physically daunting, thinly populated, economically fragile, and culturally conflicted nation had been tenuously stitched together without great enthusiasm and in singularly unromantic and unexalted circumstances. The battle to carve a nation out of a wilderness had been won, but the battle to sustain a nation through the physical, economic, and cultural tribulations that lay ahead had only just begun.

Immigration and the Consolidation of the Dominion, 1867–1896: Fulfilling the Destiny

In 1867, the dream of the architects of Confederation, that of a robust, united Canadian nation stretching from sea to sea, was far from being realized. Although Confederation, comprising Nova Scotia, New Brunswick, and Canada (Quebec and Ontario), was a promising first step, the union itself was as yet neither a complete nor a cohesive one. Both Newfoundland and Prince Edward Island had refused to join the Dominion, the Northwest was still largely under the control of the Hudson's Bay Company, and there existed a formidable repeal movement in Nova Scotia which was a credible threat to that province's continued membership.[1] Moreover, there was the ongoing concern that the United States was interested in expanding into the Canadian West.[2] The challenges facing Prime Minister Macdonald and his new government were formidable.

Within six years, with generous financial inducements, Prince Edward Island and British Columbia had been brought into Confederation, and the Nova Scotia secessionist urges had been mollified. With the acquisition of Rupert's Land and the North-Western Territory, the process of territorial consolidation was nearly complete.[3] Nevertheless, mere land acquisition was not enough, for a successful union depended upon commercial and industrial growth. Macdonald's prescription for economic prosperity was articulated in his National Policy, upon which he campaigned in the federal election of 1878 and which was the primary focus of his subsequent administration. The essential components of this strategy included increased tariffs to stimulate local industry; the completion of the transnational railway to open the West for settlement and link the country by rail from sea to sea; and the promotion of immigration.[4]

Immigration was a key element of industrial growth, for a burgeoning population would both stimulate demand for goods and services and meet the labour-supply needs of industry. Immigration policy was therefore almost exclusively directed at promoting immigration, and in particular towards facilitating the settlement of immigrants in the Canadian West. The West offered a new hinterland, a source of natural resources, a market for Eastern manufacturing, and fertile lands to be settled by an expanding population. An essential element in this strategy of Western settlement, and a condition for British Columbia's incorporation into Confederation in 1871, was the construction of a transnational railway. In linking the country together, the railway would transport raw materials east and immigrants and manufactured goods west.[5]

Aside from being one of the keys to economic prosperity, the settlement of the West was also regarded as an essential check upon American expansionist impulses. It was believed that the resources and potential of the Canadian West were coveted by the United States, and certain events seemed to support this assumption. American congressmen had spoken publicly of the prospect of acquiring the territory.[6] As well, existing transportation and trade links between the Red River settlement and the United States raised concerns that the Red River residents could well be persuaded to join the South unless Canada acquired the territory and proceeded to develop it with the aid of immigrant settlement.

Some also saw in the development of the West a road towards Canadian hegemony in the British Empire. This grandiose picture rested on the belief that, once its enormous wheat-growing potential was tapped, Canada would become an international leader in wheat production. As the major supplier to other British dominions, Canada would hold an enhanced position within the Empire.[7] Somewhat related to this view was the vision of the West as a possible trade route to Asia, opening up new markets not only for Canada, but also for other members of the Empire.[8]

The Canadian government's efforts to attract immigrants to the West were carried out under the auspices of the Department of Agriculture. They included advertising the country's advantages, such as abundant natural resources, good soil, healthy climate, and stable political institutions. Financial inducements such as land grants and transportation assistance to overcome the competition from other immigrant-receiving countries were also offered. Given that the principal focus of immigration policy throughout this period was the promotion of immigration to Canada, it is not surprising that immigration legislation contained relatively few restrictions on entry. Canada's first Immigration Act,[9] of 1869, and subsequent amendments to it, were designed primarily to ensure the safety and protection of immigrants *en route* to and upon arrival in Canada. The few admission prohibitions that were legislated were intended to exclude those with physical disabilities or criminal tendencies, or those who were unable to support themselves upon arrival. These restrictions were not consistently enforced, and in the early years many immigrants who arrived without funds were able to avail themselves of lodging and transportation assistance provided by the federal and the provincial governments.

Despite the governments' promotional work and the relatively few restrictions on entry, the immigration policy of the day failed to reap the desired results. It is for this reason that the first thirty years of the new Dominion are commonly considered a disappointing period for immigration. The numbers certainly support this view, for, although thousands of foreigners passed through Canada every year, only a small proportion settled here. While the exact figures are not known,[10] modern estimates place the number of immigrants who entered Canada between 1867 and 1892 at close to 1.5 million.[11] Yet, most of these arrivals were actually in transit to the United States. In passing through Canada, they were joined by hundreds of other immigrants and Canadian residents who, disillusioned with their prospects in Canada, were attracted by the relative prosperity experienced by the nation to the south. So prevalent was this emigration trend that, in every decade until the turn of the century, more people left Canada than arrived.[12] Even after twenty-five years of vigorous attempts to attract newcomers, the population of Canada was growing at a rate below that of the natural increase.

There were many reasons why Canada was unable to attract and sustain significant new settlement. An economy which, through most of this time, was fragile in part explains the phenomenon, as does the lack of efficient transportation to settlement areas that characterized the early years of the period. Yet, even with the completion of the transnational railway in 1885, Canada did not experience the great surge in immigration that had been anticipated. Stiff competition from other immigrant-receiving countries, such as the United States and other British dominions, was often cited as a principal reason, as was the Canadian land-grant system, which tended to isolate people and make prairie homesteading more difficult. And while all these factors help explain the modest settlement throughout this period, it is also probably the case that, given the state of farming knowledge, not too much more settlement could be expected. For it was painfully evident that settlement in Canada was not just a difficult endeavour, but often a disastrous one. Hundreds of farmers in Manitoba and the Northwest saw their efforts disappear in floods, early frosts, drought, and grasshopper plagues. Prosperity would not come to the prairies until new strains of wheat and new cultivation practices were adapted to the region's particular climate and terrain. It was no coincidence that the great boom in Western wheat growing and in settlement came at the turn of the century, when new grains and cultivation techniques, more suitable to the semi-arid prairies, were introduced.[13]

Because this period was not one of high rates of immigration, its role in the evolution of immigration policy is sometimes overlooked. And while it is true that, measured in numbers of immigrants to Canada, or in terms of the sophistication of the regulatory legislation, the period was less than notable, the policy pursued during this time nevertheless did have an impact on subsequent periods. Many of the promotional strategies that were developed in these years were relied upon later. Moreover, although relatively few in number, the immigrants who came during this time established ethnic communities which helped to attract other immigrants in more prosperous times. Finally, the economic and social difficulties encountered by so many newly arrived immigrants throughout this period sparked debate regarding what type of immigration policy it was in the country's best interest to pursue.

Between 1867 and 1892, various interests could be discerned in the immigration debate, and these interests would remain relatively constant over time. At one end of the spectrum were entrepreneurs and industrialists who favoured a relatively open and flexible immigration policy – one which would ensure a steady supply of workers. Included within this group were the major railway and steamship companies, which viewed immigrants not only as potential labourers, but also as important passengers on their lines and the source of future traffic in terms of goods and materials. At the other end of the spectrum were Canadian workers who, through their union representatives, advocated a tightly controlled immigration policy, one which would ensure that their jobs and wages would not be adversely affected by incoming labourers. Canadian unions were generally not impressed with arguments that a larger consumer base meant more employment opportunities for all.

Others advocated a middle ground, the shape of which depended upon their particular interest. Emigration societies, for example, favoured assisting immigrants, arguing that admitting farmers, child labourers, and female domestic workers not only was a charitable act, but served the best interests of Canada by supplying the country with workers in areas where there was excess demand. As the societies operated almost exclusively out of Britain, their support for an open immigration policy did not necessarily extend to those beyond the British Isles. Canadian expansionists also advocated a relatively open immigration policy and one that favoured British immigrants believed to have the moral character appropriate for the forging of a unique Canadian identity in the West. Amid the various conceptions of the ideal immigration policy, the government pursued a fairly permissive policy on the basis that it was necessary to populate the Dominion with settlers and to support industrialization through the provision of immigrant labour and capital. In this it shared the view of industrialists and entrepreneurs that to place restrictions on immigration would adversely affect economic development, upon which the viability of the country depended.

Promoting the Dominion

LAND POLICIES

Opening Up Lands for Settlement

As discussed in the previous chapter, several leading scientific explorations of the Western frontier during the 1850s had helped to transform the image of the West from wasteland to promised land.[14] With the weight of such scientific conclusions behind it, the Canadian government's purchase of Rupert's Land and the North-Western Territory in 1869 was regarded as a prudent and necessary move. For the next twenty years, the government was intent on consolidating its hold on the West and drawing from it the rewards upon which the decision to purchase it had been based. To be settled, however, the land had to be free of any encumbrances on immigrant occupancy, and that inevitably brought the government into conflict with the First Nations and Metis inhabitants.

At the time the government started negotiating with the Hudson's Bay Company for the purchase of Rupert's Land, there were approximately 25,000 First Nations and 15,000 people of mixed ancestry inhabiting the Canadian West. Within the Red River colony, the latter group made up over 82 per cent of the population, Europeans and First Nations comprising 13 per cent and 5 per cent, respectively. Those of mixed ancestry were not a homogeneous group. The minority of nearly 4,000, mainly Protestant farmers were of British and Indigenous ancestry, while the majority of approximately 6,000 Catholic Metis were of French and Indigenous descent, and were involved in farming as well as trapping, freight carriage, buffalo hunting, and interpreting.[15] Both groups were relatively prosperous and had been represented on the colony's governing council. Neither group, however, was invited to join in the negotiations over the sale of the colony to the government of Canada, a fact they bitterly resented.

Concern over English Canada's intentions with respect to their territory had existed for some time within the Metis community. In the previous decade, the arrival of central Canadian expansionists, who not only openly extolled the manifest destiny of English Canada in the West, but also ridiculed the Metis in the process, was cause for hostility and alarm. Frustrations peaked in 1869, when the newly appointed lieutenant-governor, William McDougall, was sent to establish authority in the colony before the actual legal transfer had taken place. McDougall was met at the border by a group of defiant Metis, led by Louis Riel. MacDougall was refused entry, and Riel and his followers subsequently occupied Fort Garry and established a provisional government.

Macdonald was besieged with requests from English Canada that he suppress the revolt militarily, which became more vehement after Riel's provisional government executed one of their prisoners, Thomas Scott. Macdonald, however, chose instead to negotiate a compromise, influenced in part by the belief that, with the onset of winter, a military expedition would fail. In the end, the government met most of the Metis demands, which were incorporated in the Manitoba Act of 1870. The Red River settlement became the Province of Manitoba, with most of the same rights as other provinces of Canada, except that public lands and natural resources remained under the jurisdiction of the Dominion government. French was recognized as an official language, public support was guaranteed to Roman Catholic schools, and the Metis were guaranteed title to their river lots in addition to a large reserve of land for subsequent generations.

Notwithstanding the protections afforded in the Manitoba Act of 1870, the Metis of Manitoba saw the rights they had won quickly eroded. Having objected to the act while in Opposition, the Liberal government of Alexander Mackenzie proceeded to amend it after winning the federal election of 1874. Guarantees of Metis river-front lots were weakened by more stringent title requirements, which fewer than 20 per cent of the Metis were able to satisfy.[16] In the face of this dispossession, and the influx of English settlers from Ontario, within a few years close to two-thirds of the Metis population had moved farther west or into the United States.[17]

The Metis soon found that their hold on land was no more secure in Saskatchewan. As more and more settlers moved west, the Metis petitioned the government for recognition of their land claims, many of which were located on the Saskatchewan River. The refusal of the federal government to recognize security of tenure led the Metis to form an alliance with other aggrieved settlers of the region and to invite Louis Riel to once again lead their resistance in 1885. Within a month, more than 3,000 troops were dispatched and the rebellion was crushed. The subsequent trial, conviction, and hanging of Riel for treason was applauded in Ontario as a just reward for a renegade revolutionary, and condemned in Quebec as the unjust slaying of a French-Canadian martyr. Not only did the event further polarize the French and English in Canada, but it also cost the Conservative government the support it had once enjoyed in Quebec.[18]

According to government reports, the Metis rebellion had a negative impact upon immigration to the West. For example, in his annual report for 1885, the minister of Agriculture wrote that the North-West Rebellion was a factor in the falling number of arrivals:

> The breaking out of disturbances in the Northwest, of which the most exaggerated and sensational reports were published, both in the United Kingdom and on the Continent, had a very serious effect in hindering the immigration movement. And this was particularly the case as these disturbances took place just at the time the booking season for immigrants was about to begin, and lasted during the whole of the active or spring season. The effect thus produced was disastrous to the immigration interests of Canada, as a whole, and was not by any means confined to the whole of the Northwest.[19]

The quick resolution and imposition of federal authority was regarded as imperative for the restoration of confidence in the Canadian West. In conjunction with other reforms and financial inducements offered to immigrants, it was assumed that peace would be followed by more rapid settlement.

The subjection and dispossession of the Metis in the Canadian West were not the only bitter land-acquisition legacies of the period. Land reform was designed in a way to divest the indigenous population of their holdings on prime settlement lands as well. During the first ten years of Confederation, the Canadian government succeeded in acquiring most of the First Nations lands between Ontario and British Columbia. According to the terms of the treaties, the First Nations gave up all rights, titles, and privileges they held in their lands in return for annuities, reserves, and the right to hunt on Crown land. The unfavourable terms of settlement are explained in part by the fact, that in many instances, the First Nations believed they were selling only temporary use of their land in return for peace, and federal assistance when necessary. Others were compelled to forego their land claims, weakened as they were by disease and starvation. Smallpox had a particularly devastating impact in the West, claiming nearly half the First Nations population of Saskatchewan and Alberta by the early 1870s.[20] In the end, the agreements that the First Nations concluded gave them far less than they had anticipated. Moved to reserves, legally defined as 'minors' whose lives were regulated and controlled by federal agents under the authority of the Indian Act of 1876 (as amended in 1880), Canada's indigenous people saw their independence rapidly eroded. The results, which were to persist throughout the next century, were a bitter legacy of the government's desire to obtain prime agricultural land for new settlement, and its disregard for the rights of those who were its first inhabitants.[21]

Facilitating Homestead Acquisition

Reforms to the land grant system were also designed to facilitate the orderly and expeditious settlement of the West. For most of the eighteenth century, land was given away in large blocks, generally as a reward for military or political service. The recipients often had no intention of settling the land, or no means to do so. As a result, huge tracts of land stood idle, and new settlers often could find available land only at considerable distances from others, depriving them not only of a community of friends, but also of accessible markets.[22] As a way of encouraging a more orderly development of the prairies, the Dominion government divided up the land in the fertile belt into townships, each of which consisted of thirty-six sections. Within each township, two sections were reserved for school lands, the proceeds of the sale of which would go to the province for educational purposes. Another section of the township was reserved for the Hudson's Bay Company. The remaining sections were numbered; odd-numbered sections were reserved for sale or for railways, while even-numbered sections were to be used for homestead grants.[23]

According to the provisions of the Dominion Lands Act of 1872, any male twenty-one years of age or older, and any sole head of a family, upon the payment of a $10 registration fee, could obtain a quarter-section consisting of 160 acres of public homestead land. Title to the land would pass upon the fulfilment of settlement conditions, which included continuous residence on the land for six months of each of the first three years.[24] Over the years, the act was amended to modify the residence and cultivation requirements necessary before a patent would be issued. In 1874, homesteaders were given the option of pre-empting an adjacent quarter-section at government prices.[25] This right of pre-emption was designed to work in the homesteader's favour by providing the opportunity to enlarge the homestead before it was purchased by others. Often, however, it led to speculation, with settlers availing themselves of the pre-emption, often mortgaging their homesteads to do so, in the expectation that the value of the land would rise. Unable to pay for it when due, the farmers lost both the pre-emption and their homesteads. It was primarily for this reason that the option was removed in 1890.[26]

The exclusion of women from acquiring homesteads on the same terms as men under the act[27] led to serious inequities, which are chronicled in the memoirs of Georgina Binnie-Clark, one of the country's early pioneers. Unlike men, only women who were the sole head of a household could acquire a free homestead. The act therefore effectively barred many women from acquiring homesteads and made it more difficult for those who had purchased them for full value to realize a profit as readily as their male neighbours. Observing that homesteading was not as highly profitable a means for independence and wealth for women as for men, Binnie-Clark explains: 'on every side my neighbours had obtained their land as a gift from the Government, or at least one hundred and sixty acres of it, and a further hundred and sixty had been added on the condition of pre-emption, which is by payment of three dollars an acre in addition to the performance of the homestead duties; in this way a farm in every way equal to the one which had cost me five thousand dollars was to be obtained by any man for nine hundred and seventy dollars.'[28]

The discriminatory eligibility criteria in the Dominion Lands Act was the focus of the homesteads-for-women movement, which gained momentum after the turn of the century. Notwithstanding the growing support the movement garnered from grain growers' associations, women's organizations, the Winnipeg Board of Trade, farmers, and journalists, successive federal administrations refused to remove the discriminating provisions in the homesteading legislation. It was not until 1930 that the problem was finally addressed, when the Prairie provinces assumed control over their public lands. Manitoba and Saskatchewan eliminated the provision of homestead grants. Only Alberta amended its legislation and removed the sexual discrimination in eligibility criteria that had frustrated women settlers for decades.[29]

Historians differ as to whether the Dominion government's land-grant policy was a prudent one. At the time, there was a debate within the government as to whether free grants were necessary. Some immigration agents were of the opinion that, without such grants, Canada would be unable to compete with other colonies offering land to immigrants. Critics, however, argued that, as with passage assistance, the land-grant incentive did not necessarily attract the most desirable settler. Subsequent debates have not resolved the issue. Traditionally, the free-land-grant scheme was considered an important promotional tool of the Dominion government, while more modern analysis suggests that the system encouraged premature settlement. Those who support the latter view argue that, because the settlement conditions required continuous residence, homesteaders were forced to commit too much capital and labour to their lands before the tracts were economically viable.[30]

The wisdom of setting aside lands for railways to colonize has similarly been debated. At the time the practice was promulgated, it was argued that it would be in the railways' best interest to promote their settlement lands vigorously and price them competitively, because settlers meant more rail traffic. Settlers sometimes complained, however, that the practice left them 'land-locked,' bordered on either side by railway land which was often unoccupied. It was also said that railway lands were frequently sold to speculators who held their properties until they could make a handsome profit through resale. More often, however, the railway reservation system was considered a prudent policy.[31] In his history of the Canadian Pacific Railway's (CPR's) land and colonization policies in the West, James B. Hedges writes that, throughout the 1880s, the company actively promoted the settlement of government land, recognizing that the value of its own land would be enhanced once the government's homesteads had been purchased. Hedges also claims that the CPR was genuinely committed to selling its lands to settlers rather than to speculators, and did what it could to ensure that this was done.[32] While exact figures are not known, Hedges's research suggests that, of the CPR's land sales during this period that were not made to large colonization companies, most were made to homesteaders, who, having already established themselves on free homesteads, were able to increase their holdings by purchasing adjoining railway lands.

One issue that is not in dispute is that the government's practice of reserving lands for colonization companies was an unqualified disaster. By 1881, it was clear that the costs of the CPR were spiralling. The government, seeking to avoid committing further public tax revenues to the endeavour, needed alternative sources of income. One such source was the sale of public lands outside the CPR belt to colonization companies for $2 per acre. The purchase price was payable over a five-year period, during which time the companies undertook to construct communication links between their lands and already-existing settlements, and to promote the settlement of the area. Once the land was settled, the companies would receive a rebate of $1 per acre. By 1883, twenty-six colonization companies, many of them owned by friends of Macdonald's government, held close to 3 million acres of land.[33]

Almost from the beginning, the scheme was criticized. Companies that did engage in immigrant promotion were accused of using dishonest recruitment techniques, distributing false information about settlement in Canada by highlighting the success that settlers could look forward to and failing to mention the hardships that were involved. Many companies simply did not engage in promotion at all, preferring to hold the lands themselves in expectation that their value would rise. So disappointing was the scheme that, three years after its inception, the government decided to discontinue it.

According to Norman Macdonald, in the end only one of the twenty-six companies had fulfilled the conditions of their agreement; the rest defaulted and were liquidated. Although speculation was clearly a problem with the scheme, it was not the only one. Many companies fully expected that the completion of the CPR would attract more immigrants than actually came. The expenses involved in attracting immigrants and in making the agreed-upon improvements to the land were more than anticipated and were not offset by sales. Moreover, the fact that the lands were isolated made them unattractive to potential immigrants, and particularly so as long as railway companies sold their land at prices below those that the colonization companies had paid.[34]

Other colonization schemes undertaken for chiefly charitable reasons bore mixed results. Throughout the 1880s, several attempts were made to assist indigent persons in Britain settle on Canadian land. An amendment to the Dominion Lands Act in 1881 provided that organizations and individuals could advance money to assist in the travel and initial homesteading expenses of needy immigrants. These funds would then become a charge upon the homestead, up to an amount of $500. The debt and the interest had to be discharged before the government would issue title to the land. Those who participated in this scheme included the British government, charitable organizations, and private philanthropists.[35] Although the exact number of participants is not known, these schemes probably attracted several hundred immigrant families, many of whom were unsuccessful in establishing themselves on the land as intended.

Some argued that the primary reason that the philanthropic schemes generally bore disappointing results was that giving people the opportunity to homestead simply on the basis of their impecuniosity was not, in the long run, beneficial. Poverty did not in itself mark a person with the characteristics necessary to become a successful settler. And while it was undoubtedly true that many of these assisted immigrants were not prepared for the rigours of Canadian farming life, it is also probable that, like many other failed homesteaders of the period, they were simply worn down by the vagaries of the climate, the isolation of the settlements, and unfamiliarity with the grains and cultivation techniques necessary to make farming on the prairies a success.[36]

Group Settlement

As Aboriginal people were being divested of their title to lands in the West, other settlers were entering the area to take their place. Western settlement throughout this time was made up of both migrants from eastern parts of Canada and new immigrants, primarily from Britain and other European countries. In its efforts to attract newcomers, the government promoted group settlement, with the result that, throughout this period, several relatively substantial land reserves were set aside for particular immigrant groups. Those who took advantage of these efforts included Mennonite, Scandinavian, and Hungarian immigrants.

The setting-aside of large tracts of land for immigrant groups bore mixed results. The Mennonite group-settlement schemes were among the more successful. From its beginnings in the sixteenth century, the Mennonite sect had experienced persecution and consequent migrations in search of areas where they could practise their faith freely. Those who came to Canada in the nineteenth century were originally from Prussia and had migrated to southern Russia in the eighteenth century, assured by Catherine the Great that their religious practices and beliefs would be respected. There they developed prosperous theocratic communities whose viability was put in jeopardy by the Russification policies imposed by Tsar Alexander II in 1871. Many saw emigration to the New World as the only option for maintaining their faith and independence. For its part, Canada did its best to secure as many of these agriculturalists as possible, offering generous reserves of land in Manitoba, passage assistance, settlement loans, and sectarian freedom, including the right to control their own education and to affirm rather than swear oaths. Although the lands available in the United States were reportedly more attractive than those in Canada, the American refusal to grant religious concessions was determinative for the more orthodox members of the sect. While most of their compatriots chose the United States, the more conservative Mennonites decided to immigrate to Canada. In addition to

Canadian government assistance, the Mennonites also received loans from Mennonite colonies throughout the world, as well as from other sympathetic religious sects and Russian exiles. By 1874, more than 1,400 families had settled in southern Manitoba. Three years later, more than 7,000 had established themselves in the province.[37]

While they initially experienced hardship, resulting from grasshopper plagues and heavy rains in some regions, by the 1880s the Mennonite communities were thriving. The success of those who had settled in treeless areas west of the Red River reinforced the expansionists' belief in the West, for the Mennonite prosperity challenged the old assumption that the open prairie was not conducive to agriculture. Their self-reliance and industry were praised by government officials and noted in the Western press. In one article, published in the *Manitoba Free Press* in 1876, the Winnipeg land agent described the Mennonites as the best settlers that had so far come to Manitoba: 'No man could believe what these people have done in so short a time ... In my three weeks travel over the Province I have seen nothing as regards the industry equal to the Mennonites.'[38] Equally impressive was their commitment to discharge their government loan of $100,000, which they managed to do, including interest, within the ten-year prescribed period. This led the minister of the Interior to comment that 'in all the history of our country there is not to be found a case in which a company or an individual has more faithfully met his obligation to the government than has been the case here.'[39]

Although the Immigration Committee of the House of Commons was in favour of bringing to the Canadian West all the 60,000 Mennonites in southern Russia,[40] by the end of the 1870s the movement had slowed down. According to Department of Agriculture reports, Russia's war with Turkey had led to a severe depreciation of Russian currency. Many Mennonites were not able to leave, unless willing to sustain heavy losses in the sale of their properties. Additionally, as the financial situation of the more well-to-do worsened, they were less willing to aid their indigent brethren by providing assisted passage.[41] Mennonite emigration would not resume again in significant numbers until the next decade.

The granting of land reserves and religious concessions to the Mennonites was the first such arrangement the Canadian government had adopted for a particular immigrant group. At the time, these inducements were regarded as necessary, for the Mennonites, considered to be austere, hard-working agriculturalists, represented exactly the type of settler Canada wanted but would be unable to secure unless granted the concessions that Canada's more competitive neighbour refused to offer. As successful as these inducements were in attracting thousands of Mennonite pioneers, they also sowed the seeds of conflict. By 1881, at which time the Mennonite land reserves were expected to have been filled, only seven of the eighteen townships set aside for them were occupied. The government came under increasing pressure to open up the reserves for sale to other settlers. The reserves, it was argued, not only tied up land which could be used for settlers immediately, but also discouraged people from remaining in the province of Manitoba. As James Trow, chairman of the House of Commons Select Committee on Agriculture, explained, 'a very large proportion of this Province is set apart by reservations of various kinds which retard its progress and development seriously. I am persuaded that hundreds of intending set-tlers will not remain in the Province on account of these reserves. Leaving the settled portions and travelling through the reserves for miles to new settlements, without roads, cannot but be very discouraging.'[42]

The Mennonites objected to the opening-up of the reserves, and for years the federal government vacillated on the issue. Norman Macdonald speculates that the Cabinet was caught between Parliamentarians repre-senting Mennonite regions and those who represented other districts in the province.[43] Eventually the land was sold to other settlers. However, the sale of the land did not mark the end of controversies arising from the special concessions granted to the Mennonite immigrants of the 1870s. Forty-five years later, objections would be raised over military exemptions provided to some Mennonite groups which released them from compul-sory military service during the First World War.[44]

Hundreds of Jews were among the other refugees from Russia who availed themselves of group-settlement opportunities in the Canadian West. Following the assassination of Tsar Alexander II, in March 1881, violent pogroms took place throughout Russia, and hundreds of Jews were massacred, while others were systematically turned out of their homes and ordered from their villages. Prime Minister Macdonald was receptive to the admission of Russian Jewish refugees on the basis that those with farm-ing experience could help populate the West, and wealthy Jewish entre-preneurs could put their capital and expertise to use in the development of the Canadian economy. Having authorized immigration officials to set aside some land for the Russian Jews, the prime minister revealingly ex-plained that a 'sprinkling of Jews in the Northwest would be good' for they would 'at once go in for peddling and politicking, and be of as much use in the new country as cheap jacks and chapmen.'[45]

The first party of more than 200 Russian Jewish refugees to arrive in Canada in 1882 faced formidable obstacles to their resettlement. The land grants promised to many who intended to settle in the West were not made; leaving them stranded in temporary immigration sheds in Winnipeg. The federal government refused to accept any responsibility for their maintenance, and the small Jewish community in Winnipeg was left to provide for them as best as they could. A downturn in the economy limited the refugees' employment prospects, and violence from other workers threatened those who sought employment on the CPR outside Winnipeg.[46] When the federal government and the Jewish community finally settled on an appropriate piece of land for the new arrivals, the plan was abandoned after neighbouring Mennonites objected to living beside Jews. Of the settlements that were established, one was abandoned within six years, owing to a combination of circumstances, including early frosts, summer droughts, and the farming inexperience of many of the refugees. Eventually a number of settlements succeeded, most notably in Wapella and Hirsh, Saskatchewan.[47] The latter was purchased with the financial assistance of German financier Baron Maurice de Hirsh in response to the plight of many American-bound Jewish refugees who had been stranded in Canada because of lack of financial means and the imposition of more stringent American admission criteria in 1891.[48] By the turn of the century, the Jewish population of Canada was approximately 17,000, almost ten times that in 1880.[49]

Hungarian immigrant colonies were also established in the West throughout this period. The first groups came from the United States, where, through the efforts of Count Paul d'Esterhazy, several hundred decided to leave the mines and the iron foundries of Pennsylvania for the promise of the Canadian West.[50] Although the initial settlement in Manitoba was unsuccessful, others which formed in Saskatchewan did manage to survive the initial hardships of unusually cold winters and prairie fires.[51] The Hungarian settlements in Canada were augmented by new settlers from Hungary throughout the 1890s and, as was the case with other eastern European groups, their numbers were to rise substantially throughout the subsequent decade.

Land reserves were also set aside in Manitoba and the Northwest for Scandinavian communities. Scandinavian immigrants were considered to be among the most desirable immigrants for their reputed rugged, hard-working, and frugal natures. Despite the high emigration rates of Scandinavians and Canada's efforts to induce them to the Canadian West, the United States was the most preferred destination for Scandinavian immigrants, whose numbers started to decline in the 1890s as employment opportunities in the developing areas of their own countries improved.

The most significant Nordic immigration to Canada during this period came from Iceland. Several thousand Icelanders immigrated to Canada in the 1870s, discouraged by the conditions in their homeland, where farming involved severe adversity and meagre rewards. The difficulties associated with farming in Iceland were exacerbated in 1875, when volcanic eruptions on the island destroyed many farms and resulted in significant losses of human and animal life. Throughout the 1880s, emigration rates were high, as the Icelandic economy suffered from losses in its farming and fishing industries, as well as from low prices for its exports, and relatively high prices for imported goods. Canada was eager to secure a significant share of this emigration movement because Icelanders were considered prime settlers. As one Canadian immigration agent in Scandinavia described them, 'they are a hardy, industrious, frugal race – the oldest type of Scandinavians,' who were excellent herdsmen and fishermen and 'well inured to a northerly climate.'[52] By way of inducement, Canada offered reduced ocean-passage rates, free rail transportation to Winnipeg, and land reserves for colonization.

Having unsuccessfully attempted settlement in the Muskoka and Ottawa regions of Ontario, the initial Icelandic immigrants moved to the Red River area of Manitoba, where they were provided with a reserve on the west shore of Lake Winnipeg, which they named 'New Iceland.' The descriptions of their initial settlement years not only illustrate the rigours of the Canadian West, but also provide eloquent testament to the stamina of those who endured them: 'Deaths were frequent among both grown-ups and children. It was a miracle that anyone survived the hardships and the suffering to which we were subjected: hardship of travel; poor accommodation; food generally unsatisfactory and particularly for the children and the ailing. Nor was there a doctor available in the case of need. It was, indeed, rashness thus to endanger the peoples' lives.'[53]

In addition to these initial hardships, the Icelandic colony was devastated by an outbreak of smallpox in 1877. The colony was cut off from the outside world by an enforced quarantine, which added to their misery. Neighbouring Aboriginal villages were also decimated by the outbreak of the disease: in one case, an entire community of 200 people died. In the Icelandic settlement, one-third of the population of approximately 1,500 contracted the disease, and 100 people died.[54]

The passing of the smallpox epidemic did not signify the end of adversity for the colony, for a series of unusually wet seasons, and the consequent destruction of crops, prompted many to leave the settlement. By 1881, over half the colony had left for the United States, while many of the remainder settled on higher ground or moved to Winnipeg, leaving behind approximately sixty families in the original settlement. Gradually, however, the settlement began to prosper as a steady stream of immigrants entered the colony, raising its population to about 1,500 by 1884. Four years later, the population of the settlement was reported to have been more than 5,000, with most of the settlers involved in fishing, stock raising, and agriculture.[55] By this time, several other Icelandic settlements had been established in other parts of Manitoba and in the Northwest. In addition, throughout the 1880s, the Icelandic population of Winnipeg grew substantially. By the end of the decade, it had become an important centre of Icelandic community life, where several Icelandic newspapers were published, and cultural, literary, and religious societies were established. In 1893, the commissioner of Dominion lands estimated that more than 10,000 Icelanders had settled in Manitoba and the Northwest.[56]

ADVERTISING THE WEST

At the same time that it was pursuing land policies to facilitate Western settlement, the government also dispatched immigration agents to the United States and overseas to proclaim the relative advantages of Canada and to solicit, in particular, agriculturalists with enough means to establish themselves in Canada, farm labourers, and domestic workers. Agents were instructed to discourage the immigration of clerks, merchants, and professionals. Industrial labourers and workers in resource-extraction activities were assisted in immigrating to Canada, according to the demand for their labour.[57]

Initially both the federal and the provincial governments employed overseas immigration agents, both levels of government having been accorded joint responsibility over immigration by the terms of the Constitution Act, 1867 (formerly known as the British North America Act).[58] By 1874, however, it was clear that the practice involved considerable duplication, waste of resources, and in some cases actual conflict, which reportedly had an 'injuriously prejudicial effect on the minds of intending immigrants.' It was therefore decided at a dominion-provincial conference in that year that the federal minister of Agriculture would be vested with the sole responsibility for promoting immigration to Canada from abroad. The provinces were to discontinue their independent agencies in favour of appointing subagents to the Canadian government offices in London to represent their respective interests.[59]

In Britain, permanent immigration agents were appointed in London, Dublin, Belfast, and Glasgow. When the office of the Canadian high commissioner to London was established in 1880, all immigration work done in Britain and on the Continent came within his jurisdiction. It was thought that the involvement of the high commissioner would add prestige to the work.[60] Immigration agents within Britain travelled extensively, giving lectures on Canada, setting up displays at local fairs and markets, putting up posters of Canada in post offices and railway stations, sending maps of Canada to schools, and distributing pamphlets describing the country's many attractions. Paid advertisements were also placed in British newspapers, and a news service was established to inform the British press about events in Canada. Immigration agents also wrote letters to the press documenting cases of those who had successfully emigrated to and settled in Canada. These letters were frequently intended to counteract the negative image of Canada conveyed by unhappy British immigrants who had returned home after experiencing difficulties in the Canada. The work of the immigration agents was aided by representatives of steamship companies, who engaged in promotional work of their own. Booking agents were also involved in the promotion of Canada, receiving commissions not only from the Canadian government, but also from the transportation company upon whose line they booked passengers to Canada. Promotional work in Britain, although not garnering the volume of immigrants the government desired, nevertheless was relatively successful. Of the one million immigrants who are estimated to have come to Canada between 1867 and 1890, approximately 60 per cent were from the British Isles.[61]

Promotional activities in the United States were similar to those in Britain, although the focus of immigration agents was somewhat different. In the United States, Canadian agents focused on attracting agriculturalists and repatriating Canadians, particularly French Canadians, who had moved south. Initially their work was concentrated in the East and the Midwest. Immigration agents were assigned specific territories, which they, in turn, consigned to subagents, who were given commissions for every agriculturalist they persuaded to come to Canada. Immigrations agents were responsible for giving lectures, distributing information, providing advice on available settlement lands in Canada, and protecting settlers *en route* to Canada from being persuaded by American immigration agents to remain in the United States.

Although there was some movement from south to north, it did not compare with that in the opposite direction. As long as land remained available in the American Midwest, there was very little incentive to leave for Canada, where the climate was more severe, and employment opportunities generally less abundant. Other factors also militated against American immigration. One of these was the clause in the CPR charter which gave it an exclusive monopoly on the territory south of its main line for twenty years. This prevented the opening of connecting rail lines between the CPR and American railways, with the result that Americans interested in going to the Canadian Northwest had to travel by way of Winnipeg, which was not a direct route. Another factor which reportedly discouraged American immigration was the Riel Rebellion of 1885, which was reported in the American press in lurid and exaggerated terms comparable to the depiction of Aboriginal massacres in the American West.[62]

While American emigration to Canada was generally not very popular, it nevertheless was attractive to a few groups of people. Among these were American labourers, who came to Canada, usually on a temporary basis, in response to employment opportunities. For example, construction of the western leg of the CPR attracted American labourers and skilled workers such as carpenters, bridge builders, and mechanics. As well, with the increased tariffs imposed by the Macdonald government, many American enterprises decided to establish themselves in Canada, and brought in skilled workers to do so. In the early 1890s, however, depressed economic conditions in both Canada and the United States resulted in very little movement in either direction across the international frontier.[63]

Cattlemen were among the other Americans who came to Canada throughout the 1880s. According to Marcus Lee Hansen, stock raising was a profitable exercise, and in the early part of the decade American ranchers settled in the southern regions of present-day Alberta, where the land and climate were well suited to year-long grazing. For twenty-five years, ranchers dominated this area until crowded out by incoming settlers. Although the owners of the farms were often Englishmen or Canadians, the cowboys and the herds were generally from the United States, and the American cow towns on the other side of the border were supply areas as well as marketing points for Canadian stock.[64]

While the Canadian Northwest appealed more to American cattlemen than to American farmers, there was one notable exception. A series of American anti-polygamy laws and attempted prosecutions under these laws near the end of the century led to a migration of Mormons north to Canada. One of the first pioneers was Ora Card. In 1887, he brought with him eight families to settle in Alberta, near present-day Cardston. In several months, the colony had grown to close to 100 people; within a few years, several hundred had settled in the area. One of the reasons for the success of the colony was that the Mormons were familiar with farming in dry conditions and, in particular, were experienced in irrigation techniques. They developed a sugar-beet industry, which found many markets in Canada and the United States. The growing prosperity of the colony attracted other immigrants with the result that, by the turn of the century, there were more than 3,000 Mormons in southern Alberta. In 1902, Cardston was incorporated into a village. Over the next thirty years, the Mormon community in Canada continued to grow, so that, by 1914, the community numbered more than 13,000 persons, the majority of whom were in Alberta.[65]

Canadian promotional activities in Europe required a different approach from that which was pursued in Britain and the United States, because many European states were opposed to their nationals' emigrating. Although only Russia expressly forbade the emigration of its citizens, other European governments either prohibited or limited the dissemination of emigration literature and the work of foreign immigration agents. Germany was particularly restrictive, as one Ontario agent learned in 1873, upon being incarcerated there for violating German emigration laws. Emigration propaganda was also prohibited in Austro-Hungary, Switzerland, Italy, and the Scandinavian countries, and was restricted in Belgium and France.[66]

The first Dominion immigration agents posted in Europe were stationed in Antwerp and Paris in 1872. Their work was aided by travelling agents who were responsible for disseminating information on Canada throughout the Continent. Permanent agents often complained about the work of the travelling agents, alleging that they were inexperienced and ineffectual, and often harmed the work of promotion more than they aided it. According to Norman Macdonald, frequently these complaints were justified. The travelling agents often were political appointees who used their assignments as a way of securing a European holiday at public expense. Unlike permanent agents, they generally were not familiar with the areas they travelled in and were more inclined to give an overly positive image of life in Canada: 'In time they came to be regarded as a bunch of "noisy, boasting, bragging, blustering and flatulent story-tellers" who "cracked and chattered through the country and in the press" to the discredit of the Dominion Government. They raved about the few who succeeded ... but ignored the thousands who failed.'[67]

Gradually the government relied less on the travelling agents and fa-voured less flamboyant types of promotion, such as the use of booking agents. Booking agents were provided with literature on Canada, which they then passed on to subagents to distribute more or less inconspicu-ously. In later years, beginning around 1890, the government adopted another promotional scheme. It combined with railway and steamship companies to offer financial assistance and free transportation to immi-grants who had succeeded in Canada and who were willing to return temporarily to their countries of origin and promote the advantages of the Dominion. Within a few years of the plan's initiation, however, it was felt that these 'return men' had not appreciably affected the flow of im-migrants to Canada. Since their return passage and expenses were guar-anteed, regardless of their work, there was little incentive to use the trips as anything more than free vacations. A new plan was thus adopted which provided free transportation one way only, the return ticket and further compensation depending entirely on the person's success in soliciting settlers for Canada.

Other forms of abuse facing the government in its promotional en-deavours involved the agents of steamship companies, who, in an effort to secure their commissions, falsely represented conditions in Canada to prospective immigrants. Inland immigration agents reported that, as a re-sult, immigrants were coming to Canada without funds and, not having occupations for which the country was in need, were often unable to find employment. In 1879, an order-in-council was passed, in part to address these concerns; it prohibited the landing in Canada of indigents or pau-pers, unless the master of the ship deposited sufficient funds to provide temporary assistance and cover inland travel expenses.[68] In addition, the termination of commissions paid by the government to steamship agents was credited, in 1882, with reducing the number of poor immigrants and those unfit for life in Canada.[69] In 1890, commissions were partially re-sumed for those who were booked to Manitoba, the Northwest Territories, and British Columbia.

False representations of conditions in Canada were not made solely by the agents of steamship companies. Promotional material, in general, whether issued by private concerns or by the federal and provincial gov-ernments, frequently exaggerated the ease with which immigrants could establish themselves in Canada. In their enthusiasm to attract settlers, the writers of promotional pamphlets were inclined to turn the country's rela-tive disadvantages into strengths. It was frequently asserted that the harsh Canadian climate would strengthen both mind and body. Only the strong could endure its rigours, giving rise to an energetic, self-reliant, healthy race.[70] The clear, crisp air supposedly invigorated the mind, and the long winters encouraged people to pursue intellectual activities. It was even alleged that, compared with the moisture-laden air of the British Isles, Canada's dry air heightened perception and mental acuity.[71] In his book on the resources and possibilities of Canada, the Reverend F.A. Wightman even went so far as to suggest that the 'bright, crisp, frosty air of winter' actually was 'most conducive to agriculture,' for the frost on the soil acted almost like a fertilizer 'in a manner more complete than any chemical or mechanical appliances could possibly be made to do at any cost.'[72]

According to George Parkin, who also wrote on the comparative advantages of Canada, the rigours of Canada's northern climate protected the country from those who were lazy and unmotivated. It 'squeezes out for a part of the year the "tramp" and "swagger" class, – the incorrigible loafer,' who in winter generally 'shift[ed] to a warmer latitude' in the United States. The United States, he continued, provided a 'permanent barrier to the influx of the weaker races.' Unlike Canada, the United States was bound to be held back by the inevitable 'black zone across the South, and the increasing attraction of the warm Middle States for the races of Southern Europe.' These groups in the United States, he predicted, would 'indefinitely complicate the processes of national development, and qualify the undoubted industrial advantage of varied production.'[73] In an attempt to counter competition from the United States, some promoters suggested that the milder climate there was actually harmful to human health. Stagnant ponds, which were prevalent in American Western states but rare in the Canadian West, were said to be a source of noxious effluvia which 'poison the atmosphere, and fever and death frequently result.' Charles Mair warned people of breezes from the United States which arrived carrying the 'dim edge of fever, the dread of pestilence and famine.'[74]

Other points of comparative advantage mentioned in the literature of the day were both the size of Canada and the superior quality of its soil. The fact that so much of the country remained to be settled was used to tout the enormous possibilities awaiting those interested in tapping its mineral and agricultural wealth. The soil was heralded as being superb for cultivation, and no mention was made of the infertile belt identified by Hind and Palliser. Surpassing Wightman's claim that the frost provided a natural fertilizer, George Grant wrote of lands that were so rich as to not need fertilizer.[75] Areas with little rainfall were depicted as having soil with incredible retentive abilities that, together with the abundance of rivers, ensured adequate irrigation. Treeless areas, while admittedly lacking in lumber for building and firewood, were portrayed as being capable of supporting trees so that, once a settler had become established, trees could be planted and expected to grow well.[76]

The effect of such inflated claims concerning the climate and soil conditions of the West was that immigrants were led to believe that they could establish themselves with ease and readily profit from their homesteads within the first few years of arrival. The approach would eventually prove counter-productive, as hundreds of settlers ill-prepared for the rigours of Canadian homesteading left in bitterness for the United States.

TRANSPORTATION POLICIES

Improving Ocean Travel and the Reception of Immigrants

In the early nineteenth century, the conditions of cross-Atlantic travel were often appalling because of the great demand for transportation by many anxious to leave their depressed conditions at home and a corresponding unwillingness of ship owners to provide anything but the barest of necessities to their desperate passengers. As a result, ships were typically overcrowded, and often unseaworthy, and passengers were not provided with the necessary provisions to sustain good health, such as clean drinking water and adequate food. Successive regulations governing the safety of ocean travel enacted by the British Parliament and colonial legislatures had, by the middle of the century, helped to reduce the incidence of death aboard ships. Nevertheless, regulations continued to be circumvented. Captains often did not provide sufficient amounts of food, and there were reports of shipmasters that showed inspectors good food stocks only to exchange them, after embarking, for unsound ones in ports along the coast of Ireland. Moreover, passengers were harassed by the captain and crew and charged exorbitant rates for basic foodstuffs.[77] Deaths on board were not uncommon, especially among babies, who died from dysentery brought on by lack of nutrition.[78]

The introduction of steamship travel contributed to the marked reduction of deaths in transit. In 1870, more than 90 per cent of those coming to Canada were arriving on board steamships rather than on sailing vessels. Although passage on them was more expensive, steamships cut the travel time across the ocean by a month and were generally more spacious and sanitary than sailing ships. As the reports of the medical officer at Grosse Isle, Quebec, illustrated, however, too many ships were still able to evade inspection, with the result that more deaths were occurring than reported, and noxious diseases such as cholera, yellow fever, smallpox, typhoid, and measles were entering the country undetected.

One of the first steps the Dominion government took towards ensuring the safety of passengers on board immigrant ships, and preventing the spread of contagion in Canada, was to incorporate many of the ship-safety regulations of the British Parliament and of colonial legislatures in the Immigration Act of 1869.[79] Canada's first immigration legislation focused primarily on the protection of immigrants from the health hazards of ocean travel and from exploitation by unscrupulous ship captains, inn-keepers, merchants, and others providing services to immigrants. Included in its provisions were limits on the number of passengers ships were per-mitted to carry, and a requirement that passenger lists be provided to quarantine officers before embarkation. Other provisions in the act were designed to protect passengers from extortion by shipmasters and their crew. There were few restrictions on entry, although ship captains were to indicate on their passenger lists those who were insane, deaf, blind, or infirm. If such a person was considered likely to become a public charge, the collector of customs was authorized to collect a $300 bond from the shipmaster for any expenses that might be incurred on that person's be-half within three years of landing. The act also contained a provision authorizing the Cabinet to prohibit the landing of destitute immigrants unless the captain of the ship transporting them deposited a sum suffi-cient to cover the destitutes' temporary support and travel expenses within Canada.[80]

To further improve passenger safety, in 1872, the government passed An Act Relating to Quarantine.[81] This act required all vessels (except Canadian mail steamers) that had come from an infected port, or that had experienced a death or outbreak of disease on board, to report for inspec-tion at Grosse Isle. Together with the provisions of the Immigration Act, the quarantine regulations helped to check the abuses and risks long associated with ocean travel. For years, however, the medical officer in charge of Grosse Isle complained that they simply were not sufficient be-cause exemptions, circumvention of the regulations, and insufficient fines weakened their effect.[82] Finally, in 1887, the quarantine regulations were amended to require all vessels entering the St Lawrence to be inspected by a medical officer before landing.[83]

In addition to making ocean travel safer, the Dominion government also endeavoured to make immigrants feel both secure and welcome upon their arrival. Typically, immediately after their landing, immigrants were accosted by porters, tradesmen, innkeepers, booking agents, and others intent on exploiting their vulnerability through fraud, extortion, or excessive rates for services rendered. The Immigration Act of 1869 attempted to prevent these abuses by requiring, among other things, that those soliciting business from immigrants first obtain a special licence to do so. Inns and boarding-houses had to have a list of their prices clearly displayed and were not allowed to place a lien on the property of an immigrant for payment of a bill exceeding five dollars.[84] In addition, the government assigned agents to meet immigrant ships and assist immigrants in finding temporary lodging and making their travel connections to other parts of the country.

Eventually, reception centres were constructed in major cities such as Halifax, Montreal, Quebec, Kingston, Toronto, and Winnipeg. Here immigrants could stay upon arrival for a few days and prepare for their final destination. Meals were offered at reasonable rates, and advice was provided on such things as the localities where work could be found and the best route to take to get there. Permanent immigration officials were appointed in the chief immigrant-receiving centres to oversee the settlement of immigrants within their region and to report annually on their progress. These officials were required to keep lists of all immigrants coming to their jurisdiction and were responsible for advising newcomers on available lands and employment opportunities. In addition, immigration agents were posted on trains to provide information and to ensure that the needs of passengers were being met and that they were not exploited *en route*. Agents were also provided to help settlers select homesteads.

Special initiatives were undertaken with respect to the reception of female immigrants coming to Canada as domestic workers. Throughout this period, there was an unfulfilled demand for domestic workers. The major reason was that Canadian women preferred higher-paid factory work to the poor pay, long hours, and low status of domestic employment. To fill the demand for domestic help, private Canadian recruitment agencies worked with the Canadian government and English benevolent organizations[85] in the recruitment of domestic workers from Great Britain. The government provided reduced passage rates for women so selected; and private agencies, in addition to identifying prospective employers, also advanced money to cover the remaining fare, which was later deducted from the women's wages. Steps were taken to ensure that the overseas journey was free from sexual harassment. Amendments to the Immigration Act in 1892 prohibited seduction and sexual intercourse between ship's officers or seamen and female immigrants.[86] As well, matrons were required to be on board ships to protect female passengers, and special immigration agents were assigned to help women disembark and find accommodation and employment. Women who were destined for other parts of the country were transported in special railcars accompanied by a travelling agent who was responsible for ensuring that the women were met by a government representative, whose duty it was to see that they were placed in respectable employment situations.

Throughout the 1880s, the protection of women immigrants was an issue frequently raised in the Department of Agriculture's annual reports. In 1882, a sensational story in the Toronto *Globe* which suggested that women arriving in Montreal were being lured into prostitution prompted an investigation. The investigating committee, consisting primarily of representatives of several English benevolent societies, received testimony from the Montreal chief of police, the chief of the Montreal Detective Force, immigration agents stationed in Montreal, and the general manager of the Grand Trunk Railway, all of whom denied that any 'girls' had been 'seduced from the path of virtue.' Given the testimony of the law-enforcement officials and immigration agents, the committee concluded that the report was erroneous and that all 'immigrant girls' to Canada were well protected 'as to morality.'[87]

The issue of the protection of women immigrants continued to be of concern, however, as reflected in the 1884 annual report of the Canadian high commissioner in London. He recommended better reception and supervision of female immigrants in the cities and the large towns until they were able to secure employment, as well as the provision of a home they could go to in the event that they lost their jobs.[88] Several private organizations undertook to assist in these ways, among the most prominent being the Women's National Immigration Society, which had offices in Montreal and in Quebec City. Also, in 1887, the federal government established the position of superintendent of female immigration to oversee the settlement of single women in Canada.[89]

Overseas- and Inland-Travel Assistance

Throughout this period, there were various public and privately funded schemes to overcome the financial disincentives facing immigrants to Canada. Within the publicly funded sphere, overseas and inland transportation assistance was offered to certain groups of immigrants. The former was provided by the warrant system, whereby the federal government entered into arrangements with shipping lines to provide for reduced passage for approved immigrants. The reductions were usually applied to agricultural labourers and domestic workers, of whom the country was in need for the entire period, and were occasionally applied to other labourers in years when their services were in great demand.[90] The warrant system did not involve repayment at a later date. It was open to all immigrants coming within the appropriate occupations, with the exception of those who were sick, blind, criminal, or 'otherwise undesirable.'[91] Applications for assistance had to be accompanied by an attestation of the applicant's intention to settle in Canada and a certificate of good character signed by an official such as a clergyman or magistrate.

Inland-passage assistance also offered aid to those immigrants in need of travel funds within Canada. Prior to Confederation, passes covering inland travel from points of embarkation to points of destination were given rather freely by colonial governments as an inducement to settlement. Abuse of the system, particularly by those who used the funds to travel to the United States, led to the restriction of the practice to those immigrants who were in need of funds and who intended to settle in Canada. The problem, however, was in determining the validity of such claims. Immigration agents had no means of checking whether recipients actually settled in Canada. Abuses of the system continued as booking agents, in particular, were known to advise their clients to claim poverty so as to qualify for an inland-travel pass. To curtail these abuses, in 1868 the federal government directed that passes be given only in exceptional cases and upon official authorization. To further reduce the costs of this scheme, in 1872 the federal government reached an agreement with Ontario and Quebec whereby these provinces assumed two-thirds of the inland transportation costs of immigrants settling within their respective borders. Within three years, Ontario had limited its contribution to paying inland transportation only for female domestics.

Within the private sphere, there were two prominent schemes that were approved by the federal government. One was an advance-passage regime whereby employers would advance money to prospective employees to cover the cost of ocean travel, which later would be deducted from the immigrant workers' pay. Dominion immigration agents acted as middlemen, selecting eligible workers and making the necessary employment contracts with them. Although the government did not advance fees for passage itself in this way, it regarded the practice as important in the promotion of immigration and encouraged employers to take advantage of the scheme. According to the minister responsible for immigration, Canada was not otherwise able to compete with other countries which offered passage assistance: 'Should the appeal which has been made fail to awaken the interests of the employers of labour in Canada ... I should feel that a great opportunity had been lost to obtain a considerable influx of population, and that the efforts which have been made by the Government would be to some extent defeated, either by the apathy of the people, or a too great reliance on what their Government can itself unaided do.'[92]

The other common form of assistance was that provided by British philanthropic organizations. As one way of relieving the distress of the rural and urban poor, funds were set aside to aid those wishing to leave Britain and settle elsewhere. Some of these institutions were involved in emigration as part of their larger mandate; others were established entirely for emigration purposes. Generally, applicants were required to establish the *bona fides* of their intention to emigrate, and to provide a certificate from a local authority attesting to their good character and their ability to support themselves once sent abroad. A physical examination was also usually part of the screening process. Once approved, emigrants would be provided with funds to cover travel expenses and, in some cases, further funds to assist their settlement.

All forms of assisted immigration were hotly contested in both Britain and Canada. In Britain, they were criticized by some as a way for the rich to dispose of the poor. In Scotland, they were condemned for their depopulating effect, and, in Ireland, Catholic bishops railed against emigration more generally on the grounds that it deprived people of their religious heritage. Others felt that it was a waste of money to send destitute persons abroad unless there was firm evidence to suggest that they would be good settlers. These critics warned that unsuitable emigrants would fail in their attempts to re-establish themselves. Their failure would come at great expense to their sponsors and lead to more restrictive measures being adopted in the receiving countries.[93]

Canadian overseas immigration agents and transportation companies tended to applaud the schemes as being necessary to secure the immigrants which the country needed. In contrast, immigration agents within Canada were among the first to complain about the arrival of assisted immigrants. According to their reports, the practice encouraged the emigration of those who could not readily adapt to the rigours of Canadian farming life. It was alleged that many were not skilled in agricultural pursuits or were so worn down by the poverty they had experienced in Britain that they did not have the stamina to succeed in their new country. Arriving in Canada without enough funds, they fell upon the mercy of the government for assistance, and, 'listless and desolate,' they were not inclined to help themselves.[94]

Several municipal authorities[95] and labour organizations also argued vigorously against financially assisted immigrants. In April 1888, for example, Toronto City Council sent a resolution to Ottawa describing the chronic state of unemployment in Toronto and arguing for strict controls to prevent the poor and the destitute of Britain from coming to Canada inevitably in need of public assistance.[96] Labour unions were also vocal in their opposition to the indiscriminate landing in Canada of British workers who were encouraged by reduced passage rates and the provision of settlement assistance.

According to Eugene Forsey, within the major unions of the day there was some divergence of views on the issue of assisted immigration. There were those within the movement who thought of the assisted immigrant as 'an impoverished, unfortunate, perhaps oppressed, even persecuted, human being who deserved a chance in a new, free, rich developing country.' Others chose to focus on the practice of spreading false information on Canada and the creation of unrealistic expectations on the part of immigrants as being more worthy of censure than the practice of assisted immigration itself. The majority of members, however, as reflected in the resolutions of national and local union councils, objected to the use of public funds to finance the importation of those whose labour it was felt would compete with that of Canadian workers.[97] They rejected claims that those being assisted were immigrants in occupations for which there was a short supply in Canada. For example, in 1892 the Vancouver Trades and Labour Council criticized the government for 'spending thousands of dollars of public money encouraging and enticing the poor of foreign countries to come to the Dominion and enter into a life struggle of competition with our people in a market always overcrowded as long as Canada is open to all and every class of immigrant.' Similarly, in 1883 the Trades and Labour Congress of Canada also objected to the practice of assisted passages, which it claimed overcrowded a labour market 'already more than amply provided for by the surplus working population.' Similar resolutions denouncing the immigration of assisted persons were adopted in almost all the congress's other conventions of the period.[98]

Ongoing complaints about the arrival in Canada of the impoverished no doubt influenced the passing of the 1879 regulation prohibiting the landing in Canada of indigents and paupers unless the master of the ship upon which they arrived deposited funds to cover the cost of their temporary support and transportation within Canada.[99] The 1879 order, however, did not put the issue to rest, for it did not squarely address the concerns of those opposed to assisted immigration. By 1888, the government seemed to be persuaded that the warrant system and inland passes cost far more than they were worth, for both schemes were terminated. Within two years, they were replaced by a bonus system which was believed to target more specifically the immigrants of whom Canada was most in need.[100] This scheme provided a $10 bonus for men who could prove they actually settled in the Northwest within six months of arrival. A further $5 was provided for the settler's wife and for his children of twelve years or older. As was the case with homesteading grants, the bonus system was not provided to women on the same terms as to men.

It has been argued that the government's termination of inland-passage assistance and the warrant system was in response to pressure from labour unions, city councils, and other charitable institutions called upon for re-lief.[101] Other actions taken by the government, however, suggest other-wise. The termination of these two schemes in favour of bonuses paid to those who actually settled in the West demonstrated that the government did not want to discourage immigration, but rather to ensure that the as-sistance it provided went to the intended groups. The main problem it identified with respect to travel assistance was not that it encouraged the admission of those who would compete with Canadian workers, but that there was no way of ensuring that those assisted remained in the country. The bonus system addressed this concern by ensuring that money was advanced only to those who actually settled in Canada. Had the govern-ment been sensitive to the demands of trade unions, it would have pro-hibited the advancing of travel funds by Canadian employers to prospect-ive immigrant employees. It would also have severely restricted the practice of importing British child workers, for whom restrictions were advocated not only by Canadian labour unions, but by other interests as well.

Private agencies which sponsored the immigration of British child work-ers to Canada were very active throughout this period. This source of in-expensive farm and domestic labour is frequently overlooked in Canadian history, yet between 1870 and 1897 approximately 40,000 British children emigrated to this country.[102] Throughout the 1870s, an average of 500 chil-dren came to Canada annually. So popular was the movement, especially in rural areas, which were the prime beneficiaries of the importation of child workers, that between 1879 and 1883 approximately 1,500 children arrived each year, and in 1888 annual admissions surpassed 2,000.[103] Even with these relatively high admission rates, the demand for British child workers invariably exceeded the supply.

Child-emigration schemes were largely organized and administered by private English charities whose work was driven by two primary objectives.

One was the desire to relieve the urban congestion of destitute children, whose concentration in big cities such as London was believed to be a threat to public safety. The other was the belief that both the material and the spiritual well-being of poor children would be served by removing them from the evils associated with British urban life and sending them to the relatively unpolluted environment of rural Canada.

The children who came to Canada ranged in age from six to fifteen. Some, particularly the youngest, were adopted by Canadian families. The large majority, however, were contracted out to farmers as labourers or house workers. As the histories of the child-immigration schemes reveal, many children brought to Canada in this way were treated in Canada as indentured servants. Unlike adult immigration, child immigration was involuntary and irreversible, at least until the child reached maturity and could control his or her own destiny. The lack of regulations ensuring that homes met minimum suitability requirements, and the absence of regular inspections to ensure that the children were treated well in the homes to which they were sent, meant that thousands of children bound by such agreements spent their childhood years in Canada in circumstances that were no less harsh and often significantly more brutal than what they had been delivered from at home.[104] In fact, this was the conclusion reached in 1875 by Andrew Doyle, a British inspector, in his report on the movement, having visited more than 400 children placed throughout Ontario and Quebec. Doyle was alarmed at the physical abuse and ill-treatment he discovered, and the inadequate, and often non-existent, supervision provided by the receiving homes. His report and recommendations for improvement were not well received in Canada.[105] At hearings held by the House of Commons Select Committee on Immigration and Colonization, Doyle's report was characterized as inaccurate and unjust.[106] Child-immigration agencies and their benefactors were particularly defensive and critical of his findings. In addition, politicians as well as other prominent citizens wrote in praise of child-immigration programs, providing, as they did, a source of needed labour in their constituencies. Others attested to the sincere motives of those who supervised the schemes, and of the great care that was taken in the placing of children, who, by and large, were sent to good people in decent communities. So overwhelming was the support for child immigration that, in the end, the committee concluded that child immigration schemes were advantageous both to the children brought to Canada and to the employers who received them. A subsequent investigation by the provinces reached similar conclusions.[107]

Official endorsement of the movement, however, did not reflect consensus within the Canadian community. As they did with other forms of assisted immigration, organized labour, particularly the Canadian Labour Union, and later the Trades and Labour Congress of Canada, objected to the importation of children on the grounds that child workers were unfair competitors, driving down wages and displacing Canadian men and women from employment.[108] Law-enforcement officials also complained that children who emigrated from the 'depraved slums' and 'ghettos' of Britain's cities perniciously corrupted Canadian youth and swelled the ranks of the country's criminal class.[109] Prominent members of the medical establishment also argued strenuously against the immigration of destitute British children, who were reported to bring syphilis and other contagious diseases arising from the moral depravity and squalor of their British existence, and who were also genetically impaired. One eminent physician, C.K. Clarke, after whom Toronto's Clarke Institute of Psychiatry was named, cited as an example a group of immigrant boys he had watched on a train whose 'asymmetrical heads' and 'stunted forms' earmarked their degeneracy. 'It is almost criminal neglect on the part of the authorities to allow this sort of immigration to be permitted,' Clarke said.[110] The warnings of law-enforcement officers and doctors did not go unnoticed and were often picked up in the press, which was quick to print stories of immigrant children charged with crimes such as robbery, assault, and prostitution. For its part, the government was very much aware of what it described as 'a pretty strong sentiment, almost amounting to a prejudice, growing up in the minds of the Canadian people in regard to this class of immigration.'[111] It claimed, however, that the fears were exaggerated, for most of the children brought to Canada were a great success. It substantiated this with reports from its own inspectors, as well as from the reports of the societies involved in the movement. Yet neither government inspectors nor those appointed by the child-emigration societies were equipped to interview all the children under their jurisdiction, and so their conclusions were largely unsubstantiated. Notwithstanding the growing opposition to the importation of children, the demand for child labourers continued unabated. This no doubt explains why the movement was allowed to continue.

While claiming that the allegations of rampant mental and physical degeneracy among child immigrants were false, the government did take steps to mollify some of the critics of the movement. In 1893, it required all societies engaged in the work to show, by statutory declaration, 'the antecedents of the members of each party brought out,' and strict medical examinations were required of every child at the port of embarkation. Children who were not certified by a department official as being desirable were to be returned to Britain immediately.[112] Regarding the welfare of the children, the first significant piece of legislation was passed by Ontario in 1897. An Act to Regulate the Immigration into Ontario of Certain Classes of Children provided for, among other things, the licensing of all child-immigration agencies, and the regular inspection of these agencies and of the children themselves.[113] Similar legislation was subsequently enacted in Manitoba, Quebec, Nova Scotia, and New Brunswick. Although these acts suggested that, in principle, the provinces were committed to ensuring that the children were provided with the necessities of life, in practice this was not the case. According to Joy Parr, the regulations were ineffective because no staff was hired to enforce them. Two decades later, the Ontario legislation was removed from the statute books altogether.[114] Throughout its sixty-year history, child immigration to Canada remained relatively unregulated, with the result that the abuses documented by Doyle in 1875 persisted until the movement was terminated in 1930.

The Trans-Canada Railway

In fulfilment of its pledge to build a transcontinental railway, Macdonald's Conservative government concluded an agreement with the Canadian Pacific Railway Company in 1880, whereby the company agreed to construct the railway for $25 million and 25 million acres of land, in alternate sections of 640 acres each, along a 24-mile-wide belt on either side of the railway line. The company also received approximately 720 miles of government railway lines in the West, and a monopoly on the territory south of its main line for twenty years.[115] In 1883, the CPR requested an additional $22.5 million, an amount close to the entire annual federal revenue, to complete the project. The loan was granted, as was another loan request made two years later, thereby ensuring the government's interest in seeing the line completed. By the time the railway was finished in 1885, it is estimated that it cost the federal government more than $60 million dollars in grants and $35 million dollars in loans.[116]

The building of the railway stimulated movement West. People were lured to Manitoba and the prairies in search of employment opportunities in the construction of the line and in search of land, the value of which was expected to rise with the completion of the transnational route. But employment on the railway was temporary, and the true value of the land was commensurate only with the productivity of its soil. In 1879, the West experienced a land boom. It was short-lived. Beginning in 1882, land prices plummeted as settlement proved to be arduous and often unproductive. Persistent crop failures throughout the 1880s, together with the inability to market grain at remunerative prices, discouraged settlement and immigration, as did the Metis rebellion of 1885.

Given that the completion of the railway was an important concession to British Columbia in the negotiations leading up to that province's entry into Confederation, it is ironic that, in fulfilling this obligation, the government alienated the province in a manner unanticipated in 1871. For, in its efforts to have the railway completed, the federal government endorsed the entry of thousands of Chinese immigrants, most of whom settled in British Columbia, provoking the ire of many of that province's inhabitants and setting the tone of immigration-policy discourse in that province for the next thirty years.

During the 1880s, an estimated 15,000 Chinese labourers were brought to Canada to work on the western leg of the CPR. Andrew Onderdonk, the railway contractor, favoured the importation of Chinese labourers because there were not enough workers in the West to do the job, nor were there enough American navvies willing to move north for the wages that were being offered. The Chinese had the advantage over other immigrant workers of arriving on the West Coast, where transportation to worksites was a much simpler endeavour than for most other immigrants who, upon landing in the East, then had to be transported across the entire country. Equally important, however, Chinese workers were relatively easy to secure, were more servile than most other workers, and were willing to work at wages 30–50 per cent lower than those paid to white labourers. The advantages of Chinese workers were not lost on other employers as well.

The Chinese immigrants who came to Canada at this time were from the Guangdong Province of China, where crushing poverty was endemic. Generally they were recruited through labour agencies that would arrange for their employment and pay their passage to Canada, which later would be deducted from their wages. Most commonly, board was also deducted from wages or the workers were required by their employment contracts to buy supplies from company-owned stores at inflated prices. So onerous were the transportation and lodging debts that, after several years of employment, many workers found that they did not have enough savings to return to China, as they initially intended.

Almost from the beginning of the movement, there was controversy regarding the entry of Chinese labourers. In the construction of the CPR, the arrival of Chinese navvies was not welcomed by white labourers, who on several occasions attacked neighbouring Chinese work gangs.[117] Moreover, a number of anti-Chinese groups were formed in the province to formally protest against Chinese immigration.[118]

In response to the complaints voiced by such groups, the prime minister emphasized that Chinese labourers were necessary for the completion of the western leg of the CPR. As he assured the House in 1882, he, too, objected to the 'Mongolians becoming permanent settlers' but said that nothing could be done until the railway was completed, at which time he would 'join to a reasonable extent in preventing a permanent settlement in this country of Mongolian or Chinese immigrants.' In the meantime, he felt that the choice was clear; 'either you must have labour or you can't have the railway.'[119] Left unstated but equally clear, however, was the fact that, given the enormity of the government's investment in the railway, much more was at risk than simply the completion of the line. Land grants, loans, direct subsidies, and tax concessions provided to railway promoters had placed a heavy burden on federal resources. In fact, at one point, three-quarters of the national debt was related to expenditures on the railway and other transportation facilities.[120]

Protest against Chinese labourers gained momentum with the completion of the railway and as West Coast cities saw the arrival of hundreds of impoverished, unemployed Chinese labourers. Although some went back to China, assisted by Chinese benevolent societies, and others remained temporarily employed in railway work within the province or migrated east, most gravitated to the major urban centres of British Columbia. Their situation was particularly severe through the winter of 1885–6, when, without employment and without savings, many found themselves homeless and destitute. Any charity they received tended to come from local Chinese merchants; both the federal and the provincial governments disclaimed any responsibility for them.[121]

Although the government had refused to limit Chinese immigration, in the face of growing public opposition, Macdonald agreed to appoint a royal commission to examine the issue. The commission began its deliberations in the summer of 1884.[122] A wide cross-section of witnesses, including politicians, lawyers, police officials, judges, clergymen, businessmen, and workers, testified that the Chinese were dirty, disease-ridden, dishonest, immoral, and totally incapable of integrating within the larger community. Their uncleanliness was reportedly evident in almost all aspects of their lives, from the raw sewage that ran through their residential areas to their use of human excrement as manure for their vegetable gardens. Their habit of living in crowded dwellings, and sleeping several to a bed, was offered as additional evidence of their disregard for personal hygiene as well as of their lack of moral scruples. The Chinese way of living, it was claimed, compromised the safety of other communities. The noxious diseases alleged to be carried by large numbers of the Chinese, such as smallpox, cholera, and leprosy, brought with them from Asia, could spread quickly in their overcrowded, unsanitary living areas, contaminating other residential districts and putting the health of the general public at great risk. It was also alleged before the commission that the Chinese gambled compulsively and kept gaming-houses for this purpose and for the purposes of prostitution. One Nanaimo justice of the peace went so far as to assert that 'nearly the whole of their females that leave China are professed prostitutes, from children ten or twelve years of age to old hags.'[123] Their use of opium was advanced as further evidence of their moral depravity. The fact that these vices were purportedly attracting white people was regarded as reason enough for the termination of Chinese immigration lest more Canadian youth be corrupted by such practices. Union representatives and other workers appearing before the commission complained that the competition provided by Chinese workers drove wages down and put whites out of work.[124]

In his book, *White Canada Forever*, W. Peter Ward examines the many allegations raised against the Chinese and the validity of the stereotypes that were advanced at the commission, and in public debate more generally. He notes that, while it was true that Chinatowns were overcrowded and lacking in proper sanitation, this was equally true of other residential areas in the cities and not simply confined to those dominated by the Chinese. Although prostitution and gambling were prevalent in Chinese areas, Ward claims that this was not a function of the moral depravity of Chinese society, but, rather, was a reflection of the fact it was predominantly a male and transient one. The allegations of secret Chinese societies engaged in lawlessness, according to Ward, were often exaggerated, for most of the Chinese societies established at this time performed voluntary social and support functions. Ward also claims that the argument that the Chinese appropriated employment opportunities from whites was not supported by the evidence, since Chinese workers offered a source of manpower at a time of heightened demand. Moreover, in some industries the jobs in which the Chinese were concentrated were those for which the whites did not want to compete. 'The assumption that the Chinese would usurp the white labourer's place was more often based on anticipated competition than on open economic conflict.' Finally, with regard to the argument that the Chinese were unassimilable, and hence unfit to remain in Canada, Ward states that this was hypocritical, since their entry into white society was barred by white nativism.[125]

As for the commissioners, they were persuaded by the arguments raised by employers that Chinese workers were an advantage to the economy. One commissioner stated in his report that many of the complaints against the Chinese were based on ignorance and prejudice, claiming that the Chinese were no less moral or clean than the same classes of other nationalities and that the sanitation of their living quarters was something that could be supervised through municipal regulations.[126] Nevertheless, the commissioners concluded that, while Chinese workers tended to be an asset to the economy, their inability to assimilate into the larger white community, and the prevalence of white antagonism towards their continued presence, made some restrictions advisable. In particular they recommended that a poll tax of $10 be imposed on every Chinese resident, and that immigration admissions should be tightened so that the diseased, deformed, and impoverished would be prohibited entry. Subsequently, the federal government passed the Chinese Immigration Act in the summer of 1885, at the time that the CPR was reaching completion. The act imposed a $50 head tax on all Chinese immigrants, except for diplomats, students, tourists, and merchants, and it limited the number of Chinese persons a ship could carry to one for every fifty tons of cargo, as compared with one European for every two tons of cargo as prescribed under the Immigration Act.[127]

Macdonald continued to refuse to restrict entirely Chinese immigration, explaining that, with the completion of the CPR, Canada was planning to enter into a trade relationship with China, and to adopt a distinctly hostile policy might 'be the means of killing future business with that country.'[128] He was, however, prepared to ensure that Chinese immigrants would not have a political voice in their new community. In 1885, the federal government passed the Electoral Franchise Act, which excluded all Chinese persons, whether naturalized or not, from the federal franchise. Although a few members of Parliament opposed the measure on the grounds that those Chinese persons who bad been born in Canada or who were naturalized British subjects ought to be accorded the right to vote, most of those who debated the act were in favour of its adoption. Macdonald justified the denial of the franchise on the basis that the Chinese worker in Canada was merely a sojourner, and while 'valuable, the same as a threshing machine or any other agricultural implement,' the Chinese immigrant to Canada 'has no British instincts or British feelings or aspirations, and therefore ought not to have a vote.'[129]

In British Columbia, these measures were not enough. Throughout the period, the province passed many laws restricting the right of Chinese immigrants to enter, live, and work within the province. While the federal government and the courts were willing to let many discriminatory statutes stand, they were not so inclined when it came to provincial legislation aimed at driving Chinese persons from the province or at denying them entry in the first place. In 1878, for example, the legislature passed the Chinese Tax Act, which imposed a quarterly poll tax of $10 on every Chinese resident over twelve years of age as a condition of working in the province. The act was subsequently declared unconstitutional in the case of *Tai Sing v Maguire* because it was beyond provincial jurisdiction.[130] Similarly, in 1884, prior to the passage of the federal Chinese Immigration Act, the province passed its own Chinese Immigration Act,[131] which prohibited the immigration of Chinese persons into the province. Within six months the act was disallowed by the governor general.[132] Also in that year the provincial legislature passed the Chinese Regulation Act, which imposed a $10 poll tax on all Chinese residents. The act was subsequently declared unconstitutional by the B.C. Supreme Court on the same grounds adopted in the case of *Tai Sing*.[133] Judicial rulings and federal disallowances, however, were not sufficient to discourage the B.C. government from continuing its efforts to legislate Chinese residents out of the province. In 1885, immediately following the federal disallowance of the B.C. Chinese Immigration Act of 1884, the province passed another identical piece of legislation.[134] This act was also disallowed by the governor general, as were six other provincial exclusionary acts passed before 1908.[135]

Yet, while the federal government and the courts were loath to permit provincial acts which restricted the immigration of workers whose labour was in demand, many of the more than 100 acts or bills passed by the B.C. legislature between 1872 and 1922 which discriminated explicitly against Chinese and Japanese immigrants were upheld.[136] As the outcomes of legal challenges to racist legislation throughout the next period were to illustrate, the courts were more inclined to protect the economic interests of entrepreneurs and financiers than the human rights of Chinese residents.[137]

The Constraints on Immigration

Reformed land polices, advertising campaigns, transportation improvements, and assisted passages were not sufficient to ensure the rapid settlement of the Canadian West. With the exception of the land-speculation boom around Winnipeg in the early 1880s, the rate of settlement was consistently disappointing. Between 1874 and 1896, homestead entries averaged around 3,000 per year, yet cancellations, in some years, exceeded this amount.[138] The trend was alarming, especially in light of the fact that, in the United States, available farm land was rapidly being developed, a significant amount by emigrating Canadians.

At the time, the inability of Canada to attract and keep large numbers of immigrants was attributed to a variety of factors. Immigration agents claimed that disorganized promotion, coupled with an insufficient supply of promotional literature, prevented them from advertising Canada as widely as necessary to meet the government's desired immigrant quotas. Others suggested that misleading advertising, which induced people to settle with unrealistic expectations of what was required, led to inevitable disappointment. These negative experiences not only prompted people to leave Canada, but also were communicated to other potential immigrant, who were then dissuaded from coming. Most commonly, however, immigration agents attributed the disappointing number of arrivals to intense competition from immigrant-receiving countries, together with the minimal financial inducements offered to would-be emigrants to Canada.

FOREIGN EMIGRATION CONTROLS AND COMPETITION
FOR IMMIGRANTS

Among the impediments facing Canadian promotional work overseas were foreign emigration controls. For example, Canada was desirous of securing German settlers, considering them to be among the most solid and hard-working immigrants.[139] However, in an effort to discourage its nationals from leaving, Germany prohibited advertising that encouraged people to emigrate, and it forbade steamship agents from booking passengers to North America on any other than German-owned ships proceeding directly to North America. The only direct lines to North America were by way of the United States, which put Canada at a strong disadvantage. Canada's special passage rates from Liverpool, and inland-travel assistance from Quebec ports, simply were not enough to overcome this initial disincentive.

This is not to suggest that Canada was without any German immigration, for German settlements were established throughout this period, many through the colonization efforts of land companies and railways. While the first German settlements in Canada tended to be concentrated in the Ottawa and Waterloo areas of Ontario, with the opening of the

Northwest more German communities were established there. In addition to land reserves set aside for German immigrants, in 1890 Germans were permitted to administer their own schools and churches and to form their own municipalities in accordance with provincial laws.[140] As more Germans established in Canada, they encouraged others to join them. Nevertheless, it would not be until the turn of the century, when Canada's economic position improved and available lands in the United States diminished, that Canada would become an attractive destination for significant numbers of emigrating Germans.

France, too, placed restrictions on emigration promotion, which also contributed to Canada's inability to secure immigrants from this source, despite the efforts of its agents in various regions throughout the country. The French government was generally opposed to emigration, largely because it felt it needed its population, and, in particular, a strong army, to defend itself against German expansionism. Those who wanted to leave the country were encouraged to immigrate to French colonies. The absence of a direct route to Canada, and the lack of financial incentives such as reduced passage rates that were offered to British immigrants, probably also undermined Canadian efforts to secure French immigrants at this time.

The other major impediment to Canadian promotional work was the intense competition for immigrants among other immigrant-receiving nations. Apart from the United States, Brazil, Argentina, New Zealand, and Australia were among the most significant competitors faced by the Canadian government. In their bids to attract settlers, they, too, offered financial incentives such as overseas-travel assistance, inland-passage money, land grants, and loans to cover initial set-up expenses. Their more attractive climates, coupled with more favourable terms of settlement, rendered them formidable rivals in the quest for settlers throughout the period.

As attractive as these other immigrant-receiving countries were, the United States exerted an even greater pull on prospective immigrants. According to one study, of the approximately 13 million immigrants who went to the seven major receiving countries between 1870 and 1990, more than 70 per cent went to the United States.[141] Chief among its attractions were its larger market, relatively advanced and vibrant economy, and more diversified employment opportunities. In addition, the American legislation was said to provide more favourable terms of settlement.[142]

Despite the United States' apparent advantages over Canada, Canadian immigration agents frequently attributed its appeal to an aggressive promotional campaign and to cutthroat immigration agents. It was claimed that the United States was particularly effective in disseminating its promotional literature, so that its attributes were widely known throughout Britain and Europe. This disturbed A.B. Davey, a Canadian immigration agent in Britain, leading him to report in 1873 that 'all the talk seems to be about America': 'America is everything, and appears to be everywhere ... The prevailing idea seems to be that the United States is America, and Canada and other parts of America are small out of the way places, destined soon to be absorbed by the States.'[143] This was a common complaint of immigration agents throughout the period. Canada simply was not well known, and they argued it would not be until the whole system of advertising was better organized and supported by more promotional material available for wide distribution.[144]

Another grievance frequently aired by Canadian agents was that American agents engaged in misrepresentation of both their own country and Canada. It was alleged that they disseminated false reports of the rigours of life in Canada as a way of diverting people to the United States. Similarly, Canadian agents claimed that American agents provided a deceptively false picture of their own country, promising abundant employment opportunities for workers of all descriptions. American land speculators and immigration and colonization agents were reported to board trains at the major distributing points for the purpose of diverting Canadian-bound passengers to American destinations. The practice was reportedly rampant in St Paul and Chicago. As the Canadian immigration agent in Duluth described the situation in 1883:

> while *en route,* especially in Chicago and St Paul, they [passengers] are likely to hear very little in praise of Manitoba, and very much in praise of Minnesota and Dakota. Vague rumours of depression and hardship in Manitoba are freely circulated, and the condition of the settler there contrasted with the reported prosperity of settlers on the American side of the border. And all this in the face of the fact that the American settlers have actually been severe sufferers this year, both from natural causes and combinations of capital which have weighed heavily upon them ...[145]

It was also alleged that American booking agents were deliberately impeding immigration to Canada by booking passengers intent on settling in Canada, and sending them through parts of the United States before they reached their final destination. Why else, asked one Montreal agent in 1870, were immigrants being sent, systematically and with unnecessary expense and delay, from American ports to Montreal 'by way of Buffalo and elsewhere, 600 to 700 miles out of their route?'[146]

American immigration agents were also accused of engaging in aggressive campaigns to convince Canadians of the advantages of moving from their rural communities to the United States. Norman Macdonald claims that the 'ceaseless drive for immigrants' by U.S. agents 'almost depopulated whole counties in Nova Scotia alone.' Nor did they confine their efforts to the Maritimes: 'Agents of American land and railway companies in their predatory search for immigrants invaded every rural district of Ontario in the 1880s and 1890s, using every form of plausible inducement known to their class, particularly those of high wages, mild climate and enormous crops. American consuls, stationed in the larger urban centres of Canada, were more assiduous and persuasive in spreading the gospel of the "orange grove mania" and other delusions among gullible Canadians.'[147]

Yet it clearly was not the work of agents alone that caused the enormous exodus south. Nor could it be said that their depictions of the United States were entirely false or that Canadians were particularly gullible. At the root of the high rates of emigration from Canada throughout this period was the promise of better economic opportunity in the United States, which thousands of Canadians and immigrants later found to be true.[148]

In the Maritimes, for example, the United States was a magnet for those who suffered from the loss of trade occasioned after the United States abrogated the Reciprocity Treaty in 1866. In Prince Edward Island, the end of reciprocity and the increase in American tariff barriers were disastrous for the sale of Island fish, potatoes, wood products, gypsum, and coal. At the same time, the Island was faced with a decline in fish exports to the West Indies and a drop in the demand for its wooden ships. Moreover, high interest rates that the provincial government imposed on farm mortgages, which had originally been offered to tenant farmers to help them buy their land, turned out to be more onerous than the rents they used to pay. Many farmers abandoned their lands and sought employment in the United States. They were joined by other workers facing dislocation in their struggling industries.[149]

In addition, the end of the American Civil War had repercussions in the Maritimes. New England fishermen returned to their trade on the St. Lawrence equipped with improved technology which gave them a competitive edge over Canadian fishermen. Relatively poor returns, resulting from both their less efficient methods and the tariff barriers they faced, led many Canadian fishermen to transfer to American ships, where the catches were greater and where they had the benefit of a larger market. New Brunswick's wooden-shipbuilding industry, an important facet of the province's economy, suffered because it could not keep pace with technological advances, especially the development of steamships.

Canadian coal production faced devastating competition once the Pennsylvania coal mines became active again following the Civil War. Nova Scotia was particularly hurt by this competition, as well as by the fact that American inland-transportation rates were relatively low, which made Canadian coal less attractive. Several coal fields in the province were shut down, and unemployed miners moved south. Emigration from the Maritimes remained significant for almost thirty years as young people, faced with limited future prospects, left for the United States, because employment opportunities were more numerous and the attractions of American city life were more compelling than those of the rural Maritimes. Their exodus left a shortage of labour which the provincial governments tried to fill with immigrant workers. It soon became apparent, however, that immigrants were just as susceptible to the lure of the United States as were Canadians. It would not be until the 1890s, when Canada experienced an economic revival that the rate of emigration would slow down.[150]

French Canadians in Quebec also immigrated to the United States, although for different reasons. One cause was related to the system of land tenure in the province. Large tracts of land were held by seigneurs, who did not fulfil their settlement obligations with respect to the construction of roads or the sale of land at reasonable prices to prospective settlers. As the already-settled areas became even more densely populated, young French Canadians, unable to acquire land of their own, moved to the United States to accumulate savings. Most went to New England, where they were employed in textile mills, brickyards, railways, logging enterprises, and construction. They often supplanted Irish and English workers and formed their own enclaves, where they spoke their language and practised their religion freely. Initially they intended to work on a seasonal basis and return home. However, the willingness of employers, especially in the textile industry, to hire women and children eventually led to the emigration of entire families and the establishment of French communities in New England. In 1873, it was estimated that one-quarter to one-third of the farms in Quebec had been deserted.[151]

The exodus from Quebec abated somewhat in the 1870s as U.S. textile mills reduced hours and laid off workers in response to falling exports, and as railway construction declined. Several hundred French Canadians returned home, aided by the establishment of land reserves set up by the federal and the Quebec governments for the purpose of encouraging the repatriation of French Canadians. As with other colonization schemes of the day, these, too, failed to achieve the desired results. Significant French Canadian emigration to the United States resumed in the early 1880s as farmers, already burdened by debt, faced rising prices for farm implements. As in earlier years, their exodus was usually intended to be temporary, until they had accumulated enough money to repay their debts and return to their farms. Yet the continued prosperity in the United States, together with the growth of vibrant French-Canadian communities there, meant that, in the end, the migration south was, for most, a permanent move.[152]

The migration of people from Ontario to the United States was of a different character from that of people from Quebec. Those leaving Ontario in the 1870s generally did so for the American prairies, where treeless plains freed them from the arduous task of clearing land, and where cattle and dairy farming was far less labour-intensive than wheat and barley production. In addition, American laws which permitted an immigrant to bring in household effects and a team of horses duty-free also were powerful inducements to abandon debt ridden farms in Ontario and strike out on the new frontier. As a result, hundreds of settlers left Ontario for Kansas, Nebraska, Minnesota, and the eastern districts of Dakota.[153]

The economic upturn which was experienced in American commercial centres in the East in 1879 was also felt in the American West. In the 1880s there was a great increase in the westward movement of farmers, trades people, and merchants, and Canadians were eager participants. Prominent among the emigrants were Ontario residents. In Ontario, available farming land was diminishing, and farmers' sons, faced with the prospect of being landless, chose instead to try their fortunes in the United States. Ontario business people and professionals also left Canada, because demand for their services was greater in American cities than in their own.[154]

Also attracted to the American Western boom were farmers from Manitoba and the Northwest. As a result of the increase in tariffs imposed by Macdonald in 1879, Canadian farmers faced higher costs than American farmers for such goods as American farm machinery. In some cases the price differential was as much as 30 per cent, making farming in the United States a more attractive proposition. Higher implement prices, Canadian land-distribution policies which tended to isolate farmers and in some cases prevent expansion, and years of climatic hardships and devastating yields led to growing dissatisfaction. Other causes for complaint included the absence of herding regulations, which forced farmers to erect expensive fencing to protect their fields from cattle, and uncertain titles, which meant that, if farmers found they had cultivated land that was not technically theirs, they were forced to quit the land without any compensation for the improvements made to it. While some of these problems were eventually corrected, that alone could not stem the emigration tide.[155]

The Canadian government, while it tended publicly to downplay the volume of emigration south, nevertheless was deeply concerned about it. As early as 1872, the minister of Agriculture sent P.E. Gendreau to the United States to ascertain the type and extent of emigration from Canada. Noting that it was difficult to obtain accurate figures, Gendreau nevertheless estimated that a total of 800,000 people in the United States had emigrated from Canada, half of whom were French Canadian.

The government's sensitivity to the fact that immigrants were pouring through Canada to the United States was evident in the way it assessed annual immigration arrivals. Frequently, in departmental reports, a comparison was made between the change in the number of arrivals to Canada and the change in the number of departures. So, for example, in 1874, the minister of Agriculture claimed that, although the number of arrivals had fallen over the previous year, the 'decline in the number of immigrant passengers passing through Canada for the United States during 1874 was very much greater than that in the number of settlers in Canada.' Canada's improved performance was credited to good Canadian overseas recruitment techniques.[156]

Throughout the 1880s, the government, while not attempting to keep emigration figures of its own, took great pains to establish that the emigration rates were not as high as the United States claimed or as publicized in the press. A special Canadian agent was appointed to assess the situation in the United States, and his annual reports on the 'Alleged Exodus on the Western Frontier' attempted to disprove the American statistics pointing to massive emigration from Canada to the United States, frequently emphasizing that the numbers often quoted included people who were only temporarily travelling to the United States and who had every intention of returning home. In 1885, Canada seemed to have won its point, for American custom-house officials were instructed to discontinue the collection of statistics of immigrants arriving in the United States from Canada and Mexico since 'it appears to be impracticable to procure, under existing laws, accurate statistics.'[157]

While the Canadian government formally complained about exaggerated emigration reports, it nevertheless continued to take steps to attract

Canadians who had moved south. The Quebec land reserves were one measure, as were reserves that were established in Manitoba for French Canadians relocating from New England.[158] In addition, special agents were sent south to promote Canada among expatriates, and reduced travel rates were established to assist their return home. While these efforts did encourage some people to return to Canada, at no point did the movement north approximate the movement in the other direction.

THE CONSTRAINTS OF FARM TECHNOLOGY

Settlement in the Canadian West proceeded very much the way it did in the United States, with humid areas being populated before semi-arid ones. One reason for the success of the Red River settlement was that, because it did not suffer from frequent frosts or droughts, the land was suitable for cultivation with traditional farming techniques. In contrast, conditions in the Prairie West were characterized by low annual rainfall and relatively short growing seasons, and thus the land required other cultivation practices in order to be productive. As long as lands in the humid areas were available, settlers chose them over semi-arid ones. In the mid-1880s, the fact that land in humid areas was more readily available in the United States for settlement than in Manitoba was a major reason that more settlers were attracted south. Canada's provision of free homesteading land on railway lines was not sufficient to curtail this movement.

As the availability of land in the humid areas in both Canada and the United States was rapidly diminishing by the late 1880s, there was a stronger incentive to try to develop appropriate cultivation techniques for semi-arid regions. In Canada, the government set up experimental farms for this purpose, and it was here that dry-farming techniques suitable to semi-arid lands were first developed. In dry farming, crops are selected that need the least amount of rainfall, and cultivation methods are used which conserve precipitation. It generally involves leaving a portion of land fallow as a way of conserving moisture, which is reserved for the following year. According to Kenneth Norrie,[159] although dry farming was known in the 1880s to increase the yields of prairie land, there were several reasons why it alone did not prompt a significant increase in settlement there. In the first place, dry-farming techniques had to vary according to the exact soil type, nature of subsurface soil, annual precipitation, and length of growing season. A settler would thus have to experiment with several different methods over several growing seasons before profitable results could be expected. As well, the practice of leaving land fallow was costly, for not only was it more likely to erode and suffer mineral depletion, but, while fallow, it did not generate any income. In parts of the United States, this problem could be overcome by the planting of certain crops such as corn and sorghum, which had the same beneficial effects as fallow land but which yielded marketable produce. In Canada, the short growing season and relatively smaller market prevented this technique from being employed.

The widespread adoption of dry-farming techniques on the Canadian prairies was impeded by its relatively high cost, which was not offset by favourable wheat prices. Only when the world depression in wheat prices lifted in 1896, followed by an increase in returns for wheat production, would farmers be encouraged to settle in the West and to adopt the more costly cultivation techniques demanded there. The fact that sub-humid land was no longer available on the American frontier, and that transportation routes were expanding throughout the Canadian West, also contributed to this movement, sparking the great Canadian wheat boom of the next period.[160]

The End of an Era

In these early years of immigration policy, ensuring the maximum number of immigrants to Canada was the overriding objective. The location of immigration agents and the focus of financial incentives indicated the groups of immigrants which the government preferred. Throughout these years, Britons, northern Europeans, and Americans received the most attention and the most generous offers of assistance in immigrating to Canada. And while formal barriers to entry on the basis of race did not exist until the passing of the Chinese Immigration Act in 1885, the manner in which promotional activities and incentives were distributed exhibited strong racial preferences.

The open posture towards immigration that predominated in the first thirty years after Confederation has led one commentator to characterize the period as the 'Golden Age' of Canadian immigration, in which the immigrant to Canada enjoyed a 'charmed status.'[161] Not only were there few entry prohibitions, but the government offered inducements by way of travel assistance to selected immigrants, and affordable homesteads to intending settlers. As well, once in Canada a person was permitted to remain without fear of removal.[162] The highest status one could achieve was that of a British subject, which was relatively easy to obtain by becoming naturalized after three years of residency. Upon naturalization, a person was entitled in Canada to all the rights enjoyed by other British subjects.[163]

It has been suggested that the open immigration posture assumed not only by Canada, but also by Britain and the United States at this time, was informed by liberal values. Describing the American experience, Peter Schuck writes:

> The liberalism of America's first century conceived of persons as autonomous, self-defining individuals possessing equal moral worth and dignity and equally entitled to society's consideration and respect. This entitlement was in principle universally shared, a natural right deriving not from the particularities of one's time, place or status, but from one's irreducible humanity. The good society, in this view, was one in which each individual enjoyed maximum liberty to pursue his or her own conception of the good by deciding whether, and on what terms, to enter into contractual relationships with other equally free individuals. Liberal ideology was reflected in a policy of essentially open borders, one that strongly encouraged, indeed actively recruited, mass immigration to the United States.[164]

Similarly, Shin Imai writes that liberal ideology played a key role in the formulation of British immigration policy. British immigration law throughout the nineteenth century imposed few restrictions on the movement of people in and out of the United Kingdom. The historical lack of general legislation in the area was reinforced, according to Imai, by an intellectual climate which recognized the right of asylum and opposed controls on aliens. Although several exclusionary statutes were passed in Britain in response to specific disturbances, these statutes were never used, so that, from 1825 to the beginning of the twentieth century, no alien was excluded or expelled from the United Kingdom.[165] Imai asserts that this strong ideological tendency against immigration controls made itself felt in Canada as well.[166]

While liberal values may have played a role in determining the direction of American and British immigration policy throughout the nineteenth century, there is little to suggest that it exerted great influence in Canada. Although business interests were in favour of economic liberalism in so far as bringing in immigrant labourers was concerned, they were not fully committed to liberal values in other areas of economic endeavour. Government intervention in the economy through the erection of protective tariff barriers and the provision of extensive loans and subsidies to major enterprises like the railways were welcomed by industrialists and entrepreneurs who, as recipients of government largesse, were not avid supporters of laissez-faire liberalism.

Similarly, throughout this period there is no evidence to suggest that there was any more support for political liberalism. Liberal values which held that each individual possessed equal moral worth and was equally entitled to society's respect held little currency at this time, as evidenced by the limitation of the franchise to non-Aboriginal, non-Chinese males and as illustrated by the community's treatment of Asians, Aboriginal peoples, and other 'inferior' races. A commitment to liberal values, when expressed, was more likely to be used as a rhetorical flourish rather than an accurate reflection of genuinely held principles. Thus, while Macdonald resisted outright exclusion of Chinese immigrants on the grounds that it was 'contrary to the laws of nations to stop people coming in and excluding them,'[167] he nevertheless could prohibit them from voting on the basis that the Chinese were mere sojourners of an inferior race, lacking British instincts or aspirations.[168]

It is not surprising that the government pursued an immigration policy that favoured the interests of business and industry, given that many who held public office at this time were part of the Canadian corporate elite.[169] Moreover, according to Wallace Clement, industrialization throughout this period was largely funded by immigrant capital. In 1885, for example, one half of the industrialists who dominated Canadian manufacturing were immigrants, and four-fifths had fathers born outside Canada.[170] The fact that policy was designed to serve the interests of big business was true in other areas of public policy as well. Macdonald's tariff policy favoured central Canadian industrialists, as did many of his land-grant schemes. Most of the companies which were assigned large areas in the West to colonize were controlled by friends of the Conservative government, as were the ranching conglomerates that were given favourable leases on vast tracts of land in southern Alberta. These ranchers were also given preferential treatment in contracts concerning the sale of cattle and beef stock to the federal government. The largest of these ranchers was the Northwest Cattle Company, controlled by Sir Hugh Allan of the CPR and the Allan steamship line.[171]

This is not to imply that the government was unresponsive to other interests in the immigration debate, but only to suggest that, where interests conflicted, the government was apt to favour entrepreneurial concerns over all others. Thus, as long as Chinese labour was needed to construct the western leg of the CPR, the government resolutely refused to impose any limitations on Chinese immigration. Once the line was completed, however, it was quick to enact the Chinese Immigration Act, although careful not to be so exclusionary that trade with China would be adversely affected. Similarly, as long as industrial enterprises were benefiting from the importation of American labourers, the government was unwilling to enact restrictions to impede the flow. Nor was it prepared to respond to the demands by labour unions that advance-passage schemes be terminated and immigrant workers be prevented from accepting employment in Canada for wages below the prevailing rate.

By the late 1880s, the influx into Canada of thousands of Chinese immigrants, pauper British children, and others whose religion and customs were quite dissimilar from the Canadian norm had stimulated debate on the kinds of immigrants Canada should be admitting and the dangers of admitting those whose racial characteristics rendered them unassimilable. Doctors such as C.K. Clarke warned the country of the dangers of admitting British pauper children whose base hereditary characteristics threatened the health of future generations. Residents of British Columbia claimed that, given the burgeoning population of China, the West was in danger of being overrun by Chinese immigrants whose moral depravity, poor hygiene, and willingness to work for low wages threatened the physical health and economic well-being of the white race. Labour unions also warned of the perils likely to befall a country who, in admitting the paupers, waifs, and degenerates of this world, not only hurt its own indigenous workers, but threatened the vitality of the community as a whole.[172]

While racial exclusions incorporated into the Immigration Act await a subsequent period, there was growing official recognition that racial barriers to entry were desirable. Macdonald himself had demonstrated his sensitivity to such an approach with the Chinese Immigration Act and the Chinese-voter exclusion in the Electoral Franchise Act. He also seemed eager to avoid 'the mass of ignorance and vice that has flooded into [the United States] with socialism, atheism and all other isms,' a situation he attributed to liberal immigration policies.[173] Or as F. Clement Brown expressed it in his 1897 magazine article 'Canadians Abroad,' the Americans had suffered in their physical pedigree from contamination by the influx of the 'poisonous dregs of Europe': 'the moral and intellectual standards of Americans are bound to fall by reason of the immoral, illiterate, restless and degraded human importations from the eastern world. The Canadian race is favoured in that it is not corrupted in this mischievous way, and its chances for advancement in every respect are just that far augmented.'[174]

The view that Canada's population should remain homogeneous was also beginning to be voiced in the government's annual immigration reports at the end of this period. In words that were to be repeated forty years later by Charles Blair, who was the director in charge of the most exclusionary immigration policy in Canadian history, A.M. Burgess, the deputy minister of the Interior, wrote in 1893 that, 'if the Government of Canada cared merely for numbers, for quantity rather than quality, there would be little difficulty, even now, when the governing conditions are so extremely unfavourable, in producing an enormous volume of immigration to this country at comparatively little expense.'[175]

Industrialization, Immigration, and the Foundation of Twentieth-Century Immigration Policy, 1896–1914

As the nineteenth century came to a close, Canada, like many other Western nations, enjoyed an industrial boom that was to alter irrevocably the economic, demographic, and social landscape of the country In fact, the enormous transformations that occurred in Canada from the turn of the century until the outbreak of the First World War mark this period as one of the most distinctive in its history. After years of disappointing economic growth, Canada was propelled into a period of dramatic economic expansion in agriculture and other resource industries, as well as in manufacturing and the service sector. Among the factors that both stimulated and sustained the economic development during this period were: improved prices for Canadian staples; the introduction of new forms of wheat suitable for prairie cultivation; technological innovations which opened up new industries for profitable development (such as hydro-electric production, and pulp-and-paper manufacturing); and declining transportation rates which, coupled with increased foreign demand for Canadian exports, improved Canada's trading position.[1]

Just as immigrants had been essential to the progress of the nation in the first thirty years of its existence, so, too, were they central to the industrialization and resultant changes that occurred in the next fifteen years of its development. Initially attracted by Canadian prosperity and encouraged by aggressive Canadian promotional campaigns, immigrants poured into the country in unprecedented numbers. Between 1896 and 1914, Canada experienced six of the ten largest annual immigration levels ever registered. More than 3 million people immigrated within this eighteen year period, twice as many as were recorded to have come within the preceding thirty years.[2] In 1896, close to 17,000 immigrants arrived in Canada; in 1913 that number had increased to just over 400,000.[3] Yet immigrants were not simply attracted by Canada's economic growth; they also fuelled it: by their demand, immigrants helped spur industrial activity and, by their labour on farms and the railways, and in the mines, factories, and service sectors, they supported it.

Nearly 50 per cent of the immigrants who came to Canada settled in the cities and worked in industrial employment.[4] Approximately 30 per cent of all immigrants purchased homesteads in the West,[5] and the bulk of the remainder were employed in the mines or in bush camps as railway navvies, labourers for the lumber and logging industries and in agriculture, or workers on hydro-development projects.[6] Thus, in virtually every area of economic expansion throughout this period, immigrant workers were found in substantial numbers.

While the government sanctioned, and even participated in, the re-cruitment of foreign labourers, immigration policy continued to be formally articulated in terms of attracting agriculturalists to Canada. A preference for British and American immigrants was frequently expressed, while Continental Europeans and Asians were permitted entry to fill the gaps that preferred groups were unable to meet. In this regard, the goals of immigration policy during this time were not markedly different from those of previous decades. The period is notable, however, for several rea-sons. The first is that immigration had an enormous impact on the size and composition of the Canadian population. In 1911, there were ap-proximately 7 million people living in Canada, which was more than 30 per cent higher than the figure reported a decade earlier, an increase largely attributed to immigration.[7] Not only did the size of the Canadian population increase substantially throughout this period, but the distribu-tion and composition of the population throughout Canada also changed dramatically. The period saw a steady drift of the rural population to the cities, which were also attractive to recently arrived immigrants because of the industrial employment opportunities offered there. In 1891, one-third of the population lived in towns with populations of more than 1,000 people. Twenty years later, close to 50 per cent of the population was considered urban.[8] Between 1901 to 1910, Canada's largest centres experienced expo-nential growth; Montreal grew by 50 per cent, Toronto by 81 per cent, Winnipeg by 200 per cent, Edmonton by 600 per cent, and Vancouver by 300 per cent.[9]

Although urban areas experienced gains in population relative to rural areas during this period, development in Canada's agricultural heartland was no less spectacular. Hundreds of thousands of people poured into the Prairie provinces, which saw an increase in population of close to

1 million people in the first decade of the century.[10] As more people purchased farms, agricultural output increased enormously, and with it grew the demand for more rail lines, freight cars, transatlantic steamers, construction materials, grain elevators, agricultural implements and machines, and all manner of consumer goods. The rate of growth was astounding as towns and cities mushroomed across the West. Some of those which started as simple railway terminals were transformed into bustling commercial centres almost overnight.

Another feature of the changing demographic landscape was the shift in the ethnic composition of the population. Not only did immigrants flow into the country in unprecedented numbers, but they did so from more diverse sources than previously. Early emigration to Canada had been primarily from the British Isles, which was the source of approximately 60 per cent of all the Dominion's immigrants between 1867 and 1890.[11] While more British immigrants were to come to Canada over the next twenty years than ever before, their percentage of the total was to decline. By 1914, British immigrants accounted for 38 per cent of admissions, American immigrants represented 34 per cent, while approximately 25 per cent came from other European countries, most arriving from the central, eastern, and southern parts of the Continent.[12] This shifting pattern of immigration resulted in a change in the country's ethnic composition. At the time of Confederation, 60 per cent of the Canadian population was of British origin, 30 per cent of French descent, and approximately 7 per cent of other European origin. By 1911, the British proportion had fallen to 55 per cent, and the French to 29 per cent, while the other European component had risen to approximately 9 per cent. Given the increasing proportion of Europeans in the total immigration flow, this shift in the ethnic composition of Canada was to continue, so that, by 1921, 15 per cent of the population was of neither French nor British origin.[13]

In addition to these dramatic demographic shifts, this period is also distinctive from an immigration-policy perspective because the legislative changes that were implemented, in part as a consequence of the demographic and social repercussions of massive immigration, laid the foundations for twentieth-century immigration policy. In particular, the Immigration Acts of 1906 and 1910 provided the framework upon which subsequent immigration legislation was patterned.[14] At the core of the immigration policy that evolved during the eighteen years between 1896 and 1914 was the principle that the absolute right of the state to admit and exclude new members was an essential feature of state sovereignty. From this basic premise, a system of immigration regulation emerged which was largely controlled by the executive branch of government. From this point forward, immigration would be tightly regulated: those deemed undesirable were defined explicitly in the Immigration Act and regulations; formal procedures for determining admissibility and deportation were legislated; and the requirements governing the acquisition of citizenship were made more rigorous. To ensure that the government retained sufficient flexibility to respond to changing social and economic conditions within Canada, the Cabinet was legislatively empowered with enormous discretion to set the exact contours of immigration policy at any given time. Thus, the executive branch of government was free to determine – unencumbered by judicial or parliamentary scrutiny – those who would be permitted to enter the country, those who would be accorded citizenship, and those who would be excluded or expelled.

It was this flexibility in the execution of immigration policy that makes this period important from a third perspective. Both the rapid pace of development and the entry of unprecedented numbers of newcomers created problems and tensions that were often revealed in the public discourse concerning immigration policy. Since the legislation conferred so much power on the executive branch of government, Cabinet was able to alter its admissions and removal policies relatively quickly in response to the economic and political realities of the day.

The various ideas and interests that were reflected in the immigration policy of this period are best understood in relation to the circumstances that often generated them. The transformation of Canadian society came at a price. The wealth that both produced and was a product of dramatic economic expansion was paralleled by the poverty that accompanied such growth. City life was typically marred by pollution, poor sanitation, inadequate housing, crime, and disease. The plight of the urban worker was often quite desperate. Most worked ten to twelve hours a day, six days a week, in grim factories where the work was often dull and monotonous, discipline harsh, the rate of industrial accidents high, and compensation for injuries uncommon. Generally, workers had no job security and no unemployment insurance, and so could be laid off or fired at will without redress or benefits. Since labourers were in abundant supply, wages were low and did not keep pace with the cost of living. As a result, families often needed more than one wage-earner to survive, women and children being paid one-half to one-quarter of the wages men received.[15]

Urban labourers endured not only bleak working environments, but, for many, appalling living conditions. Living in overcrowded, poorly serviced tenement housing, without the benefit of purified water, pasteurized milk, adequate sanitation, and medical vaccines, they were particularly vulnerable to disease. Montreal, for example, had one of the highest infant mortality rates in the world: one in four children there died before the age of one year.[16] Within the cramped, foetid environment of most lower-class city slums, frustrations borne out of wretched living and working conditions were often channelled into racial rather than class wars. The blame for intolerable living and working environments was frequently directed at the immigrant population rather than at local and federal governments which encouraged massive unregulated industrial growth without attempting to ensure an acceptable quality of life for all citizens.[17]

In the mines, lumber and logging areas, and railway work camps, life was also harsh, and the racial tensions evident in the major urban areas were also present. As was the case with industrial workers, those engaged in resource extraction and on the railways were paid low wages, and worked long hours in physically demanding and dangerous jobs with no job security, accident compensation, or unemployment benefits to protect them. Frequently they lived in company-run camps or towns, where the cost of their lodging was deducted from their pay, and where they were charged exorbitant prices for their supplies, purchased at company-run stores. In such towns, the company often controlled the newspaper, the police, and the magistrates, with the result that worker dissention was dangerous, and frustrations were frequently channeled into violence and alcohol abuse. Sanitation was poor, government safety inspection infrequent and medical services often inadequate and expensive. It was not uncommon for workers to leave their employment as poor as when they started.[18]

While workers in general, and, in particular, the unskilled, were subjected to many forms of exploitation, the foreign-born were among the most exposed. Left largely unrepresented by trade unions, lacking political leverage, often unable to speak English, and desperate for work, foreign labourers were vulnerable to severe forms of exploitation, abuse, and discrimination. Indeed, the history of the period is replete with examples of the federal and provincial governments' deliberate ignorance of exploitive recruitment and employment practices in relation to immigrant labour.[19] In primary industries and construction, where safety standards were not imposed and/or safety inspection was infrequent or inadequate, high accident rates were often attributed to immigrant workers' unfamiliarity with English, their lack of skills, or their mental deficiencies.[20]

In light of the severity of the living and working environments that faced most Canadians, it is not surprising to find that tensions towards newcomers grew throughout this period, and that immigration became a more contentious issue than it had been in the past. In fact, aside from industrialists and entrepreneurs, no other visible group applauded the immigration policy of the day. Most of those who espoused non-materialist interests argued for more selectivity. Law-enforcement officials registered their alarm at the growing incidence of crime, which they attributed to the rapid influx of people who did not share British customs and values. Church organizations and social-service providers, overwhelmed by the demands for their assistance and appalled at the poverty and health conditions characteristic of the growing urban ethnic ghettos, cautioned against an immigration policy that paid little heed to such realities. Many physicians joined their voices to the calls for greater immigration restrictions, arguing not only that the admission of so many immigrants of 'inferior' stock would have an adverse social impact immediately, but that their negative traits, genetically transmitted, would cause irreparable harm to future generations.[21]

Given the hundreds of thousands of immigrants pouring into the country annually, a relatively small portion of whom were French-speaking, French Canadians became increasingly alarmed at the dilution of their presence within the country. Throughout this period of great immigration, the absence of aggressive recruitment of French-speaking immigrants was raised by Quebec MPs, who protested at what they regarded as the 'conspiracy against French immigration which is carried on in the Department of the Interior.'[22]

Organized workers also became increasingly vocal in their objections to the admission of those who, it was claimed, competed unfairly with Canadian workers and were used to break strikes.[23] In their calls for the exclusion of the 'tramps,' 'loafers,' and 'ex-convicts' assisted by British organizations, and for the prohibition of the 'servile,' 'criminal,' and 'morally degenerate' Asian immigrants, labour unions were joined by many other Canadians who worried that the future health of the country was in jeopardy unless greater selectivity was imposed on immigrant admissions. Whether it was Anglo-Canadian farmers in the Midwest, miners and fishermen in British Columbia, law-enforcement officials and public-service providers in Ontario, or French-Canadian nationalists in Manitoba and Quebec, the concern for a more homogeneous society was ardently felt and strongly debated throughout the period.

In 1892, the responsibilities for immigration were transferred from the Department of Agriculture to the Department of the Interior. Since the Department of the Interior was in charge of settlement of public lands, and, given the large proportion of immigrants intending to settle in Manitoba and the Northwest, it was considered advisable to bring both the settlement of public lands and immigration within the same department. The visions of the two ministers in charge of the Department of the Interior during the Liberal government under Sir Wilfrid Laurier (1896–1911) reflected to a degree the divisions that were played out in the public domain regarding the appropriate immigration policy for Canada. Clifford Sifton, the minister of the Interior between 1896 and 1905, was committed to the relatively unregulated importation of British and European farmers into the largely unsettled prairies of the Canadian West. The reforms he instituted throughout his tenure were aimed primarily at achieving this end. His successor, Frank Oliver, who ran the department until 1911, was also committed to Western settlement. He, however, favoured a more selective immigration policy, and the legislative changes enacted during his period of office reflected this concern.

As influential as the ministers of the Interior were, they alone did not shape immigration policy. Both Sifton and Oliver were opposed to the mass importation of unskilled labourers to Canada. Nevertheless, throughout this period, the proportion of unskilled workers to total annual immigrant arrivals steadily rose. Estimates place the number of unskilled male immigrants at 30 per cent at the beginning of the period, and as high as 43 per cent by 1914.[24] The divergence between the priorities articulated by the ministers in charge of immigration and the practice that emerged is explained by the influence large employers of immigrant labour wielded in both the Laurier and Borden Cabinets. The fact that foreign workers were admitted to Canada in large numbers despite the stated official preference for agriculturalists did not mean that the government had surrendered control of immigration policy to big business; for it was also true that the interests of big business and the interests of the government in furthering its larger political agenda frequently coincided. The building of railways, for example, was an essential precursor to prairie settlement. To the extent that foreign labour was needed for railway construction work, the government was willing to override the vehement objections of trade unions, nationalist organizations, immigration officials, and even members of its own party, and permit the entry of workers from what were generally regarded as 'inferior races.' Describing the Cabinet discussions on the issue, Mackenzie King wrote how he, as minister of Labour, and Frank Oliver were the only Cabinet members who opposed the admission of foreign navvies: 'Oliver is strong in his opposition to labour being brought into the country to work on the railways that ultimately is not going to be of service for settlement and favours making restrictions on virtually all but northern people of Europe. I agree with him, but we are about alone in this, others preferring to see the railway work hurried.[25]

The Focus of Admissions Policy

SIFTON'S REVITALIZATION OF PROMOTIONAL ACTIVITIES

In 1902, the key to Canadian prosperity was summarized by Clifford Sifton in these words: 'Here, then, we have the situation in a nutshell – a vast and productive territory becoming quickly occupied by a throng of people who will be called upon to take up the duties of citizenship almost at once, whose successful pursuit of agriculture will make them financially independent, and who in a short time will constitute a most potent factor in the national life of Canada.'[26] In holding this view, he was not unusual, for his vision of prosperity resembled those of the ministers who had preceded him. It was premised on the conviction that, once Western settlement was secured through the immigration of agriculturalists, industry and commerce would follow. Where Sifton differed, however, was in the energy, resources, and unusual methods he used to reach this end.

Immediately upon assuming office, Sifton reorganized his department in a manner that centralized decision making in Ottawa and afforded the minister and his officials' broader discretion in setting policy. He also endeavoured to free encumbered settlement lands by, among other things, persuading the Hudson's Bay Company and the Canadian Pacific Railway (CPR) to sell lands that had been reserved to them. To make homesteading more attractive and feasible for would-be immigrants, he simplified the homestead-acquisition procedure and provided for the pre-emption of adjacent sections at reduced rates. These reforms apparently bore strong results, for, of the close to 200,000 homestead entries made between 1874 and 1905, more than 55 per cent were made in the first five years of the century.[27]

In addition to these administrative reforms, Sifton embarked upon an extensive promotional campaign. He increased the number of Canadian immigration agents in Great Britain and the United States, and armed them with more promotional material and literature than ever before produced by the Canadian government.[28] In Great Britain, the Canadian advertising budget was raised from $12,000 in 1901 to more than $16,000 six years later. Likewise, the number of immigration agents and support personnel was increased from eighteen in 1901 to almost fifty by 1911.[29] In addition, advertising techniques were vastly improved throughout both Sifton's and Oliver's tenures, and included the widespread use of marketing surveys; stylized brochures and promotional pamphlets; large advertisements in the British popular press; billboards in prominent locations; and the exhibition of Canadian grains and produce at agricultural fairs, Canadian government offices, and the offices of leading steamship booking agents. The government also publicized the attractions of Canada in schools by distributing wall maps, atlases, and textbooks on Canada, and by sponsoring essay contests on the subject of Canada. The agents of steamship companies, colonization organizations, and railways were offered bonuses for every agriculturalist, farm worker, and domestic worker they assisted in emigrating to Canada. Their interests in recruitment were myriad and included the sale of transatlantic tickets, increased passage and freight on Canadian rail lines, potential land purchasers, and, in the case of rail companies, possible workers for their burgeoning construction projects.

In the United States, immigration offices were opened throughout the Midwest, with as many as twenty-four offices in operation at a given time.[30] Canadian immigration agents, supported by a well-financed publicity campaign,[31] were instructed to disseminate information on Canada through mailings, lectures, personal interviews, advertisements in newspapers and farm journals, and exhibitions of Canadian produce at state and county fairs. Immigration agents were also authorized to help prospective settlers choose among available homesteads, and to coordinate their movement to Canada by selecting routes, arranging tickets, and assisting those whose family head had moved to Canada in advance of other members.

In addition to promotional work in the United States, the Canadian government, in partnership with the railways, sponsored guided tours of Canada for prospective settlers, farm delegations, and the press. These tours were often offered on the understanding that the participants, upon their return to the United States, would write reports or articles about their journey, with the assistance of information and press releases provided by the government of Canada, Favourable reports were then used by the government to further advertise the advantages of the Canadian West. One particularly successful excursion was undertaken in 1899, when members of the American National Editorial Association, representing 1,000 newspapers, were brought to Canada as guests of the federal government and the CPR. That same year, more than 6,000 American papers carried an illustrated article on Canada written by a senior official of the Canadian Department of the Interior.[32]

Sifton's commitment to aggressive promotional work extended throughout Europe, including countries which had not previously been the focus of Canadian promotional strategies. One of the lessons of the previous period was that the most preferred immigration source countries – namely, Britain and the United States–would not yield the number of immigrants required for successful prairie settlement. Sifton therefore initiated promotional efforts for the recruitment of Eastern and central European agriculturalists. In later years, he defended his policy in words that are among the most quoted of any immigration minister. Central and Eastern European farmers were, according to Sifton, among the most qualified to emigrate to Canada. 'When I speak of quality I have in mind something that is quite different from what is in the mind of the average writer or speaker upon the question of immigration. I think that the stalwart peasant in a sheepskin coat, born to the soil, whose forefathers have been farmers for ten generations, with a stout wife and half-dozen children, is good quality.'[33]

Since many countries on the Continent had emigration restrictions, Sifton attempted to circumvent them by entering an agreement with a secret organization of European booking agents known as the North Atlantic Trading Company. Under the agreement, the company received $15,000 annually to secure immigrants from northern, central, and Eastern European countries, and booking agents were given bonuses of £1 for every female domestic worker, farmer, and farm labourer, and accompanying family member, whom the agents sent to Canada.[34] The scheme was cancelled in 1905[35] amid condemnation by the Opposition that the arrangement not only attempted to circumvent illegally the emigration restrictions of foreign countries, but, in doing so, encouraged the mass immigration of undesirable immigrants at great public expense.[36] Between 1901 and 1906, the arrangement was believed to have resulted in the entry of approximately 50,000 immigrants at a cost to the public purse of close to $250,000.[37]

Sifton's commitment to the immigration of agriculturalists was matched by his antipathy towards almost any other kind of immigrant. In 1902, he explained the department's policy as follows: 'The test we have to apply is this: Does the person intending to come to Canada intend to become an agriculturalist? If he does we encourage him to come and give him every assistance we can. But we give no encouragement whatever to persons to come to work for wages as a rule ...'[38]

Although Sifton acknowledged that there might be a need for foreign labour in industry, he preferred to reserve such employment for recently arrived farmers desirous of accumulating savings necessary to begin their homesteading. He was therefore a staunch advocate of measures such as the Chinese head tax[39] and the Alien Labour Act of 1897,[40] which were designed to restrict the admission of contract labourers to Canada. Yet, aside from these measures, the immigration policy of the Sifton era, like those pursued in the thirty years following Confederation, was one of minimal regulation. Although Sifton introduced more rigorous medical examinations at ports of entry and the erection of more detention facilities for those who were infectious,[41] he resisted imposing tougher controls on the grounds that they either were impracticable or would discourage immigrants from choosing Canada over other countries. For example, in 1899, upon being questioned as to why Canada did not require medical examinations of all prospective immigrants, Sifton explained that it would be impossible to institute examinations in foreign countries without prior agreement with the authorities there. Using Hamburg as an example, which was the port through which most European emigrants passed on their way to Canada, Sifton claimed that port authorities were responsible for examining immigrants 'and my information is that it would be difficult, if not impossible, to get any arrangements made that would be satisfactory.'[42]

Sifton was also not in favour of rejecting immigrants who, upon arriving in Canada, were found to be destitute. To do so, he claimed, 'would place ourselves in antagonism with the steamship agents, and after an examination of the question I am satisfied, that would stop people from coming here at all.[43] As he later explained more generally: 'there is no Exclusion Act in the Dominion of Canada at the present time, and there never has been, so far as I am aware. Therefore, it is no part of the duty of the Government, under the law to appoint agents for the purpose of keeping people from coming to Canada.'[44]

When Sifton resigned in 1905, approximately 650,000 immigrants had entered Canada during his nine-year term of office, more than 60 per cent of whom had come in the three years prior to his departure. Annual admissions, which stood at close to 17,000 in 1896, exceeded 146,000 in 1905. This eightfold increase in yearly admissions corresponded to a similar rise in government expenditures on immigration. In 1896, $120,000 was spent on immigration. Within four years, Sifton had increased this amount to $434,563. In 1905, close to $1 million was spent on immigration, over eight times the amount spent nine years earlier.[45]

Britain continued to be largest immigrant source country and would remain so throughout the entire period. Between 1900 and 1914, well over 1 million British immigrants settled in Canada. Although their percentage of total annual admissions declined from their peak in these years of 45 per cent between 1906 and 1908, nevertheless, at the close of the period, British immigrants still accounted for approximately 38 per cent of yearly immigration flows, continuing to comprise the single largest immigrant group of the period.[46]

There are several reasons for the large number of British immigrants to Canada at this time. Agricultural depressions, unemployment, urban overcrowding, and lack of social mobility in Britain made its citizens more receptive to the allure of Canada so actively promoted by the Canadian government. The favourable economic climate in Canada, the abundance of available homesteads, and the improved transatlantic and transcontinental travel also combined to make Canada an inviting destination.

There is some controversy over whether the 'push' factors in Britain – namely, economic conditions and the rigid class system – were the greatest influence behind the large British exodus to Canada, or whether the 'pull' factors in Canada – economic prosperity and aggressive promotion – were more influential.[47] It was probably a combination of factors which prompted so many people from the British Isles to leave their homeland for a relatively uncertain future. As one young immigrant who decided to make the move to Canada in 1910 explained,

> when I went to school, on my way home every day I stopped to look at a big coloured poster of a wheat field in stook. On it was printed '160 acres land free.' I made up my mind, 'That's what I want' and I got all the pamphlets on it and read all about it ... The result was I left home, worked in a hotel and saved my money and sailed in March on the Allan liner 'Corsican.' I arrived in Winnipeg with thirty cents which I spent on some pork and beans and coffee. I went to work on a farm south of Boissevain for $10.00 a month. After two years I went to Saskatchewan for a homestead.[48]

British immigrants continued generally to be considered the most preferred essentially because they were of the same stock as most Canadian-born citizens, and would therefore be the least likely to have adjustment problems and be the most likely to make an enduring contribution to the country. By the turn of the century, another argument was added in their favour – namely, that, in the absence of significant immigration from the British Isles, other immigrants of 'inferior classes' would come to meet the population needs of the country. As Rudyard Kipling urged Canada during his visit in 1907, 'immigration is what you want in the West. You must have labourers there. You want immigration, and the best way to keep the yellow man out is to get the white man in. If you keep out the white then you will have the yellow man, for you must have labour. Work must be done, and there is certain work to do which a white man won't do so long as he can get a yellow man to do it. Pump in the immigrants from the Old country. Pump them in; England has five millions of people to spare.'[49] At the time that Kipling was making his speeches across the country, and perhaps even influencing his remarks, a great deal of controversy was being aired in the press over the quality of British immigrants arriving in Canada. One of the most frequently voiced concerns was that, compared with other immigrants, the British did not take to farming, only 18 per cent having purchased homesteads between 1897 and 1913, as compared with 33 per cent of American immigrants and 29 per cent of Continental immigrants.[50] Many Canadian farmers complained that the British were among the least desirable farm hands owing to their inexperience and their unreliability, often leaving farms, complaining that the work was too strenuous and the pay too low. As well, Canadian workers protested the arrival of thousands of British skilled workers and assisted labourers through their representatives such as the Trades and Labor Congress. They alleged that these immigrants competed unfairly with Canadian workers, who were available and able to meet employer demand. Even many employers, particularly within the railways and the primary-resource extraction industries, voiced complaints about British labourers. Unlike many European and Asian workers who did not speak English, British workers earned the reputation of being intolerant of the low wages and harsh working environments that characterized these labour-intensive industries.

In several areas of employment, however, the demand for British workers often exceeded supply. For example, the immigration of British female domestic workers, milliners, dressmakers, nurses, and teachers was generally below demand, in part because many such occupations did not offer better wages and more steady employment than in Britain.[51] Although domestic work was often better paid than in England, it, too, did not attract enough British women to meet demand since it was considered harder than similar work at home. Finally, the loneliness associated with the work, being far removed from family and friends, was an additional disincentive for many prospective female immigrants.[52]

As in previous years, the promotion of female immigrants continued with the help of various charitable societies in England, who generally operated in a similar fashion, first identifying those women who were interested in emigrating, then selecting those deemed appropriate, and advancing loans for passage and initial settlement. While *en route*, women were escorted by matrons, who accompanied the new immigrants to their destinations in Canada. The work in Canada was aided by specially appointed immigration agents as well as by charitable women's organizations such as the Young Women's Christian Association (YWCA) and the National Council of Women of Canada. These organizations helped the new arrivals find jobs and become settled. Sometimes the women proceeded to Canada with prearranged employment, offered through the Canadian Manufacturers' Association, individual companies, or Canadians in need of domestic help.[53]

The demand for British child workers also consistently exceeded supply throughout this period. More than 33,500 children emigrated to Canada from Britain between 1901 and 1915 as compared with close to 300,000 applications for their services.[54] Nearly half of the children who came did so under the auspices of Dr Barnardo's Homes.[55] Despite the ongoing revelations of cases of gross neglect and child abuse,[56] the government continued to approve of the movement and insist that it was, on the whole, a success.[57]

As in the previous period, American farmers were also much sought after by the Canadian government. Their common language and customs, their knowledge of prairie farming, and their familiarity with modern farming techniques made their adjustment relatively easy. These characteristics, coupled with the fact that many brought more cash and 'settler goods,' including horses, cattle, and farm implements, than any other group, made American farmers particularly attractive.

In addition to intensive government promotional activities, American land companies were also active in promoting the Canadian West, several having purchased by 1900 vast areas of land previously granted to railway companies. Since railway lands were adjacent to government lands,[58] settlers could acquire the 160 acres offered by the government with the option to buy a neighbouring quarter-section from the land company. One of the more prominent companies operating at this time was the Canadian-American Land Company of Minneapolis, whose agents worked in cooperation with Dominion agents. In 1901, the company purchased 170,000 acres of land in eastern Saskatchewan, which, within five months, was sold in homesteading parcels to American farmers. The Luse Land

and Development Company was equally successful in bringing thousands of American settlers to the Canadian West, employing 500 agents within the United States to help do so. Perhaps most noteworthy were the activities of the Saskatchewan Valley Land Company, which acquired 839,000 acres in 1902 between Regina and Saskatchewan. Within two years, more than 1,700 land entries were made and three new towns had been founded within its tract of land.[59] These land sales were enormously profitable for the land companies. For example, the Saskatchewan Land Company purchased its land at $0.24 an acre and then sold it to settlers for between $1.30 and $1.95 per acre.[60]

There was some concern expressed across the country over the rate of American settlement across the West. In 1902, immigration from the United States was recorded to be around 26,000, after which time it steadily increased, averaging 55,000 per year for the rest of the decade, and 125,000 annually until the outbreak of the First World War. Between 1910 and 1914, departmental figures suggest that more than I million Americans emigrated to Canada.[61] Some people complained that the profits realized by American land companies were unconscionable. Others were concerned that, given their numbers, Americans would dominate the development of the West, controlling most of its industry and drawing the prairies away from Britain and the Canadian confederation and into the American sphere of influence.[62] Judging from the ongoing promotion of American immigration throughout the entire period, and the explicit and implicit encouragement given to American companies to invest in Canada at this time, it is clear that the government did not share this concern. B.E. Walker, the general manager of the Canadian Bank of Commerce, probably voiced the views of many of the country's leading entrepreneurs as well as politicians when he dismissed the concerns of those who feared American domination: 'All we want is population, and let the Americans come, as many as will. If they do bring in American capital to erect factories, it is not likely that they will bar Canadian labour.[63] D.R. Wilke, the general manager of the Imperial Bank of Canada, concurred, stating that 'the immigration of Americans in great numbers I consider a decided benefit to the country.'[64]

Another subject of debate concerning American immigration was group colonization. The movement of Mormons to the West was one example. Having begun in the late 1880s, the movement gained momentum in the following decade. Sifton, impressed with the early Mormon achievements in Alberta, granted them an additional 125,000 acres of land in 1899, upon which they began to cultivate sugar beets, and, by 1902, a beet-processing plant was in operation. Frank Oliver was also supportive of Mormon settlement, and, by 1914, there were more than 13,000 Mormons in Canada, most of them concentrated in Alberta.[65] In response to criticism from some Protestant clergymen for allowing the group settlement of the Mormon sect in Alberta, Frank Oliver defended the government's policy: 'They have given an object lesson in agriculture in the south-western corner of the Canada's prairies which has increased the value of the whole semi-arid region of southern Alberta and south-western Saskatchewan ... Nothing can be said against their citizenship. They are sober, orderly, law-abiding, intelligent and progressive. They take an active and intelligent part in all duties of citizenship as well as agriculture and commercial life.'[66] Apart from the reservation of land for the Mormons, and later for Finnish immigrants arriving from both the United States and overseas, the Canadian government did not as a rule set aside land for group colonization. It did, however, permit various ethnic and religious groups to purchase large tracts of contiguous land for group settlement. One of the most prominent of such groups was the Catholic German Americans, the bulk of whom came to Canada in the period from 1900 to 1907. In 1902, their annual admissions exceeded 6,000 persons.[67] They came to the prairies desirous of establishing homogeneous communities. They were assisted in this endeavour by the German-American Land Company, which was a joint religious-lay venture that resulted in the Saskatchewan colonies of St. Peter and St. Joseph.

It was this tendency to live separate and apart, maintaining their own customs, religions, and in some cases particular modes of farming, that irritated many Anglo farmers who lived in the vicinity of such group settlements. One group which particularly provoked resentment was the Hutterites, who came from the United States and established colonies in the southern regions of Manitoba and Alberta. Their communal way of life, and their collective and successful farming practices, were resented by neighbouring farmers.[68] Years later, their pacifism and consequent refusal to bear arms in the First World War fostered intense hostility, leading to the prohibition of Hutterite immigration to Canada in 1919 and for several years thereafter.

In regard to overseas immigration, the government continued to expend considerable resources in attracting Scandinavian and German immigrants. Despite Canada's impressive economic growth and the efforts of the North Atlantic Trading Company, Canada still was unable to attract significant immigration from Scandinavia, the most sizeable movement consisting of 21,000 Finnish immigrants who emigrated to Canada between 1900 and 1911. The bulk of Scandinavian emigrants chose the United States over Canada, attracted by reports of the more agreeable climate and the greater employment opportunities there.[69]

As in previous years, the government spent considerable amounts of money and energy in trying to induce German emigration to Canada. The number of immigrants from Germany was disappointing, however, owing to the more favourable climate and the abundant economic opportunities available in the United States, as well as the presence of large German communities there to welcome and assist new arrivals. In addition, German farmers tended to prefer the forest and lake areas in the American Midwest, which more closely resembled Germany than did the treeless Canadian prairies.[70] Moreover, German emigration restrictions continued to have a disproportionately negative effect on Canada, seriously imped-ing Canadian promotional activities there.[71]

Department statistics place the number of German immigrants to Canada at close to 39,000 between 1901 and 1914. It is likely that the number from Germany was lower than this, because many Germans re-corded in this statistic were actually from the United States.[72] Among the immigrants from Germany were farmers and skilled workers who estab-lished themselves among the various German ethnic settlements across the country.[73]

Where Sifton's stewardship bore both novel and impressive results was in the immigration of central and Eastern Europeans, who arrived in Canada in unprecedented numbers. Failing to secure the volume of immigrants considered desirable from more traditional host countries, Sifton expanded the ambit of government promotional activities to in-clude areas within Russia, Romania, and the Austro-Hungarian Empire.

Sifton's encouragement of immigration from these non-traditional source areas contributed towards the significant number of ethnic Germans who emigrated to Canada throughout this period from Russia and Austria-Hungary, settling primarily in Alberta and Saskatchewan. In Russia, Russification policies that had led to a mass exodus of Mennonites in the 1870s continued and were an important factor influencing the ethnic-German exodus at this time. In 1891, for example, German ethnic schools came under the authority of the Russian administration, and Russian be-came the chief language of instruction. Restrictive land regulations pro-hibiting the sale of land to non-Russian citizens and, in some regions, to ethnic Germans, whether they had citizenship or not, were among the chief reasons behind the decision of many Germans to leave. In the Volga area of the country, these oppressive measures coincided with years of severe famine resulting from crop failures, which served to intensify the emigration movement.[74]

The German emigration from Austria-Hungary also had economic and ethno-political roots. In Galicia, for example, overpopulation, the lack of industrial employment opportunities, and political domination by the Poles, who adopted policies which were oppressive to other ethnic groups, were reasons for German emigration. Similarly, in the Banat region of southern Hungary, the domination by the Hungarian majority of the ethnic-German minority created conditions favourable to emigration. The imposition of the Magyar language as the only language to be used in the schools, courts, and government, together with the lack of advancement available to ethnic Germans, fed dissatisfaction and encouraged Germans to look elsewhere for their futures.[75]

In 1911, the Canadian-German population was about 400,000, an increase of more than 90,000 over the figure for the previous decade. In 1911, the ethnic-German population accounted for close to 6 per cent of the total population, making it the largest ethnic group in the country after the British and the French.[76] Nearly one-half of this population was in Ontario, and over one-third in the West.[77]

Among the other sizeable European immigrant groups to enter Canada throughout this period were Ukrainian and Polish immigrants, most of whom emigrated from the Austro-Hungarian Empire. From the thirteenth century to Ukrainian independence in 1991, the Ukrainian nation was dominated by the surrounding states of Russia, Poland, and Austria. In the 1890s, when the first wave of Ukrainian immigrants came to Canada, most Ukrainian territory was under Russian control. The other portion of Ukraine, consisting of the territories of Galicia and Bukovyna in the western region, was under the control of the Austro-Hungarian Empire. Of the approximately 120,000 Ukrainians who came to Canada between 1892 and 1914, most were peasant farmers from the provinces of Galicia and Bukovyna.[78]

The Ukrainians within the Austro-Hungarian Empire were largely farmers dependent on the large landowners. Ukrainian peasant landholdings were small, and productivity tended to be low. Because the Austro-Hungarian Empire had designated Galicia as its agricultural heartland – the source of agricultural commodities and the recipient of industrial goods from other areas of the Empire – Galicia was industrially underdeveloped, offering few employment opportunities for those who could not sustain themselves on the land. While the Ukrainian populist parties were successful in developing profitable agricultural collectives, many peasants still found their economic prospects in the region limited.[79] Poverty was the norm for most peasants, who worked for low wages yet faced high rents, usurious interest rates, and steep prices for timber to meet their fuel and building needs.[80] In addition to their economic problems, they were also restricted politically and culturally. The governing Polish majority in Galicia and the Romanian majority in Bukovyna denied their Ukrainian minorities equal educational opportunities and erected barriers to their participation in the professions and civil services.

One of the first Ukrainian immigration movements to Canada occurred in the 1890s with the assistance of the Prosvita Society, a Ukrainian nationalist association. Within four years, more than 27,000 had established themselves in Ukrainian settlement colonies, ten of which were in Manitoba and three in the Northwest.[81] Many of the first immigrants arrived destitute and in need of government assistance. Both their numbers and their impoverished condition upon arrival were greeted with alarm throughout the country. The indignation of the *Calgary Herald* was representative. In 1899, expressing its outrage at the paucity of immigrants from the British Isles settling in the Northwest Territories, compared with more than 1,000 'dirty, frowsy Galicians,' it questioned the meaning of Sifton's immigration policy:

> What Sifton means by affecting not to know that there is such a place as Great Britain on the map, and ignoring Britishers as desirable immigrants, preferring to minister with the power behind him and the funds at his disposal to the importing of a mass of human ignorance, filth and immorality is only known to his immediate friends ... This policy of building a nation on the lines of the tower of Babel, where the Lord confounded the languages so that people might not understand one another's speech is hardly applicable to the present century ...[82]

Unlike many other immigrants at the time, who preferred to settle in the fertile prairie grasslands suitable for wheat cultivation, the Ukrainians favoured the forested northern parkland, where timber and fuel supplies were plentiful. However, because the land was more marginal, they experienced many difficulties that limited their economic success. According to John Lehr, their preference for wooded areas was in part a legacy of their existence in Austria-Hungary, where timber was controlled and expensive. It was also reinforced by the writings of one of the first Ukrainian organizers of Canadian immigration, Osyp Oleskiv, who advised people to settle in close proximity to one another, preferably in the wooded parkland.

Moreover, Ukrainians were looking for self-sufficiency and not agriculture for commercial gain, and so they preferred the wooded area, where fuel was accessible, and where they could sustain themselves.[83] As Sifton explained, 'they do not go into farming on a large scale; they are not what we call wheat growers nor what we call ranchers. But they start in such a way that they are able to make a living, and I have no doubt that in a very short time ... they will develop into a thoroughly prosperous agricultural community.'[84] In order to raise funds to purchase or develop their homesteads, many farmers worked as seasonal farm labourers or were employed in railway construction, or in mining. While most of the Ukrainian immigrants were farmers, a number were single men who worked in the cities and lived near one another, forming distinct Ukrainian ethnic communities in such places as Winnipeg, Saskatoon, and Edmonton.[85]

The pattern of Polish settlement in Canada throughout this period mirrored that of Ukrainians in many respects. By the end of the eighteenth century, Poland was divided and under the control of the neighbouring states of Russia, Prussia, and Austria. Over the next century, attempts at rebellion were crushed, and only in Austria, in the region of Galicia, were the Polish people, in particular the landowning class, able to maintain their economic privileges and retain a modicum of political autonomy. More than 3.5 million Poles emigrated from Eastern Europe between 1870 and 1914, two-thirds of whom settled in the United States. In Canada, 120,000 Poles arrived between 1896 and 1914, the majority of whom were impoverished peasant farmers from Galicia. Most settled on the prairies in close proximity to their Galician-Ukrainian neighbours.[86]

Because of their poverty the Poles, like the Ukrainians, initially were viewed with opprobrium by their Anglo neighbours as well as by those who believed that the Slavic 'wave' would cause irreparable harm to the development of the West and the fostering of Canadian solidarity. While lack of funds and hostility from many Anglo neighbours were among the initial difficulties facing these new settlers, their unfamiliarity with Canadian soil conditions and farming techniques was an additional obstacle to successful settlement. Most farmers sought seasonal farm employment, which helped them accumulate savings and familiarize themselves with the operation of farms on the Canadian prairies.

While the majority of Polish immigrants settled in farming areas, a sizeable number gravitated towards industrial centres, most notably Winnipeg, Montreal, and Hamilton. Many of these immigrants were single men whose immigration to Canada was arranged by employment agencies run by

Polish-Canadian entrepreneurs. Like other immigrant groups at this time, Polish workers lived close to one another, establishing their own Polish neighbourhoods, and setting up stores, social clubs, and mutual-aid societies for the benefit of their members.

Between 1896 and 1905, when Sifton resigned as minister of the Interior, more than 300,000 immigrants had entered Canada, 30 per cent of whom were from Galicia. While his efforts to secure British, American, and Scandinavian immigrants attracted relatively little criticism, his welcoming of Eastern and central Europeans was highly contentious. Sifton was accused of not being able appropriately to distinguish between 'quantity' and 'quality.' As one Conservative MP explained, Canadians welcome British, American, French, and German immigrants because 'they belong to the races to which we belong, they are men who tend to the elevation of our population, and to the progress of our country. They are accustomed to our institutions, they are suitable to our climate, and we desire to get them.'[87]

It was the arrival *en masse* of tens of thousands of Eastern and central Europeans each year that alarmed those who believed such immigrants to be inferior and unable to assimilate in Canada. In the House of Commons, MP Thomas Sproule condemned the government for being too ready to welcome the 'riff raff' and 'refuse' of every country in the world in its desire to populate the country rapidly: 'We are importing the undesirable elements of Europe ... people who know nothing of our institutions, who are not in any way to the manor [sic] born, who are aliens to the conditions of Canadian or American life, who are imbued with instincts and natures which have not in themselves any tendency to elevate humanity but rather to lower it in every particular.'[88]

Other MPs agreed,[89] as did some of the country's more conservative papers and English settlers in the West, who saw their communities changing rapidly with the arrival of immigrants who spoke no English and whose customs and social organizations were so different from the Anglo-Canadian norm. In 1899, the *Winnipeg Telegram* expressed sympathy for the English settler who found himself 'hemmed in by a hoard of people little better than savages – alien in race, language and religion, whose customs are repellent and whose morals he abhors.'[90]

Sifton persistently defended the admission of Galicians, arguing that they were solid agriculturalists, of proper moral habits, and promised to be 'as good-living a set of people as is to be found in any country.' Nevertheless, he did agree to drop the payment of the bonus for Galician immigrants[91] and he instructed government land agents to try to place new arrivals on land apart from the established Ukrainian communities. This attempt to prevent group settlements usually failed, for the agents were unable to persuade new immigrants that it was best for them to settle in areas distant from their compatriots.[92]

One of the most formidable opponents of Sifton's admission of Galicians was fellow Liberal MP Frank Oliver. Oliver was from Alberta, where most Ukrainian farmers settled, and he was generally quick to counter any praise of their achievements by Sifton and those who supported his policy. In 1899, Oliver put forward this argument: 'I have inquired whether any settlers have moved away on the account of the proximity of these people and have the best authority for saying they have ... People have left their places because the Galicians came in and settled near them.'[93]

Oliver explained that the effect of the open-door policy towards Slavs in general, and Galicians in particular, was to transplant here 'people who have no ideas in regard to our system of government or our social life, who have no ambitions such as we have, who are aliens in race and in every other respect.' To continue to do so could only pose a serious 'danger to our social system, our municipal institutions and our general progress.'[94] As to those who argued that, like the Mennonites and Icelanders before them, the Galicians would soon assimilate and contribute to society, Oliver responded rhetorically: 'Do you know what assimilate means? It is a nice sounding word. Do you know that it means that if you settle on a farm on the prairies amongst them or in their neighbourhood you must depend for the schooling of your children on the tax-paying willingness and power of people who neither know nor care anything about schools? Do you know that it means the intermarriage of your sons or daughters with those who are of an alien race and of alien ideas? That is assimilation or else there is no assimilation.'[95] While Oliver agreed that the government should promote Western settlement, he favoured a cautious approach, one which first looked to other Canadian provinces for willing settlers, and then to Britain, the United States, and the countries of northern Europe.[96] Instead of attempting to people the West with those who have not reached 'that degree of liberty, civilization, progress or prosperity which we expect to attain ... let us look to our own people and to kindred people upon whose industry and loyalty we can depend.'[97] In 1905, as the new minister of the Interior, Oliver was given the opportunity to fashion such a policy for Canada.

Exclusionary Measures

LEGISLATIVE RESTRICTIONS ON ADMISSIONS AND RESIDENCY

By 1905, when Oliver assumed the immigration portfolio, there were discernible trends in the pattern of dialogue concerning the impact of Canada's expansive immigration policy. Debates often revealed values and interests which were in conflict. Those who tended to be concerned about issues of assimilability of immigrants and the preservation of Anglo-Canadian norms and values tended to support a selective and restrictive approach to immigration, as did those who wanted to limit labour supply in the interests of preserving wage rates and improving conditions of work. In contrast, those who benefited from inexpensive labour advocated an expansive, relatively unrestricted approach to immigrant admissions.

In 1907, the country experienced a sudden, although relatively short, economic depression. As the spectre of increasing unemployment grew, the debates over immigration policy intensified. In the House, the government was assailed by members of the Opposition for permitting the arrival of those who, unable to support themselves or find employment quickly, swelled the ranks of the unemployed and exacerbated the depressed conditions of urban slums. Moreover, Conservative MPs claimed that the bonus system was a waste of public money since many immigrants did not remain in Canada but went on to settle in the United States.[98] Laurier was pressed to discontinue the practice and to prohibit the admission of immigrants whose passage to Canada was paid for by philanthropic organizations in Britain. The latter immigrants, described by one Quebec MP, Armand Lavergne, as 'tramps, loafers, ex-convicts, drunkards and hooligans,'[99] were frequently characterized as unsuitable since many of them came from impoverished urban ghettos and did not have agricultural experience or training.

The Trades and Labour Congress (TLC) of Canada, which was one of the most vocal critics of immigration policy at this time, registered similar concerns. At its annual conventions, resolutions were passed, urging Ottawa to prohibit the entry of Asians, immigrants assisted by British charitable institutions, all contract labourers, and, in particular, skilled British mechanics who competed with Canadian workers and were used to break strikes.[100] The TLC also supported an end to the bonus system, claiming that the money would be better spent on unemployment relief in Canada.[101] In labour circles outside the TLC, anti-immigration sentiment was also apparent, as Canadian workers complained that the abundant supply of immigrant labourers' depressed wages, weakened the prospects of wage increases by being used to break strikes, and contributed to unsafe work environments. As one writer on the mining industry in Cobalt, Ontario, described in 1908, mine operators imported 'Polacks, Dagoes and Finlanders,' paying them poor wages and skimping on safety precautions with the attitude that 'men are cheaper than timbers.'[102]

Other participants in the immigration debate were churches and social service agencies that worked among the poor and were overwhelmed with the volume of demands that were made on their services. Those who worked among the impoverished in the city slums became particularly alarmed at the numbers of people flooding into the cities; the absence of adequate housing, sanitation, and other public services to meet the needs of this growing urban proletariat; and the resultant problems that such overcrowding and commingling of races seemed to spark. Not only were the numbers alarming, but the arrival of so many immigrants speaking different languages, wearing foreign dress, adhering to different religions, and practicing distinct social and dietary customs led some to question whether British values and institutions would invariably be threatened. Many answered affirmatively, claiming that, if the importation of those of 'inferior' races was not checked, the intellectual and moral fabric of the country would be seriously damaged. Physicians and sociologists writing on the issue, influenced by American literature in the area, warned of the dire consequences that could befall the country if careful attention were not paid to those that were admitted as members.[103]

J.S. Woodsworth's writings and speeches are a good example of the growing concern over the racial composition of Canada. As he was one of the pioneers of the Canadian socialist movement, it is not surprising that Woodsworth was a more moderate voice in immigration debates at this time. Nevertheless, his writings and lectures reveal the degree of acceptability that notions of racial superiority held, even among those most sympathetic to the plight of the economically downtrodden and politically oppressed. For Woodsworth and others,[104] one of the greatest challenges facing the country was to ensure that the tens of thousands of immigrants coming each year were assimilated, adopting the majority's English language and British traditions.[105] The promise of a great unified nation, such proponents of assimilation claimed, depended upon it. The government had therefore to be very careful about whom it permitted to immigrate, given that the task of assimilation was believed to be much easier for some races than for others.

The inevitable conclusion to be drawn from Woodsworth's 1909 book, *Strangers within Our Gates*,[106] and one that was widely supported by others within the social-reform movement, was that assimilability and desirability of various European ethnic groups declined as one moved through Europe from north to south. Thus, Scandinavian immigrants, 'accustomed to the rigours of a northern climate, clean-blooded, thrifty, ambitious and hard working,' were certain to be a success 'in this pioneer country, where the strong not the weak are wanted.' Likewise, Germans 'are among our best immigrants,' and the Doukhobors 'have in them elements which will, in time, make of them good citizens.' The Galicians, on the other hand, 'figured disproportionately in the police court and penitentiary' because centuries 'of poverty and oppression had, to some extent, "animalized" them.' Similarly, Poles were 'invariably connected' to the police courts in this country. Far from the best class, they tended to be 'poor, illiterate, and with a code of morals none too high.' As for Levantine races, which included Greeks, Turks, Armenians, Syrians, and Persians, Woodsworth cites with approval authorities who describe them as 'a most undesirable class' who, through force of habit, 'lie most naturally and by preference, and only tell the truth when it suits their purpose' and whose 'miserable physique and tendency to communicable disease ... are a distinct menace' to the health of the community.[107]

Law-enforcement officials were also generally of the view that increased immigration had resulted in higher crime rates. According to Donald Avery, law-enforcement officials in the West were initially complimentary about the settlement of European immigrants, with police reports stressing their hard work and industriousness. As more newcomers poured into the area, however, the Royal North-West Mounted Police (RNWMP) began to register alarm at the increasing level of serious physical assaults, sexual assaults, and incest, which they often attributed to the 'low class' of the Eastern European settlers. Police also complained about their difficulty in prosecuting crimes because of the mistrust of the RNWMP in several ethnic communities and the corresponding reluctance of witnesses to testify in court. These observations were replicated in the large urban centres across the country, where foreigners were blamed for the violence and apparent lawlessness in city slums. One major concern, particularly in the Western cities, was that concentrations of disgruntled foreigners in urban ghettos constituted a threat to law and order, for, if incited to action, they could wreak havoc on the cities in which they dwelt. Incidents of mob violence during industrial disputes in several cities seemed to substantiate this fear.[108]

Frank Oliver was sympathetic to these concerns. Within one year of becoming minister of the Interior, Oliver introduced into Parliament a new Immigration Act which he openly acknowledged 'represents the ideas of the Minister who is responsible for it.'[109] While the new act retained certain earlier provisions aimed at the protection of immigrants from the hazards of ocean travel, exploitation by ship captains and crew, and harassment by merchants and by keepers at ports of disembarkation,[110] the focus of the 1906 act was entirely different. As Oliver explained, the sole purpose of the act 'is to enable the Department of Immigration to deal with undesirable immigrants' by providing a means of control which did not previously exist.[111] To this end, the list of immigrants prohibited from entering Canada was expanded to include the insane, epileptic, deaf and dumb, blind, infirm,[112] those afflicted with a 'loathsome' contagious disease, paupers, destitute persons, and those convicted of crimes of 'moral turpitude' such as prostitution, pimping, and the like.[113] Inadmissible immigrants were subject to removal from Canada, the costs of which were to be borne by the companies which transported them. The responsibility for determining admissibility was assigned to a board of inquiry comprising an immigration agent, medical officer, or any other officer or officers named by the minister. The minister not only appointed members of the boards, but also was responsible for hearing appeals from their decisions.[114]

The 1906 act also provided for the removal of any immigrant who, within two years, had become a charge upon public funds or upon any charitable institution, had committed a crime involving moral turpitude, or had become an inmate of a jail or hospital. It became the 'duty' of municipal authorities to report any such cases to the minister, who, after an investigation, could order the deportation of persons found to fall within these categories.

In addition to expanding the categories of excludable immigrants and providing for the deportation of those who were found undesirable during the first two years of residence, the act also conferred upon the Cabinet the broad authority to prohibit the landing in Canada of 'any specified class of immigrants.' The Cabinet was also empowered to establish landing-money requirements, the amount of which 'may vary according to the class and destination' of immigrants and 'otherwise according to the circumstances.'[115]

Oliver was as clear on the more selective approach he intended to take towards immigration to booking agents, immigration officials, and the Canadian public as he was to Parliament when the 1906 Immigration Act was introduced. Booking agents were directed to take the utmost care in their selection of immigrants and were warned that their bonus would be repayable to the government for every immigrant they brought to Canada who was deported or left the country voluntarily within a year of arrival. Furthermore, bonuses were expressly limited to farmers or farm labourers with one year's previous experience, railway workers, and female domestics. The North Atlantic Trading Company agreement, which had been responsible for the immigration of approximately 50,000 people during the five years of its operation, was cancelled. The Canadian public was informed that the department did not intend to promote the immigration of Continental Europeans, as it had previously. As Oliver told Calgary's *Albertan* in 1906, 'we are not pushing Continental immigration at all.'[116]

To help placate the growing concern over the arrival of indigent immigrants who became dependent upon the services of public aid and private charities in Canada, an order-in-council, approved in 1908, provided that, in addition to their ocean and inland transportation fare, all immigrants had to possess $50 if arriving in the winter, and $25 if landing at other times of the year. An exception was made for those who were going to prearranged farm or domestic employment and those who had family and friends in Canada capable of providing support.[117] Also in 1908, Oliver announced that all immigrants who were sent by charitable and philanthropic organizations in Britain would be inspected 'as to their antecedents, both morally and physically, and as their general suitability for settlement in this country.' Entry to Canada would depend upon their prior receipt of an admissibility certificate.[118] British aid societies were subsequently informed that approval would be forthcoming only for those with assured farm employment.[119]

In 1910, these regulations were incorporated into a new Immigration Act. Rather than introducing major new changes to immigration policy, this act amplified the provisions of the 1906 legislation and formalized admissibility and deportation procedures. The list of excludable immigrants was extended with the addition of those who were sponsored by charitable organizations unless prior approval had been obtained. Cabinet was authorized to enact regulations that prohibited the entry of immigrants 'belonging to any race deemed unsuitable to the climate and requirements of Canada or immigrants of any specified class, occupation or character,' as well as immigrants who came to Canada other than by continuous journey.[120] The 1910 act introduced the concept of domicile, providing that Canadian domicile was obtained once a person, legally landed in Canada, had resided here for three years. Until domicile was acquired, an immigrant could be removed from Canada for becoming a member of an undesirable class, which included pimps; prostitutes; convicted criminals; public charges; and inmates of jails, hospitals, and insane asylums. Undesirable immigrants were also defined as those who advocated the overthrow of governments by force and those who attempted to create a riot or public disorder in Canada.[121]

The duties and procedures of boards of inquiry were also expanded and more fully articulated in the 1910 act.[122] While still appointed by the minister, the boards now comprised at least three members, and heard not only admissibility cases, but deportation cases as well. Proceedings before the boards were not public, and the immigrant also could be excluded, the act only providing for the presence of the immigrant 'wherever practicable.' The immigrant had no right to present evidence or cross-examine witnesses on evidence prejudicial to his or her case, and a board could base its decision on any evidence it considered credible and trustworthy. In admissibility cases, the burden of proof rested with the immigrant to establish the right to enter Canada. An appeal to the minister in all rejection and deportation decisions was provided, except when the decision was based on a medical certificate attesting to the person's being afflicted with a disease dangerous to the public health. In determining the appeal, the minister considered a summary record of the case as provided by the superintendent of immigration, along with his written views on the case. To enhance ministerial control over the administration of immigration policy, the act contained the following privative clause: 'No court, and no judge or officer thereof, shall have jurisdiction to review, quash, reverse, restrain or otherwise interfere with any proceeding, decision or order of the Minister or of any Board of Inquiry, or officer in charge ... relating to the detention or deportation of any rejected immigrant ... upon any ground whatsoever ...'[123] While the 1906 legislation provided only for the passing of regulations governing medical inspections of immigrants coming by ship, the 1910 act provided for the inspection of those coming over land as well.[124] In practice, medical examinations were administered soon after arrival. Immigrants were scrutinized closely, and those with eye ailments, contagious diseases, nervous disorders, physical deformities, skin conditions, and other general health problems were detained and either released upon treatment or returned home. As in previous years, those found inadmissible were removed to the country from which they came at the cost of the transportation company that brought them to Canada.[125] The list of medical conditions warranting detention and/or removal was extensive and included problems as serious as tuberculosis, measles, insanity, and pneumonia, as well as less grave conditions such as conjunctivitis, neuralgia, curvature of the spine, and sore feet.[126]

Although these Immigration Acts expanded the grounds upon which a prospective immigrant could be excluded, they were not implemented in such a manner as to significantly restrict the immigration of central and southern Europeans, as Oliver would have wished. However sympathetic Frank Oliver was to the claim that the growing population of Eastern Europeans had a disruptive effect on Canadian society, it was clear that his Cabinet colleagues were not inclined to stem the flow. As in the Macdonald years, the voice of big business held considerable sway with the country's executive. For the most part, employers favoured unrestricted immigration, arguing that it was a benefit not only to them, but to the country as a whole. As the chairman of the CPR's board of directors, Sir William Cornelius Van Horne, proclaimed in 1905: 'What we want is population. Labour is required from the Arctic Ocean to Patagonia, throughout North and South America, but the Governments of other lands are not such idiots as we are in the matter of restricting immigration. Let them all come in. There is work for all. Every two or three men that come into Canada and do a day's work create new work for someone else to do. They are like a new dollar. Hand it out from the Bank and it turns itself in value a dozen times or more during the year.'[127] Among the chief beneficiaries of the mass importation of immigrant workers were mining companies, logging camps, sawmill operators, and railways. An unrestricted supply of labour ensured that wages would remain low. Moreover, the free movement of labour was a powerful weapon to break strikes. As one mine manager, Edmund Kirby, stated: 'In all the lower grades of labour especially in smelter labour it is necessary to have a mixture of races which includes a number of illiterates who are first class workmen. They are the strength of the employer, and the weakness of the union.'[128]

Many of the large employers of immigrant labour actively recruited immigrants from abroad. Also involved in immigrant-labour recruitment were hundreds of private labour agencies, generally specializing in particular nationalities. These agencies worked in both Europe and the United States. They acted as middlemen between the immigrants and employers, advancing the costs of transportation to the prospective worker, which would subsequently be deducted from the worker's wages.

The immigration of Italian workers is illustrative of how effective such recruitment practices were. Immigration statistics place the number of Italian immigrants to Canada between 1901 and 1914 at close to 119,000. Canadian census figures suggest, however, that the number was much lower, the Italian population increasing by only 35,000 between 1901 and 1911.[129] The reason for the discrepancy is that many Italians who arrived in Canada came as seasonal workers, and eventually returned home. Many of these immigrants were from the southern areas of Italy, where soil exhaustion, lack of capital, and growing indebtedness had led to economic stagnation.[130] Initially, the majority of Italians who came to Canada sought work on the railways. For example, in 1904 it was estimated that, of the 8,576 men employed on the CPR, more than 35 per cent were Italian.[131] The opening-up of the Ontario mining industry also attracted Italian workers, who, between 1906 and 1914, comprised close to 8 per cent of the immigrant miners in Canada.[132] Both Clifford Sifton and Frank Oliver were opposed to the immigration of Italian labourers, yet, despite their objections, on average more than 6,500 entered Canada annually.

The steady influx of Italian workers to Canada was in a large part co-ordinated by *padroni*, agents who supplied Canadian business with a pool of labourers recruited from Italy.[133] The system was replete with corruption, the costs of which were borne by the worker, who was often controlled by his *padrone* in return for work that was frequently dangerous, onerous, and poorly paid.[134] The largest recruitment agencies were in Toronto and Montreal, where most of the country's Italian population was concentrated. As these cities grew, Italians were recruited to help meet the demand for labour in the expanding construction industry, industrial plants, and the maintenance of urban infrastructure such as roads and sewer systems. As with other immigrant groups, the Italians formed their own neighbourhoods, where Italian businesses such as grocery stores, shops, and bakeries opened to serve an Italian clientele. The church was a central focus of community life, as were mutual-aid societies, the latter often organized along Italian regional or village lines.[135] Mutual-benefit associations were in part the result of the discrimination suffered by Italians, which hindered their professional and social advancement and barred them from many trade unions. The societies provided their members with a place to socialize, as well as assistance for those who were ill or unemployed.

Polish, Ukrainian, Bulgarian, and Russian workers were recruited in similar ways. Canadian labour unions complained vigorously that the importation of contract labourers was a violation of the Alien Labour Act of 1897, which made it unlawful for anyone to assist or solicit the importation of any foreigner for labour purposes into Canada under contract or agreement.[136] Notwithstanding this act, and the fact that the practice of soliciting immigrants for other than domestic or agricultural purposes was contrary to the official pronouncements of the government, no actions were taken to significantly impede the movement of contract labourers to Canada.

As reluctant as the government was to restrict the supply of immigrant workers to the country's major employers, it was equally disinclined to interfere with the employment contracts themselves. Mistreatment of contract immigrant workers, including fraudulent recruitment procedures, inflated agency and transportation fees, indentured-labour practices, company-enforced incarcerations of reportedly 'unruly' workers, inadequate food and insufficient medical care, were well publicized throughout the period. Even when the government accepted the accuracy of such reports, it did not undertake to prosecute those responsible.[137]

The deference to employer priorities that the government showed in its administration of immigration policy was also displayed by courts that were called upon to resolve conflicts between employer interests and immigrant rights. By the turn of the century, the pattern of judicial decisions revealed a tendency on the part of the courts to strike down legislation that adversely affected employers' economic interests and a reluctance to interfere with laws which affected aliens exclusively. Thus, B.C. statutes which restricted the right of employers to hire Asians, for example, were declared invalid as being beyond provincial jurisdiction,[138] while provincial laws regulating the right of Asians to vote[139] or to hire white employees[140] were found to be lawful exercises of provincial powers.

This tendency was illustrated vividly in two Privy Council decisions: *Union Colliery v Bryden*[141] in 1899, and *Cunningham v Tomey Homma*[142] in 1903. In the former, the court held that a B.C. statute which prohibited the employment of Chinese in underground mines was beyond the powers of the provincial government. The court found that the statute encroached upon the federal authority over 'naturalization of aliens,' which it said included 'what shall be the rights and privileges of Chinese aliens and naturalized subjects.' Finding as a matter of fact that the prohibition in question affected only aliens and naturalized subjects, the court characterized the legislation in question as centred on the imposition of a disability on Chinese immigrants rather than on the regulation of working conditions in the coal mines. It concluded that, 'in establishing a statutory prohibition which affects aliens or naturalized subjects,' the act therefore infringed upon 'the exclusive authority of the Parliament in Canada.'[143]

The Privy Council's decision in *Bryden* is noteworthy for several reasons. First, it is striking because there is nothing in the judgment that would compel one to accept that federal power over aliens and the process of

naturalization necessarily implies an exclusive jurisdiction over the rights
and privileges of aliens and naturalized subjects. Moreover, the court
completely ignored the fact that the act applied not only to aliens and
naturalized subjects, but also to British subjects by birth yet of Chinese
race, and who, under the court's analysis, could not necessarily be said to
fall exclusively within federal jurisdiction. Finally, within three years the
same court refused to be bound by the principle it had enunciated in
Bryden. In 1903, the Privy Council delivered its decision in *Cunningham v
Tomey Homma*. The case was brought by a naturalized Japanese immigrant,
Tomey Homma, who challenged the validity of the Provincial Elections
Act, which disenfranchised Chinese, Japanese, and East Indians. The
challenge was based on two grounds. It was argued that, as in the decision
in *Bryden*, the consequences of naturalization, in this case the franchise,
were within the exclusive jurisdiction of the federal government.
Moreover, since the Naturalization Act provided that all naturalized subjects shall 'be entitled to all political and other rights, powers and privileges'[144] as a natural-born British subject, the right to vote could not be
taken away by a provincial statute.

Unlike the lower courts who considered the case, the Privy Council did
not feel bound by its decision in *Bryden*. In an equally unpersuasive judgment, the court found that the federal jurisdiction over aliens and naturalized subjects did not necessarily imply exclusive jurisdiction over all the
consequences of either alienage or naturalization. Rather, it reasoned that
subsection 95(25) of the British North America Act (now known as the
Constitution Act, 1867) conferred upon the Dominion government jurisdiction only over the 'ordinary rights' of individuals in a province to reside there and earn a living. Since the Provincial Elections Act applied to
all those of Japanese, Chinese, and East Indian race, regardless of whether
they were born in Canada or whether they were naturalized, it could not
be said to deal either with naturalization or aliens. As such, the legislation
was within provincial competence.[145]

The two cases are impossible to reconcile and, indeed, later courts have
not attempted to do so. A year after the *Tomey Homma* case was decided,
the Supreme Court of British Columbia was once again faced with another B.C. statute which restricted the employment of any Chinese person
unable to speak English.[146] The Court chose to follow *Bryden* and found
the prohibition to be beyond provincial jurisdiction.

These cases lend support to the view that it was the underlying interests,
rather than the strict application of legal doctrine, that determined the
results. The fact that employer interests were rarely prejudiced by judicial

decisions suggests that the judiciary were as sensitive to business concerns as were the politicians.[147]

SELECTIVE ADMISSION RESTRICTIONS

The fact that Cabinet was unwilling to significantly restrict the immigration of contract workers to Canada did not mean that it was entirely insensitive to public pressure. Demands for a more racially selective policy were heeded, especially when the government's popularity was put in serious jeopardy. For example, in 1907, fearing a public backlash if it did not respond to demands to limit the entry of Asian workers, the government did impose landing-money requirements on East Indians, raised the head tax on Chinese immigrants, and negotiated an agreement with Japan to limit the immigration of its nationals.[148] Similarly, in 1910, faced with a possible influx of African-American settlers, which caused consternation among many prairie residents, measures were taken to ensure that the movement did not take place. Although their numbers were not significant in relation to the overall immigration picture at this time, the passions that such immigration movements aroused were out of proportion to their size. The government's response to the fervour that the admission of Asians and African Americans sparked was illustrative of its ability to deal quickly and administratively with immigration 'problems.'

Between 1900 and 1915, government reports suggest that more than 50,000 immigrants of Japanese, East Indian, and Chinese descent arrived in Canada.[149] Although comprising less than two per cent of the total immigration flow, Asian immigration sparked intense controversy, especially on the West Coast, where the majority of Asian immigrants arrived and subsequently settled. For example, approximately 16,000 Japanese immigrants were admitted to Canada during this period, of whom more than 83 per cent settled in British Columbia.[150] Despite the fact that fewer than half remained in Canada – many immigrated to the United States or returned home[151] – the presence of close to 5,000 Japanese immigrants in British Columbia by the turn of the century was enough to raise fears that a larger wave would follow. Similar concerns had led to the imposition of the head tax on Chinese immigrants in 1885. The head tax was raised from $100 to $500 in 1903, precipitating a decline in the numbers of annual Chinese arrivals from 5,000 before the tax, to fewer than 77 the following year, but within several years annual admissions were again exceeding 2,000, and demands for tighter controls correspondingly increased.[152] Beginning in 1905, East Indian immigrants also began coming to Canada in record numbers, recruited by steamship companies and encouraged by stories of their compatriots who had come to Canada and prospered. In 1906 close to 400 arrived, and the next year more than 2,000 were admitted.[153]

The kinds of prejudice Chinese immigrants experienced, discussed more fully in the preceding chapter, were also experienced by other Asians.[154] Racist stereotypes, characterizing Japanese persons as dishonest, unclean, immoral, and unable to assimilate, acquired considerable currency at this time.[155] In addition, trade-unionists charged that Asian immigrants were a menace to the aspirations of white workers, who felt that their wages and working conditions were adversely affected by the presence of Asians willing to work for less. The complaints against Japanese immigrants were particularly vociferous in the fishing industry. Prior to 1892, almost all the West Coast fishermen were white. After that year, an increasing portion of fishing licences was given to Japanese immigrants. Trade unions demanded that the practice be stopped, complaining that the Japanese fishermen were charging fish canneries less than the going rate for fish, and that they were willing to break strikes.[156]

East Indian immigration was also opposed by trade unions. Most East Indians came to work in manual-labour jobs. They did not enter into the more highly skilled occupations such as laundering and market gardening, as had many Chinese immigrants. Nor did they take an interest in the fishing industry and farming to the same extent as had many Japanese arrivals. Like all 'coolie' labour of the time, however, they were sought after by employers because they would work for relatively low wages and because they had a weakening effect on trade-union activity. The competition they posed to white workers, however, was deeply resented, and their cultural dissimilarity was considered threatening. It was rumoured that, aside from their odd appearance, different mode of living, and strange religion, the 'Hindoos' were also a seditious group intent on overthrowing British rule in India.

The demands of organized labour, various nativist organizations, the media, and other disgruntled residents attracted a warm reception in the B.C. legislature. As early as 1875, Chinese persons were prohibited from having their names on the voters' list and thereby prevented from voting in that province.[157] In 1895, at a time when the Japanese population of British Columbia was fewer than 1,000, the provincial legislature amended the Provincial Voters Act to exclude those of Japanese descent from the voters' lists.[158] Since placement on the provincial voters' list was a prerequisite for voting in federal elections, Chinese and Japanese persons in

British Columbia were denied the federal franchise as well. Disenfranchisement bore consequences beyond the inability to participate in the political life of the country. It also disqualified them from sitting on juries and entering various professions, such as law, pharmacy, and teaching. And while not legally confined to menial work, they were prevented from advancement by other discriminatory employment practices. As a result, many Chinese and Japanese persons preferred to run their own businesses. Their social ostracism, as reflected in their exclusion from private clubs and other Anglo dominated institutions, encouraged support of their own social, religious, and economic affiliations.

The B.C. legislature's efforts to discourage Asian immigration extended well beyond the franchise prohibition. As discussed earlier,[159] the provincial government regularly sent petitions to Ottawa and passed its own anti-Asian resolutions and exclusionary statutes aimed at barring Asian workers from employment on public-works projects and in companies holding Crown licences.[160] In addition, private statutes of incorporation also contained clauses prohibiting the employment of Chinese and Japanese workers. British Columbia's legislative attempts to exclude Asian immigrants were generally reserved by the lieutenant-governor, or disallowed by the federal Cabinet, or found to be beyond provincial jurisdiction by the courts.[161] Often the B.C. legislature simply responded by re-enacting them in slightly modified form, with the result that, in 1902, for example, thirteen anti-Asian bills were disallowed by the Dominion, only to be reenacted by a combative B.C. legislature.[162]

Despite the federal government's persistent refusal to accept provincial restrictions on the admission of Asians, the increase in Asian immigration from approximately 500 persons in 1904 to more than 12,000 in 1908 posed a challenge for the Laurier government. On the one hand, it was sensitive to the calls of industrialists, particularly railway promoters, that Asian workers were essential to meet labour shortages and to offset what they claimed were crippling wage increases for white labourers.[163] On the other hand, it could not ignore the growing militancy, especially in British Columbia, of those who felt economically and culturally threatened by the 'yellow peril.' The consequences of failing to respond to their calls for restrictive legislation were driven home in 1907 by the ugly Vancouver Riot.

The effects of the economic recession of 1907 and the unemployment that followed were felt acutely in Vancouver, where the population continued to grow at a rate of 1,000 a month, amid severe housing shortages.[164] Anti-Asian sentiment, which had long been smouldering in the province, reached new heights when it was reported that the state-supported Grand Trunk Pacific Railway had entered into a tentative agreement with the Canadian Nippon Supply Company to import Japanese labourers for the completion of the western leg of the railway. Exaggerated press reports of an impending 'invasion' of '50,000 Japanese'[165] fuelled anti-Asian sentiment, which was expressed in a public rally held in Vancouver in the summer of 1907. The rally, organized by the Asiatic Exclusion League, attracted thousands of people. After a series of anti-Asian speeches, an angry mob marched through the Chinese and Japanese districts of Vancouver, terrorizing people and destroying property. Following his subsequent investigation into the causes of the rampage, Mackenzie King, then deputy minister of Labour, recommended that the Chinese and Japanese communities be awarded approximately $26,000 and $9,000, respectively, in damages.[166]

In his report on the methods by which Oriental labourers had been induced to come to Canada,[167] King concluded that the tension in British Columbia was not merely confined to labour disputes, but had serious racial overtones. He recommended that, in the interests of labour harmony and racial homogeneity, measures should be undertaken to prohibit the importation of contract labour from Japan.[168] Laurier did not need King's report to impress upon him that, unless restrictions were put in place, social tensions were likely to erupt again, perhaps with more serious consequences. Nevertheless, having acceded to the 1894 Anglo-Japanese Treaty of Commerce and Navigation, Canada could not bar the entry of Japanese nationals into its territory without abrogating the treaty and risking the loss of a lucrative trading partner. As an alternative, Laurier dispatched Rodolphe Lemieux to Tokyo to attempt to negotiate an undertaking with Japan for the restriction of Japanese immigrants to Canada. The task was a difficult one, because the Japanese people were angered by the treatment that their compatriots had received in Canada and were likely to be enraged should their government make an agreement which would nullify their treaty rights to enter and reside in Canada freely.[169] The most that Lemieux could secure was an agreement by Japan to limit the number of emigration passports issued to its subjects *en route* to Canada to 400 a year, providing that the agreement was portrayed as a voluntary restraint and that the number would remain secret.[170] In the House, Lemieux refused to disclose the numerical limit, other than to say that press reports of 1,000 persons were exaggerated. In response to those who were opposed to relying on the good faith of Japan as an assurance that the limit would be respected,[171] Lemieux argued that the only alternative to the agreement was abrogating treaty rights and a consequent loss of trade with

Japan, which represented a market of 50 million people.[172] It would appear that this fact carried the day, for, within three months of the drafting of the agreement, Parliament passed a resolution endorsing it.

The Lemieux agreement affected only those Japanese coming to Canada directly from Japan, for the Japanese government disclaimed any responsibility for controlling the movement of Japanese immigrants from Hawaii, who accounted for more than 50 per cent of the Japanese who entered Canada intending to remain.[173] Several measures to control this flow were adopted. The 1897 Alien Labour Act, which was designed to prohibit the entry of contract labourers, was given new life, and was selectively enforced against contract labourers from Hawaii. Moreover, the Japanese were subjected to more rigorous medical examinations than were white immigrants. In addition, a regulation was passed authorizing the minister to prohibit the entry of immigrants unless they came to Canada from the country of their birth or citizenship 'by a continuous journey on through tickets purchased before leaving the country.' Together with the landing-money requirement, the continuous journey regulation further limited the entry of Japanese immigrants.[174] Frank Oliver's instructions to immigration agents in Vancouver left no doubt that these measures would be strictly enforced against the Japanese: 'Regarding Japanese in quarantine, exclude all who do not pass medical examination, or do not have twenty-five dollars in cash or who do not come on a direct ticket from country of birth or naturalization.'[175] In concert, these measures significantly curtailed the flow of Japanese immigrants for many years. Within one year, the number of Japanese immigrants fell from 7,601 in 1908 to 495 in 1909. Annual arrivals were to remain around 500 persons for close to twenty years, when a new arrangement was made to limit the numbers still further.[176]

In the course of his report on Oriental labourers, Mackenzie King described how many unemployed East Indians in British Columbia were suffering from poverty, hunger, and illness. King concluded that this phenomenon stemmed directly from the incompatibility of East Indians with the Canadian climate and way of life: 'The experience has shown that immigrants of this class having been accustomed to the conditions of a tropical climate are wholly unsuited to this country and that their inability to readily adapt themselves to surroundings so entirely different inevitably brings upon them much suffering and privation.'[177] In fact many of the East Indian immigrants had come from the Punjab and were accustomed to winters that were harsher than those experienced in southern British Columbia. Nevertheless, even in the absence of empirical evidence, the notion that some races were 'unsuitable to the climate and conditions of Canada' was an idea that gained considerable acceptance at this time. Inspired by King's report, the Cabinet explicitly referred to the unsuitability of certain races as a justification for raising the landing money required of East Indians from $50 to $200 in 1908.[178]

From a diplomatic perspective, the outright exclusion of East Indians was impossible because India was a part of the British Empire. Faced with growing discontent over British colonial domination in India, Britain feared that passions in India would be inflamed further if it accepted any Canadian legislation which discriminated against East Indians. Another problem facing the Laurier government was that, since East Indians were fellow British citizens, it would be difficult to bar their entry on the basis of citizenship alone. The government attempted to avoid these problems through the invocation of the continuous-journey regulation which would prove so effective in controlling the immigration of Japanese persons from Hawaii. It authorized the minister to prohibit the entry of East Indian immigrants unless they came to Canada from the country of their birth or citizenship 'by a continuous journey on through tickets purchased before leaving the country.' At the time that the order was promulgated, the Canadian Pacific Railway was the only shipping company that offered a continuous journey from India to Canada. To ensure that East Indian immigrants were unable to meet the continuous journey requirement, the government subsequently issued a directive to CPR outlets in India prohibiting the sale of any through tickets to Canada.[179] The company, annoyed at the possible loss of lucrative business, sponsored several challenges to the regulation.

The first court challenge to the continuous-journey provision involved a number of East Indians who arrived in Canada in March 1908, having come directly from India by steamer on tickets issued before the CPR had received the government directive. Immigration officers enforced the medical regulations and landing-money requirements strictly and tried to apply the continuous-journey prohibition even though the passengers had come by a direct route. According to the authorities, since there was no guarantee that the Indians who left Calcutta were the same ones who arrived in Vancouver, the continuous-journey prohibition could be said to apply. In addition, provincial authorities tried to bar their entry into the province by the application of the British Columbia Immigration Act, which imposed literacy and educational requirements on prospective immigrants.

Twelve of the arrivals were rejected for health reasons, 23 were refused for not meeting the landing-money requirement, and 142 were detained under the continuous journey prohibition.[180] This last group made a *habeas corpus* application to the B.C. Supreme Court in the case of *Re Behari Lal.*[181] The Court granted the request and ordered that the detainees be released. In its decision, the Court noted that the Immigration Act gave the governor in council the authority to prohibit the landing of certain persons. The order-in-council, however, gave the minister of the Interior the discretion to prohibit persons who had not arrived by way of a continuous-journey. According to the Court, this was an improper delegation of authority from the governor in council to the minister, and therefore the order was *ultra vires.*

Although the immigrants were released from detention, they faced rejection under the provincial statute. A challenge was therefore made to British Columbia's Immigration Act in the case of *Re Narain Singh.*[182] In its decision, also released in 1908, the B.C. Supreme Court reasoned that, because the federal Immigration Act had prohibited certain people from entering Canada and had given the governor in council power to proscribe others, the federal government had 'occupied the field' of immigration. As such, the B.C. act was beyond provincial jurisdiction.

The effect of the striking down of the continuous journey regulation was short-lived. The federal Cabinet quickly responded by issuing another order-in-council removing the discretion of the minister of the Interior and making the prohibition applicable against all immigrants.[183] To ensure that the order was not used to bar entry to Europeans who had not come to Canada on a continuous journey, Frank Oliver issued the following instructions to his officers: 'Please bear in mind that the newly issued Order-in-Council re: 'continuous journey' is absolutely prohibitive in its terms but that it is only intended to enforce it strictly against really undesirable immigrants. You will understand, therefore, that a great deal is left to your discretion with regards to the application of the particular Order.'[184]

The prohibition was subsequently modified in an amendment to the Immigration Act in which the governor in council was given the full authority to prohibit the landing in Canada of any 'specified class of immigrants who have come to Canada otherwise than by continuous journey from the country of which they are natives or citizens and upon through tickets purchased in that country.[185] The wording of the provision had been changed slightly. Whereas the old order provided that persons had to come directly from their countries of *birth* or citizenship, the new wording stipulated that persons must come directly from the country of which they were *natives* or citizens. According to government legal opinion, a person of Indian ancestry born in China, or a person of Japanese ancestry *born* in Hawaii, remained a native of India or Japan, respectively. Thus, such persons, too, could be excluded unless they came to Canada directly from their so-called native lands.[186] The day after the passing of the amendment, in a letter to Superintendent of Immigration W.D. Scott, Frank Oliver again explained that the regulation was not intended to apply against otherwise desirable immigrants; rather, it was enacted in light of 'the conditions on the Pacific Coast.' This regulation, he emphasized, 'is therefore intended as a means of excluding those whom it is the policy of the government to exclude, but not those whom the policy is to admit.'[187]

The continuous-journey provision and the landing-money requirement had an immediate effect. The number of East Indian immigrants fell from 2,623 in 1908 to six the following year. It rose to ten persons in 1910, and fell again the next year to five. Between 1908 and 1915, slightly more than 100 East Indians were admitted to Canada.[188] To ensure that this pattern continued, the continuous-journey order and the landing-money requirement were renewed following the passage of the 1910 Immigration Act.[189] Although both were successfully challenged in the courts,[190] generally on the basis that the orders exceeded the authority provided in the act, the defects were quickly remedied, and new orders were issued in which the content was retained and the technical defects corrected.[191]

The continuous journey prohibition was effective so long as there was no shipping company providing direct passage from India to Canada. In 1913, the Conservative government, under the leadership of Sir Robert Borden, confronted rumours that private interests were contemplating establishing a direct steamship line between Vancouver and Calcutta. In response, another order-in-council was subsequently passed which prohibited the landing in British Columbia of all skilled and unskilled labourers and artisans.[192] The order was clearly directed at Asians, since they made up almost all the entries at B.C. ports. More specifically, the order was targeted at East Indians. Anticipating the arrival of a boatload of Indians from China, the government instructed immigration officers in Vancouver and Victoria not to apply the order 'against trans-Pacific passengers other than Hindus.'[193]

Undeterred by the new regulation, one wealthy Indian businessman, Gurdit Singh, sponsored the arrival of 376 East Indian residents of Hong Kong, China, and Japan. Allegedly bent on challenging the entire package of discriminatory legislation against East Indians, Singh, with the support of the local East Indian community, chartered the *Komagata Maru* to sail from Shanghai to Vancouver. Upon arrival in Vancouver, the boat was not allowed to dock. Immigration authorities dragged out each inquiry regarding the passengers' admissibility and refused to permit the passengers to disembark. Food and medical provisions were not supplied until they had been paid for and shortages were allowed to develop. For two months, during which time their fate was being determined in court, the passengers were confined to the *Komagata Maru,* causing the ship to become progressively more unsanitary. As a means of further weakening the passengers' resolve, the delivery of provisions was delayed.[194]

Press reports were the most hostile in British Columbia. Bold headlines in Vancouver papers reflected the mood of the province. Headlines in the *Vancouver Sun* such as 'Hindu Invaders Now in the City Harbour,' 'Hindus are Dancing a Religious Can-Can Aboard the Komagata,' and 'Hindus Hold Meeting and Preach Sedition and Treason,' belied any attempt to report the incident dispassionately.[195] In one article a reporter purported to describe what transpired at a public fund-raiser for the passengers: 'The speakers poured out malediction and anathema against the Canadian government and the Canadian people, in the Punjabi language which is especially adapted to envenomed speaking.'[196] Accounts in other parts of the country were, on the whole, less explosive. The eastern press seemed to be ambivalent about how the problem should be resolved. The *Ottawa Citizen* took a position in line with that of the B.C. press, while the *Montreal Star* suggested that an 'Asian born under the British flag ought to feel that he gets better terms than any other Asiatic; and gets it because he is British born.' The *Toronto Star* noted that East Indians were under British domination, and it reasoned that 'we ought to recognize that the situation is one which is very difficult to justify to Hindus, who are compelled to be in the Empire in one sense and out of it in another.'[197] Despite such expressions of sympathy for the East Indian plight, however, no eastern paper unequivocally supported the demands of the passengers of the *Komagata Maru.*

As is evident from the parliamentary debates, politicians approached the problem in a very straightforward way. Concern seemed to focus, not on whether the passengers should be allowed to remain, but on the way the government could affect their expeditious departure. The East Indians were not welcome, and their attempt to force themselves on the country was, for many politicians, particularly galling. Frank Oliver, the former minister of the Interior and now an Opposition MP, expressed the sentiments of many: 'To say that we in Canada shall not be able to say who shall join us in the work of building up the country, that we must accept the dictation of other people as to who shall join in that work, places us in the position not of a self-governing state in a free empire, but in the position of a subordinate dependency not in control of its own affairs.'[198]

Ultimately the fate of the passengers of the *Komagata Maru* was determined in court. One of the passengers, Munshi Singh, had been ordered
deported on the grounds that he had violated three orders-in-council. In
particular, he had not come to Canada on a continuous journey, he could
not meet the $200 landing-money requirement, and, as an unskilled
labourer in Canada (although not in India), he was not permitted to
enter British Columbia. The refusal of a lower court to order his release
was affirmed upon appeal in 1914. The B.C. Court of Appeal held that all
three orders giving rise to Singh's deportation were valid.[199] Clearly, successful challenges to earlier orders had been instructive in the drafting of
the new regulation. Yet the tone of the reasons for judgment in *Re Munshi
Singh* suggest that members of the court, like many other Canadians,
were becoming intolerant of Asian immigrants. The words of justice
McPhillips are particularly revealing. After claiming that the 'laws of
this country are unsuited to them, and their ways and ideas may well be
a menace to the well-being of the Canadian people,' he went on to say:
'Better that the peoples of non-assimilative – and by nature properly non-
assimilative – races should not come to Canada, but rather, that they
should remain of residence in their country of origin and there do their
share, as they have in the past, in the preservation and development of
the Empire.'[200]

The decision left little hope for the remaining passengers. Escorted by
a Canadian warship to the jeering and cheering of local citizens, the
Komagata Maru left Vancouver harbour exactly two months after it had arrived. Its departure signalled the virtual cessation of Indian immigration
to Canada for many years to come. Between 1914 and 1920, only one East
Indian immigrant was admitted. Over the next twenty-five years, fewer
than 650 settled in Canada.[201]

With respect to Chinese immigration, restrictions on their entry came
in the form of amendments to the Chinese Immigration Act in 1908. In
particular, the list of prohibited persons was expanded, and the classes of
persons exempt from the head tax was narrowed. The extensive, ambigu-
ous list of prohibited persons resembled the Immigration Act's list of prohibited classes, which, to the extent that it did not conflict with the Chinese
Immigration Act, also applied to Chinese immigrants.[202] Amendments to
the head tax included a requirement that students pay the tax up front,
and then apply to be reimbursed after one year, upon proof of attendance
at an accredited institution. The merchant exemption was also tightened
by excluding dependants except minor children, by narrowing the definition of merchant, and by requiring that persons establish their identity to

the satisfaction of an immigration officer.[203] The success of these changes is reflected in the fact that the proportion of Chinese immigrants exempt from paying the tax was reduced from 33 per cent in 1909 to fewer than 5 per cent by 1914.[204]

While the number of exemptions fell following these amendments, the number of Chinese arrivals did not. Between 1908 and 1914, for example, the annual number of Chinese immigrants to Canada averaged around 4,500.[205] There are several reasons why Chinese immigration was not restricted as effectively as was that of the Japanese and East Indians. In the first place, although raising the Chinese head tax to $500 in 1903 was an effective deterrent for several years, the willingness of employers to pay the tax and subsequently deduct it from workers' wages probably helped dampen its effect, as did rising wages for Oriental labour itself.[206] In addition, the existence of the exemptions meant that those who qualified, such as students and merchants, and who may have been prevented from immigrating had they had to pay the tax, were not so deterred. These particular exemptions were considered by Mackenzie King and others to be in the interest of fostering good trading relations with China. The rationale, explained King, was that students would act as 'missionaries of trade' upon their return to China, while merchants themselves were genuine agents of trade.[207] The corollary of these exemptions was, however, that the number of Chinese immigrants remained higher than some may have hoped would be the case after the imposition of the tax. Another reason for the failure of the tax to deter significantly Chinese immigration to Canada stemmed from the fact that the tax was regularly circumvented by various means.[208]

Aside from the head tax, the Liberal government had in 1909 instructed Mackenzie King to try to negotiate a voluntary restriction of Chinese immigrants with the Chinese government. The effort was unsuccessful, for the Chinese authorities were not receptive to the idea. Notwithstanding this failed effort,[209] it has been argued that the government failed to find a more effective substitute for the head tax because the tax was too lucrative to replace. Between 1901 and 1918, close to $18 million was collected from Chinese immigrants, which exceeded the amount the government spent on promoting European immigration by more than $8 million.[210] In 1914 alone, the revenue from the head tax exceeded government immigration expenditures by more than $750,000.[211] It is also probably the case that, like Continental European workers, Chinese labourers were in demand for many of the expanding economic activities of the period, particularly for railway construction. In deference to some of the leading industrialists of the day, the immigration of Chinese contract labourers was not entirely restricted.

The fact that Chinese immigrants were not as tightly regulated as their Japanese and East Indian counterparts did not mean that they were accorded any better treatment in Canada. British Columbia continued to enact discriminatory legislation, as did the federal government. In fact, one federal amendment to the Chinese Immigration Act conferring tax exempt status on Chinese teachers was made to complement recent moves by B.C. school authorities to push the Chinese out of white schools and into schools of their own.[212] Selective criminalization of opium use was another example of the federal government's willingness to tolerate and instigate discriminatory treatment of Chinese persons. In 1908, the Opium Act[213] was passed, which made opium trafficking illegal. The act was designed exclusively to target the Chinese community, which used opium for recreational and medicinal purposes, leaving non-Chinese pharmacists and doctors, for example, free of sanction.

Continuous journey regulations and the imposition of head taxes were among the instruments used by the government to limit Asian immigration; however, the restriction of African-American immigration was largely effected through administrative directives. The entry of African-Americans had long been a contentious issue. In his book *Only Farmers Need Apply*, Harold Troper explains that the domestic aversion to African-American immigration stemmed in part from an awareness of the racial strife experienced in post-Reconstruction America and a desire that these tensions not be imported into Canada.[214] In addition, racist stereotyping, pervasive at the time, invariably placed African Americans among the 'inferior' classes of people who could not be assimilated. J.S. Woodsworth's writings are an example of these perspectives. Discussing the problems associated with the immigration of 'negroes' to Canada, Woodsworth relied on the observations of an American writer, John R. Commons, in his characterization of the Negro: 'In Africa the people are unstable, indifferent to suffering, and "easily aroused to ferocity by the sight of blood or under great fear." They exhibit certain qualities which are associated with their descendants in this country, namely, aversion to silence and solitude, love of rhythm, excitability, and lack of reserve. All travellers speak of their impulsiveness, strong sexual passion, and lack of will power.'[215]

Of the more than 1 million American immigrants reported to have emigrated to Canada between 1896 and 1911, fewer than 1,000 of them were African Americans.[216] Of these, many came to work as porters for the Canadian Pacific Railway. Others came as farmers, fur trappers, and whisky traders. The relatively limited interest in settling in Canada shown by the African-American community was primarily attributable to the fact that most were either too poor to move or unaware of the opportunities which Canada offered. As a result, African-American immigration initially was not an issue of concern to the Canadian government. The policy of the government was simply not to promote their settlement in Canada.

On those occasions when department officials or immigration agents were approached by African Americans wishing to emigrate to Canada, government policy was respected. Sometimes the requests were simply ignored by Canadian immigration agents or put 'on file' indefinitely. More frequently, however, applications were refused by Canadian authorities on the basis that, according to the department, it had been 'observed that after some years of experience in Canada [Negroes] do not readily take to our climate on account of the rather severe winter.'[217] The assertion was patently false, for several thousand African Americans, most notably in Ontario and Nova Scotia, had successfully survived Canadian winters for over 150 years. Moreover, in invoking the Canadian climate as a reason to discourage settlement, the government was being disingenuous. As Troper notes, while, on the one hand, 'the Immigration Branch was doing all in its power to convince white Americans that the Canadian west did not have a climate too harsh for productive labour, in virtually the same breath it was trying to convince the Negroes that, at least in their case, the opposite was true.'[218]

In 1910, several hundred black Oklahoma farmers expressed an interest in coming to Canada. As there was no law preventing such migration, and given the financial ability of this particular group to make such a move, fear of an imminent invasion quickly spread throughout the Canadian West. Faced with petitions by white settlers, with which he was sympathetic, Oliver sent Inspector William White to Oklahoma to investigate. Referring to the prospective immigrants as the 'Negro-Indians,' to reflect their former status as slaves of the Cree Nation, White observed that there was 'so much of the Indian blood in the coloured man of Oklahoma, carrying with it all of the evil traits of a life of rapine and murder' that they would 'not easily assimilate with agrarian life.' For the good of the Negro and for the good of Canada, he therefore recommended that it would be best for the Negro to remain in Oklahoma.[219] Nevertheless, several settlements of a few hundred black settlers emerged in Saskatchewan and Alberta as some Oklahoma farmers made their way across the border from the United States.[220]

At the time that White was writing his report, editorials and articles began to appear across the country, alerting readers to the potential 'tide of coloured immigrants' that was threatening to spill over the West. People were forewarned of consequences ranging from the displacement of white settlers by blacks to unprecedented racial violence. Local boards of trade throughout the prairies, joined by the Edmonton Municipal Council, sent resolutions to Ottawa demanding the exclusion of black immigrants to Canada.[221]

The White Report, together with the protests in the Prairie provinces and the impending election, prompted Oliver to act decisively. In 1911, under the authority recently conferred on the Cabinet by the 1910 Immigration Act, an order-in-council was drafted that prohibited the landing in Canada of 'any immigrant belonging to the Negro race, which race is deemed unsuitable to the climate and requirements of Canada.'[222] The order was not proclaimed. Historians speculate that Laurier refused to approve the order because of the potential diplomatic problems it could have provoked with the United States, and the antagonism it could generate among black liberal voters in Nova Scotia and southwestern Ontario.[223] Instead, an informal exclusionary program was adopted. The department made it very clear, both to immigration agents and to prospective black settlers, that the standard medical and character examinations made at the border would result in the rejection of most black immigrants. Oliver denied that race was being used as a criterion for rejection. Instead he characterized the government's selection procedure as being one where more desirable immigrants had a lower threshold to cross: 'there are many cases where the admission or exclusion of an immigrant depends on a strict or lax interpretation of the law, so that if the immigrant is of what we would call the desirable class they are administered laxly and if he is of the presumably less desirable class then they are administered more restrictedly.'[224]

So effective was the 'strict interpretation' policy that the number of black immigrants to Canada fell from 136 in 1907–8 to 7 in 1909–10.[225] The policy had an important deterrent effect. The impermeable border separating Canadians from African Americans became so well known that interest among potential black immigrants soon dissipated.

The same restrictions applied to prospective black immigrants from the Caribbean. Nevertheless, during this period, groups of Caribbean blacks entered the country to fill specific labour requirements. The coal mines and steel mills in Sydney, Nova Scotia, actively recruited Caribbean black workers. Between 1912 and 1914, the Dominion Iron and Steel Company sent two Barbadian steelworkers to Barbados to recruit labourers. From 1912 to 1915, more than 200 Caribbean blacks immigrated to Canada each year, most of whom went to Nova Scotia. In addition, the first Caribbean Domestic Scheme of 1910–11 brought 100 Guadeloupean women to Quebec to work as domestics.[226]

ENHANCED DEPORTATION POWERS

Expanded powers of selection were complemented in the Immigration Acts of 1906 and 1910 by enhanced deportation provisions. For the first time, the grounds for deportation were legislatively enumerated, and immigration officials were formally empowered to deport landed immigrants. Prior to this period, government policy was to deport those who, within one year of their arrival, were physically impaired or unemployed and unable to support themselves. As one official explained to the House of Commons Committee on Immigration and Colonization in 1877, 'the rule of the Department is that immigrants who have not been over one year in the country, are, in some measure, under the care of the Department; and if it has been found, after they have been unable to get their living, they have been sent back, as the simplest and cheapest mode of dealing with them.'[227] Generally immigrants were returned at the expense of the transportation company which brought them to Canada. Such individuals usually were brought to the attention of federal immigration authorities by municipalities and private charities whose financial assistance the immigrant had requested.

As the number of immigrants to Canada increased, the number of deportation cases also rose. Amendments to the Immigration Act in 1902 contributed to this pattern because they provided for the deportation of immigrants who were medically inadmissible, or had landed contrary to the provisions of the act.[228] Of the approximately 125 deportations effected annually between 1902 and 1906, more than two-thirds were for medical reasons.[229]

Coincident with the increase in deportations was a rise in the number of deportation orders that were challenged successfully in the courts on *habeas corpus* applications.[230] The 1906 amendments, which, in addition to expanding the grounds for deportation, also provided for boards of inquiry to make such decisions, were thus designed to introduce more formality into deportation procedures. The 1910 act tightened the process still further by expanding the grounds for deportation, extending the probationary period to three years after arrival, and outlining more clearly the jurisdiction of the boards as well as the rules governing board proceedings.[231] The act also provided that, where the deportation of a head of a family was ordered, all dependent members of the family could be deported at the same time.[232]

These successive changes to deportation policy and procedures reflected the growing concern that Canada's open posture towards immigrants was bringing in a host of persons who were unable or unwilling to provide for themselves. At the forefront of this issue were municipalities and private charities, to whom sick and unemployed immigrants looked for assistance. Given their limited resources, these institutions petitioned the government for more effective measures to remove those who were a drain on the public and private purse. The increase in unemployment caused by the economic downturn of 1907 exacerbated the problem. The rise in deportations from approximately 200 in 1907 to more than 800 in 1908 reflected government sensitivity to these concerns. Between 1908 and 1909, the number of deportations doubled, despite the fact that immigrant admissions fell by 50 per cent. Whereas previously medical causes were the chief grounds for removal, during the recession public-charge grounds were cited in more than 50 per cent of the cases. Once prosperity resumed by 1910, public charge removals fell to 38 per cent. Deportations for medical reasons also fell to 27 per cent as compared with 70 per cent of all deportations eight years earlier. Medical inspectors explained that the decline in the proportion of deportations for medical reasons was largely the result of more thorough inspections at ports of embarkation and ports of entry, which prevented many medically unsuitable immigrants from gaining admission.[233]

While the proportion of deportations for medical and public-charge reasons fell after 1910, the proportion of removals for criminal reasons rose. In 1903, criminality accounted for 3 per cent of annual deportations. This proportion had risen to 1I per cent by 1906, and to 33 per cent by 1913. Because statistics were not kept on the particular crimes for which people were deported, it is difficult to know exactly how this provision was invoked. Some historians have speculated[234] that the increased use of the criminality provision reflected the growing insecurity and unrest within the metropolitan areas and the corresponding willingness on the part of the authorities to use crimes such as vagrancy, watching and besetting (picketing), being a nuisance, obstructing the police, and political subversion as grounds for removal. As the interwar years were to witness, deportation for such criminal acts was a powerful tool in silencing foreign labour agitators and political activists.[235]

By 1914, deportation had developed from a relatively *ad hoc* procedure to a more organized and formal one. Just as the Immigration Act was amended to provide a greater degree of selectivity in the admission of immigrants, so, too, was it changed to provide wide latitude to the minister and his officials to deport those who did not meet the requirements of 'good citizenship' within three years of their arrival. The fact that their illness or poverty may have been caused by forces beyond their control was immaterial, provided that their infirmity or their reliance on public funds occurred within the three-year probationary period.

RESTRICTING THE RIGHT TO NATURALIZATION

The prevailing view that certain races were inassimilable and therefore not desirable permanent residents seems to have informed naturalization cases of the period. In contrast to the strict-interpretation approach taken by the courts in regard to exclusionary orders, judicial interpretation of naturalization legislation was strikingly less rigid. Judges displayed a willingness to go beyond the face of the legislation, and impose conditions which exposed aliens to a greater likelihood that their naturalization applications would not be granted.

Canadian citizenship was defined in the Immigration Act as meaning: a person born in Canada; a British subject with domicile; and a person naturalized under the laws of Canada.[236] Following Confederation, and continuing through the Laurier era, naturalization was a relatively easy process. Immigrants with three years' residence in Canada could bring an application for naturalization before a court official, who, having heard the applicant swear an oath of allegiance and swear to have fulfilled the three-year residency requirement, and upon being satisfied that the applicant was of 'good character,' would issue a naturalization certificate. The certificate was then posted in court and, if no valid objection was filed, the act provided that the court, on the last day of sittings, 'shall direct' that the certificate be filed.[237] Despite the mandatory language of the legislation, and despite an earlier court ruling to the contrary,[238] in 1908 the B.C. County Court held that the intent of the legislation was to require the judge, when objections were filed, to look behind the certificate to determine whether the evidence of residency and good character was sufficient. The case involved naturalization applications of twelve Japanese persons against whom objections had been filed on the basis that they had 'no conception of the nature of the oaths of residence and allegiance.' The court found in favour of the objectors.[239]

The following year, the court went further and held that it had the power to go behind the certificate even where no objection had been filed. Moreover, Judge Grant ruled that future applications to the court would have to be accompanied by statements of 'at least two credible natural-born Canadian subjects' attesting to good character, residency, and the applicant's intention to reside in Canada.[240] This was clearly in excess of the court's authority, given that the Naturalization Act required only that the applicant provide such evidence as required by the court official who administered the oath in the first instance.[241]

Two years later, in the case of *Re Cabulak*, the Alberta District Court refused to grant certificates of naturalization to 100 Eastern European applicants against whom objections had been filed. The basis of the objections was that, in some cases, the naturalization certificate had not been properly posted or, where posted, was not properly completed. In finding for the objectors, the court reasoned that the proper completion of the certificate was mandatory and that the defects could be remedied at a later time without injustice or inconvenience to the applicants, provided they were applying 'for the privilege on legitimate grounds, and not solely for the purpose of exercising some particular right at a particular moment.' Apparently speculating that the applications in question had been brought by individuals who had been bribed to do so by politicians desirous of their votes, the judge went on to remark: 'In this connection it is noticeable that there are a number of aliens who make no application to be naturalized until an election is imminent, although for a long period they may have been qualified to apply; and if they delay their applications and then employ agents who put forward defective papers (which cannot be made good in sufficient time before the election takes place to enable such aliens to obtain a certificate of naturalization), any resulting inconvenience must lie at their own door.'[242]

The judge's comments reflected the growing concern over the practice of offering bribes and arranging for the naturalization of foreigners in return for their votes. The Conservatives had long accused the Liberals of engaging in such vote-getting exercises. It was an issue important enough for the Conservatives that, when they were returned to power in 1911 under the leadership of Sir Robert Borden, amending the naturalization laws was one of their priorities.

After a series of Imperial conferences and negotiations aimed at harmonizing the Naturalization Acts of Britain and the dominions, a new Naturalization Act was passed in 1914. Among other things, the new act tightened the requirements for naturalization. Immigrants were now required to have lived in Canada for five years before applying to be naturalized. In addition, the applicant not only had to provide evidence of good character, but also to have sufficient knowledge of English or French. Where satisfied that the applicant qualified for naturalization, the court was required to send its decision to the secretary of state, who, with 'absolute discretion,' was authorized to grant or withhold the certificate without 'assigning any reason,' and whose decision was not subject to appeal. Similarly, the secretary of state was authorized to revoke naturalization certificates where it appeared that the certificate was obtained by false representation or fraud.[243]

These changes to naturalization law were significant, for, as with admission and deportation decisions, the granting of naturalization certificates and the revocation thereof was governed by executive discretion, beyond the purview of judicial review. Since naturalization not only enabled immigrants to vote in federal elections, and thereby to have a voice in the political life of the country, but also protected persons from deportation,[244] the refusal or loss of such status increased their vulnerability. As illustrated in the hundreds of cases of Asian immigrants who were regularly denied naturalization certificates, and political and labour activists who were stripped of their naturalized status, naturalization law was, from then on, an important tool for ensuring that undesirable immigrants were not accorded membership in the Canadian polity. As with the immigration legislation of this period, the Naturalization Act of 1914 laid the foundation upon which subsequent acts were based.

Conclusion

Amendments to the naturalization laws were among the few changes that the Conservative government made to the laws affecting immigrants and foreigners prior to the war. For all their criticisms of immigration policy throughout the Laurier years (1896–1911), once in power the Conservatives did little to change it. In fact, the Conservative government of Robert Borden oversaw the admission of more immigrants in one year than in any previous or subsequent year in Canadian history. In 1914, more that 400,000 immigrants were admitted to Canada, at which time the government spent close to $2 million on immigration, almost twice what the Liberal government had expended in 1910.[245] The main admissions-policy initiative undertaken by the Conservative government was its 1913 closure of Western sea ports to immigrant labourers in an effort to prohibit the entry of East Indians. As in the Liberal era, however, the order, although drafted broadly, was limited in its application so as not to prejudice employer interests too severely. Immigration officers were instructed that the regulation was not to apply 'against trans-Pacific passengers other than Hindus.'[246] Similarly, in most other respects, the Conservative immigration policy, was, as the minister, W.J. Roche, admitted in 1914, 'in the main ... the policy that had been enforced for some years, and is being continued under the auspices of myself as Minister of the Interior.'[247] That policy continued to be one officially directed at the promotion of agriculturalists, farm labourers, and domestic workers, yet it remained open to the large-scale importation of immigrant workers for industrial employment.

In 1907, Chief Medical Officer for Immigration P.H. Bryce wrote eloquently on the industry, success, and good citizenship of the new immigrants to Canada and of their rapid absorption, particularly in the Northwest: 'Canada, is ... receiving and welcoming more largely than ever a population ... who are being absorbed so rapidly into our several communities that a few years only will have passed when ... they will be known only by their industry, success and good citizenship, be amenable to the laws of the country, proud of her history and traditions and loyal, enthusiastic supporters of her institutions and labouring to realize to the fullest, the splendid promise of the country of their adoption.'[248]

Seven years later, his writing reflected a change in mood. While still convinced of the value of immigrants, Bryce was also very much aware of the controversy surrounding the massive immigration movement of the period and sensitive to the fact that immigrant adjustment to Canada was not automatic, nor a necessarily painless endeavour. Unlike those opposed to the immigration policy of the day, Bryce was of the opinion that the problems associated with immigration simply highlighted the communal responsibility for the adjustment process: 'In every part of Canada the conscience is being aroused as to its duty to the immigrant, and his ills become apparent, because his needs are being more inquired into. To distribute the immigrants, to fit the man to the work needing him, to realize that he may become a drag on the market or an asset to the country, are so obviously both the work and the duty of our communities...' The fulfilment of this obligation, predicted Bryce, would benefit not only newcomers but also society as a whole: 'as the immigrant becomes more recognized as a factor in the social problems of our communities so will our people more and more develop methods whereby he will no longer be a stranger within our gates, but as a strand to be woven into the social fabric, making it stronger ... more extended... more picturesque ... and more precious.'

Bryce was, in these respects, a harbinger of modern multicultural policy, for he adhered to the view that society was enriched by the presence of those with different 'manners and customs ... developed separately in their own environments, each having elements of truth and beauty.'[249] In 1914, however, his voice was a lonely one. Most people, whether they were in favour of an expansive immigration policy or opposed to it, adhered to the view that it was up to the immigrant to adjust to the Canadian way of life. For some, failure to do so warranted deportation. For others, it demanded less than removal, yet no more than rights to residency, for full citizenship and all it attributes should be denied those who were unwilling or unable to assimilate into the Canadian norm.

In 1906, the Privy Council delivered its judgment in the case of the *Attorney General for Canada v Cain.* The words of Lord Atkinson were particularly relevant, for they reflected a view of the state's rights and obligations towards aliens that had taken root in Canada and that was to inform Canadian immigration policy for decades to come: 'One of the rights possessed by the Supreme power in every State is the right to refuse to permit an alien to enter that State, to annex what conditions it pleases to the permission to enter it, and to expel or deport from the State at pleasure, even a friendly alien, especially if it considers his presence in the State is opposed to its peace, order, and good government, or to its social or material interests.'[250]

The immigration and naturalization legislation of the day reflected this prevailing view of the rights of the state *vis à vis* the rights of the immigrants. The right of immigrants to enter Canada was conditional upon the country's willingness to accept them, a decision which, in practice, rested with the Cabinet, according to its assessment of the needs and desires of the Canadian community. Similarly, as amendments to the Naturalization Act made clear, the granting of citizenship was also conditional and discretionary – ultimately dependent on ministerial approval. Judicial review, which could circumscribe the exercise of these discretionary powers, was legislatively restricted. Courts, on the whole, respected the limitations imposed upon them, particularly where the harm was individualized to the immigrants and did not involve any competing entrepreneurial interest. Like the executive branch of government, the judiciary was influenced by the industrial and entrepreneurial concerns of the day and so was more likely to interfere with legislation that adversely affected such interests than an immigrant's right to remain or claim full membership rights.

It is ironic that, at a time when the country was admitting more immigrants than in any preceding or subsequent eighteen-year period, it was also introducing an unprecedented degree of selectivity aimed at ensuring the effective exclusion of all undesirable immigrants, whether it be for racial, political, economic, or other reasons. While the degree of discretion vested with the minister and department officials would ultimately diminish in later periods, selectivity and exclusivity were features of immigration policy that would prove enduring. They were rooted in the unwavering belief, for the first time widely articulated in Canada, that the state had the ultimate discretion in determining who would gain admission and full membership in the Canadian community. As Mackenzie King stated in 1914, immigration laws were the manifestation of the state's right to determine membership:

> This I take is not because of any declaration of individual or national superiority on the part of the people of Canada over the people of any other national, country or race ... The country is the people; the people are the country, and it is the first duty of the country ... to take such measures as may be right and expedient to prevent, if prevention is necessary, the occupation of the country by a population that shall hamper and deter in any material degree the development of those ideals of civilization which we believe ourselves to be here for the purpose of working out to their highest degree.[251]

CHAPTER FIVE

The War and the Recovery, 1914–1929: The Dominance of Economic Interests

The economic prosperity of the pre-war years, which was stimulated by great waves of immigrants, and which in turn had supported a burgeoning population base, began to suffer a serious decline just prior to the outbreak of the First World War in 1914. Industrial production and expansion dropped dramatically, in large part as a result of a tightening in overseas credit, principally by the London money market. The rumblings that war was imminent on the Continent and a growing distrust of Canadian securities led foreign financiers to become more cautious in advancing credit to Canadian industries whose returns on investment had been disappointing. The first to feel this contraction in credit were industries such as real estate, housing construction, and railway expansion, where foreign capital had largely been concentrated. As these industries cut back and laid off workers, the production of lumber, bricks, steel, and other related products fell off markedly, with a consequent rise in unemployment across the country. Land prices plummeted and the number of bankruptcies soared. The West was particularly hard hit, because of the effect of the failing transcontinental railways, and previous land speculation which had led to considerable overcapacity in the construction industry. Poor crop yields in 1914 further exacerbated the depressed economic climate in the West.[1]

The country's economic fortunes were soon to turn again, however, following Canada's entry into the war in the summer of 1914. At that time, few people would have predicted the long duration of the war, or its immense cost in death and human suffering. Of the 650,000 men Canada sent to the battlefields, more than 60,000 died there. At the close of the conflict, more than one-quarter of the country's young men of military age were either dead or wounded.[2]

Just as the costs of the war effort were not generally anticipated in 1914, neither were the tremendous economic changes set in motion by Canada's involvement in the war. The war generated demand for such things as tanks, aircraft, sea vessels, and explosives, which stimulated existing industries in Canada and induced the development of new ones. Although this economic boom was interrupted in the recessionary years that followed the cessation of hostilities, it nevertheless revived by the mid-1920s, and continued until the close of that decade. By that time, the Canadian economy, once dominated by agriculture and the iron, steel, and coal industries, was now more diverse. Although wheat remained a staple product, other resource and manufacturing sectors – such as the production of pulp and paper; the mining of silver, gold, nickel, lead, and zinc; and the generation of hydro-electric power – outstripped in import-ance the iron, steel, and coal industries upon which the country had relied in earlier years.

In terms of immigration policy, the years between 1914 and 1930 were very much transitional, bridging the most expansive period in Canadian immigration history and the most restrictive and exclusionary one. Straddling these two extremes, the immigration policy of this period, not surprisingly, exhibited several of the characteristics that distinguished the periods on either side of it. For example, economically recessionary years such as those immediately before and immediately after the First World War were characterized by more selective admission criteria and the cessa-tion of most promotional activity. Economically more prosperous times, such as during the war and throughout the mid to late 1920s, witnessed a relatively more open immigration policy.

In terms of numbers, annual admissions, which were extraordinarily high in the first decade of the century, fell considerably during this period, yet did not reach the unprecedented lows of the Depression years. For ex-ample, 1929 admission levels peaked at approximately 168,000 persons, as compared with more than 400,000 in 1913 and 11,000 in 1936. Similarly, annual deportations between 1914 and 1929 were on average higher than in previous times but considerably lower than during the Depression years. In the eleven years between 1902 and 1913, approximately 7,000 persons were deported from Canada. In the next fifteen years, more than 36,000 were expelled, as compared with more than 23,000 persons in the four years between 1930 and 1934.[3]

In contrast to the immigration policies throughout the first forty years of Confederation, which were primarily driven by the need to populate the West, immigration policy throughout this period was also designed to meet domestic labour-market needs. Economic considerations tended to be paramount, and large employers of foreign labourers had considerable influence over the formation of immigration policy. The need to select the 'right kind' of immigrants, persons who would contribute towards the growth of a great nation, continued to be voiced throughout this time. Government policies reflected prevailing public concerns that immigrants should be of a racial and political character that ensured their ready assimilation into Canadian society. The Immigration Act and regulations provided the government with enough flexibility to prevent admission, to prohibit naturalization, and to effect the removal of those who were perceived as lowering the standards of acceptable citizenry, by their nationality, race, or political opinions. Thus, nationals of countries with which Canada was at war ('enemy aliens') were interned and refused entry; African and Asian immigrants were almost entirely prohibited; and those suspected of communist or socialist sympathies were denied admission and/or deported throughout these years.[4]

The manner in which immigration policy was administered remained the same as it had in the previous period. Successive amendments to the Immigration Act continued to give the Cabinet broad discretion in determining those who would be admitted to Canada and those who could be expelled. Permissible classes of immigrants were specified in orders-in council which changed in response to the labour-market conditions within the country. The deportation of the ill, the unemployed, political activists, and criminals was effected largely as before. Immigrants who fell within one of the prohibited or undesirable classes were brought before administrative boards of inquiry, where their cases were reviewed. Deportation decisions were reviewable by the minister, but not by the courts. To assist in removing immigrants who were not desirable permanent residents, greater surveillance measures were undertaken, particularly of Oriental persons, labour activists, and female domestics.

In 1917, control over immigration and settlement was transferred from the Department of the Interior to the newly established Department of Immigration and Colonization. The shift represented more than a bureaucratic shuffle. It appeared to be an acknowledgment of the growing complexity of immigration policy and the increasing demands placed upon those charged with overseeing its operation. Throughout the 1920s, departmental reporting became more detailed and specialized. Extensive statistical breakdowns of immigrant arrivals and rejections were provided. As well, new subdivisions within the department were created, such as the Women's Division, which was in charge of supervising the settlement of unaccompanied immigrant women. Annual reports from these divisions were included with that of the department.

The War Years

DECLINING ADMISSIONS

During the war, immigration to Canada was greatly reduced, primarily because movement from Britain and the European Continent to North America became highly problematic. Not only was transportation scarce, expensive, and hazardous, but foreigners, needed at home to work in war-related industries or serve in their countries' armies, were faced with emigration controls that made relocating to Canada exceedingly difficult. Thus, British emigration to Canada, which in 1913 stood at more than 142,400 persons, fell by 70 per cent the following year, and averaged about 7,500 persons annually for the remainder of the war. Similarly, emigration from the Continent, which reached more than 130,000 persons in 1913, also fell by 70 per cent the next year, and averaged about 5,000 persons per year until the end of the war.[5]

Of the approximately 55,000 persons who emigrated to Canada annually throughout the war, the vast majority came from the United States. The pattern of immigration from the United States contrasted sharply with other immigration flows. Although the number of American immigrants fell by almost 50 per cent between 1913 and 1914,[6] admissions were to remain relatively constant throughout the war, averaging approximately 50,000 people per year. American arrivals were primarily farmers, labourers, and domestic servants. Although American immigration figures were significantly higher than those from any other source, the annual reports by the supervisor of the Canadian immigration agents in the United States, W.J. White, disclose a dissatisfaction with the number of migrants moving north. Reference is often made in his reports to the fact that admissions to Canada would have been higher had certain conditions outside the control of the Department of the Interior not prevailed. In particular, the decrease in the number of available homesteads near one of the transnational railways was a disincentive to relocating in Canada. Moreover, according to White, Canada's entry into the war was a concern to many prospective settlers hesitant to move to a country embroiled in an international conflict. This natural reluctance was exacerbated by rumours that conscription would soon be imposed in Canada, and a heavy war tax assessed on all Canadian lands.

Immigration agents in the United States tried to suppress false rumours and allay the fears of prospective American immigrants. Yet, despite their best efforts, annual American immigration levels remained relatively modest. Although excess labour demand in Canada attracted American labourers across the border in the initial years of the war, the effect was only temporary. Once the United States entered the war, available manpower was needed to fill labour shortages at home and enlistments for overseas duty. The subsequent imposition of the American Draft Act further inhibited immigration to Canada, for it prevented the movement of males between the ages of twenty-one and forty-five unless they received special permission.[7]

The most distinctive aspect of immigrant admissions was the dramatic drop in annual arrivals. Legislatively, however, admissions policy remained relatively unchanged. As far as changes to the Immigration Act and regulations are concerned, of more significance was the manner in which the government used the legislation to handle the 'enemy aliens' question and to deal severely with immigrants involved in labour and radical political movements in the period.

RESPONSE TO THE 'ENEMY ALIENS' QUESTION

Canada's entry into the war in 1914 served to exacerbate intense and long festering prejudices against European immigrants, especially those from countries with which Canada was now at war. The widespread patriotic endorsements of Canada's involvement in the Imperial cause were matched by sweeping calls for the suppression of the rights and liberties of enemy aliens. The government was pressed by diverse individuals and groups, including prominent Canadians and the conservative press across the country, to impose upon enemy aliens such extreme restrictions as compulsory lay-offs, forced internment, surtaxes, restricted travel to within several miles of home, mandatory registration, constant police surveillance, and mass deportation.[8]

Despite demands that it impose such harsh measures, the government's position was that, since it had no reason to believe that enemy aliens would be disloyal to Canada, and provided they violated no law of the country, they would be afforded the protection of the law.[9] The government formalized this commitment in 1914 with a series of proclamations which promised all persons in Canada of German or Austro-Hungarian birth the protection of the law and assured them that the government would not take action to deprive them of their freedom to hold property or carry on a business.[10]

Within weeks of issuing these proclamations, however, the government passed the War Measures Act, which gave the governor in council sweeping powers to authorize acts deemed necessary for the 'security, defence, peace, order and welfare of Canada.' It was explicitly given power over 'arrest, detention, exclusion and deportation.'[11] Under the authority of this act, enemy aliens were subsequently prohibited from possessing firearms, subjected to compulsory registration, required to carry identity cards, forbidden to publish or possess material in an enemy-alien language, prohibited from joining certain socialist and anarchist organizations which were declared unlawful, and prevented from leaving the country without exit permits. Moreover, thousands were interned in camps across the country and summarily deported.

The number of people affected by these measures was not small. Those classified as enemy aliens included almost 400,000 persons of German origin, more than 100,000 immigrants from the Austro-Hungarian Empire, close to 5,000 people from the Turkish Empire, and several hundred Bulgarians.[12] While many of these immigrants had been the subject of animosity before the war, the level and intensity of public hostility towards them reached new heights during these years.

No doubt a good deal of the public's antagonism stemmed from pre-war prejudices against Austro-Hungarians and Germans. As noted earlier, Austro-Hungarian immigrants were frequently reviled for their language, customs, and low socio-economic status.[13] During the war years, it was relatively easy for such contempt to be channelled into concerns that these immigrants were potential enemies of Canada. According to Desmond Morton, however, they did not pose a significant danger: 'Far from retaining an allegiance to the Habsburg monarchy, most of the Poles, Ruthenians, Slovaks, Czechs, and Croats were fugitives from the law and the economic backwardness of the ramshackle Austro-Hungarian empire.'[14]

The militarization of Germany and the tendency of German immigrants to maintain their language and culture helped breed suspicions in Canada as to their primary allegiance. The fact that the German government did not regard Canadian naturalization as relieving German citizens of their military obligations reinforced such concerns.[15] German military advances overseas and rumours of fifth-column activities added to the growing hysteria in Canada that enemy-alien residents posed a threat to internal security and the war effort. Unsubstantiated rumours of enemy invasions of Canada reinforced these fears,[16] as did the many accusations of subversive activity among enemy aliens in Canada. The presence of German spies in the country was a common fear. A commentary in a 1915 issue of the *Canadian Law Journal* reflected the sentiments of many: 'bitter experience has proven that no reliance can be placed on the word or honour of a German when the welfare of his country is at stake. The truth is that during the continuance of this war it is not desirable to have alien enemies in the country at all. It is common knowledge that there are too many spies and traitors among them and the spy system of Germany has been England's greatest danger and difficulty.'[17]

As with rumours of German invasions in Canada, allegations of rampant subversive activity were never substantiated. Throughout the war, very little genuine espionage was found to have occurred. The suspicions, however, proved to have a life of their own. Together with the fears of German attack, they were used to justify the massive firing of enemy aliens that took place across the country during the initial stages of the war. Thousands of blue-collar workers, as well as government bureaucrats, teachers, and university professors, were dismissed from their employment.

With the effects of the 1913 depression still being felt in the first few months of the war, the widespread firing of enemy-alien workers exacerbated an already severe unemployment problem and placed additional demands on public support. In an apparent move to address the desperate situation in which many enemy aliens found themselves, and within weeks of its proclamation that the rights of enemy aliens would be protected, the government initiated internment operations under the directorship of Sir William Otter. Local registrars were appointed by the minister of Justice and given the responsibility for determining who would be interned and who could remain at large. Internment decisions were based as much on relieving municipal welfare agencies of foreign-born relief recipients as they were on protecting the country from subversive activity. As the war progressed and militant labour activity intensified, internment was also a way of removing political and labour activists from the public arena.[18] Throughout the war, between 8,000 and 9,000 enemy aliens were placed in twenty-four internment camps across the country. The two largest centres were located in Kapuskasing, Ontario, and Vernon, British Columbia.[19] At the beginning of the war, several attempts were made by aliens so interned to have the cause of their detention reviewed by the courts, and orders for release made where the detention was found to be unlawful. Such requests, brought as applications for writs of *habeas corpus,* were uniformly unsuccessful.[20] The courts generally relied upon a privative clause in the War Measures Act which prohibited the release of enemy aliens 'without the consent of the minister of Justice' as precluding the courts from granting *habeas corpus* relief.[21] Even where there was reason to believe that the imprisonment was unlawful, *habeas corpus* relief was not forthcoming. As Justice Meredith of the Ontario Supreme Court explained,

> ... it should be plain to everyone that in the stress and danger to the life of any nation in war, the Courts should be exceedingly careful not to hamper the actions of those especially charged with the safety of the nation; careful, among other things, not to take up the time and attention of those who should be fighting the enemy in the field, in fighting law suits in the Courts over private rights. It is not a time when the prisoner is to have the benefit of the doubt; it is a time when, in all things great and small, the country must have every possible advantage; ... until the final victory is won; even though individuals might suffer meanwhile. Private wrongs may be righted then: while final defeat would not only prevent that but bring untold disasters to all.[22]

Although enemy aliens could be deprived of their liberty without due process, they were able to bring and maintain private rights of action in the courts. The courts interpreted the 1914 proclamation, guaranteeing enemy aliens the protection of the law, to mean that, provided they did not engage in acts of a hostile nature, they were entitled to assert their claims in court. Thus, throughout the war years, the right of enemy aliens to assert claims for personal injury,[23] death benefits,[24] protection of property,[25] and breach of contract[26] was repeatedly affirmed by the courts.

By 1916, the internment of thousands of enemy aliens began to create problems for both the government and the labour-intensive industries. When war was declared, labour was relatively abundant, and so enemy-alien workers were generally expendable. This situation was to change as the manufacturing sector expanded as thousands of men were leaving the country for service overseas. The demand for labour soon exceeded supply, a problem which worsened in 1917 with the implementation of conscription in Canada and with the entry of the United States into the war. Conscription reduced the pool of available Canadian labour. Restrictions placed upon American emigration consequent to its entry into the war meant that Canadian industries could no longer rely on American workers to meet their labour needs.

As labour became in short supply, industries began to apply pressure on the government to release interned enemy aliens.[27] The issue was extremely sensitive, because the public was opposed to such an action.[28] Debates were waged in Parliament and the press over whether the internees should be released and, if so, whether they should be conscripted to work for nominal pay. Those who accepted that current labour shortages necessitated the release of enemy aliens were nevertheless divided as to the terms under which the releases should be made. One of the more contentious issues was whether enemy aliens should be forcibly conscripted to work for less than market wages. The absence of such restrictions meant that enemy aliens could find work in Canada for wages substantially higher than those earned by Canadian soldiers overseas. This struck many as perverse in the extreme. As one member of Parliament noted, 'Men fail to see the reasons why their boys should voluntarily go overseas and work for $1.10 a day, while foreigners come in and take their places in the ordinary walks of life and earn $7 and $8 a day.'[29]

Returning soldiers were very vocal in this regard. In 1918, the Great War Veterans' Society petitioned the prime minister, demanding that all enemy aliens be interned unless they were needed 'in work of national importance or industries essential to the winning of the war' and any earnings they received over and above the pay of a Canadian soldier should 'be taken by the Government for war purposes.'[30] A similar resolution was presented in the House the following month by H.S. Clements, a Conservative MP. Noting the concerns of organized labour, which was opposed to compulsory employment for wages below the union rate, Clements proposed that enemy aliens conscripted for work 'should be given a fair wage for the sustenance of themselves and families,' and that the balance of their wages 'should be taken and applied for the benefit of the State.'[31]

The government responded to the controversy by ensuring that the employment needs of industry were met, while at the same time recognizing some of the concerns of organized labour. Internees were gradually released into the workforce, and labour conscription at fixed wage rates was not imposed on them. By the close of 1916, 6,000 enemy aliens had been released, and by the end of the war fewer than 2,500 internees remained in the camps.[32] The government defended the release of the internees, arguing that internment measures had been resorted to in a time of high unemployment, when many enemy aliens were without jobs. It thus made sense that they should be released once their labour was again in demand. As C.J. Doherty, the minister of Justice, reasoned in 1918, 'Although there was a glut in the labour market, conditions changed until there was, in this country, a crying need for labour; we had people from all parts, as loyal people as we are ourselves, asking for the labour of those men, and we discharged them and allowed them to go out where they found employment.'[33]

As for refusing to enforce labour conscription at fixed wages,[34] Doherty relied upon international and domestic law. As a signatory to the Hague Convention, Canada could enforce compulsory labour only on captured prisoners of war and not on civilian internees. Moreover, by its own proclamation in 1914, the government had promised enemy aliens that, as long as they acted peaceably, they would be accorded the protection and consideration due to law-abiding citizens.[35]

The government apparently saw no contradiction between its promises of 1914 and its subsequent restrictions on the voting rights of enemy aliens. In 1917, the Conservative government faced an election and a very divided electorate. The passage of the Military Service Act, which brought in conscription, was regarded by Borden and his supporters as essential if Canada was to honour its international commitments and prevent Allied defeat.[36] Conscription was hotly contested. Western farmers demanded that their sons be exempted on the grounds that they were needed on the farms. French Canadians, who regarded the war as an essentially British conflict, were intensely opposed to sacrificing their men for a British cause.[37] Wilfrid Laurier and his Liberal party, which tended to attract many new immigrant votes, supported the war effort but opposed the imposition of conscription, essentially because it had a deeply divisive effect on English and French Canadians. In the face of such opposition, the government formed a coalition, the Union government, with Liberals who supported conscription. It also passed the Wartime Elections Act.[38] The act enfranchised women who had sons, brothers, or husbands in active service, and disenfranchised all persons from enemy-alien countries who had been naturalized in Canada since 1902.

Members of the Opposition protested bitterly against the act, accusing the government of simply enfranchising those it felt would vote for it and disenfranchising those it thought would vote against it. The government insisted that extending the franchise to female relatives of men overseas was intended both to give representation to those unable to vote and to reward women for their service. Members of the Opposition, however, noted that the legislation did not accomplish either of those supposed objectives. One soldier might have several female relatives, or one woman several male relatives at the front. Similarly, many women served in war-related industries and charities, but had no male relatives in overseas service, and therefore had no way of exercising the franchise.[39]

In its justification for disenfranchising citizens of enemy-alien birth, the government advanced two related arguments. First, it emphasized the relationship between service and the franchise. According to Prime Minister

Borden, if enemy aliens were to be permitted to vote, then it necessarily followed that they would also have to be given the opportunity to fight with Canadian troops overseas. This, he argued, would be 'cruel' and 'unnatural,' and he asked the Opposition whether they would seriously propose that enemy aliens fight against 'their own kin, men of their own blood, men perhaps with whom they were brought up in days gone by?'[40] Fellow Conservative MP and future prime minister R.B. Bennett lent his support to the argument, adding the following observation: 'I have talked with some of them; I know something of their views ... and they tell me that the tie of blood is strong upon them, the call of the Fatherland, the call of the homeland, the call of brothers and fathers and cousins fighting in the German and Austrian armies ... the insistent call of the blood is ever upon them ... And that call, strong as it is, should be the call that deprives these aliens of the franchise in this country.'[41]

The second reason advanced by the government for disenfranchising enemy aliens was to relieve them of the burden of voting, since many would not want to exercise the right. As the prime minister said, 'I have reason to believe ... that a large number of these men will be grateful for exemption from compulsory military service on the one hand and for not being called upon to pronounce their judgment in this election on the other.'[42]

Again the Opposition challenged the government's rationales. Several members maintained that the government had no reason to believe that enemy aliens would be disloyal to their adopted country. As Laurier argued, 'when a man leaves Europe ... and comes to this country, when he swears allegiance to His Majesty the King, when he becomes a citizen of Canada, when he builds a home for himself and for his family, I am not prepared to believe that if a conflict arises between the land of that man's birth and the land of his adoption, that he will go back upon the country to which he has sworn allegiance.'[43]

That these immigrants did not want to vote was also discounted. As Arthur B. Copp reasoned, 'any elector who feels that way can refrain from voting; it is not necessary to take from him the right to exercise the franchise.'[44] The only reason for the measure, the Opposition concluded, was to ensure that the Conservatives won the election. As one Liberal MP stated bluntly, the only ground upon which enemy aliens were being disenfranchised was that they were suspected by the government of committing 'the high crime and misdemeanour of being liable to vote Liberal at the next election.'[45]

Arthur Meighen, who was to assume leadership of the Conservative party three years later, admitted as much when he declared: 'If it is true ...

that the majority of the women in this country whose near relatives are overseas, those who spend their days in anxiety and their nights in tears, will support us, and that those who, of all our population, are likely to favour the enemy will reject us, then, in the name of the Government which has been striving for three years to fight that enemy, I accept the compliment.'[46]

Borden's Union government won the election by a two-thirds majority. The Wartime Elections Act clearly helped it overcome the difficulties it may have had in carrying the West, where many enemy aliens were resident. In Quebec, however, the act was regarded as a means of rigging the election in favour of the Conservatives, thereby strengthening their conscription mandate. The act thus sealed the defeat of the Union party in that province, where it secured only three seats in predominantly English-speaking ridings.[47]

With the signing of the armistice, most of the wartime restrictions imposed on enemy aliens were lifted. Although they were no longer subject to internment, and although naturalized subjects were once again permitted to vote, aliens from enemy countries were by no means embraced as equal and desirable citizens. The extent of their undesirability was, in fact, explicitly recognized in the Immigration Act of 1919 and the Naturalization Act of 1920. The Immigration Act specifically excluded from Canada immigrants from countries with which Canada had been at war. The Naturalization Act provided that naturalization certificates could not be issued to enemy aliens until ten years after the war.[48] Both these provisions were repealed in 1922.

WARTIME REMOVALS AND LABOUR ACTIVISTS

Prior to the war, the largest single cause for deportation was becoming a public charge. Years of high unemployment, such as 1909 and 1913, were therefore characterized by relatively high levels of deportation. During the war, the number of immigrants deported fell continuously, from 1,834 in 1913–14, to nearly 1,200 in 1915–16, and to nearly half that number annually for the duration of the war.[49] While the removal of deportable Americans continued without interruption, the deportation of Europeans was hampered by the scarcity and expense of available transport. The government also claimed that it was helping the war effort by refusing to deport public charges to Britain. Canadian municipalities, it was said, were in a better position to care for the indigent than was Great Britain. Keeping them in Canada, explained Superintendent of Immigration W.D. Scott, was 'one way in which we can help Great Britain and to my mind appears to be a patriotic duty.'[50]

The fall in public-charge deportations was countered by an increase in the proportion of deportations for criminal reasons, which accounted for approximately 50 per cent of all removals throughout the war years. Included within this category were those accused of crimes 'incidental to times of war' such as being 'pro-German,' or 'anti-war,' or attempting to disrupt the war effort through labour activities.[51] The removal of labour activists and those suspected of having communist sympathies was part of a larger effort to suppress labour unrest.

Despite the excess demand for their labour, and a corresponding increase in wages, workers did not share proportionately in the economic prosperity of the war years, of which industrialists and farmers were the chief beneficiaries. Spiralling costs of living cut deeply into wages, leaving labouring people barely better off than in the pre-war years. Nevertheless, unlike the pre-war period, which was characterized by high unemployment, the shortage of labour during the war afforded workers greater confidence in pressing for more favourable terms of employment. Between 1915 and 1920, union membership grew almost 40 per cent, from approximately 143,000 persons to 378,000. Not surprisingly, within the same period Canada experienced an unparalleled wave of strikes and a high level of labour militancy.

Not only was the intensity of labour unrest new, but so too, were many of the participants. With growing frequency, foreign workers expressed their intolerance of exploitative working conditions and the lack of support received from the traditional craft unions by withholding their labour and backing more radical unions such as the Industrial Workers of the World (IWW). This increase in radical labour activity was accompanied by the growth of ethnic-socialist political organizations such as the Finnish Social Democratic Party, the Russian Social Democratic Party, and the Ukrainian Labour-Farmer Temple Association, who were sympathetic to the demands of labour.[52]

The concomitant rise in labour militancy and socialist activism led to the frequent accusation that labour unrest was being fomented by alien fanatics intent on bringing industrial capitalism to its knees. While there were many activists committed to a restructuring of political power, for the most part industrial conflict was the response of workers, both alien and Canadian-born, to employment conditions that they regarded as fundamentally unfair. As the Royal Commission on Industrial Relations found in 1919, 'though advocacy of extreme views both by speech and by the

distribution of literature may be a contributing cause to occasional outbursts, the real causes of unrest are of a more fundamental nature.'[53] The
principal causes of discord, reported the commission, were the high costs
of living, desire for shorter hours, lack of collective-bargaining rights, insufficient housing, restrictions on freedom of speech, lack of confidence
in constituted government, the wide gap between the rich and poor, and
unequal educational opportunities.[54]

Throughout the war, business leaders sent a steady barrage of reports to
Ottawa charging that, but for the alien agitators, Canadian business would
not be afflicted by the strikes that were hindering production. As a representative of the Manitoba Gypsum Company, whose enterprise was affected by work stoppages, alleged, 'all of the men who have gone out are
of alien nationality, many of them not naturalized.'[55] It was also common
to link industrial unrest with deliberate attempts to sabotage the war effort. The *Vancouver Sun* reproduced the following warning of an American
'writer and student of labour conditions' who had reportedly seen many
traces of IWW influence in Canada: 'It is the hidden, sneaky, secret propaganda that it is the hardest to reach and if the Canadian labouring man is
not careful he will find that the scheming pro-German element will have
him working for it before he realizes it. If the men who are striking had
full knowledge of German efforts to cause labour unrest they would be
mighty careful.'[56] This sentiment was also echoed by various members of
Parliament. According to H.S. Clements, the troubles in British Columbia's
forestry industry were attributable to the activities of the 'alien-enemy,
pro-German agitators who are creating disturbances in the different
camps and at the different mills.'[57]

Charges by industrialists,[58] MPs, and the press[59] that worker unrest was
being instigated by enemy aliens, foreign socialists, and revolutionaries
were supported by internal government security reports, many of which
warned of an impending socialist revolution in Canada. Russia's withdrawal from the war had raised suspicions in Canada towards Bolsheviks
and heightened hostility towards communism and socialism. The federal
government's growing concern with these developments led it to appoint
a wealthy Montreal businessman, C.H. Cahan, to conduct a special investigation in 1918. After consulting with business leaders, representatives of
the more conservative unions, various members of ethnic communities,
and Canadian and American security officials, Cahan informed the minister of Justice that the manifestations of unrest 'among our alien peoples'
was not 'directly due to German propaganda.' Rather, it was 'directly attributable to the dissemination in Canada of the Socialist doctrines,

espoused by the Russian revolutionary element.' Viewing the Bolsheviks as the most serious threat to economic and political stability, Cahan recommended a series of repressive measures aimed at silencing the IWW, the Social Democratic Party, and 'any other society or organization inculcating the same doctrines or teachings.'[60] The government responded promptly and, by order-in-council, declared fourteen socialist and anarchist organizations unlawful.[61] The order was drafted broadly to include any association 'one of whose professed purposes is to bring about any governmental, political, social, industrial or economic change within Canada by the use of force, violence or physical injury to person or property.' In addition, another order-in-council made it illegal to print, publish, or possess literature in an enemy-alien language.[62] The penalties for breach of these regulations were very severe, ranging from fines of up to $5,000 to a maximum prison term of five years.

The censorship regulations were used to silence foreign activists, while immigration regulations were directed at excluding and removing them. Although there was no law or regulation explicitly prohibiting socialists from coming to Canada, immigration officers were repeatedly instructed to find reasons for barring the entry of such persons. IWW organizers were specifically targeted. As Superintendent of Immigration W.D. Scott assured the minister of Labour in 1917, 'For some time past – in fact for years – our officers have been alive to the danger of the IWW movement ... Although it may not be possible to reject one of these men solely on the ground that he is a member of that organization, yet there are usually other circumstances ... and our inspectors are, as a rule, very careful to do this.'[63] For foreign activists already in the country, the threat of deportation was both a real and a constant one. In the case of foreigners from countries with whom Canada was at war, deportation could be effected expeditiously and relatively inconspicuously. Wartime regulations left enemy aliens open to internment, and once interned they could be summarily deported. According to Donald Avery, there was considerable public support for the mass deportation of enemy aliens, especially those who were affiliated with socialist organizations. He writes that the reason the government did not adopt such a policy was 'both because of its likely international repercussions and because of the demands it would make on the country's transportation facilities at a time when the troops were returning from Europe.'[64]

In dealing with activists from neutral countries, or countries with which Canada was an ally, immigration officers were instructed to pick them up for breaches of the Immigration Act, whereupon they could be removed from Canada. Since the act authorized the deportation of foreigners convicted of a criminal offence within three years of entering Canada, Scott instructed his officers to arrange for the arrest of radicals, such as members of the IWW, 'who in any way lay themselves open to arrest even though their breaches of the law be technical rather than serious.'[65] Following the passage of the censorship regulations, simple possession of prohibited literature was enough to expose a person to expulsion from Canada.

Censorship, entry restrictions, and deportations were three techniques employed by the government to suppress labour activity. In addition, the government passed several regulations to ensure that industries would not be fettered by labour shortages. In 1916, the Alien Labour Act was suspended to permit the entry of American labourers into Canada.[66] In the same year, all persons between the ages of sixteen and sixty were required to register with the Canadian Registration Board. This registration requirement was a precursor to the Anti-Loafing Law, proclaimed in 1918, which provided that 'every male person residing in the Dominion of Canada should be regularly engaged in some useful occupation.'[67] Within two months, the government announced its War Labour Policy, which prohibited strikes and lock-outs for the duration of the war.[68]

The government's attempts to silence labour without addressing the grievances that generated labour unrest led to a growing radicalization of the labour movement, especially in the West. Workers in Western cities generally worked for lower wages than those in central Canada, and so were harder hit by rising costs of living. Forced registration, censorship laws, limitations on strikes, and the harassment of labour activists were seen as further insults to the legitimate interests of working people. Nor was the most dominant union, the Trades and Labor Congress (TLC), representative of the majority of aggrieved workers. Its close association with the American craft unions and its failure to recognize the more radical movements left it open to criticism from Western activists. So, too, did its tacit support for conscription and its willingness to work within the traditional party system.[69]

In 1919, Western labour leaders convened a Western labour convention in Calgary. The disaffection among the delegates with government policy and TLC representation was clearly manifest. There was broad consensus that the most effective way for working people to ensure that their voices were heard, and their demands met, was through the power of the general strike. Delegates agreed to urge their membership to break with the TLC and join an industrial organization of all workers under the banner of One Big Union (OBU). The appeal for working-class solidarity under the OBU was a popular one with Anglo and non-Anglo workers alike. In fact, at the convention in Calgary, a resolution was passed declaring 'the interests of all members of the working class being identical that this body recognize no alien but the capitalist.' Avery observes that the resolution was not empty rhetoric — the OBU organizers paid attention to alien workers, and in return garnered substantial support from them.[70]

To the government, the growing popularity of the OBU was further cause for alarm. In April 1919, fearing an outright rebellion in the West, the acting prime minister, Thomas White, cabled Prime Minister Borden in Paris, suggesting that British warships be stationed in Vancouver or Victoria in the event of a violent outburst. Although Borden refused to endorse such a move on the grounds that 'as far back as 1885 we attended to our own rebellions,'[71] the fact that the suggestion was made illustrates how serious some perceived the threat of rebellion to be.

The general strike that virtually paralysed the city of Winnipeg in May 1919 provoked further alarm. More than 30,000 workers walked off their jobs in solidarity with the Metal Trades Council when employers refused to recognize it as the bargaining agent for its affiliated unions.[72] In a city of 200,000 persons, it was estimated that the strikers and their families represented more than 50 per cent of the population.[73] Despite the obvious solidarity between foreign and Canadian-born workers, the strike was characterized by business leaders, the press, and government officials as further evidence that a Bolshevik revolution was under way, and it was primarily upon foreigners that the full force of the Immigration Act and Criminal Code was brought to bear.

John Dafoe, editor of the *Manitoba Free Press,* claimed that five foreigners on the strike committee had gained power only through 'the fanatical allegiance of the Germans, Austrians, Huns and Russians.' The surest way of breaking their hold upon labour, Dafoe maintained, was 'to clean the aliens out of this community' and ship them back to their 'happy homes in central Europe, which vomited them forth a decade ago.'[74] Various politicians also claimed that the strike was Soviet-inspired. A Conservative MP, M.R. Blake, opened one parliamentary debate by declaring that the 'heart of Labour is all right but many of the leaders are all wrong.' He continued by supporting the minister of Labour 'when he said that he had no doubt that while the strike in Winnipeg arose over a definition of collective bargaining, it was at heart really an attempt at revolution and the establishment of a Soviet government.'[75]

Some historians have argued that this fear was simply used by members of the establishment to generate support for the outright suppression of worker unrest.[76] Others maintain that, in the wake of the Russian Revolution, the 'Red Scare' was a sincere one.[77] What is not in serious dispute, however, is that, as a matter of fact, the strike was primarily over employment issues.[78] Contrary to the allegations made by the business community, nearly all the strike leaders were British-born and educated and not central European Bolshevists. Moreover, the strike enjoyed broad support both from foreign and Anglo-Canadian workers, including many war veterans previously hostile to alien labourers.

It is clear that the strikers themselves regarded the accusations against aliens as propaganda designed to inflame fears of a revolution, and thereby provoke government repression. The *Western Labour News* reminded its readership that it was members of the business elite who had been the strongest advocates for the entry of foreign workers. 'So long as they were ... abject slaves, they were desirables; now they have become a little better off and a little better informed they are aliens.'[79]

As sympathy strikes started to spread across the country and as rumours of an impending railway strike circulated, the federal government decided to intervene. At its disposal was a recently amended Immigration Act which extended the time an immigrant had to wait from three to five years before acquiring Canadian domicile. This meant that a person could now be deported any time within five years of arrival for becoming a member of an inadmissible class, such as a convicted criminal, a recipient of public charity, or a patient of a hospital or mental institution.[80] In addition, the scope of section 41 of the act, which authorized the deportation of those who advocated the overthrow by force of the government of Canada or Great Britain, was widened considerably. The section was amended to include one who 'advocates or teaches the unlawful destruction of property' and one who 'is a member of or affiliated with any organization entertaining or teaching the disbelief in organized government.'[81] The section exempted only Canadian citizens by birth or naturalization in Canada. Thus, British subjects who had Canadian domicile[82] could be deported if they were found to engage in the activities set out in section 41. British-born residents were deliberately not exempted to ensure that British labour activists could legally be deported from Canada whether they had acquired domicile or not.

Parallel amendments to the Naturalization Act provided that naturalization certificates could be revoked by Cabinet where the holder 'has shown himself by act or speech to be disaffected or disloyal to His Majesty' or where the person 'was not of good character at the date of the grant of the certificate.'[83] A person whose naturalization certificate had been revoked was then open to removal if it could be shown that the person fell within the prohibitions set out in section 41 of the Immigration Act. The net effect, then, was to expose all immigrants, regardless of how long they had been in Canada, and regardless of whether they had become naturalized subjects, to expulsion for engaging in the anti-government activities described in section 41.

Armed with increased powers under the Immigration Act, the Royal North-West Mounted Police was authorized to carry out the deportation of more than 100 persons across the country. In Winnipeg, among those arrested were ten of the strike leaders, six of whom were Anglo-Saxons and the other four foreign-born. The government proceeded to charge the British leaders with seditious conspiracy, and instituted deportation hearings against the other four.[84] It was the beginning of the end of the strike. A parade organized by war veterans to protest the government's unwillingness to listen to labour turned ugly as Mounties charged the crowd, leaving one person dead and many others wounded. Thirty-one foreigners were arrested, sent to internment camps in Northern Ontario, and then deported.[85] The incident, known as 'Bloody Saturday,' marked the effective end of the strike.

Shortly after the end of the strike, the Criminal Code was amended, expanding the provisions relating to sedition. The definition was broadened, and the penalties upon conviction were increased from two years to a maximum of twenty years in prison. In addition, the amendments outlawed any organization that advocated or defended the use of force or the threat of physical injury 'as a means of accomplishing any governmental, industrial or economic change.' It was illegal to wear any insignia indicating a connection with such an unlawful association. The normal presumption of innocence was removed. Anyone who attended a meeting, advocated the principles, or distributed the literature of an unlawful association was, in the absence of proof to the contrary, presumed guilty.[86]

Amendments to the Immigration Act and Criminal Code, and the official intimidation that was employed under the authority of these two statutes, severely dampened radical labour politics in Canada. In 1919 alone, the government attempted to deport more than 200 'anarchists and revolutionaries.'[87] Throughout the next decade, immigration officials worked closely with employers to remove immigrants who had become troublesome from a labour-relations perspective.[88] Moreover, the homes and offices of union activists were regularly raided, as were those of left-leaning

political writers and organizers. At the same time, the increase in unemployment that followed in the wake of the war also contributed to the
decline in strength and militancy of organized labour. Industries responded to new market conditions with lay-offs and wage cuts, and often
resorted to force when confronted by striking workers. By 1925, union
membership had fallen more than 30 per cent from 1919 levels.[89] The
OBU was one of the largest union casualties,[90] and the hardest hit by the
lack of effective representation were unskilled workers. The loss of some
of the more radical leaders following the wartime purges, subsequent
high unemployment, and the high turnover of the workforce in many industries where unskilled workers were concentrated, all militated against
effective union organizing. The unwillingness of the TLC to make any
substantial efforts towards organizing these sectors contributed to their
lack of effective representation.

Postwar Recession and Recovery

RESTRICTIVE ADMISSIONS POLICY

The end of the First World War marked the beginning of a difficult transitional period for Canada. The fact that the demand which had fuelled
war related industries dramatically fell off had repercussions throughout
the economy. This situation was exacerbated by the return of a quarter of
a million soldiers who needed to be reabsorbed into the national economy. The challenge this posed was substantial, given that an equal number of workers in war-related industries were facing lay-offs. Added to this
was the fact that, throughout the war, the government spent considerably
more than it raised in revenue, forcing it to borrow at high rates of interest, thereby contributing to inflationary conditions at home.[91] Among
the additional demands on federal funds were disability allowances, pensions, and other payments to veterans. The economy was quickly transformed from one of expansion to one characterized by rising prices and
growing unemployment.

   Following the advice of the country's leading bankers, the government
pursued a policy of rapid deflation. Interest rates rose, credit was tightened, and the country plunged into a deep depression, the effects of
which were borne disproportionately by workers, farmers, and small businesses. In the autumn of 1920, the *Labour Gazette* reported that 10.2 per
cent of organized workers were out of work. Within six months, the figure
had climbed to 16.3 per cent.[92] Between 1920 and 1922, the value of

Canadian exports fell significantly, commercial bankruptcies doubled, and the total income earned by workers fell by 25 per cent.[93]

The 1919 amendments to the Immigration Act and the orders-in-council passed pursuant to its provisions reflected these new economic realities. The amendments expanded not only the grounds on which a person could be deported from or denied entry to Canada, but also Cabinet's authority to limit admissions to specified classes of immigrants. The new legislation, explained J.A. Calder, the minister of Immigration and Colonization, was necessary because it enabled the government to better screen out undesirable immigrants and to protect it from increased unemployment occasioned by the arrival of too many newcomers.[94]

Accordingly, the amendments extended the list of inadmissible and undesirable immigrants beyond the diseased, criminals, and those likely to become a public charge, to include alcoholics, persons of 'psychopathic inferiority,' physical and mental defectives, illiterates, persons guilty of espionage or treason, enemy aliens, and those who believed in the overthrow by force of the government of Canada or who were opposed to organized government.[95] In addition, section 38, which authorized Cabinet to declare immigrants of certain races inadmissible owing to their being unsuited to the climate and requirements of Canada, was extended so that Cabinet was empowered to prohibit any race, nationality, or class of immigrant by reason of 'economic, industrial, or other condition temporarily existing in Canada'; or because such immigrants were unsuitable, given the social, economic, and labour requirements of the country; or simply because of their 'peculiar habits, modes of life and methods of holding property' and their 'probable inability to become readily assimilated or assume the responsibilities and duties of Canadian citizenship within a reasonable time.'[96]

In the years immediately following the war, Cabinet availed itself of its broadened authority and prohibited the immigration of enemy aliens[97] as well as Mennonites, Hutterites, and Doukhobors, who were considered 'undesirable' because of their customs and the unlikelihood of their 'becoming readily assimilated.'[98] Additionally, the 1913 prohibition on the landing of skilled and unskilled workers in Western seaports was renewed,[99] and substantial landing-money requirements were imposed on other immigrants to Canada. For example, adult immigrants were required to have $250, and children $125, before being permitted to land in Canada, as well as sufficient money to pay for their travel expenses to their Canadian destinations. Farm labourers and domestic workers with assured employment, and the immediate families of Canadian residents, were exempted from the landing-money requirement.[100]

At a time when war veterans were returning to an economy that was struggling from both the loss of war production, and the burden of wartime debt, the restrictive immigration policy was justified politically as a prudent one. Parliamentary debates show that there was a substantial degree of support for this approach. It was widely believed that immigration policy should be governed by economic realities, and that immigrants should be selected carefully to prevent 'any lowering of the standard of civilization in Canada.'[101] Even the Canadian Manufacturers' Association, formerly a strong advocate of a liberal immigration policy but whose membership was smarting from radical labour activity, supported the government's postwar immigration restrictions. As the association's president, W.J. Bulman stated in 1919, 'We have enough problems on our hands now without encouraging the influx of Europeans who want to leave their own countries in order to escape the burden of war taxation. We should not encourage the immigration of those whose political and social beliefs unfit them for assimilation with Canadians. While a great country such as Canada possessing millions of vacant acres needs population, it is wiser to go slowly and secure the right sort of citizens.'[102]

In part as a result of the postwar economic slump and the consequent immigration restrictions, arrivals from the United States fell from approximately 48,000 in 1921 to around 29,000 in 1922.[103] The imposition of the $250 landing-money requirement was prohibitive for many American labourers intending to come to Canada. In addition, the exclusion of Mennonites, Hutterites, and Doukhobors prevented the migration of members of these sects, and the ban on enemy aliens, according to Inspector White, also considerably lessened immigration flows: 'While they had the desired effect of keeping out many undesirables, the precautions were so sweeping that there were those who, able to qualify as far as farming experience, character, finances, etc., were denied admission, owing to the legal obstructions that it was not deemed advisable to remove. These restrictions were a means of deterring a great many who would have become a profitable addition to Canada's farming community.'

Lest he seem unpatriotic, however, White was quick to endorse the restrictions, despite their dampening effect on numbers: 'While the restrictions have been drastic, and while their operation were the cause of keeping from our farming lands numbers who would have made good settlers, there is no doubt that they produced a good moral effect, which will, if it has not already done so, show that Canada's gates are open only to those who will be factors in the building up of a great nation, unspoiled by anarchism or bolshevism.'[104]

The fact that the annual number of American immigrants did not increase even after these restrictions were lifted suggests that the restrictions in themselves were only marginally significant. The large number of Canadians emigrating to the United States throughout the 1920s indicate that conditions in that country were as determinative of immigration flows as were conditions in Canada. During this time, the American manufacturing sector expanded, and American cities and towns grew correspondingly. The relatively high wages enjoyed in the industrial sector attracted not only Canadian immigrants, but also American farm labourers, one of the groups that the Canadian government sought to attract. Canadian farm employment could not compete with the more lucrative work available in factories and building trades in the United States.

Another contributing cause of the modest scale of American immigration was that many American farmers, especially in the first half of the decade, experienced financial difficulties that made it impossible to move. Sustained low prices for agricultural produce coupled with high interest rates left many in a situation where it was impossible to liquidate their holdings and pay off their debts without incurring severe financial losses.[105] Those who could cover their debts upon sale of their lands were not necessarily more likely to move. Although the prices of farmland were lower in Canada than in the United States, they were not sufficient to attract American farmers in great numbers. Had free homesteads been available, the story no doubt would have been different. However, that time was now past. Thus, it was across the ocean that Canada increasingly had to look for prospective new citizens to support its ongoing development.

With respect to European Continental immigration, the postwar restrictions also had an effect. The imposition of the $250 landing-money requirement in 1921, and the restriction of admissible immigrants to agriculturalists, farm labourers, and domestics in 1923, created barriers to entry that many Europeans were unable to surmount. Nevertheless, the fact that many thousands continued to arrive in Canada each year[106] reflected the relatively loose control the Immigration and Colonization department had over departures from the Continent, and the influence that Canadian business wielded in the political arena.

The annual reports of the Department of Immigration and Colonization between 1919 and 1924 disclose the department's frustration at not being in complete control of immigration originating from the Continent. Canadian immigration agencies on the Continent were closed during the war, and no regular agency was reopened before 1924. A Canadian immigration agent in the Canadian High Commission office in Paris continued to do immigration work from France, and an inspection office was opened in Antwerp for emigrants passing through that port. But, as the superintendent of emigration for Canada in London, J. Obed Smith, noted in 1923, 'emigrants are passing out of Europe through a dozen other ports besides Antwerp, so that the whole question of inspection etc., on the Continent is one that will have to be faced at an early date.' He continued by emphasizing that 'the question of proper inspection of continentals, and disinfection of their persons and clothing, is one of vital importance.'[107]

Smith's report notes the movement of 'many thousands of cosmopolitan and alien nationalities, for the most part not of a class Canada calls for.'[108] Although the government had extensive authority to exclude 'undesirables' that were able to reach Canada, and the authority to order their deportation, it was frequently persuaded not to by businesses desirous of European workers. Avery cites numerous examples where the government succumbed to such pressure. In 1919, for example, the Dominion Coal Company successfully requested the admission of large numbers of Continental European miners for work in Cape Breton, despite objections raised by both the miners' union and local immigration officials. Similarly, in the same year, the Shepard & Morse Company of Ottawa was able to secure Finnish immigrant workers over the objections of immigration officials.[109]

These examples are not to suggest that the government was entirely insensitive to the demands of organized labour, war veterans, and many others who called for tight restrictions on the immigration of European workers. Had it not imposed the 1921 landing-money requirement and the occupational guidelines in 1923, emigration to Canada from the Continent undoubtedly would have been higher than it was in the postwar years. Nor was the government insensitive to the warnings of doctors, psychologists, and others in the medical profession that, unless more stringent examinations were put in place, the social character of Canada would be seriously compromised. By 1925, nearly all immigrants from the Continent were required to pass a medical inspection before departure to Canada.

SELECTIVE EASING OF ADMISSION RESTRICTIONS

In 1921, Arthur Meighen lost the federal election to Mackenzie King, leader of the Liberal party, which retained power for the rest of the decade. Within three years, the Canadian economy began to recover from the postwar recession. An increase in international trade and improved prices for agricultural products and minerals stimulated industrial growth. During the last half of the decade, the production and export of pulp and paper, wheat, and base metals soared. Between 1921 and 1929, for example, Canadian production of newsprint tripled, to more than 2,000 million tons per year, 90 per cent of which was exported, mostly to the United States.[110] American demand for Canadian natural resources also stimulated production and exports, including nickel, zinc, and asbestos. Similarly, the production of hydro-electric power skyrocketed, and, with it, demand for Canadian copper used in electrical devices. In 1930, four times as much power was being generated as in 1921, and the products of new technologies such as radios, electric stoves, and refrigerators were common household items.[111] To meet the growing demand for hydro-electricity, new generating stations were constructed throughout the 1920s, which in turn created jobs and stimulated investment.

As the economy showed signs of recovery, the government faced increasing pressure to ease postwar immigration regulations.[112] The situation was given added urgency by the high numbers of workers leaving Canada every year for the United States. Demand for Canadian labour in the United States had increased with the 1921 changes to American immigration policy, which imposed quotas on European immigrants but left immigration from Canada unrestricted. Both agricultural and industrial skilled and unskilled workers left Canada in large numbers. During the 1920s more than 1 million people emigrated from Canada to the United States.[113]

Initially the government moved cautiously in opening the doors to more immigrants. In 1922, Mennonites and Hutterites were once again permitted to immigrate to Canada.[114] In the same year, the $250 landing-money requirement was revoked, except for Asians, and the list of admissible immigrants was extended to include British subjects coming from the British Isles who were able to support themselves, American citizens whose labour or services were required in Canada, farm labourers and domestic servants with reasonable assurances of employment, and the immediate families of Canadian residents.[115] In 1923 the list of those who could immigrate without satisfying occupational requirements was extended beyond those from the British Isles to include American citizens and British subjects from the United States, Newfoundland, Ireland, New Zealand, Australia, and South Africa.[116] British subjects from the West Indies and other African nations were not included, presumably on racial grounds.[117] Also in that year, the prohibition on the entry of enemy aliens was revoked.[118] At the same time, however, other controls were put in place to help regulate the flow of immigrants. Passports were required of all immigrants other than American citizens and British subjects from specified countries,[119] and visas were required of all other immigrants.[120]

With respect to Continental Europeans, the lifting of the ban on enemy aliens, Mennonites, and Hutterites, and later on Doukhobors, lowered the impediments to European immigration, as did the revoking of the landing-money requirement. By administrative order, independent immigrants of means from the 'preferred countries' of northern Europe were admissible, although those from the non-preferred countries had to satisfy the occupational requirements before being permitted entry.[121] Beginning in 1924, immigration barriers were lowered further as the government entered into numerous arrangements with the British government, several provinces, various railways, and ethnic organizations for the selection, transportation, and settlement assistance of British and European immigrants. Two years later, the doors were opened even wider when the government provided for the entry into Canada by special permit of any person whose labour or service was required.[122]

Thus, by 1926, there was essentially a four-tiered immigration-admissions system. British and American citizens were permitted to enter Canada relatively freely, provided they either had employment or could support themselves, and were not black. Immigrants from the preferred countries of northern Europe and Scandinavia could enter Canada provided they had valid passports, were sponsored by Canadian relatives, or had of an occupation of which Canada was in need. Immigrants from the non-preferred countries of Eastern and southern Europe were admitted through special permits, and those from Asia and Africa were virtually excluded.

The progressive easing of admission requirements throughout the mid to late 1920s, with respect to British, American, and European immigrants, led to a considerable increase in annual admissions over the period. Between 1920 and 1923, on average 100,000 persons were admitted to Canada each year. Over the next three years, annual admissions averaged around 120,000 persons. In the last three years of the decade, this figure rose to 160,000 persons per annum.[123]

SPECIAL IMMIGRATION SCHEMES

The Empire Settlement Agreement

Throughout the 1920s, British immigration did not to reach its pre-war levels. In fact, between 1920 and 1930 British immigration was to average approximately 54,000 persons per year, as compared with approximately 99,000 annually in the ten years preceding the First World War. Several factors militated against British immigration. The relative prosperity in Britain during the 1920s removed some of the incentive to emigrate. In addition, relatively high transportation costs also made the transatlantic journey less appealing. In Canada, free land close to the railways was no longer in abundant supply. Although free grants of government land were available in areas far from rail services, few people cared to settle in these remote areas.

The Canadian government initiated several schemes throughout the 1920s to counteract the disincentives facing potential British settlers. In 1922, it entered into an arrangement with the British government known as the Empire Settlement Agreement.[124] The agreement, which was renewed and modified over the years, provided transportation assistance to four classes of immigrants: agriculturalists and their families, farm labourers, domestics, and juvenile immigrants. It was, to some degree, a more detailed and refined version of the various transportation-assistance schemes that had been offered at the turn of the century.[125] One of the features of the agreement was that any British subject residing in Canada could nominate a relative, friend, or acquaintance for farm or domestic work in Canada. Transportation assistance was complemented by various other inducements, the features of which depended on the targeted group. By 1931, approximately 127,654 persons had come to Canada under these schemes.[126]

Farm family settlement schemes were designed to promote the settlement of British families on farms in Canada. Under the 3,000 Family Scheme, the Canadian government offered assisted passage, the sale of land on a credit basis, and agricultural training and supervision. The British government agreed to provide each family with a loan for the purchase of stock and equipment. The loans were repayable in yearly instalments over a period of twenty-five years at a low rate of interest. Provincial governments were also involved in similar schemes. By 1927, both New Brunswick and Nova Scotia had entered into an agreement with the Canadian and British governments for the placement of 500 British families in each province under terms similar to those of the 3,000 Family Scheme. In the end, the farm family schemes were a disappointment. More than 1,000 families who were approved under the 3,000 Family Scheme withdrew from the plan after having contracted their loans. By 1941, only seventeen families had repaid their loans, while more than 50 per cent had abandoned their farms.[127]

Under the Empire Settlement Agreement, British farm workers were encouraged to come to Canada by the establishment of a special transportation rate. As Avery notes, the effect of the passage assistance was dramatic. Rates from Liverpool to Winnipeg, for example, were reduced from $120 to $30.[128]

In 1928, in response to demands of transportation companies and agrarian organizations, the Canadian government entered into another agreement with Britain for the emigration of 10,000 unemployed British miners to harvest Canadian wheat. Transportation assistance was guaranteed, and the Canadian government agreed to find the miners jobs on farms in Western Canada. The scheme was an unqualified disaster. Seventy-five per cent of the more than 8,000 persons who were recruited returned to England. According to the government, the plan failed because the men had to be hastily selected over a two-week period, with the result that certificates of character were dispensed with and only medical certificates required. The result was the movement of those who, 'while generally physically fit, were not of the type to take a serious view of the value of work in the scheme of life; but were rather attracted to a free trip across the ocean.' The fact that they were given assurances that they would be cared for and returned to England, if it was their wish, 'created a feeling amongst a great many that the trip was worth taking anyway, for it cost them nothing and they were sure of a return voyage.'[129] For their part, many British workers claimed that they had been discriminated against in employment. As one worker alleged, 'we were engaged by a German farmer or a Pollack but the minute one of their own people could be secured, we were fired and our jobs taken by those who could speak the language of this bunch.'[130] Their lack of farm experience was also cited as a reason for the scheme's failure.

The Empire Settlement Agreement met with considerably more success with respect to the emigration of British household workers. Under the terms of this arrangement, household workers from the British Isles were given passage assistance and guaranteed work at standard wages. The Canadian government also agreed to arrange for adequate care and supervision until suitable work situations were found, and as long as such care was necessary. Canadians were able to apply directly to the Department of Immigration and Colonization for a domestic servant or nominate a relative or friend for domestic work. Between 1923 and 1929, more than 22,000 women came to Canada under the Empire Settlement arrangement.[131]

In 1920, the Women's Division of the Department of Immigration and Colonization was created. Although the division was in charge of overseeing the arrival and settlement of all unaccompanied women immigrants, it was formed primarily to ensure that 'special care might be given to un-accompanied women coming to Canada from the British Isles.'[132] To this end, female immigration officers were stationed in Britain to conduct interviews with prospective immigrants and select the 'type of girl who will settle here and become a good Canadian.'[133] A system of permits was insti-tuted, attesting to the applicant's good health and legitimate purpose in coming. Receipt of a permit was a precondition to admission. Greater se-lectivity was seen as necessary to prevent the migration 'of girls who will ultimately become public charges or unsatisfactory citizens.'[134]

In addition to imposing more stringent selection requirements, the Women's Division also instituted measures to ensure the supervision of women from the moment they embarked for Canada until their assump-tion of domestic employment. Arrangements were made with steamship companies for the employment of 'ships' conductresses' to exercise super-vision over unaccompanied female travellers. Upon arrival, the women were met by female immigration officers, who guided the new arrivals through their medical examinations and who placed them on trains for transportation to other parts of the country. Train conductresses were em-ployed by the department to supervise the journey and to link women up with voluntary organizations once they reached their destination.[135]

The work of the Women's Division expanded throughout the 1920s. As it assumed more responsibilities for the settlement of immigrant women, the division's work became more institutionalized, and the division itself grew to meet the increasing demands upon it. While voluntary organiza-tions continued to provide settlement assistance, more of the ongoing follow-up work was assumed by the staff of the Women's Division itself.

There were various ways in which the division kept track of the women brought to Canada for household work. Hostels and local welfare agen-cies would send regular reports to the division on newly arrived women whom they had assisted. In addition, the division sent letters to employers of foreign domestics to monitor how their employment was proceeding, and the division maintained close contact with the Women's Branches of the Employment Bureau to see how many women accepted for domestic work assumed other employment following their arrival. Finally, women investigating officers were employed in several immigration offices across the country. These officers would send quarterly reports to their super-visors on problem cases.

The close supervision of women immigrants was instituted as much to ensure their suitability for Canada as for their own protection. Women who were unable to establish themselves or who transgressed moral conventions were liable to be deported. According to departmental records, close to 700 British female domestics were deported between 1926 and 1931.[136] Department records reveal that offending public mores, such as bearing an illegitimate child, contracting venereal disease, living with a man out of wedlock, and having more than one sexual partner, were often the underlying cause for expulsion.[137] That there appears to have been no corresponding accountability for the men associated with such transgressions reveals the discriminatory treatment more generally faced by immigrant women. By 1936, notwithstanding efforts at careful screening and supervision, 12 per cent of the more than 18,000 women who came to Canada under the Empire Settlement Agreement had gone back to the British Isles by deportation and voluntary return.[138]

The Empire Settlement Agreement also contained provisions to promote the continued emigration of British child immigrants to Canada. This movement already had a long history, commencing in 1868, when the first boatload of British immigrant children arrived in Canada. Over the next sixty years, close to 100,000 'home children' would follow.[139] Despite the well-known deficiencies with child-immigration schemes, including reports that children were vulnerable to, and not infrequently suffered from, emotional deprivation and physical and sexual abuse, the government failed to introduce any significant restrictions or regulations to ensure the well-being of child immigrants.[140] In fact, in his annual reports, the supervisor of juvenile immigration, G. Bogue Smart, consistently maintained that the children, almost without exception, were well cared for and managing well in Canada. The number of unsatisfactory cases was regularly reported as being less than 1 per cent of the total, and generally the result of 'faulty traits of character' on the child's part.

Perhaps the best explanation for the government's refusal to carefully regulate and supervise the movement was the enormous demand for the services of child immigrants. According to the 1921 annual report of the Immigration and Colonization department, applications for juvenile immigrant workers consistently exceeded supply by 10,000 to 30,000 per year.[141] As organized labour noted bitterly, the children were a ready form of inexpensive labour. Lacking representation, mobility, and financial resources, children were an attractive alternative to adult Canadian workers.

By the time the government entered the Empire Settlement Agreement, objections to the existing child-immigration schemes were being voiced with more regularity, and by a wide spectrum of the public. Organized labour continued to demand that the movement be stopped on the grounds that it resulted in unfair competition for Canadian workers.

Physicians, social-service providers, and others also called for the cessation of the movement, arguing that it was a conduit for the importation of the lowest castes of British society. These children, they maintained, poorly bred, and steeped in criminality, pauperism, and mental deficiencies, were a serious threat to the stability of Canadian society. Social reformers also campaigned for a halt to the movement. Some objected to it on purely compassionate grounds, driven by a genuine concern for the protection of the children themselves. Others seemed moved as well by fears that the importation of these children would lower the mental and physical health of the Canadian population.[142]

It is clear that the Department of Immigration and Colonization was aware of the growing concern regarding child-immigration schemes. In his annual reports, Supervisor Smart became increasingly insistent that the children were being properly placed and supervised, and that few unsatisfactory cases existed. He went further to claim that each child received a personal interview by inspectors on a regular basis: 'Each child is privately interviewed and a careful survey made of his home surroundings, personal appearance and general progress. When complaints are received the child and his employer are brought together with a view of healing any trivial differences that have been found to exist between them.'[143]

Smart's assurances were misleading. The statistics produced by his office reveal that annual inspections covered only a fraction of the children residing in the country. Moreover, by their own testimonies, the children were often unable to talk to the inspector, or unwilling to speak frankly because of fear of reprisals: 'Even when the visiting lady would visit me every six months I never complained about this woman. I would not dare complain for this foster woman would drill into me that I would be severely punished.'[144]

It was only upon the publication of a disturbing report by a British parliamentary commission which pointed to the abuses of child-immigration schemes, and which recommended the prohibition of child immigration for those of statutory school age,[145] that the Canadian government restricted the admission of British immigrant children to those fourteen years of age or older. Under the Empire Settlement Agreement, such children were guaranteed passage assistance. In several provinces, training farms were established which received a number of British boys each year, gave them some instruction in agricultural practices, and then distributed them to farms in need of labourers. An additional scheme provided selected British men between twenty-one and twenty-five years of age who had sufficient farm experience and accumulated savings with loans from the British, Dominion, and provincial governments for the purchase of a farm, stock, and equipment. The scheme was intended to induce young settlers to remain on the land, and thereby counteract the drift to the cities.[146]

Although the restrictions of 1924 put an end to the importation of the very young, they did not affect the overall number of children who continued to come to Canada. In fact, throughout the 1920s admissions consistently ranged between 1,000 and 2,000 children annually, rising in 1930 to a total of more than 4,000 children.[147]

The Railway Agreement and Permit System

Despite the progressive easing of the postwar immigration restrictions throughout the first half of the 1920s, and the inducements provided by the Empire Settlement Agreement, by the middle of the decade it was apparent that Canadian immigration policy had not achieved its objectives. In particular, the government's promotional strategies aimed at attracting British agriculturalists and farm labourers were revealed to have fallen far short of their desired goals. The 1931 census disclosed that immigrants from the British possessions were the least inclined to go into farming, and fewer than 10 per cent went into agriculture.[148] Nor could the labour-intensive industries rely on British workers to meet their growing labour needs. British immigrants were, by and large, not inclined to work in lumbering, railway construction, mining, or unskilled urban employment. By 1925, the failure of British immigrants to meet the labour demands of the Canadian economy, coupled with the fall in immigration from the United States, meant that European workers were becoming more attractive prospects than they had been in the first half of the decade.

The transportation companies were the strongest lobbyists for more relaxed immigration controls governing Continental Europeans.[149] More emigrants to Canada translated into more passenger and commercial traffic on their lines. In 1924, the Canadian National and the Canadian Pacific Railways successfully negotiated an agreement with the federal government which permitted them to bring in more than 6,700 farm labourers from the Continent. The following year, they negotiated a more far-reaching agreement which gave them a virtually free hand in the recruitment and selection of European farmers and agricultural workers. Known as the 'Railway Agreement,' it authorized the CNR and the CPR to recruit *bona fide* agriculturalists and farm labourers from non-preferred countries in southern and Eastern Europe. Those who were not settled on the land or employed in farm work within one year could be deported at the cost of the transportation companies. The agreement ran until 1928, at which time it was renewed for an additional two years.[150] Between 1925 and 1929, more than 185,000 central Europeans came to Canada under this arrangement.[151]

The 1926 decision to allow the entry under permit of any immigrant 'whose labour or service was required in Canada'[152] further opened the doors to European immigrants from the non-preferred countries. Under this regulation, employers made requests to the government for permits based upon their employment needs. With the assistance of various ethnic organizations and immigrant-aid agencies, individuals were selected abroad for immigration and brought to the Canadian immigration authorities; if they satisfied the employment requirements and successfully passed their medical examinations, they would be issued visas permitting their emigration to Canada. As did the Railway Agreement, the permit system facilitated the entry of thousands of Eastern and Southern Europeans in the latter half of the decade.

Among those groups to benefit from these arrangements were German immigrants. Estimates place the number of Germans entering Canada in this decade at close to 90,000, well over half coming from Russia and Eastern Europe, 20 per cent from the United States, and just over 10 per cent from Germany.[153] The arrival of ethnic-German immigrants commenced after 1923, when the prohibitions on the admission of enemy aliens and Mennonites were lifted. German speaking Mennonite refugees from Russia came to Canada to escape the hardship they experienced in Russia. During the Russian revolution, their refusal to take up arms alienated and angered both sides of the conflict. Mennonites were the victims of brutal assaults and intimidation, which continued after the civil war ended. Throughout the 1920s, land expropriation, official intolerance of their religion, and the threat of being sent to Siberia prompted thousands to seek a safe haven elsewhere.

Between 1923 and 1930, close to 20,000 Mennonites from Russia were permitted to settle in Canada. They were admitted on the understanding that no special privilege would be accorded the refugees other than selective exemption from military duty. The expectation was that their settlement and adjustment in Canada would be the responsibility of the Canadian Mennonite community through its agent, the Canadian Mennonite Board (CMB). The CPR, which was anxious to encourage the immigration of the Mennonite farmers to the prairies, provided passage, and settlement loans guaranteed by the CMB. The flow of Mennonites to

Canada slowed at the end of the decade as it became harder for many to leave Russia and as Prairie governments, beginning with Saskatchewan's, became increasingly opposed to the continuation of the movement.

While the Mennonites represented the largest group of German speaking immigrants to come to Canada, 10,000 Catholic and Lutheran Germans also fled Russia and settled here. As was true of the Mennonites, the majority of these immigrants were farmers whose settlement in the West was facilitated by the immigration boards of their denominational churches with the assistance of the railways. Among the other Germans to come at this time were close to 20,000 from countries in Eastern Europe, many of whom were political refugees. While the majority of the German immigrants from outside Germany were agriculturalists, most of the approximately 12,000 immigrants from Germany tended to be skilled workers and entrepreneurs in search of work in the industrial centres.[154]

One of the salient features of the German immigrant community in the interwar years was its reluctance to foster and promote German cultural and political institutions in Canada. The war had left a bitter legacy of hostility and mistrust towards German Canadians. Many were thus hesitant to declare their German heritage, as evidenced by census data which illustrate that, following the war, German Canadians tended to report their ethnic affiliations as being something other than German.[155] Similarly, unlike in earlier years, Germans were more cautious about the use of their language in public, there were a more limited number of German-Canadian papers, and German-Canadian organizations were careful to confine their activities to social events, staying clear of political discourse.[156]

Although not as numerous as German immigrants, more than 68,000 Ukrainians settled in Canada throughout the 1920s.[157] The genesis of this wave of immigration is found, as was the case for so many European immigrants, in the events of the First World War. In 1918, the Ukrainian goal of independence was achieved. It was a short-lived victory, however, for within four years the republic had been incorporated into the Soviet Union. Although the majority of the population of Ukraine came under Soviet rule, large segments became sizeable minorities under Polish, Czechoslovakian, and Romanian domination. While many Ukrainians in the Soviet Union would have preferred to leave and escape the economic devastation there, they were not permitted to emigrate. In Poland, however, where 8 million Ukrainians constituted the country's largest minority, they were encouraged to leave. This was particularly true in Galicia, where the large Ukrainian population was seen in official circles as an obstruction to the Polonization of the territory. Thousands of Ukrainians left Poland in an effort to escape both the severely depressed conditions of life there and political persecution.[158]

Most of the Ukrainian immigration to Canada came in the latter half of the decade, once the prohibitions on the entry of enemy aliens had been lifted, and the Railway Agreement and permit system were instituted. These immigrants benefited from the great wave of Ukrainian immigration to Canada in the first decade of the century. Their settlement was thus aided by the established Ukrainian-Canadian community, whose churches, schools, and community centres were available to the newcomers. Although, like the first wave of Ukrainians to Canada, most of the interwar immigrants were agriculturalists, the 1920s movement had a larger component of educated skilled workers and political émigrés. As in previous decades, the majority of Ukrainian arrivals went to the Prairie provinces, the largest concentration being in Manitoba. Like other immigrant groups at this time, however, many Ukrainians settled in Ontario, attracted by the employment opportunities available there.

Poles were among the other sizeable immigrant groups to be recruited under the Railway Agreement. Between 1921 and 1931, approximately 50,000 Poles came to Canada.[159] Like many immigrants from Eastern Europe, they came as a result of impoverished conditions in their home country. In 1918, after more than 100 years of Poland's being partitioned and ruled by foreign powers, the Polish Republic was proclaimed. The new republic was beset with problems, ranging from the economic dislocation suffered throughout the war to the many difficulties involved in forging a new constitution and integrating three regions which, before independence, had been ruled by other countries. The years following the war were a time of significant upheaval characterized by high rates of inflation and political instability. The Polish government encouraged emigration, regarding it as one way to help alleviate the tensions and frustrations that were mounting as a result of the poverty endemic in the country.[160]

Although their admission to Canada was predicated on their being agriculturalists, most of those who immigrated sought semi-skilled industrial employment. Many worked in mines and in bush camps, while others gravitated to the cities in central Canada. Their settlement was aided by the Polish government, which set up consuls in Canada to assist the new arrivals and maintain contact with them. The Polish government also helped to foster Polish cultural life and the maintenance of ties with Poland by providing financial aid to Polish-Canadian organizations and newspapers.[161]

Of the approximately 28,000 Hungarians who came to Canada in the 1920s, most came in the latter half of the decade. Following the war, Hungary was reduced to less than a third of its former size. One-quarter of its former population of 12 million were now within the borders of Romania, Czechoslovakia, Yugoslavia, and Austria, as were many of its most valuable natural resources. In addition to these losses sustained after the war, the country also suffered considerable political uncertainty, having experienced two revolutions between 1918 and 1920. Although the country's economic and political life would stabilize by the end of the 1920s, the experience was a difficult one for many thousands of the country's poor.[162] Emigration was seen by many as a welcome opportunity to secure a brighter future elsewhere. In addition, those Hungarians who became minorities in the states now occupying former Hungarian territory faced hostility and discrimination, and many sought emigration to North America as their only hope for freedom.

The Hungarian government assisted the emigration of its nationals. It established the Immigration Protection Bureau in Hungary to help emigrants obtain passports, travel documents, and foreign currency, and to protect them from unscrupulous agents who, for a substantial fee, promised to secure immigration to Canada and elsewhere by circumventing immigration regulations. A similar organization was also established in Winnipeg, which provided Hungarian immigrants with information, links to the Canadian community, and protection from corrupt land agents and others who might try to take advantage of the new arrivals.[163]

As in the case of the Polish immigrants to Canada, most of the Hungarian immigrants were listed as agriculturalists; yet, in fact, many of the newly arrived went into industrial employment. While most of the pre-war Hungarian immigrants settled in the farming communities of Saskatchewan, the majority of the interwar immigrants were attracted to central Canadian cities, where the growth in manufacturing and in public works offered greater employment opportunities. As occurred in many other ethnic communities at this time, the increase in the size of the Canadian-Hungarian community was accompanied by the establishment and growth of a diverse array of Hungarian-Canadian presses; ethnic schools; and mutual benefit societies, and other social, cultural, and political organizations.[164]

SELECTIVE ADMISSION EXCLUSIONS

The progressive easing of immigration restrictions which commenced around 1923 was not evenly applied to all immigrant groups. Controls vested in it by the Immigration Act continued to be used by Cabinet to control the composition of immigration to Canada.

British immigrants from the predominantly non-white dominions, such as those from the West Indies and certain African countries, unlike other British immigrants, had to satisfy occupational criteria and meet the passport and visa requirements. Since the latter requirements were a discretionary matter, their immigration could be easily prevented. Immigration statistics reveal that there was virtually no immigration to Canada from Africa other than slightly more than 200 persons coming from South Africa. Immigration from the West Indies was reported as being approximately 250 persons during the 1920s. 'Negro' immigration to Canada in this decade is reported as being fewer than 500 persons.[165] Moreover, during the twenty-five years that followed the 1923 order-in-council excluding Asians, other than Chinese or Japanese persons, from the list of admissible classes,[166] fewer than 800 East Indians entered the country.

Other means of controlling the entry of those deemed 'undesirable' was through the refusal to grant permits under the system established in 1926. Jewish refugees were among those to feel the discriminatory effect of the discretionary granting of such permits. While Ukrainians in Poland sought political freedom and economic opportunity through emigration to Canada, thousands of Jews sought safety from the brutal pogroms and ensuing persecution that swept Ukraine following the First World War. In 1920, it was estimated that 100,000 Jews had been killed in Ukraine, and thousands had fled into neighbouring Romania.

The story of interwar Jewish immigration to Canada is an important one, for, although approximately 40,000 Jews were permitted entry, the impediments placed in the way of Jewish immigration would be used with even greater vigour during the Second World War, with devastating results.[167] According to Simon Belkin, who was the director of the Canadian Jewish Colonization Society and directly involved in the immigration of Jews throughout the 1920s, most of those who came to Canada were admitted by special permit. The Immigration and Colonization department was generally hostile to the admission of Jews, and any special concessions won by the Canadian Jewish community and their parliamentary representatives were restricted in application and not easily adapted to changing circumstances.[168]

Among the first requests made by the Canadian Jewish community in the 1920s was for the entry of 1,000 of the reported 50,000 Jewish orphans languishing in Ukraine. Although the Canadian Jewish community agreed to finance the entire cost of the movement and assume full responsibility for the children once they were admitted, the Canadian government agreed to admit only 150 children. The community was, however, more successful in obtaining the government's consent to the admission of 5,000 Jewish refugees in Romania, and, between 1923 and 1924, 3,000 came to Canada. When the government was asked if the remaining allotment of 2,000 could be used to resettle Jewish refugees displaced in other areas of Europe, the government refused, claiming that, since many had left Russia with the consent of the authorities, they could not be considered refugees. In addition, according to the deputy minister of Immigration and Colonization, W.J. Egan, the government had received too many complaints from sectarian associations, labour organizations, and others for it to risk changing the terms of the original agreement.[169]

Similarly, while the Railway Agreement facilitated the immigration of thousands from the non-preferred countries, it, too, was not very helpful to Jews. According to Belkin, the railways were instructed not to accept applications from Jewish farmers. It was the position of the government that Jews were not farmers and that any who came would not stay on the land. Finally, in 1927, after considerable lobbying, the Canadian Jewish Colonization Society was permitted to bring in thirty farm families on the condition that the immigrants possess valid passports, arrive from their country of origin (thereby excluding refugees), and be in good health and literate. Literacy was required of every member of the family, although a similar stipulation was not required of those coming under the Railway Agreement. Belkin claims that Canadian immigration officers abroad created so many difficulties for prospective Jewish immigrants that it was difficult to fill the allotment within one year. By February 1929, only sixteen families had arrived, and only eighteen by 1930, when the movement was suspended.[170]

Many of the Jews who came to Canada in the latter half of the 1920s were sponsored by Canadian relatives. Others were admitted under special permits, which became more restrictive in the closing years of the decade. At this time Deputy Minister Egan's assistant, F.C. Blair, was open in his criticism of the permit system generally, and of the admission of Jews in particular. Blair was opposed to Jewish immigration, claiming that Jews were not farmers, of which Canada was most in need. His view, which he would reiterate years later as director of the department and a major influence on Canadian immigration policy during the Second World War, was that Jewish immigrants had succeeded in being admitted to Canada because 'the Jews have been able to organize public opinion in their favour, creating the impression that they are the most oppressed people, deserving of special consideration.'[171]

Armenian refugees also felt the full impact of Canada's exclusionary policies. Beginning in 1915 and continuing during the First World War, the Ottoman Empire embarked on a crackdown on its Armenian population characterized by mass killings, relocations, and deportation. Forced marches claimed many thousands of lives, not least due to famine, disease, exhaustion, and exposure to the elements. More than 1 million Armenians died in the purge, and more than 500,000 were displaced. In Canada, the plight of the Armenian people was well publicized, particularly in 1920, and this publicity helped to raise between $200,000 and $300,000 in aid. It was not enough, however, to persuade the Canadian government to join international efforts to resettle Armenian refugees.

Armenians fled in the tens of thousands to the neighbouring states of Syria, Lebanon, and Soviet Armenia, as well as to Egypt, Ethiopia, Greece, and the Balkan states. Many refugees survived the rigours of their escape only to face death in refugee camps rife with starvation and disease. Although 80,000 refugees would receive sanctuary in France, and 23,000 were provided permanent refuge in the United States, fewer than 1,300 were admitted to Canada. In her moving article 'Armenian Refugees and Their Entry into Canada, 1919–30,' Kaprielian-Churchill documents the government's exclusion policy with respect to Armenians and the ways in which those who qualified under its narrow admissibility criteria were often rejected.[172] In particular, despite their Indo-European language and their Christian faith, Armenians were classified, for the purposes of Canadian immigration, as members of the Asian race. The classification was not based on racial or ethnological grounds, but, rather, on the geographical fact that they came from Asia Minor. As 'Asians' they faced exceedingly high barriers to entry, having to meet the restrictive occupational requirements, narrow family-class definition, passport provisions, continuous journey stipulation, and $250 landing-money regulations. Each of these on its own was sufficient to impede the admission of most Armenians, and together they formed an insurmountable obstacle. For example, since most of the Armenians seeking resettlement were outside Turkey, they could not meet the continuous-journey provision without re-entering Turkey at enormous personal risk. Nor could they meet the passport requirement, since they were outside their own state and unlikely to persuade the Turkish government to provide them with documents. Despite appeals to the Canadian government to relax these requirements, it refused to do so, and even refused to recognize the identity documents provided by the League of Nations High Commission for Refugees. According to Kaprielian-Churchill, Canada wanted to be able to deport immigrants who became inadmissible within the three-year domicile period. Since the League of Nations documents did not allow the return of the individual to a particular country, Canada was unwilling to accept these in lieu of passports.[173]

Many Armenian residents in Canada petitioned the government to change the classification of Armenians from 'Asians' to 'Europeans.' In this way the refugees would not have to meet the $250 landing-money requirement.[174] In addition, many Canadian Armenians had family members trapped abroad who did not come under the family-class regulations applicable to Asians but would qualify under those governing Europeans. For example, Canadian residents were permitted to sponsor only their Asian wives and their children under eighteen years of age. In contrast, residents could sponsor their European wives, parents, unmarried brothers and sisters, and unmarried children of any age. Reclassification of the Armenians, however, was not seriously considered until the end of the decade, and only for a brief period of time.[175] Given the enormous impediments in the way of Armenian immigration it is likely that most of the approximately 1,200 Armenians who came to Canada were admitted on special permits.

Selective admission restrictions also targeted immigration from the Orient, which, like other overseas movements, was reduced substantially during the war. Nevertheless, in 1919 the issue once again became prominent and considerable time was spent in Parliament debating a resolution introduced by New Westminster MP W.C. McQuarie, which called for the complete cessation of Oriental immigration to Canada. Their exclusion advocated by the B.C. legislature, the Trades and Labor Congress, provincial trade unions, teachers' associations, farm organizations, various war veterans' associations, the Retail Merchants' Association of Canada, and racist groups such as the Asiatic Exclusion League and the Ku Klux Klan of Canada. The resolution also enjoyed wide support in the House.[176]

Prime Minister Mackenzie King voiced the sentiments of many of his colleagues when he stated that it was 'impossible ever to hope to assimilate a white population with the races of the Orient.' To even contemplate assimilation would bring Canadians 'face to face at once with the loss of that homogeneity which ought to characterize the people of this country if we are to be a great nation.' Making it clear that his government was 'anxious to bring about an effective restriction of this Oriental immigration,' King nevertheless was careful about how the policy would be labelled. Perhaps for diplomatic reasons, his government's support for the resolution was predicated on the condition that the policy be labelled 'effective restriction,' rather than 'exclusion,' of Oriental immigrants.[177]

In fact, 'effective restriction' came to mean 'exclusion.' In 1923, a revised Chinese Immigration Act was passed which effectively put an end to Chinese immigration to Canada for over twenty years. The act did away with the head tax in favour of very broad exclusionary provisions. Chinese persons were prohibited from landing in Canada unless they were merchants, students, diplomats and their staff, or Canadian-born Chinese children who had left for educational or other purposes. Chinese students were permitted to remain in Canada only for as long as they were pursuing their education.[178] The definition of 'merchant' was left for the minister to prescribe, which he subsequently did in July of that year. The provision was so tightly worded that, as one commentator has noted, it essentially defined a merchant out of existence, since virtually no Chinese person could meet all the criteria.[179]

Those who fell within the admissible classes were required to obtain a visa from an immigration official stationed in Hong Kong. Although a written appeal of a refusal was permitted to the minister, it was of little practical consequence. Moreover, the visa itself did not ensure admission. Upon arrival in Canada, the immigrant was subjected to a separate examination to determine whether he or she fell within one of the prohibited classes. Although the prohibited classes were much the same as those found in the Immigration Act, the procedure for making and contesting the determination was not. An examination was conducted by a special inquiry officer rather than before a board of inquiry, as for all other immigrants. The examination was to be held 'separate and apart from the public but in the presence of the person wherever practicable.' Unlike other immigrants, who were guaranteed a right to counsel before a board of inquiry if evidence or testimony was received by the board, Chinese immigrants were entitled to counsel at their examinations only if they could afford one. There was a limited right of an appeal to the minister on certain grounds. Where an appeal was permitted, the appellant and dependants could be kept in custody at the discretion of an immigration officer.[180]

Other discriminatory provisions of the act and its regulations included the mandatory registration of all Chinese immigrants and the carrying of photo identification cards.[181] Ships were prohibited from bringing in more than one Chinese person per 250 tons of tonnage, as compared with one person per 50 tons for other immigrants.[182] Most important, a Chinese person who changed status to one that would have rendered him or her inadmissible upon arrival was subject to deportation.[183] Thus, a merchant, for example, who ran into hard times, was prohibited from seeking employment as a labourer to support himself. Should he do so, he would be liable to expulsion. The 1923 act was exceedingly effective in achieving the objectives for which it was drafted. During the next twenty-four years, only fifteen Chinese persons were permitted to emigrate to Canada.[184]

Although the McQuarie resolution also called for the exclusion of all Japanese immigrants from Canada, the Canadian government was unwilling to pass legislation to give effect to this demand. There were several reasons for its reluctance. First, Japan had been an ally of Canada's during the war. Not only had the two countries fought together, but Japan had also sent its warships to Vancouver harbour to defend the Canadian government against the rumoured German invasion from the United States. Additionally, by 1925 Japan was Canada's sixth most important trading partner.[185] Legislative exclusion of Japanese nationals was considered too great a threat to the ongoing goodwill that had developed between the two nations.

The government decided instead to limit Japanese arrivals through diplomatic means. Beginning in 1922, the Canadian government once again entered into negotiations with the Japanese government for modifications to the Lemieux agreement. Within three years, the Japanese government agreed to reduce the quota of Japanese covered by the Lemieux agreement from 400 to 150 persons annually.[186] This agreement governed immigration from Japan until the Second World War.

Court decisions involving the right of the provinces to limit or circumscribe the entry and employment rights of Oriental immigrants are revealing, for, as in previous periods, they disclose a traditional sympathy by the judiciary for the prevalent social, political, and economic order. This is perhaps best illustrated in two cases arising out of the Oriental Orders in Council Validation Act,[187] passed by the B.C. legislature in 1921. The act retroactively confirmed certain orders-in-council which stipulated that no Japanese or Chinese persons were to be employed in connection with undertakings involving provincial licences, contracts, or leases. Two years later, in the case of *Brooks-Bidlake and Whittal v British Columbia (A G.)*,[188] the Privy Council held that an anti-Asian labour clause in timber licences issued by the B.C. government was valid in so far as it applied to Chinese persons. The court dismissed the contention that the restriction fell within the exclusive right of the Dominion to legislate on the subject of 'naturalization and aliens,' characterizing it as within the purview of the provincial rights to manage their property as provided by sections 92(5) and 109 of the British North America Act.[189]

The decision in *Brooks-Bidlake*, however, did not entirely resolve matters. A collateral issue, not dealt with in that case, was whether the provincial act was *ultra vires* in so far as it was in conflict with the Treaty of Commerce and Navigation,[190] which afforded Japanese subjects resident in Canada the same treatment as subjects or citizens of the most-favoured nation. Before the issue was heard by the Privy Council, the governor general disallowed the provincial statute. The court nevertheless considered the matter in order to ascertain the limits within which the legislature of the province could pass further legislation on the subject. Writing for the majority in *Re Oriental Orders in Council Validation Act*,[191] Viscount Haldane stated that their Lordships entertained 'no doubt' that the provincial statute violated the principle laid down in the Japanese Treaty Act. The statute having been disallowed, the court was of the opinion that, if re-enacted, it would have to be drafted so as to exclude from its operation all Japanese subjects.[192]

In 1899, the Privy Council, in *Bryden*[193] struck down provincial legislation that restrained the ability of the Chinese to find work in the province. Twenty-four years later, in *Brooks-Bidlake*, it was to uphold provincial legislation that had a similar effect. Both cases had been decided on the interpretation of the division of powers between the Dominion and the provincial governments. Radically different results emerged, despite the fact that there had been no constitutional changes to the division of powers to warrant such divergence. What had changed, however, was the economic environment within which both judgments had been rendered.

At the time the Privy Council rendered its decision in *Bryden*, there was a huge demand for Oriental workers, primarily on the railways and in the resource industries. *Bryden*, and cases that followed, helped to ensure that employers' access to this abundant, malleable, and relatively inexpensive source of labour would not be impeded by provincial restrictions. By 1923, however, when *Brooks-Bidlake* was decided, the demands of industry were considerably different from those at the turn of the century. The railway boom was over, and new production processes had been introduced that were less dependent on an abundant supply of unskilled labour.[194] As well, the economy was just starting to emerge from the postwar depression, characterized by high levels of unemployment. Finally, anti-Asian sentiment was at its height, not only among labourers, but among prominent members of the business community as well.

Seen in this light, it is perhaps not surprising that the Privy Council in 1923 was more disposed to find provincial laws that imposed employment restrictions on the Chinese as within provincial competence than it had been in 1899. Moreover, in concluding that similar restrictions on Japanese persons were in violation of the Japanese Treaty Act and therefore outside the powers of the province, the court was sensitive to the consideration that led the government not legislatively exclude Japanese immigrants, as it had Chinese persons. Unlike China, which did not command an imposing presence on the world stage, Japan had emerged as a leading power and, in addition to having been an ally in the war, was now one of Canada's major trading partners. The government was careful not to upset this relationship. The Privy Council's decision in *Re Oriental Orders in Council Validation Act* suggests that the court was sensitive to this relationship as well.

DEPORTATION

Given the greater control over who entered Canada, a drop in the number of persons subsequently expelled would perhaps have been expected. This was not the case. Deportations throughout this period exceeded those of any previous period. Between 1920 and 1930, for example, more than 1,700 people on average were deported every year. By comparison, approximately 900 persons were deported annually between 1905 and 1915, a period which was characterized by the unprecedented volume of both admissions and deportations that took place.[195]

There are several reasons for this increase. In the first place, regardless of how careful the initial scrutiny of an immigrant was, it could never be enough to ensure that the person would be free of disabilities beyond his or her control. Loss of employment in times of general economic hardship, sudden illness, or a disabling occupational accident could not be predicted by the simple application of racial criteria or by a cursory medical examination prior to admission. In addition, admissibility requirements were frequently flouted. This was particularly evident with many immigrants who were admitted under the permit system and the Railway Agreement. Finally, deportation came to be seen as a legitimate means for removing those who may have satisfied the technical criteria for admission but who, on closer examination, were seen as undesirable.

The increased latitude to deport activists that was provided by the 1919 amendments to section 41 of the Immigration Act was used extensively throughout the 1920s. So, too, were the provisions that authorized the deportation of those who fell within the inadmissible classes as defined in section 3 of the Immigration Act – namely, the physically or mentally disabled, the sick or diseased, alcoholics, criminals, paupers, and those who relied on public charity for support. Generally those who fell within these categories were liable to deportation only within five years of their arrival. If it could be shown, however, that immigrants were members of an inadmissible class at the time of entry, then they were deemed not to have legally landed in Canada and therefore could not have acquired domicile;[196] thus, they were open to deportation, regardless of the length of their residence here. For example, in 1921, a woman who had been in Canada for seven years, had borne an illegitimate child, and was receiving treatment for venereal disease was deported, despite her long residence. Having received a medical report stating that the woman was 'feeble-minded' at the time of her entry in Canada, one senior immigration official justified her deportation on the basis that she 'could never have legally entered, and thus could not have fulfilled the requirements of domicile.[197] Thus, in expanding the list of inadmissible persons, the 1919 amendments also increased the circumstances in which the department could effect such removals.

As in earlier periods, the numbers of those deported for becoming a public charge were particularly high during periods of economic hardship. Thus, between 1920 and 1925, deportations for this cause accounted for approximately 40 per cent of all removals. Deportation continued to be regarded as a means of easing the demands placed on social assistance, which remained a low priority for government spending. For example, in 1926, despite the increased needs for social assistance of a more urban, industrial society, public-welfare spending accounted for approximately 12 per cent of expenditures, the same level as in 1896.[198] As Henry Drystek explains, faced with chronic underfunding 'municipalities and public institutions felt compelled to request deportations to reduce the costs of outside relief, overcrowded asylums and overburdened hospital wards.'[199]

Just as the number of deportations did not decline with greater admission controls, neither did the rate fall with the economic recovery of 1926. The proportion of public-charge cases, however, did decline from 40 per cent to approximately 22 per cent of the total for the remainder of the decade.[200] Removal seemed to be effective for an increasing array of reasons beyond the traditional grounds of being a threat to public health and security, or a burden to the public purse. An examination of departmental deportation records for this period is particularly illuminating, for they give a fairly accurate picture of what was behind the thousands of deportations that took place at this time. The reports themselves, as with reports on other areas of the department's work, became more detailed, and tended to be supported by more statistical analyses than in earlier years.

With respect to its deportation activities, the greater emphasis on record keeping followed from the fact that the department was handling more cases per year than ever before, and more of its deportation decisions were being challenged in the courts. The records reveal that often the statutory causes for deportation were merely a label applied to support deportations for a host of seemingly unrelated concerns. For example, regularly listed under the statutory causes were reasons such as illegitimacy, immorality, child desertion, contributing to delinquency, bad conduct, attempted suicide, and feeble-mindedness. Even seemingly treatable and relatively inoffensive ailments such as varicose veins and foot trouble were listed in support of deportation orders.[201]

Throughout the 1920s, immigration officials continued to work closely with employers to remove those immigrants who had become troublesome from a labour-relations perspective. In 1924, for example, in response to a request from the Mountain Lumber Manufacturers' Association 'to rid the country of agitators,' the department asked the association to provide more information about foreigners 'advocating or participating in strike agitation among the lumber camps.' The same year, upon expressing reservations over the practice of arresting and examining IWW members after they had been legally admitted to the country, an immigration officer was informed by his superior that it was the 'desire of the Department that men of this type be carefully examined and the Act be strictly applied.'[202]

The power of the courts to review deportation decisions was circumscribed by a privative clause in the Immigration Act which provided that courts did not have jurisdiction to 'review, quash, reverse, restrain, or otherwise interfere' with a proceeding or order relating to the detention or deportation of an immigrant 'upon any ground whatsoever, unless such person is a Canadian citizen or has Canadian domicile.'[203] The courts largely deferred to the privative clause, rarely interfering with a deportation decision. The general principle was that the court's right of review was limited to cases where the authorities had exceeded their jurisdiction by exercising powers outside those authorized by the Immigration Act or over persons not within its purview. The test of excess jurisdiction turned out to be a subjective one. Although there was some willingness to find jurisdictional errors of a technical nature, such as a failure to state reasons in full on a deportation order[204] or failing to disclose on the order any jurisdiction in the officer making it,[205] there was a clear reluctance to interfere with substantive decisions. As stated by one Quebec Superior Court judge in reference to the privative clause,

... what Parliament intended, and what Parliament actually provided in the language of this statute, was that all questions as to the entry of immigrants into Canada should be determined exclusively by the machinery of the Department of Immigration, namely, by the board of inquiry and immigration officers, subject only to an appeal to the Minister, and without any powers of review or control by the Courts ...

... no Court or Judge may interfere with the proceedings of a board of inquiry, either on the ground of misunderstanding or misrepresentation of the law, or of the regulations, nor on account of admission of illegal evidence, nor of error in weighing the evidence heard, nor on account of any informality or omission which may fairly be classed as a matter of procedure, or of departmental regulation.[206]

Pressures for Change

Noted annually in *The Canada Year Book* was the observation that Canadians preferred immigrants who were readily assimilable. Assimilability carried with it racial, economic, and social connotations. The most desirable immigrants remained those from Great Britain and the United States. Others were assessed on a graduated scale, placement upon which depended on their similarity to the Anglo-Saxon norm:

... preferable settlers are those who speak the English language – those coming from the United Kingdom and the United States. Next in order of readiness of assimilation are the Scandinavians and the Dutch, who readily learn English and are already acquainted with the working of free democratic institutions. Settlers from Southern and Eastern Europe, however desirable from a purely economic point of view, are less readily assimilated, and the Canadianizing of the people from these regions who have come to Canada in the present century is a problem both in the agricultural Prairie Provinces and in the cities of the East. Less assimilable still, according to the general opinion of Canadians, are those who come to Canada from the Orient.[207]

Despite these preferences, however, the proportion of most-preferred immigrants among arrivals continued to decline throughout the period. In 1914, for example, British, American, and European immigrants comprised 37, 35, and 27 per cent, respectively, of the country's immigration intake. In 1929, British immigrants made up 35 per cent of the total, immigrants from the United States had fallen to fewer than 15 per cent, while those from Continental Europe had risen to approximately 46 per cent of the total.[208] Thus, shift in composition was often attributed to the relatively free hand that railways and other large entrepreneurs were able to wield over the immigration process, and in particular through the operation of the Railway Agreement and permit system.

Both the Railway Agreement and the permit system were the subject of considerable controversy. In the case of the former, while many who came to Canada under its terms were employed in farm labour, it was often short-term and seasonal. Generally farm labourers were required from April to September. Once their contract was completed, they were left to search the country for alternative employment. Some went to work in mines, on the railways, or in lumbering, while many others migrated to the cities in search of construction or industrial employment. It often took many years before an immigrant worker could secure enough capital to settle on the land or return home.

Another frequently cited problem with the Railway Agreement was the railways' practice of employing the recent arrivals on section gangs and other railway jobs despite having certified that the immigrants were intended for farm work. For example, in 1927 the Land Settlement Branch reported that 75 per cent of the Continental European immigrants who had arrived in Calgary under the terms of the Railway Agreement had obtained jobs with the CPR. Moreover, the branch also indicated that companies who dealt with the CPR were expected to give preference in hiring to those who had come to Canada 'on CPR ships.'[209]

The permit system was also criticized as being open to flagrant abuse. Workers brought into the country on permits were often charged excessively for their transportation, paid less than the promised wage, and employed only temporarily, leaving them unemployed and dependent on public relief. In addition, both the Railway Agreement and the permit system were seen as having a particularly detrimental effect on Canadian workers. Labour unions charged that the schemes were depressing local wages, displacing already employed workers, and being used to break unions through the employment of strike-breakers.[210]

Immigration officials also opposed the schemes on the grounds that they took the selection of Continental immigrants almost entirely out of the hands of the government with the result that thousands of non-preferred immigrants were entering the country every year. Calling for the termination of the permit system, F.C. Blair, the assistant deputy minister, wrote: 'If there is any present day desire close to my heart, it is the desire to wipe out this cursed business at one strike ... With unemployment ... it seems a terrible thing to have to issue Permits day after day for the admission of Italians, Greeks, Jews, and others of the less desirable classes of immigrants, and merely because some member of Parliament or other influential gentleman demands that it be done.'[211]

Similarly, Professor A.R.M. Lower warned in 1928 that the 'gradual displacement of the English-speaking farmers from the small farms and soils by Central Europeans who demand less from life' is but one example of how 'cheap' men will always drive out 'dear' men.[212] And W.A. Carrothers cautioned the following year that, unless Canada exercised stricter selection criteria in admitting European immigrants, the stability of Canadian 'political, social and economic institutions and life' would be threatened.[213] Western farm associations, religious societies, nativist groups, and others concerned about racial homogeneity complained along similar lines. As one Ku Klux Klan organizer advocated most explicitly, 'we are a great melting pot, but let us see that the slag and scum that refuse to assimilate and become 100 percent Canadian citizens is skimmed off and thrown away.'[214]

Those who warned of the dire consequences that could befall a nation that was not selective in its immigration policy found support for their views in eugenics theory, which garnered considerable popularity in the interwar years. Eugenics was pioneered by an English scientist, Francis Galton. At the heart of Galton's theory was the belief that humans were primarily defined by their hereditary composition. Characteristics such as intelligence and feeble-mindedness, traits such as alcoholism and criminality, as well as numerous diseases were passed in the blood plasma from one generation to another. Progress necessarily depended on the reproduction of those of superior stock and the restriction of the inferior castes. The term 'eugenics' was coined by Galton to refer to the study of policies to improve the behavioural and biological qualities of future generations.[215] Among the prescriptions advocated was highly selective immigration policies.

Eugenics was far from an exact science. In fact, proponents of eugenics based their beliefs on highly speculative propositions and observations. It was primarily through physical observation, examination, and the use of intelligence testing that the undesirable classes could be identified. Galton himself claimed that he would categorize individuals by observing them in passing on the street: 'Whenever I have occasion to classify the persons I meet into three classes, "good, medium and bad," I use a needle mounted as a pricker, wherewith to prick holes, unseen, in a piece of paper, torn rudely into a cross with a long leg. I use the upper end for "good," the cross arm for "medium," the lower end for "bad." The prick holes keep distinct, and are readily read off at leisure.'[216]

The crude measurements afforded by simple observation and examination were not enhanced by the use of intelligence testing. Low scores on the intelligence tests offered to immigrants were frequently cited as proof that immigrants were disproportionately genetically defective, yet the effect that factors such as the foreigners' linguistic and cultural differences had on these scores was not adequately addressed in the medical and psychological literature.[217] In large measure, the criterion used to distinguish between the fit and unfit was adherence to accepted cultural norms. Any deviation was loosely attributed to 'feeble-mindedness.' Hence, it was common to label as defective the foreign-born, the poor, the diseased, and the criminal, and others engaged in anti-social acts.

Eugenists and geneticists shared a common belief in the importance of heredity in understanding the human character. By 1915, however, advances in genetic theory, which pointed to the innumerable complexities of heredity, led many geneticists to turn away from eugenics entirely. In fact, during the interwar years, the most prominent advocates of eugenics were those in the helping professions – namely, doctors, psychologists, and social workers – with little understanding of genetics at all. The most prominent among them believed that eugenics provided the answer to the innumerable ills that seemed consequent upon high levels of immigration and industrialization, such as increases in poverty, unemployment, crime, disease, and mental breakdown. It was commonly asserted that a high proportion of alcoholics, criminals, prostitutes, and the like were feeble-minded. Feeble-mindedness, in turn, was overrepresented among the foreign-born. And so the link between social problems and immigrants was made. As W. Burton Hurd, a professor of political economy at McMaster University and a leading Canadian demographer, claimed in 1928, the country was 'paying for its immigrants through increased insanity and crime.'[218]

It was not just their tendency towards degeneracy that made immigrants such a threat to the country's future, but also their disproportionately high fertility rates. The medical literature of the interwar years contained reports of the declining fertility of native Canadians and the disproportionately high fertility rates of the foreign-born. Some went so far as to assert that the high fertility of the foreign-born had the effect of lowering the fertility of the Canadian-born. According to W.S. Wallace, confronted with increasing competition from immigrants, the indigenous population endeavours to maintain its standard of living and relatively higher social position, and voluntarily checks its own procreation. 'The native-born population, in the struggle to keep up appearances in the face of increasing competition, fails to propagate itself, commits race suicide, in short: whereas the immigrant population, being inferior, and having no appearances to keep up, propagates itself like fish of the sea.'[219] Others attributed the declining fertility of native Canadians to their need to restrict family size so as to be able to pay taxes in support of the unfit who were dependent on the state.[220]

C.K Clarke, after whom the Toronto Clarke Institute of Psychiatry was named, was one of the most prominent doctors of the period who campaigned vigorously for controls to prevent 'the dumping of the defective and diseased classes on Canadian soil.' Clarke was a professor of psychiatry at the University of Toronto and superintendent of the Toronto General Hospital. In 1911, he established a social-service clinic in Toronto, where he examined young people suspected of being mentally defective who were referred by schools, the Juvenile Court, charitable organizations, and private individuals. According to his observations, immigrant children were disproportionately feeble-minded and/or insane when compared with the host population, and it was from this group that future classes of thieves and prostitutes would be drawn. Although the country had been able to assimilate some of the worst elements in the past, Clarke warned that 'the forced feeding she has been subjected to in former years will have its effect.' The rigorous inspection of immigrants by 'competent men specially trained in psychiatry' had to be implemented to prevent the supply pipe from 'tapping streams reeking with insanity, crime and degeneracy.'[221]

Clarke's recommendations help in part to explain the popularity of eugenics among professionals such as doctors, teachers, and social workers. The application of eugenics to social policies would necessarily entail an enhanced role for those qualified to put such policies in place. As explained by Angus McLaren, the argument was increasingly made that 'only experts adequately schooled in the importance of heredity could possibly cope with the complex problems of rationally planning and controlling immigration, education, and a range of programs supporting the birth and rearing of healthy, fit children.'[222]

This is not to suggest that all proponents of eugenics were self-serving. Many saw in eugenics a way of combating the serious problems that were especially prevalent in urban centres. Eugenics seemed to offer a scientific explanation for the rise in crime, poverty, criminality, and disease, as well as a program for alleviating such distress. Although eugenics was attractive to those whose racial prejudices could be wrapped conveniently in eugenic language, it also appealed to those genuinely committed to social reform. Seen in this light, it is not surprising to find among its adherents leading progressives of the day. Many women's groups across the country, who were fighting for political emancipation, were, at the same time, pressing for policies such as sterilization of the mentally ill and impaired, and restrictions on the entry of foreign defectives. Even socialist political reformers such as Tommy Douglas initially were drawn to eugenics theory. In fact, as McLaren documents, 'the average Canadian was schooled to be as accepting of the notion of "race improvement" as of the idea that Canada was a Christian nation.'[223]

In terms of social policy, eugenicists met with some success. By the 1930s, several provinces had in place legislation permitting the forced sterilization of the mentally ill and mentally handicapped. Some statutes were to remain on the books until the 1970s. In immigration policy, eugenics theory both influenced and was invoked to justify the increasingly restrictive policies that were adopted at the close of the decade.

By the close of the 1930s, transportation companies seemed to stand relatively alone in their support of an expansionary immigration policy.[224] In 1928, the Select Standing Committee on Agriculture and Colonization recommended restrictions on the application of the Railway Agreement and tighter controls over the permit system.[225] Following the report, more stringent controls were placed upon the issuing of permits, and in 1928 transportation companies were instructed to reduce by 30 per cent the number of immigrants they had recruited. Growing unemployment led to a further restriction and the cancelling of all permits to prospective immigrants in 1929. By this time even prominent members of the Canadian Manufacturers' Association were questioning the necessity of bringing in unskilled workers in light of the progress in mechanization that was being made. The following year, the association president, R.J. Hutchings, was unequivocal in his support for the cessation of central European emigration to Canada: 'Large numbers of unemployed and illiterate people are liabilities and not assets. Employment, at fair remuneration, should be the keynote of our immigration policy. It is not economic to import farmers to compete with those now on the land ... nor is it wise to congest cities with people unless industry is encouraged to expand and provide them with employment.'[226]

With the collapse of the New York stock market in 1929 and the deepening economic depression in Canada, the new Conservative government under the leadership of R.B. Bennett moved to close Canada's doors once again. Admissible immigrants were restricted to agriculturalists with means, immediate relatives of Canadian citizens, and immigrants from Great Britain and the United States with sufficient capital to support themselves. By the close of 1930, all immigration promotional schemes were discontinued.

CHAPTER SIX

The Depression Years, 1930–1937: Exclusion and Expulsion

In 1930, R.B. Bennett won the federal election with promises to end unemployment by 'blasting' Canada's way into international markets and to stamp out communism with the 'iron heel of ruthlessness.' From an immigration-policy perspective, both his promises are revealing, for they reflected priorities which were adhered to in the formation of immigration policy. Within months of coming to power, Bennett's Conservative government had initiated a series of immigration restrictions that were to culminate the following year in the tightest immigration admissions policy in Canadian history. By March 1931, admissible immigrants were limited to: Americans and British subjects from the predominantly white parts of the Commonwealth such as Britain, Ireland, the Irish Free State, Newfoundland, New Zealand, Australia, and South Africa who had sufficient money to sustain themselves until employment was secured; agriculturalists with sufficient means to farm in Canada; and wives or minor children of Canadian residents.[1] In addition to narrowing the admissible classes, the government adopted a series of other measures to control immigrant arrivals. All government promotional activities were stopped, health requirements were strictly enforced, and a number of immigration offices in the United States were closed. The minister explained Canada's tighter immigration controls in the following words: 'We regard the present situation as temporary, but we propose to apply an effective remedy until employment conditions have improved and to control any immigration movement in the future so that immigration will not again be a contributing factor to unemployment conditions.'[2]

Depressed economic conditions and tight immigration controls resulted in a dramatic fall in immigrant arrivals, from 88,000 in 1931 to fewer than 26,000 the following year.[3] Annual admissions continued to decline, reaching a trough in 1936, when they stood at 11,000 persons, a drop of more than 93 per cent from the 1930 level.[4] During the next three years, admissions would slowly increase, only to plunge further with the outbreak of the Second World War.

Admission statistics, however, point to only one aspect of the immigration picture of this time. More remarkable are the number of deportations that occurred throughout this period. Between 1930 and 1937, more than 25,000 people were deported from Canada, far exceeding the level experienced in any previous seven-year period.[5] As admission levels fell and removal rates rose, the proportion of deportations to annual admissions (over 50 per cent in 1936) was greater than in any preceding or subsequent period in Canadian history. In a country facing unprecedented rates of unemployment and bankrupt municipal and provincial coffers, deportation was the most inexpensive and expedient method of clearing from the welfare roles those of foreign birth. It was also the most decisive way of removing from Canada those immigrants who challenged the status quo by advocating, among other things, better wages, improved working conditions, and adequate unemployment relief. Deportation was an effective 'weapon' in the Bennett administration's 'war' on communism.

In terms of admissions policy, the restrictive approach implemented by Bennett, and continued by Mackenzie King upon becoming prime minister in 1935, was not seriously contested by any group at this time. The Depression was not a short-lived phenomenon. In 1933, four years after it began, more than 32 per cent of Canadian wage earners were unemployed, and 15 per cent of the population was dependent on public relief.[6] During the next three years, the economy gradually improved, although recovery was very uneven. While gains were made in business, manufacturing, and metal mining, other sectors of the economy, such as agriculture, construction, and transportation, lagged behind. In 1937, the country suffered another setback as a severe recession commenced, not to end until Canada's involvement in the Second World War invigorated the economy.[7]

Given the economic environment throughout most of the 1930s, it is not surprising to find that limitations on immigration admissions were imposed without the controversy that characterized restrictions in earlier periods. The same, however, cannot be said of deportation policy, which was the subject of intense, although localized, controversy throughout the period.

In light of the size of annual removals, the absence of significant public opposition to the deportation of indigent immigrants revealed that there was probably considerable support among the general public for the government's efforts in the early years of the decade. Considering the magnitude of the dislocations caused by the Depression, from which few Canadians escaped unscathed, many people were simply too overwhelmed by their own financial difficulties to consider the plight of indigent foreigners. Moreover, as immigrant accounts of this period reveal, and as letters to the prime minister from the public confirm, many who searched desperately for employment, and waited hours in line for relief, supported the removal of those who placed additional demands on shrinking resources and whose relatively short residence in Canada was seen as not entitling them to public assistance.[8] And for those who already resented and feared the changing ethnic complexion of Canada brought about by previous permissive immigration policies, the disparagingly called 'hunkies,' 'bohunks,' 'ukes,' 'dagos,' and 'kikes' were easy targets. As one Grimsby, Ontario, resident reasoned in a letter to the prime minister: 'Why not put some of these foreigners and indians in their own country and give the white man some show, as they are taking the work away from the Canadian men and I would think that the Government could do something to prevent this.'[9]

This call for the removal of foreigners was not an isolated one. In fact it was one that received a sympathetic hearing from a government which tended to see unemployed foreigners as a troublesome and unstable element in society. A report prepared for the Prime Minister's Office reflects the prevailing view: 'The number of single men, foreigners on relief, is unduly large, and in several centres, officials report them as among their troublesome clients. Language differences, their tendency to segregate, their corporate loyalties, their susceptibility to seditious propaganda, their known proclivity to hoard money, and the consequent difficulty of ascertaining their actual need of relief, all greatly complicate an already difficult problem in these cities.'[10]

It was precisely this type of adverse characterization that was at the root of job discrimination as well. In the large city centres, where the major concentration of immigrants was to be found, discrimination in employment was rife. Winnipeg was a prime example. As one journalist at the time recalls, life there was particularly difficult for Ukrainians, Poles, and Jews:

None of the city's chartered banks, trust companies, or insurance companies would knowingly hire a jew, and anyone with a Ukrainian or Polish name had almost no chance of employment except rough manual labour. The oil companies, banks, mortgage companies, financial and stock brokers and most retail and mercantile companies except the Hudson's Bay Company, discriminated against all non Anglo-Saxons. For the young Ukrainians and Poles there was one possible solution if they could beat the accent handicap. They could change their names ... But for the Jews, a name change was not enough.[11]

Among those who urged the removal of unemployed foreigners were municipalities who were overburdened by the crushing welfare demands that the swelling ranks of urban workers made on insufficient municipal resources.[12] Provincial premiers were also vocal in their insistence that the provision of support for immigrants was not within their responsibilities. Several premiers, in response to the growing labour militancy in their provinces, were also supportive of the government's efforts to remove labour radicals and political activists.[13]

There were a few groups during this time that protested the government's removal policy. Among the most vocal was the Cooperative Commonwealth Foundation (CCF), which consistently challenged the government's deportation practices in the House of Commons. Formed in 1932, the CCF drew its support from farm groups, labourers, and white-collar social democrats. Its ideological foundations came largely from the League for Social Reconstruction, comprising left-wing intellectuals who denounced what they characterized as the monopolistic capitalist system and the repressive state tactics that were its guardians.[14] The CCF grew in popularity over the next decade, becoming the official Opposition in Ontario in 1943, forming the first socialist government in Saskatchewan the following year, and electing twenty-eight members to the House of Commons in 1945. Although its influence in the 1930s was much more limited, it was important in so far as it became the voice of the oppressed, including immigrants.

Although many municipalities welcomed the removal of foreigners, some, Winnipeg and Brandon, Manitoba, for example, regarded the government's removal strategy as being excessively sweeping and harsh, and refused to cooperate fully with the deportation of foreign indigent residents. More influential in tempering the practice, however, were the complaints made by countries whose nationals were being removed. Britain, for example, also beleaguered by the Depression, admonished Canada not to return immigrants who, like many Canadian nationals, were down on their luck, owing to circumstances beyond their control. The Canadian government took such complaints seriously and tempered its deportation practices accordingly.[15]

The deportation of communists and radicals was both urged and supported by those who increasingly came to view political and labour activists as the most serious threat to political democracy. Counted among these groups were political leaders, law-enforcement officials, members of the judiciary, entrepreneurs, and representatives of the Conservative press. Also sharing a deep antipathy to communism were the various fascist organizations that grew in size and number throughout this period.[16]

Most fascist organizations were patterned along Nazi Party lines. In the West, the Canadian Society for German Culture, Inc. (Deutscher Bund, Canada) was the largest, drawing its membership from Germans citizens and Canadians of German descent. Although it was more a cultural group than a political organization, it nevertheless declared support for the New Germany and restricted membership to those of Aryan descent, expressly prohibiting those of Jewish or 'negro' ancestry. At the peak of its activities, the Bund had approximately 2,000 members.[17] In Ontario and Manitoba, the dominant fascist movement was the Canadian Nationalist Party, led by William Whittaker, which patterned itself after the German National Socialist Party. Although the leadership tended to be primarily Anglo-Saxon Protestants, its membership came largely from Eastern European immigrant communities.[18] In 1937, it joined with the National Social Christian Party in Quebec to form one national movement, the National Unity Party.

In some respects, the National Social Christian Party in Quebec, led by Adrien Arcand, was the most disturbing fascist movement in the country. Although the party could not boast a substantial membership, it drew considerable attention across the province. As noted by one reporter at the time, 'a crowd of 2,000 people with an overflow listening to Arcand's pyrotechnic oratory through loudspeakers, is a commonplace today in Quebec.'[19] Given that Arcand's orations were typically full of vitriolic slurs against Jews, the degree to which he was tolerated by the public, and indeed by the government, was a cause of great concern to the Jewish community.[20] Equally alarming was that many prominent members of Quebec society, including politicians, clerics in the Roman Catholic Church, and nationalist organizations such as Jeune-Canada and the Ligue d'Action Nationale, shared Arcand's assessment of Jews as 'dirty,' 'thieving' 'communist conspirators,' who had, through the manipulation of politicians, monopolized the commercial interests of the province.[21]

Also centred in Ontario and Quebec was the Italian Fascist Party – the Fascio. It was formed in the mid-1930s with the assistance of the Italian government, essentially as a means of eliciting financial support for Mussolini, and in particular his war in Ethiopia. The party was attractive to many Italian Canadians who, faced with economic exploitation and discrimination, took great pride in the achievements of the leader of their homeland.[22]

Those attracted to fascism believed that only a fascist state could steer the country out of the Depression. Germany and Italy appeared as prime examples of this. Fascism drew on deeply held nationalist feelings within the German, Italian, and French-Canadian communities also helps to explain its popularity at a time when such communities felt particularly beleaguered by the economic collapse. In addition, all fascist movements were ardently anti-communist, a platform that attracted those who firmly believed that communism constituted one of the most serious threats to Canadian society.

Even at its peak in the early 1930s, however, fascism attracted a relatively small number of supporters, far fewer, for example, than the Communist Party, which itself could not boast a huge following.[23] Yet, as far as immigration policy is concerned, the rise and fall of fascism in Canada is interesting in several respects. In the first place, the fact that fascist groups could publish anti-Semitic tracts with impunity shows the degree to which the government and society as a whole was tolerant, and even complacent, about such attacks upon Jews. Second, fascism, like communism, drew some of its strongest adherents from immigrant groups, primarily those from Eastern Europe. This reflected the lack of homogeneity of immigrant communities. Immigrants brought with them diverse political loyalties and racial prejudices that found expression here in Canada. Political diversity and racism were certainly not confined to the Anglo-Canadian community. As James Gray describes,

> ... ours was a society with a well defined pecking order of prejudice. On the top were the race proud Anglo-Saxons, who were prejudiced against everybody else. On the bottom were the Jews, against whom everybody discriminated. In between were the Slavs and Germans. By the mid-thirties the Germans had become deeply infected with Hitler's poison and discriminated against Ukrainians, Poles and Jews. The Poles hated the Russians, Ukrainians and Jews, and both the Ukrainians and Jews subdivided again into 'reds' and 'whites' who endlessly refought the Russian revolution.[24]

Finally, the fascist movement is significant from the perspective of immigration policy in so far as many of the same methods that were used to crush communism in the 1930s, and that were applauded by the fascist movement, were subsequently employed in the 1940s to suppress all fascist organizations in Canada.[25]

Although immigration policy between 1930 and 1937 was formulated around a different set of issues than in preceding periods, and attracted a distinctive constellation of interests, its implementation was the same as in previous decades, with one notable exception. As the aggressive immigration-promoting objectives of previous periods were abandoned, the Department of Immigration and Colonization lost its independent status. In 1936 it became the Immigration Branch of the Department of Mines and Resources. Notwithstanding this change, however, the Immigration Act was not significantly amended during this time, changes to admissions policies being effected through orders-in-council. The minister in charge of immigration, in consultation with the Cabinet, continued to wield enormous control over immigration policy and immigration regulations, and ministerial directives were enforced by immigration officials relatively free of parliamentary or judicial scrutiny.

Admission Restrictions

The 1931 restriction of immigrants admissible under the Immigration Act to agriculturalists with means, immediate relatives of Canadian residents, and immigrants from Great Britain and the United States with sufficient capital, immediately affected not only the size, but also the composition of the flow of immigrant arrivals to Canada. For example, throughout the 1930s, the majority of immigrants who came to Canada were wives and minor children of Canadian residents, and more than two-thirds of all arrivals were of British or northern European descent.[26] Although the admission of contract labourers had been prohibited in 1929, employers were still able to secure admission of skilled workers by special permit where the minister was satisfied that the workers' labour or services were required in Canada.[27] While the exact number of permit entries were not recorded in the annual immigration data, department reports of the period suggest that employers continued to use the permit system to admit immigrant workers, although not nearly to the extent that it was used in the previous decade.[28]

Regulations limiting the entry of Chinese immigrants, passed pursuant to the provisions in the Chinese Immigration Act,[29] remained in force and restricted immigration from China so effectively that, between 1930 and 1935, only three Chinese persons emigrated to Canada.[30] In order to discourage Chinese residents who had temporarily registered out of the country from returning during the Depression, the time-frame permitted for re-entry was extended from two to four years. As explained in the regulation, the minister was of the opinion that, with this extension, many Chinese visiting China would extend their visit, and many Chinese in Canada would return to China until employment conditions improved. This, in turn, would 'relieve the unemployment situation in Canada as well as reduce the number of Chinese persons who would otherwise apply for relief.'[31]

Japanese immigration continued to be governed by the special agreement that Canada had renegotiated with Japan in 1928, which limited Japanese immigration to 150 persons annually. The entry of all other persons of 'any Asiatic race' was expressly prohibited, with the exception of wives and minor children of Canadian citizens who were able to care for their dependants.[32] Citizenship was regularly denied to those of the Asiatic race[33] and consequently relatively few Asians could avail themselves of this exception.

One interesting feature of immigrant arrivals during this time is that juvenile immigration continued, although in much smaller numbers than in previous periods,[34] despite the controversy that had always surrounded the movement. As of 1931, the government discontinued the practice of advancing passage assistance, and, while this contributed to a 50 per cent fall in annual arrivals of juvenile immigrants, to 2,000 in 1932, it is clear from records of the Department of Immigration and Colonization that the demand for juvenile workers among Canadian farmers remained relatively high. The British child labourer was reportedly 'easier to teach and more likely to remain in his position than is the case when a young fellow has had experience on the road or in the relief camp.'[35] As in previous periods, the department seemed sensitive to the accusations of exploitation that had long been levied at child-immigration schemes. Particularly during the early 1930s, in his annual reports, the supervisor of child immigration regularly mentioned the difficulties youths had in collecting wages, and that many left their placements. Yet these problems were never discussed in any detail, and often the blame was placed upon the children's lack of moral fibre rather than on the economic situation in general, and the failure of their employers to meet their obligations. As explained by Supervisor G. Bogue Smart in his 1931–2 report,

> while the majority of boys were found well placed and settled in their work, there was some unrest chiefly among those who arrived in 1930 and 1931,

a number taking advantage of the general depression and leaving good, comfortable homes to travel about the country and swell the ranks of the unemployed. Efforts to get these settled were not satisfactory as relatively a small number remained in the places to which they were sent and exhibited a disinclination to work preferring rather to impose on the sympathy and credulity of the public in towns and cities. Some succeeded in working their passages home and others deliberately became public charges and were finally deported. The industrious and better class have remained in farm jobs, even at reduced wages for the winter, and Inspectors' reports show that many are making favourable progress.[36]

Smart's information was derived from the regular investigations he claimed his inspectors conducted into the welfare of child placements. As he asserted in 1930, 'each child is dealt with individually and made to feel that the Department has a direct and personal interest in his welfare.'[37] Yet subsequent testimonies by many of the children themselves indicate that this was not the case.[38] In fact, statistics provided by both Smart and his successors reveal that an individual assessment of each child under supervision would have been exceedingly difficult. For example, in 1931 the inspection staff reportedly consisted of one woman to look after the girls, and five men to inspect the situations of the boys. According to the figures provided by Smart, close to 7,000 visits and inspections were carried out in that year alone.[39] With only six inspectors on hand, this meant that each inspector would have had to make on average more than 1,000 personal visits a year, which was logistically implausible, given that the children were most often placed in rural areas.

While the investigation of the employment conditions of child immigrants may not have been assiduously pursued in this period, it is clear that other aspects of the department's investigative work were. Department reports of the period consistently refer to the heavy burden of its investigative activities, which were described as including: responding to general complaints, establishing the actual settlement conditions of those applying as dependent members of families, investigating reports of illegal entrants and others who had allegedly violated the Immigration Act, and examining the status of immigrants who had become public charges or inmates of public institutions.[40] The sheer magnitude of its deportation efforts confirm that a considerable proportion of the department's time must have been focused on its investigational work.

Restrictive and Punitive Naturalization Practices

Just as admission controls were tightened, so too, did it become harder for some to acquire citizenship, and for others to retain their status once naturalized. As discussed earlier,[41] naturalization was available to immigrants who had acquired Canadian domicile by residing in the country for five years. For British immigrants, naturalization was automatic upon five years' residency. All other immigrants had to file an application for naturalization in court. Where the presiding judge determined that the applicant met the requirements of the Naturalization Act, the application was forwarded to the secretary of state, who could grant the certificate at his discretion. The minister was not required to give reasons for his decision, which was final and not reviewable by any court.[42]

Not only did naturalized Canadians enjoy more political rights than other immigrants, such as the right to vote in federal elections and to sit in Parliament,[43] but they also could not be excluded from entering the country unless their certificates had been revoked. Similarly, unlike immigrants without domicile who could be deported from Canada for engaging in a wide range of activities, including criminal acts and having received public charity,[44] naturalized Canadians could be removed only if their naturalization certificates were revoked, and only within a narrower set of circumstances. Section 9 of the Naturalization Act set out the circumstances for which naturalization certificates could be revoked by the governor in council. These included situations where a person was considered to have obtained the certificate by fraud or concealment of material circumstances; demonstrated disloyalty or disaffection to the Crown; communicated with the enemy; been sentenced to a term of incarceration for over a year or to a fine of $500 or more; resided outside of the British dominions for seven years without retaining a substantial connection to them; or was not of good character at the time the certificate was issued. So, for example, persons who were naturalized yet who were subsequently found to be inadmissible at the time of landing could have their certificates revoked. They would also be considered not to have acquired domicile[45] and could therefore be deported for the same reasons as those immigrants with less than five years' residence. Those whose certificates were revoked, yet had not lost domicile, could be removed only on the more limited grounds enumerated in section 41 of the Immigration Act, which included engaging in rebellious acts such as advocating the overthrow by force of the government or attempting to cause public disorder.[46] The importance of naturalization, then, lay in the fact that it accorded the person certain political rights, provided unrestricted entry into the country, and reduced the person's vulnerability to being expelled.

One of the striking features of the Depression years was that the rate of naturalization refusals went up, as did the number of naturalization revocations. Because the naturalization process was highly discretionary, it was not uncommon for applications to be denied without apparent reason. The Oriental population had experienced this most dramatically, such that since 1923 few, if any, naturalization applications from Chinese or Japanese residents had been approved.[47] While the reasons may not have been evident on the face of the records, the pattern of rejections made it clear that such refusals often were made on racial grounds. In 1931, this became even more explicit when an order-in-council was passed limiting the issuing of naturalization certificates to those persons of Chinese or Japanese origin who could produce evidence of having renounced their former allegiance.[48] Not only was this requirement unique, having no application to other nationalities, but it had the effect of making it impossible for Japanese citizens to become naturalized, since Japanese law did not provide for revocation of citizenship.[49]

Among the others who were affected by the discretionary nature of the naturalization process were those who were unemployed or who engaged in labour advocacy or radical politics. As part of the naturalization procedure, the applicant was investigated by the RCMP, whose assessment of the individual, along with information provided by the Immigration and Colonization department, was considered by the secretary of state before a decision was made. These assessments were confidential, leaving the applicant unable to disprove false or exaggerated reports. They were also often determinative, such that police or Immigration and Colonization department reports of bad character, as evidenced by unemployment, involvement in labour disputes, or support of communist or socialist organizations, led to rejection. It is thus not surprising that, in 1934, a time of both high unemployment and increased labour militancy, close to 94 per cent of the 18,000 naturalization applications made were rejected.[50]

Naturalization revocations also increased during this time. A person's naturalization certificate could be revoked by the Cabinet on several grounds, including evidence that the person had obtained the certificate by fraud or misrepresentation, was not of good character at the time the certificate was granted, had shown disloyalty to the Crown, or had been sentenced to imprisonment or fined over $500 within five years of the granting of the certificate. The secretary of state was given discretionary authority under the Naturalization Act to refer a case to a commission of inquiry, provided that the proposed revocation was not based on criminality or discontinued residence.[51] The act did not provide the person concerned the right to be present or to submit evidence. Naturalization revocations, particularly when followed by deportation proceedings, bore very harsh consequences, not only for the person involved, but for the person's family. Section 10 of the Naturalization Act provided that, where a person's certificate of naturalization was cancelled, the Cabinet could also revoke the citizenship status of his wife or minor children.[52] In addition, the group could be left stateless if their former nationality was lost upon their becoming Canadian citizens.[53] The severity of these consequences, however, did not temper the practice of resorting to naturalization revocation. In fact, during periods of relatively active labour and political advocacy, the revocation of naturalization certificates appeared to be used as a form of social control. Between 1930 and 1936, there were 461 naturalization revocations, more than half of which occurred in 1932, following the crackdown on the Communist Party.[54]

Enhanced Deportation Activities

The use of deportation to remove from Canada recipients of public assistance and political and labour activists had been a characteristic of immigration policy for decades. What set the 1930s apart from all previous, and indeed subsequent periods, was the sheer magnitude of the removals. Between 1902 and 1928, for example, on average approximately 1,000 persons were deported annually. In 1931, by contrast, more than 7,000 immigrants were removed from Canada. Between 1930 and 1935, there were on average more than 5,700 deportations per year. According to department records, becoming a public charge accounted for just over 60 per cent of this number, while criminality and medical reasons accounted for approximately 15 per cent and 10 per cent, respectively. Family members accompanying deportees accounted for almost 10 per cent of the total, and those deported for 'other causes' made up the remaining 5 per cent. As the economy improved and as the government's deportation policies came under increasing censure both at home and abroad, deportations eased off considerably, to fewer than 500 persons annually for the remainder of the decade.[55]

That the government could engage in extensive deportation practices stemmed from the wide latitude provided by the Immigration Act to the minister responsible for the administration of the act, and the reluctance of the courts to limit the exercise of discretionary power in any significant way. As will be recalled,[56] according to the Immigration Act, municipal officers and immigration officers were charged with the 'duty' of filing a complaint with the minister regarding any person believed to be in violation of the act.[57] Upon receipt of the complaint, the minister could order that the person be detained, at which point the person was required to be brought before a board of inquiry, comprising three immigration officers, to determine whether the person was an undesirable immigrant and liable for deportation. The conduct of deportation proceedings was the same as admission determinations, so that all evidence the board considered trustworthy was admissible, and the normal burden of proof was reversed, leaving the immigrant responsible for establishing his or her right to remain in Canada. A negative decision could be appealed to the minister, provided the finding was not based on the person being diseased or mentally defective.[58] In practice, appeals to the minister were rarely successful, accompanied as they were by a summary record of the board's proceedings made by an immigration officer along with a statement of the officer's own views of the case. Nor did the courts offer a more promising prospect of impartial review. The act specifically excluded the courts from reviewing any admission or deportation order of the minister or any such decision by a board of inquiry, 'upon any ground whatsoever' unless the person was a Canadian citizen or had Canadian domicile.[59]

Although the jurisdiction of the courts was greatly circumscribed by statute, challenges to the detention of persons subject to deportation orders were brought before the courts by way of *habeas corpus* applications. Through these challenges, a body of case law was established confirming that immigrants facing deportation, regardless of the consequences that such forced removal could bring upon their lives and security, had far fewer rights than litigants or alleged criminals in the civil and criminal courts of the country. For example, immigrants did not have to be fully informed of the allegations against them: a general outline and, in some cases, oral notice would suffice.[60] Immigrants believed not to be legally resident in Canada could be apprehended without a warrant, and the burden of proof was upon the immigrant to establish the contrary. Moreover, the immigrant did not have the right to cross-examine testimony prejudicial to his or her case.[61]

The lack of procedural protections afforded immigrants in deportation hearings and the absence of judicial review left the entire process open to severe abuse. In the case of public-charge deportees, the facts supporting the removal were relatively easy to obtain and substantiate, based, as they often were, on municipal welfare records. Coupled with a summary deportation procedure, people could be and were quickly rounded up and deported by the thousands. With respect to deportation for political reasons, generally the government's case rested on information received by police spies and informers. The lack of procedural safeguards, enabling the immigrant to challenge the validly of such accusations, or to establish mitigating circumstances where appropriate, meant that these cases, too, could be decided relatively quickly in the government's favour.[62]

REMOVING THE UNEMPLOYED AND INDIGENT

Under the terms of the British North America Act, welfare assistance was primarily a provincial and municipal responsibility. Nevertheless, the extent of the destitution occasioned by the Depression and the unprecedented demands for social assistance were simply more than either the provinces or their municipalities could bear. In Toronto, for example, the budget for relief increased twenty times between 1929 and 1933.[63] Similarly in Winnipeg, relief costs, which had amounted to $31,000 in 1927–8, skyrocketed to more than $1.5 million three years later.[64] Faced with spiralling expenditures, falling tax revenues, and burgeoning debt, municipalities turned to the federal government for assistance.

For its part, the federal government resisted requests that it assume a greater responsibility for the provision of relief. The government's refusal was based primarily on the belief that to do otherwise could bankrupt the treasury. This belief was in turn influenced in part by the British Poor Law tradition. The traditional view was that the unemployed could remedy their situation by agreeing to accept lower wages. From this basic premise, it followed that those who were unemployed were voluntarily so. As Prime Minister Bennett stated in 1931, 'The people are not bearing their share of the load. Half a century ago people would work their way out of their difficulties rather than look to a government to take care of them. The fibre of some of our people has grown softer and they are not willing to turn in and save themselves.'[65]

In order to discourage laziness, it followed that relief rates should be set at levels just below the lowest wage paid to workers. In this way people would not be deterred from seeking any type of work to improve their situations. The rationale also supported the government's insistence that relief should primarily be a local responsibility. Since wage rates varied across the country, municipalities were best able to determine and justify relief rates in their area.[66]

As the threat of municipal and provincial bankruptcy became more real, however, the federal government was forced to step in, lest the provinces default on their loans, which would in turn seriously damage the country's credit rating.[67] Federal assistance was provided by way of loans to the provinces, which were then used to subsidize municipal relief efforts. Throughout the Depression, the federal government spent ten times the amount on relief than it had in the previous decade.[68]

Even with provincial loans, most cities continued to struggle with the demands for welfare assistance. As a way of cutting costs, eligibility criteria were tightened, such that, to qualify, applicants had to meet various requirements such as: continuous residence within the city for a given number years; the absence of family relations who could provide support; and evidence that, although out of work, the applicant was ready and willing to accept employment if offered. Very strict rules were imposed on those collecting relief, violation of which could terminate assistance. For example, some cities prohibited the owning of phones, the driving of cars, and/or the consumption of alcohol. As well, immigrant claimants in some districts were required to sign voluntary deportation requests as a precondition for receiving assistance.[69]

The duty of municipal officers, imposed by the Immigration Act, to notify the government of persons without domicile who had received public assistance was vigorously discharged during this time. Thousands of names were sent to Ottawa, and thousands of arrest warrants were returned, followed by detentions, board of inquiry hearings, and deportation. Being on relief was a statutory ground for removal for those without domicile with the result that there was very little an immigrant could do once it was established that he or she had been in Canada less than five years and had received public assistance.

While most of the deportations were based on becoming a public charge, the government did try to ground many removals on the basis that the person had been inadmissible at the time of entry and therefore could not have acquired domicile regardless of the length of time resident here. Where this could be shown, it was incumbent on the transportation company that brought the person to Canada to bear the cost of removal. It was a process that bore tremendously harsh consequences, as illustrated in several widely publicized cases involving long-time residents of Canada who were deported on account of physical ailments. One such case involved a woman who was deported after eighteen years' residence on the grounds that she suffered from epilepsy at the time of her admission to Canada. Since this would have put her in an inadmissible class, her entry was deemed unlawful. It was said to follow therefore that she could not have obtained legal residency, and so she was subject to removal. The case was raised in the House by the CCF leader J.S. Woodsworth, who, despite his earlier stated preferences for immigrants from Britain and northern Europe, nevertheless vigorously criticized the summary-deportation practices affecting all European immigrants at this time. He used this case, and others like it, to support his motion that there should be no deportation after ten years' continuous residence.[70] The controversy that such cases generated prompted the minister to order that all proposed deportations of persons with over five years' residency for mental or physical reasons be first reviewed by the deputy minister. Notwithstanding this concession, however, according to Barbara Roberts, the practice of deporting long-time residents continued.[71]

Within the House, the CCF continued to raise the issue of deporting the unemployed. It frequently censured the government for a policy that it described as being as irresponsible as it was unjust. As Woodsworth argued,

> whilst I agree that it is a considerable relief to the individual municipalities to have these men deported, I think it is a serious state of things when men who have come to this country in good faith to settle here, and who have attempted to get work, should be deported just because they are unable to get work ... I think it is hardly fair to the immigrants we have begged to come to this country. Many of them have broken all their home ties in the old country. Many of them have spent all they had in order to pay for their passage to this country and many of them will be excellent settlers if they got half the chance. I would say that after we have spent millions of dollars to advertise this country in Great Britain and Europe, it is, to say the least, very poor policy for us to return a great many of these disgruntled people to the old country suffering from what they regard, and I think rightly, as a substantial injustice.[72]

For its part, the government insisted that in no case was deportation taken solely on account of the person being a public charge. 'Canada is not deporting immigrants because they are unemployed but mainly because they are unemployable.' It was 'illness and in some cases inability or unwillingness to find work' that were reportedly the 'main causes.'[73] As minister of Immigration and Colonization W.A. Gordon stated categorically: 'I know of no case where deportation has taken place of a desirable citizen simply because he has become a public charge through inability to find employment. I do not know of any such case.'[74]

Despite the adamant denials, government records show that deportations were carried out by the thousands simply on presentation of evidence that the person in question had been a recipient of public support. And, as the deportation activities of the department continued, so too, did the protests against it. In 1932, a CCF MP, Mr. Reid, rose in the House to once again condemn the government's 'unfair' deportation practice, wondering 'what the feelings will be in the old country when those hundreds arrive back with the stigma on their names that they were ejected from Canada for what under our law is termed a crime.'[75] As a matter of fact, the reaction in the 'home countries' was far from complacent. Britain was particularly disturbed by the large number of immigrants that were being deported there, and it made its concerns well known to Canadian officials. This was also true of Germany, Sweden, Hungary, Norway, Poland, and Denmark, who through their consulates inquired as to why so many of their nationals were being deported solely because of their inability to find work at a time of general economic hardship.[76]

As the number of deportations mounted, other groups also added their voices to the growing protest, including several unions, unemployed associations, and churches. Even the Canadian Legion, traditionally not generally sympathetic to immigrant grievances, protested against the way municipalities were allegedly threatening veterans with deportation.[77] As criticism increased and the hardships encountered by immigrants faced with deportation were more widely publicized, some cities decided to moderate the number of public-charge cases they reported to Ottawa. In a move that annoyed the Immigration and Colonization department, Winnipeg City Council decided in 1934 not to report for deportation every immigrant who was on relief solely on account of unemployment. As this was contrary to the compulsory reporting obligation set out the Immigration Act, the department simply retaliated by deciding that it would no longer deport any public-charge cases from that city.[78]

The situation became the subject of debate in the House. CCF MP Abraham Heaps proposed that the law be changed so as to give municipalities the option of whether to report public-charge cases or not, noting that the compulsory provision in the Immigration Act had been enacted before the First World War, when unemployment itself was considered a crime.[79] The minister rejected the proposal on the grounds that it would lead to a situation where 'control would be transferred from the federal to the municipal level.' Not only would this be contrary to immigration law and policy, but it would create a situation where, in the absence of centralized control, the law would be inconsistently applied across the country. It was the duty of the minister, which he claimed to fulfil, to review all deportation cases to ensure that there were no abuses and to authorize removal only if satisfied that the individual could not find employment: 'I can assure hon. members that if on review of the facts – it is my duty to review the facts in such cases, and I do it – it is found that there is even a possibility of the alien being absorbed into gainful occupation, this section will not be invoked.'[80]

Despite the minister's assurances that he reviewed the facts of each case, given the magnitude of the numbers involved it is unlikely that he was able to do so. Nevertheless, sensitivity to criticism of its deportation activities was revealed in the department's desire to characterize increased deportations as a familiar phenomenon in times of economic weakness: 'During the past few years there has been increasing interest on the part of public in the subject of deportation. Some appear to be unaware of the fact that deportation has been going on for many years... When times are good and employment plentiful, deportations decrease but they increase when the conditions are reversed. This is equally true of Canada, the United States and other immigration countries which make a practice of deporting immigrants.'[81]

While keen to have the public see the relatively large number of deportations as being a natural consequence of a depressed economy, the department was also eager to characterize most deportations as being voluntary. For example, in its 1933–4 report, the department claimed that more than 50 per cent of the British public-charge deportees had approached the department, requesting deportation, before any complaint or request had been received from any other source. A large percentage of the rest, it noted, expressed at their hearing a desire to be returned to their former homes. 'The combined total of these two classes was 92% of British public charge deports,' leaving only 8 per cent returned involuntarily.[82] As for the foreign public-charge cases, the department alleged that only 20 per cent were sent home contrary to their own wishes.[83] Three years later, the commissioner of immigration asserted that, of all the public-charge deportations conducted between 1931 and 1937, only 11 per cent were sent home against their wishes.[84]

These statistics, however, seem highly contrived. In its internal documents, the department recorded other reasons accompanying public-charge deportation decisions, in addition to voluntarily requesting deportation, which also tended to point to the culpability of the immigrant. Such explanations included 'refused to consider employment,' 'demanded impossible wages or working conditions,' 'illness,' and 'anticipated employment in native country.' Yet Barbara Roberts's research reveals that these reported reasons were deduced from board of inquiry hearings, which were reported inaccurately and sometimes in a deliberately misleading manner:

> There were manipulative questions asked at Boards. Immigrants who had been assured that they would be deported were asked if they looked forward to seeing their families and friends; if they agreed their response was counted as a request to be deported or as a desire to go home. The Department included numbers of those who 'did not appeal' in its voluntary deportation figures. Similarly, if during the Board of Inquiry immigrants made any statement indicating a lack of enthusiasm for a specific job or work experience (saying that they preferred an industrial job they once had, to farm work, because the former paid better) or a field of work, or even if they expressed discouragement about their ability to find a job, the Department made use of such statements in their statistics showing that public charge deports were unemployable, unwilling or undesirable.[85]

While the government continued to deny that it summarily deported recipients of public welfare, it did take steps which demonstrated that it was nevertheless attentive to adverse publicity. By 1932, certain practices were adopted, such as putting in abeyance deportation orders of persons who had found employment by the time the order was issued, and suspending the deportation orders of British subjects. Roberts claims, however, that such practices were not widely followed. When, in 1934, it was apparent that British immigrants were still being deported solely on account of their inability to find work, the department issued a directive to all its offices, ordering them not to carry out deportation orders of British public-charge cases where the order was based solely on the person's unemployment.[86] This directive was significant since British immigrants were the largest single group of public-charge deportees throughout the Depression. Once their removal was no longer automatic, public-charge deportations fell off the following year.[87] While protestations, particularly from Britain, no doubt influenced the government's relaxation of it deportation practices, the fact that the economy was emerging from the Depression was equally, if not more, determinative.

REMOVING POLITICAL RADICALS AND LABOUR AGITATORS

In terms of numbers, the expulsion of Communists and labour agitators through deportation was not nearly as large as the removal of relief recipients. Nevertheless, the vigour with which the purge was undertaken was comparable and was subject to similar kinds of excesses and abuses. Unfortunately the exact number of immigrants who were removed from Canada on the basis of their political beliefs and activities is not known, since the government did not record deportations in this way. Politically motivated deportations were statistically concealed in the other categories, most commonly under 'criminality' and 'public charge.' Records kept by legal advocates, trade unions, and civil-liberties associations, however, suggest that the number of political deportees was well into the hundreds.[88] So thorough and sweeping was the government's war on communism and labour radicalism that the Communist Party of Canada (CPC) and the main radical trade unions of the time lost many of their leaders and a significant number of their supporters through deportation.

The Communist Party of Canada was formed in 1921, and almost from the moment of its inception was the subject of intense political surveillance. The success of the Russian Revolution had proved the potential potency of communist doctrines, particularly among those who considered themselves most oppressed by an economic system whose benefits largely eluded them. It was for this reason that leading politicians and security officials felt that it was essential for the government to keep close watch over a party whose very existence was premised on the assumption that a proletarian revolution was inevitable. It was a belief that fuelled the close surveillance of radical leaders throughout the 1920s as well as the ongoing information exchange with the intelligence arms of the British and American governments concerning the movements of foreign radicals. It was also the concern behind the denial of naturalization certificates to those suspected of communist leanings.[89]

For those who regarded communism as the single most important threat facing the country, the increase in militant labour activity in the early 1930s seemed to underscore the dangers inherent in permitting communists to operate freely within the community. The fact that the party and its labour-union affiliate, the Workers Unity League (WUL), drew much of their membership from Polish, Russian, and Slavic communities, who increasingly faced unemployment, job discrimination, and deportation, further underscored fears that they were essentially foreign movements that threatened the stability, and indeed the entire democratic structure of the country.

Within one year of its formation in 1929, the WUL had a membership of eleven unions, most of which represented previously unrepresented workers within the resource-extraction industries.[90] By 1933, the WUL claimed responsibility for one-third of the strike activity across the country.[91] Most of the strikes initiated under WUL leadership were 'desperation strikes' in protest against reduced wage rates and lay-offs resulting from the Depression. They were met with employer intransigence and police repression. As WUL strikes were characterized as being 'communist inspired,' their suppression often had the support of the general public, who regarded communism as being as much an evil force as did the politicians.

Since communists did not limit their activities to the labour arena seemed to confirm for many that, if left unchecked, it would only exacerbate the severe social disruption already precipitated by the Depression. In the major metropolitan areas, communists worked among the unemployed, organizing marches, demonstrations, and meetings. As described by Stewart Jamieson, such demonstrations and riots 'brought civil disturbance generally to a new high and provoked the most widespread, severe, and in many cases brutal measures of repression by police forces since the Winnipeg General Strike.'[92] Within the relief camps established by Bennett and under the control of the Department of Defence, the communists were also active. Set up to keep unemployed men busy and distant from the influences of communism, the camps turned out to be dens of frustration and despair, where the Relief Camp Workers' Union (RCUW) of the WUL garnered considerable support. Although its leaders were often expelled from the camps, the RCWU succeeded in organizing several major strikes within the camps for better conditions, improved wages, and the recognition of camp committees.

In this climate of economic collapse and increasing militancy among the employed and the unemployed, appeals across the country were made to the government to silence the Communist Party and the foreign agitators who were behind it. With respect to foreigners, deportation was the most sought-after response. As Ontario premier G. Howard Ferguson advised Prime Minister King in 1929, deportation was most expedient, since criminal convictions of communist agitators for sedition were difficult to obtain and 'a jail term merely makes martyrs of these individuals and stimulates them to greater action.'[93] Ferguson's appeal was followed by similar requests from other municipal and provincial governments.

Members of the judiciary were no more sanguine about foreign communists than were many politicians, as illustrated in 1931 in a speech by Ontario Chief Justice Sir William Mulock at a Canadian National Exhibition banquet in Toronto. Addressing a gathering which included the federal minister of Labour, the chairman of the Toronto Board of Police Commissioners, the Toronto chief of police, and the chairman of the University of Toronto Board of Governors, Mulock said of the threat of foreigners, many of whom he claimed were communists:

> If Canada is content to have her laws made by those who deny the existence of God, who would suppress religion, would destroy the sacredness of marriage and who would nationalize women, who would extinguish the love of parents who would deprive children in their tender years of a mother's care and expose them to the imminent danger of growing up as criminals; who would rob all citizens by any degree of force up to that of murder, of all their worldly goods and leave them penniless; who would make it a crime for one to save; would deprive people of liberty and would make slaves of them to the State.
>
> If, I say, those are the conditions which Canada is content to have established in Canada then let her open her doors wide and admit into full citizenship the millions of people of that class.
>
> But if Canada does not wish to become a hell on earth she should rid herself at once of all those who would, if they could, make her such, and let her prevent any of that kind of people ever setting foot on Canadian soil.[94]

The police and RCMP, who were charged with the responsibility of enforcing the Immigration Act and regulations, were directed by individuals who tended to see foreigners in the same light as did Chief Justice Mulock. In a speech given in Toronto in 1932, Major-General James H. MacBrien, commissioner of the RCMP, also articulated the view that many of the country's current problems would disappear if the foreign element were removed: 'It is notable that 99% of these fellows [the unemployed] are foreigners and many of them have not been here long. The best thing to do would be to send them back to where they came from in every possible way. If we were rid of them there would be no unemployment or unrest in Canada.'[95]

Four years later, in a speech to the Synod of the Presbyterian Church and reprinted in the *RCMP Quarterly*, Colonel C.E. Edgett, the former chief of the Vancouver Police, warned that communism was the greatest threat to world peace. He called attention to the fact that, in Canada, there were a large number of communists within the mainstream churches, particularly the United Church of Canada. Communism, according to Edgett, was a Jewish conspiracy dating back to the eighteenth century, whose aim was the destruction of 'all cherished feelings of patriotism, nationalism or race conscience.' Fascism, in contrast, had arisen precisely to preserve those values that communism was bent on destroying. 'And if fascism had not arisen and conquered in Italy, and subsequently had not Nationalism arisen and conquered in Germany, then today these two great countries would have been obliterated from the map in a flood tide of Bolshevism.'[96]

In light of the ardent anti-communist sentiments that were so popular at this time, official attempts to suppress the movement are perhaps not surprising. One of the first major moves in this respect came in Toronto in 1929. Following the chief of police's announcement that public meetings were to be held in English and no aspersions on the government or the King would be allowed, the licences of many public halls which had been the venue for meetings in foreign languages were revoked. Street meetings of communist sympathizers were also brutally dispersed. The crackdown elicited strong support from such staunchly patriotic organizations as the Orange Lodge and the Canadian Legion. It was also sympathetically reviewed in the press. As the *Mail and Empire* observed, 'the majority of those who have made a noise about police interference ... are not Canadian by birth or persons who have lived here all their lives under British institutions. These need reminding that ... the laws of Canada are binding upon them. No sovietism or other form of anarchism they have been indoctrinated in alien countries or by alien teaching will find footing here.'[97]

In the House of Commons, the Toronto measures to suppress communism were criticized by the CCF as being far too sweeping and an abrogation of the British rights of freedom of speech, freedom of the press, and freedom of assembly. Several other members also warned that the greater the efforts by the state to suppress these fundamental rights, the more people would be driven to communist ideology. As stated by independent MP A.W. Neill: 'I believe the best method of dealing with extreme views is to afford them the greatest publicity ... The surest way of propagating a doctrine is to make a martyr of somebody in connection with it.'[98]

Henri Bourassa agreed, arguing as well that it was ill advised to prevent the use of foreign languages in publications or in public speech. Moral and political unity, he claimed, would not be achieved 'by making foreign born Canadians English-speaking or French-speaking by force; it will not be achieved by days of imprisonment, by fines or by threats of what may happen if they dare use ... other languages, or if they dare oppose a certain social or political theory which may be held by other people.' The state would achieve better results, he predicted, if it was impressed upon foreigners that 'there is a place in Canada for every group of people to grow according to its racial or intellectual tendency provided the whole community is united in a few basic principles of national unity.'[99]

Despite these impassioned arguments, they did not persuade the majority of MPs. Woodsworth's later attempt in 1931 to amend the Criminal Code prohibitions on unlawful assemblies so as to protect the right of people 'to peacefully assemble' and to 'discuss any matter of public interest' was soundly rejected.[100] One month later, the federal government moved even more decisively. On 11 and 12 August, the RCMP and the Ontario Provincial Police raided the CPC headquarters, the offices of the WUL and its official paper *The Worker*, as well as the private homes of prominent party leaders. Eight party officials were arrested, including Tim Buck, the political secretary of the party, and charged under section 98 of the Criminal Code with being members of an unlawful association and with seditious conspiracy.[101] Of the eight, one was Canadian-born, two were British, and the remaining five were from Eastern Europe. All the foreign-born had been in Canada for close to twenty years, with the exception of Sam Carr, the party organizer, who had come to Canada in 1924.

At their trial, the men were found guilty on all charges brought against them. They were given prison terms ranging from one to five years, and all the foreign-born, with one exception, were recommended for deportation at the expiration of their imprisonment. The basis for their conviction of being members in an unlawful association rested on evidence that the CPC defended the use of force or the threat of physical injury as a 'means of accomplishing any governmental, industrial or economic change' and as such was, by the terms of section 98, unlawful.[102] Upon appeal, the conviction for criminal conspiracy was quashed, but the other convictions for being members of an unlawful association were upheld.

The judgment of the Court of Appeal was delivered by Chief Justice Mulock, whose views on the threat of communism had been well publicized in his address at the Canadian National Exhibition dinner one year earlier.[103] Referring to passages from *The Worker* as well as to the theses and statutes of the Communist International of Russia which were binding on the CPC, Mulock found that these extracts 'bristle with incitements to bring about a change in the governmental and industrial life of Canada by violence.' These, together with evidence to the same effect given at trial by a police informer, led Mulock to conclude that there was sufficient reason to find that the CPC was an unlawful organization.[104]

The Court of Appeal ruling affirmed the illegal status of the CPC and gave legitimacy to the arrests of its supporters, which continued throughout the next few years. For those without domicile (having been in Canada less than five years), a criminal conviction under section 98 was sufficient to initiate deportation proceedings once the sentence had been served.

For those with domicile, however, association with the CPC could also be grounds for removal, since section 41 of the Immigration Act authorized the deportation of domiciled aliens who advocated the overthrow of government by force or attempted to create a public disturbance. In such cases, a criminal conviction was not necessary.

Also included in the purge were those involved in disruptive practices such as unemployment demonstrations and labour strikes. Here the government relied upon other sections of the Criminal Code to secure a conviction before initiating deportation proceedings. Among the offences most commonly relied upon were: unlawful assembly, disorderly conduct, distributing communist literature, inciting a riot, and vagrancy. Least problematic for the Immigration and Colonization department were the activists who had received public relief. In such cases a criminal conviction was not necessary to secure deportation; simply presenting evidence before the board that the person had received public assistance was enough.

With the exception of those found to have been involved in seditious activities, those who had domicile could not be deported on criminal or public-charge grounds. Where there was no evidence of seditious activity, the government was thus limited in its ability to deport a person with five years' residence. Although limited, however, it was not entirely constrained. As Roberts documents, the charge of 'entry by misrepresentation' was used by the department to deport those who undertook work in Canada at variance with the person's stated intentions upon admission. Where this could be shown, the person was considered to have entered the country illegally, and therefore unable to have acquired domicile. Having violated the Immigration Act, the person could be deported. The case of Mikolaj Dranuta serves as one example:

> Mikolaj Dranuta was brought over under the auspices of the Ukrainian Colonization Board in 1926 to do farm work. Instead, according to an RCMP spy report, he took a job in an Edmonton meat packing plant, joined the Ukrainian Temple and taught in a Ukrainian school, helped to organize cultural activities such as the visit of a dance troupe and so on. The Mounties described him as a communist, and noted that while he had not made any speeches ('yet'), he was open about his views. After reviewing the spy report an Immigration official perused Dranuta's photograph ... and decided on that basis that Dranuta was not a farming peasant type. 'Under the circumstances' wrote the official, the Department would take 'action ... with a view to deportation on the ground of entering Canada by misrepresentation.'[105]

The Dranuta case is also an example of how immigrants were targeted for deportation on the basis of unsubstantiated evidence, such as the personal opinions of immigration officers, which the immigrant could not properly contest at the board of inquiry hearing. The lack of procedural protection afforded by the act and the latitude given to adjudicative officers meant that contesting a deportation decision was often a frustrating and ultimately unsuccessful activity.

This was the experience, of the Canadian Labour Defence League (CLDL), which was established in the mid-1920s to raise funds for striking miners and their families. As the crackdown on radicals grew in intensity, so, too, did CLDL efforts to represent the persecuted. It set up a fund to pay bail, fines, and legal expenses for those arrested because of their labour or political activities, and it set out to mobilize public opinion against the government's heavy-handed approach. In 1931, it had 123 branches. Within two years, it had grown to have more than 350 branches, with a total membership of more than 20,000 persons.[106] In its defence of political detainees, including those who had been ordered deported, the CLDL was crippled by a lack of financial resources to meet the legal expenses involved. As well, in the case of deportees, there was very little that even a defence lawyer could do, given the procedures set out in the act and the latitude provided to the board of inquiry members.

The lack of success in contesting deportation proceedings was amply illustrated in May 1932 with the arrest of eleven more leading radicals from major centres across the country following May Day demonstrations. The men were detained under the Immigration Act on the grounds enumerated in section 41 – namely, that they advocated the overthrow by force of the government and, by word or act, had attempted to create public disorder. They were swiftly sent to Halifax, where they were to await board of inquiry hearings regarding their deportation. The manner in which they were spirited away provoked a storm of protest, not only among their advocates, but also in Parliament and in the press.

J.S. Woodsworth rose in the House to notify members of the manner in which three men arrested in Winnipeg had subsequently disappeared. One of the men, Daniel Holmes, had been in Canada twenty years; another had resided in the country for five years; and the third man, Orton Wade, was believed to be Canadian-born. Authorities had refused to produce warrants and had refused to disclose to legal counsel the reasons for the arrests or the detainees' whereabouts. According to the detainees' lawyer, the RCMP assistant commissioner said the men had been put on trains for the east coast for deportation purposes, yet the immigration commissioner denied all knowledge of the case, claiming that it was not a matter for his department. Woodsworth himself had called the department, who instructed him to call the minister. The minister claimed that the case had not come to his attention.[107]

In a bid to bring his clients before the court, the lawyer for the men made applications in Winnipeg for writs of habeas corpus. The motions were denied, since the men had been removed to Halifax and the writs could not be issued outside provincial boundaries.[108] In his reply to Woodsworth's queries, the minister of Justice, Hugh Gutherie, said that the detention and removal of the men had all been done under the authority provided by the Immigration Act. Moreover, he assured the House that, if the detainees were unable to obtain necessary evidence on their behalf, facilities for doing so would be extended to them. The minister of Immigration and Colonization, W.A. Gordon, further explained that the men had been taken to Halifax simply as a matter of convenience: 'There are very few places in Canada – the necessity has not arisen – where boards of inquiry composed of three members are set up, and there are very few places where proper detention quarters are available for the detention of aliens until such times as their cases can be reviewed and their appeals heard.'[109] The minister's explanation, however, was not supported by the annual reports of his own department, which claimed that Winnipeg had adequate detention facilities. According to the annual report of 1931–2, 'overseas deports in the West' were brought forward to Winnipeg, where parties are assembled and sent forward to Montreal in the summer and Halifax in the winter months for embarkation. 'At both Winnipeg and Montreal the department maintains suitably equipped buildings for the accommodation of these people where they are comfortably housed and fed.'[110]

Among the other radical leaders arrested in May 1932 were Arvo Vaara, editor of the Finnish daily paper *Vapaus,* and its translator, Martin Parker. Both men were arrested in Sudbury and also sent immediately to Halifax. As described by the *Ottawa Citizen*:

> Mystery surrounds the whereabouts of Arvo Vaara, editor of the Finnish Daily *Vapaus* at Sudbury, and Martin Parker, translator. The two men were arrested when police raided the newspaper office yesterday, bundled them into a large automobile with five plainclothesmen, and the car left immediately heading south.
>
> Today the Royal Canadian Mounted Police at Ottawa said the raid was carried out by the provincial police, while the Ontario provincial police headquarters here said that they had 'no report.'[111]

In explaining its actions in the House, the government maintained that, since the men were arrested under the Immigration Act, procedures regularly followed in criminal cases were not applicable. As reasoned by the minister of Immigration and Colonization, 'The men are not snatched away from their homes; they are not under arrest, although they are in detention, it is quite true … They have not been convicted of an offence: they are not on trial; but their conduct as aliens is under review to determine whether or not they have the right to stay in Canada.'[112] According to Woodsworth, regardless of whether they were convicted of a criminal offence or not, the men simply by virtue of their long residence in Canada were entitled to certain procedural protections: 'If they are communists, and if the decision given by the court of appeal stands, I presume it is possible to bring them up for trial as communists and deport them. But my contention is that there should be a trial. I do not think men should be deported from this country simply after an investigation by the Immigration Department. As residents of this country for a considerable numbers of years certainly they ought not to be deported without a full, fair trial.'[113] Another CCF member, Edward J. Garland, accused the government of behaving like the Russian secret police and, in doing so, threatening the very basis of democracy. 'To persist in a course of that kind is to destroy the democracy concerning which so many proud protestations have been made.'[114]

Despite the objections raised in the House and elsewhere, the deportation hearings against the radical leaders arrested in May proceeded, with the exception of Orton Wade, who was released upon the discovery that he was a Canadian citizen. Of the remaining ten, four had been in Canada for approximately twenty years, five since the late 1920s, and one since 1923.[115] All denied that they were members of the CPC or that they advocated the overthrow of the government by force. All were ordered deported, and all appealed to the minister. While the ministerial appeal was still pending, eight men applied to the court for release from custody by way of a *habeas corpus* applications. The applications were refused. An appeal to the Supreme Court of Nova Scotia was dismissed, as was a further appeal to the Supreme Court of Canada. The final appeal was based on two grounds. The first was that the complaints against the men were invalid since they did not set out the full particulars of the offences alleged, such as dates and places where acts complained of had taken place. The second argument on appeal was that the evidence before the board did not warrant the board's conclusion.

The Supreme Court rejected the first ground of appeal on the basis that the appellants had not challenged the sufficiency of the complaint in earlier proceedings. It did make clear, however, that there was 'no analogy between a complaint under the *Immigration Act* and an indictment on a criminal charge.' Unlike the latter, a complaint under the *Immigration Act* need not set out the particular place or the time when the act alleged against the immigrant took place. All that was necessary was that immigrant be made aware of the conduct which was considered in violation of the act.[116] The Court also dismissed the second ground of appeal, on the basis that it could not weigh evidence in *habeas corpus* proceedings.[117] All of the ten men were deported. One man, Hans Kist, reportedly died of torture in a German concentration camp.[118]

Kist was not the only deportee who would face persecution upon being returned home. Many activists sent to fascist countries such as Italy, Germany, Finland, and Croatia were in danger of losing their lives. It was a fact which caused great concern within the Canadian Labour Defence League, who petitioned the government to refrain from removing those who would be persecuted in their home countries. According to Roberts, the department was unmoved by such appeals, and in several cases responded by taking steps to ensure extra security so that the deportations could take place as intended.[119]

Aside from the appeals marshalled by the CLDC and some isolated press comment,[120] such removals attracted little public concern. This response may in part be attributable to their lack of visibility. What is clear is that it was not so much the fate that awaited political deportees that attracted the public's attention, but more the excessive force with which the government was arresting alleged radicals of all persuasions. In this the CLDL had some success, in so far as it kept up an aggressive campaign, publicizing government actions and eliciting support for the repeal of the sedition provisions (section 98) of the Criminal Code and the reform of deportation procedures. The RCMP's crushing of a coal miners' strike in Estevan, Saskatchewan, in 1931, in which three miners died and many more were injured and arrested, lent credibility to the CLDL's campaign.[121] As well, the raiding of public meetings by the police in search of subversives in major centres also attracted the ire of many Canadians. In Toronto, for example, the ambitious anti-subversive campaign by the police, which included the surveillance of a passivist ecumenical group, the Fellowship of Reconciliation, served to raise public awareness of the dangers of such actions for freedom of speech.[122] Similarly, in Regina, an RCMP raid of a Roman Catholic parish in search of Communist Party organizers enraged many, including the archbishop's council, which called the move a 'gross insult to common decency and to the Roman Catholic Church.'[123]

An incident in 1933 that attracted nationwide attention and called into question the government's commitment to the rule of law involved a prison riot in Kingston, where Tim Buck was serving his sentence. The riot involved more than 400 prisoners and was in protest against prison conditions whereby prisoners had to work nine to ten hours a day without wages and with only a fifteen-minute recreation period in open air. During the course of the riot, shots were fired at Buck in his cell. The CLDL immediately launched a campaign, demanding a review of the prison system in Canada. According to the minister of Justice, following the riots his office was 'flooded with telegrams and petitions from every quarter of Canada.' Inferring that the petitioners were simply CLDL sympathizers, who had neither Anglo-Saxon nor French-Canadian names 'but names of foreigners, unpronounceable names for the most part,' he advised the House that he disposed of their petitions as follows: 'I merely hand them over to the Mounted Police in order that a record may be kept of the names and addresses of the people who sign them, and I make this statement so that the petitioners may know what I do with them.'[124]

Several months later, the head of the CLDL, A.E. Smith, led a delegation to Ottawa to meet with the prime minister. Among the requests that the delegation submitted was that there be an investigation into the Canadian prison system, that section 98 of the Criminal Code be repealed, and that those incarcerated for their communist associations be released. Bennett refused.

The government's response to the Kingston riot, including the minister of Justice's assertion that it was the work of communist sympathizers, provoked editorial comment throughout the country and from diverse political affiliations. For example, the generally conservative *Winnipeg Tribune* castigated the minister for his dismissive attitude towards the event: '... the people of Canada are not going to be thrown off the track of penal reform by his excited cries of 'Red, Red'... If it is the communists who have brought it to a head, then it is the first and only contribution they have made to the advance of civilization in Canada.'[125]

The more liberal *Winnipeg Free Press* agreed, noting that, in this regard, the Communists were supported by 'strong public opinion demanding a more enlightened prison administration.' In a later comment, the paper warned that the government's attitude towards the inmates and the attempt on Buck's life showed such a disregard for basic human rights that the public would do well to question the government's commitment to protecting human rights in general.[126]

When, several months later, Smith was arrested and charged with sedition for alleging that Bennett gave the order to shoot at Buck in his cell, a new wave of protest erupted. Smith had made the comment in a speech he gave condemning the Toronto police for closing the play *Eight Men Speak*, which was a critique of the handling of the Estevan strike, prison conditions, and the attempt on Buck's life. Smith's arrest and trial aroused national attention and were the subject of criticism from mainstream labour, church, and civil-rights leaders. His acquittal further damaged the government's credibility.[127]

The following year, Bennett was once again challenged to respond to the grievances of the marginalized. In that year, thousands of relief-camp workers left camps in British Columbia and, led by the Relief Camp Workers' Union, converged upon Vancouver to demand better wages, the recognition of camp committees, and the abolition of military control over camp life. The federal government refused to respond. As the strikers' occupation of the city stretched into several weeks, citizens became hostile to the strike, especially when strikers engaged in parades down aisles of department stores, 'snake walks' through the streets, panhandling, and finally a sit-in the on the third floor of the public library to demand financial strike assistance for the duration of the strike. The city agreed to provide six-day strike aid, while the federal government remained intransigent. Because of the lack of response from Ottawa, a massive trek to Ottawa was initiated, in which 1,000 men participated. They left Vancouver in June, making their way across the country in freight cars, picking up supporters as they went. By the time they reached Regina, their numbers had increased twofold.[128]

The prime minister, fearful of similar movements being organized in Winnipeg and Toronto, agreed to meet with a delegation of the strikers. The meeting was unproductive, and the prime minister remained steadfast in his resolve to prevent the strikers from moving beyond Regina. The movement, which had been peaceful and well disciplined, ended in a riot as the RCMP and the Regina Police attempted to arrest the Trek leaders for sedition while they were addressing a large gathering of supporters in the city's Market Square. As described in the *Toronto Globe*, 'the first outbreak occurred when the helmeted mounted police swooped down upon the strikers and supporters meeting in the market square. They appeared as a spokesman began a plea for funds to aid the strikers ... A score of men were taken into custody as police reinforcements were rushed by truck and on horses after the meeting broke up.'[129] The ensuing panic was graphically described in the *Montreal Gazette:*

> The mob rushed for the streets as police swooped down on them. Women raced for cover, hauling children after them. Men, women and children ducked behind automobiles parked on the market square ...

Strikers and citizens scattered down lanes with police following them across streets touching the square. When the crowd at the last side of the square surged back onto the meeting ground, police lines were reformed and attacked, scattering them once again.

Stones and other missiles found in the street ... were hurled at the police.[130]

The result of the Trek was the incarceration of its leaders, many of whom were subsequently deported. One person died, and approximately 100 were injured in the riot. Property damage was estimated to amount to more than $25,000.[131]

Although Bennett's response to the striking reliefers was supported by the conservative press,[132] the general response was not so favourable. In a stinging attack by the *Toronto Star,* Bennett was compared to a dictator: 'It is particularly unfortunate that at a time like this the government of Canada should be in the hands of a man who holds such views, whose arbitrary and non conciliatory actions in the face of a grave crisis are those of a dictator rather than the head of a great and free people.'[133] The *Vancouver Sun* also called his leadership into question: 'When Prime Minister Bennett told the delegates of subsistence camp workers in his office to go back to their camps and forget their appeal, he did the cruellest and least worthy thing ever done by any leader anywhere.'[134]

As to Bennett's claim that it was a communist conspiracy, the *Winnipeg Free Press* once again argued that the public would not be so fooled:

The more the story is clarified, the plainer it becomes that the federal authorities showed bad judgement and that the rioting at Regina last Monday could easily have been avoided.

Mr. Bennett's speech in Parliament on Tuesday was devoted largely to saying, in rather hysterical language, that the strike was really a 'revolutionary movement' prompted by Communists ... His picture was complete with the usual melodramatic features of a master mind in Moscow and an international conspiracy. But this account of the strike appears to be pure surmise on Mr. Bennett's part. He produced nothing any judicially minded person would recognize as evidence.[135]

In the end, although Bennett succeeded in preventing the Trekkers from reaching their Ottawa destination, his accomplishment failed to help in the general election several months later. Judging from the public criticism that his suppression of the Trek attracted, it is in fact likely that his handling of the Trek contributed to the general disillusionment with his leadership.

Conclusion

During the 1930s and continuing throughout the Second World War, immigration policy receded to the periphery of public-policy priorities, reflecting the enormous shift in attitudes towards immigration that had occurred over the previous thirty years. At the turn of the century, immigrants were regarded as one of the essential elements in the prosperity of the new nation. Their central place in national-policy priorities resulted in close to 3 million immigrants being admitted to Canada in the first fifteen years of the century.[136] With the economic downturn of 1913 and the outbreak of the First World War, new concerns dominated political agendas, not the least of which was the maintenance of social harmony. Since the relatively unrestricted flow of immigrants to Canada was seen as a threat to this end, immigration policy shifted from one aimed at *attracting* potential settlers to one directed at *selecting* the most desirable future members of the country. The shift in emphasis was accompanied by a shift in numbers such that, between 1915 and 1930, only one-half the number of immigrants arrived as had come in the first fifteen years of the century.[137]

In the 1930s, immigration policy was to shift in nature and emphasis once again. Throughout this decade, immigration policy was reduced to an essentially explicit concept of *exclusion*. Although the extensive deportation practices of the Bennett years were to ease off in the latter half of the decade, admission restrictions remained in place and were explained as being necessary until full economic recovery was realized.

The shifting focus in immigration policy was in response to the changing priorities that successive government administrations faced. In the Depression years, the preservation of democracy and the fostering of economic recovery demanded, in the government's view, a policy that restricted admissions and that facilitated removal of those who were a drain on public finances and/or a threat to established economic and political interests.[138] The policy attracted relatively little controversy, primarily because the concerns of the government reflected those of the general public. Opposition, when voiced, was largely limited to those groups, like the CCF, WUL, and CLDF, whose political orientation was shared by only a minority of Canadians, as evidenced in the 1935 elections.[139]

While the government could afford to ignore their interests in the way immigration policy was administered, it could not ignore the wider demands for more restrained expulsion practices that these organizations helped to marshal. Shortly after he was elected prime minister in 1935, King closed the relief camps, repealed the controversial sedition section

(section 98) of the Criminal Code, and eased deportations. Yet, as significant as these developments were, the fact was that the Immigration Act remained unchanged. As long as the enabling legislation, and the restrictive manner in which courts reviewed its application, remained unaltered, the discretionary manner in which immigration policy was administered in the past continued to carry the potential for abuse.

In 1930, Mackenzie King lost the federal election largely because of his failure to read the public mood accurately. It was a mistake that he would not repeat. Throughout his next two terms in office, King would be ever vigilant in assessing the general temper of the times and refraining from taking initiatives that would cost the Liberal party support at the polls. While his re-election in 1935 may have been positively received within certain immigrant communities that felt harshly treated throughout the Bennett years, many would soon be disabused of any hope that King would be a better guardian of their rights than his predecessor had been. For, in the absence of a groundswell of support for a more accountable immigration system, and one which guaranteed that admission and deportation decisions be made in accordance with principles of fairness and due process, no change would be initiated by King. Widespread support for such a system still lay a long way in the future; Canadian policies affecting immigrants continued to be designed and implemented in the same highly discretionary and largely unaccountable manner as in the past.

CHAPTER SEVEN

The Recovery and the Second World War, 1938–1945: Closure and Internment

By 1935, the Canadian economy began to recover from the Depression. Although buffeted by a brief recession in 1937–8, the economy was soon stimulated as a consequence of the outbreak of war on the Continent. As in the First World War, demand for Canadian agricultural and industrial products rose rapidly and ushered in a new period of economic prosperity. In response to increased demand, the manufacturing sector underwent dramatic changes, with the construction of aircraft, navy vessels, merchant ships, tanks and other motor vehicles. An enormous amount of investment also went into the manufacturing of arms, explosives, and ammunition, and into a diverse array of war-related industries, from the making of chemical explosives and bomb casings to the manufacturing of optical supplies.[1] Within two years of Canada's entering the war, the gross national product increased by almost 50 per cent,[2] and unemployment, which had claimed one in five members of the workforce before the war, literally disappeared.[3] By the end of the war, for the first time industry rather than agriculture dominated the economy.

With the rapid transformation of the Canadian economy, one might have expected that, as in previous times, the immigration restrictions imposed during the Depression years would have been eased. This, however, did not happen. Throughout this period, admission to Canada continued to be limited to American and British subjects with adequate capital, European agriculturalists with sufficient means to farm in Canada, wives and minor children of Canadian residents capable of caring for their dependants, and those who had received permission to enter through special orders-in-council. In 1938, the criteria were broadened somewhat to include the fiancées of male residents of Canada who were able to support their intended wives. In 1944, the regulations were similarly widened to permit the immigration of European wives and dependent children of members of the Canadian armed forces.[4] Reflecting the sexual inequities of the times, family sponsorship was not available to Canadian women with adequate means.

In 1937, approximately 12,000 persons emigrated to Canada. The succeeding years saw the numbers rise gradually, to more than 17,000 in 1939. And while this increase was significant when compared with numbers in the Depression years, as noted in the annual report of the Department of Mines and Resources, Immigration Branch, it was 'insignificant when viewed against the extent of Canada and the restless millions of Europe and is in strange contrast to the peak of 382,841 new arrivals of 1913.'[5] With Canada's entry into the war, immigration levels began to plummet to unsurpassed lows, reaching a trough of 7,445 in 1943.[6] Not only were potential immigrants unable to meet capital requirements imposed by the department as a precondition to admission, in many cases because their property and finances had been confiscated by the Nazis, but the conditions of war made the whole application and re-settlement process exceedingly difficult. As war spread throughout the European Continent, and as more and more countries fell to the invading Nazi armies, travel became increasingly difficult, and many application centres were closed. Immigration personnel were withdrawn from Germany and Poland. By 1941, offices in Paris, Antwerp, and Rotterdam were closed, followed by those in Liverpool, Glasgow, and Belfast. In the end, all Canadian immigration work on the Continent was coordinated out of the London office.[7]

An expanding economy did not affect immigrant admissions in this period, but it did affect the number of deportations, which declined dramatically from the Depression years, averaging fewer than 400 annually for the period. Although deportations decreased in number, the manner in which they were effected did not change throughout this time. In fact, during the late 1930s and 1940s, the basic framework of Canadian immigration legislation changed very little. With few exceptions, the regulations passed at the onset of the Depression remained in effect. And, while new restrictive orders-in-council and administrative directives were issued throughout this period, the implementation of these ordinances was very much in keeping with past practices. Immigration policy continued to be a low priority for the government, as exemplified by the fact that, in 1936, the Department of Immigration and Colonization became the Immigration Branch of the newly created Department of Mines and Resources.

What distinguishes this period from the Depression years are how immigration policy was determined and what consequences it carried. During the Depression, immigration policy was largely shaped in response to internal pressures brought about by the collapse of the Canadian economy. In contrast, post-Depression immigration policy was almost entirely fashioned in response to events overseas. Successive restrictions on admission criteria, together with the incarceration of enemy aliens and others deemed dangerous to society in times of war, were justified in relation to the international circumstances of the period. Ironically, it was also external realities – namely, the devastation of Europe and the creation of unprecedented numbers of refugees – that in the end lent credence to the criticisms that Canadian immigration policy had reached new extremes of exclusion and unchecked exercise of discretion.

The genesis of Canada's post-Depression and wartime immigration policy are found in the election of Adolf Hitler as chancellor of Germany in 1933. Shortly after he assumed office, Hitler's government passed several hundred anti-Semitic laws and decrees which severely limited the educational, employment, and professional opportunities of Germany's Jewish population. Together with the passage of the Nuremberg laws in 1935,[8] they sparked an exodus of thousands of Jews from Germany. Hitler's military manoeuvres over the next four years led to more mass migrations. Within six years of his coming to power, Hitler's domestic policies and foreign offensives had created a movement of more than 300,000 mostly Jewish refugees, fleeing into the neighbouring countries of Poland, France, Britain, Belgium, Switzerland, and The Netherlands.[9] For their part, these countries of first asylum sought the assistance of the rest of the Western world, insisting that permanent sanctuary within their territories for all present and prospective refugees was not possible.

In 1938, President Roosevelt convened a thirty-nine-nation conference in Evian, France, to discuss solutions to the refugee dilemma. Canada, like other nations in attendance, was not prepared to commit the country to the provision of substantial assistance.[10] The outcome of the Evian conference was a grim forewarning of the reception that future appeals on behalf of Jewish refugees would receive. The apparent hypocrisy of the Western democracies' condemnation of Hitler's practices towards the Jews while themselves refusing to provide permanent sanctuary was used in German propaganda. As one Berlin publication, *Weltkampf*, observed in 1939, 'We are saying openly that we do not want the Jews while the democracies keep on claiming that they are willing to receive them – then leave the guests out in the cold. Aren't we savages better men after all?'[11]

As the refugee crisis was building overseas, the Canadian economy was slowly recovering from the Depression, and industrialists were once again pressing the government for a more relaxed admissions policy. Immigrants, they argued, were necessary for the development of the country's natural resources and for the expansion of its productive capacity. More immigrants would enlarge Canada's consumer base, leading to an increase in demand for goods and services, and a consequent rise in employment and investment to meet the needs of the larger community. Moreover, in order to be economically viable, the country's immense transportation network and costly government bureaucracies needed to serve and be supported by a larger population.[12]

While the government was prepared to use the permit system to meet the labour requirements of various businesses and industrial enterprises, it was not prepared to make any other exceptions to the general admissibility requirements. Its reluctance to relax immigration restrictions more generally initially stemmed from its concern that the economic upswing that had emerged by 1935 could be temporary, making any significant changes to immigration policy premature. In the early 1940s, once recovery had occurred and full employment was attained, the government refused to relax admission restrictions on the basis that the country had to guard against admitting more members than could be absorbed in an uncertain postwar economy. While this official justification was no doubt a consideration in the refusal to widely liberalize Canada's entry restrictions, it does not account for the country's failure to respond in a more meaningful way to the refugee crisis abroad. As revealed in the public debates of the period and in internal government documents and memoranda,[13] the dominant motive behind Canada's refusal to liberalize entry restrictions was to ensure that the country did not become a haven for the displaced, and mainly Jewish refugees from Nazi aggression.

Within Canada, support for a more humanitarian policy with respect to refugees came from a few members of Parliament, the Jewish community, various church groups and humanitarian organizations, and a small segment of the press. In the House of Commons, it was the Co-operative Commonwealth Federation (CCF), along with two Jewish Liberal MPs, who were the spokespersons for refugees and their relatives in Canada. In the years leading up to and during the war, these MPs consistently demanded, in the House and in meetings with members of King's Cabinet, that Canada join with other democracies of the world in providing sanctuary to the refugees of Fascism.[14] Despite their efforts, they had virtually no influence on the direction of Canadian immigration policy. Nor were the

various religious and humanitarian groups that worked tirelessly on behalf of European refugees any more influential. The Canadian Jewish
Congress, which regularly received appeals from refugees abroad as well
as from family members within Canada, was unsuccessful in its attempts
to influence Canadian attitudes or government policy. The same was
true of the Canadian National Committee on Refugees (CNCR), which
was formed in 1938 and drew its membership from individuals as well as
non-governmental organizations throughout the country.[15] For ten years,
it carried on an educational campaign across the country to promote
public awareness of the refugee issue. It succeeded in setting up a fund
to assist refugees overseas and to help provide settlement assistance to
those who were permitted to come to Canada, but, aside from these efforts, which unquestionably helped individuals, the CNCR was unable to
generate the public support necessary to persuade the government to
ease its restrictive policies.[16]

Press commentary on the immigration issue tended to be uneven and
divided. Generally, throughout the war years, there was little sympathy to
be found in press editorials for the suggestion that Canada open its
doors to refugees. While certain atrocious events overseas, like the brutal
1938 pogrom in Germany known as 'Kristallnacht,' did elicit widespread
calls for a more humanitarian attitude towards refugees and a relaxation
of admission restrictions, these calls were not sustained as the events
and their consequences became old news and faded from the pages of
the press.[17]

There were exceptions. Both *Saturday Night* and the *Winnipeg Free Press*
were consistently critical of the government's policy. The costs of Canada's
exclusionist policy, they claimed, were borne not only by the refugees that
Canada rejected, but also by the society which made it possible: the racial
prejudices reflected in Canadian immigration restrictions ran counter to
the ideals for which Canadians were fighting in the war and kept from the
country those who not only needed protection, but also could contribute
to the country's political capabilities.[18]

Running counter to such appeals and warnings were influential politicians and several high-ranking public servants at home and abroad[19] who
counselled against any easing of immigration restrictions, and a prime
minister who, ever sensitive to public sentiment, concluded that, regardless of their expressions of sympathy, most Canadians would not be willing
to open their doors to Europe's outcasts.

Admissions policy was only part of the total immigration-policy picture.
As relevant, and as revealing, was the treatment of immigrants in Canada

and the limited rights to remain and to live freely that were accorded them. As in the Depression years, an immigrant's right to remain was qualified by his or her ability to be self-sufficient and steer clear of radical politics. During the war, the tenuous nature of Canadian residence was further underscored by the incarceration of thousands of individuals of enemy-alien descent. Canada's involvement in a war brought with it emergency legislation designed to ensure that the war effort was not threatened from within. Security measures included the internment of immigrants from countries with which Canada was at war, as well as the incarceration of those whose political philosophies were seen as a threat to internal security. Wartime exigencies were used to justify the suspension of civil liberties, and thousands of German and Italian immigrants, as well as those with allegedly dangerous fascist, communist, and/or radical-labour sympathies, were summarily incarcerated. Like other aspects of government policies with respect to immigrants, internment was carried out excessively and arbitrarily. Nowhere was this more dramatically displayed than in the forced internment of those of Japanese descent. More than 22,000 Japanese immigrants and Japanese Canadians were removed from their homes along the coastal regions of British Columbia. The majority were relocated to camps in the interior of the province, and most evacuees never returned to the homes and businesses they had worked hard to acquire and maintain. The most massive forced relocation of any group in Canadian history was carried out, despite strong reservations by leading members of the RCMP and armed forces that the Japanese Canadians posed any serious threat to the security of the country. The subsequent confiscation and sale of their property at bargain prices masked far more unsavoury reasons for their internment, such as the economic benefits to be reaped with the removal of the relatively successful Japanese community of British Columbia.[20] While there can be no doubt that Japan's entry into the war sparked fears of a west-coast invasion, it was not the legitimacy of these fears that prompted the government to strip the Japanese Canadians of their properties and their rights to reside freely in the country. The war ignited deep prejudices against those of Japanese ancestry that bad been smouldering in British Columbia since the turn of the century.[21] Their removal *en masse* was justified as the most expeditious way of eliminating any subversive threat that some members of that community might pose and, more important, would pre-empt vigilante action that was threatened against them within the province.

Just as the refusal to admit Jewish refugees was largely rooted in bigotry, so, too, was public support for the extensive internment operations, although not exclusively so. While the invective launched against those of Italian, German, and Japanese ancestry revealed racial prejudices, it is also true that many people genuinely believed that, in times of war, ancestral ties commanded strong allegiances. In other words, a deep communal tie to their countries of origin was believed to predispose those of enemy alien descent to loyalty to the countries against which Canada was at war. Internment was seen as a legitimate way to avoid subversive activity. As for those interned because of suspected communist sympathies, the lack of public condemnation reflected the distrust of communism that was widely shared throughout most segments of Canadian society. Even after Russia became an ally in the war, there remained a deep public antipathy towards those who did not adhere to and promote democratic and liberal economic values.

Canada's exclusionary immigration policy of this period was not without its costs. Most immediate were the costs imposed upon those directly affected by it. Those, who were refused entry, those who were deported, and those who were detained for years suffered undoubtedly the most, many at the cost of their lives. But perhaps more enduring was the legacy that Canada earned as a result of the policies pursued at this time. Canada's acceptance of fewer than 5,000 refugees during the war was one of the worst records of any democracy in providing assistance to the persecuted Jews of Europe.[22] In addition, the massive internment of enemy aliens left a long legacy of bitterness, which, in the case of the Japanese community, has only recently been addressed.[23]

If the period between 1930 and 1945 can accurately be described as the blackest cloud in Canadian immigration history, then its silver lining was undoubtedly the changes that such excesses eventually provoked. At the end of the Depression and during the war, a growing number of individuals and groups registered their concern over the extreme actions of the government. The courts were more frequently called upon to rule on the legitimacy of the government's discretionary policies. And, while most judges were willing to defer to the authority of government officials, a minority increasingly demanded more stringent adherence to statutory provisions and a more limited exercise of discretion. In addition, a growing number of people became disillusioned with traditional parties and turned to the more radical left, with its insistence on respect for individual liberties. The rise in popularity of the CCF[24] helped to bring issues of human rights, which included treatment of immigrants, more to the fore. Perhaps most important, however, was the fact that Canada's treatment of immigrants was inconsistent with the ideals which it supposedly fought for during the war. The blatant denial of admission, citizenship, or residence to those of races and political leanings at odds with the Anglo-Canadian norm came to be seen in later years as entirely inappropriate, given the implications of notions of racial superiority exemplified so grotesquely by the Nazis.

Admissions Policy

In federal politics, immigration policy, although hotly debated from time to time, generally commanded relatively little attention. When the issue was raised, usually by one of the refugee advocates noted earlier, those who spoke against easing Canada's regulations generally punctuated their remarks with expressions of deep concern for the plight of refugees in Europe, yet, at the same time, voiced their opposition to providing sanctuary in veiled and sometimes not so veiled racist terms. The speech of one MP Herve-Edgar Brunelle, in 1939 is but one example. While expressing sympathy for the Jews who were being persecuted in Europe, he wanted to be 'placed on record as one who objects strongly to the entry of Jews, *en masse* or otherwise, into our country.' He continued: 'I hasten to say that I have no brief against the Hebrew race; but since through all the ages they have been the cause, justly or unjustly, of great difficulties in various countries, I say we must take care. History repeats itself.'[25]

For his part, Mackenzie King had a number of responses to questions concerning Canada's position on providing asylum. One of the most common replies was to say that the matter was under consideration and no commitment of any kind had yet been made. As the war progressed, however, and the extent of Nazi atrocities became widely known, King was obliged to explain Canada's position more fully. In the summer of 1943, at which time the Nazi concentration camps and crematoria were fully operational, King, in a lengthy address to the House, explained his government's policy with respect to refugees. In the first place, he noted that most of the refugees were to be found within the ring of territories controlled by the Axis armies. While a few of these 'unfortunates' may be able to escape into neighbouring neutral countries, for the rest, he said, the only deliverance from persecution was in the victory of the Allied armies. 'There is nothing that the allied governments can do to save these hapless people except to win the war as quickly and as completely as possible.' As for those who already were in neutral territories, King could say only that the problem was an international one which demanded an international solution. Until then, Canada would not undertake any bold initiatives of its own. Nor would King state how many refugees Canada would be prepared to receive if an international agreement was concluded, for he indicated that it would depend on such things as: the availability of transport, the possibility of repatriation at the war's conclusion, the employment possibilities in Canada, and internal security concerns such as the need to protect Canada from the admission of German spies and secret agents. And while he could not give exact figures for the number of refugees Canada had admitted since Hitler's rise to power, because immigration statistics did not distinguish between refugees and immigrants, King nonetheless asserted that, between 1932 and 1943, most of the 39,000 immigrants who entered Canada were refugees.[26]

King's position with respect to the refugee issue was influenced by several factors. Largely determinative was his assessment of public opinion with respect to the refugee question. The lack of support for the easing of immigration restrictions found in the press was one indication that any liberalization of the current policy would not be welcomed by the Canadian public. Supporting this assumption were the results of a number of public opinion polls conducted throughout the war years which revealed a widely held belief that European Jews would not adapt well to Canada.[27] There was ample other evidence available to King which pointed to the fact that Jews were not welcome immigrants to Canada. Across the country Jews faced restrictions in where they could work, live, and spend their recreational time. There were restrictions on entry into certain teaching and nursing professions; bars to their advancement existed in many business enterprises, most notably in real estate, brokerage houses, banks, and loan companies; and there were few Jews in management positions of major industrial enterprises. They also faced restrictive covenants prohibiting their purchase of certain lands and houses, their use of various recreational centres, and their membership in many private clubs.[28]

King was also fully aware of the public mood in Quebec, where the most strident anti-immigrant sentiment was found. The issue of immigration had always been an inflammatory one in that province, since many French Canadians worried that anything other than a highly restrictive policy would lead to their being overwhelmed by the weight of numbers of non-French immigrants. Within the context of the European refugee crisis, the issue took on a particularly ugly face, given the widespread anti-Semitism that flourished within the province.[29]

Approximately one-third of the Canadian Jewish population of 60,000 lived in Quebec. Anti-Semitism within Quebec had been visible since the mid-nineteenth century, although Lita-Rose Betcherman maintains that, until the 1930s, Jews and French Canadians lived in relative harmony. Antagonism towards Jews intensified, however, as the number of Jews increased and competition in shopkeeping and the professions grew. Jacques Langlais and David Rome explain the rise in anti-Semitism in the 1930s within the context of the economic crisis and the growing fear, especially within the Catholic Church, of a social revolution within Quebec. The latter was fuelled by the rise in popularity of the Communist Party of Canada. In their inability to stem the economic Depression and the growth of communism, the political and religious leaders 'sought a scapegoat- in this case the Jews.'[30]

Anti-Semitism in Quebec was revealed in many different ways throughout the 1930s, in public debates, in the exclusions of Jews from various organizations and clubs, and in the widely supported movements to boycott Jewish businesses and to prohibit the admission of Jewish immigrants. As early as 1933, one ultra-nationalist group, Ligue d'Action Nationale, had petitioned the government to exclude Jewish immigrants who were characterized as an 'element accused of Marxism and Communism by Germany, and which itself cannot be an asset for Canada, being by its faith, its customs and its character unassimilable, a source of division and dispute, and thus of weakness for the Canadian people.'[31]

Quebec MPs were acutely sensitive to the anti-immigration sentiment that was widely held within their province, and in representing their constituencies they were resolutely opposed to any suggestion that Canada relax its immigration policy.[32] Within his Cabinet, King was advised by his Quebec caucus that he simply could not afford to open Canada's doors more widely, regardless of how isolated or exceptional the case. Should he waver on this, he risked losing their support, and also electoral support within Quebec, upon which the future electoral success of the Liberal party depended.[33]

While public attitudes favouring the maintenance of a restrictive immigration policy to a large extent accounts for the government's persistent refusal to relax immigration regulations, it does not explain why thousands of refugees who did qualify for admission under the narrow requirements were nevertheless denied it. Here one must look to the Immigration Branch, and in particular its director, Frederick Blair. Blair had been involved in the various departments charged with the administration of the Immigration Act for more than thirty years before he was appointed director of the Immigration Branch in 1936.[34] He had always been a strong proponent of a selective immigration policy, one that encouraged the immigration of 'preferred' immigrants from Britain and other areas of northern Europe, and limited those of the 'unpreferred class.' Jews, in his estimation were clearly in the latter category, for in his opinion they had a tendency to lie, and force themselves upon others, and therefore the Canadian government had to be particularly vigilant in resisting their attempts to enter Canada. In 1938, Blair personally assumed the responsibility of processing many of the Jewish applicants that had been approved by immigration officers and railway colonization agents overseas. Of the thousands of such applications he received, relatively few passed his scrutiny. As he acknowledged, it would have been easy to obtain tens of thousands of immigrants simply by relaxing the barriers erected in 1930 to protect the Dominion from an influx of surplus labour: 'If quantity rather than quality was the objective sought, its attainment was simplicity itself.'[35] The many directives he sent to officers overseas made it clear that regulations were to be strictly interpreted to ensure that as few Jews as possible met the legislative requirements. Blair's influence over admissions policy was considerable largely because the minister responsible for immigration, Thomas Crerar, was not particularly interested in such matters. Several senior bureaucrats, such as Norman Robertson, under-secretary of state for External Affairs, and his assistant, Hume Wrong, objected to Blair's intransigence towards the admission of refugees, but, in the absence of support within Cabinet, they exerted relatively little influence.[36]

RAISING THE IMPEDIMENTS TO ENTRY

It is difficult to determine the precise character of admissions to Canada just prior to and during the Second World War, for the immigration statistics provided by the Immigration Branch veil or simply fail to illuminate the true immigration picture at this time. For example, neither branch statistics nor its annual reports distinguish between immigrants and refugees, making it possible for both King and his senior immigration officer to claim from time to time, in the absence of corroborating statistics, that the majority of immigrants were refugees. Despite these assertions, however, close examination of the Immigration Branch's own figures reveal that, between 1938 and 1945, the vast majority of immigrants who entered Canada were British and American nationals. In fact, between 1938 and 1940 these groups made up approximately 57 per cent of admissions, and in each of the following five years their proportion increased to 98 per cent of all those entering.[37]

The discrimination that these statistics expose on their face is more graphically illustrated in the history of the individual movements of immigrants that the country readily admitted and embraced and those that it resisted. While the Canadian government, with the full' support of most of the electorate, would in 1939 welcome the entry of more than 6,000 British women and child war evacuees, and would later, in 1944, readily admit without restriction discharged U.K. service personnel and their dependants, it would delay, obstruct, and simply reject thousands of requests for the admission of Jewish refugees whose systematic annihilation was otherwise inevitable. Between 1939 and 1945, while more than 40,000 British nationals, more than 30,000 American citizens, and 15,000 nationals from other countries were admitted to Canada, fewer than 5,000 Jewish refugees were offered sanctuary.[38]

Of the approximately 100,000 immigrants who arrived in Canada between 1937 and 1945, the majority were wives and dependent children of Canadian residents, and not, as the government frequently contended, refugees. Farmers with capital comprised the next largest group, accounting for approximately 30 per cent of admissions during this time. A large proportion of the remainder were made up of industrialists with the capital to set up new industries in Canada, and technicians and skilled workers admitted by special permits. In 1944, by which time the fortunes of war had turned in the Allies' favour, the largest group of arrivals to Canada were the dependants of Canadian service personnel abroad.[39]

As restrictive as admission regulations were, it soon became apparent that additional measures would have to be imposed to ensure that the flow of refugees was kept to an absolute minimum. One of the first of such measures was the raising of the capital requirement for prospective immigrants, a measure that was effected simply by direction from the Immigration Branch. In 1938, the capital requirement for Jewish applicants was raised from $5,000 to $20,000, and by the end of the year even that amount was insufficient. Jewish agriculturalists who met the capital requirement were routinely rejected because, according to Blair and his officials, 'experience had shown that the Jewish people do not ... take to farming.' Jewish industrialists also faced insurmountable obstacles. Frustrated immigration agents reported that Jewish industrialists with as much as $170,000 to invest in Canada regularly were being denied admission.[40]

A further barrier to Jewish immigration was erected in 1940 with the passing of an order-in-council prohibiting the entry of people who were nationals of countries with which Canada was at war.[41] Although the order was probably not intended to have this effect, Blair nevertheless made it clear that his department would not consider applications of German nationals or nationals of German-occupied territories, regardless of whether they were refugees or not. Thus, although the regulation was passed to keep out possible spies and foreign agents, Blair's own directive had a much wider ambit, excluding those who had been victims of enemy oppression.[42] Even refugees intending to merely transit Canada *en route* elsewhere, such as the United States and countries in Latin America, faced insurmountable barriers. It was Blair's position that, should Canada issue transit visas to refugees, it would simply be the thin edge of the wedge. Once in Canada, they would not want to leave. Moreover, he reasoned, once some took advantage of the ability to transit through Canada, word would get out of this possibility, and then there would be many more people 'clamouring for entry.'[43]

The extent to which Jewish applicants were routinely rejected, regardless of their abilities or financial worth, has been well chronicled by Irving Abella and Harold Troper.[44] It is clear from their work and from memoirs of the period that not all immigration bureaucrats shared Blair's antipathy towards the entry of Jewish refugees. The manner in which even the most qualified refugees were refused was deeply disturbing to those within Canada acting on their behalf, and also various immigration officers who recommended such applicants for admission.[45] Nevertheless, the Immigration Act invested the minister responsible for immigration with extensive authority over the implementation of policy, which was in turn delegated to the director of the Immigration Branch, Frederick Blair. Given such delegation of responsibility, and in the absence of any legislative or judicial check on the exercise of such authority, there was little that those working on behalf of Jewish refugees could do other than to try to secure the entry of Jewish exiles through their inclusion in special groups and movements authorized through branch directives and specific orders-in-council.

SPECIAL APPEALS AND MOVEMENTS

The Sudeten Refugee Movement

In September 1938, the Sudeten area of Czechoslovakia was ceded to Germany, precipitating the exodus of 80,000 people. The majority of those displaced were Czechoslovakian citizens who proceeded to seek accommodation and employment in the part of the country still under Czechoslovakian control. Approximately 15 per cent of those displaced, however, were German-speaking Sudeten people, most of whom were Roman Catholics and/or social democrats unwilling to live under German

Fascist domination, yet at the same time unable to live in the remainder of the country under Czechoslovakian leadership. For them, Czechoslovakia was not a realistic place of refuge not only because of the overcrowding endemic there, but also because of the anti-German hostility that was widespread within that community. For its part, the strongly nationalistic and conservative Czech government committed itself to helping its own Czech nationals by seeking British assistance in the permanent resettlement elsewhere of the Sudeten Germans.[46] Britain responded by providing a £10–million loan to Czechoslovakia, a portion of which was to be used for the overseas resettlement of the 10,000 to 20,000 displaced Sudetlanders. It then commenced discussions with the dominions as to the possibility of their accepting a portion of these refugees. Canada answered the request by sending to Prague agents of the two major Canadian railways, the CNR and CPR, to inquire into the suitability of the Sudeten refugees for immigration to Canada. These agents reported favourably on the prospective immigrants, describing the Sudetlanders as good workers, anxious to make a home in Canada, but unlikely to qualify under existing admission regulations since few of the refugees had adequate agricultural experience and/or sufficient financial resources. The Canadian high commissioner to Britain, Vincent Massey, also endorsed the acceptance of a sizeable number of Sudeten refugees on the basis that their professional skills and farming experience would be of benefit to Canada and, being predominately Roman Catholic, they were more 'desirable' than other refugees. In accepting them, he reasoned, Canada would be in a better position to reject the others.[47]

After protracted negotiations, the Canadian government offered to accept 1,200 Sudeten families, providing that the cost of their resettlement was borne by Britain and coordinated by the CNR and the CPR, who would be responsible for soliciting the approval of the Western provinces within whose territories the refugees would settle. The Western provincial governments were not enthusiastic about the plans, most refusing to sell Crown land for the purpose of settling the refugees, and all opposing the settlement of the refugees in block communities.[48] In the end, the Sudeten refugees that finally made their way to Canada were settled on railway lands in northern Saskatchewan and in the Peace River district of British Columbia.

Despite the urging of the initial investigatory team that Canada quickly evacuate as many refugees as possible from Czechoslovakia, the Canadian government insisted on proceeding cautiously until all financial and land arrangements were in place. The decision proved to be disastrous for those refugees willing and able to come, for, in March 1939, Germany moved into the remainder of Czechoslovakia, closing off all access routes to the country and making it impossible for the Sudeten Germans within to be resettled elsewhere. Although several hundred Sudeten refugee families had been temporarily admitted to Britain the previous year, most of these families did not qualify for the Canadian Sudeten family resettlement scheme since many were missing family members and Canada insisted that only complete family units would be eligible. Consequently, only 303 refugee families and 72 single men were admitted to Canada under the Sudeten refugee movement.[49]

At the same time as Sudeten Germans were on their way to Canada, another smaller group of destitute refugees was at the gates, requesting admission. The group consisted of slightly more than 900 refugees, mostly German Jews, who in the spring of 1939 had embarked on the ocean liner *St Louis,* bound for Cuba. Upon their reaching Cuba, however, the Cuban government would not honour their visas and prohibited them from landing. In a desperate attempt to find sanctuary, they made appeals to several countries in Central and South America, all which of which refused them refuge. A month later, forced out of Havana harbour, the *St Louis* headed for Canada. The United States made it clear that the passengers would not be welcome in its harbours and, to underscore this fact, a gunboat was sent to monitor the ship as it made its way north.[50] Despite appeals made by several leading Canadians, the Canadian government also refused to relax regular admission requirements. The last possibility of refuge having being extinguished, the *St Louis* was forced to return to Germany.

Child Refugees

Throughout the course of the war, several major appeals were launched by various voluntary organizations for the admission to Canada of children in danger overseas. The warmest and most generous response to such appeals was given to British children, while Jewish Continental child refugees faced the same obstacles to their admission as their elders.

In 1939, the Canadian National Committee for Refugees (CNCR) and the Canadian Friends Service Committee successfully petitioned the government to provide sanctuary for 100 Jewish child refugees temporarily residing in Britain. The government agreed to the request on the understanding that the costs of the program would be borne by various voluntary organizations, and not by the federal government. The entry of Britain and Canada into the war the following year, however, disrupted the plans for the acceptance of the Jewish children. This movement was soon overshadowed by appeals within Canada and Britain for the temporary admission of British women and children to remove them from the dangers of war at home. The scheme won widespread support from families across Canada and, according to the Immigration Branch, more than 50,000 Canadians offered to house the war guests until the cessation of hostilities.[51] Against this backdrop of public sympathy, the government soon agreed to the admission of 5,000 British children and their mothers, the costs of ocean travel to be borne by the British government, and the resettlement expenses in Canada to be assumed by the Canadian government.[52] And although the Canadian Jewish community had already undertaken extensive preparations for the reception and care of the 100 Jewish refugee children, government officials made it clear that Continental children would not be part of the British evacuation scheme. One of the reasons, according to Blair, was that many of the refugee children in Britain may have had surviving parents elsewhere in Europe. The admission of such children would thus inevitably result in the later admission of their families, something that Canada was unwilling to undertake.[53] In the end, more than 4,500 British children and 1,000 mothers came to Canada.[54] While some British-born Jews were included in the movement, Continental refugee children were not. The movement was abruptly terminated in 1940, when two ships carrying children to Canada were torpedoed.

Although their initial appeal for the admission of Jewish refugee children had met with disappointing results, the Jewish community was not deterred from seeking government assistance on behalf of Jewish children on several other occasions. In 1942, it appealed to the Canadian government to accept Jewish children in Vichy-controlled France who were destined for concentration camps. The Canadian government agreed to accept 500 children with the proviso that their entry would be temporary and that all the resettlement costs would be borne by the Canadian Jewish community. Once the community proved able to meet its commitments, a further 500 children would be admitted on the same terms. The movement was unable to proceed, however, owing to the severing of diplomatic relations with the Vichy government in November 1942 and Germany's move into unoccupied France. Subsequent requests to rescue twenty children of the several hundred who had escaped into neighbouring Spain and Portugal were denied by the Canadian government. In contrast to the American government, which offered asylum to all who were under sixteen years of age, the Canadian government refused to admit any of the older children as part of the French child-admission scheme. Blair withheld his approval on the grounds that the children were probably with their parents, and the French children's movement was limited to those whose parents had died or who had been deported. As an exasperated Hume Wrong, deputy under-secretary of state for External Affairs, pointed out to his colleague Norman Robertson, 'Mr. Blair resolutely sticks to his point that the Jewish children now in Spain and Portugal do not come within the terms of our agreement of last September. He is technically right but his only argument against modifying the terms of the agreement is that it is the settled Canadian policy to deal with European families as family units and not to separate children from their parents. We did exactly this of course in taking British children as "war guests" in 1940.'[55]

The children's rescue scheme, however, was not totally abandoned, for in 1943 the British government and the International Committee for Refugees began negotiations concerning the possible evacuation of the remaining Jewish children in France to Switzerland, where they could then be moved to other resettlement countries. The American government endorsed the plan and provided 4,000 entrance visas for any children who might be able to leave France for Switzerland. Canada refused to participate on the grounds that the children would be unable to meet health requirements, and therefore could be a threat to public health, and because it could involve Canada's accepting other family members at a later date.[56] The children were, in the end, unable to leave France because of the Vichy government's refusal to issue exit visas.

Canada's response is illustrative of its approach to the refugee crisis more generally. Between 1939 and 1945, Canada was approached numerous times to provide sanctuary to children in life-threatening situations. Within a six month period, the country had warmly accepted 4,500 British children. During the next five years, it would commit itself to accepting only 1,000 Jewish children from the Continent and, in the end, provided sanctuary to none of them. And, while the failure of the French child-rescue scheme cannot be blamed on Canada, its minimalist response to the crisis of Continental Jewish children more generally can be contrasted with its response to the British child-evacuation scheme.

British Internees

Shortly after the British child-evacuation scheme was under way, the British government once again approached Canada with an immigration request. This time it concerned enemy aliens who had been interned in

Britain and were now considered a threat to its security. In the spring of 1940, during the Nazi assault on Holland, Belgium, and France, Britain interned more than 30,000 residents of German and Austrian descent. Included within this round-up were both Nazi sympathizers and refugees from Nazi oppression. In approaching Canada, Britain requested that Canada admit for the duration of the war 7,000 of the internees considered to be dangerous Nazis. The Canadian government accepted the request. In proceeding with the arrangements, however, it became clear to British officials that they would not be able to fill the quota with dangerous aliens. Having rounded up 2,500 suspected German civilians and 3,000 German prisoners of war, the officials decided to make up the remainder with 2,000 refugees. The mixing of refugees with those who were, or sympathized with, their oppressors was at best an insensitive mistake and one which would not be quickly remedied.[57]

Upon their arrival in Canada in July 1940, the internees were sent to Canadian internment camps which had been set up to hold enemy aliens and suspected Axis sympathizers in Canada. Even after becoming aware of the inclusion of refugees within the British movement, the Canadian government refused to release them from the camps, or to treat them differently from the other prisoners held there. It did, however, request that the British government send a representative to investigate the situation. Accordingly, Alexander Paterson, the former commissioner of prisons in England, came to Canada in the spring of the following year. After conducting interviews with all the refugee internees, Paterson concluded that half would prefer to return to Britain, while the other half preferred to wait in Canada until entry into the United States could be secured. For its part, the Canadian government was not inclined to release any of the internees until their passage elsewhere was guaranteed.

In his moving memoir of the years spent in Canadian internment camps, one Jewish refugee, Eric Koch, recalls the difficulties that the refugees encountered there.[58] One of the most difficult things for them to accept was having to live in the same quarters as those they considered their grievous enemies, and, moreover, to be treated as enemies themselves. Particularly when the consequences of Nazi atrocities were well publicized, the presence of Nazi sympathizers in the camps became unbearable for the refugees. In one camp, the authorities' attempt to remedy the situation by announcing that Aryans would be separated from others simply displayed insensitivity to the composition of the refugee population that was equally intolerable. As noted by one internee, Paul Heller, the fear among the refugees was that 'Aryan' anti-Fascist refugees would be carted off to a Nazi camp. 'Then the people who left Germany for reasons of principle, and not because as Jews they had no choice, would be locked up with their mortal enemies.'[59] In the end, the planned separation was not effected, primarily because of the inmates' refusal to cooperate in their classification as Jews or Gentiles.

The camps were run along military lines. Interned refugees were treated the same as those considered enemies of the state, and generally special concessions were not made for refugees whose religious beliefs, for example, made working on particular days sinful. Added to the difficulties of camp life was a persistent anti-Semitism among some of the officers, which Alexander Paterson found particularly disturbing. As he reported, 'sitting day after day in a small cell through the open window came the shouts of the guards and sometimes of the officers, alluding to the fact that the internees were Jews and commenting, not infrequently, upon the correctness of their birth.'[60]

For over a year, the Canadian government refused to release any of the refugee internees who had not returned to England. Their continued incarceration was not for security concerns, but because the Cabinet envisioned a negative reaction should the mostly Jewish refugees be released into Canadian society. Finally, in May 1941, the Cabinet agreed to consider individual releases, providing sponsors were available to guarantee their maintenance. Priority was given to students, and men qualified to work in industry or agriculture.[61] Students were paroled into the custody of individual sponsors who offered to care and financially support them. Workers were released to firms engaged in war-related production or to farmers in need of farm help. Blair scrutinized every application with the same rigour and attention to detail he showed to Jewish refugee applications more generally. According to Koch, 'if anyone said he had seventeen years of experience as an *animal raw produce sorter* he only may have had sixteen years. If Blair found out, that was the end of it and the man was declared unreleasable. If anyone wrote down that he was a farm labourer with considerable experience, Blair's immigration officers would inspect his hands to see whether they showed traces of manual labour.'[62]

After two years, half the refugee internees had returned to Britain, and 600 had been released into Canadian society as 'friendly aliens enjoying temporary liberty in Canada.' By December 1942, more than 300 were still incarcerated, a hundred of whom were scheduled to return to Britain, and many of the remainder being people with specialized skills not needed by Canadian industry. Finally, in December 1943, two and a half years after they had been shipped to Canada, an order-in-council was passed authorizing the issuance of temporary immigration permits to all the refugees transferred to Canada from Britain.[63]

Refugees in Europe and Japan

As the situation in Europe became more desperate for the victims of Nazi persecution, and as the countries of first asylum became more burdened with their burgeoning refugee populations, Canada was increasingly pressed to relax its immigration criteria in favour of providing sanctuary to at least relatively small groups of refugees. And, although for the most part the Canadian government refused to assent to such requests, it did make a few concessions over the years in order to appease its allies, and in particular to accommodate Britain. Thus, in 1941, in response to a request from Britain that Canada take 3,000 to 4,000 Allied nationals, primarily Polish and Czech officials and their families in Europe, Canada agreed to accept 1,000 persons, providing that the costs of their resettlement were borne by their governments, and that not too many of the complement were Jews.[64]

The Canadian government similarly responded to a plea made in 1940 by the Polish government-in-exile requesting that Canada accept 2,000 Polish refugees. After considerable deliberation, King and his Cabinet decided the following year to permit the temporary admission into Canada of 1,000 Polish refugees, providing that the Polish government-in-exile assumed the costs, agreed to their repatriation after the war, and offered assurance that the number of Jews would be limited.[65] Within weeks of this decision, the Canadian government was approached by Japan, not yet allied with Germany, to join with other nations in relieving it of its refugee population. By 1941, the number of refugees arriving in Japan from Europe was increasing at a rate that alarmed the Japanese authorities. With 2,000 refugees within its territory and hundreds more on their way, the Japanese government threatened to close its doors until those within Japan had been given sanctuary elsewhere. It also threatened to deport those within Japan who did not have exit permits for other countries.

Of the 2,000 refugees in Japan, most were Jews. One-quarter of the total were Jews who had fled eastern Poland in order to avoid being sent to concentration camps in Siberia. Despite Blair's concern that to admit any of the refugees inevitably meant Canada would have to take in many more later, the Cabinet decided to accept seventy-nine Polish Jewish refugees, stipulating, however, that the refugees would come under the 1,000 Polish refugee program, subject to its terms and conditions, and would not be considered as an additional refugee movement.[66]

Several hundred refugees admitted to Canada at this time were selected as much on the basis of their usefulness in Canada as on their desperate need for refuge. In fact, the speed with which refugee requests were processed in large part depended on the need Canada had for their particular skills. A case in point involved seventy Polish engineers and technicians and their dependants who had fled Poland and were temporarily resident in Vichy France. In September 1941, the Polish government-in-exile, in consultation with various Canadian industries, approached the Canadian government, requesting that these refugees be admitted into Canada. Within several weeks, the proposed movement was approved. Interested industries agreed to advance funds to pay for the costs of transportation, these amounts later to be deducted from the refugee workers' wages. The Polish government-in-exile agreed to support those refugees who were not employed within four weeks of their arrival.

Despite the relative speed with which the negotiations were concluded, it was not fast enough to save those who became trapped in France following the Vichy government's decision in January 1942 to prohibit the emigration of all men under the age of forty-five. Unlike the French children's movement, which also was thwarted by the Vichy government's unwillingness to issue the necessary exit permits, the Polish skilled-technicians program was not altogether abandoned by the Canadian government. Unable to secure the needed labour from France, the Canadian government subsequently admitted several hundred Polish scientists and engineers temporarily resident in Britain. These refugees came to Canada under the same provisions as those intended for their compatriots in Vichy France.[67]

The government's quick and positive response to the admission of several hundred skilled Polish refugee workers is to be contrasted with its response to the plight of Jewish refugees who managed to flee from France to the Iberian countries of Spain and Portugal. In 1943, estimates of the number of exiles within these territories varied from 1,300 to 3,000 mostly Jewish refugees. Although the Iberian countries were neutral at this time, there was considerable concern that they could in future be annexed by Germany. The security of the refugees within these territories was therefore in jeopardy, and so the Jewish community in Canada, along with other refugee activists, requested that the Canadian government provide these refugees with sanctuary, the costs of which would be borne by the voluntary sector.

The request to assist the refugees in Spain and Portugal coincided with the prime minister's speech in July 1943 in which he reported to Parliament on the conclusions reached at a recent international conference held in Bermuda on the refugee problem. Although the conference provided no concrete promises of sanctuary by the participating Allied governments, broad statements of principle were endorsed, to which Canada agreed. On the problem of refugees in neutral countries, the conference made recommendations designed, according to King, 'to maintain the refugees in their territories whose removal could not be arranged.' King went on to say that Canada would participate in international efforts to provide temporary sanctuary for such refugees where transportation was available, although the exact number of refugees it would assist, he maintained, could not be determined at that time.[68] Following King's statement in the House, Cabinet agreed to the admission of up to 200 refugee families from the Iberian Peninsula, of whom 75 per cent would be Jews, on the understanding that the costs of the movement were to be borne by the Jewish community or international refugee-relief organizations. It was also agreed that the exact number of families permitted to enter under the program should not be publicly revealed, lest there be a negative response to the initiative.[69]

The effort to keep the numbers secret was not successful and, as feared, public controversy erupted. The strongest reaction came from Quebec, and one of the most vocal opponents was Maurice Duplessis, leader of the Union Nationale and soon to become premier of the province, who railed that Liberal candidates were being financed by Zionists in return for the admission of 100,000 Jewish refugees in Quebec.[70] The controversy was also aired in the House of Commons. According to Donald Avery, the RCMP registered its concerns, particularly with respect to those refugees sponsored by the Montreal Jewish Labour Committee, who had alleged subversive tendencies.[71]

Despite this protest, the government continued with the implementation of the project. The guidelines established by the Immigration Branch, however, were sufficiently severe to ensure that the movement of refugees would not be a significant one. And unfortunately for the refugees, the immigration officer sent to Lisbon to coordinate the program, Odilon Cormier, was no more inclined to see it work effectively than were some of his superiors within the branch.[72] Although the screening of applicants was eventually relaxed from the very rigid approach initially applied, in the end fewer than 200 families eventually made it to Canada. In his annual report, the minister, A.L. Jolliffe, observed that 162 families were admitted to Canada under the scheme. Jolliffe did not elaborate on the failure to reach the target of 200, other than to say that it 'is understood the numbers of families available is comparatively small.'[73]

Internal Security Measures

Among the myriad concerns facing the government upon Canada's declaration of war in 1939 was how to deal with the tens of thousands of residents who were from countries with which Canada was now at war. The government pursued two avenues. It launched a massive propaganda campaign to enlist support for the war effort and, in doing so, targeted ethnic communities as a means of fostering their cooperation. It also passed regulations pursuant to the War Measures Act,[74] empowering it to compel the registration of all residents of enemy-alien birth and to incarcerate those considered to be a potential security risk.

THE PROPAGANDA CAMPAIGN

The propaganda work of the government throughout the war had several objectives. Not only was it aimed at generating support for the war effort generally, but it was also designed to foster loyalty to Canada among immigrant groups and to encourage tolerance among native Canadians of the foreigners in their midst. The latter objective was a pressing one for the government, since public hostility towards enemy aliens was made manifest immediately upon Canada's entry into the war. Not only had hundreds of enemy aliens been fired from their jobs following Canada's declaration of war, but vigilante groups started forming throughout the country, threatening to take unilateral action against immigrants suspected of subversive activity. The situation became particularly acute following the German invasion of Holland and Belgium in the spring of 1940, which was rumoured to have been aided by fifth columnists. Senior government ministers were warned by security officers that the mounting public hysteria could erupt into serious riots, and possible loss of life. Information was thus disseminated to assure Canadians that not all enemy aliens were disloyal to Canada. Promotional work among immigrant communities was also undertaken to counteract what was believed to be the dangerous dissemination of communist ideology. Some government officials felt that far too many immigrants were becoming enamoured with communist doctrine and, if left unchecked, these individuals could undermine public support for the war effort and might even become enemy agents. One way to counteract this was to distribute widely, in several different languages, information about the principles Canada stood for and the reasons for its commitment to the war effort.[75]

The government's propaganda work was carried out at several levels. Through the Bureau of Public Information, replaced by the Wartime Information Board in 1942, news stories, radio broadcasts, articles, and pamphlets in different languages were disseminated across the country, aimed at explaining the war and Canada's role in it. These efforts to mould public opinion also urged unity in the fight for democracy and emphasized that different ethnic groups in Canada posed no threat to Canadian solidarity.[76] Moreover, following the anxieties unleashed in the spring of 1940, the government established the Department of National War Services, which was also given the responsibility for disseminating government information. The department's Nationalities Branch was created to undertake extensive information work among Canada's ethnic communities, generally to encourage ethnic minorities to identify more closely with the rest of the Canadian community, and more particularly to lend their support to the war effort.

According to historian N.F. Dreisziger, the significance of the creation of the Nationalities Branch and its advisory body, the Committee on Cooperation in Canadian Citizenship (CCCC), was that it marked 'a perceptible watershed between an age when "ethnics" or "ethnic populations" were generally ignored, and the post-war era when increasing attention was paid to them, not only at election time but on an ongoing basis.'[77] Dreisziger goes on to suggest that these bureaucratic developments were a small but vital aspect of 'the general process whereby ethnic minorities in Canada have acquired a higher profile and greater influence in the country's national affairs.'[78]

Dreisziger's conclusions are not without controversy. William Young maintains that the government's attempt to foster Canadian solidarity did not enhance the influence of ethnic minorities, and was, by and large, a failure for several reasons. He claims that paternalistic attitudes and an anti-communist bias prevalent within the Nationalities Branch and the CCCC undermined their credibility with various ethnic communities, and at times exacerbated divisiveness among rival groups. This partiality was evident in the provision, with Cabinet approval, of secret subsidies to those segments of the ethnic press considered loyal to the government and in the attempts that the Department of National War Services made to secure private contributions to these periodicals. Such favouritism drew the ire of other ethnic groups, as did the refusal of the Nationalities Branch to accept new Canadians onto its advisory committee.[79]

In addition to the partisan way financial support was given to various ethnic organizations, Young maintains, often the information publicly disseminated by the government agencies was contradictory and counter-productive to its overall aims. In particular, he cites warnings issued by the Bureau of Public Information regarding the possibility that German fifth columnists might have escaped detection and internment. Young contrasts this with other circulars emanating from the bureau aimed at counteracting public hostility towards those of German and Italian descent.[80] As well, government-sponsored information, which character-ized the Japanese as a race which could not be trusted, also reinforced negative stereotypes.[81]

That government's efforts failed to solicit the ethnic support in the war effort as intended seems to be borne out by the small amount of ethnic contributions to the Victory Loan drive.[82] That it failed to temper anti-alien sentiment also seems evident from responses to public-opinion polls and from the Wartime Information Board's own conclusion in 1943 that prejudice towards foreigners had grown.[83] Nevertheless, while the government's propaganda endeavour may not have bridged the gap that divided segments of the Anglo- and French-Canadian populations from many ethnic communities, its efforts revealed a willingness to work with ethnic communities rather than merely attempting to marginalize or silence them. This approach was one that would be developed in the post-war years.

INTERNMENT

Unlike during the First World War, Canadians had no illusions that the second Continental conflict would be swift and decisive. Too many lives had been lost in the first conflagration, and too many from that time were still alive to remember the enormous personal sacrifices that war entailed for there to be much heady optimism about the current confrontation. As they had in the First World War, however, many people immediately iden-tified with the Allied cause. Canada's adversaries became their personal foes. Germans were the enemies, be they in Europe or at home, and the government was soon inundated with demands to intern them lest they sabotage the war effort in favour of their fatherland.

It was within this context that the Defence of Canada Regulations (DOCR) were passed under the authority of the War Measures Act on 3 September 1939, a week before Canada formally entered the war. There were a total of sixty-four regulations within the DOCR, which in their entirety conferred upon the government enormous powers to restrict and control the rights and liberties of both Canadians and resident immigrants. Under these regulations, the government was given authority to arrest without warrant and intern without trial persons suspected of subversive intent; to declare certain religious, political, and community organizations illegal; to censor the press; and to confiscate property.[84] Regulation 21 gave the minister of Justice the authority to detain 'any particular person' in Canada to prevent the person from 'acting in any manner prejudicial to the public safety of the State.' The government was thus empowered to detain without trial both immigrants and Canadian citizens on the mere suspicion of hostile intent, rather than on proof of such.[85] Under regulation 24, all immigrants from enemy countries were required to report monthly to the local police. In 1940, this regulation was broadened to include all Canadian citizens from enemy countries who had been naturalized after September 1922.[86]

The DOCR were invoked frequently during the war years to detain both immigrants and other persons who were believed to be members of organizations deemed hostile to the war effort, such as various Nazi, Fascist, and Communist organizations and clubs. Also under the DOCR, used in combination with other regulations, many of these associations were banned, their publications stopped, some of their properties confiscated, and many of their alleged supporters detained.[87] Restrictions on freedom of speech and freedom of association experienced by radical political activists were applied to others as well, for the DOCR also authorized the internment of those whose statements the authorities considered 'would or might be prejudicial to the safety of the state or the efficient prosecution of the war.'[88] So it was that Camillien Houde, the mayor of Montreal, was taken into custody in 1940 after having publicly denounced the compulsory national-service registration as simply a prelude to conscription. Houde remained interned for three years.

Not only were the regulations sweeping in scope, but they also were free from judicial or parliamentary scrutiny. The right to legal counsel and *habeas corpus* relief were suspended so that the detention was not open to review by any court.[89] Moreover, unlike the Emergency Powers Act of Britain, in which every order under it had to be submitted to Parliament for approval, and which itself lapsed after one year unless renewed on recommendation of Parliament, the DOCR and its enabling legislation, the War Measures Act, contained no such safeguards.[90] In fact, the War Measures Act had been on the statute books since 1914, when it was first introduced by the Conservative government of Sir Robert Borden.[91]

Under the terms of the act, the Cabinet was authorized to make a proclamation which 'shall be conclusive evidence that a state of war, invasion
or insurrection, real or apprehended, exists,' and it was given the power
to make such orders and regulations as it 'may deem necessary or advisable for the security, defence, peace, order and welfare of Canada.'[92] The
regulations promulgated pursuant to the Canadian emergency legislation
could be revised simply by Cabinet fiat. As a result, the DOCR were often
amended, sometimes weekly, which made it almost impossible for local
enforcement agencies to interpret or exercise them consistently across
the country. The absence of review only exacerbated the problem, as well
as leaving the DOCR vulnerable to abuse.[93]

There were essentially two waves of internment activities throughout
the war. The first followed directly upon Canada's declaration of war and
involved the incarceration of nearly 2,500 people. According to government records, close to two-thirds of these were persons of pro-Nazi or
pro-Italian sympathies, the majority of whom were of German and Italian
descent, respectively. Another third were reportedly interned for being
pro-Japanese, and, of the remaining five per cent who were incarcerated
for their alleged communist activities, one-third were of Ukrainian origin.[94] In 1942, just as most of those in the first wave were being released,
the government embarked on a more massive internment operation
which resulted in the forced relocation and incarceration of 22,000 persons of Japanese descent.

In 1940, there were more than half a million people of German descent living in Canada, comprising the largest single ethnic group, apart
from those of British or French extraction, in the country. Two-thirds of
Canada's German-speaking residents originated outside of Germany.
Many had come as refugees from Russia and other Eastern European
states, and fewer than 15 per cent had not been naturalized as Canadian
citizens.[95] Of those who had not been naturalized, many were recently
arrived immigrants, including, as Minister Thomas Crerar noted in 1940,
Jewish refugees and Sudetan social democrats, groups who shared a common antipathy to Hitler.[96]

Despite these facts, German-speaking people tended to be regarded as
a more or less homogeneous group, and their various cultural and political organizations were seen as representing the community as a whole.
Several of these organizations had been supported by the National
Socialist Party in Germany. It is therefore not surprising that the internment committee, headed by Norman Robertson and appointed by King to
determine which persons were possible threats to the nation's security,

used the membership lists of such organizations for internment purposes.[97] The committee also relied upon names provided by local police officers and other citizens at large. The day after the DOCR were proclaimed, more than 300 German aliens and Canadians of German descent were arrested.[98] By 1941, approximately 1,500 people were reported to have been interned in camps in Petawawa, Ontario, and Kananaskis, Alberta.[99]

It was soon apparent that the information which formed the basis of internment decisions was not reliable in ascertaining those who legitimately could be considered disloyal or a threat to national security. A review procedure was therefore implemented, which shortly thereafter was denied to immigrants who were not naturalized, whereby internees would come before a judge to determine whether their continued incarceration was necessary.[100] The judges reviewing the cases, however, frequently had little more to rely on than what was provided to the internment advisory committee. Their decisions thus were often based on subjective assessments gleaned from an internee's statements and general deportment. And while the review proceedings fell far short of what normally would be considered fair in *habeas corpus* applications, they nonetheless resulted in the release of about seventy persons within the next six months.[101]

Through these proceedings, it also became clear that mere membership in one of the targeted German associations did not necessarily imply disloyalty to Canada. As many internees testified, people often joined these associations for cultural rather than political or ideological reasons. This prompted some members of the judiciary, the bureaucracy, the press, and civil-liberties groups across the country to argue for a liberalization of the DOCR.[102] The most organized public opposition to the emergency measures emanated from three civil-liberties associations centred in Montreal, Toronto, and Winnipeg. During the 1940 general elections, they pressed local candidates to support the establishment of an inter-parliamentary committee to recommend changes to the DOCR. All of the associations argued for the repeal of regulation 21, or at the very least its amendment to provide safeguards against abusive exercise of authority.[103] In addition, the founding members of the Winnipeg association, the first chairman of which was A.R.M. Lower, drafted a detailed critique of the regulations which was signed by seventy-seven leading Canadians and presented to King in May 1940.[104] Less detailed and condemnatory, yet nevertheless still somewhat critical in tone, were several press editorials which appeared in the winter of 1940, urging the government to exercise moderation in acting pursuant to its emergency powers.[105] Within the government, one of the most persistent critics of the

DOCR was C.J. (Chubby) Power, the postmaster general, whose criticism of the arbitrary and potentially abusive regulations may have been influential in securing Cabinet approval of the parliamentary committee demanded by the civil-liberties associations.[106]

Given these pressures upon King, it has been speculated that he may have liberalized the DOCR had events overseas not prompted a new wave of hysteria across the country over the potential alien menace.[107] The most significant of these events was the German Blitzkrieg across northern and Western Europe in the spring of 1940, which culminated in the fall of France in June of that year. The second event was Canada's declaration of war against Italy, also in June 1940. Calls once again went out from the public, the press, the RCMP, municipal and provincial governments, and Opposition MPs to tighten the DOCR and intern those residents of enemy-alien descent.

The fear of enemy infiltration may not have been substantiated by facts, but it was nevertheless widely felt throughout the country. R.B. Hansen, the leader of the Opposition, seemed to speak for thousands of Canadians when he asked members of the House whether they were 'aware of the extent of the danger to which we in Canada may be subject because of the presence in our midst of persons of German and Italian origin and nationality.'[108] Hansen warned the House that many recently arrived Germans may have come here on the direction of Hitler to further the aims of their fatherland overseas. Hansen supported his admonition with the following quotation, reportedly taken from a 1934 speech by Hitler delivered to a conference of Nazi leaders from overseas countries: 'It is a good idea to have at least two German societies in every country. One of them can always call attention to its loyalty to the country in question and will have the function of fostering social and economic action. The other one will be radical and revolutionary. It will have to be prepared to be frequently repudiated by myself and other German authorities.'[109]

Having regard to the number of Germans who had arrived in Canada since the beginning of the Nazi regime; 'having regard to the Nazi theories with regard to the penetration of foreign countries; above everything else having regard to what we have witnessed on the continent of Europe, in Norway, in Denmark, in the Netherlands and even in Belgium itself,' Hansen expressed his astonishment that more enemy aliens had not been interned.[110] He strongly urged the government to retain regulation 21 and not submit to the pressures for its repeal. He also argued for giving the RCMP even greater authority than they already possessed, enabling them to have the entire discretion, with few exceptions, as to who should or should not be interned. As for those who objected to the extent of the DOCR, Hansen dismissed them as intellectuals who had nothing better to do than engage in abstract exercises and who, if they mixed with 'common people,' might find their 'pink colouring will fade to a more orthodox white.'[111]

Hansen's comments did not go unopposed in the House. The minister responsible for immigration, Thomas Crerar, argued that the majority of Germans who had entered Canada in the past several years had been refugees from the Third Reich and not its supporters. Moreover, he tried to temper Hansen's alarm by showing that the figures upon which Hansen relied were misleading. Hansen claimed that more Germans had entered Canada in recent years than Scottish, Welsh, and Irish settlers put together. Crerar, however, countered with the fact that, in the preceding three years, more than 20,000 immigrants had come to Canada from the British Isles and the United States, as compared with 1,240 immigrants of German birth.[112]

While the government tried to put Hansen's remarks in perspective, the CCF went further and challenged the moral legitimacy of many of the provisions under the DOCR. While acknowledging that the government in times of war 'must have ample and adequate power to prevent sabotage, espionage, and any subversive activity,' the CCF nevertheless held that such power had to be exercised consistently and with due regard to individual rights. Contrary to giving the RCMP expanded powers, as advocated by the Conservatives, the CCF was of the view that the regulatory powers ought to be exercised by the minister of Justice and his department, and not left to uneven application by the provincial attorneys general. Failure to observe these basic recommendations, according to the CCF, left the country open to an erosion of democracy, precisely at a time when the country was at war with those who would do the same.[113]

It seemed to the government, however, from the volume of petitions it received, that the majority of Canadians were much more disposed to the thinking of the Conservatives on this issue than they were to that of the CCF. Security reports seemed to suggest the same. Entries in King's diaries reveal the prime minister's concern over reports that paramilitary organizations were being formed by groups such as the Canadian Corps and the Legion of Frontiersmen to take matters into their own hands if the government failed to take more decisive action against enemy aliens still at liberty within the state.[114] And so, in June 1940, the DOCR were toughened. Nazi, Fascist, and Communist organizations were banned, their offices, ordered closed, and their printing presses shut down. Registration

requirements were expanded, and internment operations were intensified, as Germans were joined by Italians suspected of having fascist
sympathies and others who were accused of communist activities. By
the end of 1940, the interned population had increased four times, to
1,200 persons.[115]

At this time, the ethnic Italian community of Canada consisted of approximately 150,000 persons, 80 per cent of whom resided in Ontario and
Quebec.[116] Within hours of the Cabinet's authorization of the RCMP to
intern all residents of Italian origin whom it believed might endanger the
safety of the state or engage in activities prejudicial to the prosecution of
the war, close to 1,000 RCMP police officers and specially sworn-in civilians attended to the task. They bore down on Italian communities in
Canada, conducting warrantless searches of homes and offices, arresting
without the laying of formal charges scores of individuals, interrogating
them at local police stations, and sending hundreds off to internment
camps.[117] Within two days, approximately 500 people were detained.[118]

For some time, the RCMP had been gathering the names of individuals
belonging to pro-fascist groups in Canada. Those of Italian descent who
were subsequently arrested tended to come from the membership lists of
three of the more prominent associations: The Fascio, the Italian Fascist
Party; the Sons of Italy, a lodge and mutual benefit society; and the Dopo
Lavaro, an after-work club for recreation and study, which recruited for
the Fascio. Like many of the German associations that had been aided
with money from overseas, these Italian groups had connections with the
Italian fascist government, yet many of their members had joined for
other than political reasons.[119] Moreover, even those who respected
Mussolini, and admired the benefits they believed he had brought to Italy,
saw themselves as no less loyal to Canada. In explaining the attraction of
fascism for many Italian Canadians, Bruno Ramirez writes: 'Fascism, as it
was imported into many immigrant communities of the humble and uneducated, served several purposes at the same time. It brought a sense of
respect towards the social hierarchy that played very well into the hands of
the community's *prominenti*. It brought an elaborate system of public cer-
emonial that many Italian immigrants could easily appropriate for themselves in their longing for ethnic respectability.'[120]

Accounts of the round-up of suspected Italian subversives show the sur-
prise with which the offensive took the community, and the alarm that it
caused as relatives and friends were whisked away from their homes
throughout the day and during the night, their whereabouts often not
revealed for several weeks. As one Montreal resident recalled, one of the

worst memories of the experience was the constant sound of sirens going off in her neighbourhood, as though it was under siege.[121] The panic and apparent overreaction of the RCMP is well illustrated in the description given by Kay Pavia of the Mounties coming to her house to arrest her father: 'They searched upstairs, downstairs. We had this closet in the kitchen and they looked in there and they saw these wires. They asked if these wires were a direct line to Italy. I said "No, it's the front door bell." They said they didn't believe me. I went with one of them and I rang the front door bell. "There you go," I said.'[122]

Despite the arbitrariness of the RCMP's actions, they received very little adverse criticism, aside from that expressed by several academics, civil-libertarians, and others who maintained a critical view of the DOCR for the duration of the war. It may be that most Canadians, unaffected by the internment regulations, simply did not appreciate the extent to which the regulations were being used against those for whom there was no firm proof of subversive activity. It is also probably true, however, that, even if they had been fully aware of the circumstances, they might well have supported the government's actions as being necessary in time of war. In fact, many felt entirely justified in wreaking their own discipline on the Italian community, as illustrated in Toronto where, following Italy's entrance into the war, hordes of demonstrators took to the streets, smashing the windows of Italian establishments and vowing to boycott Italian businesses. As described in the *Globe and Mail*, 'plate glass windows of dozens of stores went smashing inwards as demonstrators roamed the streets looking for opportunities to vent their feelings against "Jackal" Italy.'[123] Similar events took place in other parts of the country. Moreover, job dismissals were almost immediate for many Italian workers, and in some areas those of Italian origin were denied welfare relief.[124]

The round-up of suspected communist sympathizers also began in June 1940 with the passing of P.C. 2363, which declared the Communist Party of Canada illegal, along with ten of its associated groups. Although the manner of their arrest and the conditions of their incarceration were similar to those experienced by other internees at this time, the impetus behind many alleged communist incarcerations was different. While public demands for the suppression of the communist menace, in part explains why suspected communists were interned, the desire simply to silence labour activists was equally compelling.

It is perhaps arguable that the initial communist opposition to the war, coupled with the Soviet Union's signing of a non-aggression pact with Hitler in August 1939, led to a concern among some RCMP and other

officials that Canadian communists might try to subvert Canada's war efforts.[125] Yet, as several historians have pointed out, the RCMP opinions
were not based on in-depth investigative work, let alone revelations of
acts of communist sabotage or espionage. Rather, they were premised on
the suspicions of those who had a deep antipathy of communism and
who tended to react ideologically rather than in keeping with the normal
requirements of their peacekeeping functions.[126]

Nevertheless, had the RCMP been the only ones to sound the communist alarm, King may have heeded the advice of Jack Pickersgill and
others within his administration[127] to demand restraint and full accountability from the RCMP in regard to its anti-communist campaign. As Reg
Whitaker has documented,[128] King was urged to contain the communists
from several different quarters. At the same time as the RCMP was warning King about the severity of the communist menace, Ontario Tory
leader George Drew was publicly calling for the establishment of the
Canadian equivalent to the American House Committee on Un-American
Activities, and city officials in Kitchener and Timmins were promising
that raids would be made on the homes of all those who had communist
sympathies. Within King's own caucus, leading members also advocated
a strong stand against communists in Canada. Included in this group
were Ernest Lapointe, the minister of Justice, and his successor, Louis
St. Laurent, who vigorously opposed the lifting of the Communist Party
ban after the Soviet Union's entry into the war on the side of the allies.
C.D. Howe also took a hard line on communists and pressed for decisive
action against them and, in particular, labour activists whose strike activities, he argued, were seriously impeding the war effort. The Canadian
Manufacturers' Association, whose interests Howe often represented in
Cabinet, went so far as to demand that King declare the industrial unions
unlawful and have their leaders arrested.[129] While King was unwilling to
go that far, he was prepared to use the DOCR to ensure that industrial
production proceeded relatively unhindered.

There were approximately 133 people interned for their communist
sympathies during the war. Among the first to be arrested were the leaders
and organizers of the Communist Party and several of its affiliated groups.
But, as the purges continued, the net was cast more widely to encompass
many individuals who were picked up in the course of contract negotiations, strike organizing, and other union activities.[130] In his memoir,
William Repka recounts his feelings upon being arrested in September
1940, just after having won a wage increase for his union, the Beet Workers'
Union of Canada: 'It is a frightful feeling to be shown a prison cell, to be

pushed in and then to hear the steel door close and the key turned. I was being told that I was a menace to society – that at 25 years of age I was not safe to have around.'[131]

As an added injustice most of the communist internees were sent to Kananaskis, where they were initially put in bunkers with German internees. Camp rules required that the internees select a spokesperson who acted as a liaison between the internees and the camp administration. Because German internees were more numerous, the spokesperson was generally selected from among their ranks. According to the reminiscences of the interned anti-fascists, the Germans assigned the best jobs and hoarded the choicest food for themselves, which only heightened the anti-fascists' grievance at being incarcerated with those whom they considered enemies of the people. As one internee, Peter Krawchuk, recalls, 'therein lay our misfortune: Canadian citizens, avowed anti-fascists, were dependent on the Nazis and had to comply with their orders. Thereby the federal Minister of Justice, Ernest Lapointe, did us the greatest harm, which we could never forget nor forgive.'[132]

While the anti-fascists eventually obtained their own bunkers, they continued to protest their ongoing internment with fascists in Kananaskis, and later in Petawawa, where most of them were transferred. According to the anti-fascists, the military police favoured the fascists over the communists.[133] Krawchuk writes that, in Petawawa, the French-Canadian military were not only hostile to the communists, but particularly helpful to the Quebec fascists among Adrian Arcand's group.[134] This led to great frustration among the communist internees, who continued to demand that they be removed from the camp and sent to a location where there were no fascist sympathizers. In August 1941, following a strike by communists and other anti-fascists which threatened to get out of hand, the decision was taken to remove the strikers to an empty, and apparently derelict, prison in Hull, Quebec. There, despite its physical shortcomings, the communists and anti-fascists had more influence on the internal administration of the centre.[135]

As far as review hearings were concerned, few of the communist internees held out any hope that such a review would lead to their release. The communists claimed that the review hearings were far from objectively determined and that there was a perceptible bias on the part of the reviewing judges against anyone suspected of communist sympathies.[136] Seeing very little hope of being released through the review process, the anti-fascist internees, with help from their advocates outside the camps, kept up a steady barrage of petitions to Prime Minister King, the minister of Justice, and other MPs. Once the Soviet Union entered the war against Germany in June 1941, these appeals gained new vigour. The internees sent the government affidavits attesting to their loyalty to Canada and their support for the war effort, and letters offering their services in the armed forces or other war work. Their continued incarceration, they argued, could not be justified on the grounds of national security, and its continuance was simply a form of persecution on the basis of class and political prejudice.[137]

Throughout 1941 and 1942, criticism of the government's internment policies intensified. The CCF and civil-liberties associations continued to press for liberalization, and were joined by others who demanded a more accountable process. Included among these individuals and groups was Liberal MP and former Ontario attorney general A.W. Roebuck, who, in 1942, recommended specific amendments to the DOCR which would narrow their scope, and provide for less arbitrary and more accountable means of enforcement.[138] The labour movement was particularly agitated over this issue, having had many of its union organizers incarcerated in the midst of labour disputes or contract negotiations.[139] B.K Sandwell, the editor of *Saturday Night,* continued to caution the public against becoming too complacent over the suspension of democratic rights.[140] The *Toronto Daily Star* was also critical of the government's detention of people in a cloud of secrecy for long periods of time without any formal charges being laid and without the benefit of a prompt hearing into the validity of their incarceration: 'In some instances there may be reasons for a certain amount of secrecy, but it is too much like Nazi Germany under a Nazi government, and too little like Canada under a Liberal government, to have men like this spirited away and held incommunicado, without a hearing and without any hint as to their supposed wrongdoing.'[141]

In 1942, the leader of the CCF, M.J. Coldwell, once again called for a meaningful review of cases involving those who may have been initially opposed to the war but who were now 'anxious and willing to assist in every way possible to carry forward our war effort.'[142] Some prominent bureaucrats were also urging the same. In the Department of External Affairs, as early as October 1941, Lester Pearson wrote to Norman Robertson that he could not understand why 'we should keep the communists interned when their views towards the war which necessitated such internment must now have changed.'[143] Several months later, Walter J. Turnbull, King's principal secretary, similarly argued that some officials were 'too concerned with pursuing their own prejudices ...

I would think that a change of policy might well be indicated to them, with Russia a valiant ally.'[144]

A parliamentary committee examining possible modifications of the DOCR in 1942 also considered the matter and, according to Whitaker, most of the public representations made before it recommended the lifting of the ban on the Communist Party of Canada. The RCMP and the Department of Justice, however, stood resolutely opposed, on the grounds that the Communist Party's highest loyalty was to Russia and its essential war aim was the victory of communism over democracy. In the end, the committee recommended that the Communist Party and several other banned organizations be removed from the prohibited list. Cabinet, however, refused to follow the recommendation.[145]

King appeared to be sympathetic towards the arguments in favour of relaxing the regulations. After receiving a delegation from the Toronto Civil Liberties League in February 1942, he noted in his diary: 'I thought the delegation made out a strong case for need of less rigid interpretation of the Defence of Canada Regulations; also for greater justice in manner of trials and of appeals of those interned, and danger of using the Defence Regulations to thwart labour organization, collective bargaining, etc.'[146] Whitaker suggests that the reason King's government did not lift the ban on the Communist Party and release the communist internees earlier was because of the strong anti-communist feeling prevalent in Quebec. Thus, in 1942, Mackenzie King prevented the issue from going to the House, arguing that, since Quebecers were already feeling betrayed over the conscription issue, to lift the ban on the Communist Party would be 'too much for them' and would leave them feeling like they were 'being deliberately attacked.' As a result, Canada maintained its ban on the Communist Party throughout the war – the only Allied nation to do so.[147]

Although the government was not to budge in lifting of the ban, it could not remain so intransigent in regard to the release of the communist internees. Several rather sensational cases had raised the profile of the communist internees and, together with the rising popularity of the CCF, and the mounting criticism of internment policies more generally, contributed towards the decision to release the communist internees in 1942 upon their undertaking not to participate in the Communist Party or any other affiliated organization. By the middle of 1942, as Italy's fortunes were faltering, most of the ethnic Italian internees were released, nearly all of the remainder to follow the next year with Italy's surrender. Similarly, the release of German internees began in 1942 after a series of Allied victories, and by the end of the year more than half were discharged. In 1943, enemy aliens of Italian or German descent were permitted to serve in the armed forces, provided their applications for naturalization had been accepted and they had cleared security checks.

During the war, there was no incidence of sabotage committed by a Canadian resident of German or Italian descent, nor was any fifth-column activity discovered.[148] Whether there was credible evidence to justify the initial internment of enemy aliens is the subject of spirited debate.[149] Less controversial is the charge that using the membership lists of pro-Nazi organizations was too blunt a tool to discern real from perceived threats to state security. Once it was revealed that many people joined such organizations for the economic and social benefits they offered, the government could have taken more decisive steps to rely less on such lists and release those for whom there was no other evidence of subversive activity. Its refusal to do so seemed to be motivated largely by its desire to meet public expectations regarding the incarceration of the 'alien menace.' The continued incarceration of communist sympathizers after Canada and Russia became allies also seemed to serve no other purposes than responding to the public aversion to communists and effectively immobilizing labour activists.

There were other costs of Canada's initial internment strategy. The bitter legacy of the wartime internments was to live on within the Canadian Italian community for years to come. On a personal level, many people felt intense pain and embarrassment at having been unjustly labelled as enemies of the state. For example, as one former internee told Mario Duliani, a well-known Italian playwright, this type of humiliation did not pass: 'The deprivation of my freedom, being torn from my family, being robbed of the time, the loss of my money, all this I might learn to live with without complaint. But what I cannot come to terms with is the idea that my wife, a Canadian, and my Canadian-born children, may suspect that I have betrayed my country.'[150]

The stigma suffered by the internees affected the younger generation, who, according to Kenneth Bagnell, began to shy away from their culture. Some, who might have 'assumed leadership in the years immediately after the war, avoided doing so, in favour of simply getting by, making a living, forgetting the past.'[151] Perhaps even more damaging were the deep divisions within the Italian community that the wartime experience exacerbated. The fact that many of the arrests were made on the basis of information supplied to the police by others within the Italian community itself 'engendered a climate of mutual suspicion,' writes Ramirez,

'which had the immediate effect of paralysing public activities and reducing social intercourse to a bare minimum.'[152] In the long term, the
use of anonymous informers who had been passionate opponents of the
pro-fascist faction 'transformed bitter dissension and rivalries into
hatred and profound divisions that were never reconciled in the subsequent history of the community.'[153] According to Ramirez, it took a new
wave of Italian immigrants in the 1950s to revive associational life. Until
then, however, those associations and newspapers that did exist with
the financial assistance of the federal government 'were the preserve of
anti-fascist leaders and informers, and as such their presence in the community stood more as a reminder of victors and of vanquished, of pride
and of humiliation than as attempts to heal an ethnicity that had been
gravely wounded.'[154]

The incarceration of communist sympathizers had similar ramifica-
tions and affected both individual lives and community life. The most
stark example of the latter was within the Ukrainian-Canadian community. Ever since the Russian Revolution, the Ukrainian-Canadian community had been sharply divided between pro-communist Ukrainians who
supported Russia, and nationalist Ukrainians who denounced the Soviet
occupation of their homeland and called for an independent Ukraine.
Both sides of the communal divide posed problems for the Canadian government on the eve of the Second World War. On the one hand, there was
the concern that the left-leaning Ukrainians, who had expressed their opposition to the war, would disrupt the war effort. On the other hand, there
was concern that the nationalist Ukrainians' hope that Hitler would fulfil
his promise of creating an independent Ukraine would also lead to their
disloyalty to Canada in the event that Canada declared war on Germany.

The government had two approaches for dealing with these potential
problems. In an attempt to ensure the loyalty of the nationalist Ukrainians,
it set up an umbrella organization, the Ukrainian-Canadian Committee,
representing all the non-communist Ukrainian groups and associations in
the country. The purpose was to use the committee as a vehicle for making
sure that Canada's involvement in the war was fully understood by the
Ukrainian population. And as Lubomyr Luciuk and Bohdan Kordan point
out, 'access to the leadership also offered an opportunity to keep abreast
of current developments within the community.'[155]

As far as the pro-communist groups were concerned, the government
took a more direct approach, declaring many of them illegal, closing
down their publications, disposing of their property, and interning many
of their leaders and members. The most severe attack was launched

against the Ukrainian Labour-Farmer Temple Association (ULFTA). While the ULFTA had long been associated with the Communist Party, its several hundred branches were centres of cultural, not political, activities. Reg Whitaker estimates that total membership in the ULFTA was around 10,000 persons, and that about 50,000 Ukrainians participated in its activities. And while the culture fostered in the temples 'was a left-wing culture,' he claims that was 'merely a reflection of a certain reality of Ukrainian working-class and farming experience.'[156] Nevertheless, consistent with its wartime measures more generally, the government did not discriminate between the cultural services the temples provided and the political philosophy their central administration apparently espoused. As a result, in addition to having its leaders and various members of the ULFTA interned, its libraries were burned, and its temples were closed down and the contents confiscated. Adding to the sense of injury felt within the ULFTA community was the fact that many of its seized properties were subsequently sold to rival nationalist organizations at a fraction of their real value.[157]

The Second Wave

On the eve of the Second World War, there were approximately 22,500 persons of Japanese descent living in Canada, the majority of whom were Nisei, Canadian-born and Canadian-educated citizens. Immigrants from Japan and Hawaii, Issei, accounted for about 8,500 persons, one-third of whom had been naturalized in Canada prior to 1923 after which time naturalization became exceedingly difficult for Asian immigrants to obtain. Nevertheless, the majority of the remaining 5,000 non-naturalized Issei had resided in Canada for over twenty-five years.[158]

Canada's Japanese community was heavily concentrated in British Columbia, where more than 95 per cent of the total population of Japanese descent lived. Although their roots in Canada dated back to the turn of the century, the Japanese community had not become well accepted and integrated into the larger community. Fifty years of restrictive and exclusionary laws and practices had kept the Japanese on the margins of the social and political life of society at large. Their continued marginalization was underscored with the 1937 report of the Parliamentary Committee on Elections and Franchise Acts which recommended that the provincial franchise not be extended to Japanese residents on the grounds that they would otherwise have too much influence in the political life of British Columbia.[159] At the same time, Japan's increasing military incursions into China were engendering considerable concern and negative publicity in Canada, which did little to arouse any sympathy for disenfranchised Japanese Canadians. Reports of Japan's brutal attack on Nanking, where 200,000 persons were believed to have died, and accounts of the Japanese army's assaults on Canadian missionaries stationed there, were followed by a renewal of anti-Japanese sentiment expressed both in the press and in the House.

In 1938, seizing on the growing alarm occasioned by the Japanese government's military ambitions in Asia, A.W. Neill, an independent MP from British Columbia, introduced a resolution in the House calling for the cessation of all Japanese immigration to Canada.[160] In explaining his resolution, Neill reiterated the problems that white British Columbians faced in the presence of a sizeable Japanese population. The arguments against Japanese people that had been well aired for the previous fifty years were once again brought forward. In particular, Neill reminded the House that the Oriental population were 'all of alien thought and mind and tendency; they are all one body, acting and thinking as a unit.'[161] H.C. Green, a Conservative MP from Vancouver, followed by drawing attention to the fact that, since intermarriage was opposed equally by the whites and the Japanese, assimilation of the latter was impossible. Most serious, according to Green, however, was their alleged unfair competition in many areas of economic enterprise within the province. Claiming that their lower standard of living and their willingness to accept wages below the prescribed minimum rendered Japanese entrepreneurs and labourers unfair competitors, Green went on to speculate that in addition they probably received loans from the Japanese consulate at 'rates of interest far lower than those obtained by a white man.'[162] Added to these grievances were allegations that the Japanese population of British Columbia had exceedingly high birth rates. This fact, together with the reported illegal entry of hundreds of Japanese had, in Neill's opinion, rendered the gentlemen's agreement reached with Japan in 1917, and amended in 1928, 'a gentleman's joke as far as one party to the bargain was concerned.'[163]

Former prime minister and leader of the Opposition R.B. Bennett also rose and spoke in sympathy with Neill's resolution. Bennett reasoned that 'to be fair to both the Chinese and the Japanese' the entry restrictions that applied to Chinese immigrants should similarly be imposed on Japanese immigrants. He preferred, however, that an agreement be worked out with Japan, and only failing that should exclusionary legislation be proclaimed. In addition, Bennett raised concerns that were to dominate the question of the Japanese-Canadian population in the next several years.

Noting what he conceived to be the national ambition of the Japanese Empire in the Pacific, Bennett warned rather obliquely that Canada had to be prudent in protecting its own coast and remember that its residents of Japanese descent were knowledgeable about that coastline, its ports and harbours, and other resources of British Columbia.[164]

For his part, Mackenzie King took great care in expressing his empathy with the citizens of British Columbia, 'who have had to carry pretty much of the whole burden of one of the greatest national problems with which our country is faced.'[165] Nevertheless, having acknowledged this 'grave and acute problem,' King continued to maintain that the best way to deal with it was by the present agreement with Japan. Noting that the Chinese government was aggrieved over Canada's exclusionary policy towards Chinese nationals, he argued that it would be imprudent to enact similar legislation in regard to Japanese immigrants. King claimed that the gentlemen's agreement had been kept, citing figures which suggested that annual admissions had been well below the 150 persons agreed upon in 1928. These figures, together with the sensitive international situation developing in Europe and Asia, argued against the acceptance of Neill's resolution. Nevertheless, King did appoint a board of review the following month to inquire into the Japanese problem in British Columbia and the question of illegal entry into Canada of Japanese nationals.[166]

The Board of Review consisted of three government officials, Hugh Keenleyside of the Department of External Affairs, F.W. Taylor, district superintendent of immigration in Vancouver, and C.W. Fish of the RCMP in Vancouver. The board received information through interviews, by representations by telephone, and by written submissions. Among the allegations it investigated were: rumours of widespread Japanese illegal entry at points in northern British Columbia and the Queen Charlotte Islands; gun-running operations at Port Alberni; and the surveillance and mapping of the B.C. coast by Japanese residents. Included within the suggestions put before the board were: that all Oriental persons within the province be required to register, that further Japanese immigration be prohibited, and that the concentration of Japanese persons within the province be eased through their mandatory relocation to other parts of Canada. Some people, including apparently British Columbia's premier, Duff Patullo, even supported the suggestion that Oriental persons within the province be forcefully repatriated to their countries of origin.[167]

The board found that most of the allegations concerning illegal entry of Japanese persons were false. It did note, however, that an interpreter for the Japanese consulate had been arrested in 1931 and subsequently convicted of aiding approximately 1,500 people to enter Canada illegally. The board estimated that, in addition to this number, a further 1,500 had entered the country surreptitiously, more than 75 per cent of whom had left the country voluntarily and about five per cent of whom had been deported. There remained, it concluded, approximately 400 illegal entrants still at large.

As for espionage by residents of Japanese descent, the board found no evidence to support the allegations. 'In general it was noted that assertions of this nature came most frequently from witnesses who were distinctly below average in intelligence, experience and judgement.' In fact, the board found that, once it had proceeded with its investigations, there was a noticeable drop in the number of anti-Oriental speeches within the province, leading the board to remark that, if its work 'has done nothing else, it has at least put a stop (it is perhaps too much to hope that it will be permanent) to the charges regarding illegal entries which were formerly so prominent a part of the anti-Oriental campaign in the province of British Columbia.'[168]

While the board's work may have quelled the rumours of illegal immigrants, it did not allay concerns over Japan's growing militarization and the possible threat that persons of Japanese descent could pose on the West Coast, should the Imperial Army decide to invade. At the forefront of the campaign to strengthen B.C. defences and remove the province's Japanese population was Ian Mackenzie, the minister of Pensions and Health. Mackenzie was himself from British Columbia. He was also an ardent anti-Japanese activist who, according to Ann Gomer Sunahara, throughout his twenty-one years in politics had, with one exception, 'endorsed every anti-Asian proposal raised in the Legislative Assembly, in Parliament and in the Cabinet.'[169] Within the Cabinet, Mackenzie ceaselessly raised the spectre of a Japanese invasion, and warned of the growing hostility and likely violent outbursts that would be occasioned against the Japanese population unless their removal was promptly undertaken.

Following the Japanese bombing of Pearl Harbor in December 1941, rumours were widely circulated that the invasion had been aided by fifth columnists in Hawaii. Although the rumours were soon after discredited, and although the Japanese population of Hawaii remained free throughout the course of the war, within British Columbia calls for the removal of Japanese residents became more intense. So did the animosity directed against the Japanese population there as thousands were dismissed from their jobs and menaced by angry white residents. With the fall of Hong

Kong, and the death and imprisonment of Canadian soldiers stationed there, internment demands escalated.

For several years, King had been advised by senior RCMP, military, and navy personnel that, in the event of war with Japan, it would be unlikely that Japan would invade the West Coast and, moreover, that the Japanese residents did not pose a serious security risk. Yet, while King's senior military advisers may have been convinced of the loyalty of B.C.'s Japanese community, and confident that a Japanese invasion was unlikely, other military commanders on the West Coast disagreed. In the summer of 1941, the Joint Service Committee for the Pacific Coast recommended that the Japanese population resident around key defence areas and air bases be evacuated in the event of an emergency.[170] Following the bombing of Pearl Harbor six months later, the committee recommended the removal of all persons of Japanese racial origin.[171]

Judging from King's diaries, he tended to agree with the assessments coming from his Ottawa-based security officials. In February 1942, he wrote that, in his opinion, the threat of a possible Japanese invasion was not immediate and would arise only if Japan succeeded in gaining control of the entire Far East.[172] He nevertheless deemed it advisable to authorize the mandatory registration of all Japanese enemy aliens. They were required to guarantee their good behaviour, not to move to another locality without permission, and, as with the Italian and German aliens before them, they were required to report regularly to the registrar. Ten days later, the registration requirement was widened to include all persons of Japanese ancestry, regardless of whether they were born in Canada or had become naturalized Canadian citizens.[173]

Also in December 1941, the Royal Canadian Navy was authorized to seize Japanese fishing vessels along the coast. All of the 1,200 boats subsequently taken were owned by Japanese Canadians; the owners were not informed as to when and if they would be returned. The vessels were roughly strapped together and towed to New Westminster, suffering considerable damage along the way, and more as they lay in anchor. Several months later, Cabinet passed two orders-in-council directing that the boats be turned over to non-Japanese operators and sold at prices which turned out to be not only less than their value at the time of seizure, but also less then the value appraised after their damaging trip down the coast.[174] Their Japanese owners were thus left with poor compensation for their property and no means to secure a livelihood.[175]

In January 1942, King convened the Conference on Japanese Problems, where the views of the different advocates could be aired. The conference, held in Ottawa, was chaired by Ian Mackenzie and attended by several B.C. politicians, who called for the mass evacuation of persons of Japanese origin within their province. It was also attended by representatives from the Department of External Affairs, the armed forces, and the RCMP, who counselled moderation, given their assessment that the resident Japanese did not pose a security threat to the coast. The central military officials, the RCMP, and the federal civil servants continued to maintain that adequate measures were already in place to ensure the safety of the West Coast and that other discriminatory measures against the Japanese population would gain nothing except to expose Canadian prisoners of war to possible retaliation.[176]

For their part, the B.C. delegates were united in their mistrust of the Japanese population and they were enraged at the opposition emanating from the Ottawa delegates. Even if the RCMP and central military command were correct in assuming that there was no significant threat of a Japanese invasion, the B.C. MPs claimed that the populace of their province simply would not be convinced of that, and the longer the Japanese population remained within the province, the greater the threat of a violent backlash against them. So explicit were the B.C. representatives in their opposition to the continued residence of those of Japanese descent that Escott Reid, a participant from the Department of External Affairs, likened the way they spoke of the Japanese to the way the 'Nazis would have spoken about Jewish Germans.' Reid claims that he felt 'in that committee room the physical presence of evil.' Similarly, Lieutenant-General Maurice A. Pope, recalling a conversation with a B.C. delegate who said 'that for years his people had been telling themselves that war with Japan would afford them a Heaven-sent opportunity to rid themselves of the Japanese *economic* menace for ever more,' wrote that he left the conference 'feeling dirty all over.'[177]

Although a consensus could not be reached, King was prepared to strike a compromise between his Ottawa advisers and the delegation from British Columbia. On 16 January 1942, Cabinet passed another order-in-council empowering the minister of National Defence, with the concurrence of the minister of Justice, to declare any area in Canada a 'protected area' from which enemy aliens could be excluded.[178] The government also announced that it intended to remove from the protected areas, soon to be defined in British Columbia, all Japanese aliens of military age and to create a Japanese civilian corps to work on projects deemed to be of national interest. The evacuation, which would involve more than 1,700 persons, was explained as being a necessary precaution to protect the security of the West Coast.[179] It was greeted warmly by B.C. politicians and press. Yet, putting the plan into action proved to be no easy task. Communities in the B.C. interior and in other provinces east of the Rockies protested vehemently against the relocation of any Japanese persons to their environs. Moreover, the setting-up of work camps took time to plan and carry out, such that no coordinated movement of Japanese aliens could take place for many weeks.

This delay in acting on its announced partial evacuation plan led to a growing sense of outrage among many B.C. residents and their representatives. As Sunahara explains, 'Ottawa's apparent inertia aggravated West Coast insecurities. By agreeing to remove Japanese aliens "for reasons of national security," the government had confirmed the "big lie" of a Japanese conspiracy to overthrow British Columbia. Having confirmed B.C.'s fears, Ottawa's disinclination to act only magnified those fears and reinforced B.C.'s traditional complaint that Ottawa really did not care about the West Coast.'[180] Added to this were renewed fears of an imminent West Coast invasion, fears that were in part fed by false rumours emanating from the United States of sightings of Japanese ships off the coast and radio signals transmitted by Japanese nationals. In the House of Commons, B.C. MPs pressed the government to authorize the internment of all B.C. residents of Japanese descent, while officials within the Department of External Affairs grew more alarmed by the hysteria mounting in British Columbia.[181]

In the end, King sided with his B.C. advisers and, on 24 February 1942, the minister of Justice was authorized to remove and detain any persons from designated protected areas.[182] Within Cabinet, it was understood that all persons of Japanese ancestry were to be evacuated from the West Coast. Subsequently, the British Columbia Security Commission was established, with authority to order the removal and detention of any person of Japanese descent from designated protected areas.[183] All property that evacuees were unable to take with them would be placed with the custodian of enemy property. In the meantime, all residents of Japanese descent within the province were to remain in their homes from sunset to sunrise and to turn in all their radios, cameras, and automobiles. According to the authorizing regulation, the confiscation of restricted articles was a 'protective measure only' and the owners were assured that their property would be returned at a later time.[184] The crowd that assembled to watch the impoundment of motor vehicles in Hastings Park in Vancouver, however, was itself a grim forewarning of their ultimate destination. As Ken Adachi described, 'joining the throng of RCMP officers and press and movie news cameramen were a clutch of used car dealers.'[185]

Almost half of the people evacuated from the West Coast also passed through Hastings Park exhibition grounds in Vancouver, which was turned into a temporary internment centre. Cattle and horse stalls were used to house entire families, while rudimentary sanitation and mess halls were erected to service a population which, at its peak, reached close to 4,000 persons.[186] Maryka Omatsu describes the experience of one family who, along with hundreds of others, were transported by train down the coast to Vancouver:

> The train came to a stop at its destination in Vancouver. Mysteriously, all the doors and windows were suddenly locked. Sealed inside their cars, unable to go to the toilet or move around within the train, the passengers felt tensions escalate as the temperature rose and the hours passed. Just as abruptly the car doors opened and the cool night air rushed in. In the twilight, six hundred Japanese Canadians from the north-coast settlements formed a line and silently walked towards the gates of the Hastings Park exhibition grounds. The group was herded towards some low buildings and Kimiko, clutching her youngest son's hand, was shown to a horse stall that would be home for her and her three youngest children for six months. Her husband and her oldest son, Henry, were taken away to be housed in a separate all-male dormitory building.[187]

The movement to internment camps in the interior of B.C. took eleven months to complete. Frequently cabins were not ready when internees arrived, leaving them to sleep in tents regardless of the weather and with only the crudest of sanitation facilities. Like other internment camps across the country, those for the Japanese were isolated and enclosed with high barbed-wire fencing. Each family was forced to share a small, poorly insulated three-room cabin with another family that generally they did not know. Again the experience of Kimiko and her family is illustrative: 'Initially they lived in a tent while the cabin they would share with another family for the next four years was being completed. Kimiko remembers the intense cold in the winter as the green lumber of the new cabin dried and the icy winds blew through the chinks. She says the heat from the pot-bellied stove made the walls steam and the floors 'were like a river' as the water came out of the wood.[188]

While in the camps, the internees were provided with food, fuel, medical care, and primary-school education at the government's expense. Although those who were employed within the camp and on projects outside of it were required to deduct their expenses from their earnings, this alone was not enough to slow down the spiralling costs of internment. Within a year, the government was looking for alternative ways to finance the mass incarceration so as to lessen the drain on the public purse. The federal minister of Labour favoured the sale of the evacuees' properties, the proceeds of which could then be used to offset the costs of their internment. Several B.C. MPs and local politicians had been lobbying for such a move since the evacuation itself was announced. Most notable among these lobbyists was Ian Mackenzie, who, as minister of Pensions and Health, viewed the prosperous agricultural properties of the interned Japanese as appropriate for returning war veterans. Other B.C. politicians also saw merit in the sale of Japanese properties as a way of ensuring that the internees would not return to the province and as a means of opening up areas previously inhabited by the Japanese community to more desirable development opportunities.[189]

In January 1943, the Cabinet took a major step in this direction by passing an order-in-council authorizing the custodian of enemy property to dispose of Japanese-Canadian property without the owners' consent.[190] Empowered to sell the properties entrusted in his care, the government's custodian of enemy property, G.W. McPherson, made it clear that he intended to sell both the real estate and the personal possessions of the evacuees. This news was not calmly or passively received by internees, a group of whom retained legal counsel to challenge the forced sale in the courts. At the same time, several advocates acting on behalf of Japanese Canadians registered their concerns with the prime minister. Among the most prominent was Henry Angus, a professor at the University of British Columbia and a long-time critic of discriminatory practices against Asian minorities. In 1940, he was appointed by King to the newly created Standing Committee on Orientals, established to advise the government on issues involving Asians. After passage of the dispossession order-in-council, Angus wrote to King, arguing that the order was contrary to British justice and regarded by some as analogous to the dispossession provisions of the Nuremberg laws passed by Hitler against the Jews.[191]

Neither Angus's appeal nor the subsequent court challenge was to prove effective. The challenge against the custodian of enemy alien property itself illustrated how deeply marginalized and disenfranchised Japanese Canadians were. Petitions on behalf of the Japanese complainants were filed in the Exchequer Court in 1943. According to Sunahara, hearings in this court generally took place within four to six weeks of filing. In this case, however, the hearing did not commence until almost a year later, at which time it was delayed on the question of whether the custodian of enemy alien property was a servant of the Crown, and therefore accountable in Exchequer Court. The presiding judge, J.T. Thorson, who just two years earlier was the minister of National War Service and part of King's Cabinet which had authorized the mass evacuation, suspended the case while he considered the issue. Three years later, he issued his judgment that the custodian was not a servant of the Crown, and therefore not accountable in his court.[192]

Throughout Thorson's three-year deliberation, Japanese properties and personal possessions were being sold. By 1947, property which had been estimated by the Office of the Custodian of Enemy Alien Property as worth $11.5 million had been sold for less than half that amount.[193] Not only did the evacuees lose their lands, houses, businesses, and personal possessions, but their meagre remuneration was immediately applied to their upkeep in the internment camps. The capital they received from the sale of their property was kept in the trust of the custodian of enemy property at no rate of interest. Withdrawals of capital were strictly controlled, such that families were permitted to draw only $100 per month. Work within the camps was prohibited for single men without dependants and those who had capital in the care of the custodian. Both by limiting employment opportunities within the camps and by forcing the internees to assume the cost of their maintenance, the government hoped to induce many to leave the camps and move east in search of employment.

By 1943, a serious labour shortage had developed both in British Columbia and in other provinces, such as Ontario, where industry was booming in response to wartime demands. Faced with an interned population whose maintenance was far more costly than the government felt it could assume, a decision was made to induce and to compel Japanese workers out of the camps and into areas where their labour was required. In February 1943, the cabinet passed an order-in-council giving the minister of Labour the power to order 'any person of the Japanese race in any place in Canada to proceed to any other place in Canada at such times and in such a manner as he may prescribe.'[194] In British Columbia, at the request of representatives of the lumbering industry, which was in need of workers, a ban that had prohibited persons of the Japanese race from being employed on Crown timber lands was lifted. The opening of B.C. Crown timber lands was well received in the camps in British Columbia because it meant that men could work at sites not far removed from their families. The Department of Labour's ban on the employment of single Japanese men in the province was, however, bitterly received by the internees, as were attempts by the government to force Japanese workers east to fill job vacancies there. In reserving the sawmilling and lumbering jobs for men with families, the Ministry of Labour hoped to induce those without such ties to move east. But the experience of other Japanese people who had made such moves was well known and not eagerly embraced by those who remained in internment camps.

While moving east meant that persons could take possession of their capital being held by the custodian of enemy property, as Sunahara explains there was little people could do with their resources. An order-in council passed the previous year, in February 1942, prohibited Japanese persons from buying or leasing land or business premises without the permission of the minister of Justice. The minister, Louis St. Laurent, was not inclined to give his consent. Although, in 1944, St. Laurent relaxed his restrictive approach and permitted Japanese Canadians to lease business premises for one year, the change often had little practical effect since many cities had by-laws which prohibited the holding of business licences and residences by persons of Japanese ancestry.[195]

Despite the considerable disincentives towards moving east, many internees were simply compelled to do so by the poverty of their circumstances. Although the government had, in the end, decided not to force the evacuees to accept jobs elsewhere against their will, the restriction on employment in the camps and their rapidly dwindling personal resources compelled many to move. Farmers and property owners who had previously been able to survive on the income from their properties now had to live off their capital. The prohibition on employment in the camps of those with capital and those without dependants created additional financial pressures, as did the denial of relief benefits to single adults. Gradually an increasing number of people left in search of employment in the industrial areas of the east, most notably in Winnipeg, Toronto, and Montreal.

Neither internment nor relocation was regarded as the final solution to the problem of Canada's resident Japanese population. For the government and the leading B.C. federal politicians, the preferable resolution to the situation was the repatriation of Japanese persons to Japan once the war was over. Ian Mackenzie had advocated such a solution as early as 1942, although the option was not considered seriously by King until August of the following year. At that time senior civil servants in the Department of External Affairs were considering ways to effect the voluntary return of Japanese aliens to Japan after the war, along with the removal of Japanese Canadians and aliens who were deemed disloyal to Canada.[196]

While the deportation of Japanese aliens provoked little debate, the deportation of Canadian citizens of Japanese descent was fraught with controversy. Aside from the legal question involved as to whether the government could deport its own citizens, public opinion on the issue was divided. In British Columbia, where calls for evacuation had been the loudest, two-thirds of those questioned favoured the deportation of Japanese aliens, but not of Canadian citizens. A national poll reflected a similar split.[197]

Pressed in the House to articulate the government's post-war plans for persons of Japanese ancestry, King responded with a policy statement in the summer of 1944. While confirming that 'no person of Japanese race born in Canada has been charged with any act of sabotage or disloyalty during the years of war,' King nevertheless proceeded to outline the government's plan, which was designed to effect the removal of those deemed disloyal and to discourage the rest from remaining in Canada. Thus, Japanese residents would be able to remain in Canada, provided that they dispersed themselves across the country and were considered 'loyal' by the Loyalty Commission. Those judged to be disloyal would be deported to Japan 'as soon as this is physically possible,' and those among them who were Canadian citizens would be stripped of their citizenship. In addition, those persons who wanted to go to Japan following the war would be encouraged to do so, and immigration from Japan would be terminated.[198]

In furtherance of this policy, the following year all persons of Japanese race over sixteen years of age were required to indicate their intention concerning relocation to Japan. According to Sunahara, the survey was designed to encourage as many as possible to opt for removal.[199] Those who did so were told that they could remain in British Columbia until transportation to Japan could be arranged. While they waited, they would be able to collect relief benefits, regardless of their own personal savings. In addition to free transportation back to Japan, each person would receive funds equivalent to his or her remaining Canadian assets. For those who did not have assets in Canada, the government promised it would provide resettlement assistance of $200 per adult and $50 for every child. Internees in one camp were also assured that, if they opted for removal, this would not be seen as evidence of disloyalty to Canada.

The inducements facing those considering removal to Japan compared highly favourably with those offered to those wishing to remain in Canada. Internees who chose the latter were to be removed to a camp in Kelso, British Columbia, where they would wait until the government found them employment opportunities elsewhere in the country. Refusal to accept such employment would be seen as a 'lack of willingness to cooperate' and would disqualify the person from receiving relief. The resettlement allowance they were promised was less than 25 per cent of the amount promised to those who left for Japan. Moreover, it was made clear that employment, when found, would be only of a temporary nature, and even resettlement locations could not be guaranteed as permanent.[200]

Aside from the obvious disincentives offered by the government for remaining in Canada, other pressures also inclined many to sign the voluntary-repatriation request. Among these was the knowledge that life in Eastern cities would be extremely difficult for them, primarily because discriminatory employment practices would ensure that veterans took precedence in terms of job opportunities and, where employed, Japanese persons would be relegated to the most menial, low-paying work. In addition, Japanese patriots within the camps both urged and coerced others to sign the voluntary-repatriation forms, convinced that Japan would come out the victor in the war and provide better life opportunities for its descendants. Moreover, misinformation in some camps, such as the assurance that Canadian citizenship would not be lost until deportation was effected, and promises that persons could later revoke their request, also led many to sign the voluntary-removal undertaking, believing that there would be no adverse consequences in doing so. Finally, there were those who, because of age or illness, simply could not expect to work elsewhere and, devoid of capital, could not hope to re-establish themselves in another part of the country.[201]

In the end, close to 7,000 Japanese Canadians opted for removal to Japan. Together with their 3,500 dependants, they represented more than 43 per cent of the Japanese-Canadian population.[202] While the numbers alone suggested that the way was clear for the government to commence removal as soon as the war was over, other developments both within and outside the country worked to forestall immediate action. One of these developments was the groundswell of critical opinion that began to form once the circumstances of the removal requests were publicized. Individuals and groups who had traditionally protested discriminatory practices against Japanese residents were now joined by a host of others who regarded the government's deportation plans as fundamentally unjust.

Churches, social-service agencies working with Japanese Canadians, various professional associations, civil-liberties groups, labour unions, the National Council of Women, and the Canadian Jewish Congress worked together in publicizing the abuses to which the Japanese community was being subjected. As well, Japanese persons in the camps in British Columbia, and in other Japanese communities outside the province, banded together to protest their maltreatment. Then, in 1945, an umbrella organization was formed – the Cooperative Committee on Japanese Canadians (CCJC) – representing more than thirty organizations drawn both from within and outside the Japanese-Canadian community.[203]

In addition to the grass-roots action that developed, a court challenge was launched by several Japanese camp committees contesting the validity of the survey. However, the challenge was brought against the previous administrator of the camps, the B.C. Security Commission, whose authority had been transferred to the Department of Labour in 1943. The case was thus dismissed.[204]

The growing opposition to its deportation policy was but one obstacle facing the Canadian government. Once the end of the war was declared in August 1945, new impediments arose. One of these was the position of General MacArthur, Supreme Allied Commander in Japan, who was not in favour of immediate removal to Japan, given the devastation that gripped that country. Faced with the enormous problems associated with administering a country where disease, malnutrition, and starvation were rampant, he was not enthusiastic about swelling the already-burgeoning ranks of the dispossessed. Another impediment facing the Canadian government was the wave of revocations of removal requests that soon poured in following the armistice. Within eight months, more than 65 per cent of those who had signed such requests had applied to remain in Canada.[205]

Confronted with applications to revoke removal requests, the Cabinet sought means to make them binding. At this point, the Cabinet's power to issue orders-in-council free from parliamentary scrutiny was coming to an end, for the War Measures Act was to be declared inoperative in four months' time. It was to be replaced by the National Emergency Transitional Powers Act (NETPA), which was introduced into the House in the form of Bill 15. All orders-in-council under its authority would be reviewable by Parliament. In an effort to exclude deportation from such scrutiny, the government inserted a clause giving the Cabinet power over the 'entry into Canada, exclusion and deportation, and revocation of nationality.' The clause became the subject of heated debate within the House and within the press. Somewhat cowed by the controversy, the government agreed to remove the clause, while at the same time retaining another section in the bill which made all outstanding orders issued under the War Measures Act valid and non-reviewable by Parliament. To take full advantage of this, the Cabinet, just three weeks prior to the expiration of the War Measures Act, passed an order-in-council authorizing the deportation of four classes of Japanese residents. The first included all Japanese aliens who had signed repatriation requests. As for naturalized and Canadian-born Japanese residents who had signed requests and since revoked them, different criteria were imposed, depending on citizenship status. All naturalized Japanese Canadians who did not revoke their request prior to 2 September 1945 could be deported. Canadian-born Japanese Canadians could be deported only if their revocation was made after the minister had issued an order for their deportation. Finally, the wives and minor children of these three classes of persons could also be deported. Another order-in-council stripped deported naturalized Japanese Canadians of their Canadian citizenship, while yet another regulation established a loyalty tribunal to determine the loyalty of any person referred by the minister of Labour.[206]

These orders-in-council were greeted with opposition in the House, especially from the CCF, who argued that deporting those who had signed removal requests was particularly unjust, given the way such requests were solicited. The prime minister countered that it was entirely appropriate that Canada deport those who, at a time Canada was at war with Japan, illustrated their sympathy with the enemy by voluntarily agreeing to be removed there. Despite the objections of the CCF and other MPs, however, King was not prepared to back down. Since the orders-in-council were passed under the authority of the War Measures Act, they were not subject to parliamentary approval. King and his Cabinet were free to act on them, pending any judicial restraint on their authority to do so.

Although the debates within the House ended with the Christmas recess, the debate within the community did not. The Canadian Cooperative Committee on Japanese Canadians (CCJC) was particularly vocal in its criticism.[207] Not willing to dismiss outright its objections, given that the committee counted among its members several prominent Canadians, the government did agree to refer the regulations to the Supreme Court of Canada for a ruling on their validity.

Within a month, the Supreme Court heard arguments challenging the legality of the orders-in-council from the CCJC and submissions in their defence from the attorneys general of Canada and British Columbia.[208] The CCJC noted that the orders were enacted pursuant to the War Measures Act, which empowered the Cabinet to authorize such acts as it deemed necessary in times of war or other proclaimed emergency. The committee argued that, since the war was over, and indeed since the War Measures Act was now inoperative, the orders enacted under it were invalid. Moreover, it was submitted that, even if the Court found that an emergency was still in existence, the War Measures Act restricted the powers of the Cabinet to 'arrest, detention, exclusion and deportation,' the latter being defined to mean the 'return of an alien to the country from whence [sic] he came.' It did not therefore authorize the deportation of naturalized subjects or Canadian-born citizens. Furthermore, the CCJC claimed that the Cabinet was not empowered to revoke naturalization certificates solely on the basis that a person had signed a request for removal to Japan. Nor, it submitted, could a national emergency be used to support the forced return of the dependants of persons who had signed repatriation requests.

Within four weeks, the Court issued its decision. All of the seven justices who heard the case were agreed that orders passed pursuant to the War Measures Act were not necessarily invalid by virtue of the fact that the war was over and the act was inoperative. In the first place, the National Emergency Transitional Powers Act provided for the continuance of all orders made under the War Measures Act, and NETPA itself contained a clause declaring that the national emergency occasioned by the war 'has continued since the unconditional surrender of Germany and Japan and is still continuing.'[209] The Court further held that it was not within its jurisdiction to decide whether the measures were advisable or necessary; rather, it had to determine whether the Cabinet deemed them so by reason of a real or apprehended emergency. The majority were of the view that the fact that Cabinet had considered them necessary was apparent from the words of the orders themselves.[210]

The justices were further in unanimous agreement as to the validity of the deportation orders with respect to Japanese aliens and naturalized subjects of Japanese birth. As Chief Justice Rinfret stated, whether 'Canada possessed the power to expel an alien from its territory, or to deport him to the country whence he entered it, is a question that may now be regarded as settled since the judgment of the Privy Council in *A.G. Can. v Cain.*'[211] The Court was, however, divided as to whether the government had authority to revoke a naturalization certificate by virtue of the person's signing a request to be removed to Japan. Four of the seven judges felt that the government was within its powers to do so, noting that the Naturalization Act empowered Cabinet with the authority to revoke certificates where the 'person has shown himself by act or speech to be disaffected or disloyal to his Majesty.' According to justice Estey, the signing of a removal request 'provides evidence that with respect to such a person his affections are not with Canada, the land of his adoption, but rather with the country from which he originally came.'[212]

On the issue of whether the orders were valid as regards the Canadian-born, again the justices were divided. Five of the seven members felt that deportation was not limited to aliens, but applied equally to naturalized subjects and Canadian-born citizens. They found support for this view both in dictionary definitions of 'deportation' and in a section of the War Measures Act which gave Cabinet the power of exclusion and deportation, the former power governing removal of Canadian citizens. Justices Hudson and Estey went further to stress the voluntary nature of the request and the fact that, in carrying through with the person's expressed wish to go to Japan, the deportation order was 'no more than a compliance with such a request.'[213] Viewing the formal written request as a contract between the person and the government, Justice Hudson said that, if there is no revocation of the request before the deportation order is issued, then it would seem that, in the language of commerce, there was a 'firm contract,' so that the 'deportation order when made and carried out will be in fulfilment of the promise made on behalf of the government.'[214]

Finally, as to whether the order-in-council authorizing the involuntary repatriation of wives and dependants of those who had signed repatriation requests was valid, the Court was split four to three against its validity. The majority of the Court held that the compulsory deportation of wives and dependants was invalid in so far as the order authorizing it did not say that such deportation was necessary or advisable for the defence, security, peace, order, and welfare of Canada. The fact that it may be advisable for the welfare of the families, by ensuring that they would not be separated, was not enough to make the order constitutional.[215]

In its entirety, the Supreme Court of Canada's decision illustrated the willingness of the judiciary to accept the relatively unfettered discretionary power conferred on the Cabinet by the legislature over a matter of fundamental importance to individual security – namely, the right to remain in Canada. With respect to aliens and naturalized subjects, the decision was an affirmation of previous legal precedents and executive actions. The right of the government to deport, at its pleasure, aliens within its territories had been firmly entrenched since 1906 with the Privy Council's decision in *A.G. Can. v Cain*. The tenuous hold that naturalized Canadians had on their adopted country had also been underscored for years, particularly with the amendments to the Naturalization Act following the Winnipeg General Strike of 1919, which were later revised and consolidated in 1927.[216] The Naturalization Act gave the Cabinet wide powers to revoke naturalization certificates on grounds which included engaging in conduct exhibiting disloyalty or disaffection to the Crown. It was a power that had been readily relied upon in times of labour unrest, such as that experienced in the 1930s.

While the Supreme Court's decision confirmed the relatively weak claim that aliens and naturalized citizens had on permanent residence in Canada, it charted new waters in so far as it affirmed the right of the government to expel its own Canadian-born citizens, in effect creating refugees and stateless persons. It did this by essentially not looking beyond the form of the orders or the deportation requests, accepting both that an emergency necessitated the actions and that the requests were voluntarily signed, evincing a disloyalty to Canada. It is a striking decision, given, as Sunahara observes, that deportation of citizens was a crime for which the Nazis would soon be tried and convicted.[217]

The effect of the Supreme Court's decision complicated matters for the government. Although it authorized the removal of more than 6,000 aliens and Canadian citizens who had signed repatriation/relocation requests, it prohibited the forced removal of their 3,500 wives and dependants. Meanwhile, opposition to involuntary expulsion of Canadian citizens had gained momentum in the community, as evidenced by the letters of protest reaching the Prime Minister's Office and by editorials in the press. Upon the recommendation of the Special Cabinet Committee on Repatriation, the Cabinet agreed to refer the matter to the Privy Council for a final determination of the issues.[218]

By the time the Privy Council delivered its unanimous judgment affirming the validity of the orders-in-council, the government was no longer committed to using them. Instead of implementing forced removal to Japan, King chose to offer new incentives to the remaining Japanese population in British Columbia to induce their resettlement in the East. While employment continued to be denied them in that province, resettlement allowances were raised to assist people in buying or leasing property in the East, and hostels were established to aid in their resettlement. Most of the resident Japanese in British Columbia responded to these incentives, leaving in the province only the sick, elderly, and unemployable, and those who refused on principle to be removed to other provinces.

In the end, more than 4,000 people were removed to Japan, most of whom had no choice but to leave, either because their age or unemployability left them unable to avail themselves of job opportunities elsewhere in Canada or because their close family members had been trapped in Japan during the war and would not be permitted to rejoin their relatives in Canada. Of those that were removed to Japan, more than 50 per cent were Canadian-born citizens.[219]

By 1947, more than 13,000 people of Japanese decent had resettled in places east of British Columbia, leaving fewer than 7,000 remaining in that province, representing one-third of the pre-war Japanese population.[220] Although in that year the wartime restriction prohibiting Japanese persons from returning to their homes in B.C. was finally lifted, few could avail themselves of the opportunity, having had their homes and businesses confiscated and their savings consumed with the costs of their own internment. As Maryka Omatsu noted, unlike prisoners of war, or enemy nationals under the Geneva Convention, or American Japanese, 'Canadians of Japanese ancestry were forced to pay for their own internment.'[221]

Recent commentary on the internment and relocation of British Columbia's population of Japanese descent, and the subsequent confiscation and sale of their possessions, has been critical of the government's measures and the motivations behind them. Most commentators reflecting on the decision to intern Japanese Canadians agree with the assessment of Jack Pickersgill that it was made primarily in response to pressures from within B.C.[222] Other factors such as conscription and the American decision to remove 110,000 persons of Japanese ancestry from its coastal regions are also cited as having undoubtedly influenced the Canadian government's internment decision.[223] In assessing the legitimacy of the declared Japanese threat to Canadian coastal security, it has been pointed out that a greater threat to Canada at this time was on the East Coast. The American entry into the war left the East Coast vulnerable to attacks by German submarines, yet the government did not attempt to intern the entire population of German ancestry resident there.[224] In the end, the assessment of King's Ottawa-based military commanders turned out to be correct, for the only attack on Canada occurred when a Japanese submarine fired on a lighthouse and wireless station at Estevan Point on Vancouver Island, causing little damage.

According to J.L. Granatstein and Gregory Johnson, however, contrary to the conventional view that 'there was never any threat from Japan to the coast and hence no justification on the grounds of national security for the evacuation of Japanese Canadians, there *was* credible – if limited – military threat into 1943.'[225] In support of their position, they point to the fact that the RCMP and military were generally ill equipped to spot a subversive threat among Japanese Canadians and so, if one existed, they would most probably have been unable to uncover it. Moreover, they claim that the information that was supplied to the RCMP, and which formed the basis of Assistant Commissioner Mead's judgment that the Japanese population would remain loyal, was supplied from a noted underworld operator not generally known for his credibility. In addition, Granatstein and Johnson note that the government had information suggesting that the Japanese consulate in Vancouver had been instructed to recruit Nisei for intelligence gathering.[226] As well, these writers argue that the government may have legitimately questioned the loyalty of the Japanese-Canadian population, given that many Japanese Canadians supported the war against China prior to 1941, and, even after the bombing of Pearl Harbor, some still expressed loyalty to Japan. Finally, they observe that, while Ottawa's central military advisers were of the opinion that the Japanese population of B.C. posed no threat to national security, senior officers and staff planners of all three armed forces within the province disagreed. And while the writers acknowledge that 'Japanese Canadians were victims of the racism of the society in which they lived and an uncaring government that failed to defend the ideals for which its leaders claimed to have taken Canada and Canadians to war,' they nonetheless conclude that there were military concerns that 'could have provided Ottawa with a justification for the evacuation of the Japanese Canadians from the coast.'[227]

Yet, even assuming that Granatstein and Johnson are correct in accepting that there was a 'limited' threat of invasion, it would seem that the removal of 22,000 persons was nevertheless excessive under the circumstances. As Howard Palmer questions, if security was the motivating factor behind the evacuation, why were orphans and the blind removed along with the more plausible subversives?[228] One could also legitimately ask why, instead of embarking on an exceedingly expensive internment operation, the government did not direct its resources to significantly increasing its surveillance of the Japanese community, especially those people that it viewed as potential saboteurs. The fact that Japanese internees were not afforded the right of review of their internment, like other war internees, suggests that the government simply did not have any evidence to support their incarceration other than the fact that their racial origins could dispose them to treasonous activity.

In 1988, less then two weeks after the American government had announced its $1.25-billion compensation package for Japanese Americans, the Canadian government announced that it would compensate each survivor in Canada with $21,000 and provide $12 million to the Japanese community for educational, social, and cultural programs. In addition, it pledged $12 million for a Canadian Race Relations Foundation to foster racial harmony.[229] It took almost fifty years for the Canadian government to publicly acknowledge and apologize for the fact that, during the war, the government had 'wrongfully incarcerated, seized the property, and disenfranchised thousands of citizens of Japanese ancestry.'[230] It was an admission greatly appreciated by the Japanese community, whose wartime experiences had, until then, largely remained beyond public scrutiny. The fact that it had been omitted from standard Canadian history texts, or at best referred to superficially, meant that most Canadians were largely ignorant of the fact that, during the war, the government had incarcerated its own citizens, confiscated their properties, and attempted to deport them in a way that reflected the same racial intolerance that it had fought against through its participation in the Second World War.

Conclusions

The immigration policies followed by Canada throughout the war years were largely supported by the general public. The mechanisms for setting policy, primarily through executive orders and Immigration Branch directives, enabled the prime minister, Cabinet, and bureaucrats within the Immigration Branch to shape immigration policy quickly and relatively easily in response to public and personal biases, in the absence of parliamentary scrutiny. Certainly, as far as admissions were concerned, Prime Minister King, his French-Canadian caucus members, and the director of the Immigration Branch, Frederick Blair, wielded considerable influence. King's steadfast reluctance to open Canada's doors was motivated by his assessment of what the public would tolerate. His concern not to alienate French Canadians further, particularly after his reversal on the question of conscription, led him to pay special heed to the advice of his French-Canadian ministers, who ardently argued against the provision of sanctuary to European refugees.[231] And while he may not have had as much sway with King as did his French-Canadian ministers, Frederick Blair's own aversion to assisting European Jewry was played out daily in the directives that he issued to his immigration officers and in the hundreds of requests he personally rejected among the eligible applicants.

From a broader perspective, however, the reluctance to admit European refugees was not isolated to Quebec, or to a few key ministers, but was expressed throughout the country. Canadians in general felt that they were doing their share overseas, and while many were undoubtedly moved by the atrocities committed against the Jews, relatively few felt that it was their responsibility to provide the persecuted with sanctuary. Their attitude towards European refugees nonetheless contrasts with their attitude towards British war evacuees. While the former would be resisted, the latter were embraced enthusiastically. The British were considered to be among 'our own,' while, as public-opinion polls demonstrated, Jewish refugees were regarded as an alien race, incapable of assimilating into the Canadian way of life.

This divergent response to requests for assistance to some extent mirrored the way diverse racial groups were viewed in society as a whole. British immigrants had always been the most preferred group, quickly accommodated within the Canadian polity. Jews, on the other hand, had traditionally been a marginalized group, facing numerous forms of discrimination in both their personal and their professional lives, That Canadian immigration policies appeared racist was simply a reflection of deep ethnic divisions existing within the society as a whole.

The same can be said about internment policy. Canada's massive wartime incarcerations were largely undertaken in response to public clamour and hysteria. Here again King was ever mindful of the mood of the electorate. Certainly the first wave of internments of Germans, Italians, and alleged Communists was undertaken mostly in response to unsubstantiated fears of subversive activity. The public animus directed at Germans and Italians illustrated the deep ethnic divisions that existed within the country. As for alleged Communists, their internment was undertaken in response to security officials who distrusted Communist sympathizers, and powerful business interests; including the minister of Munitions and Supply, C.D. Howe, who argued that, unless decisive action was taken against radical workers, wartime production would be immeasurably harmed. In the absence of a large constituency to defend their interests, and initially in the face of considerable public hostility towards communism, radical leaders were incarcerated without public exposure or outcry.

The internment of Canada's Japanese population was also primarily a response to public pressure. There was a strong demand in British Columbia for the removal of what for years had been considered an alien and undesirable race. It was also an expedient move to justify conscription on the basis that troops were needed for the security of the West Coast. And while B.C. military leaders argued in favour of internment on the grounds that Japanese residents there might aid the enemy, these leaders also were concerned that, in the absence of evacuation, serious race riots would erupt.

According to Donald Avery, it would be a mistake to see Canadian immigration policy as primarily a result of racist public pressure. While racist attitudes on the part of politicians, bureaucrats, and the public help to explain the poor response to Jewish refugees, he argues, other factors also

significantly affected Canada's wartime admissions and internment policies.[232] One of these was an anti-left-wing bias among both immigration
and security officials that worked to exclude refugees and immigrants
with communist or socialist affiliations and that similarly provoked the
incarceration of hundreds of Canadians with suspected radical tendencies for the duration of the war. Avery points to Canada's refusal to assist
250,000 Spanish refugees from the Franco regime on the grounds that
they would be an economic burden and a disruptive influence.[233] Avery
maintains that, in addition to nativist and anti-left-wing biases, the concern for safeguarding the country against the infiltration of spies and
saboteurs was also a driving force behind the immigration and internment policies pursued during the war. This was equally true of Britain
and the United States, Canada's closest allies, for whom tight immigration policies and extensive internment measures were also features of
their wartime experience.[234]

While security concerns no doubt help to explain immigration and
internment policies pursued in times of war, they do not explain why, if
admitting refugees was considered a threat to national security, Canada
nevertheless admitted more than 600 Polish engineers and technicians
and their families as soon as it was clear that the expenses associated with
their immigration would be assumed by other governments. These immigrants were given more favourable treatment than equally qualified, and
sometimes more financially secure, Jewish refugees. Nor can security reasons account for Canada's refusal to release the British Jewish refugee internees after Britain had assured the Canadian government that they were
not considered risks to the war effort. Similarly, the massive nature of the
evacuation of Japanese residents along the west coast, the sale of their
properties, and the attempts to remove them to Japan following the war,
point to the fact that government policy was motivated by other than wartime security concerns.

Perhaps the best way to understand Canada's wartime treatment of
aliens, both refugees and residents, is to acknowledge that the government's policies were motivated by an amalgam of factors, some of which,
like national security, are understandable within the context of war, and
others, like racism, more enduring and pervasive. What is particularly
striking about Canada's wartime policies, however, with respect to prospective immigrants and resident aliens, is that they were formalized in
statutes that were sweeping in scope, that sanctioned extensive delegation
of authority, and that were relatively free from parliamentary or judicial
scrutiny. Thus, immigration policies adopted pursuant to the Immigration

Act, and internal security measures effected under the War Measures Act, were subject to uneven application and abuse of authority, which caused great hardship to immigrants and Canadians alike.

As far as Japanese Canadians are concerned, the official recognition of wartime abuses was a milestone in Canadian history. However, this, and the informal acknowledgment by the federal government that many egregious excesses were condoned that affected other Canadian ethnic groups,[235] came over forty years after the fact. Nevertheless, while there was no immediate recognition of wartime abuses, postwar immigration policy reflected a growing awareness on the part of both the Canadian government and the public that the exclusionary immigration policies of the Depression and war years were no longer acceptable in a postwar society. Although the shift would not be immediate, a perceptible change in government policies and public attitudes was taking place. The days of defining the national identity in terms of an Anglo-Saxon norm were coming to a close, to be replaced by the more modern concept of a multicultural society. There were several factors which contributed to this shift. In the first, place postwar prosperity itself tended to mute racial conflicts which generally surfaced in times of economic distress. Additionally, however, and more directly related to the wartime experience, was the fact that many different ethnic groups were represented in the Canadian forces overseas. As Anglo-Canadians fought alongside Chinese, Ukrainian, and later Japanese-Canadian soldiers,[236] a new respect emerged for ethnic minorities among the veteran community. As well, as the atrocities of Hitler's policies became well known, people developed a heightened awareness of the consequences that notions of racial superiority could entail, and public expressions of racial intolerance became less acceptable.

CHAPTER EIGHT

The Postwar Boom, 1946–1962:
Reopening the Doors Selectively

During the postwar period, two prevailing trends had a strong impact on the formation of immigration policy. First, the period from 1946 to 1962 saw the beginning of a significant economic boom in Canada that, with minor fluctuations, endured until the early 1970s.[1] Large-scale private investments in the natural resources and manufacturing sectors, and government investments in physical infrastructure and educational facilities, combined with pent-up consumer demand from the Depression and war years, fuelled the boom. Canada's gross national product rose from $5.7 billion in 1939 to $36 billion in 1962. The unemployment rate through to 1958 ranged from about 2.8 to 5.9 per cent, and over the period average real incomes almost doubled, initiating nearly thirty years of almost uninterrupted prosperity. In urban centres, manufacturing industries continued to expand, requiring new capital investments in plant and machinery, and new types of skilled labour. Low birth rates during the Depression and war years also led to shortages of many forms of skilled and unskilled labour and created ample job opportunities. Between 1941 and 1962, Canada's population increased from 11.5 million to 18.5 million. Extremely high domestic birth rates from the end of the war through to 1960 largely accounted for this population increase, although the large scale of postwar immigration also had a significant impact. The strong performance of the postwar economy favoured the opening up of Canadian immigration policy. As we will see, this period was marked by the admission of more diverse groups of immigrants, and by a relative absence of controversy over immigration issues – a notable difference from policies in preceding periods.

Another factor influencing immigration policies was the international environment, which was also undergoing dramatic changes in this period.

Following the end of the Second World War, Canada played an active role in the creation of the United Nations in 1945 and in the United Nations Relief and Rehabilitation Administration (UNRRA), designed to restore and rebuild those countries devastated by the war. Canada was also involved in the promotion of a multi-racial Commonwealth following the granting of independence to India, Pakistan, Ceylon, Burma, and Israel in 1947–8, and to many other former colonies in succeeding years. Canada also played a prominent role in U.N. peacekeeping efforts throughout the 1950s. As well, the Canadian government participated in the negotiations that led to the formation in 1947 of the General Agreement on Tariffs and Trade (GATT), which provided the basis for a multilateral, non-discriminatory international trading regime. However, there was increasing pressure during this period to strengthen the Western Alliance in the face of growing threats from the Communist Bloc. As the era of the Cold War began, Canada became a signatory to the North Atlantic Treaty Organization (NATO) in 1949, and to a bilateral joint defence arrangement with the United States (NORAD) in 1957. Canada's increasingly active participation in world affairs led politicians, interest groups, and the general public to favour a selectively more open immigration policy.[2]

In terms of immigration policy, a widely quoted speech by Prime Minister Mackenzie King in 1947 suggested little change:

> The policy of the Government is to foster the growth of the population of Canada by the encouragement of immigration. The government will seek ... to ensure the careful selection and permanent settlement of such numbers of immigrants as can advantageously be absorbed in our national economy ... I wish to make it quite clear that Canada is perfectly within her rights in selecting the persons whom we regard as desirable future citizens. It is not a 'fundamental human right' of any alien to enter Canada. It is a privilege. It is a matter of domestic policy ... The people of Canada do not wish, as a result of mass immigration, to make a fundamental alteration in the character of our population ... Any considerable Oriental immigration would ... be certain to give rise to social and economic problems ...[3]

This speech affirmed some of the key principles of earlier immigration policies: admission was a privilege, and therefore properly left to the discretion of the government, with few due process protections; immigrants were to be viewed in terms of their potential contribution to the economy; and immigration was not to change the fundamental demographic character of the community, which necessitated continued restrictions on Asian immigration.

The federal government, probably reflecting broader public apprehensions, was also concerned that Canada might experience the same kind of postwar recession that had occurred after the First World War. At the same time, the country faced the immediate task of reintegrating its returning servicemen and women back into Canadian civil life, as well as dismantling the highly centralized role played by the government in the economy in mobilizing wartime resources.

However, as the postwar economic boom got under way in the late 1940s, these apprehensions receded, and the need for both skilled and unskilled labour in many of the growth sectors of the economy became obvious and widely acknowledged. Strong 'push' factors in the devastated countries of Western Europe also contributed to a change in immigration policy. Thus, the economic and political context of the postwar period led to a gradual liberalization of admission policies and a dramatic increase in immigration. Over the sixteen-year period between 1946 and 1962, the total intake of immigrants was 2,151,505, averaging 126,559 on an annual basis (almost 160,000 between 1951 and 1960) – almost as many as in the large immigrant waves of the first decade of the twentieth century and the 1920s. Canada also responded to pressure from its allies to assist with the resettlement of displaced persons and other refugees in Europe. Nearly a quarter of a million refugees were admitted between 1947 and 1962. Of the 165,000 refugees admitted between 1947 and 1953, Poles (23 per cent), Ukrainians (16 per cent), Germans and Austrians (11 per cent), Jews (10 per cent), Latvians (6 per cent), Lithuanians (6 per cent), Magyars (Hungarian) (5 per cent), Czechs (3 per cent), Dutch (3 per cent), and Russians (3 per cent) comprised most of the intake.[4]

Immigration patterns over the period increasingly reflected an emphasis on skilled trades people and professionals, instead of agricultural workers, who settled, not in rural areas, but in urban centres. In 1948, about one in five workers arriving in Canada was a farmer or agricultural worker. By 1961, this figure was closer to one in twenty. Unskilled blue-collar workers in manufacturing industries also declined, while the percentage of skilled trades people and professionals rose significantly.[5] Approximately half of all immigrants settled in Ontario; about 20 per cent in Quebec; about 10 per cent in British Columbia; 17 per cent on the Prairies, declining to 12 per cent by the end of the period; and only about 2 per cent in the Atlantic provinces.

There was also a dramatic change in the demographics of immigration during this period. A 1956 order-in-council continued the practice of giving preferential status to Western European and some Commonwealth source countries. However, immigrants from Britain declined from 44 per cent of the intake in 1946–50 to 27 per cent in 1956–61, while Italian immigrants increased from 4.5 to 18 per cent of the intake over the same period. With the exception of a small Chinese intake between 1952 and 1955, non-European immigrants were not represented at all in the top ten source nationalities.[6]

National security concerns, heightened by the advent of the Cold War, played a prominent role throughout the period with respect to both admission and deportation of immigrants suspected of having communist sympathies and in monitoring immigrants' activities including ethnic organizations and the ethnic press for evidence of communist sympathies.[7] Security screening not only caused delays, but served as the grounds for rejection of a large number of prospective immigrants. From 1946 to 1958, more than 29,000 prospective immigrants were rejected as 'security risks,' and deportations or refusals of temporary visas to visitors on security grounds were also quite common.[8] There were a total of 8,572 deportations over the period. On the other hand, this antipathy to perceived communist sympathizers led to lax admission policies towards a number of fascist or Nazi sympathizers, a number of whom, it subsequently transpired, were war criminals.

Immigration policy rarely attracted serious parliamentary debate and did not play an important role in any of the federal elections that occurred during this period. The Immigration Branch, which at the beginning of the period was housed in the Department of Mines and Resources, was a minor backwater of the federal bureaucracy, and executive discretion was central to the formulation and administration of immigration policy. However, coinciding with the postwar rise in immigration, the Canadian Citizenship Act (S.C. 1946, c.15) extended Canadian citizenship to certain non-Canadian residents in Canada. This marked the first time that a Commonwealth nation had created its own class of citizenship separate from that of Britain. Prior to this time, the highest status that immigrants could attain was British subject status, which was conferred by naturalization. British subjects who had lived in Canada for five years, women who had married Canadians, and naturalized Canadians could now acquire Canadian citizenship. Women who married non-Canadians were now permitted to preserve their citizenship status.[9] The Chinese Immigration Act was repealed in 1947, although Chinese immigration continued to be subject to an order-in-council that mostly restricted Asian immigrants to close relatives of sponsoring Canadian citizens. In 1950, a separate Department of Citizenship and Immigration was created.

A new Immigration Act was passed in 1952. While the act set out requirements for admission, it mostly codified existing executive practices and included provisions which maintained the broad discretionary powers of the Cabinet. Nevertheless, a growing awareness emerged in this period of the importance of due process and public accountability in the administration of immigration policy, which resulted in a gradual strengthening of the procedural rights of immigrants, including an enhanced role for immigration appeal boards in deportations. Admission policies which explicitly discriminated on the basis of race or country of origin were largely eliminated by 1962 and were replaced by criteria for independent immigrants that emphasized skills, education, and training. Residual restrictions limited the ability of non-European residents to sponsor more distant relatives, and very restrictive quotas applied to independent immigrants from India, Pakistan, and Ceylon. As well, most immigration offices continued to be located in Europe.

In the immediate postwar years, the Senate played the lead parliamentary role in reviewing immigration issues. The Senate Standing Committee on Immigration and Labour was established in 1946 to explore policy options in immigration, specifically regarding what types of immigrants were desirable and on what terms, as well as Canada's absorptive capacity for immigrants. The committee continued to meet until 1953 with the major stakeholders, including ethnic groups, community organizations, labour unions, transport companies, and business associations. The ethnic groups heard from included the Finn, Czech, Ukrainian, and Polish communities. Almost all called for Canada to expand sponsorship rights to include extended families, including adult married nephews/nieces and cousins, and sometimes even friends. Most delegations attacked the government's designation of classes of immigrants as preferred or non-preferred for being racist. Ethnic delegations were generally politely received, yet most senators favoured a selective immigration policy based on both race and skill.

The Senate committee also heard from organized labour in 1946. Organized labour had traditionally opposed mass immigration into Canada, viewing immigrants as cheap workers flooding local labour markets and causing unemployment, reduced wages, and poorer living conditions. However, after the war, organized labour began cautiously to embrace expanded immigration. The two main national labour bodies were the Trades and Labor Congress (TLC), the largest union, with 356,121 members at the end of 1946, and the Canadian Congress of Labour (CCL), slightly smaller, with 314,025 members.[10] The TLC had traditionally been strongly opposed to large influxes of immigrants and was opposed specifically to assisted immigrants from Europe and to Orientals. The CCL, on the other hand, grew out of the All Canadian Congress of Labour (ACCL), which represented less-skilled industries with a large immigrant membership. The CCL and its forerunners had traditionally been more sympathetic to foreign workers. Some union leaders (specifically those of the CCL) were clearly ideologically opposed to racism.[11] At the Senate hearings, A.R. Mosher, president of the CCL, stated his unequivocal opposition to racial classifications in Canada's immigration policy. The following exchange took place with Walter Aseltine, a long-time Conservative appointed to the Senate by Prime Minister Bennett:

HON. MR ASELTINE: You do not believe in bringing in Negroes do you?
MR. MOSHER: I believe Negroes may be brought in with no more discrimination against them than any other colour, class or creed.
HON. MR ASELTINE: I do not agree with you.[12]

In contrast, in TLC president Percy Bengough's presentation, he called for 'exclusion of all races that cannot be properly assimilated into the national life of Canada. It must be recognized that there are citizens of other countries who may be good brothers and sisters, internationally, but yet would not be acceptable as brothers and sisters-in-law to Canadians. Experience has clearly demonstrated that because of this fact certain nationals who have in the past been admitted into Canada remain as a distinct race and will remain a problem for future generations.'[13]

The much smaller Canadian and Catholic Confederation of Labour (CCCL), the major French-Canadian trade union, continued to oppose immigration on the grounds that standards of living would fall if large numbers of new immigrants were admitted.[14]

The railway companies also testified before the Senate committee in 1946. Canadian National Railways (CNR) had an optimistic outlook regarding economic expansion and called for an aggressive immigration policy. The Canadian Pacific Railway (CPR) urged Canada to follow Australia's lead, stating Canada could readily double or triple its population.

For the first three years, the Senate committee issued annual reports which called for Canada to adopt a more open immigration policy. The committee acknowledged that Canada had 'a non-Immigration Act, [whose] main purpose [was] ... exclusion.'[15] It stated in 1946 that 'intelligently selected immigrants in managerial, technical and artisan classifications would increase employment, rather than taking work from those already here.'[16] The committee also strongly advocated a more humanitarian immigration policy: 'It is not right that we should entirely close our doors against the victims of world upheaval and particularly the children.'[17] The committee recommended an extension of the regulations regarding sponsored immigrants to include married sons and daughters, brothers, sisters, and nephews/nieces over the age of sixteen.[18] It called for preference to be given to family groups over single men and women, and more extensive discretion for officials when interpreting otherwise restrictive regulations.[19]

Each of the three Senate committee's annual reports (1946–8) was presented to the full Senate and received approval with minimal debate. The reports were then forwarded to Prime Minister King and his Cabinet for their consideration.[20] The government did not formally respond to them, and it is not clear that they had any direct impact on government policy making.

Like most editorial, political, and business leaders, most academics in the early postwar era were optimistic about Canada's future. The 'displacement theory,' made prominent in 1939 by W. Burton Hurd, based on his own work and that of M.C. MacLean,[21] became discredited in academic circles and the popular media by the end of the first postwar decade. This theory sought to explain the low net migration trends for Canada historically and claimed that high levels of immigration into Canada caused emigration of Canadian-born citizens to the United States. If emigration were to become impossible (e.g., because of changes in U.S. immigration policy), then immigration would lead to an increase in unemployment for Canadians because immigrants were a cheaper source of labour and would take jobs away from Canadians. After the war, Hurd continued to advance his theory and was supported by Canadian historian Arthur Lower.[22] In 1946, Professor Angus, head of the Department of Economics, Political Science, and Sociology at the University of British Columbia, and an enthusiastic supporter of immigration in the early postwar period, rejected the theory. He wrote: 'Canada has won a position of great importance in the World. Without a very substantial increase in her own population it will be impossible for Canada to retain her relative importance when other nations of equal or greater population rebuild their shattered lives.'[23] Angus called for an end to restrictions based on race or nationality, in part because he considered that the scale of immigration by particular groups was likely to be small, reflecting the views of many academics of this period. He argued that, if it was necessary to limit immigrants from ethnic groups, the government should adopt a quota system similar to that of the United States.[24] In his view, immigrants were needed to perform jobs Canadians would not do.[25] B.K. Sandwell, the editor of *Saturday Night* magazine, who was well known for his keen interest in immigration, agreed with Angus: 'The immigrants were muscle, the emigrants were skills and judgment. The immigrants were European, the emigrants were Canadian. The Canadians left, not because they wanted to do the jobs which the immigrants were doing, but because they wanted to do much better jobs, and because even with the immigrants working at the muscular jobs there still were not enough of the better jobs to employ all the ambitious Canadians.'[26]

In 1953, economist Mabel Timlin mounted a vigorous attack on the 'displacement theory.' In her book entitled *Does Canada Need More People?*,[27] commissioned by the deputy minister of Citizenship and Immigration, Dr. Hugh Keenleyside, Timlin analysed in detail different theories surrounding immigration, and strongly rejected the 'displacement theory.' She called Lower's analysis 'oversimplified' and an example of theory in its most primitive form.[28] She attacked Hurd's methodology, stating that what he called 'absorptive capacity' was a misleading combination of a number of short-term factors.[29] For Timlin, emigration was not a response to immigration. For example, Canada's pre-war population may have been smaller than what it was had it not been for immigration; immigration sustained the level of population by both increasing the net-migration figure and expanding the economy to keep more Canadians from leaving.[30] Timlin wrote: 'The notion that immigration is usually, in any direct sense, the main cause of emigration seems to me to have even less to recommend it than the notion that deaths are mainly caused by births ...'[31] She also argued that emigration from Canada might have encouraged immigration by opening up job opportunities.[32] She concluded that, in the long term, immigrants created more wealth for Canada and expanded the economy. Timlin argued that Canada should relate its immigration policy to its labour-market needs. Her views appear to have been influential with the Gordon Commission, which in 1957 took a similar position,[33] and more generally in the increasing focus of admissions policy on education, skills, and labour market needs.

Although immigration was not generally considered a matter of 'high politics' during the postwar-boom period, the politics of Canadian immigration policy nonetheless changed in important ways. Business interests pressed hard for an expansionary immigration policy, including contract labour schemes.[34] While labour interests opposed such schemes, they adopted a sharply more supportive attitude to increased immigration generally than in previous periods. Labour groups were largely persuaded that immigration was an important ingredient of domestic economic growth. Church and community groups became influential advocates of more humanitarian immigration policies, especially with respect to refugees. Broad, albeit belated, public awareness of the horrors of Naziism and its racist implications led to increasing receptiveness to these humanitarian views. Ethnic groups of former immigrants often supported similar positions. They also promoted liberalization of family sponsorship policies and resisted efforts to curtail existing sponsorship rights. By the end of the period, these groups had become politically salient in their own right in a number of urban electorates. For example, the government's perceived attempt in 1959 to curb Italian immigration by restricting family sponsorship rights was abandoned in the face of protests from Opposition political parties, and ethnic and community groups. Anti-Semitism, anti-Orientalism, and anti-black racism continued to affect policy development. However, by the end of the period, there was a recognition that explicitly racist immigration policies were no longer defensible. This change in perspective reflected both the growing domestic political influence of church, community, ethnic, and other public interest groups, and international considerations whereby Canada's credibility in a multi-racial British Commonwealth of newly independent nations, and its role as an honest broker, middle power, and peacekeeper in the larger global theatre, made many of its former immigration policies increasingly anachronistic, and indeed an embarrassment.[35]

Major Changes in Immigration Policy, 1946–1962

The principal legislative changes in the period were the passage of the Canadian Citizenship Act in 1946, the creation of the Department of Citizenship and Immigration in 1950, and the enactment of a new Immigration Act in 1952. However, most of the major changes in immigration policy in this period, following long-standing tradition, occurred as a result of executive policy changes implemented through regulations or administrative practice. Major developments included changes in the definition of admissible classes, special movements, and contract labour programs, refugee policy, and deportation procedures. From

1945 to 1962, immigration policy was not the focus of extensive debates in the House of Commons. Only three discrete events, the repeal of the Chinese Immigration Act in 1947,[36] a Canadian Bar Association's subcommittee report in 1954,[37] and a change in an order-in-council in 1959,[38] attracted serious parliamentary debate. As members of the Opposition noted in 1955, the Department of Citizenship and Immigration had a habit of producing the annual immigration figures and estimates on the last day of a parliamentary session, thereby avoiding debate altogether.

ADMISSION POLICIES

Admissible Classes, 1945–1952

Until 1945, the admissible classes of immigrants were restricted by a 1931 Privy Council Order (P.C. 1931–695) to:

1 British subjects, as defined in P.C. 1923–183 – 'British by reason of birth or naturalization in Great Britain, Newfoundland, New Zealand, Australia and South Africa';[39]
2 U.S. citizens;
3 the wives and unmarried children under eighteen and fiance(e)s of legal residents of Canada;
4 agriculturalists having sufficient means to farm in Canada.[40]

The only preconditions to admission for members of preferred classes were that they be in good physical and mental health, of good character, and not likely to become a public charge. Anyone not falling within one of these four classes had to apply for an exemption through a special order-in-council. Chinese immigrants were almost completely prohibited by the 1923 Chinese Immigration Act. The one exception to this prohibition was a provision that permitted the immigration of Chinese merchants, a term narrowly defined in the legislation. Thus, a Chinese Canadian could not bring his wife or child to Canada. In addition, Asians and Africans were excluded from Canada by P.C. 1930–2115, which prohibited the landing of 'any immigrant of any Asiatic race.'[41]

According to Freda Hawkins,

Asia meant almost everything in the Eastern Hemisphere outside Europe. Its northwest frontier ran along the southern border of the Soviet Union and the Black Sea and round the eastern and southern coasts of the Mediterranean. All Turkey and lands to the south, including Egypt, were in Asia. Only the Armenians managed to slip out of the Asian net. Thus, by excluding Asians and, by association and extension, Africans also (except South Africans), Canada was prepared to accept only one kind of immigrant from the Eastern Hemisphere – the European immigrant.[42]

The only exception to this restriction was the wife or the unmarried child under the age of eighteen of a Canadian citizen (or British subject). In 1946, government regulations extended admissible classes for non-Asians to include brothers, sisters, parents, and orphaned nephews and nieces under eighteen years of age of Canadian citizens as long as the Canadian citizen agreed to sponsor them, which entailed rather nebulous obligations 'to receive and care' for them.[43] This gave some members of immediate families who were refugees the right to enter Canada.[44]

Several regulations in early 1947 signalled important changes in Canada's immigration policy. The first of these was an order-in-council which widened the admissible classes to include farm workers, miners, and loggers as long as they had secured employment in Canada. This same regulation permitted the immigration of any agriculturalist with a Canadian relative. Whereas, under the 1931 order (P.C. 1931–695), only 'agriculturalists having sufficient means to farm in Canada' were eligible to immigrate, this new regulation stated that a farmer who could not afford to purchase a farm was eligible to immigrate if he either had a relative (as defined by the order) who was also a farmer and promised to assist him, or was assured of employment on a farm.[45]

The second and more significant order was a direct reaction to the booming Canadian economy: the adoption of the contract labour scheme (discussed below.)

A third order widened the admissible classes to permit the landing of fiance(e)s, husbands, wives, and unmarried children of people legally residing in (but not citizens of) Canada.[46] In addition, in 1947 the Chinese Immigration Act was repealed.[47] There had been considerable criticism of the Chinese Immigration Act by various interest groups, including the Roman Catholic Church of Toronto, the Canadian Council of Churches, and the Canadian Congress of Labour, who formed the Committee for the Repeal of the Chinese Immigration Act.

The press gave the government's decision to repeal the act guarded endorsement. However, the plan to repeal the Act received sharp criticism from all B.C. members of Parliament who spoke, regardless of party affiliation (with the notable exception of CCF member Angus MacInnis). They voiced fears of great influxes of Asian immigrants that would cost Canadian jobs. One Liberal member stated that Canadian Congress of Labour (CCL) leader A.R. Mosher,[48] who supported repeal of the act, did not understand British Columbia's problems: 'Ontario is very generous in that matter, of course, so long as the Japanese and Chinese all stay in British Columbia.'[49] Howard Green, Conservative MP from B.C., supported his Liberal colleague:

> Always underlying the public uneasiness and unrest has been the threat of a large influx. With that removed in 1923, the friendly feeling for the Chinese people steadily increased in Canada. The Chinese are scrupulously honest … The feeling has improved to such an extent that in British Columbia at the coming session of the legislature, which opens today, it looks as if the vote will be given for the first time to the Chinese and the East Indians. I suggest that it would be unwise to destroy this good relationship and opening the gates to an influx would probably do that.[50]

Another member was more blunt about his beliefs when he stated: 'I would warn every hon. member that we have a solemn responsibility toward the generations that come after us to see that we keep this Canada white. I do not say that in any derogatory way, because I believe that a man with a yellow skin or a black skin is just as good as I am in every respect.'[51]

The government's response was that Chinese immigrants would still fall under P.C. 1930–2115, which limited any Asian-Canadian citizen's sponsorship to his wife and his children under age eighteen.[52] In addition, P.C. 1378 still required the government of China to approve any Chinese seeking Canadian citizenship. Conservative John Diefenbaker stated that the government had not eliminated discrimination as it had claimed; CCF leader Coldwell called this turn of events a 'cruel hoax.' Under heavy fire, the government revoked P.C. 1378 but retained P.C. 1930–2115. The *Globe and Mail* criticized the government's choice to retain PC 1930–2115 and the *Toronto Daily Star, Ottawa Citizen, London Free Press*, and *Quebec Chronicle-Telegraph* all ran editorials calling for its repeal.[53]

With a federal election pending in the fall of 1948, the Cabinet approved a regulation that gave French citizens the same preferred status as British subjects.[54] This regulation was designed to avoid a backlash to increases in immigration from French Canadians who had traditionally viewed immigration as an Anglophone plot to overwhelm the French population with numbers, given the absence of any significant French immigration.[55] However, departmental officials took the view that a large proportion of prospective French immigrants were Communists or former Nazi collaborators. Between 1946 and 1950, fewer than 5,000 French immigrants entered Canada. While prospective immigrants besieged Canadian consular offices in Paris, and the Canadian consul made urgent requests for more resources, Keenleyside advised the deputy minister of Labour to channel 'all efforts in the same direction, that is to say, the encouragement of British immigration to Canada.'[56]

Political sensitivities in this context were further illustrated by an episode involving the Count de Bernonville, the former military governor of Lyons during the Vichy regime in France and an assistant to Klaus Barbie, the 'Butcher of Lyons.' Sentenced to death in absentia by the postwar French government, he entered Canada with three accomplices in 1946, dressed as a priest. He was warmly welcomed in Quebec, and a chorus of powerful Quebec figures, including Premier Duplessis, the mayor of Montreal, and the hierarchy of the Catholic Church, rose to his defence to prevent extradition to France and to delay deportation proceedings for four years. As a result, the Count was able to escape in 1950 to a Nazi haven in South America. He was found strangled to death in Rio de Janeiro in 1972.[57]

In 1950, with the creation of the Department of Citizenship and Immigration to replace the Immigration Branch of the Department of Mines and Resources, there was now a minister whose primary responsibility was immigration, although he or she was also responsible for citizenship and Indian affairs. Also in 1950, the admissible classes were further widened to include any European who could 'satisfy the Minister that he is suitable, having regard to the climatic, social, educational, labour and other conditions or requirements of Canada.'[58] This regulation gave the minister wide discretion and was inserted almost verbatim in the Immigration Act of 1952 (s.61 [g]).[59] In particular, this power resulted in the admission of a large number of Italian and German immigrants, with the removal of the former from the enemy alien list in 1947, and the latter in 1950.[60] Italians became so significant a percentage of the new immigrants that, by 1957, the backlog of sponsored cases in the Department of Citizenship and Immigration's Rome office had reached 52,000.[61]

In February 1951, the Department of Citizenship and Immigration implemented the Assisted Passage Loan Scheme to financially assist immigrants from Europe whose services were urgently needed and who could not afford their own transportation.[62] A fund of $9 million was established by regulation, and loans made to immigrants were repaid over the two years following landing, by pay deductions if the immigrant had come to Canada to be employed as a salary or wage earner.[63] This program was largely a response to the 1949 devaluation of the British pound, which substantially raised the cost of transportation for British immigrants.[64] By 1955, 32,600 people had taken advantage of the program, which boasted a remarkably high repayment record.[65] The department's *Annual Report, 1955–56*, announced that the program was expanded in 1956 to include all immigrants 'likely to become successfully established.'[66] Nonetheless, immigrants from Africa and Asia were excluded from the program until 1970.[67]

The early 1950s also saw some shift in the Quebec elite's attitude towards immigration. W. Greening noted in 1951 that Quebec academics and editorialists had realized that the new non-British immigrants shared much in common with the Quebecois. They both considered themselves Canadians first, and subjects of the British Commonwealth second. In addition, Eastern European immigrants were mostly Roman Catholics. Although the French still feared mass immigration, Greening argued, the selective immigration policy of the Liberal government, which included immigrants from beyond the British Isles, 'is no longer looked upon with complete disfavour.'[68]

The Immigration Act, 1952

In 1952, the first new Immigration Act since 1910 was enacted by Parliament within a month of being introduced.[69] In most important respects, the 1952 act was similar to its predecessor in that it provided a skeletal statutory framework within which the government of the day could adopt orders and regulations that reflected prevailing immigration priorities.

For the most part, the new Act simply legislated procedures that had developed administratively over the forty-two-year period since the last Immigration Act was passed. As Liberal Minister of Citizenship and Immigration Walter Harris pointed out in introducing the 1952 Act, the proposed legislation entailed no significant changes to immigration policy. For example, the Act made provisions for an assisted-passage loan scheme (s.69), which had already been instituted through orders-in-council in 1951. Similarly, the new Act stated specifically that all persons seeking admission to Canada must be examined in order that their admissibility could be established.[70] As with the 1910 Act, the new Act's major feature was the enormous discretion over the admissibility and deportation of aliens vested in the federal Cabinet, which in practice devolved to the minister responsible and his officials. The key section which permitted the Cabinet to set the criteria for admission to the country was subsection 61 (g). The Cabinet was empowered to limit admission of people by reason of

(i)   nationality, citizenship, ethnic group, occupation, class or geographical area of origin,

(ii) peculiar customs, habits, modes of life or methods of holding property,

(iii) unsuitability having regard to the climatic, economic, social, industrial, educational, labour, health or other conditions or requirements existing ... in Canada ... or

(iv) probable inability to become readily assimilated or to assume the duties and responsibilities of Canadian citizenship ...

A 1952 letter from Citizenship and Immigration minister Walter Harris, which was put on the record in the House in 1953 by CCF member Joseph Noseworthy, illustrated that these provisions were designed to exclude non-white immigrants:

In the light of experience it would be unrealistic to say that immigrants who have spent the greater part of their life in tropical or sub-tropical countries become readily adapted to the Canadian mode of life which, to no small extent, is determined by climatic conditions. It is a matter of record ... that natives of such countries are more apt to break down in health than immigrants from countries where the climate is more akin to that of Canada. It is equally true that, generally speaking, persons from tropical or sub-tropical countries find it more difficult to succeed in the highly competitive Canadian economy.[71]

The list of prohibited classes was little changed, and continued to exclude idiots, imbeciles, morons, epileptics, beggars, as well as the insane, the diseased, and the physically defective (unless they would not be a public burden or a danger to public health), individuals convicted of crimes of moral turpitude,[72] and those advocating subversion of democratic processes.[73] Dropped from the previous act was an exclusion against feeble-minded persons. Although prostitutes continued to be excluded, the prohibition in the previous act of 'women and girls coming to Canada for any immoral purpose' was eliminated. Finally, the 1952 Immigration Act added some new classes of excluded people. Subsection 5(e) excluded homosexuals, and subsections 5(j) and (k) excluded drug addicts and traffickers.[74]

The immigration regulations that accompanied the new act imposed a literacy test,[75] but this new test was given in the language of the potential immigrant's country of origin. By 1962, literacy tests were eliminated altogether.

Section 39 of the 1952 Immigration Act retained an important feature of the 1910 act by denying courts' jurisdiction 'to review, quash, reverse, restrain or ... interfere with any ... decision or order of [any] immigration officer ... made ... in accordance with ... this Act relating to the detention or deportation of any person ... unless such person is a Canadian citizen or has Canadian domicile.' The 1952 Immigration Act did, however, strengthen the appeals system by providing for the creation of immigration appeal boards (IABs; s.12) to hear appeals from decisions of special inquiry officers (SIOs) to deport aliens. Each board would consist of at least three members selected by the executive from officials of the department.[76]

With a few exceptions,[77] all those subject to deportation orders made by SIOs were given the right to appeal the decision.[78] All appeals were to be heard by the minister unless he or she directed the appeal to an IAB. Both the IAB and the minister were given full powers to overturn the SIO's decision, and the minister in turn could reverse any decision by an IAB.[79] They could also reopen an inquiry and order the SIO to admit new evidence.[80]

The 1952 Immigration Act was proclaimed into law on 1 June 1953, along with Order-in-Council P.C. 1953–859, entitled 'Immigration Regulations.' Section 20 of the new regulations stated that a person was eligible to emigrate to Canada if the immigration officer found him or her to be a member of one of the following classes:

20(1) (a) British subjects by birth or by naturalization in the United Kingdom, Australia, New Zealand or the Union of South Africa and citizens of Ireland;

(b) citizens of the United States of America; and

(c) citizens of France born in France or in Saint-Pierre and Miquelon Islands if such a person has sufficient means to maintain himself until he has secured employment.

Subsection 20(2) limited Asian immigrants to the wife, husband and unmarried children under twenty-one years of age, of any Canadian citizen.[81]

However, the most important provision was subsection 20(4), which was designed to reinforce subsection 61(g) of the new Immigration Act (the provision that allowed the government to limit admission on the basis of race or nationality). Subsection 20(4) conferred this power in unqualified form on SIOs. It prohibited admission 'where in the opinion of a Special Inquiry Officer such a person should not be admitted' because of the customs 'or methods of holding property' in his country of origin or because of his 'probable inability to become readily assimilated' after his admission.

By vesting such a wide range of discretion in SIOs, the Canadian government did not have to pass regulations which blatantly discriminated against non-preferred immigrants. This reduced the potential for embarrassment in international relations, and explains the adoption, at least on paper, of the apparently more expansive regulations first passed in 1950.

The administration of the 1952 act was criticized in a 1954 report of a subcommittee of the Canadian Bar Association (CBA).[82] The subcommittee was created in 1952 and examined 200 cases involving allegations of improper or arbitrary exercise of bureaucratic discretion. Among its other recommendations, the final report called for the creation of a quasi-judicial immigration appeal board. This report was the focus of a Conservative attack on the minister of Citizenship and Immigration, Jack Pickersgill, in the 1955 session of Parliament,[83] including a motion for censure brought by Conservative MP Davie Fulton.[84] Fulton stated that the 'proposition that Canada needs more people is undisputed and is supported by statements made by government spokesmen, chamber of commerce spokesmen and by labour leaders themselves.'[85] However, both Fulton and Diefenbaker were critical of the level of discretion granted to officials under the 1952 Immigration Act and how it was exercised.

Fulton criticized P.C. 1953–859, which empowered departmental representatives acting as special inquiry officers to make their own assessments of potential immigrants,[86] for giving too much discretion to departmental officials.[87] He also echoed the CBA report's criticism of the government's policy of withholding reasons for rejection from 'everyone, including members of parliament,' stating that 'immigrants are tried and condemned without even knowing that their trial is taking place.'[88]

Diefenbaker described the appeal to the minister provided for by the act as 'an appeal to Caesar, to the Minister himself. An appeal from the hired man to the hired man's boss.'[89] He also quoted the deputy minister, who had defended the limited appeals process by arguing that 'the danger in giving the rejected applicant recourse to the courts is that a court may reach a final decision. The beauty of the department's present system is that the civil service can review and review and review and the applicant always has the hope that some day he may be admitted.'[90]

In an editorial, the *Globe and Mail* welcomed the debate. It stated that, although Pickersgill and former Citizenship and Immigration minister Harris tried to defend their government's policy, 'they failed, because no defence of it ... [was] possible.'[91] The *Globe* went on to describe Prime Minister King's statement in 1947 as nothing but a 'vague collection of generalities ... the fact is that the present government has no definite immigration policy.'[92]

The Conservative motion of censure was defeated, and the Liberal government refused to alter its policies. However, in 1956, in the *Brent* decision,[93] the Supreme Court found that the discretion given to SIOs by subsection 20(4) of the Immigration Regulations exceeded the provisions of the Immigration Act. The government was compelled to pass new regulations that specifically divided countries into different categories of preferred status. The result was an obscure order-in-council, P.C. 1956–785.

Preferred Classes under P.C. 1956–785

Section 20 of P.C. 1956–785 divided admissible immigrants into four classes. The section allowed British subjects born or naturalized in the United Kingdom, Australia, New Zealand, or the Union of South Africa to be admitted if they were able to support themselves until they found employment. Citizens of Ireland or the United States and citizens of France (born or naturalized in France or the islands of St Pierre and Miquelon) were also admissible under this category.[94] It has been suggested that the distinction in the section between those who were 'born or naturalized' and those who were 'citizens' was designed to ensure that British or French subjects who were born in countries that the Canadian government might consider less desirable (such as India, Hong Kong, the West Indies, and French North Africa) were not automatically eligible for admission.[95]

Under the second category, citizens (by birth or naturalization) of Austria, Belgium, Denmark, West Germany, Finland, Greece, Iceland, Italy, Luxembourg, The Netherlands, Norway, Portugal, Spain, Sweden, or Switzerland could emigrate to Canada if they undertook either to find employment under the auspices of the Department of Citizenship and Immigration or to establish themselves in a business, trade, or profession, or in agriculture. Refugees from Europe were also eligible for admission under these criteria.[96]

Under the third category, citizens (by birth or naturalization) of any country of Europe or the Americas, or of Egypt, Israel, Lebanon, or Turkey, could emigrate to Canada if they had relatives in Canada who were legal residents and were willing to sponsor them. The sponsor had to reside in Canada, apply to have his or her relatives admitted, and be able to 'receive and care for these relatives.'[97] In this context, 'relatives' referred to the spouse, child, or sibling of a legal Canadian resident. Further, if the legal resident's child or sibling had a spouse or children (under age twenty-one), they, too, could be admitted. Finally, the legal resident's fiancé(e) or spouse, parents, grandparents, unmarried orphaned nephews or nieces (under age twenty-one) were also admissible as 'relatives.'

Under the fourth category, citizens of any countries other than those enumerated in the preceding paragraphs (e.g., Asian countries) could be admitted if they were the husband, wife, or unmarried child (under age twenty-one), the father (over age sixty-five), or the mother (over age sixty) of a Canadian citizen residing in Canada who had applied for their entry and was in a position to sponsor them. Further, a child under age twenty-one from any country other than those listed in the previous three categories could be admitted only if his or her father or mother, as the case may be, was landed in Canada concurrently with him.[98]

It should be noted that falling into one of these categories did not guarantee entry. Admission also depended on whether or not the applicant fell within one of the prohibited classes outlined in the Immigration Act. This left immigration officials with considerable discretion to exclude potential immigrants. Section 20 thus established a hierarchy of preferences, reflecting an immigration policy that was highly selective with respect to country of origin.

The same order-in-council limited immigration from India, Pakistan, and Ceylon to 150, 100, and 50 people per year, respectively, apart from those admissible under the fourth category of immediate family sponsorship.[99] These small quotas, established by treaties, were viewed as a 'gesture for the improvement of commonwealth relations,'[100] since none of these countries, which had recently become fully self-governing members of the Commonwealth, had previously enjoyed the privilege of having independent immigrants admitted into Canada.[101]

From 1956 until 1962, there were only minor changes made to these regulations. The quota for India was doubled in 1958 by P.C. 1958–7. P.C. 1957–1675 extended the fourth category to apply to the relatives of Canadian residents in addition to Canadian citizens. Another order-in-council eased the procedure for prospective immigrants who wished to marry a Canadian citizen (P.C. 1960–372).

By the late 1950s, immigration officials had developed a conviction that there were substantial domestic benefits to immigration.[102] An internal departmental memo called for a steady immigration policy that would facilitate the planning and admission of immigrants every year in a number equal to 1 per cent of Canada's population, with an emphasis on independent immigrants.[103] The report of the Royal Commission on Canada's Economic Prospects (the Gordon Commission) in 1957 took a similar position, arguing that a stable immigration policy best served the nation's interests:

> It is our conviction that the economic advantages of continued immigration are substantial enough to justify an attempt to maintain a stable immigration policy, even through periods of mild recession in Canada. Inevitably, and rightly in our opinion, if there were to be a deep and widespread drop in employment in Canada, immigration would either be drastically reduced or suspended altogether. But, as we have suggested, there may be difficulty over the next two or three decades in obtaining as many suitable immigrants as it would be to Canada's advantage to have. The task would be made harder if our immigration policy, as expressed through regulation and administrative instructions, were to fluctuate with every minor fluctuation in business activity in Canada.[104]

By contrast, the Department of Labour believed that immigration should serve the country's labour needs, and should be severely restricted in times of high unemployment – the so-called tap-on/tap-off approach to immigration. Generally, the Department of Labour had the stronger voice in Cabinet.[105] According to the leader of the Ontario Federation of Labour (OFL), unions took a similar position. While acknowledging that 2 million immigrants had been successfully absorbed into Canada since the war without long-term problems, the OFL suggested that immigration should be curtailed during hard economic times because new immigrants are the most vulnerable to economic vicissitudes.[106]

Beginning in 1947, the Immigration Committee – made up of representatives of the Departments of Immigration, Labour, Health and Welfare, and External Affairs; the Unemployment Insurance Commission (UIC); the National Employment Service (NES); and the U.N. International Refugee Organization (IRO) – would meet each year to set the quota of immigrants for that year, based on requests and estimates. (There were no limits for Britons, Australians, New Zealanders, South Africans, and Americans.) For example, in 1952, with a surplus of workers in the textile and other industries, the committee reduced the quota for total immigration for that year.[107] Although the director of Immigration, Dr Keenleyside, admitted in 1948 that no one knew the real absorptive capacity of Canada, he claimed that the committee's annual compromise was the best way to determine an estimate.[108]

In 1958, in the light of declining economic conditions, a new policy was announced to prevent visitors from accepting unauthorized employment. All visitors to Canada were required to sign a statement promising not to work illegally, on penalty of deportation. Also, a decision was taken that prospective immigrants must apply from their own country for landed immigrant status.[109] As a result, emigration to Canada dropped from 282,164 in 1957 to 124,851 in 1958. However, the Citizenship and Immigration department also began to view professionals and 'capitalists' as potential sources of employment and encouraged people in these categories to emigrate.[110] Thus, the department's 1958–9 Annual Report noted that, 'although total opportunities for foreign labour were down, nevertheless there were still many vacancies for professional, skilled and service workers which could not be filled by Canadians.'[111]

Although overall immigration began to decline in 1958, it was not falling in equal proportions by ethnic group. By mid-1958, British immigration had dropped to 5,000 from 23,000 during the same period in the previous year.[112] However, southern and central European immigration was steadily increasing. By 1959, Italian immigration alone was about to overtake British immigration. At this point, most southern European and Central and South American immigrants were admitted under P.C. 1956 785, which restricted immigrants from those countries to mostly sponsored relatives.[113] Municipalities had also become increasingly concerned that sponsors often did not honour their commitment not to allow sponsored relatives to become a public charge, thus increasing the burden on municipal welfare budgets,[114] and the federal government was increasingly concerned that family sponsorship undermined efforts to relate immigration more closely to labour-market needs. In 1959, the government passed a new order-in-council, P.C. 1959–310, which limited the class of sponsored immigrants from these countries by excluding married children, brothers, and sisters from the list of eligible relatives.[115] However, the measure was seen by many, including Pickersgill (now the Opposition's immigration critic), as aimed primarily at excluding Italians. The ensuing outcry both in the House and in the media forced the government to revoke this measure.[116]

In August 1959, Hong Kong police arrested thirty-five people involved in a large-scale illegal immigration scheme that took advantage of the sponsorship rules permitting the emigration of immediate relatives to

Canada. Thousands of Chinese immigrants had entered under fictitious names and relationships as part of complex 'paper families.'[117] In the spring of the following year, the RCMP allowed Hong Kong authorities to assist in gathering evidence in Canada against the illegal immigration movement. More than thirty Chinese homes and businesses were raided, from Vancouver to Montreal.[118] On 9 June 1960, Minister of Citizenship and Immigration Ellen Fairclough announced the Chinese Adjustment Statement Program, involving measures to curtail the illegal entry of Chinese while at the same time legitimizing the status of those already in Canada illegally.[119] Chinese people illegally in Canada would be given landed immigrant status, provided they were of good health and character. They were also required to make a statement to immigration officials concerning their family backgrounds and how they had arrived in Canada. Attempts to restrict illegal migration through police investigations and increased enforcement were largely unsuccessful; the problem was too widespread. The adjustment program was continued throughout the 1960s, as it had strong support from the Chinese community; 11,569 Chinese had taken advantage of the right to have their status normalized by July 1970.[120]

Internationally, Canada's list of approved countries had not gone unnoticed. Canada's unofficial ban on black immigrants cost it diplomatic legitimacy with newly independent former colonies.[121] In 1954, a local organization, the Negro Citizenship Association,[122] complained to the Citizenship and Immigration minister that British subjects from England, Australia, New Zealand, and South Africa received preferential treatment. It argued that there was no scientific proof that people from the West Indies could not adjust socially or climatically to Canada. By 1961, Britain began to pressure Canada to change its policies.[123] Any British subject was allowed to emigrate to Britain; 60,000 a year were arriving from the West Indies alone, and Britain could not provide adequate housing or employment. Canada, however, would take only enough immigrants from these countries to supply its needs for domestic workers.

The 1962 Regulations

In 1962, Minister of Citizenship and Immigration Ellen Fairclough tabled new immigration regulations in the House of Commons.[124] The regulations were the culmination of a long process of review instituted by the Conservatives following their election in 1957, originally intended to lead to a new Immigration Act, and marked a major watershed in Canadian immigration policy. The goal of the government was to reduce the number of unskilled workers entering Canada, and correspondingly increase the number of skilled workers. At the same time, the government sought to eliminate discrimination based on colour, race, and creed.

The first step was to change the non-sponsored class of immigrants so that, for the first time in the history of Canadian immigration policy, race and nationality were no longer to play a role. Thus, there were no longer provisions for preferred countries for independent immigrants. Instead, subsection 31 (a) of the 1962 immigration regulations called for a person to be admitted to Canada 'who by reason of his education, training, skills or other special qualifications is likely to be able to establish himself successfully in Canada' and has either sufficient means to support himself or has secured employment.[125] However, SIOs were still vested with the discretion to determine what skills were relevant, despite the *Brent* decision in 1956. Not until 1967 would the extent of this discretion be substantially reduced, with the creation of the points system that identified and weighted various categories of credentials and skills.

The second step taken by the government was to open the class of eligible relatives for sponsorship by Canadians, whatever their country of origin. In this area, the government took only a half-step. The new regulations did expand the sponsorship categories so that now all Canadians could sponsor their parents whatever their age (previously, Asian and African Canadians' mothers had to be over the age of sixty, and their fathers over sixty-five). However, fearing an influx of non-European (principally Asian) unskilled relatives, the government at the last minute instituted subsection 31(d), which still discriminated on the basis of nationality.[126] Thus, whereas any Canadian could sponsor his or her parent, grandparent, spouse, or unmarried child under the age of twenty-one (s.31 [c]), only Canadians from preferred nations could sponsor children over the age of twenty-one, married children, siblings and their corresponding families, and unmarried orphaned nieces and nephews under the age of twenty-one (s.31 [d]).

The regulations also enlarged the jurisdiction of the Immigration Appeal Board (IAB) to include appeals from all deportation decisions under the Act.[127] However, Canadian sponsors whose applications for relatives abroad had been rejected could not appeal to the IAB.[128] These changes to the structure of the IAB were effected through executive order so that the Immigration Act did not have to be amended. For this reason, the provisions of the Immigration Act that permitted the AB's decisions to be overridden by the minister continued to apply. Other minor changes included a provision which allowed for illegitimate children under twenty-one years of age to be admitted if their mother was a legal resident in Canada. Finally, the 1962 regulations eliminated the rarely used literacy tests.[129]

The new policy did not affect the quotas limiting the number of South Asian immigrants to Canada because these were the result of international treaties between Canada and the governments of India, Pakistan, and Ceylon. Fairclough informed the House that discussions were under way to eliminate these quotas, but that they would likely remain in effect for some time.[130] Despite the fact that, by this time, it was clear that Asia and Africa were experiencing the most severe refugee problems in the world, the Department of External Affairs took the position that at 'this stage it would seem unrealistic to us to consider taking in African and Asian refugees, at least until such time as the necessity of such efforts is apparent and other countries have begun to share our concern.'[131]

Special Movements

The first orders-in-council after the Second World War provided for the repatriation of Canadian armed forces members and their dependants, many of whom were not Canadian citizens.[132] Another Cabinet decision granted landed immigrant status to 2,500 German and Austrian nationals, many of them Jews, who had been interned in Britain after the outbreak of hostilities and then sent at Britain's request to Canada for temporary asylum for the duration of the war. About 1,000 chose to stay.[133] Although the Immigration Branch had plans to round them up and remove them from Canada, the federal Cabinet decided that a possible public outcry and the administrative inconvenience caused by numerous appeals to the minister rendered such a move inexpedient.[134] The King government had also planned to repatriate Japanese Canadians after the war, but under pressure from civil liberties organizations such as the Cooperative Committee on Japanese Canadians and newspapers such as the *Toronto Daily Star* and *Winnipeg Free Press*, the government stopped its efforts in 1947 after removing several thousand people.[135]

In the early postwar years, the Immigration Branch sought to increase the population of Canada's rural areas. To this end, they found an attractive match in the Dutch government, which had a surplus of farmers after the retreating Germans destroyed dykes and left much of Holland's farmland flooded. As a result, a special movement of 15,000 Dutch farmers occurred in 1947.[136] This was so successful that the Immigration Branch continued to encourage farmers from Holland to emigrate throughout the 1950s.

Another special movement of immigrants consisted of 500 Maltese and their dependants, who left their country in the late 1940s after the British dockyards in Malta closed, creating high unemployment.[137]

Contract Labour

In 1947, the government adopted a contract labour scheme in order to respond to the increasing need for skilled and unskilled workers. In the wake of the war, after lobbying by the British government, 4,527 Polish ex-servicemen in Britain and Italy arrived on a special plan designed to assist farmers in urgent need of help. Britain paid the transportation costs. The Department of Labour had planned for each ex-serviceman to sign a two year labour contract, but farmers protested that they wanted to guarantee employment for only a year. The government described the workers as qualified agriculturalists' and granted them landed-immigrant status.[138]

The Departments of Justice, Health and Welfare, and Labour screened the first 1,700 Poles prior to departing for Canada. Of these, only one was Jewish. Upon their arrival it was discovered that several had tuberculosis (TB) and could not work, which resulted in a subsequent regulation, Order-in-Council 1947–2951. This required all applicants from countries with a higher incidence of TB per capita than Canada to submit themselves to a chest x-ray and to receive a clean bill of health from a radiologist before leaving Europe for Canada.[139]

After the success of the Polish farmers' program, the government abolished its ban on contract labour (which had existed since 1929) by P.C. 1947–1329, and began to promote contract labour schemes. The schemes worked as follows: an industry in need of labour would approach the Department of Labour, the Department of Citizenship and Immigration, or the National Employment Service (NES). Departmental officials would then review the application to determine that it was genuine and that the employer was suitable.[140] The employer had to show that the job could not be filled locally and had to guarantee a year's labour at the prevailing rates in the locality and accommodation for the new immigrants. At this point the request was transmitted to immigration officials in Europe, who had the U.N.'s International Refugee Organization (IRO) select two or three times as many potential immigrants from among available refugees as there were jobs. Often, companies would send their own representatives to help in the selection process. If chosen, a worker signed a contract guaranteeing a year's labour; the cost of his or her voyage was advanced by the employer and deducted from the worker's pay.

In its 1947 Annual Report, the Senate Standing Committee on Immigration and Labour adopted the position of the TLC and CCL, who called for the elimination of the role of private enterprise in selecting contract labour.[141] Both unions reiterated the view that immigration was entirely a public responsibility. Jean Tweed, in a series of articles in *Saturday Night,* wondered how this form of so-called controlled immigration could really be as beneficial as claimed. These labourers, she predicted, usually would stay on the job only for the length of the contract, resulting in both an unemployed immigrant and a renewed shortage in that field.[142] However, with a flourishing economy and many labour shortages, the contract labour program was attractive on both self-interested and humanitarian grounds. It also had the enthusiastic support of the business community and the media, although an editorial in the *Globe and Mail* argued that a program motivated only by the need for a rapid supply of labour could not even constitute the beginning 'of an intelligent program of immigration.'[143]

In a statement in 1952, Minister of Citizenship and Immigration Harris explained that, although Canada could choose to deport those who broke their contracts, this would violate the Canadian ideals of freedom of the individual. Thus, once in Canada, the immigrants were able to break their contract, but they had to reimburse the full cost of the voyage to their employer. Between 1947 and 1951, 100,000 refugees entered Canada by way of sponsored-labour movements. A married man was prohibited from bringing his family to Canada until he had sufficient capital to support them, at which point he could sponsor their admission.[144] The government contract labour programs were so successful that some companies decided to implement their own contract labour schemes for Eastern and central European immigrants by offering free transportation to British workers in return for eighteen-month contracts.

In the mid-1950s, a shortage of domestics in Canada prompted the Department of Citizenship and Immigration to implement a special form of contract labour scheme for 'coloured' domestics from Jamaica and Barbados.[145] Before 1955, the stereotype of black women as promiscuous and lazy had been used to restrict the immigration of Caribbean domestics; section 61 of the 1952 Immigration Act was strictly applied to exclude black immigration. In the early 1950s, Canadian trade commissioners in Jamaica and Trinidad warned that Canada's discriminatory immigration policies might affect Canadian-Caribbean trade. There had also been considerable negative publicity surrounding the exclusion of Caribbean domestics, including articles in the *Financial Post* and *Maclean's* magazine.[146]

After it became clear that European domestics could not meet the demand, the Cabinet agreed to allow a small number of Caribbean domestics 'of exceptional merit' to enter Canada as landed immigrants. This program was so successful that it was expanded in the following years, until several hundred domestics from the Caribbean were admitted annually as landed immigrants.[147] Only 'healthy' single women between the ages of eighteen and forty, with no dependants and with at least a grade-eight education, were eligible for the program. The women had to promise to remain as live-in domestics for at least one year.[148] Although the Department of Citizenship and Immigration referred to the 1956 group of domestics as the best to enter Canada from any country since the Second World War, the women who came to Canada under the scheme were often very disappointed with their jobs. They were paid much less and were required to work longer and harder than they had expected.[149] The scheme was often criticized as a type of indentured labour and for causing a 'brain drain' out of the Caribbean. The program 'reinforced the racial, class and gender stereotypes about black women being inherently suited to domestic work;'[150] however, the program remained popular in the Caribbean and was approved by orders-in-council each year until the points system was introduced in 1967.[151]

REFUGEE POLICY

All told, Canada admitted nearly a quarter of a million refugees between 1946 and 1962. Some were sponsored by Canadian relatives; many came under contract labour schemes; others were selected and sponsored by the government; and still others were selected by church groups.

In the late 1940s, the Senate Standing Committee on Immigration and Labour heard testimony from the Canadian National Committee for Refugees (CNCR), formed in October 1938 in anticipation of the thousands of opponents of Naziism who were to be driven from recently occupied Czechoslovakia. The CNCR was funded by contributions from national groups, including the National Council of Women, the Council for Social Service of the Church of England in Canada, the YWCA, and the Board of Evangelism and Social Service of the United Church. Before the Senate committee, CNCR representative Senator Cairine Wilson,[152] along with the CNCR's honorary chairman, B.K Sandwell, editor of *Saturday Night*, described Canada's immigration policy as 'self-destructive' because it did not admit immigrants in a period when Canada required a greater population and 'internationally dangerous' because of the foreign policy consequences of having a racist immigration policy. In addition, they called on Canada to expand its immigration policy to help the displaced persons (DPs).[153] Labour groups such as the CCL and the TLC were also supportive of the admission of refugees to Canada as long as this did not adversely affect the standard of living of Canadian workers. The Canadian Association of Social Workers (CASW) told the Senate committee in 1947 that it supported the admission of selected DPs with their families, on the basis that refugees who had survived hardships during and after the war were excellent prospects as Canadians.

In 1947, there were one million displaced persons living in or outside of the U.N.'s International Refugee Organization (IRO) camps, many of whom had refused to be repatriated to their homelands.[154] Twenty per cent of these DPs were Jewish, and half of them were living in Germany and desperate to leave. In the first three years after the war, the government had been reluctant to open its doors to the DPs, prompting criticism from some of the most vocal Opposition members, including Frederick Zaplitny (CCF member from Manitoba), Gladys Strum (CCF member from Saskatchewan), Lawrence Skey (Progressive Conservative member from Ontario), and Anthony Hlynka (Social Credit member from Alberta).[155]

In April 1947, almost two years after the war ended, the first group of displaced persons set sail for Canada on board the *Aquitania*.[156] Fifty berths had been reserved for first-degree relatives of Canadians, but they were mostly empty. Only 12 out of 900 applicants had been approved by immigration officials.[157] Beginning in 1947, several special orders-in-council permitted the admission of thousands of war refugees from Europe.[158] The Canadian Jewish Congress was able to lobby for 1,000 orphaned children to be admitted in 1947; this was matched by the Catholic Immigration Aid Society's success in lobbying for 1,000 Catholic refugees in the same year.[159] In the following five years, Canada accepted 166,000 DPs, as well as 1,000 Baits fleeing Stalinism in small boats[160] and hundreds of desperate European refugees stranded in Shanghai.[161]

In July 1947, the railways and shipping companies were anxious to reestablish their privileged position with ethnic groups as sources of transportation and finance, and as their liaison with government.[162] Thus, the Department of Immigration and Colonization of the Canadian Pacific Railway Company (CPR) and its counterpart at Canadian National Railways (CNR) set up the Canadian Christian Council for Re-Settlement of Refugees (CCCRR) in collaboration with various religious and ethnic groups.[163] The council was financed by community and religious groups and designed so that the railways could coordinate activities. The CCCRR was created to assist some of the approximately 500,000 displaced persons who were not eligible for the U.N. International Refugee Organization's (IRO's) assistance. Soon after, the CPR purchased and renovated a German supply ship. It began operations by shipping 700 new emigrants from Europe.[164]

The relationship between the Department of Citizenship and Immigration and church groups was not always amicable.[165] In 1953, the department issued a directive to its overseas offices which sought to curb church participation in immigrant selection in Europe. The church groups responded through political pressure, and the directive was withdrawn. The church groups and the department reached a compromise by setting up the Approved Church Program (ACP) in 1953. The ACP officially recognized four groups: the Canadian Council of Churches (CCC), an umbrella organization for the major Protestant churches formed in 1951;[166] the CCCRR; the Jewish Immigration Aid Service (DIAS), a subsidiary of the Canadian Jewish Congress; and the Rural Settlement Society of Canada. These groups could not only process and approve sponsored immigrants, but also select non-sponsored immigrants.

The conflict occurred over the type of immigrant each group preferred. Religious groups often sought to promote the admission of unemployed, desperate people, whereas the department favoured skilled or unskilled labourers. In addition, the volunteer agencies would often ask the Department of Citizenship and Immigration to move a candidate to the top of the list, despite a substantial backlog of applicants. The privileges granted by the department to the churches under the ACP required the department to comply. Finally, in 1958, a departmental directive, while acknowledging the religious groups' nominal status, removed their privileged position in selecting immigrants.[167]

The selection of refugees by immigration officials came under fire in the House. Social Credit member Anthony Hlynka told the House that Canada's immigration officers were rejecting as 'unfit' underweight refugees, people missing a finger, and persons with naturally formed moles on their bodies.[168] These may have been extreme examples, but Canada was clearly selecting the most healthy candidates. It was not interested in accepting 'hard core' cases of injured, sick, and old displaced persons. John Holmes, an External Affairs officer, claimed that Canada selected refugees 'like good beef cattle'.[169]

Despite the generally, albeit belatedly, positive attitude towards refugees, at least one tradition remained from the previous era: blatant anti-Semitism. Jews were not accepted in several industries participating in the contract labour program,[170] and plans by Jewish-dominated industries, such as the needle trades, to select primarily Jewish labour were resisted by Cabinet and the Immigration Branch. For example, the minister for Reconstruction, C.D. Howe, was fearful of a backlash from Quebec if it were perceived that part of the contract labour program was a guise for getting more Jews into the country. He informed recruiters representing the needle trades that no more than 50 per cent of the DPs brought to Canada by any industry could be Jewish.[171] These federal policies apparently reflected public opinion. An October 1946 public-opinion poll found that 49 per cent of Canadians objected to Jews emigrating to Canada.[172] However, in April 1947, the federal Cabinet reactivated an unused order-in-council from 1941 that authorized the immigration of 1,000 Jewish orphans from Vichy France.[173]

In 1951, Canada did not adopt the U.N.'s International Convention Relating to the Status of Refugees because the RCMP believed it would restrict Canada's right to deport refugees on security grounds.[174] This reflected the government's suspicion that organizations such as the U.N.'s International Refugee Organization (IRO) were infiltrated by Communists.[175]

In the mid-1950s (ten years after efforts had started), Canada gave 23,000 stateless people landed immigrant status as part of a concerted international effort to clear the DP camps in Europe.[176] Then, as a result of the Soviet invasion of Hungary in October 1956, more than 200,000 Hungarians, representing two per cent of that country's population, fled their homeland for Austria and Yugoslavia. Although the first few hundred refugees had been Communist officials fearing reprisals from the dissidents, the masses that left following the Soviet invasion were from all walks of life, seeking freedom from communism.

As Western countries began to open their doors, Minister of Citizenship and Immigration Jack Pickersgill announced on 6 November 1956, that all eligible Hungarian applicants would have priority over all other immigrants and could take advantage of the assisted-passage loan scheme.[177] He stated that the government had not changed its general policies, but merely moved the Hungarians to the top of the waiting list, as long as they met all other immigration requirements.[178] However, that announcement was greeted with criticism, and several religious groups (especially JIAS, the CCC, and the Catholic Immigration Aid Society – a member of the CCCRR) placed considerable pressure on the government to admit greater numbers of the refugees. Ethnic groups along with the two major Opposition parties (the CCF and Conservatives) were also quite vocal. The nation's newspapers were highly critical of the government's stance; a *Globe and Mail* editorial criticized Canada's refusal to help the refugees under the headline 'For Shame.' In late November, the minister announced a new policy.[179] Pickersgill stated that the Canadian government would open its doors to the refugees: 'Our position is, as it has been throughout this matter, that we intend to take these people as long as they want to come here and it looks as though we can find accommodation for them and, in a reasonable time, find work for them.'[180]

To facilitate the refugees' transportation, the assisted-passage loan scheme was dropped and replaced by guarantees of a free voyage to Canada for all Hungarian refugees.[181] Plans were made for an airlift of the refugees to port cities. Canada promised to house and feed them.[182] Perhaps the most important aspect of the announcement was the minister's decision personally to fly to Vienna to take charge of the movement, having been authorized by Cabinet to make on-the-spot decisions.[183] Seeing that Austria was unable to handle the massive number of refugees it had received, Pickersgill quickly made arrangements with both the British and the Dutch governments for them to take in more refugees temporarily who would later be transported to Canada. In order to expedite the application process, Pickersgill told his officers in Vienna to make only preliminary examinations of applicants, and then to approve them. He ordered the RCMP not to delay any application without a solid reason.[184] More than 37,000 Hungarian refugees were admitted to Canada in less than a year. The entire operation cost $14.4 million. By March 1960, only six of these immigrant families remained on the welfare rolls.[185] In July 1957, the government, concerned with the high immigration figures for 1956–7, withdrew the additional sponsorship privileges for Hungarians which it had granted the previous year.[186]

The business community responded enthusiastically to the Hungarian crisis and was particularly interested in the skilled labour available. By 1956, businesses were bidding for the services of Hungarian engineering students (who were absorbed by the University of Toronto) and forestry students (who were relocated to the University of British Columbia).[187] Meanwhile, organized labour restricted itself to seeking assurances that the new immigrants would not be 'dumped' on the labour market, and that they would receive immediate training in English.[188]

According to Dirks, 'of the states accepting Hungarian refugees for permanent resettlement, none surpassed Canada. This country opened its doors and lowered its barriers for refugees more quickly and generally behaved more magnanimously than during any previous refugee emergency.'[189]

The press reaction to Pickersgill's November announcement was overwhelmingly positive. The *Winnipeg Free Press* welcomed it by stating that 'we have a month of paralysed inhumanity to make up for.'[190] However, motives were not exclusively humanitarian. First, it was clear that the refugees could supply needed labour in both the industrial and the service sectors. Moreover, the Hungarians were a relatively more attractive group of refugees than those who sought entry over the previous decade, since they had not been physically and emotionally ravaged by years in internment camps. All except 5,000 of the refugees were under forty-five years of age, with a high concentration between nine and twenty-nine years of age.[191] In addition, approximately two-thirds of those admitted were Roman Catholics; Jews constituted only one-fifth of the total. One document from the Immigration Branch's director argued that many of the 'refugees were not bona fide,' but 'Hebrews who had taken advantage of the situation,'[192] reflecting the anti-Semitism that continued to exist in the Immigration Branch.

Despite this anti-Semitism, the JIAS was able to lobby successfully for some special movements of refugees. For example, when the Jewish community in Egypt was in peril following the 1956 war, the JIAS convinced Cabinet to approve without security screening the admission of 400 Jews from Egypt with relatives in Canada.[193]

When the United Nations declared 1960–1 as World Refugee Year in an attempt to resettle the remaining 'hard-core' DPs still in camps in Europe, Canada responded by exempting refugees from age and occupational criteria, although good health and character requirements were maintained. As an exception, for humanitarian reasons, the Canadian government, as a contribution to the Year of the Refugee, agreed to take in persons infected with tuberculosis in order to treat them. By 1960, the first 100 families under the program arrived.[194] Initially, the government budgeted $600,000 for these 100 infected persons and their dependants. But by June 1960, 75 of the 100 had been released from hospital, and Canada had spent only $185,000. As a result of the program's success and underbudgeting, Canada admitted 100 more infected immigrants in July 1960. This second movement cost $130,000, thereby permitting a third and final movement of

100 TB-infected immigrants. Thus, by year end, the program had admitted 300 infected immigrants, along with 526 of their dependants. The year also marked the reinstitution of private sponsorship of refugees, as several hundred were admitted under the auspices of Canadian organizations.[195] In 1961, almost 3,000 refugees were admitted as the special policies from World Refugee Year were extended.[196]

The Canadian Committee for World Refugee Year was formed in the early fall of 1959 and consisted of forty-four organizations, ranging from the non-sectarian Canadian Red Cross to the sectarian Canadian Council of Churches (CCC). This committee raised funds for the U.N. effort to permanently resettle hard-core refugees still living in camps in Europe. The $1.8 million that it was able to raise during its short lifespan helped the U.N.'s high commissioner for refugees to resettle more than 1,200 displaced persons in Western European states.[197]

SECURITY SCREENING

Security considerations played a major role in Canada's immigration policy in this period, initially in seeking to screen-out Nazi complicitors (not always effectively) and then Communist agitators and sympathizers. In the late 1940s, Soviet-led communism gained momentum as country after country from Eastern Europe to China – became the subject of Communist takeovers. In 1946, the Gouzenko affair, which revealed the existence of a major Soviet spy ring in Canada, brought the Communist threat close to home.

This year also marked the creation of the Security Panel, a group of senior civil servants, RCMP, and military officers who oversaw RCMP operations and advised the government on internal security policy.[198] The panel was successful in convincing Cabinet of the necessity for stringent security measures, such as the time-consuming RCMP screening of prospective immigrants in overseas visa offices.[199] In 1948, with the Berlin blockade and a Soviet-backed coup in Czechoslovakia, Stalin consolidated his grip on Eastern Europe. As a 'Red Scare' swept Canada, the Cabinet met secretly to decide that 'known Communists seeking admission to Canada for the purpose of engaging in subversive propaganda' were considered to fall under subsection 3(n) of the Immigration Act, 1910, which barred the entry of advocates of the violent overthrow of government.[200] Screening requirements frequently resulted in massive backlogs, such as the 52,000 applications by sponsored relatives in Canada's embassy in Communist influenced Italy in 1957.[201]

Security screening not only caused delays, but served as the grounds for rejection of a large number of prospective immigrants. The RCMP reported in 1958 that, from 1946 to 1958, 29,671 applications for admission had been rejected on security grounds.[202] In 1956–7, 5 to 6 per cent of Italian applicants were rejected on security grounds.[203] Visitors, such as union leaders, academics, and performers, were also often denied temporary entry visas if they were viewed as a security risk, including W.E.B. Du Bois, a distinguished black scholar, in 1952, and Paul Robeson, in 1956, because of their alleged Communist sympathies.[204]

The denial of entry by leftists to Western countries was an international effort, led by Britain and the United States. In 1948, Canadian diplomatic posts were informed that they were to consult with the U.K and U.S. embassies in gathering information about Communist subversives who might seek to enter Canada.[205] On the other hand, any liaison with Soviet-bloc police was ruled out. Because of the need to establish a clean security record, prospective East Bloc emigrants had to live in another Western country for two years and apply for landed-immigrant status from there. As a result, from 1949 when the two-year rule was introduced, emigration from Communist countries was drastically curtailed.[206]

The possession of Canadian citizenship was insufficient to gain entry for one group of would-be immigrants. Groups of Yugo-Canadians moved to Yugoslavia after Tito's victory to help build a socialist society. After enduring the realities of communism for several years, many sought to return to Canada. Although the Department of External Affairs – generally more liberal in security matters – supported their right of return, the Department of Citizenship and Immigration and the RCMP did not. By the mid-1950s, many remained in Yugoslavia, their applications for readmission rejected on security grounds.[207]

DEPORTATIONS

The immigration appeal boards provided for in the 1952 Act played a very minor role in immigration decisions. The boards had jurisdiction only to decide questions of law and could not consider the non-legal merits of a case, such as humanitarian and compassionate grounds. In view of the large discretionary powers granted to the Department of Citizenship and Immigration, errors of law were quite rare.[208] David Lewis, MP, gave the following revealing description of the appeal process:

If a person came to Canada without 'a visa' and applied for landed immigrant status, he went through the silly exercise of a special inquiry. An officer would ask, 'Have you a visa?' knowing perfectly well that the applicant did not ... When he said he did not have one ... [he was] told, 'In that case you cannot stay.'

After that followed the equally silly exercise of going to the old appeal board ... [which] would look at the situation and say: 'You do not meet the requirements because you have no visa ... therefore out you go'... If security matters were involved ... you could only guess that the refusal was for security reasons because you would not be given any reason at all.[209] When you inquired into the matter ... you faced a blank wall. You had no information. You did not know what the source of the evidence was ... you argued as if you were punching a pillow... I have had that kind of experience dozens of times.[210]

Originally, the IABs may have been established with the objective of reducing the number of appeals to the minister. However, given the IABs' relative powerlessness, it is not surprising that cases were dealt with quite quickly at the appeal level.[211] A prospective immigrant's best hope lay with the minister. Unfortunately, there are no published figures that show the number of appeals granted by either the IAB or the minister.[212]

The regulations introduced in 1962 provided that all those subject to deportation decisions made under the Immigration Act had the right to appeal to the Immigration Appeal Board.[213] Previously, the IAB had the jurisdiction to deal with only cases directed to it by the minister.[214] However, the provisions of the Immigration Act that permitted the IAB's decisions to be overridden by the minister continued to apply.

Between 1946 and 1950, 1,872 immigrants were deported from Canada; from 1951 to 1955, 3,003; and from 1956 to 1961, 3,197. The principal causes of deportation were 'stealth or misrepresentation' (46 per cent), criminality (28 per cent), mental and medical (11.6 per cent), public charges (2.9 per cent), and 'other' (8.8 per cent). This last category is of interest since it appears principally to relate to security grounds.[215]

Conclusions

By 1962, a new era in immigration policy was beginning. The basic elements of Mackenzie King's statement on immigration policy in 1947 were already undergoing major transformation. In the case of independent immigrants, potential economic contribution was to weigh much more heavily than race or country of origin, although family sponsorship was assuming a larger role relative to independent admissions. The demographic profile of immigrants began to change significantly. British immigration had declined substantially, while southern Europe, especially Italy, and central Europe became much more important sources. Canada had also opened its doors, albeit belatedly, to a considerable number of refugees from Europe. King's promised restrictions on Asian immigration had been, for the most part, eliminated. In addition, even if admission to Canada was still considered a privilege and not a right, basic due process protections were coming to be seen as properly extended to aliens in the sense that the rules governing their admission or deportation should be reasonably well specified and transparent, and deportation decisions made in particular cases by immigration officials should be open to challenge before a neutral tribunal. Thus, with respect to both substance and process, immigration policy was beginning to take a shape that was sharply different from that which had obtained throughout most of Canada's history.

Community interest groups had assumed an important role in policy development. These groups, along with many parliamentarians, academics, and members of the press, promoted policies based on the recognition of the individual equality of applicants from all countries. The increasingly internationalist role that the country chose to assume during this period militated in the same direction. Business and labour interests adopted the position that liberal admission policies would create economic benefits for most Canadians as well as for immigrants. The legal community and others also argued that the rights of immigrants ought not to be subject to arbitrary determination without respect for due process. Thus, the values and the interests that were driving immigration policy had taken on – politically, economically, and legally – a much more liberal complexion.

CHAPTER NINE

Immigration Policy, 1963–1976: Democracy and Due Process

The period that is the focus of this chapter (1963–76) was, for the first ten years, marked generally by a strong economy. The recession that had begun in 1958, which was accompanied by significant restrictions on immigration and a sharp fall in the number of immigrants admitted, was largely over by the end of 1961. Recovery began in 1962 and led to an extended economic boom, fuelled in part by a similar boom in the United States that was sustained, with some minor fluctuations, until 1973. Most of the period was characterized by high rates of economic growth (in the 5 to 7 per cent range) and low levels of unemployment (in the 4 to 6 per cent range). By the end of 1973, the good times were beginning to come to an end. The inflation rate, which had been at 1 per cent in 1961, increased to over 10 per cent by the mid-1970s, in part as a result of the first OPEC oil-price shock in 1973, and the unemployment rate rose to about 7 per cent. These changes heralded the advent of what economists came to call the phenomenon of 'stagflation,' with excess capacity in the economy, significant levels of unemployment, yet rapidly rising prices – a phenomenon that defied conventional macro-economic thinking at the time. In response, the federal government took several measures to control prices and wages.[1]

As 1976 came to a close, the almost 30-year wave of rising prosperity, with minor fluctuations that Canadians had ridden from the end of the war until the mid-1970s, was over. The economy had lapsed into a deep and persistent recession, the government had largely lost control of its expenditures as the bills for the social activism in areas such as pensions, health care, unemployment insurance, and welfare policies of the 1960s and early 1970s came in, and budget deficits began to spiral. The ominous economic storm clouds that began to gather in the mid-1970s presaged an extended period of economic turbulence, dislocation, and stress. Just as seriously, the Front de Libération du Québec (FLQ) crisis in Quebec in October 1970 and the election of a Parti Québécois government in Quebec in the fall of 1976 led to concerns on the part of many Canadians that the political fabric of the country was unravelling. The 'peaceable kingdom' had, at least temporarily, lost some of its lustre.

The strong postwar economic conditions that continued to prevail in Canada until near the end of the 1963–76 period and the increasing social and political commitment during the 1960s to concepts of equality and non-discrimination, yielded high levels of immigration for most of the period and an increasingly more diverse composition of the immigrant intake.[2] Annual admissions increased approximately threefold, from 76,000 in 1962 to 222,000 in 1967, and then declined unevenly to 149,000 in 1976. Total intake for the period 1963–76 was 2.25 million people, representing, on average, more than 160,000 immigrants annually (at the very high end of the historical range). The decline in numbers after 1974 was attributable to the stringent labour-market criteria imposed at that time on independent immigrants. Thus, while the annual number of sponsored immigrants almost doubled from 1972 to 1976 (from 33,000 to 60,000), the number of independent immigrants fell by almost 60 per cent between 1974 and 1976 (from 109,000 to 44,000).

The proportion of immigrants in the nominated category (which applied to distant relatives of status Canadians) was close to a quarter of all arrivals between 1969 and 1976. The nominated category, created in 1967, applied to distant relatives of status Canadians who were subject to a lower threshold for admissibility than independent applicants. However, unlike sponsored immigrants, these relatives had to meet skill and education standards set by the Canadian government. As of 1976, the sponsored and nominated classes together accounted for 62 per cent of all immigrants, the independent class 29.6 per cent, and refugees 7.9 per cent.

The proportion of refugees in Canada's total immigration intake ranged widely throughout this period, from lows of 600 (0.5 per cent) in 1971 to highs of 10,000 (11 per cent) in 1968 and 11,000 (7.9 per cent) in 1976. However, throughout the fourteen year period, the number of refugees entering Canada was relatively small, yielding an average of about 3,600 per year, for a total of fewer than 60,000, or fewer than one in every forty immigrants. In 1968–9, 12,000 Czechoslovakian refugees were admitted after the Soviet suppression of the Czech uprising in 1968; slightly more than 200 Tibetans were admitted in 1970–1 following China's occupation of Tibet; 7,000 Asians, primarily East Indians, were admitted from Uganda in 1972, following Idi Amin's expulsion of the Asian population of Uganda; and, in 1973–4, about 7,000 refugees were admitted from Chile, after a military coup ousted the democratically elected socialist government of Salvador Allende.

The dominant trend in immigrants' place of origin was the steady, but steep, reduction in emigration from Europe as a proportion of total immigration. This change reflected, in part, the adoption of the points system in 1967. In 1962, 78 per cent of all immigrants came from Europe, a figure that fell to 38 per cent in 1976. British immigration fell from 28 to 16 per cent, and Italian immigration from 17 to 3 per cent, over this period. In the late 1960s, the proportion of immigrants coming from Asia and the Caribbean increased dramatically, from 10 per cent in 1965–6 to 23 per cent in 1969–70.[3] By 1976, more than a quarter of all arriving immigrants were Asian in origin.

In terms of intended work sectors, manufacturing, mechanical, managerial, professional, technical, and clerical occupations grew in importance, while service, labour, and agricultural occupations became less common. The impact of immigrants on the labour force was substantial, although not as large as that of the immediate postwar movement. The 725,000 immigrants who entered the labour force from 1961 to 1970 represented an 11 per cent increase in the number of the employed, more than half the total growth during the decade. Intended destinations of immigrants by province did not change significantly from the previous period, with Ontario accounting for 53 per cent, Quebec 18–20 per cent, British Columbia 11–13 per cent, the Prairie provinces 9–12 per cent, and the Atlantic provinces 2 per cent.

Deportations jumped substantially in the 1967–71 period, rising to 11,766 (compared with about 3,500 for each of the previous three five-year periods); the causes of most deportations were classified as stealth or misrepresentation (57 per cent) and criminality (32 per cent).

A White Paper commissioned by the Liberal government and issued by the Department of Manpower and Immigration in 1966 recommended a curtailment in family-sponsored immigrants and an increased emphasis on admission of independent or economic immigrants. This led to joint Senate–House of Commons Committee hearings in 1967. A new points system adopted in 1967 explicitly identified and weighted factors to be assessed in admitting independent immigrants, although it left existing sponsorship rights largely untouched. As was the case with the 1962 regulations, the 1967 points system assigned no explicit weight to country of origin, but reflected continuing efforts to integrate immigration policy more closely with labour-market conditions. This orientation was also reflected in the Government Organization Act of 1966, which created the Department of Manpower and Immigration (merging the Departments of Citizenship and Immigration and Labour).

Following inquiries by Toronto lawyer Joseph Sedgwick commissioned by the federal government, a new Immigration Appeal Board Act was passed in 1967 to provide for an independent administrative review process for all deportation decisions taken by immigration officials and for denial of Canadian citizens' family sponsorship applications. In 1974, as a precursor to the preparation of a new Immigration Act, the government released a Green Paper on immigration that identified a range of policy options, but generally adopted a negative view of the domestic impacts of large-scale immigration. This led to a further and extensive set of public Joint Senate–House of Commons Committee hearings in 1975, where the Green Paper generally met a critical reception. The committee's report and recommendations substantially influenced the new Immigration Act, which was passed in 1976 with scarcely a dissenting vote in Parliament (reviewed in the next chapter).

One of the most striking features of this period is the democratization of the process of policy formulation. The publication of the White Paper in 1966 by the Department of Manpower and Immigration, followed by the Joint Senate–House of Commons Committee hearings, attracted broad participation and attention by politicians, special interest groups, church groups, ethnic groups, individual Canadians, academics, and the media. Many of these groups were influential in successfully resisting any significant curtailment of family sponsorship entitlement.

This precedent was followed in the publication of the Green Paper in 1974, and the ensuing extensive joint Senate–House of Commons Committee hearings across Canada, leading to the passage of a new Immigration Act in 1976. This process elicited an even broader range of political and public participation than the White Paper. The almost unanimous support in the House of Commons for the new Immigration Act suggests that the process succeeded in achieving a broad public consensus.

Also to some extent reflecting the democratization of immigration policy making, the 1967 Canada Manpower and Immigration Act provided for the creation of councils to advise the minister of Manpower and Immigration on matters relating to the development of manpower resources. Only one of the five councils established dealt specifically with immigration: the Advisory Board on the Adjustment of Immigrants. Although this advisory board took a broad view of its mandate, its effective functioning was hampered by structural problems. Its mandate did not include inquiries into the desirable number and composition of immigrants, and the council was provided with no independent research staff. Moreover, this body did not have direct access to the minister. Instead, any recommendations had to be conveyed through the Canada Manpower and Immigration Council, an umbrella consultative body to the minister that met semi-annually[4] and apparently had little impact on policy.[5]

In terms of the politics of immigration policy, a broad range of private and public interest groups participated extensively in the political and consultative processes surrounding policy formulation. Church, ethnic, and community organizations began to play a particularly vocal and prominent part in these processes. Since most post-war immigrants had acquired citizenship, sizeable ethnic political constituencies had developed, particularly in Toronto, Montreal, and Vancouver. Consequently, members of Parliament from these ridings were apt to take a closer interest in Department of Manpower and Immigration practices than were other MPs. For example, after the 1974 election, the Liberals held thirty-six swing seats that contained high ethnic concentrations.[6]

Perhaps reflecting the economic buoyancy of the period, at least until near its end, many of the long-standing cleavages between different interest groups substantially narrowed or disappeared. Business and employer interests tended to advocate a very liberal immigration policy, and organized labour was also at least qualifiedly in favour of a liberal immigration policy, in contrast to earlier periods, provided that there was sensitivity to prevailing labour market conditions. In turn, business interests largely abandoned demands for the preservation of contract labour schemes. A consensus emerged among business, labour, ethnic, religious, and community groups over the generous treatment of refugees, although the extent of this generosity was not pressed very severely during this period.

The other process issue that emerged strongly in this period was an enhanced concern over the rights of individual immigrants, at least those present in Canada, to some basic due process protections in the determination of their status. Prime Minister Mackenzie King, in his oft-quoted speech on immigration policy in 1947, had declared that immigration was a privilege and not a right – a view that had been reflected during most of the history of Canadian immigration policy in the enormous discretion vested in immigration officials and relevant ministers. However, the Immigration Appeal Board Act of 1967 proceduralized and judicialized this aspect of immigration policy to an unprecedented extent and presaged subsequent calls for similar due process protections in other areas of immigration policy, most prominently in the determination of refugee claims.

The 1967 regulations that instituted the points system reflected a significant shift of thinking with respect to both matters of process and matters of substance. With respect to process, by assigning a set of publicly announced weights to different factors to be evaluated in determining the admissibility of non-sponsored immigrants, the regulations attempted to confine and structure the exercise of administrative discretion by immigration officials. This again contrasts sharply with discretionary admission policies that had prevailed throughout the history of Canadian immigration policy to this juncture.

With respect to substance, the 1967 regulations finally removed all explicit traces of racial discrimination from Canada's immigration laws. This position was supported by all political parties and most public and private interest groups that participated in public debates throughout this period. It is probably fair to note that pragmatic considerations combined with considerations of principle to yield a rejection of race or nationality as a relevant selection criterion: by the early 1960s, Canada's traditional sources of immigrants, in particular Britain and Western Europe, were drying up as the European economies recovered from the Second World War and as the European Economic Community began to gather momentum. However, as critics fairly pointed out, despite the racially neutral selection criteria adopted in the 1967 regulations, the emphasis on skills and education disqualified most immigrants from developing countries. The government's decision as to where to locate its overseas visa offices also meant that it was practically very difficult for even skilled immigrants in most developing countries to apply for admission to Canada.

The 1967 regulations, and the political and public discourse that surrounded them, stand in marked contrast not only to Mackenzie King's insistence in 1947 on preserving the basic demographic characteristics of Canada, but also to the entire history of Canadian immigration policy dating back to before Confederation. The regulations of 1962 and 1967 quickly led to a dramatic change in the composition of Canada's immigration intake, with Asia becoming the leading source of immigrants by the end of the period.

In other respects, the points system adopted in 1967 reflected a compromise among contending schools of thought as to appropriate selection criteria, even setting aside race or nationality. Throughout the 1950s and early 1960s, the Department of Citizenship and Immigration and the Department of Labour had held divergent views as to the appropriate basis for selecting independent immigrants: the Department of Citizenship and Immigration tended to argue for reliance on long-term factors bearing on adaptability, such as age, education, and training, while the Department of Labour tended to take the position that selection criteria should be adjusted on a regular basis to reflect current labour-market shortages and surpluses. In the private sector, employer groups tended to favour the first position, while organized labour tended to favour the second. In the result, the point system included both sets of criteria. Restrictions adopted on independent admissions in 1974 with the downturn in the economy revealed the government's continuing sensitivity to short-run economic considerations over long-term factors bearing on the desirability of immigration.

Another compromise reflected in the 1967 point system related to treatment of sponsored relatives. The 1966 White Paper proposed to restrict sponsorship privileges for landed immigrants to their immediate family, while permitting Canadian citizens to sponsor a wider range of relatives. This proposal elicited sharply critical reactions from ethnic groups, church groups, and other community organizations. This reaction, which followed equally negative reactions to Conservative minister Ellen Fairclough's abortive attempts in 1959 to restrict sponsorship rights, seemed to persuade the government that these rights were now largely inviolable. The 1967 regulations abandoned any distinction between the sponsorship rights of Canadian citizens and Canadian landed immigrants, but confined the sponsorship category to a relatively limited range of relatives. It also created a new category of nominated immigrants, comprising more distant relatives of Canadian citizens or landed immigrants, who were required to pass a relaxed version of the point system.

In most cases, refugee intakes occurred without major controversy, and they appear to have been widely endorsed by all political parties and a broad cross-section of the Canadian public. There was, however, a growing criticism of the essentially *ad hoc* nature of the government's responses to refugee crises, and an emerging view that refugee issues should be separated from general issues of immigration. As we shall see, this issue became much more pressing in the post-1976 period.

Major Changes in Immigration Policy, 1963–1976

ADMISSION POLICIES

The 1966 White Paper

Following a decision by the Liberal government to re-evaluate Canada's immigration policies, a policy document was commissioned from the Department of Manpower and Immigration. The White Paper on Immigration was tabled in Parliament in 1966 by Jean Marchand, the minister of Manpower and Immigration,[7] but the content of the report was largely the responsibility of the deputy minister, Tom Kent, who sought to reform the sponsorship system in order to avoid the 'potential for explosive growth in the unskilled labour force' without inciting political controversy.[8] The White Paper's major thrust was that government should increase the integration between immigration policy and Canada's labour needs. As the document stated, 'to remain of positive value ... immigration policy must be consistent with national economic policy in general and with national manpower and social policies in particular... '[9] According to the White Paper, this new direction meant that Canada should cease orienting its immigration policy to short-term factors and base its admission standards on long-term needs. 'A selective immigration policy today must be planned as a steady policy of recruitment based on long-term considerations of economic growth.'[10]

The press evinced mixed responses to the White Paper. Under the headline 'An Uninspiring Document,' the *Globe and Mail* attacked the White Paper, stating that 'we see nothing in the document that would plant in [immigration officials'] minds the notion of a Canada that is grateful for human resources and aggressive in their pursuit in any land.'[11] The *Montreal Gazette* welcomed the White Paper for suggesting that the extent of ministerial discretion be curtailed,[12] while the *Vancouver Sun* applauded the White Paper for proposing that the minister retain his or her discretionary power to permit entry of an applicant who might otherwise be prohibited: 'The triumphs of humanity have always been achieved by ignoring the letter of the law and future ministers will have every opportunity to triumph if this provision is approved.'[13]

The first of the two joint House of Commons–Senate committees created during this period was established in 1966 after the publication of the Sedgwick Report and the White Paper. Its task was to convene hearings to gauge public and interest-group opinions on immigration policy and to issue a final report with the committee's recommendations to Parliament. Delegations representing religious organizations, ethnic groups, community-based groups, organized labour and business organizations, and professional organizations, all testified on the White Paper and other immigration issues. This committee was disbanded at the time of the 1968 federal election without having issued a final report. During the hearings, many groups and the committee members themselves demonstrated a strong aversion to the White Paper, particularly its proposals to curtail unscreened family sponsorship in favour of more screened independent immigrants.

The linkage of manpower goals with immigration (reflected in the creation of the new department) required an assessment of Canada's labour needs. According to the White Paper, the best employment opportunities existed for immigrants who possessed education, training, and skills.[14] Since sponsored immigrants were frequently unskilled and uneducated, the White Paper advocated reducing the number of immigrants who were admitted in this category. The solution advanced in the White Paper, and advocated by the deputy minister, was to control the influx of sponsored immigrants by limiting sponsored admissions to spouses, unmarried offspring under the age of twenty-one, orphaned relatives under sixteen years of age, and parents or grandparents, who would not be allowed to work in Canada.[15] Both landed immigrants and citizens would have the right to sponsor a relative who met these criteria. However, only a Canadian citizen would be given the additional privilege of sponsoring his or her children, regardless of their ages, with their accompanying spouses and unmarried children under twenty-one; brothers or sisters, again with their spouses and unmarried children; unmarried nephews or nieces under the age of twenty-one; and parents or grandparents who would be permitted to enter the labour force. These extended sponsorship privileges were subject to certain literacy or employment requirements.

These recommendations generated considerable criticism in the House of Commons and before the Joint Committee by groups favouring generous family sponsorship policies although some business interests supported a tighter linkage between immigration policy and labour market needs.

The 1967 Points System

The debate that the White Paper provoked in Parliament and the media eventually led the new department to re-evaluate its policies. The result of

Table 9.1
Immigration Selection Factors under the Point System, Canada, 1967

Independent applicants	Range of points assessment
Short-term factors	
Arranged employment or designated occupation	0 or 10
Knowledge of English and/or French	0–10
Relative in Canada	0–5
Area of destination	0–5
Long-term factors	
Education and training	0–20
Personal qualities	0–15
Occupational demand	0–15
Occupational skill	1–10
Age	0–10

Source: Manpower and Immigration Canada, *The Immigration Program: Canadian Immigration and Population Study* (Ottawa: Information Canada, 1974), as reprinted in Economic Council of Canada, *Economic and Social Impacts of Immigration: A Research Report,* ed. Neil Swan et al. (Ottawa: The Council, 1991), 15.

this re-examination was the implementation of the Norms of Assessment points scheme in 1967, which achieved the same objective as the White Paper proposal, but in a more direct fashion.[16]

The 1962 regulations essentially granted admission to 'a person who by reason of his education, training, skills or other special qualifications is likely to become successfully established in Canada ...'[17] Immigration officers could decide how these criteria were to be interpreted and applied in individual cases, although they were given an 'Immigration Counselling Handbook' to guide them about occupations in demand.[18] Consequently, there were widespread criticisms that, given such unchecked discretionary power, some immigration officers were acting arbitrarily.[19]

As indicated in table 9.1,[20] in the 1967 regulations the standards for immigrant selection were explicitly spelt out with the creation of a 'points system' that assigned prospective immigrants a score in the following categories: age; education; training; occupational skill in demand; knowledge of English or French; a personal assessment made by an immigration official in an interview; relatives in Canada; arranged employment; and employment opportunities in area of destination.[21]

The new regulations also addressed the sponsorship controversy by creating three categories of immigrants: independent, sponsored, and nominated. The sponsorship issue was a continuing source of concern to immigration officials because, allegedly, too many unskilled workers were being sponsored by relatives, a process which was largely beyond the department's control.[22] Although immediate relatives could continue to be sponsored, the new regulations subjected more distant 'nominated' relatives to five factors in the points system – education, personal assessment, occupational demand, occupational skill, and age – that assessed the long-term suitability of an applicant.[23] The other factors affecting an applicant's ability to become established initially in Canada were waived for nominated applicants, since it was expected that the nominator would assist his relative in getting established in Canada.[24] Finally, it is important to note that there was no formal quota in the points system. This meant that, if an immigrant passed the points criteria, he or she would be admitted to Canada regardless of the number of immigrants that Canada had already admitted in that year.

The 1967 points system ostensibly reduced immigration officers' discretion. However, two methods for adjusting an applicant's result remained. Under 'Personal Qualities,' up to fifteen points out of one hundred could be assigned by the officer, based on 'adaptability, motivation, initiative, resourcefulness and other similar [subjective] qualities.'[25] Second, an immigration official had the discretion, with the approval of a superior officer, to deny admission to applicants who had a 'pass' mark, and to admit those who otherwise failed.[26]

The points system was welcomed by the Canadian media. After describing how the White Paper had been criticized as placing too great an emphasis on skilled labour, the *Winnipeg Free Press* approved the points system because it allowed other factors to play a role. The *Globe and Mail* acknowledged that the new system could be criticized for dehumanizing applicants because of its mechanistic approach to evaluation. Yet the newspaper insisted that the points system be given a fair chance because there was a need for a non-discriminatory procedure to screen applicants. Perhaps the most enthusiastic response came from the *Montreal Gazette*: 'Canada needs more immigrants, and it has needed more humane methods for selecting them. These changes in the rules should help to meet both needs.'[27]

Reflecting the government's desire to eliminate explicitly racist immigration policies, the Cabinet amended the Assisted Passage Loan program during this period. The Assisted Passage Loan Scheme, created to assist urgently needed immigrants who could not afford to pay for their transportation, was open only to Europeans from its inception in 1951 until its extension to immigrants from Caribbean countries in 1966.[28] The department's Annual Report for 1969–70, states that, on 1 April 1970, loans were made available on a worldwide basis.[29] Despite this ostensible expansion, the number of loans granted fell from 58,000 in 1966[30] to 1,155 in 1970.[31] An explanation for this dramatic change is given in the 1969–70 Annual Report, which mentions in passing that, beginning in 1967, loans were made at a 6 per cent interest rate, and only to immigrants with skills in strong demand in Canada.[32]

The worsening economy in the early 1970s led to increased restrictions on immigrants and visitors intending to work in Canada. In 1973, the Immigration department made employment visas mandatory for all non-immigrants wishing to work legally in Canada. These visas, valid for up to one year, were granted only to fill specific job vacancies for which no Canadian workers were available. Also, in an attempt to keep better track of foreigners, all visitors intending to stay for more than three months had to register with the department on entry.[33] The government met the demand for cheap labour without recourse to increased immigration by issuing visas for temporary work to migrant workers, many of whom were seasonal workers from Mexico and the Caribbean,[34] or domestic workers, a class which previously had been able to enter the country as landed immigrants.[35]

In 1974, new economic pressures emerged to restrict immigration by tying it more closely to employment conditions. In February, the regulations were changed so that all independent immigrants (including nominated relatives) intending to enter the labour force had to have a firm job offer or occupation in demand in order to be admitted.[36] In October, the points system was adjusted so that ten points (out of a possible hundred) were subtracted from an independent applicant's total unless he or she had arranged employment (for which no Canadian was available) or had an occupation in demand.[37]

Despite the new points system, the Immigration Act gave the minister ultimate discretion in determining the right of individuals to stay in Canada. The practice of lobbying the minister after all other avenues had failed was described in the previous chapter. Over the current period, temporary or permanent admissions by ministerial orders-in-council of immigrants otherwise ineligible to enter Canada would typically run in the 4,000–7,000 range each year.

Special Admission Policies

From 1960 until 1962, the Chinese Adjustment Statement Program to deal with illegal immigration (described in the previous chapter) was largely unsuccessful.[38] Only 86 people had their status adjusted. However, in

November 1962, a simplified procedure was announced by the minister. As a result, the program began to function more effectively, and almost 2,000 applied for status adjustment in 1963.[39] The program was extended several times, and, by July 1970, 11,569 Chinese had their status adjusted.[40]

In 1966, Canada hosted the Commonwealth-Caribbean-Canada Conference (CCCC). In affirming its willingness to accept immigrants from the Caribbean on a non-discriminatory basis, Canada agreed to double the number of domestic service workers admitted from the Caribbean and to begin a movement of seasonal agricultural labourers from Jamaica on an experimental basis. Also, as mentioned above, the Assisted Passage Loan Scheme was extended to immigrants from Commonwealth-Caribbean countries.[41]

Although immigration standards for arrivals from the Caribbean were supposedly non-discriminatory, the nature of these programs for temporary domestic and agricultural workers indicates the sorts of immigrants Canada expected to admit from this part of the world. Indeed, the 1967–8 Annual Report refers to the 'moral issue' of whether Canada can take well-qualified people from developing countries that 'can ill-afford to lose them.' Consequently, the department 'will not actively seek immigrants in the developing countries,'[42] although Canada opened visa offices in Jamaica and in Trinidad and Tobago in 1967, making selective immigration in significant numbers from these countries possible for the first time.[43]

Provincial Initiatives

The 1963–77 period marks the emergence of the province of Quebec as a key participant in immigration policy. Between 1946 and 1971, Canada admitted more than 3.5 million immigrants. Of these, only 15 per cent settled in Quebec; of those who did move to Quebec, only 5 per cent were francophones prior to immigrating. The vast majority of immigrants to Quebec chose to educate their children in English rather than French. For example, in 1962–3, only 25 per cent of the children of Italian Quebecers were attending French schools; by 1971–2, this number had fallen to 10 per cent.[44] Only 2.1 per cent of Jews claimed French as their first language, compared with 55.1 per cent who claimed English.[45] Projecting these trends forward, it was likely that, by the year 2000, a majority of residents of the city of Montreal would be English-speaking. As well, beginning in the 1960s fertility rates in Quebec began to drop to levels that, by the 1980s, were the lowest in Canada and the third-lowest in the industrialized world.[46]

As a result of these apprehensions, the Quebec government began to develop an active and independent presence in the immigration field. In 1968, it created its own Department of Immigration to 'facilitate the adaptation of immigrants to the Quebec environment.'[47] The new department sent representatives to Paris, Brussels, Beirut, and other areas with large French-speaking populations to promote emigration to Quebec. In 1969, Bill 63, a controversial French-language bill, was passed by Quebec's National Assembly. The Immigration Minister became responsible for ensuring that immigrants to Quebec acquire knowledge of French.[48]

In October 1975, the Andras-Bienvenue agreement was signed between Quebec and the federal Department of Manpower and Immigration, under which Quebec immigration officers were given a greater role in recruiting and settling immigrants, reflecting Quebec's concerns regarding the impact of English-speaking immigrants on the province.[49]

REFUGEE POLICY

Refugee policy during this period was reactive in nature, with no evidence of a stable, long-term approach towards assisting victims of war and persecution. Most of the refugees arrived as part of special programs that Canada set up for political, economic, or humanitarian reasons. The first such program was established in 1962, and involved 100 families from Hong Kong who were part of a sudden mass influx of Chinese escaping the People's Republic of China.[50] This movement represented the first time that Canada served as a haven for non-European refugees.

From 1962 to 1967, about 2,000 refugees, the majority of them from Europe, arrived in Canada annually. Instead of creating special programs, the Immigration department interpreted educational and occupational requirements with leniency for refugees on an *ad hoc* basis. To be admitted, refugees had to have 'reasonable prospects for employment.' Also, a program for disabled refugees who had means of supporting themselves, or sponsors in Canada, was continued from World Refugee Year.[51]

Canada was a major financial supporter of the United Nations High Commissioner for Refugees (UNHCR). For example, in 1965 Canada contributed more than $500,000, making it the fourth-largest donor.[52] In June 1969, Canada finally acceded to the 1951 U.N. Convention Relating to Refugees and the 1967 Protocol. Prior to 1969, Canada adhered in practice to the terms of the convention and also was a member of the UNHCR's executive committee.[53] Canada did not sign the convention earlier, primarily because of the RCMP's belief that it would constrain Canada's ability to deport refugees on security grounds.[54]

In August 1968, thousands of refugees fled Czechoslovakia as Warsaw Pact troops crushed an uprising designed to take Czechoslovakia out of the Soviet sphere of influence. Newspaper editorials urged the government to give assistance to the Czecheslovakians. In response, Allan MacEachen, the minister of Manpower and Immigration, announced on 6 September 1968 that relaxed admissions standards and transportation grants would apply to these refugees. The Department of Manpower and Immigration dispatched a team of officials to Vienna, Austria, in an attempt to attract the most desirable refugees.[55] By the end of 1969, some 12,000 refugees had arrived, a third of whom were highly skilled trades people or professionals.[56] Most adjusted well to their new country.

The first group of refugees entering Canada as a result of the Vietnam War were not Vietnamese. From 1965, Canada served as a favourite haven for American draft evaders and military deserters. Until 1968, however, it was departmental policy to refuse admission to those who could not prove they had been discharged from military service.[57] In January 1968, Canada responded to criticism from those who sympathized with the resisters by changing its policy to permit deserters of foreign armies to gain landed immigrant status.[58] In May 1969, the minister, Allan MacEachen, announced that 'membership in the armed services of another country, or desertion ... will not be a factor in determining ... eligibility... for landed immigrant status.'[59] Because draft dodgers and deserters were not formally classified as refugees and were selected under standard immigration regulations, no official estimates exist of how many emigrated to Canada. Some reports placed the number of 'exiles' at approximately 60,000 by the fall of 1969.[60] However, annual reports from the Department of Manpower and Immigration indicate that, from 1965 to 1969, the number of draft age male immigrants from the United States grew from approximately 2,360 to 4,700, for a total of 17,000 over five years. The percentage of such immigrants, compared with the total number of immigrants from the United States during this time, steadily increased from 15.6 to 20.6 per cent.[61]

In the late 1960s, the Canadian High Commissioner in India learned about the plight of some 60,000 Tibetan refugees who had escaped to India after China had seized their homeland in 1959. Since the Indian government was not able to provide assistance to all the refugees, the High Commissioner suggested that some be allowed to emigrate to Canada. Through his efforts, the Canadian government accepted 226 of these refugees in 1970 and 1971. Unfortunately, they encountered difficulties adjusting to their new environment, in part because they were dispersed to various provinces owing to a policy disfavouring group resettlement. Many felt lonely and bereaved because of a lack of contact with their spiritual and cultural leaders.[62]

On 4 August 1972, the Ugandan dictator Idi Amin Dada gave all Asian holders of British passports (who were mainly of East Indian descent) ninety days to leave the country. The 50,000 people affected formed a large part of Uganda's managerial, professional, and commercial classes. They were Ugandans of Indian descent who had lived in Uganda for lengthy periods and had chosen to retain British citizenship after independence. The British government appealed to other countries to assist it in resettling the Uganda 'expellees,' and Canada reacted with alacrity. On 24 August 1972, despite a worsening economic situation and a federal election in the offing, Prime Minister Trudeau announced that Canada would accept some of the refugees.[63]

An immigration team was swiftly dispatched to Kampala to process applications, and thirty-one aircraft were chartered to bring them to Canada.[64] By the end of 1973, more than 7,000 arrived to well-organized receptions in Canada. Much of the resettlement assistance was provided by *ad hoc*, largely volunteer committees funded by the federal government.[65] The Liberal government's response to the Ugandan crisis received praise in the House. New Democrat John Gilbert congratulated the Liberals for their quick response to the crisis, since it occurred at a time when popular opinion was sceptical of such an intervention in light of the worsening economic situation reflected in rising unemployment and housing shortages.[66] These refugees quickly established themselves in Canada. In a follow-up interview a year after arrival, 89 per cent of respondents wishing to enter the labour force were employed, and more than 90 per cent intended to stay in Canada permanently, regardless of developments in Uganda.[67] The major criticism of this movement was that Canada skimmed the cream of the crop, not taking any of the less desirable or less skilled refugees. Nonetheless, the United Kingdom was committed to accepting all the expellees because they were British passport holders.

The final major refugee crisis during this period was prompted by a military coup that displaced Chile's democratically elected Marxist government of Salvador Allende on 11 September 1973. General Pinochet's new regime began a brutal crackdown against the former Allende government's supporters. Many fled to other South American countries or sought asylum in embassies. Immediately after the coup in Chile, church organizations began pressing the Canadian government to take action by granting large number of exiles and asylum seekers refugee status. As public awareness of the coup and its aftermath grew, more groups joined the churches in their call for action. Finally, in October 1974, a delegation representing Amnesty International, the Canadian Council of Churches, the Canadian Labour Congress, the Confederation of National Trade Unions, the Canadian University Service, and Anglican, Lutheran, United and Presbyterian churches met with the minister of External Affairs, Allan MacEachen, and the Manpower and Immigration minister, Robert Andras. The delegation presented a brief detailing the crisis, but this had little or no effect.[68] Despite pressure from church, labour, and Latino groups, the Canadian government was slow to react out of a desire to avoid antagonizing the United States, which supported the new government and because of concerns over the possible implications of permitting hundreds of alleged Marxists into Canada.[69]

Intensive security screening, a lack of translators, and no relaxation of immigration standards were the major factors that caused only 780 visas to be issued in the six months after the coup.[70] Independent observers judged Canada's record one of the worst among Western nations.[71] Although 6,990 Chilean refugees were ultimately admitted,[72] Dirks, in his history of Canadian refugee policy, lamented that 'ideological considerations have replaced racial criteria as a discriminatory factor in determining Canada's refugee admissions policy.'[73]

The Opposition attacked the government for its response to the Chilean crisis. During question period, New Democrats Andrew Brewin and John Harney persistently inquired as to the government's plans to assist the refugees. Manpower and Immigration Minister Andras responded with promises of action and details of those assisted by Canada already. Brewin welcomed the government's promise to relax selection criteria, 'although I do not know exactly what that means.' He agreed that security checks were necessary, 'but I hope these background checks will not result in long delays.'[74] Conservative Jake Epp demanded an explanation as to why it took four weeks to complete security checks, whereas it had taken less than two days during the Hungarian and Czechoslovakian crises.[75] By 1974, the New Democrats no longer accepted Liberal promises of action after reports appeared describing the treatment that refugees had received from Canada. John Rodriguez, a New Democratic MP, described the situation: 'Three common complaints from UN refugee camps have been that the Canadian immigration officials presume the clients to be guilty as criminal terrorists until proven innocent. The refugees have also spoken bitterly of police-type interrogation. Thirdly, the manner in which the Canadian officials have gone about assisting these refugees appears contrary to what the minister of Manpower and Immigration in his statement referred to as humanitarian considerations.'[76] Even Liberal MPs, such as Jim Fleming, began to question the government's lukewarm response.[77]

However, not all members of Parliament opposed the government's policy. Conservative Ian Arrol wondered why '… the government of Canada [felt] it necessary to facilitate the entry into this country of these communists.'[78] He was supported by Social Credit member Réal Caouette, who asked: 'Is the department considering the advisability of suggesting to Chilean immigrants to go rather to the USSR, Cuba, the People's Republic of China, and Algeria where ideologies would be more in keeping with their deep convictions and yearnings?'[79]

The different treatment given to Hungarian and Chilean refugees was criticized by the Canadian Council of Churches (CCC) before the joint committee studying the Green Paper in 1975. The CCC began its testimony by congratulating Canadians on the assistance offered to the Hungarian refugees. However, it strongly criticized the Canadian government's reaction to the Chilean situation, and the security establishment for its overzealousness: while Canada took six to eight months to screen an applicant for security reasons, people were forced to flee, were imprisoned, or were killed.[80]

DEPORTATION

While statistics on deportation are available only until 1971, perhaps their most striking feature is the very large number of deportations from 1967 to 1971. The figure of 11,766 is triple the number in the previous five years, and even larger than the number in previous five-year periods going back to 1947. Very few deportations were undertaken on the basis of the public charge criterion, the major cause during the Depression. Most fell into the 'stealth and misrepresentation' (57 per cent) or 'criminality' (32 per cent) categories; 860 (7 per cent) fell in the 'other' category, which presumably primarily covered deportation for security reasons.

Although the reasons given for the deportations conceal more than they disclose, there is some evidence that the RCMP cooperated with the FBI in returning military deserters to the United States, many without the benefit of legal proceedings. The RCMP raided one hostel for draft dodgers and deserters ten times in 1969 alone.[81] Part of the explanation for the increase in deportations between 1967 and 1971 presumably also lies in the 1966 regulation (withdrawn in 1973) that permitted visitors to apply for landed-immigrant status from within Canada – negative decisions on such applications would sometimes be followed by deportation proceedings in the absence of voluntary departures.

A large proportion of those deported in the 'stealth and misrepresentation' category under the 1952 Immigration Act involved ship jumpers who were caught and returned. More than 2,000 such deserters were arrested and deported between 1966 and 1970.[82] This practice became controversial in 1964, when allegations were made in Parliament and the press that foreigners were being detained illegally and denied access to counsel. Much of the outcry arose over cases of Greek sailors who were ordered deported after entering Canada illegally and marrying Canadian women.[83]

Guy Favreau, the minister of Justice, appointed Joseph Sedgwick, a Toronto lawyer, to investigate the allegations. Sedgwick's report,[84] released in April 1965, was generally supportive of existing deportation procedures, concluding that the right to counsel was not violated, nor were the sailors detained for an unduly long period, pending hearings. Sedgwick criticized the media's selective reporting of the facts in these cases and accused members of Parliament of cynical catering to ethnic groups in raising the matter in the House.[85] The government was pleased with the tenor of the report, and in 1965 Prime Minister Pearson asked Sedgwick to enlarge his investigation to include the issue of ministerial discretion in the immigration process. In his report, Sedgwick largely endorsed the government's immigration procedures. However, part II of his *Report on Immigration*[86] made the following recommendations: (1) vest final authority in the IAB in deportation decisions, subject to an appeal to federal courts; (2) repeal section 39 of the Immigration Act, 1952, which barred judicial review of immigration decisions; and (3) eliminate the practice of issuing special orders-in-council to permit ineligible immigrants to circumvent the act.[87] The first two of these recommendations were accepted in 1967 and 1973, respectively. The third has never been implemented.

Perhaps the most important aspect of Sedgwick's report was his call for an independent IAB, specifically an appeal tribunal that was no longer controlled by immigration officials. This recommendation was incorporated into the new Immigration Appeal Board Act passed in March 1967. The Immigration Appeal Board Act was welcomed by all sides of the House when it was introduced.[88] The act made the IAB into a quasi judicial body, independent of the Department of Manpower and Immigration.[89] Under the 1952 Immigration Act, the IAB consisted of Immigration

Branch officials who made recommendations to the minister, which he or she could accept or reject in his or her discretion.[90] Under the Immigration Appeal Board Act, anyone facing a deportation order could appeal to the IAB on issues of law or fact, or a combination of law and fact.[91] Section 17 of the Act extended this right to persons who made an application for the admission of a relative. However, section 17 included the proviso that appeals under this section could be restricted by order-in-council. In the House, Richard Bell stated his support on behalf the Conservatives for section 17, but voiced the fear that the Cabinet's ability to restrain these rights was prone to abuse.[92] His fears were in part justified: after the Act was passed, the House passed P.C. 1967–1956, dated 12 October 1967, which stated that the word 'persons' in section 17 referred only to Canadian citizens (thus landed immigrants whose relatives were denied admission were not given a right to appeal) and that this right of appeal applied only to sponsored relatives, and not to nominated relatives.[93]

IAB decisions were final, subject to an appeal with leave to the Supreme Court of Canada on questions of law, including jurisdiction.[94] As a quasi judicial body, the IAB had to give reasons for its decisions, if asked. The most important innovation in the new act was an extension of IAB powers to include areas of equitable jurisdiction. This new power allowed the IAB to consider humanitarian and compassionate arguments if the appellant was about to be deported under the strict terms of the Immigration Act.[95] Richard Bell opposed placing such equitable powers in the hands of an administrative tribunal, preferring that the political arm of government continue to exercise it. However, as he himself acknowledged, his view was not one widely shared by his colleagues: 'without question, sir, the majority opinion is against me.'[96]

The minister of Manpower and Immigration and the Solicitor General could pre-empt an IAB decision if they jointly filed a certificate with the board that 'based upon security or criminal intelligence reports ... the national interest' required that a deportation order proceed.[97] Such a certificate was considered 'conclusive proof of the matters stated therein.'[98] Otherwise, the minister could not interfere with IAB decisions. New Democrat David Lewis stated in the House that this provision 'carries forward in the new law an idea which is vicious, basically undemocratic in every sense of the word, and destroys much of the good which the minister intended to achieve through this legislation.'[99]

With the creation of an independent IAB, the courts became more willing to review immigration decisions. For example, until *Gana v MMI*[100] in 1970, Special Inquiry Officers (SIOs) and the Immigration Appeal Board did not vary the original assessment on the points test given a prospective immigrant because this was perceived to be solely the immigration officer's responsibility. In *Gana*, however, the Supreme Court of Canada ruled that, because an applicant's score was bound up with his or her right to remain in Canada, the SIOs and IAB must have the power to vary the assessment.

Soon after the independent IAB was established in 1967, it was swamped with cases. This increase was spurred by a 1966 regulation permitting people to apply for landed immigrant status from within Canada.[101] Immigration officials were not supportive of the 1966 regulation and sought to subvert it by holding applicants within Canada to the requirements for a valid medical certificate, which was only obtainable abroad. In *Podlaszecka v MMI*,[102] the applicant was ordered deported solely on the grounds that she lacked the necessary visa and medical certificate. Mr. Justice Laskin, speaking for the majority, ruled that the rejection of potential immigrants must be based on substantive evidence, not technical non-conformities.[103]

In *Leiba v MMI*,[104] the Supreme Court insisted that immigration officials conform to procedures in the Immigration Act. It had been departmental practice to issue 'check out' letters to people who applied for admission within Canada but failed to satisfy the required standards. These letters informed recipients that they had to leave the country or deportation proceedings would be launched against them. Mr. Justice Laskin rejected this practice by insisting that the only correct procedure was a proper section 22 inquiry before a special inquiry officer and a right of appeal to the IAB prior to enforcing a deportation order.

In 1970, the Minister asked Sedgwick to examine the causes of the backlog and make recommendations. Sedgwick reported that many visitors were coming to Canada with the intention of applying for landed immigrant status and then using all means of appeal to stay for as long as possible.[105] In particular, many took advantage of the practice of not deporting anyone who had filed a notice of appeal. Delays in the appeals process of up to seven years began to develop.[106]

The huge backlog of cases that developed in the Immigration Appeal Board in the late 1960s and early 1970s revealed two contrasting problems with the new due-process protections. First, the process could be abused by immigrants without meritorious claims who delayed an ultimate determination in the hope that they might benefit from an amnesty or humanitarian or compassionate treatment following the establishment of roots in Canada. Second, even with respect to *bona fide* claims, due process protections proved extremely costly and time-consuming and could result in serious injustices by delaying and impeding applicants' effective integration into their new society.

Various measures, both legal and administrative, were taken to address the problem of excessive delays. In November 1972, with the problem becoming increasingly severe, Cabinet passed an order-in-council revoking the 1966 regulation that gave visitors a right to apply for landed status from within Canada.[107] In 1973, the Manpower and Immigration Minister, Robert Andras, introduced amendments to the Immigration Appeal Board Act to increase the size and modify the procedures of the IAB to help it cope with the backlog. The previous legislation allowed all people facing a deportation order a right to appeal to the IAB; under the amendment, only permanent residents, valid visa holders, and persons claiming to be refugees or Canadian citizens were given a right of appeal.[108] Thus, people in Canada illegally and those from countries with no visa requirement, such as the United States and Great Britain (which constituted a high proportion of deportees), lost their right of appeal to the IAB. An illegal immigrant who did not claim to be a refugee or Canadian citizen, or permanent resident, and who did not hold a visa to enter Canada, could be deported after losing a hearing before a special immigration officer.[109] The original proposal to eliminate appeal rights for visitors attempted to deny these rights retroactively to visitors who had entered Canada before the regulations changed, but pressure from Opposition members caused the minister to withdraw this provision.[110]

On 15 August 1973, with a backlog of more than 17,000 cases which the IAB was dealing with at the rate of 100 cases a month, Andras introduced the Adjustment of Status Program, under which people in Canada illegally had sixty days in which to regularize their status. Applicants would be judged on the basis of how well established they were in Canada, and on compassionate grounds. The program was supported by all the political parties, and received a great deal of publicity in the media. Thirty-nine thousand people took advantage of this selective amnesty to obtain landed status.[111] By giving the benefit of the doubt to individuals whose status had been subject to substantial delays, this *de facto* amnesty involved the exercise of executive discretion in a massive way – precisely the kind of decision making that the process was initially designed to avoid. Formulating both fair and administratively feasible due process requirements for the determination of individual immigrant status thus became one of the most vexing policy issues both in this period and in the period to follow.

A major legal issue that remained unresolved during this period was whether or not a Special Inquiry Officer (SIO) was bound by the principles of natural justice, particularly fairness and impartiality, in making initial deportation decisions. Although the courts, with hesitation, leaned towards requiring SIOs to adhere to the principles of natural justice,[112] the structure of the inquiry was inherently inconsistent with this. For example, the SIO served as both a prosecutor and judge in the inquiry.

The Beginnings of a New Immigration Act: The Green Paper, 1974

In November 1972, Robert Andras became minister of Manpower and Immigration. Managerial problems and an illegal immigration backlog spiralling out of control caused deep morale problems among immigration officials. Andras brought in a senior bureaucrat, Alan Gotlieb, as deputy minister to assist in devising new policies to address these problems.[113]

Andras's first step towards formulating a new Immigration Act was to commission a Green Paper to be prepared under the supervision of department officials and to canvass options for a fresh approach to immigration. All the major parties supported the commissioning of the Green Paper.[114] This comprehensive review was announced in September 1973 and was intended to take only six months. In fact, it was not submitted to Cabinet until the fall of 1974, and it was finally published in December of that year, under the title: *A Report of the Canadian Immigration and Population Study*.[115]

Unlike a White Paper, which is intended to be a government statement of its position on an issue, a Green Paper is designed merely to provide factual background on policy issues and present policy options with a view to forging a consensus on new legislation.[116] Although the Green Paper upheld that tradition by not formally advocating its preference for any one policy option, its tone clearly evinced a negative attitude towards an active immigration policy. As two commentators noted, 'while the Green Paper reads like some verbal tennis game, it is still possible to hazard a guess at the score.'[117]

The Green Paper described the problems that the country faced, including the negative effects of increased urbanization and the decline of francophones as a percentage of the population. According to the Green Paper, since Canada's population was not increasing without immigration, and all the problems described were caused by a growing population, it was appropriate to conclude that immigrants were the cause of these problems.[118] In addition, the Green Paper went on to detail the increase in racial tensions that accompanied the changing ethnic composition of Canada as a direct result of the 1962 and 1967 changes to immigration policy.[119] The Green Paper argued that immigration should be tied primarily to labour market needs. However, the Green Paper went further by suggesting that Canada should steer '... immigrants against prevailing population currents.'[120] Thus policies should be considered that would induce immigrants to live in designated areas of Canada outside large urban centres.

RESPONSES TO THE GREEN PAPER

The Green Paper achieved its objective of provoking wide public debate; reaction to it was swift and critical. Entire academic journals were devoted to critiquing it, a Joint Senate–House of Commons Committee was appointed to tour the country and canvass opinions about it, and a national conference was held to examine it.[121]

The publication of the Green Paper provoked the most lively academic debate about Canadian immigration policy in the country's history. Academics such as Freda Hawkins and Gerald Dirks (who published important books in 1972 and 1977, respectively) participated in the debates surrounding the Green Paper.[122] Two journals, *Canadian Ethnic Studies* and *Canadian Public Policy,* devoted entire issues to critiques of the Green Paper,[123] inviting virtually every academic in the country with an interest in immigration to contribute to their fora.

While many academics criticized the Green Paper's recommendations, especially its negative views on the social and economic effects of immigration, others reserved their criticism for the process entailed in its formulation. Hawkins described the Green Paper as a superficial study that paid lip-service to the consultation process in policy making. In contrast to Canada, both Australia and the United States had conducted extensive public hearings into immigration. She called on Canada to establish a royal commission to examine immigration policy,[124] although the subsequent joint-committee hearings largely served this function.

On the other hand, York University sociologist Anthony Richmond criticized the government for having commissioned the Green Paper in the first place. For Richmond, immigration policy was a Pandora's Box not to be opened in difficult economic times. Although the immigration issue could be expected to act in part as a diversion, it also threatened to be confused with the issues Canadians were worried about in 1975: unemployment, housing shortages, and inflation. Richmond documented how public opinion polls showed declining support for immigration among the middle class. In 1959, 57 per cent of university-educated Canadians supported immigration; by 1973, this figure had fallen to 39 per cent.[125]

The Green Paper also recommended that refugees should be recognized as a separate category within the act. However, the paper suggested that the definition of who qualified for refugee status, and thereby became eligible for admission to Canada, should be left to governmental regulations. The Green Paper implicitly rejected any suggestion that the definition of refugees in the U.N. Protocol of 1967 be adopted in the new Immigration Act.[126] Although Canada acceded to the protocol in 1969, the authors of the Green Paper were concerned about giving the U.N. definition the status of domestic law in Canada. Gerald Dirks criticized the Green Paper's flattering portrayal of the history of Canada's responses to refugee crises. He stated that, although Canada's refugee policy was no longer driven by racism, it was now governed by ideology.[127]

The Green Paper received a large amount of media attention compared with the more carefully considered and influential report of the joint committee of the following year.[128] Surprisingly, the Green Paper, which was widely criticized in most other quarters, was favourably received by many of the media.[129] The *Montreal Gazette* greeted the document as a chance for Canadians to participate in the policy-formation process. 'Canadians have been given a sound overview of immigration trends, problems and some alternatives without any definite answers.'[130] While recognizing the risks of an immigration debate (namely, that racists would be given a forum to express their views), the *Globe and Mail* welcomed the document, stating that immigration policy needed a proper review. Both the *Globe and Mail* and the *Vancouver Sun* approved of the Green Paper's call to lower the level of immigration by the establishment of an annual quota (it appears that the *Globe and Mail* had changed its position on immigration between 1967 and 1975), but they rejected the Green Paper's suggestion that quotas should be set for each continent or region of the world.[131]

The Cabinet wished to avoid any form of parliamentary review of the Green Paper, fearing that the publicity generated could exacerbate ethnic tensions. However, the Liberal caucus, along with Opposition MPs, insisted on the creation of a joint committee,[132] which was established in the spring of 1975 to examine the Green Paper. Co-chaired by Senator Maurice Riel and former minister of Labour, Martin O'Connell,[133] the committee held fifty days of public hearings over thirty-five weeks in twenty-one cities. It received more than 1,800 briefs from both individuals and organizations. Unlike its 1967 predecessor, this committee produced a comprehensive final report which was to become the basis of the new Immigration Act in 1976.

The government had initially allocated five months for the committee to conduct hearings and issue a report. Under intense pressure from interest groups, the government gave the committee an additional three months. Almost every ethnic delegation testifying before the 1975 joint committee disapproved of the Green Paper's pessimistic tone and viewed the document as racist. Beyond this, there was little agreement.[134] Some welcomed the chance to participate in the policy-making process, while others chastised the government for providing opportunities for racially motivated objections to immigration to be ventilated.[135]

The Canadian Bar Association (CBA), the professional association of Canadian lawyers, argued before the joint committee that the inquiries conducted by Special Inquiry Officers (SIOs) should be independent of the Department of Manpower and Immigration.[136] The CBA called for a new Immigration Act which incorporated and expanded the principles of natural justice and due process embodied in the Immigration Appeal Board Act, 1967.

The joint committee of 1975 was heavily influenced by the CBA's call for a radical change in the deportation system. Prior to the enactment of the new Immigration Act in 1976, if an applicant already in Canada was denied the right to remain, he or she received a deportation order. This order not only returned the applicant to his or her country of origin, but prevented him or her from ever seeking admission to Canada again without a minister's permit. Applicants began to withdraw their admission applications voluntarily and to leave Canada prior to receiving this order.[137] However, in the 1974 case of *Morris v Minister of Manpower and Immigration,* the Federal Court of Appeal stated that this option was foreclosed once the inquiry process began.[138] The CBA recommended that Canada institute different levels of deportations, with less drastic consequences. The deportation order could still be utilized for those who did not comply with the first dismissal order. The 1975 joint committee adopted this recommendation in its final report.[139]

THE JOINT COMMITTEE'S FINAL REPORT

The Joint Senate–House of Commons Committee issued its final report to Parliament in the fall of 1975. After describing the modern urbanization problems that Canada faced, the committee's report stated that '... all these are problems faced by rapidly growing cities, but concluded that they are caused by the economic, social and cultural dynamism of cities and their attractiveness to Canadians and immigrants alike.'[140] This was a clear rejection of the Green Paper's conclusions, which had blamed these problems on immigration.

Among its many recommendations, the committee called for a global quota for the total number of immigrants admitted to Canada in a given year. The quota would be set by departmental officials in conjunction with the provinces and would be subject to approval by the House of Commons. Immigrants would be admitted on a first-come-first-served basis: any potential immigrant satisfying the points requirements would be admitted to Canada until the quota for that year had been filled.[141]

The committee also proposed changes to the points system. It proposed to eliminate the nominated class but expand the sponsorship category to allow a Canadian citizen over the age of twenty-one to sponsor his or her parents regardless of their age. In addition, the report recommended that the number of points allotted to an independent applicant with a relative in Canada should be doubled, from five to ten. It also stated that the point system should be redrawn to place less emphasis on education and personal assessment, and a greater emphasis on life experience and personal competence.[142] Other recommendations included a separate regime for refugees,[143] independent special inquiry officers,[144] and the removal of the ban on homosexuals.[145]

The committee's final report was well received both in Parliament and in the media. Sixty of its sixty-five recommendations were implemented in the 1976 act. However, three members (Liberal Monique Begin, New Democrat Andrew Brewin, and Conservative David Macdonald), along with two other MPs closely associated with the committee (Liberal Peter Stollery and New Democrat David Orlikow), issued a short statement, noting points of dissent. This statement called for widening the IAB's jurisdiction and an extension of sponsorship rights of landed immigrants equivalent to those of Canadian citizens.[146]

Conclusions

The period 1963–76 is characterized by two important features. First, immigration policy formulation became a much more democratic process with the publication of the White (1966) and Green (1974) Papers and the appointment that followed of the two joint Senate-House of Commons Committees to undertake a broad public consultation process. Second, the enactment of the Immigration Appeal Board Act in 1967 and the elimination of much administrative discretion in the application of admission policies as a result of the adoption of the points system, also in 1967, reflected a recognition on a much broader scale of the importance of due process protections.

The increased emphasis on public consultation combined with the changing political importance of ethnic constituencies to ensure that ethnic groups played a major role in policy development, as is demonstrated by the government's compromise on the issue of family sponsorship in the 1967 regulations. Religious and community organizations also exerted an influential voice in this period, in resisting curtailing of family sponsorship rights, supporting generous refugee policies, and rejecting the negative characterization of the effects of immigration in the Green Paper.

By the end of this period, the groundwork was laid for the new Immigration Act, which was enacted in 1976 and proclaimed in 1977 with near unanimous support from politicians of all parties and with the broad support of private and public interest groups, academics, and the media. Based on the consultations which followed the 1974 Green Paper, the new Act would further curtail administrative and executive discretion, increase due process protections for immigrants, and create a relatively generous refugee policy (as detailed in the following chapter).

In less than thirty years, the country had seen a remarkable shift from Prime Minister Mackenzie King's vision in 1947: race and concerns about preserving Canada's demographic character were no longer major considerations for admission, while increasing respect for due process demonstrated that immigration was now seen as something more than merely a privilege; on the other hand, the points system institutionalized the 'tap on/tap off' approach to immigration by making short-term labour-market considerations an important, albeit not exclusive, determinant of admissibility for independent immigrants. An unprecedented political and public consensus had emerged during this period on the basic elements of a generally liberal immigration policy. However, this consensus was to be severely strained in the period that followed by the dramatic increase in the influx of refugees from non-traditional source countries.

CHAPTER TEN

Regulating the Refugee Influx, 1977–1994: The Fraying of the Consensus

From the mid-1970s, economic growth in Canada fell off sharply, inflation and unemployment rose, and government deficits soared.[1] Thereafter the country experienced two recessions. One, beginning in 1981, was the most severe recession since the Depression of the 1930s. After a modest but uneven recovery, in 1991 Canada was leading other industrialized countries into yet another worldwide recession, with unemployment reaching almost 12 per cent, interest rates rising to the 14 to 15 per cent range, and federal and provincial government deficits rapidly escalating.

The period closed with the resumption of a healthy rate of growth in gross domestic product and inflation at minimal levels. However, the unemployment rate remained obdurately high (in excess of 10 per cent) and federal and provincial budget deficits were still at historically high levels.

Immigration levels matched the economic climate with annual numbers falling by over 60 per cent from 1974 to 1978 (210,000 to 86,000 persons). Although they rose significantly in subsequent years, they plunged again with hard economic times in the 1980s such that in 1985 annual admissions were 84,000 persons – the lowest intake since 1962.

Declining numbers reflected in part the adoption of more restrictive admission policies in the recessionary environment of the late 1970s and early 1980s. With more buoyant economic conditions in the latter half of the decade, levels rose steadily again. By 1992 annual admissions were 212,000. The relatively low levels of the first part of the period were therefore counterbalanced by higher levels in later years, such that the total number of immigrants admitted to Canada between 1971 and 1992 was 2,268,161, an average of 141,160 a year.

One of the marked features of the period was the significant change in the country of origins of immigrants. Prior to 1961, 90 per cent of all immigrants to Canada came from Europe and only 3 per cent originated from Asia and the Middle East. By 1990 these figures had dramatically changed: European immigrants accounted for less than 25 per cent of the total, while those from Asia and the Middle East represented over 50 per cent of all arrivals.[2] As in the previous period, the proportion of Francophone immigrants continued to decline, with long-term implications as the influence of French Canadians as a percentage of the Canadian population also fell. This was made much of by the Quebec separatist party, the Parti Québécois, during the debates surrounding the 1980 Quebec separation referendum. It added increased urgency to Quebec's demands for greater autonomy in immigration selection and admission – an autonomy that was progressively accorded throughout the period.

Ontario and British Columbia attracted proportionately more immigrants than other provinces, with close to 50 per cent of the total going to the former compared to 12 per cent to the prairies, whose share had fallen considerably. By 1991 the proportion of immigrants to total populations in the provincial capitals of Toronto and Vancouver was 38 per cent and 30 per cent, respectively.[3]

The shifts in immigrant composition were in part brought on by more expansionary policies regarding the immigration of family members as well as, in later years, more favourable conditions for business immigrants, many of whom came from Asia. Interestingly, both these movements sparked considerable controversy during the period, but not as much as was occasioned by the dramatic rise in refugee arrivals. The latter occurred amid a global surge in the number of refugees uprooted by civil war and religious, ethnic, and/or political persecution. Between 1970 and 1993 the global refugee population soared from 2.5 million to more than 18 million.[4] In Canada, the number of refugees selected overseas for admission correspondingly rose from 7,300 in 1977 to 52,300 in 1991: 23 per cent of the total immigrant intake. Most dramatic and controversial was the rise in spontaneous arrivals of refugees making claims for protection at Canadian borders or from within the country. These went from a few hundred annually in the 1970s to several thousand in the 1980s, peaking at more than 37,000 in 1992.[5]

In terms of immigration policy, the Immigration Act of 1976 marked a bold directional shift. The act was passed following extensive political and public debate that led to an unprecedented consensus – embodied in the new act – on central issues such as generous family reunification policies, transparent admission criteria for independent immigrants embodying a revised form of the point system, deportation procedures that provided some significant measure of due process protection to immigrants, and a reasonably generous refugee policy.

Importantly, for the first time the Immigration Act clearly set out the objectives of immigration law and policy. These included attaining Canada's demographic goals, fostering a strong and viable economy, facilitating family reunion, fulfilling Canada's international obligations with respect to refugees, and upholding its humanitarian tradition with respect to the displaced and persecuted.

Another significant change introduced in the new act was the requirement that the minister consult with the provinces as well as with other individuals and institutions regarding future levels of immigration. In 1993, this was amended to include the requirement that the minister submit an annual immigration plan to Parliament setting out the total number of immigrants and the breakdown of the various classes of immigrants to be admitted the following year.

Canada's immigration policy following the passage of this act was significantly more expansionary, from both an admissions and a due-process perspective, than in previous decades. Nevertheless, the dramatic and sudden increase in refugee claims in the late 1980s led to the fraying of the consensus reached at the beginning of the period. The relatively open posture that characterized the first part of this period gradually shifted in the second half, with an increased focus on security issues and with broader powers conferred on the minister to exclude and remove those found inadmissible.

The nearly unanimous parliamentary endorsement in 1976 of major revisions to the Immigration Act might have been expected to herald the beginning of a period of relative calm and stability in Canadian immigration policy. In fact, the debates over immigration policy that occurred in Parliament and other fora during the 1980s were as bitter and fractious as in any previous period. On a planet both torn by escalating civil strife and shrunk by increasingly accessible global travel, much of this controversy surrounded the highly emotional issue of refugees. However, issues surrounding appropriate levels of annual admission and the relative proportion of family class to independent and business class immigrants were also vigorously debated within Parliament and other public arenas, as were changes to admissibility provisions, including expanded grounds for exclusion and removal.

Ethnic, religious, and community-based groups (NGOs) were extremely active in their attempts to influence both government policy and public opinion. They were particularly vocal about measures by the government to tighten borders against unauthorized entry, expand grounds for deportation, and reduce numbers of sponsored refugees. They argued that the government's implicit agenda was to close Canada's doors to deserving and undeserving refugee claimants alike. They were joined in their opposition to more restrictive measures by lawyers and their associations, including the Canadian Bar Association, the Refugee Lawyers Association, and the Quebec Lawyers Association. However, the effectiveness of their opposition was limited by the extent to which the Conservative government, with a large majority, was already strongly committed to a particular policy, and by the short time frames provided for responses.

In contrast, most of the major organizations representing business interests, with the exception, perhaps, of the Chamber of Commerce, were not especially active in immigration debates. When they did become involved, business interests often focused on immigration as a means of improving the quality of Canada's workforce. In 1990, for example, representatives of the Chamber of Commerce wrote to Minister Barbara McDougall that Canadian immigration policy could be employed 'as a major policy instrument for increasing the size of, and improving the quality of, the labour force.'[6] They argued for an 'expansionary' immigration policy 'aimed at allowing for more immigrants in the business and independent workers classes rather than planning only moderate increases in immigration.'[7] They noted that shortages of labour in specific sectors such as the service sector could be addressed through an immigration policy that would increase the supply of young people entering the workforce for the first time.

The views of organized-labour interests on immigration issues varied somewhat. The 'Canadians First' policy adopted by the federal government in 1978, under which Canadian citizens and residents were given priority in all jobs, reflected continuing political sensitivities of organized labour to the threat of foreign workers. Nevertheless, the crackdown on refugee admissions initiated in the late 1980s garnered criticism from labour leadership. For example, in a brief presented to the parliamentary committee studying proposed amendments in 1992, the president of the Canadian Labour Congress (CLC), Bob White, argued against the 'mythology' of Canada's generosity to immigrants. White challenged the government's position that Canada was being overrun with refugee claimants,[8] and, while admitting that some individual CLC members might assert otherwise, he rejected unequivocally the contention that immigrants took jobs away from Canadian citizens: 'When you look at the

numbers of refugees, for example, when you look at the numbers of immigrants coming to the country ... in most cases, once they get established
here they contribute enormously to economic growth and to the availability of jobs for other people.'[9]

Members of the media frequently commented on the benefits and
drawbacks of immigration. Some members of the media called for a reduction in immigration levels, arguing that it was becoming increasingly
difficult for the Canadian economy to absorb large numbers of underedu-
cated and poorly skilled immigrants.[10] In 1992, Toronto freelance journalist Daniel Stoffman published a series of articles in the *Toronto Star* and the
Ottawa Citizen on various immigrant communities in Canada, highlighting
problems of adjustment and settlement, and tensions with other groups in
the community. In 1993, he published, through the C.D. Howe Institute,
a paper arguing for a more conservative immigration policy.[11] Others, in
contrast, advocated virtually unrestricted immigration, on both economic
and moral grounds.[12]

There was a plethora of academic research on the effectiveness of immigration policy and the impact of immigration on the Canadian economy in this period, including a paper by W.L. Marr and M.B. Percy,
'Immigration Policy and Canadian Economic Growth,' prepared for the
Macdonald Commission in 1985,[13] which presented a view of immigration
as a blunt and comparatively ineffective instrument of economic policy.
The Institute for Research on Public Policy subsequently published
'Immigration and Employment Effects,'[14] which concluded that 'econ-
omy-wide there is no modern evidence as of 1980 that the post-war stock
of immigrants significantly displaced workers born in Canada.'

In 1991 the Economic Council of Canada (ECC) published the findings
of its major study of the economic and social impacts of immigration. Its
report, *The Economic and Social Impacts of Immigration,* examined a wide
variety of issues and perceptions associated with immigration, attempting
to separate myth from reality and to lay a foundation upon which a more
rational discourse over immigration might take place. It was the product of
a wide review of available literature as well as new empirical work. The report observed that 'immigration hardly ever has any effect on the
employment rate' and therefore did not lead to higher levels of unemployment. Moreover, it found that immigration has small but positive economic
benefits for the host community. In addition, it highlighted empirical evidence supporting the 'contact hypothesis,' which suggested that increased
contact between persons of different races would reduce, not increase, racial discrimination and animus over time. The ECC concluded that any

decision as to whether to increase immigration levels was likely to be influenced more by social and political implications than economic ones.[15]

A series of studies published by the C.D. Howe Institute largely confirmed these findings, although noting some deterioration in the economic performance of recent immigrants and arguing for more restricted family-sponsorship rights and a larger role for independent immigrants screened for labour-market skills.[16]

Consultation and Planning

The increased public participation introduced into immigration policy formulation in the previous period was expanded further under the 1976 act. Section 7 required the minister to consult with the provinces and other relevant persons, organizations, and institutions annually.[17] Amendments in 1993 required the minister, after such consultations, to table before Parliament an annual immigration plan for the following year.[18]

Three years prior to the 1993 amendment, the government had tabled in Parliament its five-year immigration plan. According to the minister of Employment and Immigration, the Five-Year Immigration Plan presented by the federal government to Parliament in 1990 was based on the most extensive consultations ever undertaken, involving 4,000 individuals representing business, labour, all levels of government, and various other community groups, and departed from the prior departmental practice of presenting merely annual estimates of, or targets for, various classes of immigrants in annual reports to Parliament. The consultations apparently indicated considerable support for moderate increases in immigration over a five-year period, which were also supported by all the major federal political parties at that time.[19]

The plan was predicated upon the total immigrant intake rising from 200,000 in 1990 to 250,000 in 1992 and being maintained at that level until 1995 (almost 1 per cent of the existing population).[20] For the first time in Canadian immigration history, the government – supported by most of the major political parties – committed itself to a longer-term view of immigration less influenced by current stages in the business cycle, and to a significant increase in immigration at a time of serious economic recession. This policy represented a sharp departure from the Department of Labour's view in the 1950s and 1960s that immigration levels should be adjusted frequently to reflect the current state of the economy, although the government's reduction of the intake target from 250,000 to 200,000 in 1995 suggested some continuing sensitivity to these concerns.

The plan contemplated that the family class would constitute 34 per cent of the total intake, refugees 21 per cent, independent immigrants and their dependants 25 per cent, assisted relatives 12 per cent, and business immigrants 8 per cent.[21]

Another feature of the plan was the increase in the proportion of skilled workers in the independent class.[22] Moreover, it provided for the establishment of a list of 'designated occupations,' in consultation with the provinces and private sector, that would identify occupations in short supply in particular provinces. Applicants qualified for those positions would receive extra selection points.[23] Interestingly, despite its disavowal of short-term micro-management of the immigrant intake, the government continued to adjust its designated occupations list on a regular basis.

The plan was not without its detractors. Under the plan, Ontario found itself facing an estimated 85,000 more immigrants in the following four years, and the provincial government complained about the costs (i.e., of education, health, welfare, etc.) associated with such an influx. Despite the protestations of Ontario premier Bob Rae and other representatives of the provincial government, Employment and Immigration minister Barbara McDougall refused to provide additional funds, arguing that 'if there is a provincial benefit to immigration, then I think there should be some provincial responsibility.'[24]

Some academics argued that these increases in immigration were ill-timed. Basing much of the argument on the recessionary environment of the period, one policy analyst asserted that a country like Canada is incapable of effecting any major change in global economic disparities by accepting 'a few more thousand immigrants.' She also challenged the benefits of economic migration, arguing that certain immigrant groups are concentrated in declining industries, and suggested instead maintaining both the pre-five-year-plan levels of immigration, and the prevailing balance among the three major classes of immigrants.[25] Another author also criticized the government's announcement of the higher immigration levels in the five-year plan, arguing that the move was poorly timed, given the large refugee backlog and uncertain economic conditions. He also contended that there was a historical relationship between immigration and the unemployment rate, and questioned the wisdom of increasing immigration levels during an economic downturn.[26]

Enhanced Provincial Responsibility

Another important development in the 1976 act was the increased latitude for the provincial governments to shape immigration into their provinces. The minister was not only required to consult with provinces on immigration but was further authorized to enter into special agreements with the provinces in regard to immigration policy formulation, coordination, and implementation. This was the first recognition in immigration legislation that under section 95 of the Constitution Act, 1867 (formerly known as the British North America Act), immigration is a concurrent jurisdiction, albeit with federal paramountcy.[27]

Prior to the new act, Quebec had already been in negotiations with the federal government for increased autonomy over immigration to the province. Immigration minister Bud Cullen and the Quebec Liberal government had begun to define their respective governments' roles with regard to such issues as the housing, education, training, and counselling of Quebec's immigrants.[28] These negotiations gathered renewed momentum with the election of the Parti Québécois (PQ) government in 1976. A strong and widespread belief in the province that immigration was flooding Quebec communities with anglophones or 'allophones' (persons whose first language is neither English nor French) led the PQ government, as one of its first moves, to terminate English-language classes for immigrants.[29] That same year it set up an immigration committee that undertook extensive consultations with more than eighty-one ethnic groups across all regions of the province.[30] The chair of the committee recommended that Quebec push for a full range of powers in the area of immigration, arguing that Quebec's requirements for immigrants were distinct from those of other Canadian provinces.[31]

In 1978 the federal government and the government of Quebec reached an agreement permitting the latter to establish its own point system for independent immigrants that would work concurrently with the federal system, and that would allow Quebec to recruit more francophone immigrants to the province. While the Cullen-Couture Agreement, as it came to be known, still accorded ultimate responsibility for immigration to the federal government, the Quebec government described the powers granted to Quebec as 'decisive.'[32] Federal officials, meanwhile, hailed the agreement as 'proof of the flexibility that exists in the current federal system.'[33]

This was followed in 1979 with the introduction of Quebec immigration legislation. The provincial legislation included its own point system, which, like the federal system, awarded up to a maximum of 100 points to prospective immigrants. However, whereas the federal system allowed only 10 points' discretion in the area of 'personal suitability,' the Quebec system allowed for 22 points' discretion in determining 'personal qualities, motivation and knowledge of Quebec.'[34] Furthermore, while the federal test awarded a maximum of 5 points each for knowledge of either official language, the Quebec legislation provided for 12 points for French-speaking immigrants, and only 2 for English.[35]

Quebec continued to strive for greater control over immigration policy, and to this end sent its own immigration officers abroad to represent its interests. Hoping perhaps to minimize the political fall-out from the rejection of the Meech Lake constitutional accord in 1990, the federal government and Quebec premier Robert Bourassa immediately began bilateral negotiations designed to transfer additional immigration powers to Quebec.[36] In December 1990, Quebec and Ottawa concluded a five-year agreement,[37] the Quebec Accord, which expanded the province's powers in the area of immigration. Specifically, while the federal government retained responsibility for establishing immigration levels and national standards, Quebec gained sole responsibility for the selection of independent immigrants destined for that province, as well as full responsibility for linguistic, cultural, and integration services for permanent residents of Quebec.[38] The accord compensated Quebec for the federal withdrawal from settlement and immigration services in the form of federal transfers over the life of the agreement of an estimated $332 million.[39]

The federal government also entered into immigration agreements with other provinces. In fact, Nova Scotia signed an immigration agreement with Ottawa prior to the completion of the Quebec agreement, and Saskatchewan signed an agreement soon afterward. Neither of these agreements, however, was as extensive as those with Quebec.[40]

Notwithstanding the successful negotiation of several federal-provincial immigration agreements, this period also saw conflicts between the federal government and provincial governments over a variety of immigration issues. In Quebec, a large and unexpected influx of refugee claimants saw the province take in as many refugees in 1986 as it had in the previous three years, and the burden of providing resettlement assistance for all the claimants was left largely up to the province. Quebec Immigration minister Louise Robic claimed, much as Bob Rae would argue in later years with increased immigration to the province of Ontario, that the lack of additional assistance from Ottawa to pay for settlement costs was an abdication of federal responsibility: 'This has nothing to do with Quebec immigration,' Robic asserted. 'We're paying for a federal jurisdiction here. We're talking about Canadian borders.'[41]

Admissions

The 1976 Immigration Act provided for four classes of admissible immigrants: family; assisted relatives; independent; and humanitarian. Several years later a new business class was also added. Regulations promulgated in 1978 provided a revised point system that placed greater emphasis on practical training and experience.[42] The use of the point system was applied to varying degrees depending on the class of immigrant. Members of the family class and certain categories of the humanitarian class were not subject to the points assessment. The latter could be adjusted without parliamentary approval.

The act also preserved the ability of the minister and the executive to exercise their discretion to make exceptions – through the use of ministerial permits and Orders-in-Council – to the admissibility requirements or the conditions of stay for particular individuals. The minister was not, however, authorized to issue a permit to someone who was subject to a removal order unless an appeal from such an order had been allowed.[43]

While ministerial permits and Orders-in-Council had long been a feature of immigration legislation since at least the 1910 act, they were particularly important under the 1976 act because of the large number of detailed rules governing admissibility of immigrants.[44] They enabled the minister and Cabinet to exercise the discretion necessary to deal with 'hard' cases and to respond quickly to humanitarian crises in other parts of the world.[45] Exceptions on humanitarian grounds were effected largely through regulations creating special designated classes and special programs (described below). Individual requests for exceptions to admissibility requirements were delegated to immigration officers, and the Immigration Department developed detailed guidelines setting out applicable criteria for exercising discretion in different circumstances.

Family Class Immigrants

Members of the family class included spouses; fiancé(e)s; unmarried children under twenty-one years of age; aged (over sixty) or disabled parents; and orphaned sisters, brothers, nieces, nephews, and grandchildren if under eighteen and unmarried.[46] Sponsorship of family class members was open to both Canadian citizens and permanent residents. Those sponsoring, however, had to establish their ability to provide lodging, care, and maintenance of the sponsored individual and dependants for up to ten years.[47] This latter requirement imposed a more formal commitment on sponsors in response to past experiences where, if a sponsor failed to provide the support needed, the federal government was responsible for providing support for the first year, after which the responsibility fell to provincial and municipal governments.[48]

Despite the more formal undertaking by the sponsor, however, the inadequacy of enforcement mechanisms made the commitment of limited practical significance. Even if inclined to do so, the sponsored relative could not sue the sponsor for support, not having been party to the agreement between the sponsor and the federal government. The federal government had little incentive to keep track of sponsors' failure to fulfil their obligations because the municipal and provincial governments shouldered most of the burden.

The lack of enforceability of sponsorship obligations was seen by some as a weakness with the category. The expansion of the class to include parents of any age in 1978 also sparked some controversy. According to Daniel Stoffman, this change in the regulations was 'a monumental blunder'[49] that opened the flood-gates of family class immigration, because parents could then sponsor other relatives in turn. In practice, however, the widening of the category did not lead to any significant increase in the proportion of family class immigrants as compared to other categories. After 1980, the percentage of all immigrants constituted by family class admissions remained relatively constant.[50]

A further expansion of the family class category to unmarried children of any age in 1988 was relatively short-lived, followed as it was in 1992 by further restrictions. Under the new rules, parents of any age were eligible to be sponsored, but the sponsorship of children was limited to those under the age of nineteen. Exceptions were made for children older than nineteen but 'dependent' on their parents for reasons of full-time study or a disability. The government claimed that the changes were designed to 'capture more effectively the concept of family.'[51] However, they were also intended to limit the potential for excessive growth of the family class (thus increasing the proportion of immigrants who must qualify under the point system).[52]

The family class was also affected by important changes to the definition of adoption. Under the 1976 act adopted children were admissible under the family class provided the adoptions took place before the child reached thirteen years of age. The previous age limit of eighteen was believed to have resulted in 'adoptions of convenience,' undertaken solely for immigration purposes rather than to provide a child with a new family. However, the use of the age limit ran the risk of being inconsistent with the Canadian Charter of Rights and Freedoms (the Charter), which came into affect in 1985, and specifically section 15, which prohibited discrimination on the basis of age. It was also inconsistent with the 1990 U.N. Convention on the Rights of the Child, which recognized children as being eighteen years of age or younger and which Canada had ratified although not yet implemented into national law. Moreover, the provisions were inconsistent with negotiations on international adoption conducted under the auspices of the Hague Conference on Private International Law.

As a result, in 1993 the immigration regulations were amended so that adopted children were eligible for admission provided that the adoption had occurred before the child reached nineteen years of age, involved a genuine parent-child relationship, and was not solely for immigration purposes.[53] In March 1994, a further amendment applied the new regulatory provisions retroactively, so that most sponsored adoption cases not finally decided on 1 February 1993 would receive the benefit of the new criteria, subject to the provisions regarding adoptions of convenience.[54]

ASSISTED RELATIVES

The 'assisted relative' class included brothers, sisters, aunts, uncles, nieces, nephews, and grandparents.[55] Those who fell within this class had to satisfy some although not all of the selection criteria of the independent class. The sponsoring relative also had to be willing to provide an undertaking of assistance for up to five years.[56]

In 1993, along with other measures restricting admissions, the assisted-relative class was abolished as a separate category. Those who would have qualified under previous provisions were now assessed as independent immigrants, although they received bonus points for being a relative of an eligible family member in Canada.[57]

INDEPENDENT IMMIGRANTS

The point system as applied to the independent class was intended to ensure admission of those immigrants of whose skills Canada was in need, and was amended over the years to give preference to immigrants with occupations in demand in Canada.[58] In addition, in 1978 a 'Canadians First' policy was implemented to ensure that Canadian citizens were given first priority in all jobs. As a result, employers wishing to hire a foreigner had to demonstrate that there were no suitable Canadian or permanent-resident candidates for the position before a foreign candidate would be admitted to take the position.

In 1982, with the country mired in the depths of a recession, the 'Canadians First' policy took an even stronger form: all independent immigrants (excluding those in the business class) had to have firm offers of jobs for which no Canadians or permanent residents were available.[59] Consequently, the number of independent immigrants (excluding dependants) dropped sharply from 18,143 in 1982 to 6,558 in 1984.[60] When economic conditions began to improve in the mid-1980s, the government announced the lifting of the 'firm offer' policy for 1986. Any increase in independent immigrants, however, would have to be 'moderate' and 'controlled,' so as not to result in, or create the perception of, domestic labour dislocation.[61]

Also introduced (in 1981) was the Foreign Domestic Worker Program, following 'extensive consultations' with provincial governments, NGOs, and specialists in the field of immigration.[62] It reflected a more selective approach to the admission of domestic workers. Applicants were assessed according to a set of suitability criteria and could only acquire permanent-resident status after two years' residency in Canada and proof they had the skills to successfully establish themselves.[63]

The stringent assessment criteria applied to domestic workers were challenged in the 1990 *Pinto*[64] case. The applicant, a primary-school teacher from India, had been rejected by the immigration officer on the basis that she lacked related experience. The Federal Court ruled that the immigration official had used his discretion unreasonably. According to the court, the policy guidelines that had been drafted to assist officers in assessing the potential of a foreign domestic to settle permanently in Canada had been applied too stringently.[65] The court ruled that other factors – the applicant's experience as a single parent, and as a teacher for sixteen years, and her ability to speak the language of the elderly persons in Canada who were to be under her care – should be assessed in the context of the requirements of the specific employment offer, and ordered a reconsideration of the case.[66]

The government responded with the imposition of more stringent and precise criteria.[67] In 1992 the program was replaced with the Live-in Caregiver Program, designed to permit the temporary entry of foreign domestics when there existed a shortage of Canadians to provide live-in care to children, the elderly, or the disabled. Employers who wished to participate in the program had to be private households, and had to provide proof that they had attempted to hire a caregiver in Canada before approval to employ someone through the program would be considered.[68] Applicants seeking employment as live-in caregivers had to possess the equivalent of a Canadian grade-twelve education; six months' formal training related to the job; and the ability to speak, read, and understand

French or English 'at a level sufficient to communicate effectively in an unsupervised situation.'[69] The program still permitted its participants to apply for permanent-resident status from within Canada after two years of uninterrupted employment as live-in caregivers.

The more stringent requirements facing domestic workers were criticized by immigrant groups, advocacy organizations such as Intercede, the Women's Committee of the Canadian Ethnocultural Council, the media, and academics.[70] Many argued that the requirements would unfairly discriminate against women from the developing world.[71] The new rules were equated with the 'covertly racist' motives of the earlier Chinese head tax regulations and continuous-journey provisions aimed at halting Chinese and East Indian immigration.[72]

In 1994, the new federal government, in response to a reported shortage of live-in caregivers, relaxed some of the conditions adopted in 1991. In particular, it eliminated the requirement for foreign 'nannies' to have six months of formal training in order to enter Canada. This change was in part a result of pressure by employers faced with an inadequate supply of domestics as well as the advocacy of immigrant groups. The new plan still required foreign domestics to have attained the equivalent of a grade-twelve education and, in the absence of formal training, at least a year of related experience.[73]

A much more short-lived independent class program was the retiree program introduced in 1990. This program permitted wealthy people over the age of fifty-five to resettle in Canada. The program was intended for retirees who had been born in Canada and wished to return. However, those who made the most use of the class were not Canadian-born but immigrants to Canada who had subsequently left and now wished to return.[74] The program was discontinued in 1992.[75]

BUSINESS CLASS IMMIGRANTS

Within two years of the passage of the Immigration Act 1976, a new business class of immigrants was introduced which was subsequently expanded over the next decade. Initially, this class recognized 'entrepreneur' and 'self-employed' as categories of business immigrants. Viewed by the government as creating economic and employment benefits, both these categories were evaluated under a variety of selection criteria that attempted to gauge the likelihood that an applicant would be successful in a particular venture.

Potential entrepreneurs were required to submit a detailed business plan outlining their intention to establish or purchase an interest in a business venture in which they would involve themselves on a daily basis and in which five or more Canadians would be employed.[76] Similarly, self-employed applicants were obliged to submit a business plan, employ four or fewer Canadians, or contribute to the 'cultural and artistic life of Canada.'[77]

The numbers of immigrants admitted under these programs generally followed an upward trend. For example, 1,282 entrepreneurs and self-employed workers were admitted to Canada in 1979, and while these accounted for little more than 1 per cent of all applicants in that year, the Immigration Department claimed that their collective financial contribution to the Canadian economy was estimated at more than $216 million.[78] By 1985, Canada admitted more than 2,100 entrepreneurs and self-employed persons, and these immigrants declared investments in Canada of approximately $1.2 billion.[79]

In 1986 the business class was expanded further to include the 'investor' category. This was created for those individuals who, unlike members of the entrepreneurial class, did not wish to be involved in the day-to-day operation of a business.[80] Persons falling within this class would be required to have a net worth of more than $500,000 and to invest at least $250,000[81] for a minimum of three years in a project in Canada that would create employment and contribute to business development.[82] The investment had to be in a project or investment fund approved by the federal government and submitted as well to the province concerned. Generally, the investment would not receive federal approval unless it was acceptable to the province in question.

Some in the business community argued that the 'entrepreneur' and 'investor' categories created benefits in the form of increased employment and investment in Canada.[83] By 1986, provincial officials were not only encouraging the federal government to increase the numbers of immigrants admitted to the country under the program,[84] but many provinces had themselves set up offices abroad to lure potential business and investor immigrants to their respective provinces.

Nevertheless, despite this enthusiasm, and the ostensible benefits claimed for the various business-immigration programs, they often came under criticism. The government was accused of using them to 'sell Canadian passports with the wealthy being the only eligible buyers.'[85] The programs were also criticized for lax monitoring that allowed some business immigrants to avoid compliance with their undertakings.[86]

In response, the government in the mid-1980s introduced a monitoring system to attempt to ensure compliance with the conditions of the business immigrants' entry. However, by March 1991 only three entrepreneurs had been ordered deported for failing to meet the conditions of their entry.[87] Continuing dissatisfaction led the government in 1994 to announce a moratorium on new investor fund offerings, pending a redesign of the program.[88]

REFUGEES

It was significant that for the first time in Canadian immigration history one of the explicit objectives of the act was to fulfil 'Canada's international legal obligations with respect to refugees and to uphold its humanitarian tradition with respect to the displaced and the persecuted.' This objective was to be met by providing for the admission to Canada of Convention refugees as well as those who were members of a class specifically designated by the Cabinet as admissible for humanitarian reasons.[89]

Convention refugees were those who met the definition of refugee as set out in the Convention Relating to the Status of Refugees 1951 and the Protocol of 1967. Specifically, this meant that the person had to be outside his or her country of origin and unwilling or unable to return because of a well-founded fear of persecution for reasons of race, nationality, religion, political opinion, and/or membership in a particular social group.

Convention Refugees Selected Abroad

Convention refugees who sought admission to Canada from overseas generally had to satisfy the immigration officer that they met the Convention refugee definition and that they would be able to successfully establish themselves in Canada. Ability to meet the latter criterion most often depended on sponsorship by the government or by a private group.[90] Sponsorship entailed a written undertaking to provide refugees with lodging, care, maintenance, and resettlement assistance for one year.[91] Exceptions to the definitional or sponsorship requirements could be made if the person fell under a special class designated by the Cabinet.

Each year the government established immigration levels for the different admissible classes, including levels for refugees sponsored by government and private groups. However, after peaking in 1989, at 36,745, the number of both government-assisted and privately sponsored overseas refugees fell sharply to 11,801 in 1993.[92]

The Department of Citizenship and Immigration explained that the drop in government-sponsored refugees was the result of the preference of the U.N. High Commissioner for Refugees (UNHCR) for repatriation or resettlement in a neighbouring country over third-country resettlement. While the UNHCR had requested third-country resettlement for less than 1 per cent of the world's refugees, there still were many eligible refugees who could have been included in Canadian annual plans either through direct referral by the UNHCR or from Canadian overseas consulates and embassies. The main motivation for reductions in the government-sponsored category was probably fiscal, for the settlement costs associated with the movement were significant. Refugee, humanitarian, and other advocacy groups, however, saw the federal government's diminished commitment to the sponsorship program as a reflection of its declining commitment to humanitarian immigration more generally.

Designated Classes

In 1979 three designated classes of refugees were created: the Indochinese, the Eastern European Self-Exiled Persons, and the Latin American Political Prisoners and Oppressed Persons.[93] The admissibility requirements varied according to the class, reflecting ideological influences that were particularly salient during the Cold War. The most liberal criteria applied to those in the Eastern European Self-Exiled Persons class,[94] who only had to establish that they were outside their country and willing to emigrate to Canada. With the collapse of Communist regimes in Eastern Europe, the Eastern European class was eliminated in 1990. Those falling under the Indochinese class had to have been outside Vietnam since the taking of control by the Communist government in 1975 and be able to show that they could successfully establish themselves in Canada (a criterion usually met through government or private sponsorship).[95] In contrast, those within the Latin American Political Prisoners and Oppressed Persons class had to meet the Convention refugee definition, or establish that they had been detained as a result of the legitimate expression of free thought or for exercising civil liberties, as well as demonstrate that they could successfully establish themselves in Canada.[96] In effect, therefore, individuals fleeing Communist regimes had a lower threshold for admission than those in need of protection from right-wing authoritarian regimes. This was particularly galling for families and groups advocating for the rights of refugees from Latin America during the 1980s and early 1990s, given the extent of political repression in that region.[97]

Of the three designated classes, none compared in terms of its size and degree of public involvement to the 'Indochinese' class. After forty years of fighting major imperialist powers (including Japan, France, the United States, and China), Vietnam was devastated. Almost immediately after the Communists gained control of the entire country in 1975, Vietnamese citizens opposed to (or fearing persecution from) the new regime began leaving the country in a steady flow. In autumn of 1978, the flow began to increase, and by the spring of 1979 it had become a torrent. By midsummer, the total number of refugees exceeded 290,000.[98] Many thousands were languishing in overcrowded camps in circumstances that fell far below international standards. Known as the 'boat people' because of their exodus by boat, new arrivals faced increasing intolerance in the region (including being prevented from landing) and risks of pirate attacks at sea. Many died in the process of trying to flee.

Initially, Canada accepted relatively few Vietnamese refugees, and in 1978 this prompted considerable public criticism in the media and elsewhere.[99] Prime Minister Trudeau responded by pledging to accept 5,000 in the coming year.[100] By then the movement was very much on the international stage, and an international conference was organized to address the growing humanitarian crisis in the region. Canada participated and, along with several other resettlement countries, agreed to resettle new arrivals from Vietnam on the condition that the first-asylum countries would permit them to land and be properly processed. In parallel the UNHCR helped establish an Orderly Departure Program from within Vietnam. This was aimed at stemming clandestine departures and the great risks involved in them by matching those who had been selected by resettlement countries with those the Vietnamese government had authorized to leave.

The Indochinese designated class, therefore, was a means to help Canada deliver on its international commitment. The requirement to be able to successfully establish in Canada could be satisfied through a government or private sponsorship.

Following the conclusion of the international conference, Canada under a new Conservative government, announced that it would resettle 12,000 Vietnamese, of whom 4,000 would be privately sponsored.[101] As media reports continued to highlight the enormous dimensions of the problems in South-East Asia and in particular the living conditions of refugees and the losses of life occasioned by those who attempted to flee Vietnam, public opinion rapidly changed. From being initially opposed to accepting a substantial number the public mood swung dramatically and expressed itself in unprecedented private commitments to sponsor the refugees.[102]

Government commitment changed accordingly. Within months of setting an annual intake of 12,000 refugees, Immigration minister Ron Atkey announced that Canada would increase this to 3,000 a month, with 50,000 to arrive by the end of 1980. He further committed the government to sponsor one refugee for every private sponsorship.[103] A Canadian Foundation for Refugees was established to receive financial contributions to assist the refugees, and the contributions and expressions of commitment it and other organizations received were far more than anticipated.[104] In fact by the end of 1979, so many offers of private sponsorship had been received that the government was unable or unwilling to live up to its commitment to match them on a one-for-one basis. In the spring of 1980, the new Liberal government was able to honour the commitment of the previous government by increasing its target intake of Vietnamese refugees.[105] Within two years, more than 60,000 refugees from Vietnam, Laos, and Cambodia had been resettled in Canada, most of whom subsequently integrated well into Canadian society.[106]

International efforts, including those of Canada, helped to stabilize the situation in South-East Asia. As the crisis there subsided, and with the onset of a recession in the early 1980s, both federal and private sponsorships fell in number. A renewed exodus from Vietnam in the mid-1980s prompted a second international conference in June 1989. A Comprehensive Plan of Action (CPA) was adopted that terminated blanket resettlement and introduced a screening mechanism to determine those in need of resettlement for Convention refugee reasons or for other compelling reasons such as family reunification. Other provisions of the CPA were designed to deter further departures from Vietnam through media campaigns and to assist those who were not qualified for resettlement to return.

In Canada, the 'Indochinese' designated class was accordingly amended. Claimants arriving in Hong Kong after 16 June 1988, or in any other South-East Asian country of first asylum after 14 March 1989, would be screened to determine if they met regular Convention refugee criteria.[107]

SPECIAL PROGRAMS

As has been noted, the act conferred on the minister and Cabinet the discretion to make exceptions to normal admissibility requirements. This they could exercise on a group basis, as with the designated classes, or on an individual basis. While the creation of the designated class was one mechanism to effect a group exception, other means were also used, such as suspension of visa requirements, relaxed application of selection

criteria, and/or exceptions to the requirement that applicants for permanent residence status make their applications outside Canada.

One of the first special programs was in response to the humanitarian
needs arising from the outbreak of civil war in Lebanon in 1976. Canada
created a special measures category for Lebanese that permitted the
granting of 11,010 immigrant visas by 1979. After Canada's Beirut embassy
was closed because of heavy fighting, a small office was opened at
Jounieh, north of Beirut, to continue to process applications.[108] In June
1982, following the Israeli invasion of Lebanon, additional measures
were announced that permitted assessment under relaxed immigration-
selection criteria for Lebanese relatives of both Canadian citizens and
landed immigrants who were directly affected or displaced by the fighting.
Additionally, the measures provided visitors from Lebanon who were unable to return because of the war the opportunity to apply for permanent-
resident status from within Canada.[109] The flow of Lebanese refugees
continued throughout the 1980s, peaking at 6,100 arrivals in 1989.[110]

A special measures class was also introduced in December 1980 for
Poles, following the imposition of martial law in Poland in an attempt to
suppress the Solidarity movement. Between 1981 and 1983, immigration
rules for visiting Poles were eased, permitting several thousand to gain
landed-immigrant status from within Canada.[111] Poland was also included
as one of the countries prescribed under the Political Prisoners and
Oppressed Persons Designated Class. Even after the victory of the
Solidarity movement over the Communist regime, the Canadian government continued to admit large numbers of Poles.

Other examples of special measures included a policy, announced in
March 1981, for Salvadorans fleeing the threat of persecution in their
homeland.[112] In 1982, the program was expanded to include Salvadorans
in the United States who were facing deportation to El Salvador because
the U.S. government did not recognize them as *bona fide* refugees.
Canadian consulates in the United States, with the knowledge of American
authorities, began issuing entry visas to such applicants.[113]

In June 1989, following the Tiananmen Square Massacre in Beijing,
Canada relaxed immigration rules for Chinese citizens in Canada.[114] Some
8,000 took advantage of this program to acquire permanent-resident status.
Those who subsequently arrived and requested refugee status, however,
were assessed according to the Convention refugee definition, although
the removal of those who were denied status was put on hold. The latter
number grew to more than 4,500. In 1994, Citizenship and Immigration
minister Sergio Marchi announced a new measure, applicable to all failed

refugee claimants but principally motivated to resolve the issue with respect to the Chinese. Specifically, a Deferred Removal Order Class (DROC) was introduced that permitted failed claimants who had been in the country for more than three years to apply for permanent-resident status. Applicants could not have a criminal record, pose a threat to Canadian health or security, or have evaded deportation officials during their time in Canada.

Not every refugee-producing event led automatically to the introduction of a special measure in Canada. For example, shortly after the passing of the 1976 Immigration Act, Afghanistan was plunged into a civil war that killed more than 1.5 million people, displaced an additional 5 million people, and devastated the country's infrastructure and fragile economy. By 1990 there were an estimated 6.3 million Afghan refugees, nearly all of whom were in neighbouring Pakistan and Iran.[115] This enormous humanitarian disaster did not lead to special measures for Afghan refugees. Nor did the government-sponsorship category respond specifically to the needs of Afghans. They did not even merit a mention in Canada's annual refugee quotas. In 1986, for instance, the number of government-assisted refugees was set at 12,000. 'Other World Areas,' which included refugees in India and Pakistan, received a tiny quota of 300.[116] Some claimed that the unresponsiveness of the Canadian government and immigration organizations was attributable to an anti-Muslim bias.[117]

In 1983, when internecine violence prompted tens of thousands of Sri Lankans to leave their homeland, Canada made it easier for some to gain landed-immigrant status,[118] while simultaneously imposing a visa requirement on all Sri Lankans wishing to visit the country.[119] This had the effect of making it more difficult for the great majority of Sri Lankans without immigrant visas to enter Canada, including those in need of international protection.

Displacement crises in Africa also failed to lead to an easing of restrictions facing Africans. Like Afghanistan, Africa was also a major source of refugees, with some 5 million refugees throughout the 1980s, 3 million in the Horn of Africa and 1 million in southern Africa.[120] Despite these numbers, Canada's refugee and humanitarian admissions policies were not used to admit a significant number from that continent. In April 1981, at the International Conference on Assistance to Refugees in Africa, External Affairs minister Mark MacGuigan argued that solutions to the continent's problems 'can only be found in Africa, by Africans.'[121] This stood in stark contrast to the efforts to resolve the problems occurring at the same time in South-East Asia.

Canada consistently maintained its restrictive stance towards the admission of Africans on refugee or humanitarian grounds. In 1981, only 200 African refugees were selected from overseas, and no more than 1,000 were selected in any year in the 1980s, despite a continually worsening refugee situation.[122] Even this meagre quota was rarely met, owing to what were described as 'considerable difficulties in processing refugee applications,' and problems with obtaining exit permits in some countries.[123] In 1989, only three immigration officers were available to service the entire African continent.[124]

INLAND REFUGEE CLAIMS PROCEDURE

The 1976 act explicitly provided for the granting of permanent-resident status to refugees who claimed asylum in Canada and could establish that they met the Convention refugee definition. The procedure set out in the act and regulations was cumbersome, and soon was strained by the large increase in asylum flows throughout the 1980s.

Those who sought refugee status in Canada had first to present themselves to an immigration officer. Generally found to be inadmissible, they were then sent to an immigration inquiry to determine whether they should be removed from the country. At that point the refugee could request refugee status, in which case the removal order was stayed and the person was brought before a senior immigration officer for an interview regarding the substance of the refugee claim.[125] The senior immigration officer then sent the transcript of the interview to a newly created Refugee Status Advisory Committee (RSAC). RSAC reviewed the application and made a recommendation to the minister as to whether to accept or deny the claim for protection.

If the claimant did not qualify, his or her application was considered on humanitarian and compassionate grounds by the Special Review Committee, which acted in an advisory capacity to the minister.

Those who did not receive a favourable determination by the minister could appeal the decision to the Immigration Appeal Board (IAB). The IAB reviewed the documentary record and was authorized to grant an oral hearing on the merits of the claim for any applicant who, on the basis of the documentary record, showed that there were reasonable grounds to believe that the claim could be established.[126]

Claimants who received positive determinations either initially or following an oral hearing by the IAB, would be permitted to remain in Canada provided there were no medical or security grounds on which to find them inadmissible.[127] This determination was made at the resumed removal order inquiry. A rejection at this stage could also be appealed to the IAB.[128] All IAB decisions were subject to judicial review by the Federal Court of Appeal on questions of law or jurisdiction.

The Immigration Department's inability to handle the backlog of inland refugee claims is the dominant theme in Canada's immigration history in the 1980s, when increasing numbers of claimants arrived in Canada and requested asylum.[129] In the late 1970s, between 200 and 400 people arrived in Canada each year and claimed refugee status. These relatively small numbers were handled by the system without difficulty. However, between 1982 and 1984, 3,400 to 5,200 claimants arrived annually.[130] A serious backlog started to develop, prompting a series of reports, recommendations, and amendments aimed at better management of the influx.

As early as 1981 the Task Force on Immigration Practices and Procedures submitted its report on the procedure for determining refugee status to the minister.[131] The report (known as the Robinson Report) recommended several changes in the system to ensure procedural fairness. These included a new refugee-determination system with a centralized, independent tribunal and a full hearing process at the earliest level of refugee determination. It also recommended the imposition of a visa requirement on citizens of countries responsible for a 'significant volume of frivolous refugee claims.'[132] A report prepared by University of Ottawa Law School professor Ed Ratushny, three years later, *A New Refugee Status Determination Process for Canada,* echoed many of the concerns expressed in the Robinson Report, including the lack of oral hearings in refugee determinations.[133]

In 1985 the government commissioned yet another study. Written by Rabbi Gunther Plaut, *Refugee Determination in Canada* (the 'Plaut Report'),[134] received a great deal of public attention, being subject to examination by legislative committees as well as commentary by academics, lawyers, refugee organizations, and members of Parliament. The report outlined different models for refugee determination. These models shared certain features, such as oral hearings, an independent decision-making body, regional decision making in the first instance, and a full appeal process.[135]

The procedural fairness of the inland refugee determination process was the central focus of the Supreme Court of Canada's landmark decision in *Singh v Minister of Employment and Immigration.*[136] The case involved refugee applicants whose claims the minister had rejected and who subsequently were denied a hearing by the IAB. They argued that the procedure was unconstitutional. Specifically, they claimed that it violated their section 7 right to 'life, liberty, and security of the person and not to be denied thereof except in accordance with the principles of fundamental justice' because the procedure did not provide them with a meaningful opportunity to present their claims and know the case they had to meet.

Both the majority and minority reasons of the court found for the claimants: the minority found that the procedure violated the Canadian Bill of Rights, while the majority found it in violation of the Charter. Madame Justice Wilson, writing for the majority, reasoned that the rights in section 7 extended to 'everyone,' including refugees who were present in Canada and amenable to Canadian law. The right to security of the person was engaged in the refugee-determination process because security of the person encompassed freedom from the threat of physical punishment as well as punishment itself. Given the potential consequences to applicants denied status if in fact they did have a well-founded fear of persecution, it was unthinkable, she wrote, that 'the Charter would not apply to entitle them to fundamental justice in the adjudication of their status.'[137] Madame Justice Wilson also rejected the government's argument that administrative considerations, such as the costs and delays of a more elaborate process, were relevant to the constitutional calculus. The guarantees of the Charter would be 'illusory,' she wrote, 'if they could be ignored because it was administratively convenient to do so.'[138]

The Supreme Court's decision in *Singh* prompted Parliament in 1985 to pass Bill C-55, which provided for oral hearings on appeals to the IAB and expanded the maximum number of IAB members from eighteen to as many as fifty, and the number of vice-chairs from five to thirteen.[139] This was, the House was assured, merely a temporary measure before a major overhaul of the system was introduced.[140]

Not surprisingly, the imperative consequent on the *Singh* decision to ensure an oral hearing for all refugee applicants led to delays in processing and increased the backlog of claims yet to be finally determined. To help alleviate pressures, in 1986 a partial amnesty was implemented, giving landed status to those refugee claimants who were likely to establish themselves successfully in Canada. Eighty-five per cent of the 28,000 applicants successfully gained immigrant status under this administrative attempt to clear the backlog.[141]

Unfortunately, the refugee claims process started to attract those without legitimate claims to persecution in the hope that there would be a future amnesty that would apply to them. Among this group were large numbers of individuals from Portugal and Turkey advised by unscrupulous immigration consultants. In a six-month period between 1985 and 1986 more than 1,000 people from Portugal claimed refugee status in

Canada.[142] Similarly, between mid-1986 and January 1987, more than 2,000 Turks made refugee claims.[143] The government delayed imposing visa requirements in order not to alienate Portuguese and Turkish Canadians. When requirements were finally imposed in January 1987, the number of claimants from both countries substantially subsided.[144]

No such fears of alienating a Canadian constituency influenced the case of Indian visitors, who lost their visa exemption on 15 October 1981. The 1981 *Annual Report* justified the action by explaining that, prior to the change, 1,500 Indians had claimed refugee status, causing an additional eighteen-month backlog in the determination system. None was granted refugee status.[145] Between 1977 and 1984, the government took eighteen countries off the visa-exempt list as part of a policy to reduce illegal immigrants and to avoid turning people back at the border.[146]

Another deterrence measure was imposed in 1987 to stem the flow of asylum seekers from the United States. Claimants arriving from the United States were given a hearing date in Canada (often several months in the future) but denied entry into the country until that date.[147] The hardship to *bona fide* claimants was severe, especially for those from Latin American countries where persecution was acknowledged in Canada but not in the United States. These claimants were at risk of being removed from the United States while waiting for their hearings in Canada. Many were reported deported despite threats of persecution in their country of origin.

Additional deterrence measures included the imposition of transit visa requirements for those who claimed they were simply passing through Canada *en route* to other destinations. The transit visa was to prevent them from disembarking in Canada to make a refugee claim.[148]

Despite these initiatives, the refugee backlog continued to grow. In the face of mounting public and media pressure, the government felt compelled to take more decisive action, which it incorporated in the long-awaited overhaul of the system it had promised following the *Singh* decision.

The new amendments, introduced in May 1987 in Bill C-55, created the Immigration and Refugee Board (IRB).[149] This was an independent, quasi-judicial tribunal consisting of the Immigration Appeal Division (IAD) and the Convention Refugee Determination Division (CRDD). The former was responsible for hearing appeals from Canadians or permanent residents whose applications to sponsor family members had been denied. The IAD also heard appeals from permanent residents who had been issued removal orders. The IAD's jurisdiction extended to issues of law and fact. Significantly, it was also given authority to determine on the basis of humanitarian and compassionate grounds whether an appeal should be allowed. This represented an important form of relief from the summary and unreviewable decisions of previous periods.

The CRDD was responsible for determinations of refugee status. Both divisions conducted oral hearings in which the persons concerned had full disclosure of evidence, the right to submit documentation of their own, the right to be heard orally, and the right to written decisions. The minister also had standing to appear as a party before the IRB.[150]

Under the new system, refugee claimants first had to appear at an inquiry jointly heard by an adjudicator within the Adjudication Branch of the Department of Immigration and a CRDD member to determine whether the person was admissible.[151] Inadmissible claimants included those who were criminals, those recognized as refugees in other countries, and those whose claims had already been determined in Canada.[152] The inquiry was adversarial in nature: both the minister and the claimant were entitled to be represented, present evidence, and cross-examine witnesses. Claimants were entitled to interpreters.[153]

Claimants found to be admissible also had to establish that there was a credible basis for their claim.[154] Where they were not able to do so, they could be removed within seventy-two hours, even if an application for judicial review was filed with the Federal Court of Appeal, unless the court granted a stay against removal.[155] Judicial review was available with leave of the court on relatively narrow grounds of error of law or jurisdiction.[156] The credible-basis hearing was intended to quickly weed out of the system manifestly unfounded claims. In practice, most claimants passed this stage, giving rise to increasing calls for its abolition.

Claimants who successfully passed the credible-basis hearing were then entitled to a hearing before two members of the CRDD.[157] Hearings were non-adversarial unless the minister chose to oppose a claim (which was rare). CRDD decision makers were assisted by refugee-hearing officers (RHOs), whose task it was to file documentary evidence, call and question the claimant and witnesses, and make written or oral submissions.[158] If the claimant did not have adequate representation, the RHO could assist the claimant in presenting his or her case.[159] In cases where the two-member panel was split, the decision went in favour of the refugee.[160] Negative decisions could be appealed to the Federal Court, with leave, on the basis of law or capricious findings of fact.[161] A further review by the Federal Court of Appeal was only permitted with leave from a Trial Division judge certifying that 'a serious question of general importance is involved.'[162]

Months after the government introduced these changes to the refugee determination procedure, public opinion was stirred by the landing of 173 East Asians off the coast of Nova Scotia. Most were Sikhs claiming religious persecution in India. They had spent three weeks at sea in a crowded vessel and had been dropped close to the Canadian coast and told to swim to shore. Their arrival touched off a national furore. The Conservative government used this as justification for an emergency recall of Parliament in August 1987 to 'deal with an issue of grave national importance.'[163] It introduced further amendments to the Immigration Act and regulations in Bill 84, principally to deter refugee claimants, impose more stringent detention provisions, and expand inadmissibility provisions.

One amendment that did not pass because of intense opposition would have empowered Canadian authorities to turn back ships suspected of carrying refugees before they reached shore.[164] But other proposed amendments did win the necessary parliamentary majority and reflected a new, more cautious and security-minded posture towards refugee claimants that was to persist and indeed grow over time. In regard to deterrence, the amendments expanded powers of search and seizure and increased fines and jail terms for smugglers and transportation companies assisting those who did not have proper documents to enter Canada. While the latter provision was broad enough to include the penalties imposed on humanitarian groups who assisted refugees to come to Canada to claim asylum,[165] in practice it was aimed at smugglers and transportation companies. Transportation companies began to check more scrupulously the documents of passengers to minimize the possibility of liability under the legislation. This was, and continues to be, an effective deterrence measure, making it more difficult for genuine refugees without legitimate documentation to seek refuge in Canada.

Other deterrence and security-related measures included permitting the detention of people who arrived without proper documentation until such time as their identities could be established. Moreover, those who in the opinion of the minister and the solicitor general posed a criminal or security threat could be immediately deported after the Federal Court determined the reasonableness of the opinion.

Criticism of the 1987 proposed amendments both within Parliament and in the NGO community was intense. There were seventy-seven motions to amend Bill C-55 upon its return from the House of Commons committee that had studied the bill,[166] and thirteen amendments to Bill C-84 proposed by the Senate. The bulk of these were defeated by the Conservative majority, and the amended act came into force in 1989.

Speaking on the government's refusal to enact the majority of the Senate committee's proposed amendments to Bill C-84, New Democrat Dan Heap accused the government of having 'had their agenda fixed' from the outset, and later argued that there existed a thinly veiled racism in many of the Tories' administrative policies: 'In other words, this Government chooses a sneaky, administrative means to shut out refugees from most of the countries of the world where refugees are being created such as Latin America, the Caribbean, Africa, Asia and the islands of the Pacific. The Government does not want those non-white refugees in Canada. They only want white anti-communist refugees or ones who are considered economically very advantageous to Canada.'[167]

Unfortunately, the new refugee determination system proved unable to adjudicate expeditiously and fairly what was becoming a steady stream of asylum applicants, and a large backlog developed with alarming speed. In 1990, 36,000 claims were received, twice as many as had been anticipated.[168] Adjustments to handle the situation included the introduction of an expedited process in 1990 for claims from acknowledged refugee-producing countries and/or where the claim consisted of relatively simple legal and factual issues. This process permitted the RHO to refer to a single CRDD member a claim for a paper review.[169] If the CRDD member found the claim to be established, a positive decision could be issued without the need for an oral hearing. In 1993 between 25 and 30 per cent of all claims were processed through this expedited process.[170]

In addition, a special Backlog Clearance Program was instituted for claims made prior to December 1988. This enabled certain claims to move forward without the need for a credible basis hearing. The program also permitted claimants who were close family members of Canadian citizens to be considered for permanent residence if they 'would suffer hardship if forced to return home to obtain an immigrant visa.' Immigration officers were to assess such applications with regard to age, linguistic ability, length of residence in Canada, occupation, and relatives in Canada. These considerations were more rigid than those normally used for humanitarian and compassionate review. As a result, the Federal Court ruled in 1990 that the 'rigid and inflexible' narrower guidelines constituted an unjust and unlawful fetter on the immigration officers' discretion.[171] Subsequently, claimants under the Backlog Clearance Program were considered in the same way as those assessed under the humanitarian and compassionate grounds of the act.[172] By the end of 1992, most of the pre-1989 claimants (totalling about 100,000) had been processed, with about two-thirds of claims being accepted.

In 1992, the Law Reform Commission of Canada (LRC) made seventy-two recommendations for the improvement of the refugee determination system.[173] Central to its proposals for reform of the refugee determination process was the concept of two 'parallel but connected' streams: the first would deal with groups of people that, absent specific evidence indicating otherwise, could be assumed to be in need of protection under the Convention refugee definition or as a member of a humanitarian class. The second stream would provide a 'flexible and more expeditious process' for the determination of individual claims not falling under the group approach or when membership in a group was challenged.[174] The LRC also recommended dispensing with oral hearings in cases of likely positive determinations,[175] the abolition of the 'credible basis' test in a first-level hearing,[176] and the clarification and enunciation of the role in the process of participants such as the refugee-hearing officer, the minister, and non-governmental organizations.[177]

That same year the government proposed amendments to the act (Bill C-86) that would streamline the claims process yet at the same time raise the eligibility bar, increase measures to deter the arrival of refugee claimants, and prohibit claimants from seeking employment until a final determination of their claim.[178] As with the previous amendments, these too were debated vigorously in the House of Commons.[179] Speaker after speaker from opposition ranks rose to condemn both the legislative process (the invocation of closure by the government on legislative debates) and the substance of the amendments. Once again, however, the Conservative majority prevailed, and the majority of the bill's provisions came into force on 1 February 1993.[180]

Exclusion and Removal

INADMISSIBLE CLASSES

The 1976 act introduced important changes regarding those who were not permitted to enter Canada. The previously 'prohibited' classes ('idiots, imbeciles and morons,' 'physically defective persons,' 'homosexuals,' 'the insane,' etc.)[181] were replaced by broader categories of 'inadmissible' immigrants. These included those who would be liable to endanger public health or security, or would be likely to place an excessive burden on health or social services.[182] The 1952 prohibition on entry of those convicted of 'crimes of moral turpitude' was replaced by a prohibition of persons convicted of crimes prohibited by Canadian criminal law.

The changes in the Immigration Act enacted in 1987 and 1992 also included changes to the admissibility criteria. In 1987 the concept of 'safe third country' was introduced. This authorized Cabinet to prescribe countries that comply with international law on the protection of refugees, and to return claimants who had passed through those countries without first determining their claims.[183] The rationale was to prevent refugee claimants from haven 'shopping,'[184] which had become the subject of increasing international concern.[185] The criticism of the provision was loud and forceful since among Western countries with good human rights records the recognition rates of refugee asylum claims still varied widely. Therefore, refugees who might be found to be in need of protection under the Canadian system might be rejected in another country. To remove such claimants to the latter, would effectively implicate Canada in *refoulement*, which it was internationally prohibited from doing.

As it turned out, a list of countries was not prescribed,[186] and the provision lay dormant only to be revived again with the amendments of 1992.[187] Factors to be considered in the formulation of a 'safe third country' list included whether the country was a party to the U.N. Convention Relating to the Status of Refugees, the country's human rights record, its policies and practices with respect to Convention refugee claims, and whether the country was a party to an agreement with Canada to share information on refugee claims and responsibility for their determination.[188] As with the previous amendment, these provisions were not implemented during the period.

Other inadmissibility provisions concerning refugees, however, were implemented. For example, all refugee claimants were required to appear before a senior immigration officer to determine whether they were admissible and therefore permitted to present their claims to the CRDD. Refugees could be denied access to the refugee-determination process if they were found to have been recognized as a refugee in another country or to fall within an ineligibility ground (e.g., for serious criminality and in the opinion of the minister a danger to the public in Canada).[189] A claimant found ineligible was subject to immediate removal from Canada, subject only to a right to apply for leave for judicial review to the Federal Court Trial Division, whose jurisdiction in these matters was limited to errors of law or perverse or capricious findings of fact.

The 1992 amendments also introduced changes to the admissibility provisions related to health and security, reflecting a much more restrictive posture than had opened the period in 1976. The 1976 provision excluding individuals suffering from any disease, disorder, or disability or other health impairment that was likely to be a danger to public health or place an excessive burden on health services[190] was replaced with more nebulous wording.[191] The amendments afforded more latitude to medical officers in excluding those who 'for medical reasons' were likely to endanger public health or safety, or be too great a burden on health or social services.[192]

Criminal inadmissibility was also extended in the 1992 amendments to deny entry where there were 'reasonable grounds to believe' that the applicant was or previously had been engaged in 'planned and organized' criminal activity.[193] Furthermore, the bill barred those who, it was reasonably believed, had committed an act or omission outside Canada that would constitute an offence under the Canadian Criminal Code.[194] The amendment did not require an actual criminal charge or conviction, and therefore had the potential to increase significantly the number of persons who were criminally inadmissible.

Other security provisions of the act were also tightened. Immigration officers were given broader search and seizure powers. They were permitted, for example, to search persons whom there were reasonable grounds to believe had hidden documents that would identify them as members of a particular inadmissible class or documents that could be used to smuggle other persons into the country.[195] In addition, broader powers were given to officials to fingerprint and photograph those wishing to enter the country, and penalties were increased for those attempting to smuggle immigrants into Canada.[196]

REMOVAL

In regard to removals, the Immigration Act set out the grounds for removal of anyone who was not a Canadian citizen. These included gaining entry by fraudulent misrepresentation of a material fact and/or having been convicted of an offence for which a term of imprisonment of more that six months was imposed, or for which a term of imprisonment of more than five years could be imposed. The latter had broad application, particularly since the act removed the concept of domicile. Prior to this time, generally those who had been in Canada for five years acquired domicile status and could not be deported. There were exceptions to this, but the exceptions were relatively few in number.[197] The 1976 act eliminated the notion of domicile and effectively extended the threat of removal from Canada to all non-citizens, no matter how long they had resided in Canada.[198]

The 1992 amendments to the Immigration Act further expanded the grounds for removal to include those for whom there were 'reasonable grounds' to suspect that they were or had been members of an organization that was suspected of engaging in criminal acts or that they were engaging or might engage in espionage or terrorism.

While introducing more expanded grounds for removal, the 1976 act also provided for different kinds of removals and expanded procedural protections. The least extreme was a twelve-month exclusion order, which prohibited the person from attempting to enter Canada for a twelve-month period following the making of the order. A departure notice prevented readmission unless permission was received from the minister. At the furthest extreme was a deportation order, which effectively barred readmission to Canada.[199]

Procedural protections set out in the act included the requirement that a removal order had to be justified before an Immigration Department adjudicator. A designated officer presented the minister's case for removal, and the person concerned was also able to present evidence and argument against the issuing of the order. The adjudicator's decision could be appealed, with limited exceptions pertaining to security, to the Immigration Appeal Board, on grounds of law or fact; also, in the case of permanent residents, the IAD had jurisdiction to consider humanitarian and compassionate considerations for quashing the removal order. In 1992 the independence of the adjudicator was further guaranteed by the creation of the Adjudication Division as part of the IRB, although adjudicators remained employed by the Immigration Department.

Persons considered security risks were subject to a different procedure with more limited procedural safeguards. The act enabled the minister and the solicitor general to file a security certificate with an immigration officer stating that they had 'reasonable grounds to believe' that the person was 'likely to engage' in criminal or subversive activities. A security certificate barred consideration by the IAD on humanitarian and compassionate grounds and was only reviewable by the Security Intelligence Review Committee (SIRC) on questions of law or fact and by the Federal Court on grounds of law. The limited review and restricted procedural protections provided to those subject to a security certificate, regardless of their length of residence, was challenged in the courts and eventually made its way to the Supreme Court of Canada in the case of *Chiarelli*.[200]

Prior to considering that case, however, the court heard a challenge against the extradition of an American citizen, Kindler, who had been ordered extradited to the United States, where he faced the death penalty.

The court's reasoning in the case of *Kindler*[201] stood in rather stark contrast to its decision in *Singh* just six years earlier. In *Kindler,* the court was asked to decide whether the minister's decision to extradite Kindler without receiving assurances that he would not face the death penalty was in violation of his section 12 right (not to be subjected to cruel and unusual punishment or treatment) and his section 7 rights (not to be denied life, liberty, and security except in accordance with the principles of fundamental justice) and if so, whether such violations were demonstrably justified as required by section 1.

One of the salient features of the majority decision in favour of the government was its finding that although Kindler's section 7 rights were engaged, he had been accorded fundamental justice. Specifically, the court found that the requirements of fundamental justice depended on a variety of factors, including the nature of the offence; the justice system in the requesting state; the consequences of having to request assurances; and whether the practice was consistent with what is fair, right, and just in Canadian society. The court adopted a very open-ended framework of analysis that was unlikely to yield consistent results, since each judge could weigh the factors differently. Moreover, by moving many section 1 considerations (regarding justification of the measures) into the rights analysis of section 7, the court effectively shifted more of the burden onto the applicant and obviated the need for the government to prove that the violation was demonstrably justified as required under section 1.[202]

The analytical methods used by the court in *Kindler* were used in subsequent cases regarding the constitutionality of the government's removal powers and procedures, as became evident the following year in the court's decision in *Chiarelli.*[203]

In *Chiarelli,* the court examined provisions pertaining to the issuing of security certificates and specifically the restricted rights of review afforded to those who were the subject of such certificates. Chiarelli had resided in Canada for ten years, since he was fifteen years of age. He had received two criminal convictions, one for which he received a suspended sentence and the other for which he received six months' imprisonment. Because both offences carried a maximum term of imprisonment of more than five years, however, he was ordered deported. The solicitor general and the minister subsequently issued a security certificate against him on the grounds that they were of the opinion that Chiarelli was likely to participate in organized crime. Chiarelli's right of appeal was therefore limited to questions of fact or law and did not include humanitarian and compassionate considerations.

Chiarelli argued that the deportation order and the removal of his right to appeal on humanitarian and compassionate grounds violated his section 7 rights. At the heart of his argument was that the deprivation therefore had to be in accordance with the principles of fundamental justice and required consideration of all the circumstances of the case. Without determining whether section 7 rights were involved, the court found that fundamental justice had been afforded. The content of the latter was to be determined with reference to underlying principles of the Immigration Act, which, according to the court, included the basic premise that 'non citizens do not have an unqualified right to enter or remain in the country.' The provision of an appeal on law or fact was sufficient, especially in light of historical practice, it said, noting that a review on compassionate grounds was only introduced in 1967 and that since then the minister had had the power to exclude that ground of appeal in cases involving security interests.

The decision was noteworthy in several respects. First, the court's willingness to consider the content of fundamental justice without considering whether section 7 rights were at stake (i.e., the impact on the claimant's life) made it easier to find that the procedure was consistent with fundamental justice. Moreover, looking to the underlying principles of the Immigration Act to determine the content of the Charter right rather than using the values in the Charter to determine the constitutionality of the provisions in the act effectively denied the supremacy of the Charter. Additionally, the reference to the ability to control admission and removal as the central principle of the act harked back to earlier periods and ignored other objectives in the act, such as social and humanitarian considerations, that also had a bearing on the case.

The court's reasoning in support of the constitutionality of the security certificate procedures also weighed in favour of the government. Chiarelli was only entitled to a summary of the case against him, although he could provide evidence before the reviewing tribunal. The government argued that the limitations were necessary to protect investigation techniques. In finding for the government, the court narrowly defined Chiarelli's interest as the right to a fair procedure, which it balanced against the national security interests of the state. There was no requirement that the government justify its actions as proportionate under section 1 of the Charter. This significantly limited the reach of the Charter and laid the foundations for subsequent restrictive decisions that would curtail the rights of non-citizens more than had been the case prior to the entrenchment of the Charter. [204]

Conclusions

The political and, to a large extent, public consensus that seemed to emerge on most major issues of immigration policy in the previous period (1963–76), culminating in the near-unanimous passage of the 1976 Immigration Act, was sharply fractured in the following decade and a half. The more open, democratic, policy-making process initiated in the previous period and expanded in this one ironically seemed to amplify divisions on immigration policy rather than reduce them.

The focus of the most intense controversy was how to respond appropriately to dramatic increases in refugee claims. Although the increases were dramatic by Canadian standards, they paled in relation to those experienced by other countries of far smaller size and wealth. Over a similar period, Malawi, one of the least developed countries of the world, received more than 1 million refugees from Mozambique, increasing its population by 10 per cent. In 1984 alone, more than 500,000 Ethiopian refugees fled into Sudan. In the two-year period between 1981 and 1982, more than 200,000 refugees from Guatemala fled into Mexico. Between 1986 and 1987, the Afghan refugee population in Pakistan increased by 300,000 and that in Iran by half that amount, peaking at more than 3 million in each country by 1991.[205]

Seen in this light, the emergency recall of Parliament in 1987 in response to the spontaneous arrival of 173 East Indians off the coast of Nova Scotia appears as an enormous over-reaction and subsequent concerns over losing control over borders equally overblown. Yet the prospect that refugees might continue spontaneously to arrive was and continues to be a galvanizing one. The fears ignited by the Nova Scotia arrivals were similar to those engendered by the Sikhs on the *Komagata Maru* sixty-three years earlier. What had changed, however, was that despite the rather insular perspective that persisted in regard to Canada's comparative responsibilities towards refugees throughout the world, the Immigration Act now firmly acknowledged humanitarian obligations in this regard. The procedures introduced in the 1976 act and subsequently amended provided for the first time clearly articulated and more transparent processes for admitting those in need of protection, both abroad and at Canadian borders. The inland-refugee process, in particular, afforded far more procedural safeguards than ever before.

Regular immigrants were also subjected to more transparent admissibility criteria, and Canadian citizens and permanent residents could challenge refusals of their family sponsorship applications on broader grounds than before. And while the ability to deport permanent residents was expanded under the act, mechanisms for review were correspondingly enlarged.

At the same time, however, efforts were made to deter unauthorized arrivals (for example, through visa restrictions, penalties on transport companies carrying improperly documented passengers, criminalization of smuggling, and policies for the return of arrivals to the United States) and to expand the grounds for removal to cover the broad area of security concerns. These developments reflected a retrenchment of sorts and an increased preoccupation with security issues that was also increasingly shared by the courts, as evidenced by the growing deference they accorded to the minister regarding whom to admit or exclude.

As global migration increased significantly in the next period, and fears of global terrorism intensified, the issues that dominated Canadian immigration policy in the 1980s and early 1990s continued to be the focal point of public debate and controversy. Coupled with these developments were the persistently large numbers of refugees uprooted by civil war and persecution, the substantial costs involved in processing refugee claims and resettling refugees, and the magnitude of the human tragedy in the absence of effective responses by more developed countries. All these factors ensured that the problems would not be transitory. No other immigration issue has the same potential for exacerbating the tension between expansive humanitarian values and material self-interest. However, in this period it became clear that the values involved now had highly effective political and public advocates.

The fractious nature of the debates over refugee policy that dominated the period risks obscuring other important trends in immigration policy about which much broader political and public consensus emerged. First, the composition of the non-refugee immigrant intake had changed dramatically over three short decades. Prime Minister Mackenzie King's commitment in 1947 to an immigration policy that would not significantly change the demographic make-up of the country could not have been more decisively repudiated by subsequent events. The diverse ethnic origins of the Canadian population by the 1990s stood in stark contrast to the ethnic composition of the population at the time of Confederation.

Moreover, the Five-Year Immigration Plan introduced by the Conservative government in 1990 marked the first time in the post-Confederation history of Canadian immigration policy that a government committed itself to an increase in immigration in recessionary economic times. This commitment to an expanded immigrant intake and a longer planning horizon was supported by major business and labour interests, and by most of the major federal political parties, not only at the time it was made but even in the severe recessionary environment that followed.

Finally, much of what had been contentious in previous times was now the subject of relatively broad political and public consensus. In 1992, Bob White, president of the Canadian Labour Congress, argued strongly and publicly that immigrants do not, in general, take away jobs from existing citizens but rather create employment, demand, and wealth.[206] His public support of this expansionary immigration policy, despite the difficult economic times, strikingly exemplifies the new consensus. This included a widely shared commitment to a relatively high and constant level of immigration increasingly detached from transitory labour-market conditions or the state of the economic cycle; a dramatically more diverse, multiethnic, multicultural immigrant intake; a fragile consensus on the moral and legal imperative for a relatively generous refugee policy; a stronger consensus on the need to preserve a generous family reunification policy; and a broad recognition that the major features of future immigration policy should be determined through open public and political debate rather than executive or administrative policy making.

CHAPTER ELEVEN

Retrenchment, 1995–2008: A Return to Executive Discretion

Introduction

The long-fought-for and finally achieved transparency in immigration policy formation and delivery that was embedded in the 1976 Immigration Act was to be seriously tested and in many areas reversed between 1995 and 2008. Beginning slowly and accelerating after the 11 September 2001 terrorist attacks in the United States, measures to invest greater latitude in executive decision making were once again to gain currency. Reforms that were embodied in the new Immigration and Refugee Protection Act of 2002 reflected several years of national study and debate concerning the economic performance of immigrants, renewed controversy over refugee policy, and, most importantly, heightened concerns over border security following the events of 9/11.

Although the contours of immigration policy were to change significantly in this period, the constellation of interests active and evident in the previous period remained largely the same. Legal advocates, trade unions, and immigrant and refugee groups continued to demand both transparent policies that respected the rights and security of immigrants and refugees and policies that did not limit the ability of families to be reunited in Canada. Business groups consistently called for streamlined and effective mechanisms to admit the workers and investors their industries needed. Academics continued to study the economic performance of immigrants, with a larger number also examining immigration policy from a national and international human rights perspective. The largely conservative posture of the judiciary in regard to challenges to executive discretion, evident in the latter years of the previous period, was to persist. Commentators on the right continued to call for a radical reversal in immigration trends, including a lowering of annual admissions, stricter selection criteria, and a much more restrictive approach to refugee admissions.

The tightening of immigration policy and the expansion of executive discretion that emerged amid these debates was not driven by the economic climate. Whereas, historically, economic downturns had provoked a more restrictive immigration policy, in this period preoccupation with security was the prime justification for the reversal of the more open and accountable immigration policy of the previous period. In fact, from the mid-1990s to 2008 the Canadian economy was in good health, with budgetary surpluses recorded each year. Even with the major shocks to the U.S. economy at the turn of the century, brought on by the dot-com crisis, the 11 September terrorist attacks, and the decline in confidence in financial reporting following the Enron and WorldCom scandals, Canadian economic performance continued to fare comparatively well.

Gross domestic product (GDP) grew faster than in other G7 countries, with inflation remaining low and stable and the debt-to-GDP ratio falling from 71 per cent in 1995 to 29 per cent in 2008.

A halt to this trend was occasioned with the credit crisis originating in the United States in late 2006 and reverberating through 2009. The effects of that crisis, implicating banking institutions around the world, were also felt in Canada, which experienced lower growth rates than had been anticipated. The slowdown of the U.S. economy, with the resulting impact on Canadian exports, led to downward predictions of economic performance for 2009, with an anticipated growth rate of less than 1.2 per cent, half that experienced in 2007, yet higher than expected for other G7 countries.

Just as the economy remained relatively robust throughout most of this period, so too did immigration rates. The upward trend in annual immigration levels experienced during the 1990s, when more than 2.2 million immigrants came to Canada, continued during the first eight years of the new millennium. Between 2000 and 2008 more than 1.6 million immigrants arrived, representing an average admission rate of approximately 240,000 persons annually – almost 1 per cent of the existing population.[1]

The shifts seen in the composition of immigrants experienced in the previous period were to deepen. In 1990 just over 50 per cent of new arrivals came from Asia and the Middle East. That percentage increased to 58 per cent by 2006, with the largest source countries being China (approximately 15 per cent) and India (12 per cent). The proportion of Europeans immigrating to Canada continued to decline from just under 25 per cent in 1990 to about 16 per cent in 2007. For the first time in

Canada's history, the proportion of the foreign-born population from Asia and the Middle East (40.8 per cent) surpassed the proportion born in Europe (36.8 per cent).[2] Moreover, as a result of high annual admissions and relatively lower rates of natural increase, the proportion of the foreign-born population reached a new high of 18 per cent of the total population, a level that had not been seen since the previous high of some 22 per cent in 1931. Near the end of the first decade of the twenty-first century, one in five residents of Canada was foreign born.

Major urban areas continued to attract the largest proportion of new arrivals, with seven out of ten immigrants settling in Toronto, Montreal, or Vancouver between 2001 and 2006. Some 46 per cent of Toronto's population in 2006 was foreign born, higher than in Miami (40 per cent), Sydney (31 per cent), Los Angeles (31 per cent), and New York (24 per cent).[3]

In terms of language, the 2006 census revealed that 80 per cent of the foreign-born population reported a language other than English or French as their mother tongue as compared to 50 per cent twenty-five years earlier. The Anglophone share of the total population fell to 57.8 per cent from a little over 61 per cent in 1981. Those who reported French as their mother tongue also declined to 22 per cent from close to 26 per cent twenty-five years earlier.

Against this changing landscape, public support for relatively high annual immigration levels was remarkably constant, as compared with previous periods when precisely these types of demographic shifts caused the most alarm. This is not to suggest that the period was without its immigration controversies, for public debate around immigration-related issues was as active as ever.

During the first few years of the period, this debate focused primarily on proposed changes to the 1976 Immigration Act, which was seen as having become too cumbersome to effectively manage immigration for the twenty-first century. At the end of 1994, Citizenship and Immigration released *Into the 21st Century: A Strategy for Immigration and Citizenship*, reflecting greater emphasis on encouraging immigrants who could contribute to the economy. The government subsequently appointed a three-member committee in 1996 to review the Immigration Act with a view to its complete overhaul. The aim was to make it less complex and to remove the inconsistencies arising from some thirty amendments made to the act over the preceding twenty years. Consistent with the controversy brewing over refugee admissions, the panel was asked specifically to consider ways to streamline the refugee process. It was also asked to study the scope and depth of ministerial discretion.

The panel's report, *Not Just Numbers: A Canadian Framework for Future Immigration*,[4] provoked a storm of controversy, focused as it was on means to ensure that those who came to Canada were those who could best adapt, prosper, and 'and help Canada grow.'[5] It was not so much this intent that sparked the controversy but the means the panel recommended to secure it, including standardized admission tests to prove fluency in English or French and requirements for a minimum level of education, work experience, and demonstrated ability to earn an income. Given that over two-thirds of all immigrants to Canada spoke neither English nor French, the proposed reforms were criticized as unsound and unworkable, with some groups arguing that they were reminiscent of more racist and shameful periods in Canadian immigration history.

The suggested reforms to the refugee system proved equally controversial. The panel proposed that the Immigration and Refugee Board (IRB) cease to have jurisdiction in determining refugee status and that this responsibility be transferred to civil servants in a faster process. It argued for more emphasis on overseas selection and for an increase in the number of overseas immigration officers to accomplish this. Refugee-advocacy groups, civil-rights groups, faith-based organizations, and law associations were among the prominent critics of the proposed loss of an independent tribunal to hear refugee claims.

The panel's recommendations for improving entrepreneurial immigration were equally unpopular, especially the suggestion that, in addition to being able to speak English or French and having a postsecondary education, immigrants admitted under the investor program should be forty-five years of age or younger and have half a million dollars to invest. Immigration counsellors predicted that such changes would lead to a complete collapse of the program.

Other more progressive suggestions seemed to get lost in the firestorm. These included the panel's recommendations that Canada issue annual immigration quotas rather than targets, expand the family class to include the sponsorship of close friends and same-sex partners, and establish a federal-provincial council on immigration to give the provinces an increased consultative role.

In regard to the acquisition of citizenship, the panel suggested that, in addition to knowing something about Canada, not being a criminal, and having lived and paid taxes in Canada for three years, prospective citizens should also be required to know an official language and actively participate in Canadian society through holding a job, going to school, raising a family, or doing volunteer work. These recommendations were labelled a combination of 'sensible and bizarre.' Two commentators noted that many native-born Canadians would not meet these standards. They further questioned,

> And what would Ottawa do with a single, 24 year old woman newcomer from Burkina Faso who owns a chain of doughnut shops in rural Saskatchewan and who pays out hefty sums in salaries and taxes but has no time to go to university or work in a women's shelter?[6]

In public debates chaired by the minister of Citizenship and Immigration across the country in the weeks following the publication of the report, the language issue attracted the most fire. In fact, so intense was the opposition that, within a month of the publication of the report, and just before she was to meet with the representatives of the Asian community on the west coast, Minister Lucienne Robillard said that she too questioned the wisdom of the language requirement, noting that it could be an unreasonable bar to entry. She further distanced herself from the report by stating that it was not government policy and that its recommendations would have to be carefully reviewed.[7]

As in previous periods, other events also strengthened calls for reform of the Immigration Act. In particular, the arrival of 123 Chinese migrants in a rusty trawler off the coast of British Columbia in the summer of 1999 brought the immigration debate prominently back into the public eye, where it remained for the next two months as another three ships arrived, bringing in total some 600 migrants. The Reform party quickly demanded a recall of Parliament to amend the Immigration Act to better prevent illegal migration, an echo of a similar demand by its predecessor, the Progressive Conservative party, eight summers earlier when 173 East Asians had arrived off the east coast.

The migrants who arrived in British Columbia in the summer of 1999 were largely from China's Fujian province. They had paid smugglers up to $40,000 (U.S.) to transport them to North America, where they believed jobs had been arranged for them. A significant proportion of the arrivals were children between eleven and seventeen years of age, some of them unaccompanied.

Against demands by the Reform party to tighten the Immigration Act and vocal protests, particularly in British Columbia, against showing any leniency to the arrivals,[8] the minister insisted that the existing procedures were able to manage the situation. She stated that the government was working internationally to combat human smuggling and trafficking and cautioned against an approach that would punish victims rather than perpetrators.[9] In that regard, nine suspected smugglers were charged under the Immigration Act for forcing a person to disembark at sea.

Nearly all the passengers of the first boat claimed refugee status, yet over 80 per cent did not show up for the claims procedure. This was largely why the government decided to detain the subsequent migrants until their identities could be established. The handling of the detainees came under criticism, particularly when children were separated from their mothers, when adolescent girls and boys were strip-searched after meeting with their lawyers, and when the provincial guardian of the unaccompanied minors advised them to return home since they had been deceived by smugglers who intended to put them to work illegally in factories or as prostitutes. Since their families had sent them on the journey in the first place and the migrants themselves alleged that they would be persecuted if they returned, the provincial guardian's advice was seen as not in keeping with his responsibility to represent the best interests of the children under his care.[10]

The RCMP also came under criticism for having failed to investigate adequately after being warned for years about smuggling rings from Fujian.[11] In the end, most of those who landed were removed back to China, where, it was reported, they were detained for several months for having left the country without permission and heavily fined. Some 5 per cent of those who claimed refugee status were granted asylum or otherwise allowed to remain on a Minister's Permit.[12]

Further pressure for reform came in the wake of a Federal Court of Canada decision involving a refugee claimant who had made repeated requests for asylum in Canada. The presiding judge was reported in the press as having been critical of the process whereby a rejected claimant could return to Canada after ninety days and make a new claim for refugee status. According to Judge McGillis, those who used this to make repeat claims placed an undue strain on Canadian taxpayers, the practice constituting 'a scandalous abuse of our border.'[13] While explaining that the provision was intended to allow a rejected claimant to ask for asylum again should the conditions in his or her country change, the minister was also quick to point out that this and other provisions were under review.

The 2000 Auditor General's Report to Parliament did little to assuage prevailing concerns over immigration policy. The report was particularly critical of how immigration applications were processed and assessed. It noted that, because of the volume of applications, overloaded immigration officers were unable to verify expeditiously the information provided in those applications, with the result that processing times were long. It observed that the medical, criminal, and security admissibility criteria were unreasonably vague and that the department did not have a framework to monitor the quality of immigration decisions. This, it said, weakened the system, since decisions were not of sufficient quality or consistency to instil confidence. The limited rights of appeal for rejected applicants – only to the Federal Court and only if granted leave to appeal – were inadequate to remedy problems with the initial decisions. The report concluded that, taken together, these failings limited 'Canada's ability to maximize the economic and social benefits that immigration affords.'[14]

It was during this time that issues pertaining to security also came more to the fore in immigration policy debate. Abuse of the border was spotlighted in February 2000 when a U.S. congressman and the chief of the Central Intelligence Agency referred to Canada's porous immigration system and its underfunded police and security services as among the chief reasons why the country had inadvertently become a haven for terrorists. This criticism was given added weight following the 11 September 2001 terrorist attacks, when American borders in general and the U.S. border with Canada in particular came under more intense scrutiny. A segment of the popular American television program *60 Minutes* entitled 'Al-Qaeda in Canada' summed up concerns that Canada's liberal immigration and refugee policies constituted a security threat in permitting easy access to North America for terrorists, who could elicit support in the immigrant enclaves of big cities like Toronto and Montreal.

Many Canadians and government spokespersons were quick to point out that the U.S. system was far from fail-safe, and that all nineteen of the hijackers involved in the 9/11 bombings had been issued with American visas by American authorities. Nevertheless, the 11 September attacks were a defining moment for much of government policy on both sides of the border, and immigration policy was no exception.

Among the immediate security measures taken in Canada was the introduction and swift passage of the Anti-terrorism Act, within months of the 9/11 attacks.[15] Like the controversial USA PATRIOT Act, the Canadian legislation gave police and intelligence forces extended powers that were unprecedented in times of peace. Among the controversial provisions were those that extended the powers of the police to preventively arrest and hold for three days without charge those suspected of being linked to terrorist activities, that facilitated the use of electronic surveillance, and that broadened the power of the judiciary to compel a person to testify. Also hotly debated and litigated were the expanded criteria for designating a group as a terrorist organization and for making it a crime knowingly to participate in or contribute to a terrorist group.

The legislation also implicated other acts, which were changed to enhance counter-terrorism measures. These included changes to the Criminal Code to expand the grounds upon which a person could be charged with terrorist activities. The Official Secrets Act (renamed the Security of Information Act) was amended to include new offences relating to threats of espionage and terrorism and expand the power of the executive to declare certain actions secret. The Canada Evidence Act was also amended to include changes to court and other proceedings to protect classified information. Amendments to the National Defence Act broadened powers to intercept communications and to protect government security networks from terrorist activity.

The government created a new Department of Public Safety and Emergency Preparedness with the aim of achieving better coordination of security agencies and improved information sharing. It also set up a National Security Plan, a Threat Assessment Centre, and four Integrated National Security Teams, which were designed to identify and prevent terrorist attacks.

Moreover, within months after 9/11, Canada signed a Smart Border Declaration with the United States aimed at making the border more secure while facilitating cross-border traffic and trade. The latter was vital, given that over 80 per cent of Canada's export trade was with the United States,[16] with the value of Canada–U.S. trade estimated at more than $1 billion per day.[17] Measures included the use of fingerprinting and iris-recognition technology to incorporate common biometric identifiers in travel documents, increased sharing of information on immigrants and refugees through the development of a joint immigration database, increased policy coordination with respect to visa waiver lists for foreign countries, the establishment of joint passenger-analysis units, and increased numbers of Canadian and American immigration officers overseas.[18]

In this climate of enhanced security-mindedness, it was not surprising that the new Immigration and Refugee Protection Act, which came into force in 2002, reflected similar security concerns. So, too, did many of the policies and practices implemented under the act and the reasoning of the courts which reviewed them.

The Immigration and Refugee Protection Act

The new Immigration and Refugee Protection Act (IRPA) came into force in June 2002. When the proposed legislation was first introduced as a bill in the House of Commons in April 2000, the minister characterized it as enabling the government to close 'the back door to those who would abuse the system,' thereby allowing it to ensure 'that the front door will remain open' both 'to genuine refugees and to the immigrants our country will need to grow and prosper in the years ahead.' She acknowledged that it was a 'tough bill' designed to stop criminals and illegal immigrants from getting into the country, to facilitate the power of the authorities to remove those who succeed despite safeguards, and to enhance measures to detect and prosecute severely those engaged in people smuggling; at the same time it sought to expand opportunities for families to be reunited and for foreign workers to immigrate to Canada.[19]

In a major departure from the previous Immigration Act, yet in keeping with much of the legislation of the previous century, the new act was largely skeletal, setting out in broad terms the framework of immigration policy while leaving the details to the executive to design and implement through regulation, with minimal parliamentary scrutiny. In this respect, it was considered by many immigration and legal advocates to be a dangerous reversal from the legislative accountability enshrined in the 1976 act.[20]

Other marked changes from the 1976 act included broadened grounds for denying prospective immigrants admission to Canada and for restricting the eligibility of refugee claimants to have their refugee claims determined. Security concerns figured largely in both these limitations as well as in the extended grounds for the removal and deportation of foreigners from Canada and the reasons for restricting access to the courts for review of those decisions.

Although the act expanded the range of those eligible to be sponsored by family members in Canada, regulations tightened up the financial requirements sponsors had to meet. In regard to economic immigrants, the act provided significant room to adjust the applicable criteria and to facilitate the entry of temporary workers.

Concerning refugee protection, the act extended protection to those who met the Convention definition of a refugee as well as those who would be at risk of torture, death, or cruel and unusual treatment if they were returned to a country from which they had fled. At the same time, however, it provided elaborated grounds for limiting access to protection-determination procedures for certain classes of refugees.

The authority of immigration officers to detain immigrants and refugees was expanded under the act and included the right to detain those considered to represent a flight risk or a danger to the public and/or those whose identity was in doubt. The results of this expanded authority were immediately apparent: between 2000 and 2003 the number of individuals detained pursuant to the Immigration Act rose by close to 70 per cent, from some 8,000 people to more than 11,500.[21]

In the years that followed the introduction of the act and its accompanying regulations (five times more voluminous than those under the preceding act), public examination and discussion of the act's effectiveness focused primarily on a few specific areas. In regard to admissions, legal advocates and immigrant and refugee organizations claimed that the tightening of criteria was unnecessarily restrictive and threatened the ability of refugees in genuine need of international protection to find it in Canada. Many of these groups were equally critical of provisions that facilitated the entry of temporary workers, arguing that the provisions undermined labour protections for Canadian workers and disregarded the rights of temporary workers, who were not protected by federal and provincial labour standards and were denied opportunities to become permanent residents in Canada.

The extensive security and medical screening necessary before selected immigrants could enter Canada were also criticized because they imposed additional burdens on immigration offices and, in the absence of enhanced capacity, led to onerous delays. This provoked calls from business and immigrant groups for measures to reduce processing times.

Enhanced removal and deportation powers were also the focus of considerable debate and litigation throughout the period. Legal advocates and human rights groups argued that the act gave far too much undefined discretion to the minister and his or her delegates to remove foreign nationals for a variety of reasons without due-process protections.

The Focus of Admissions Policy

Like previous immigration acts, the new act set out the classes of immigrants permitted to apply to immigrate to Canada. These included the economic class, the family class, and the refugee category. Immigrants (principal applicant and his or her dependants) admitted under the economic class consistently represented over 58 per cent of total annual admissions throughout this period, with the family class representing approximately 27 per cent and refugees approximately 12 per cent.

To immigrate to Canada a person had to fall within one of the admissible classes and, in addition, not be otherwise inadmissible for security, criminal, health, or financial reasons, or for misrepresentation or failure to comply with any provision of the act. Some of these categories, namely those pertaining to security, serious criminality, and misrepresentation, were also grounds for removal even after permanent residence was obtained.

Those inadmissible for security reasons included persons believed to be involved or who might become engaged in espionage, subversion, violence or terrorism, or who were members of an organization involved in such activities. Also inadmissible were persons who were members of organizations or governments responsible for war crimes and/or crimes against humanity, as well as senior officials of governments responsible for gross human rights violations or subject to international sanctions.

By contrast with the 1976 Immigration Act but consistent with trends of the latter part of the previous period, criminal grounds for being inadmissible were relatively broad and were applicable to those who had committed or been convicted of a criminal offence in any country. These grounds included relatively minor offences such as petty theft, simple assault, or possession of a controlled substance. Criminal grounds for inadmissibility also included involvement in transnational crime, such as people smuggling, trafficking of persons, and money laundering.[22]

In regard to health, the act prohibited admission of those whose condition was deemed likely to endanger public health or public safety or might reasonably be expected to cause excessive demands on the health system or social services. The factors for determining the latter included the impact of the person's health care treatment on medical or social services, whether the person would require hospitalization, and whether the condition would affect the ability of the person to be employed.

Persons who could be found to be inadmissible for financial reasons included those whom an immigration officer believed would be unable or unwilling to financially support themselves and their family members. Also included within the inadmissibility provisions were those found to have misrepresented a material fact – for example, by providing false information or withholding relevant information during the processing of their immigration application. Similarly, failure to comply with any provision of the act could be used to deny admission to those who had previously legally entered Canada, but who had left and now sought to return. This category included temporary residents who stayed longer than authorized or worked or studied without the necessary permits; permanent residents who did not comply with the residency obligation; and persons who had previously been deported and had returned to Canada without written authorization.

The process for gaining admission to Canada as a permanent resident was much the same as in the previous period. Applications generally had to be made from outside Canada; however, the new law further tightened this requirement by providing that prospective immigrants had to submit their applications to the Canadian visa office serving their country of nationality or a country where they had been legally resident for one year. Prior to this time, applications could be made at any Canadian visa office abroad, and files could be transferred from one office to another. This had provided a high degree of flexibility and helped minimize the potential delays faced by those in countries where Canada had a limited immigration presence or where its offices had significant backlogs.

The impact of the new system was significant and led critics to complain that immigration processing reflected racial preferences that had been denounced years ago. A review of the number of applications in different overseas visa offices compared with processing times revealed wide variations – ranging from one and a half years for applications made in Buffalo, New York, to less than four years on average for applications made in Europe, more than six years for applications made in Africa, and more than fifteen years for applications made in New Delhi.[23]

There were some exceptions to the general rule that applications for permanent residence had to be made from outside Canada. For example, some temporary workers could apply from within Canada, as could those who were granted an exemption for humanitarian and compassionate reasons. Those falling within the latter category had to show that unusual, undeserved, or disproportionate hardship would result if they had to leave Canada.

The decision to grant or refuse an immigration visa continued to rest with an immigration officer, who, as previously, had to assess applications on the basis of the requirements of the act and regulations and of guidelines issued by the Department of Citizenship and Immigration. Persons who did not meet those requirements continued to be able to apply for permanent residence on humanitarian and compassionate grounds.

In most cases, the decision of an immigration officer to refuse an application for permanent residence was subject to review, with leave, by the Federal Court of Canada. Leave would be granted only where the person was able to show that the application raised a serious issue involving an error in law, a serious error in fact, or a serious procedural flaw (a violation of natural justice).

The Immigration Appeal Division (IAD) maintained its jurisdiction to hear appeals of decisions to refuse family sponsorship applications, as well as decisions to have a permanent resident removed from Canada for failing to meet the residence requirements or for less serious forms of criminality. Decisions could be based on law, fact, and humanitarian and compassionate considerations. As discussed below, however, the IAD continued not to have jurisdiction to hear appeals of removal order decisions involving security and human rights violations. Moreover, its jurisdiction to hear appeals of removal orders based on criminality was further circumscribed in this period.

Economic Class

The most significant change introduced by the new act and its regulations with respect to the economic class was a stronger focus on young, highly skilled immigrants. The point system was retained but was weighted more towards general training and experience, proficiency in English or French, youth, and postsecondary education.

The economic class consisted of four categories of immigrants: (i) skilled workers, (ii) business immigrants, (iii) provincial/territorial nominees, and (iv) live-in caregivers. Skilled workers consistently made up the single largest group. Together with their dependants, they have accounted, on average, for half the total admissions in the economic class during this period.[24]

Skilled Workers

The skilled-worker class was designed to attract immigrants with the education, work experience, knowledge of English or French, and other abilities that would help them to establish themselves successfully in Canada. The previous requirement that they fit within one of the 'preferred occupations' was dropped in favour of a point system weighted more towards experience in managerial, professional, or technical and skilled occupations as set out in the Canadian National Occupational Classification. The former system was acknowledged to be ineffective, since the selection of the preferred occupations never seemed to mirror actual labour market demands.[25]

Out of a possible 100 points, the threshold for skilled workers was reduced from 72 points to 67, significantly widening the pool of eligible applicants. More than one-third of the needed points could be awarded for education and knowledge of English or French, and an additional one-third for previous work experience. Applicants between twenty-one and forty-nine years of age could qualify for 10 points, as could those providing evidence of adaptability, as indicated by their having previously worked or studied in Canada or having a family member in Canada.[26]

In addition to assessing the points to be awarded under the set criteria, immigration officers were given additional discretion to substitute their own opinion where, in their view, endorsed by another officer, the number of points was not an accurate reflection of the applicant's chances of successfully establishing him or herself in Canada.[27] The discretion could be used either to deny entry to an applicant with a qualifying score or to admit an applicant who did not meet the point threshold.[28]

Business Class

The business-class category was designed to attract investors, entrepreneurs, and self-employed persons. It accounted for only a modest proportion of immigrants, averaging fewer than 2 per cent of total annual admissions during this period.[29]

Admission as an investor required necessary business experience, a net worth of at least $800,000, and a commitment to invest $400,000 in a non–interest-bearing, government-guaranteed investment fund. The initial investment was only redeemable after five years. Admission as an entrepreneur required a minimum net worth of $300,000, earned through the applicant's own economic activity, and a demonstrated ability within three years to own a one-third equity in a business employing at least one Canadian or permanent resident. Admission as a self-employed immigrant required a demonstrated intention and ability to be self-employed upon arrival and to make a significant contribution to specific economic activities in Canada in the area of culture, athletics, or farm management.[30]

The application of points in the business-class category was similar in most respects to that in the skilled-worker category, with the exception that the threshold number of needed points was significantly less (35 as opposed to 67) and a greater emphasis was placed on experience. For example, 5 points could be awarded for each year of experience, up to a maximum of 35 points. Up to 6 points could be awarded for adaptability – demonstrated by simply making a business-exploration trip to Canada or attending a seminar on business immigration.[31]

As with the skilled-worker category, immigration officers retained the discretion to substitute their own opinion if in their view the point total was not an accurate reflection of the immigrant's prospects of successfully establishing in Canada, provided this opinion was endorsed by another immigration officer.

Before the changes introduced in the new act, the business category had come under severe criticism, most notably in the 2000 report of the auditor general. That report noted that the program was open to abuse by people engaging in fraud, organized crime, and/or the laundering of illegally obtained money and that many business immigrants did not meet the conditions required by their visa.[32] A 2003 study focusing on results of the program in British Columbia concluded that the government's assertions that the program was a success in terms of capital invested and jobs created were not well supported. The study revealed that the program had generated only modest income and very limited entrepreneurial activity. In part this was because of adjustment difficulties many entrepreneurs faced in regard to unfamiliar tax and regulatory systems and business networks, as well as language barriers. In spite of these problems and the insufficient resources committed to monitoring outcomes, the government continued to promote the program, and immigration officers were faced with pressure to fill their targets.[33]

Provincial/Territorial Nominees

The act maintained the authority of the minister to enter into immigration agreements with the provinces as a means of meeting their immigration needs and facilitating the distribution of immigrants across Canada. Under the Provincial Nominee Program, provinces signed agreements with the federal government permitting them to nominate prospective immigrants likely to contribute to the specific economic and labour needs of the province. Those nominated by the province were assessed according to the province's occupational priorities as well as the standard federal criminal, health, and security admissibility tests. All provinces participated in this program with the exception of Quebec, which had a specific arrangement with the government, the 1991 Canada Quebec Accord Relating to Immigration and Temporary Admission of Aliens. This accord was similar to the Provincial Nominee Program, with the notable exception that Quebec maintained its own immigration offices where provincial rather than federal immigration officers conducted the initial assessment. Federal officers continued to perform the necessary health and security checks and to determine permanent-residence status.

Provincial nominees made up a small proportion of immigrant arrivals in Canada for the initial years of this period, averaging less than 1 per cent between 1998 and 2004. Later years saw an increase, however, with nominees and their dependants constituting close to 9 per cent of annual admissions in 2008.[34]

One explanation for the relatively modest, albeit growing, contribution of the program was that the long processing times of up to two years limited the program's overall effectiveness in responding to economic conditions, including labour-market needs. Moreover, studies suggested that immigrants who entered a province under such a program did not necessarily stay there, prompting the House Standing Committee on Citizenship and Immigration to recommend in 2003 that incentives be offered to improve retention rates and that the criteria be expanded further to enable foreigners already in Canada – for example, under a temporary work permit – to be eligible under the program.[35]

Live-In Caregiver Program

The Live-In Caregiver Program was maintained, permitting the entry to Canada of individuals to provide private care to children, elderly persons, or persons with disabilities. The selection criteria, however, became more stringent, requiring the successful completion of the equivalent of a Canadian high school education, one year's experience in a related field or at least six months of recognized full-time training in a field related to the job, as well as the ability to speak, read, and understand English or French.[36] Unlike other economic immigrants, live-in caregivers did not enter Canada as permanent residents. They could apply for permanent residence status from within Canada but only if certain conditions were met. These included education and training requirements and the duty to live with the care receiver for at least two years over a three-year period.[37] The more onerous conditions help explain the drop in the proportion of this class of immigrants in this period. In 1991, for example, more than 16,000 caregivers were admitted to Canada, as compared to just over 6,000 in 2008.[38]

Numerous criticisms were levelled at the Live-In Caregiver Program. Some argued that the more onerous selection criteria disproportionately affected women from the developing world, who were less likely to have the formal education required to meet the criteria. Some critics further claimed that the more stringent selection criteria had the unintended effect of fuelling illegal work in the field, further increasing the risk of abuse for workers who, because of their illegal status, would be unlikely to report it. The conditions the person had to satisfy before being eligible for permanent residence were also criticized as leaving caregivers vulnerable. For example, some argued that compelling caregivers to live in the home of their employment left them open to exploitive employment conditions from which they could not easily extricate themselves. More-over, the stipulation that they work only as caregivers and in employment approved by the government, critics said, exacerbated the risk that women could be trapped in abusive situations, since any change in employment not only required government approval but also extended by a corres-ponding length of time the twenty-four-month waiting period before the caregiver could apply for permanent residence.[39]

Temporary Worker Programs

The act also provided for the admission of temporary foreign workers to Canada to support the Canadian economy. Despite this economic rationale, these workers were not included in the economic class because of the temporary nature of their admission, with no right to permanent residence.

Employers wishing to hire temporary foreign workers generally had to apply to and receive approval from the federal ministry responsible for human resources.[40] Approval depended on the ministry's confirmation that there was a genuine need for the worker and that admission was likely to have a neutral or positive economic effect on the labour market. The number of temporary workers admitted annually significantly increased over the years. In 2003 a total of 103,426 foreign workers came to Canada, a figure which rose to more than 192,000 in 2008.[41]

As with the Live-In Caregiver Program, conditions governing the entry of temporary workers were criticized for permitting exploitive and abu-sive practices. The Canadian Seasonal Agricultural Workers Program was highlighted as a case in point. The program was designed to cover the shortage of Canadian workers in the agricultural sector, permitting the admission of workers for a period of no more than eight months. Workers admitted under the program were subject to an employment contract whereby the employer retained the right to repatriate the worker for suf-ficient reason, including non-compliance and refusal to work. This, some critics argued, discouraged the worker from reporting abusive labour practices for fear of being returned home and/or not being hired for the following season. Moreover, those who attempted to report abuses could be required to leave the country before their claims were addressed. Additional areas of concern related to the exclusion of temporary workers from some provincial labour standards legislation such as the Occupational Health and Safety Act and the Employment Standards Act in Ontario.[42]

The relatively free reign provided to employers under the temporary worker programs drew the ire of labour advocates. In a critique reminiscent of complaints about the foreign contract labour system active in the late 1920s, one labour advocate summarized the concerns of human rights groups, the labour movement, immigrant settlement agencies, community-based migrant workers' advocates, and faith groups:

> These groups have been witness to how guest workers are fleeced by unscrupulous labour brokers who charge exorbitant 'processing fees' in exchange for work permits; how workers are misled with false promises about wages and working conditions; how they are exploited, intimidated and threatened with deportation by some employers unless they accept terms akin to indentured servitude; how they are faced with social isolation and separation from their families and communities; and, additionally, how they are sometimes exposed to sickening doses of racism and discrimination from the communities in which they work.[43]

Organized labour accused some companies of substituting temporary workers for permanent workers, particularly when labour negotiations did not result in desired concessions from their regular staff.[44] In a 2005 research paper prepared by the Canadian Labour Congress (CLC), the weaknesses of temporary worker programs were summarized as follows:

> Migrant workers in substandard work situations represent an underclass of workers in Canada. Their biggest obstacles are language and literacy. The jobs that they take in Canada often do not meet minimum employment or occupational health and safety standards. These jobs are the worst paid, most dangerous jobs where the workers are most vulnerable to their employers. They cannot easily switch jobs without their employers' co-operation because visas are employer-specific. Contractually they cannot change jobs at all. They must pack their bags and leave Canada immediately after receiving their notice of termination. There is no appeal process to dispute unfair and forced repatriation. Workers are very unlikely to receive any of the benefits of their

social contributions. Foreign workers are the least likely workforce to protest substandard conditions, unaware of federal and provincial legislation, vulnerable to the demands of their employers and often constrained by poor comprehension of English or French and lack of literacy in their own languages.[45]

The CLC recommended that adequately resourced monitoring mechanisms and minimum employment standards be put in place to protect and promote the rights of temporary foreign workers. Employment standards, it said, should be supported by a system to investigate all allegations of mistreatment of foreign workers, who should be advised that these systems exist. It further recommended that temporary workers be permitted to change employers and argued for a more inclusive role for organized labour, together with the business community, in the development of temporary-labour migration policy.

Other advocates of workers' rights called for greater government involvement in protecting the workers through the application of the relevant safety and employment standards and the minimization and clarification of when the repatriation clause could be employed.[46] Some who supported an expansion of the temporary foreign workers programs also agreed that foreign workers should have at least minimal rights to protection by employment standards legislation.[47]

These calls for further protections went largely unheeded. Meanwhile the program expanded over the years, making it possible to address labour needs in a wider range of industries at both the regional and national level as well as accommodating company-specific arrangements. In September 2006 temporary foreign-worker units were established in Calgary and Vancouver to make the program more efficient and accessible to potential employers.[48] The following year, the governing Conservative party introduced the Expedited Labour Market Opinion, applicable for various occupations, and reduced the paperwork and administrative approval time from months to days. In 2008, the program was further enhanced by the introduction of the Canada Experience Class, which permitted temporary workers, after one year of employment in Canada, to apply from within Canada for permanent-residence status, provided they fell within certain employment categories.[49]

Efforts to expedite the processing of entrants under a temporary foreign worker program were a prelude to a much more dramatic shift in policy in 2008 that was designed to speed up the admission of immigrants within the economic class as a whole. Business interests had long complained that excessive processing times, which grew annually, severely undercut their ability to gain access to and benefit from skilled labour that was in short supply in Canada. The Canadian Chamber of Commerce was critical of the fact that Canadian immigration services abroad were unevenly resourced, leading to excessive processing delays in some regions relative to others. It cited the example of Africa and Asia, where in 2005 it took close to three years to process 50 per cent of the cases as compared to a one-year waiting period for most cases originating in Europe. It further observed that the high demand for labour in many industries and the excessive immigrant-skilled-worker processing times encouraged many workers to enter the country illegally or overstay their visas. Rather than removing them, the Chamber of Commerce suggested, the government should regularize their status, streamline the overseas screening process, and amend the law to permit temporary foreign workers to apply for permanent-residence status in Canada.[50] Two years after these recommendations, when the backlog of immigration applications for the skilled category was close to 600,000 cases, the Canadian Federation of Independent Business issued a report calling for a reduction in waiting times and more emphasis on skilled workers.[51]

Many business associations therefore enthusiastically greeted the 2008 changes to the law that gave the minister expanded discretion in the processing of immigration applications. Previously, all immigration applications had to be processed in the order received. The new provisions waived these requirements and gave the minister the power to instruct immigration officers to fast-track applications from certain skilled occupations that were determined by the minister to be in high demand.

The provisions were introduced at a time when the backlog of immigration cases to be processed had reached 925,000, with people waiting up to six years for a decision. In the absence of change, it was predicted, the backlog would grow to 1.5 million by 2012, with waiting times of as much as ten years.

Speaking for the Independent Contractors and Business Associations of British Columbia, Philip Hochstein applauded the change, which he felt showed that the 'politicians have realized that the system was just completely broken' and that dramatic action was needed to fix an outmoded system that no longer worked.[52]

The amendments to the Immigration and Refugee Protection Act were introduced to Parliament in two pages of a much larger 136-page Budget Implementation Act. Because they were introduced in this way, the proposals were not entitled to separate debate nor to examination by a House of Commons committee. The only effective means to oppose the provisions was to vote against the budget bill, the defeat of which would be a vote of non-confidence in the government and would provoke an early election. Although opposition parties were against the proposed changes, the Liberal party members declined to vote against the bill, as a non-confidence vote would have led to an election they were not confident of winning.

Not only members of the opposition but also lawyers and advocacy groups overwhelmingly opposed the changes and the broad powers they gave to the minister to alter the immigration application process in a substantial way without the need to pass new laws or regulations. Critics argued that the changes would further shield immigration decisions from public scrutiny and would deny basic rights to foreigners seeking to come to Canada. They claimed that, rather than ensuring sufficient resources to immigration offices abroad, the provisions would result in Canada's turning away people who met the requirements to immigrate. Noting that there have always been problems with the accountability of visa officers in foreign countries, they predicted that such problems would be exacerbated.[53] Others noted that the new policy harked back to the reliance on occupational lists of the former act – a system discredited as not being responsive enough to the occupational needs of the provinces.[54]

Although the changes did not apply to family class and refugee applications, they did apply to many applications invoking humanitarian and compassionate considerations. This was another area of particular concern to advocates. The humanitarian and compassionate admission provisions, which had been used to grant permanent residence to on average 3,500 persons annually since 2003,[55] were designed to facilitate the immigration of those who did not fall strictly within the requirements of the act and regulations but who had compelling reasons for wanting to gain admission to Canada. For example, the mechanism was helpful to individuals such as refugee children who had come to Canada unaccompanied. Children were not permitted to sponsor family members, but they could be reunited with their parents under the humanitarian and compassionate provisions. The Canadian Council for Refugees predicted that the changes would affect family reunification in these and other compelling cases, since the humanitarian applications could easily be set aside based on other priorities set by the minister.[56] Others countered, however, that should the provinces wish to expedite such applications, they could do so under immigration agreements they had negotiated with the federal government.

Family Class

The act maintained the ability of Canadian citizens and permanent residents to sponsor their family members abroad. However, while the objective of the provisions remained, as in previous periods, 'to see that families are reunited in Canada,'[57] the means differed in key respects. In particular, the act broadened the categories of persons who could be sponsored, while the regulations imposed far more stringent requirements on sponsors.

The new act and regulations explicitly recognized same-sex partnerships and expanded eligibility to be sponsored to include spouses; common-law partners who had lived together for at least one year in a continuous, uninterrupted relationship; and conjugal partners who had not been able to marry or live together for reasons beyond their control.

Other changes included raising the age of dependent children from nineteen to twenty-two and including adopted children under this category. The regulations also provided for the sponsorship of members of the extended family, including parents and grandparents. Additionally, they recognized as eligible family members sisters, brothers, nephews, nieces, and orphaned grandchildren under eighteen years of age who were not married or in a common-law relationship. The regulations recognized as members of the extended family other relatives of any age and relationship provided that no other closer relatives could be sponsored and the sponsor did not have any other relatives in Canada.

As with earlier regulations, individuals wishing to sponsor their eligible relatives had to meet certain conditions. These principally were designed to ensure that the sponsored relative would be well taken care of and not become dependent upon the state. Specifically, sponsors had to show sufficient income – described as a low-income cut-off figure that was set by the government according to the size of the family. Sponsors had to sign an undertaking to provide financial support to the sponsored relative for a period of three years and up to ten years for a dependent child, or until the child turned twenty-five, whichever came first. Bars to sponsorship included having defaulted on a previous sponsorship agreement, immigration loan, or court-imposed support order; having received social assistance for reasons other than disability; and/or having been convicted of certain serious criminal offences. Persons wishing to sponsor their spouse or dependent child did not have to meet the low-income cut-off requirement, but in a departure from previous practice, they were not eligible to sponsor even immediate family members if they were in receipt of social assistance.

The more stringent sponsorship criteria did not appreciably affect the overall proportion of family class immigrants. This remained relatively constant throughout the period at approximately 27 per cent, although this was a significant decrease from the 40 per cent level of 1994. Nevertheless, some continued to claim that it was too high and argued that it should be reduced further in favour of more skilled applicants.[58]

This argument was based on evidence of the higher economic performance of skilled immigrants compared to those sponsored under the family class, as well as on the fact that sponsorship undertakings were difficult to enforce. The provincial and federal governments did not reveal the number of defaults on sponsorship undertakings, so the extent to which this was a serious problem was not clear. Nevertheless, some commentators held that there should be enhanced means to prevent default, or, in the case of default, that support should be provided by means other than the public treasury. Possible mechanisms suggested included requiring sponsors to post bonds with financial institutions to cover the costs of services that would otherwise be paid for by the state; requiring sponsors to buy annuities that would pay out annual benefits sufficient to take care of sponsored family members;[59] and/or a private insurance scheme to be paid for by the sponsor that would cover publicly funded social assistance, with the exception of education and health care.[60]

Critiques of the rules governing family class immigration from a different perspective regarded the more stringent criteria – specifically, the bar on the ability of sponsors in receipt of social assistance to be reunited with their immediate family – as particularly harsh in certain cases. For example, women with children who could not afford the child care that would allow them to work outside the home and had to resort to social assistance could be prevented from sponsoring their husbands, their best hope for ending their dependence on public relief. Additionally, some pointed to cases of women who were in Canada while being sponsored by their spouses and not permitted to work during that process as being unduly vulnerable to possible abuse by the sponsoring spouse.[61]

Refugees

As in the previous act, the new act provided for the admission to Canada of refugees selected abroad for resettlement and of those who arrived in Canada, claimed asylum, and were determined to be in need of international protection. Refugees selected abroad had also to be sponsored by either the government or a private group, either of which were obligated to provide financial assistance for at least one year. Extensions of this requirement for two to three years were possible, depending on the circumstances.

Resettlement from outside Canada

Under the act. three classes of persons could be considered for resettlement as permanent residents in Canada. The first, was the Convention Refugee Abroad Class, applied to those who met the international refugee definition: persons who are outside their country of origin[62] and are unable or unwilling to return because of a well-founded fear of persecution for reasons of race, religion, nationality, membership in a particular social group, or political opinion.

The second, the Country of Asylum Class, was for persons who had been or continued to be seriously and personally affected by civil war or armed conflict or who had suffered massive violations of human rights.

The third category, the Source Country Class, referred to those in refugee-like situations who continued to live at risk in their own country without the likelihood of a durable solution within a reasonable period of time. Applicable countries were set out in the regulations. Government sponsorships were only open to those falling within the first and the third class. Private groups could sponsor individuals falling within any of the three classes.

The Office of the United Nations High Commissioner for Refugees (UNHCR) or another organization with which the government had a special agreement could refer refugees for sponsorship. As previously, visa officers determined whether the person identified was eligible, and those selected were subject to medical and security clearances before being granted admission. In exceptional cases, for those in immediate danger or particularly vulnerable to risk, medical inadmissibility grounds could be waived and processing expedited.

The number of refugees selected from outside Canada and admitted annually remained relatively constant throughout this period. On average, some 7,500 refugees were admitted each year under the government sponsorship program and 3,200 under private sponsorships, the combined total varying from between 4 and 5 per cent of total immigrant admissions each year.[63]

Refugee Determination within Canada

The act extended protection beyond those who meet the Convention refugee definition to include as well those who may not be Convention refugees but whose lives may be at risk or who may be subject to torture, cruel or unusual treatment, or punishment. This extended definition was intended to give effect to Canada's obligations under the 1984 Convention Against Torture.[64]

While the grounds for receiving protected status were broader, so too were the grounds for finding a person ineligible to claim the protection of Canada, a determination made by an immigration officer. Ineligibility grounds included those pertaining to criminality and security that were equally applicable to others entering Canada (discussed below) as well as additional grounds relevant to refugees. For example, a person was not eligible to make a claim to protection in Canada if the person had been recognized as a Convention refugee by another country or had arrived in Canada directly or indirectly from another country that was designated as a 'safe third country.' Moreover, the right to make a repeat claim to protection was tightly circumscribed by provisions that made a person ineligible to have a claim to protection determined if they abandoned or withdrew their previous claim, if their previous claim was rejected either as ineligible or on the merits, or if their protected status under a previously successful claim was subsequently removed.

As with previous legislation, those found to be eligible to make a refugee claim were referred to the Immigration and Refugee Board, where their claims were determined in a quasi-judicial hearing. However, only one board member made the determination, rather than two as in the previous legislation. The act provided for the first time the right to appeal from a negative decision to a specialized Refugee Appeal Division. However, successive governments failed to institute the Refugee Appeal Division, leaving Canada as one of a very few refugee-receiving countries in the developed world without some form of merit-based appeal.[65]

The eligibility provisions of the act and regulations proved the most controversial, with legal advocates and civil society groups arguing that the breadth of the provisions could bar even very deserving claimants from receiving protection. They asserted that, given the risks faced by those in genuine need of international protection, the relatively broad grounds for denying access went far beyond what was actually needed to ensure the security and integrity of the system. These critics acknowledged that exclusion from international protection was justified in certain circumstances set out in the international Refugee Convention and included in the Canadian act. However, they claimed that the way the act extended the grounds and empowered immigration officers to decide whether to exclude did not accord with acceptable international standards.[66]

They cited in support of their arguments UNHCR guidelines on international protection. The guidelines, which were revised in 2003, note that the international Convention refugee definition excludes from international protection those who have been recognized in another country as having rights and obligations as a national of that country.[67] It also excludes those who there are reasonable grounds to believe have committed a crime against peace, a war crime, a crime against humanity, or a serious non-political crime, or who are guilty of acts contrary to the purposes and principles of the United Nations.[68] The first category relates to those who are not in need of international protection, while the second refers to those who are undeserving. As explained by UNHCR, the latter provisions are intended to deprive those guilty of 'heinous acts, and serious common crimes' from abusing the institution of asylum in order to avoid being held legally accountable for their acts.[69] The problem with the Canadian provisions, the critics said, was that they could also capture those who may have committed relatively minor criminal offences or who were members of an organization that was listed as engaging in terrorism even though the individual might not have known about such activities or was not a member at the time the organization engaged in prohibited acts.[70]

Critics further claimed that the Canadian process did not respect aspects of the guidelines that counselled the application of the exclusion provisions in a manner that was proportionate to their objectives, 'so that the gravity of the offence in question is weighed against the consequences of exclusion'[71] and that afforded rigorous procedural safeguards, given the grave consequences that could befall a person who was excluded. Such safeguards included dealing with exclusion issues not in admissibility or accelerated procedures but within the context of the regular refugee status determination procedure, and ensuring that the state bears the burden of proof in regard to exclusion, save in exceptional circumstances.[72]

Among the other ineligibility provisions considered by some as overly broad were those that prevented refugees who had made a previous claim and refugees who had been recognized elsewhere from having their claims determined. The problem with these conditions, some argued, was that they applied regardless of the particular circumstances in the individual case. Therefore, individuals previously denied status could not make another claim even if the situation in the country where they feared to be at risk had changed substantially or new evidence had come to light to substantiate the facts of their prior claim. Similarly, individuals who were found to have received protection in another country could be denied access to the Canadian system without being able to demonstrate that the country might not be safe in their particular case.

Individuals found ineligible to make a refugee claim in Canada could apply to remain in Canada through the Pre-Removal Risk Assessment. This was an administrative review of their case done on the basis of a written submission. It did not provide an opportunity to appear before the decision maker or to appeal the decision. It was rarely exercised in favour of the applicant.[73]

Although only a small percentage of applicants were found to be ineligible to make a refugee claim in Canada under the new provisions, advocates argued that the grave consequences that could befall an individual who was inappropriately excluded far outweighed the savings to the government provided by the screening mechanism.

Also vigorously debated was the provision that excluded from the asylum system those who had travelled through a safe third country as identified in the regulations. Although this provision had been introduced in the previous period, it was not until the implementation of the Safe Third Country Agreement with the United States in 2004 that it was actually applied.[74] The agreement provided that refugee claimants had to seek asylum (protection) in the first safe country in which they arrived. This meant that those coming to Canada from the United States would not be eligible to claim refugee protection in Canada unless they fell within certain exceptions such as persons with family in Canada, unaccompanied minors, or persons who did not require a visa to enter the country. The provision was justified by the government as necessary to 'create an effective measure of control to limit abuse of Canada's refugee determination system.'[75]

The Safe Third Country Agreement with the United States came under sustained criticism from refugee advocates, who questioned whether the United States should qualify as a safe third country, given its human rights record, its 'war on terror,' and, in particular, its perceived failure to live up to its requirements under international law, including the Convention Against Torture.[76]

Conversely, critics on the right complained that the agreement was not effective enough, noting that in 2005, of the 4,033 claims made at the border, the vast majority fitted within one of the exceptions, with only 303 refugees being returned to the United States as ineligible to apply in Canada.[77] Refugee advocates, however, countered that a far more telling measure was the number of claims that were not made because of the agreement.[78] In 2004 there were 19 per cent fewer refugee claims made in

Canada than in the previous year. The annual number dropped a further 16 per cent the following year to just 20,753 claims, the lowest annual number experienced over the previous twenty years.[79]

The drop, advocates argued, was of significant concern given the fewer procedural and substantive protections afforded to certain classes of refugees in the United States. Specifically, they highlighted the extremely high incidence of detention of refugees in the United States; the tough and comparatively broad exclusion provisions (which include denying access to refugee procedures for those who had been in the country for longer than a year); and a questionable human rights record, specifically with regard to compliance with the Convention Against Torture.[80] They also noted the difference in jurisprudence in the United States, citing as an example a much more restrictive approach than in Canada to claims based on persecution for reasons of gender, with the attendant risk that women who would be recognized as refugees in Canada could have their claims denied in the United States.[81]

The constitutionality of the Safe Third Country Agreement was challenged in the Federal Court of Canada in 2006, and again in 2007 in the Federal Court of Appeal. The lower court struck down the agreement as unconstitutional, a decision that was overturned on appeal.[82]

Before the Safe Third Country Agreement came into effect, the government extended its use of the practice of 'directing back' refugee claimants temporarily to the United States to await their eligibility interview in Canada. Previously, this measure had been used only in exceptional cases. Beginning in 2003, however, Canada experienced a surge in claims coming from the United States, as asylum seekers in that country worried that once the Safe Third Country Agreement came into effect they might be refused access to the Canadian system. In response, the 'direct back' measure was used much more routinely. Advocates alleged that this was being done without proper assurances from the American authorities. As a result, some returnees were reported to have been detained in the United States and removed to their countries of origin, where they were possibly at risk, without an opportunity for the claims to be determined in Canada. The procedure prompted a complaint in 2004 by several national and international organizations to the Inter-American Commission on Human Rights,[83] and provoked an expression of deep concern by the UNHCR in 2007 over the continuation of the policy despite a written commitment it had received from the Canadian authorities to cease the practice.[84]

Individuals found eligible to make a refugee claim were referred to the Immigration and Refugee Board to determine their claim to protection.

Although failed refugee claimants could seek leave to apply for review of the decision in the Federal Court of Canada, leave to apply was granted for only some 10 per cent of cases. Reasons for refusal of leave were not provided. An additional avenue was an administrative review under the Pre-Removal Risk Assessment procedure in which the person could present new evidence but could not argue that the original decision was wrong. It was rarely exercised in favour of the applicant. A final avenue was for rejected applicants to apply for permanent residence on humanitarian and compassionate grounds. This was a strictly discretionary ministerial decision, and the applicant could be deported before a decision was rendered.

Following the implementation of the new act, successive Canadian governments justified their unwillingness to provide an appeal on the merits for a variety of reasons, ranging from cost to a backlog of claims to plans to overhaul the entire refugee determination process.[85] Advocates have been severely critical of this lack of action. Citing statements of concern from international bodies such as the Inter-American Commission on Human Rights and the UNHCR,[86] as well as from the Canadian Parliamentary Standing Committee on Citizenship and Immigration,[87] they contended that the lack of an appeal on the merits was not only unfair to refugees but also an international embarrassment.[88]

The absence of an appeal mechanism was further aggravated, according to some critics, by the variable quality of decision making by the Immigration and Refugee Board. Appointments to the IRB had always been controlled by the minister of Citizenship and Immigration, although progressive reforms introduced in the late 1990s and early 2000s attempted to provide greater scope for the management of the IRB to participate in the selection and reappointment of members based more on merit-based criteria. These efforts were reversed in the winter of 2006 when the newly elected Conservative government introduced changes to give the minister even greater control and discretion. The chair of the IRB unexpectedly resigned at this time, eight months before the end of his mandate, leading to speculation that he did so in protest, having been a strong advocate for a more merit-based appointments process.[89]

Further controversy over the appointment of members surfaced again in 2008 when the government's failure to fill vacancies on the board increased the backlog of undecided cases to what the chair warned were crisis proportions. In 2006 there had been no backlog. In the intervening years the government had left 35 per cent of the positions for decision makers vacant, so that by 2008 the backlog of undecided cases had

ballooned to more than 62,000. Some accused the government of deliberately creating the backlog in order to justify scrapping the independent
tribunal altogether in favour of an administrative mechanism.[90]

With increased media attention given to this issue, the government
proceeded to appoint new members. Meanwhile a private member introduced Bill C-280, designed to amend the Immigration and Refugee
Protection Act for the creation of the Refugee Appeal Division. In June
2008 the bill passed third reading in the Senate, where it was amended
and returned to the House of Commons. It died on the Order Paper
when Parliament was dissolved with the federal election call in the fall
of 2008.

Deportation

Consistent with the broadening of the grounds for which a person could
be denied admission to Canada, the act correspondingly expanded the
basis upon which a person other than a Canadian citizen could be removed.[91] Grounds for removal included security (espionage, subversion
of a democratic government, terrorism), serious violations of human
rights, criminality (including organized crime), and misrepresentation.[92]

In regard to criminality, the threshold for removal of permanent residents, although relatively broad, remained higher than for other foreigners. A permanent resident could be removed for having been convicted
of an offence punishable by a possible penalty of at least ten years of
imprisonment (regardless of the actual sentence), or if the person was
sentenced to more than six months of imprisonment.[93] Other foreigners
could be removed for these and less serious offences (including some
summary offences) regardless of the length of the sentence.[94]

In addition to expanding the grounds for removal, the act also restricted the basis for appealing a removal decision. It considerably circumscribed the review jurisdiction of the Immigration and Refugee Board by
removing its jurisdiction to hear appeals by permanent residents against
removal orders based on security, human rights violations, and criminality
grounds unless the person had received a sentence of less than two years.
In that case, the IRB retained the right to review the removal order on the
basis of law, fact, and humanitarian and compassionate grounds. The
curtailment of the board's jurisdiction was a significant departure from
the 1976 act. As acknowledged by the Supreme Court in 2005, the new
act reflected a shift in priorities. Comparing the objectives of the two acts,
the court observed that the objectives of the new act 'and its provisions

concerning permanent residents, communicate a strong desire to treat criminals and security threats less leniently than under the former Act.'[95]

Critics claimed that the removal provisions were far too broad and failed to provide sufficient opportunity to take into account humanitarian and compassionate considerations that would militate against removal.[96] Long-term residents of Canada who fell within the criminality provisions, including persons with mental disabilities that may have contributed to their conviction, were cases in point. They were liable to be removed from Canada to their country of citizenship, where they might not have been for many years (including since early childhood) and where they might not have family or other support systems to help them get re-established. Similarly, the act maintained the authority provided to the minister of Citizenship and Immigration in 1994[97] to issue a danger opinion against a refugee applicant on the basis of serious criminality. This had the effect of staying the refugee proceedings, removing the case from the jurisdiction of the IRB to hear the claim to protection or to review a removal order. Advocates claimed that this enhanced the risk that a person could be removed to a place where persecution was feared without an opportunity to have the grievousness of the offence and the danger to the public weighed against the potential risk to life and security of the person being removed.

The act also reintroduced the use of security certificates and streamlined the procedures to expedite removal of those against whom they were issued. Security certificates were issued by the minister of Public Safety and Emergency Preparedness and the minister of Citizenship and Immigration, and could be issued against permanent residents and other foreign residents, including refugees. Certificates could be issued on grounds of security, violation of human or international rights, serious criminality, or organized criminality.

Once a certificate was issued, it had to be reviewed by a judge of the Federal Court. The court was restricted to considering whether the certificate was reasonable, not whether it was correct. The review process was significant, for if the certificate was found to be reasonable by the judge then the decision could not be appealed and constituted valid grounds for removal. Hearings were not open to the public, and the person who was the subject of the hearing did not have the right to be present or to receive all the evidence upon which the certificate was issued.[98] Moreover, the issuing of the certificate triggered the automatic detention of the person concerned, who could be held without a detention review for up to 120 days if the person was a foreigner, as opposed to forty-eight hours in the case of a permanent resident.[99] To be released, the person had to establish that he or she did not pose a threat to the safety of Canadians and that the amount of time in detention prior to removal would be unreasonable.[100] Detention could be indefinite, depending on when the removal could be effected, with some individuals being detained for years.

The use of security certificates was closely scrutinized and litigated. Some argued that the certificates had been overused and improperly employed as a substitute for criminal proceedings to avoid the more rigorous standard of proof and the due-process protections of such proceedings – protections that are appropriate given the risks faced by the persons concerned.[101] It was also argued that the grounds for issuing a security certificate, including membership in an organization that had committed or was likely to commit a terrorist act, were vague and liable to enmesh innocent as well as complicit individuals. The immigration act did not include the qualifiers contained in similar provisions in the Criminal Code that more clearly defined terrorism and excluded 'activity which is the result of advocacy, protest, dissent or stoppage of work that is not intended to result in harm.'[102] Commentators contended that the immigration legislation thus could include activities that would otherwise be considered lawful dissent and could also apply to individuals who, for social and charitable reasons not associated with violent activity of any kind, were members of an organization that had since been declared a terrorist organization.

These issues were canvassed in the Supreme Court of Canada decision in the case of Suresh,[103] a Sri Lankan Tamil against whom a danger opinion and removal order had been issued on the grounds that he was a member of a terrorist organization (the LTTE) and a threat to the security of Canada. The case was argued before but not decided until after the terrorist attacks of 11 September 2001.

Suresh made several arguments before the court. He claimed that the grounds of 'terrorism' and 'danger to the public' upon which his removal was based were unconstitutionally vague. He also argued that, if removed, he would face torture in Sri Lanka contrary to his Charter rights and to international law and that the process under which the certificate had been reviewed was also unconstitutional, as it denied him his right to due process.

In a unanimous decision, the court concluded that while removal to torture would almost always be disproportionate to the interests of the state, it might be constitutionally permissible in exceptional cases such as 'natural disasters, the outbreak of war, and the like.' Although the court could not find an authoritative international definition of 'terrorism' or 'danger to the public,' it nevertheless held that the terms were not unconstitutionally vague, finding guidance for the former in the international Convention for the Suppression of the Financing of Terrorism. Moreover, it said that the approach to 'danger to the public' must be flexible and that the requirement in place prior to 9/11 to provide proof of a direct threat to Canada set the bar too high.[104]

In regard to the review hearing itself, the court concluded that Suresh was entitled to more procedural protections than he was afforded. In particular, if Suresh could establish a *prima facie* case that he would be tortured if removed to Sri Lanka, then he was entitled to the reasons upon which the minister's opinion was based (except material for which non-disclosure was justified in the interests of security) and an opportunity to respond and present evidence and a legal argument. The decision as to whether a *prima facie* case was established was the minister's, a decision which the court characterized as factual in nature, largely outside the expertise of the reviewing court, and therefore justifying a higher level of deference.

The court's judgment reflected a striking shift from its earlier jurisprudence in *Singh,* where it had held that an oral hearing was required in every refugee determination case, given that serious issues of credibility were involved and the potential risks faced by a person who was returned to a country where his life or freedom are threatened. In *Suresh,* however, the burden was on the applicant to establish a *prima facie* case before certain due process protections would be afforded, and these protections did not necessarily include an oral hearing. Even more limiting was the court's emphasis that the level of procedural protections to be afforded to those who faced torture 'need not be invoked in every case.' This left open the question of what types of threats to life or security would fall short of torture and not warrant the limited protections provided to Suresh.

Legal commentators subsequently observed that lower courts have been similarly deferential to claims by the authorities that more stringent protections, such as a requirement for disclosure of confidential information, would be injurious to national security. They claimed that the normal checks and balances that form part of our justice system were more readily abrogated in the name of national security.[105]

The potential excessive use of discretion and the consequences of the increased latitude accorded to security services following 11 September 2001 came into sharp relief in the case of Maher Arar. Arar was a Canadian citizen born in Syria who was detained by American officials while in transit there and deported to Syria, where he was tortured and detained under inhumane conditions for more than eleven months.

A commission of inquiry, set up to examine the case following Arar's eventual return to Canada amid much publicity, concluded that it was very likely that the U.S. authorities had relied on information about Arar provided by the Royal Canadian Mounted Police, including unfounded suspicions linking him to terrorist groups.[106] In his final report, the commissioner recommended enhanced review and accountability mechanisms for agencies dealing with national security, including not only the Royal Canadian Mounted Police but also the Department of Citizenship and Immigration and the Canada Border Services Agency.

Following the Arar inquiry, another commission of inquiry was established to examine the actions of Canadian officials in regard to the detention and torture of three Canadians, Abdullah Almalki, Muayyed Nureddin and Ahmad Elmaati, in Syria between 2001 and 2004. Elmaati was also sent to Egypt and tortured there. The commissioner, Justice Frank Iacobucci, issued his report in October 2008, concluding that federal security officials were 'indirectly' responsible for the torture of the three Canadians. Specifically, he found that the authorities had sent inaccurate, inflammatory, and ill-considered intelligence to U.S. and Middle East agencies, wrongly labelling people who had not been arrested in Canada as 'imminent threats.' Once the men were jailed in the Middle East, he found that such messages from the Canadian authorities made their ordeal worse.[107]

It was against the backdrop of these inquiries that the Supreme Court of Canada was again asked to consider the constitutionality of the removal of persons considered to be security threats. In June 2007 it issued its judgment in the case of *Charkaoui*.[108] The decision of the court stands in contrast to its decision in *Suresh* six years earlier.

This case involved three appellants – a permanent resident, Adil Charkaoui, and two others who were recognized refugees. All had been arrested and detained on the basis that they constituted a threat to the security of Canada by reason of involvement in terrorist activities. Two were released on conditions after a number of years in detention; the third remained in detention, having been there for more than five years.

Consistent with its earlier rulings, the Supreme Court maintained that the deportation of a non-citizen in the immigration context may not in itself engage the Charter's section 7 right to 'life, liberty and security of the person and the right not to be deprived thereof except in accordance with the principles of fundamental justice.' However, it found that the 'features associated with deportation' may do so. It reasoned that in this case a section 7 right was clearly engaged because the person named in a certificate faced detention pending the outcome of the proceedings and because the process might lead to the person's removal to a place where his or her life or freedom would be threatened. As such, the procedures had to be in accordance with the principles of fundamental justice, a criterion which the procedures applied to Charkaoui did not meet.

Specifically, the court found that because the person concerned did not have a right to know the evidence on which the government's case was based, the person's right to a fair hearing was compromised. Either the person had to be given the necessary information or a substantial substitute for that information had to be found. The act provided neither. These deficiencies were not reasonably justified, since there were alternatives available to the government that infringed less on the rights of the individual concerned, such as the use of special counsel to act on behalf of persons named in the security certificates.

In regard to detention, the court concluded that the detention of foreign nationals without warrant did not infringe the guarantee against arbitrary detention in section 9 of the Charter but that the lack of a timely review did. It could find no reasonable justification for delaying a review of the detention of a foreign resident for 120 days when permanent residents were entitled to a review within forty-eight hours. While there might be a need for some flexibility regarding the period for which a suspected terrorist could be detained, the court stated that this could not justify the complete denial of a timely detention review. The court's decision confirmed that where a person was detained or was subject to onerous conditions of release for an extended period under immigration law, there had to be a meaningful and ongoing review of the individual case, including an opportunity for the person to challenge his or her continued detention or the conditions of his or her release.

The court suspended its declaration of the unconstitutionality of the provisions for one year to give the government time to make the necessary amendments. These were introduced in February 2008 and provided for the appointment of a 'special advocate' for persons who were the subject of a security certificate. The special advocate, appointed by the government, had access to the evidence against the person and the right to challenge the government's case. However, the advocate was not to disclose or discuss with the person concerned information classified as secret that might form the basis of the case against that person. Some legal observers contended that the amendments were unconstitutional and did not redress the lack of procedural safeguards found by the Supreme Court.[109]

Citizenship

The means of acquiring citizenship remained largely the same as in previous periods: birth in Canada; birth outside Canada to a Canadian parent; and naturalization, with the addition of citizenship by adoption added in 2007.[110] Naturalization was available to permanent residents who had lived in Canada for at least three years of the previous four, and who did not have a criminal record of a kind prohibited by the act.[111] Applicants had also to demonstrate a basic understanding of and ability to communicate in English or French and a basic understanding of the rights and responsibilities of citizens and of Canada's geography, political system, and social and cultural history. Those who passed the citizenship test had to appear before a citizenship judge, where they took an oath of citizenship and received their Citizenship Certificate.

Several attempts were made during the period to overhaul the Citizenship Act, with three separate bills to this effect being introduced in Parliament between 1998 and 2003.[112] None of the bills were enacted, largely because the parliamentary sessions in which they were introduced ended before the bills could be passed. The changes proposed would have made it more difficult to acquire Canadian citizenship and easier to lose citizenship once acquired.

Among the more controversial proposals were those that would have (1) tightened the residency requirements before a permanent resident could apply for citizenship;[113] (2) given the minister the authority to deny citizenship on the basis that a person had 'demonstrated a flagrant and serious disregard for the principles and values underlying a free and democratic society';[114] and (3) denied citizenship to persons who had been charged with a criminal offence or convicted of offences outside Canada.[115] Other controversial proposed changes were those expanding the grounds for revocation of citizenship for a number of reasons and by means that critics claimed were not fully transparent and did not afford the person concerned a meaningful opportunity to be heard.[116]

In 2005, the House of Commons Standing Committee on Citizenship and Immigration issued two reports on proposed reforms to the current Citizenship Act: *Citizenship Revocation: A Question of Due Process*, and *Respecting Charter Rights and Updating Canada's Citizenship Laws: It's Time.*[117]

The committee endorsed the three-year residency requirement for naturalization but not the proposed six-year limit within which the residency requirement had to be met, on the grounds that this latter requirement was arbitrary and unnecessary. It also endorsed the recommendation that protected persons should be given full credit for every day they had lived in Canada from the time they had initiated their claim. In its discussion of revocation of citizenship the committee held that, once citizenship was legally granted, any future conduct should be dealt with through Canada's criminal justice system, stating that '[i]f citizenship is legitimately awarded and there is no question as to fraud in the application process, a person who later commits a crime is "our criminal"'[118] and should not be subjected to the revocation of citizenship. It also argued against provisions that granted the minister discretion to deny citizenship, as it found that the proposed provision was too vaguely worded to warrant being included in any future bill.

One significant development in regard to citizenship that was resolved in this period concerned the uncertain status of many thousands of persons who had unwittingly lost Canadian citizenship or been denied it as a result of various changes to citizenship legislation between the 1947 Citizenship Act and the still operative Citizenship Act of 1977.[119] The 'lost Canadians,' as they were known, were those born in the years between the two acts who were often unwittingly caught by rules introduced in the intervening period of which they were unaware or which did not clearly address their particular circumstances.[120] The plight of these persons, whose numbers were estimated at close to 200,000, came to public attention in 2007 with media reports on how the application of outdated provisions in existing and former citizenship laws had left thousands of persons without Canadian citizenship and rendered a large proportion stateless.[121]

Categories of lost citizens included children born outside Canada whose father had taken citizenship of another country; European war brides and their babies who had been born abroad to Canadian fathers; border babies (children born in hospitals on the American side of the Canadian border, a common occurrence during the 1950s and 1960s); and children born out of wedlock to a Canadian father and a non-Canadian mother as well as children born in wedlock to a Canadian mother and a non-Canadian father.[122] The Supreme Court of Canada found that the provisions which treated children of Canadian mothers differently than those of Canadian fathers were unconstitutional in 1997, but a full response to the problem of lost children took another decade.[123]

Government amendments to the Citizenship Act were introduced in 2007 and passed into law in April of the following year. According to the minister, these amendments resolved the problems of close to 95 per cent of the 'lost Canadians,' enabling them to be recognized as citizens of Canada.[124] While the amendments were greeted warmly by the majority of those who had advocated a resolution of the situation for many years, some commentators remained concerned that, in not addressing the circumstances of all 'lost Canadians,' the provisions could leave some people stateless and therefore were not consistent with Canada's obligations under the international 1961 Convention on the Reduction of Statelessness.[125]

The Benefits of Immigration Revisited

In the past, the economic benefits of immigration were hotly debated, and this period was no exception. In fact the scope of the debate widened as more and more studies looked at global trends in migration and the effect of migration on countries experiencing emigration and/or immigration.[126] From a global perspective, one school of thought held that immigration was economically beneficial to the host country.[127] Making parallels between the benefits of the free movement of goods (free trade) and the free movement of people, proponents of this school argued that removing immigration barriers would lead to an increase in world income, with one study suggesting that removing immigration controls could double the size of the world economy and another positing that gains from free migration could be as high as $55.04 trillion (U.S.).[128] Those who favoured relatively unrestricted migration argued that it would increase incomes in both host and sending countries.[129] Immigrants, they said, bring net benefits, not only because they supply labour but also because they require goods and services, thus increasing the demand for locally supplied labour.[130] Moreover, these authors pointed out, immigrants and native workers often competed for different types of jobs and were more likely to complement than replace one another. In this way, increased immigration would have a net positive effect on the domestic labour market in the host country.[131]

Within the Canadian context, some studies found on balance that increased immigration tended to generate a net fiscal surplus, playing little observable role in reducing wages or increasing unemployment and not increasing the burden on the welfare state.[132] However, it was also found that immigrants of the preceding twenty years fared less well than those who had arrived in earlier periods, with a widening gap between the earnings of the Canadian born and the foreign born.[133] This prompted considerable public discussion, with debates tending to focus on a few key issues, such as whether Canada needed high levels of immigration and, if so, whether the system met that need appropriately and delivered the positive effects anticipated.

The government consistently maintained that high rates of immigration were necessary.[134] Specifically citing declining population growth rates and a need to address a slowing and ultimate reversal in labour-force growth, in 2005 the minister proposed a long-term objective of annual immigration levels of 1 per cent of the population. This represented a 45 per cent increase over the average of the preceding ten years to approximately 320,000 immigrants a year. While subsequent years did not see such a dramatic increase, annual immigration rates remained high, averaging 240,000, with annual total admissions of permanent residents, temporary workers, and foreign students reaching a historic high of more than 475,000 persons in 2007.[135]

The government's contention that declining fertility and the aging of the Canadian population required high levels of immigration to address short- and long-term labour-market needs found support in some academic studies. In fact, some suggested that the government had underestimated potential labour-market shortages and that the proportion of working-age persons needed to finance publicly funded health and income-security programs was declining.[136] They therefore called for even more robust immigration as the only way to ensure the continued growth of the Canadian labour market and economy.[137] Suggested reforms to encourage increases included de-emphasizing skilled workers in recognition of the important economic role low-skilled immigrants played and giving more power to private parties in securing immigrant workers so as to allow the needs of the labour market to indirectly determine the number of immigrants admitted each year.[138]

A more extreme view called for the complete privatization of the immigration plan, replacing the government point system with a system based on temporary work visas. Only those with a confirmed employment offer in a designated area would be eligible to enter, with either a complete elimination of the family program or, alternatively, stricter financial prerequisites for sponsors to ensure that those sponsored were not eligible to receive government-funded social services.[139]

The assertion that Canada needed high immigration levels, shared by most business associations throughout the country, did not go unchallenged. In a 2006 publication, the C.D. Howe Institute concluded that while there might be good reasons for high immigration levels for cultural and humanitarian reasons, they could not be justified on the basis of demographic arguments. The institute found that 'no conceivable amount of immigration with an age profile such as Canada currently experiences could significantly affect the coming shift in the ratio of older to working-age Canadians.'[140]

The authors of the report concluded that, while immigration could mitigate the immediate slowing down in labour-force growth, it could not relieve Canada of the challenges of an aging population except with a 'preposterously large' increase in the annual number of younger immigrants, a number that would be difficult to secure and manage.[141] These authors predicted, however, that the market would adjust to a declining supply of labour, as there would be upward pressure on wages, encouraging greater labour-market participation, higher incomes, and higher tax payments. Others suggested, moreover, that by the first decade of the twenty-first century, with baby boomers working longer and the 'echo' generation (the children of baby boomers) entering the workforce, a labour surplus was more likely than a shortage.[142] Any shortfall of skilled workers that might exist could be dealt with through further training of Canada's workforce.[143]

While there was no consensus on whether or not elevated levels of annual immigration were necessary, there was a high degree of agreement that the immigration system did not efficiently secure those with the skills Canada needed or ensure that the value of the skills and experience of immigrants was maximized after their arrival.

The long processing times were seen as a key weakness in the system, as was the reluctance of many employers to recognize foreign educational credentials and skills gained through on-the-job work experience, a factor that has a negative impact on immigrant economic performance.[144] In a 2005 address to the Canadian Manufacturers and Exporters Association, then Minister of Citizenship and Immigration Joe Volpe lamented the underuse of skilled, foreign-trained immigrant workers in Canada. He claimed that, while the government had successfully recruited the best and the brightest from abroad, their value to the Canadian economy was underutilized because many Canadian companies had a tendency to undervalue experience and education gained elsewhere. He urged Canadian companies to do more to help immigrants find jobs that use their skills. He noted that on average 14,000 engineers had immigrated to Toronto in each of the preceding five years, more than had graduated from Canadian universities. Yet many of these immigrants were not finding acceptance in their field of training. As a result, they worked in lower-skilled jobs, prompting the minister to observe that 'we probably have the best-educated taxi and limo trade in the world.'[145]

Another barrier, noted by the Canadian Chamber of Commerce, was a racial one. Pointing to reports by the Canadian Race Relations Foundation suggesting that discrimination might be a factor contributing to the underemployment of immigrants despite their relatively high levels of education, the Chamber of Commerce argued both for 'more support to leverage immigrants' skills and experience' and for 'programs and incentives to encourage employer involvement.'[146] Similarly, others argued for more investment in training or work experience for immigrants shortly after their arrival in Canada to enhance their job prospects.[147]

Other proposals made to enhance economic immigration focused on the admissibility criteria. One was to revise the application of points to give more weight to educational credentials, which would be recognized as equivalent to Canadian credentials and accompanied by a ranking scheme that would make it more difficult for employers to justify discrimination on the false ground of inferior education. This, in turn, would call for more cooperation between the Department of Citizenship and Immigration, educational institutions, Canadian professional associations, and employer groups. Another proposal advised increasing the points awarded for pre-arranged employment to help ensure that those who arrive 'hit the ground running with jobs they find attractive' and employers who recognize their skills.[148]

Conclusions

Looking back over the years between 1995 and 2008, one can see some discernible trends. The most salient was that the move towards more liberal values characteristic of the previous period was in many respects reversed. Whereas the provisions of the Immigration Act of 1976 were detailed and specific and constrained executive decision making in an unprecedented manner, those of the Immigration and Refugee Protection Act of 2002 were relatively lacking in specificity, leaving considerable discretion to the executive to determine and implement immigration admission, exclusion, and removal policies through regulations. The courts, which had played an active role in upholding individual immigration rights in the first half of the previous period, showed an increasing reluctance to intervene in executive decision making. This was particularly apparent in decisions concerned with removing individuals from Canada, where the court emphasized the century-old contention that immigration was a privilege not a right and, post-9/11, stressed that decisions based on security grounds warranted a high degree of deference.

This is not to suggest that the immigration policy of the period reverted back to the racist, exclusionary policy of old. Although admissibility criteria were tightened, they were tightened across the board, not, as in the first half of the twentieth century, primarily for particular racial or ethnic groups. In that respect, the commitment to a multicultural Canada remained relatively strong. Nevertheless, the tightening of admissibility criteria, the expanded grounds for removal, and the greater latitude accorded to the executive to alter the contours of immigration policy relatively free from parliamentary and judicial scrutiny were a reversal of the more liberal trends that had emerged in earlier periods.

Security concerns account in part for this trend. The previous period had ended with a fractious debate over refugee policy that was not resolved and that emerged forcefully again with the 1999 landing off the coast of British Columbia of the four ships carrying migrants. Public reaction to these unauthorized arrivals illustrated a relatively open hostility to unrestricted immigration and support for tighter controls on entry and streamlined removal mechanisms to secure Canadian borders and safeguard public safety. The terrorist attacks of 11 September 2001 reinforced those demands and, at least initially, contributed to a greater willingness on the part of the public and of the courts to support expanded latitude for the executive to remove suspected security threats from Canada without the level of due-process protections demanded by refugee advocates. The long and ultimately successful battle of Maher Arar tempered that support somewhat, although the basic procedures for effecting such removals remained largely intact.

While security concerns certainly played a role in this reversal, they do not explain it entirely. The new act was drafted long before 9/11, and the more conservative trends in Supreme Court of Canada judgments affecting immigrants were also evident years before.[149] Other salient factors shaping immigration policy at this time were the fact that immigrants were, on the whole, not faring as well economically as in previous years[150] and the fact that the immigration system itself was not responding effectively enough to what some employers complained was a chronic shortage of workers for their industries. Remedying these ills, the government maintained, called for a revision of admissibility criteria, greater emphasis on skills and education over family ties, streamlined procedures, and an expansion of temporary worker programs. The latter recommendation was revealing, for it reverted to a much earlier time when immigrant workers were sought for the services they could provide without any guarantees of more permanent membership in the Canadian community. That parallels were made between the lack of protection afforded to temporary workers and the turn-of-the-century treatment of other foreign workers, notably Chinese labourers, was not surprising.

In fact, the demands and debates over compensation for Chinese immigrants who had been forced to pay the head tax in the early twentieth
century and whose dependants were excluded from joining them in
Canada are a rather telling overlay on the underlying interests and values that shaped immigration policy in this period. Beginning in 1984,
the Chinese Canadian National Council (CCNC) waged a campaign for
redress on behalf of thousands of head-tax payers and their families.
They demanded compensation for the $23 million collected from the
tax, as well as an acknowledgment by the Canadian government of the
injustice and an apology for the consequences of the tax and the exclusion of Chinese immigrants effected through the Chinese Immigration
Act of 1923.

Throughout the 1990s, the Liberal government refused both demands,
and in 1999 the CCNC sued the government, arguing that since it had
apologized to Japanese Canadians in 1988 for their wartime internment,
the government should respond similarly to Chinese Canadians who had
suffered from the application of similar racist and exclusionary policies.
To do otherwise, they argued, was unjustifiably discriminatory and contrary to the Charter of Rights and Freedoms. Their legal arguments were
dismissed by both the trial court and the Ontario Court of Appeal,[151] but
their campaign did not end there. In fact, it continued to gain momentum, strengthened by the launching in 2003 of the Last Spike Redress
Campaign; by a report from the United Nations Special Rapporteur on
Racism, Racial Discrimination, Xenophobia and Related Intolerance,
which concluded that the government should provide redress; and by a
widely publicized 'ride for redress' initiated by the eighty-three-year-old
son of a head-tax payer who was also a Second World War veteran and
who, in the summer of 2005, rode across Canada on his Harley-Davidson
to bring attention to the issue. [152]

In the end, the decision to provide an apology and redress was finally
taken by the newly elected Conservative government in 2006 after the
issue had become both a very public and a very political one. Just before
losing power, the Liberal government had reached an agreement with a
Chinese Canadian group to pay $12.5 million for a non-profit foundation
to educate Canadians about anti-Chinese discrimination. The agreement
did not include any payments to victims, nor did it commit the government to an apology. Opposition within the Chinese Canadian community
was fierce and vocal, with allegations of improper dealings by the government negotiator, including the exclusion of the most active advocates
such as the CCNC. The bill died when the government was defeated, and,

not long after, the newly elected Conservative government provided what the community had waited more than twenty years to receive: an apology and compensation to those who had paid the tax.

The resolution of the Chinese head-tax dispute illustrated that, like many issues concerning Canadian immigration policy, outcomes are the result of a combination of values, interests, and institutions, which unite to produce results that reflect to some degree the temper of the times. In the end, redress came as the result of an executive and highly discretionary decision, taken after the courts had refused to recognize any right to redress in law but in the wake of a very public campaign. The amount of compensation offered was much less than had been advocated, but since it was directed at the victims and accompanied by an unequivocal apology it was largely a satisfactory resolution for a community that had been ignored for so long and most of whose remaining victims were in their nineties with little time to lose. Moreover, the compensation was not large enough to provoke a public outcry at the expense. The solution was both a safe and a publicly acceptable one.

Similarly in immigration policy, the measures that were taken throughout this period were those that received a large degree of public support, while those that were abandoned (such as the imposition of language qualifications on admissions and changes to the citizenship law) were those that met with the largest amount of public opposition. Yet as a review of the period reveals, these years were by no means free from public controversy. As in previous periods, divisions tended to open up between those who emphasized the importance of respect for individual rights on the one hand and those who argued from a more communitarian perspective on the other.

Labour unions, legal advocates, and human rights groups were highly critical of the lack of protection afforded to temporary workers, the tightening of admission criteria, the more stringent eligibility provisions pertaining to refugees, the expanded removal provisions, and the corresponding reduction in due process guarantees to those affected by such decisions.

For their part, those arguing from a more communitarian perspective claimed that too much of immigration policy was dictated by powerful interest groups to whom political leaders catered while paying insufficient heed to the negative economic, social, and cultural consequences and security risks occasioned by maintaining what they regarded as unjustifiably high levels of immigration. They claimed that an absence of debate on immigration policy was due to entrenched principles of multiculturalism, openness, and tolerance that elected officials and immigrant and refugee advocates used to support their particular interests. They continued to argue against high levels of immigration and in favour of moderate levels, with greatly enhanced screening mechanisms to keep out terrorists and others who support terrorist causes and greater discretion for immigration officers to reject applicants on the basis of traits that they perceived would hinder integration. They also called for a radical overhaul of the refugee determination process, including the scrapping of the Immigration and Refugee Board in favour of decision making vested in civil servants, and expanded grounds for denying admission to the refugee procedure.[153]

Amid these competing interests, successive governments, while maintaining high levels of immigration, in other respects pursued the most restrictive immigration policy that had been seen in more than twenty-five years. Canada, however, was not alone in its efforts to tighten border controls, expand grounds for denying admission, impose more stringent eligibility requirements for refugees resettled from abroad, and facilitate the removal of those, including refugees and asylum seekers, who were suspected of threatening national security.[154] This period witnessed an increase in such policies throughout many immigrant-receiving countries as well as enhanced cooperation to stem the smuggling and trafficking of persons,[155] to combat irregular migration,[156] and to prevent the spread of organized crime across international boundaries.[157]

The Immigration and Refugee Protection Act of 2002 was an ideal political vehicle for tightening Canada's borders and facilitating the removal of persons considered a threat to security, for it was deliberately devoid of detail, in stark contrast to the act and policies that preceded it. The new millennium therefore saw a reversal of the trend towards greater transparency. Whether this new trend will endure is unclear, although, among the many changes introduced during this period, it may well be that the one of the most recent will prove to be most problematic in the future. In vesting the minister with the power to instruct immigration officers on the types of immigration applications that should receive priority in processing, and in not requiring a review of all applications received, the government may find itself called to account in future. While expedited processing is likely for certain skilled immigrants whose entry will be strongly advocated by various provincial and business interests, the non-processing and/or processing delays in regard to other economic applications and those submitted on humanitarian and compassionate grounds is likely to be the subject of considerable public agitation in future years. Moreover, as the *Arar* case illustrated, there is a limit to public and judicial tolerance for policies and actions that place innocent lives at risk. So long as those actions and their consequences remain far from public view, history shows that there is little appetite for change. Once they become the focus of significant media attention and public condemnation, however, existing practices can often change very quickly.

CHAPTER TWELVE

Conclusion
Ideas, Interests, and Institutions

At the beginning of this book, we set out to determine the ideas, interests, and institutions that influenced the course of immigration policy throughout the different periods of Canada's history. In particular, we questioned whether special interests explained most of the major changes in Canadian immigration policy, or whether (in Keynes's words) ideas or values had a greater influence in setting and reshaping the features of immigration policy over time, and how, in turn, interests and values were mediated through institutions.

We have explored these questions in detail in each of the major periods of the history of Canadian immigration policy. In summary, the evidence suggests that economic interests, in particular the interests of capital, such as land developers, shipping companies, the railways, and other employers, were a dominant influence throughout most of the history of Canadian immigration policy, and that their interests generally prevailed over those of organized and unorganized labour and other settler interests. Labour interests, however, were increasingly influential, particularly in the post-Second World War period. Their demands contributed to the greater integration of immigration policy with more general labour-market and manpower policy, geared to relieving labour shortages and avoiding surpluses of labour in particular occupations. This led to the so-called tap-on/tap-off approach to immigration policy whereby relatively short-term manpower forecasting was a key element in the determination of annual immigration levels.

Until recent years, the weight assigned to short-term labour-market conditions in determining the levels of immigration has diminished, with major employer and organized-labour interests and most federal political parties favouring a relatively open and stable immigration policy with an annual intake approaching 1 per cent of the population (one of the highest relative rates of immigration in the world). The selection criteria, and the terms of admission, however, still tend to favour employer interests, as the surge in temporary workers at the expense of permanent immigrants in recent years illustrates. The influence exerted by economic interests – capital and, to a much lesser extent, organized labour – lends a significant measure of support to Public Choice theories of the political process that emphasize the dominant influence of concentrated economic interests in the political process.

Nevertheless, the influence of special interests in the political process cannot alone explain major shifts in Canadian immigration policy over time. Ideas or values have substantial independent explanatory power with respect to many of the major features of Canadian immigration policy over the course of its evolution: for example, narrow (nativist) conceptions of community in social and political contexts and ideological hostility to collectivism in the organization of the economy seem largely to explain the exclusion of Asian and black immigrants, the expulsion of political radicals in the 1920s and 1930s, the refusal to admit Jewish refugees before and during the Second World War, the internment of Japanese Canadians during the Second World War, the screening out of alleged Communist sympathizers on national security grounds during the 1950s and 1960s, and the disparate treatment of refugees fleeing totalitarian right-wing rather than left-wing regimes. On the other hand, the increasingly generous policy towards refugees and family members that emerged after the Second World War, the abandonment of explicit racial or ethnic criteria in the admission of immigrants beginning in the early 1960s, and the accompanying emergence of heightened sensitivity to issues of due process in the determination of the individual rights of immigrants all reflect the influence of liberal values, which in recent years have been tested by concerns for public safety posed by the increased threats associated with international terrorism.

The changing configuration of ideas or values that shaped Canadian immigration policy has never been exclusively domestic in origin. International factors, such as the evolution of a multiracial United Nations and British Commonwealth following the Second World War, the adoption of international human rights conventions, and more pragmatic international considerations such as changing 'push' factors in source countries that reduced the availability of immigrants from traditional source countries, significantly shaped domestic immigration policies, just as international cooperation in migration control and border security do today.[1]

As to the role of institutions in shaping immigration policies, three important institutional features stand out. First, for most of the history of Canadian immigration policy, policy making for the most part proceeded by way of executive rather than legislative action, in the form of regulations, policy directives, and the exercise of administrative discretion. This form of low-visibility, non-transparent policy making facilitated various forms of 'elite accommodation' and at the same time largely marginalized the impact of more diffuse, less concentrated interests in the policy-making process as a result of the higher access and informational barriers that they faced. One-party government in a parliamentary system, with the governing party often holding office for lengthy periods, tended to reinforce the effects of executive policy making by dramatically curtailing avenues for challenging many of these policies. This policy-making tradition began to change only in the 1960s, although the most recent immigration act has revived the tradition of conferring largely unconstrained discretion on the executive.

Second, reflecting the provisions of section 95 of the British North America Act of 1867 for shared federal-provincial jurisdiction over immigration policy (albeit with federal paramountcy), federalism and regional cleavages shaped Canadian immigration policy in important ways: for example, in responding to pressures from British Columbia early in the twentieth century to restrict Asian immigration and to intern Japanese Canadians during the Second World War; in responding to pressures from Quebec over non-francophone immigrants, including Jewish refugees, before and during the Second World War, and in subsequently allowing Quebec special prerogatives in choosing immigrants pursuant to federal-provincial agreements; and, on the other hand, in attempting to respond historically to pressures from Ontario, as the traditional economic engine of Canada, for high levels of skilled and un-skilled immigrants.

Third, in the absence of a constitutionally enshrined bill of rights up until 1982, and in the presence of privative clauses in immigration statutes, the courts – until the landmark decision of the Supreme Court of Canada in *Singh* in 1984[2] – historically displayed extraordinary deference to executive and administrative decision makers in the formulation and administration of Canadian immigration policy. The effect was to marginalize the role of the courts in policing substantive and procedural deficiencies in public decision-making processes, hence providing immigrants with only minimal due-process protections in decisions affecting fundamental aspects of their future welfare. Concerns in this area have re-emerged as a result of contemporary preoccupations with potential terrorist threats to national security.

Myths and Facts

Our research into the tangled history of Canadian immigration policy over the 500 years since the first European, John Cabot, claimed Newfoundland for Britain in 1497 reveals a number of persistent myths.

First, a central part of the Canadian mythology is that we are a nation of immigrants. In a literal sense, of course, this is true, at one or another stage removed. However, at the time of Confederation, despite the mass immigration of the preceding decades, 79 per cent of the population had been born in Canada. Even after the huge immigration influx between 1901 and 1911, the immigrant share of the total population increased only from 13 per cent to 22 per cent – much the same as at Confederation. By 1941, the proportion of immigrants had dropped to 17 per cent, and as of 2000 it was 18.9 per cent.[3]

Another aspect of this myth is the belief that Canada's population growth has largely been accounted for by immigration. This is also untrue. While recent trends suggest that future population growth may be largely immigrant driven, for most of Canada's history, the net migration rate (immigration less emigration) was either negative or only marginally positive, with some notable exceptions in the first and third decades of the twentieth century and in the post–Second World War era.[4] Both before and after Confederation, a persistent concern was the outflow of immigrants. Many of these were in transit through Canada to the United States, while others were longer-term residents relocating to the United States or returning to their countries of origin.

Another pervasive Canadian myth, illustrated in a wide range of historical accounts,[5] is that racism and bigotry were European, or at least American, inventions that have little part in Canada's history, tradition, or psyche, and that Canada has a long history of welcoming refugees and dissidents and has always been available to the proverbial huddled masses yearning to breathe free. In fact, for most of its history, Canada's immigration practices have been racist and exclusionary. Immigration policies immediately before and for many years after Confederation established a clear order of preference (rendered explicit, for example, in the *Canada Year Book, 1930)* as to who would be allowed into the country. British and American were the most preferred immigrants, followed by northern Europeans. When labour was needed the doors widened to include central Europeans and, finally, southern and eastern Europeans. The least preferred, and the target of racist exclusionary policies, were immigrants of colour (Asians, blacks) and Jewish immigrants.[6] This order of preference remained remarkably stable throughout most of the history of Canadian immigration policy; as a result, 90 per cent of all immigrants who came to Canada before 1961 were from Britain.

Change occurred progressively after the Second World War with the belated acceptance of an obligation to admit displaced persons from war-torn Europe, including a significant number of Jewish immigrants. The easing of racial restrictions was followed by the admission of a large number of southern Europeans, especially Italians, during the 1950s to help fill the shortages of skilled and unskilled labour experienced in the postwar boom. Finally, a non-explicitly racist set of admission criteria was adopted in 1962 that emphasized skills, training, and job experience rather than ethnic origin in selecting immigrants. This precipitated a dramatic increase in immigrants from Asia and the Middle East, who account for some 58 per cent of annual admissions in recent years as compared to just 3 per cent before 1961. According to the most recent census, published in 2006, for the first time in Canada's history the proportion of the foreign-born population from Asia and the Middle East (40.8 per cent) surpassed the proportion born in Europe (36.8 per cent).[7]

Ninety per cent of immigrants who arrived in Canada before 1961 were born in Europe, compared with only 25 per cent of those who arrived between 1981 and 1991. Between 1991 and 2001 the percentage of immigrants arriving from Europe further decreased to 19.5 per cent. In recent years the proportion of immigrants from Asia steadily increased to over 58 per cent.[8]

Another myth to which some scholars subscribe is that 'the central problem' of Canada's immigration policy for most of its history is that 'it never had one.'[9] However, as we have attempted to show, since at least the arrival of the Loyalists and the political reorganization of British North America, the federal government and its colonial predecessors and Imperial authorities quite self-consciously adopted and administered very detailed immigration policies, often micro-managing immigration down to the individual level, but always reflecting some set of policy values or objectives. A more accurate characterization of most Canadian immigration policy since Confederation, and indeed before, is that its basic elements were almost never articulated in legislation and were rarely subject to extensive parliamentary debate or approval. Rather, immigration legislation was largely skeletal in nature, and conferred vast executive discretion on Cabinet, the responsible minister, and his or her officials in formulating and in administering immigration policy, with minimal parliamentary or judicial oversight. This tradition of executive policy making was pursued by both major federal political parties and administered by a small and relatively obscure federal bureaucracy, probably largely reflecting an implicit political compact to attempt to remove immigration from the realm of 'high politics,' perhaps because of the zero-sum political nature of the conflicts that have always potentially, and sometimes actually, been perceived to be entailed.

Despite this long-standing strategy of keeping immigration policy on the political margins, another prevailing myth among contemporary Canadians is that immigration policy has only recently become contentious, as a result of the dramatic changes in the composition of the immigrant intake. In fact, aspects of immigration policy have inflamed intense passions at various junctures throughout Canada's history. Indeed, despite efforts to marginalize immigration policy politically, some of the fiercest – and ugliest – political conflicts in the country's history have related to immigration policy. In important respects, much of the history of the country can be written around these controversies.

Probably the most pervasive and persistent myth that has enjoyed currency in many periods of the history of Canadian immigration policy relates to the domestic welfare effects of immigration, in particular the negative impact of immigrants on domestic wage and unemployment levels. Most of these apprehensions have been negated by recent research, which finds that immigration increases economic growth and dynamism and has generally positive effects on domestic wages and employment levels.[10] This recent research has focused principally on the economic impacts of immigration. An assessment that included non-economic impacts of immigration would need to take account of, on the one hand, humanitarian considerations that may favour generous family reunification and refugee policies, and on the other, concerns over the potential erosion of cultural and social homogeneity and cohesiveness.[11]

Generally, a majority of Canadians have become accepting of the economic benefits of immigration, as reflected in contemporary public opinion polls. In a recent book, *Unlikely Utopia: The Surprising Triumph of Canadian Pluralism*,[12] prominent Canadian pollster Michael Adams reports that,

Canadians consistently express positive attitudes in the world toward immigration. In 2006 an International Ipsos MORI study found that 75 per cent of

Figure 12.1

Immigrant Influence (Q. Overall, would you say immigrants are having a good or bad influence on the way things are going in [country]?)

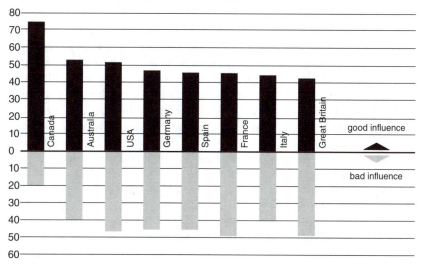

Approximately 1,000 interviews in each country

Source: 'Attitudes toward immigrants,' International Social Trends Monitor, IPSOS MORI, May 2006, www.ipsos-mori.com/istu/istu-may06.pdf

Canadians believe that overall, immigrants have a positive influence on the country. The country with the second most positive attitudes, Australia, was slightly over half (54 per cent), with the United States not far behind (52 per cent). In Western Europe, Germans (47 per cent) were the most positive about immigrants' influence on their country, with Spain (45 per cent), France (45 per cent), Italy (44 per cent), and Great Britain (43 per cent) hovering just below.

Especially striking are the 'net positive' results – the number of points by which positive attitudes toward immigrants exceed negative attitudes in each country. Australia, for example – with 54 per cent saying that immigrants overall have a positive effect on the country and 39 per cent saying they have a negative influence – registers a net positive attitude of 15 per cent. The table [above] shows the other countries surveyed as well. Canada, with a net positive attitude of 55 per cent, ranks a full 40 points higher than the next most positive country.

Adams also notes that, as of 2006, nearly three-quarters of Canadians believe that, overall, immigrants have a positive effect on the Canadian economy. Just one-quarter believe that immigrants take jobs away from other Canadians.[13]

However, evidence of the declining economic performance of recent immigrants cautions against complacency and suggests that there is a serious need for more proactive policies to facilitate their economic and social integration – for example, through facilitating the recognition of credentials earned abroad, providing widely accessible bridging programs that permit the upgrading of foreign credentials and work experience, offering enhanced opportunities for training in an official language, and encouraging greater levels of cooperation between the various levels of government and the private sector in settlement and integration policies.[14]

Thus, we conclude that the history of Canadian immigration policy exposes some clear myths concerning Canada and the role, place, and reception of immigrants over time. Moreover, the contours of immigration policy throughout various periods of history cannot be explained by an austere Public Choice model that focuses on the role of special interests in the political process, or by Keynes's view that ideas matter more than special interests. Additionally, while institutions through which ideas and interests were mediated played a significant role in determining which ideas and interests would be accommodated and which would be marginalized, institutional factors were far from decisive determinants of immigration policy. In short, the policy-making process in general, and in the immigration context specifically, is too complex to be accounted for by a single theory of the determinants of public-policy outcomes. Ideas, interests, and institutions all shape these outcomes in complex and interactive ways.

The Past as Prologue

As one reflects on the major episodes in the history of Canadian immigration policy, there is much to celebrate in the triumph of the human spirit over the daunting adversities of transshipment in often appalling conditions; a forbidding climate and geography; minimal and often incompetent, or even corrupt, governmental services; and wide cultural diversity and cleavages. There is also much cause for satisfaction in notable acts of compassion and generosity, including acceptance of large numbers of displaced persons from Western Europe after the Second World War, refugees from the suppression of the Hungarian and Czech uprisings, Asian refugees expelled by Idi Amin from Uganda, refugees from Vietnam, and refugees from many other countries in recent years.

However, the progressive exclusion of most Asian and black immigrants beginning in the first decade of the twentieth century, sweeping use of deportation powers for political or ideological purposes after the First World War, the refusal to accept Jewish refugees before and during the Second World War, thereby consigning many to the Holocaust, and the massive internment of Japanese Canadians during the Second World War reflect another and darker side of Canadian immigration policy – which most of us, from the comfortable moral vantage point of the present day, are likely to have difficulty or feel discomfort in identifying with. But moral indignation, or even revulsion, about the past is less important than what the lessons of history should teach us about the future – after all, the participants in the shaping of these policies included many of our ancestors, whose views and values we may well have shared had we shared their context. Fortunately, social progress, while never inevitable, has occurred – some of the lessons of history have indeed been learned. As the beneficiaries of this progress, we enjoy the privilege of being able to build on a more refined self-understanding than was available to many of our forebears. But this is little cause for complacency.

The racist policies with which most of us are likely to feel discomfort as we reflect on our history exemplified a community's collective resolve to attempt to define its core communal values and characteristics. As we suggested in the opening chapter of this book, while communitarianism need not *necessarily* imply these policies, a moral licence to exclude, expel, or intern individuals who are 'not like us'[15] carries a much higher risk than liberal values that majoritarian passions and prejudices will override the individual freedoms that are central to the commitment of all liberal theories to the equal moral worth of all individuals. Emphasizing commonalities rather than differences is a natural corollary of liberal values. The atrocities committed over the course of history as a result of tribalism, ethnocentrism, 'ethnic cleansing,' religious fanaticism, and ideological collectivism (e.g., Stalinism) are a tragic testament to this risk.[16] The ethnic and religious conflicts that are raging and perhaps proliferating in different parts of the contemporary world suggest that the lessons of history have not yet been fully learned.

To recall the words of Santayana, 'those who cannot remember the past are condemned to repeat it.' As we consider the future of Canadian immigration policy, we would be well advised to take this advice. Many of the more shameful past immigration policies, supported by now discredited views of racial superiority, were nevertheless enabled by ensuring that immigration policy was set largely at the discretion of the executive branch of government. The return to this type of policy making in recent years should cause us to pause and consider the lessons of history, which show the corrective value of legislative and judicial oversight in an area of public policy that plays such a central role in defining our community.

Notes

Chapter 1 Introduction: Ideas, Interests, Institutions, and Issues Shaping
Canadian Immigration Policy

1 International Organisation for Migration, 'About Migration,' 2008: http://
www.iom.int/jahia/Jahia/lang/en/pid/3; UNHCR, Global Trends 2007:
http://www.unhcr.org/statistics/STATISTICS/4852366f2.pdf. In 2007 the
number of persons internally displaced within their own countries as a result
of conflict reached 26 million, and an additional 25 million persons had been
internally displaced because of natural disasters.
2 Ibid.
3 Global Commission on International Migration, *Migration in an Interconnected
World: New Directions for Action*, October 2005, Annex II: http://www.gcim.org/
attachements/GCIM%20Report%20 Annex%20II.pdf. See more generally
Michael Trebilcock and Mathew Sudak, 'The Political Economy of
Emigration and Immigration,' *New York University Law Review* 81 (2006): 234.
4 For brief social histories of immigrant groups in Canada, see Department of
the Secretary of State, Multiculturalism Directorate, *The Canadian Family Tree:
Canada's Peoples* (Toronto: Corpus Information Services, 1979); Virginia
Knowles, *Forging Our Legacy: Canadian Citizenship and Immigration 1900–1997*
(Ottawa: Public Works and Government Services Canada, in conjunction with
Citizenship and Immigration Canada, 2000).
5 For an extensive canvassing of normative perspectives on immigration policy,
see the essays in Warren F. Schwartz, ed., *Justice in Immigration* (Cambridge:
Cambridge University Press, 1995).
6 J.M. Keynes, *The General Theory of Employment. Interest and Money* (London:
Macmillan, 1936), 384.

7 Joseph Carens, 'Aliens and Citizens: The Case for Open Borders,' *The Review of Politics* 47 (1987): 251.

8 Robert Nozick, *Anarchy, State and Utopia* (Oxford: Basil Blackwell, 1974).

9 John Rawls, *A Theory of Justice* (Cambridge, MA: Harvard University Press, 1971).

10 Joseph Carens, 'Membership and Morality: Admission to Membership in Liberal Democratic States,' in *Immigration and the Politics of Citizenship in Europe and North America*, ed. William Rogers (New York: University Press of America, 1989).

11 However, it needs to be noted that in later writing, Rawls would ascribe a very limited role to the application of principles of distributive justice among nations. See John Rawls, *The Law of Peoples, with 'The Idea of Public Reason Revisited'* (Cambridge, MA: Harvard University Press, 1999) – a position strongly contested by other philosophers: see, for example, Charles Beitz, *Political Theory and International Relations*, rev. ed. (Princeton, NJ: Princeton University Press,1999), and Thomas Pogge, *Realizing Rawls* (Ithaca, NY: Cornell University Press, 1989).

12 Peter Schuck, 'The Transformation of Immigration Law,' *Columbia Law Review* 84 (1984): 6.

13 Michael Walzer, *Spheres of Justice: A Defense of Pluralism and Equality* (New York: Basic Books, 1983). ch. 2.

14 Ibid., 61–2.

15 See Peter Brimelow, *Alien Nation: Commonsense about America's Immigration Disaster* (New York: Random House, 1995).

16 See generally Dennis Mueller, *Public Choice II* (Cambridge: Cambridge University Press, 1989); Michael J. Trebilcock, Douglas Hartle, Robert Prichard, and Donald Dewees, *The Choice of Governing Instrument* (Ottawa: Economic Council of Canada, 1982).

17 See R. Kent Weaver and Bert A. Rockman, eds., *Do Institutions Matter?* (Washington, DC: The Brookings Institution, 1993); Michael M. Atkinson, ed., *Governing Canada: Institutions and Public Policy* (Toronto: Harcourt Brace, 1983); Laurent Dobuzinskis, Michael Howlett, and David Laycock, eds., *Policy Studies in Canada: The State of the Art* (Toronto: University of Toronto Press, 1996).

18 Atkinson, *Governing Canada*, ch. 1.

19 Carolyn Hughes Tuohy, 'National Policy Studies in a Corporative Perspective: An Organizing Framework Applied to the Canadian Case,' in *Policy Studies in Canada*. ed. Dobuzinskis, Howlett, and Laycock.

20 Ibid., 321.

Chapter 2 From Wilderness to Nationhood, 1497–1867: 'The Land God Gave to Cain'

1 'Jacques Cartier's First Account of the New Land, Called New France, Discovered in the Year 1534,' in *The Voyages of Jacques Cartier*, ed. H.P. Biggar (Ottawa: PublicArchives of Canada, 1924), 22.
2 See chapter 3, this volume.
3 Olive Patricia Dickason, *Canada's First Nations: A History of Founding Peoples from Early Times* 3rd ed. (Toronto: Oxford University Press, 2002), x.
4 See Arthur J. Ray, *I Have Lived Here since the World Began: An Illustrated History of Canada's Native People* (Toronto: Lester Publishing, 1996).
5 Ibid., 34–5. A map illustrating the distribution of Native groups from A.D. 500 to the time of European contact appears in *Historical Atlas of Canada*. vol. 1, *From the Beginning to 1800*, ed. R. Cole Harris (Toronto: University of Toronto Press, 1987), plate 9. An example of a Native creation myth appears in Margaret Conrad, Alvin Finkel, and Cornelius Jaenen, *History of the Canadian Peoples*, vol. 1, *Beginnings to 1867*, 4th ed. (Toronto: Pearson Longman Pitman, 2006), 17.
6 R. Douglas Francis, Richard Jones, and Donald B. Smith, *Origins: Canadian History to Confederation* (Toronto: Holt, Rinehart & Winston, 1988), 1–6; J.M. Bumsted, *The Peoples of Canada: A Pre-Confederation History*, 2nd ed. (Toronto: Oxford University Press, 2003), 41; Dickason, *Canada's First Nations*, 63.
7 Francis, Jones, and Smith, *Origins*, 24.
8 R. Pastore, 'The 16th Century: Aboriginal People and European Contact,' in *The Atlantic Region to Confederation*, ed. P. Buckner and J. Reid (Toronto: University of Toronto Press, 1994), 22.
9 J.L. Finlay and D.N. Sprague, *The Structure of Canadian History*, 5th ed. (Toronto: Prentice-Hall Allyn and Bacon Canada, 1997), 1; the failed early settlements of Cartier are described in Conrad, Finkel, and Jaenen, *Canadian Peoples*, 93.
10 Kenneth Norrie, Douglas Owram and J.C. Herbert Emery, *A History of the Canadian Economy*, 4th ed. (Toronto: Thomson Nelson, 2008), 32.
11 Bumsted, *Peoples of Canada*, 65–68; the early French colonization plans involving deMonts are outlined in Conrad, Finkel, and Jaenen, *Canadian Peoples*, 56–7.
12 Finlay and Sprague, *Structure of Canadian History*, 26.
13 Ibid., 27–8; Bumsted, *Peoples of Canada*, 81–2; Finlay and Sprague, *Structure of Canadian History*, 50–1.
14 R. Cole Harris and John Warkentin, *Canada before Confederation* (Toronto: Oxford University Press, 1974), 32.

15 Finlay and Sprague, *Structure of Canadian History*, 49. The era of 'royal government' in New France is the subject of W.J. Eccles, *Canada under Louis XIV 1663–1701* (Toronto: McClelland & Stewart, 1968).

16 Finlay and Sprague, *Structure of Canadian History*, 43.

17 Harris and Warkentin, *Canada before Confederation*, 19. The French origins of the Canadian population from 1608 to 1759, which includes a breakdown of French immigrants by sex and decade of arrival, and the percentage who were of urban origin, are displayed in *Historical Atlas*, vol. 1, ed. Harris, plate 45. Similar information is presented in textual form in R. Cole Harris, 'The French Background of Immigrants to Canada before 1700,' reprinted in *Interpreting Canada's Past*, vol, 1, *Before Confederation*, ed. J.M. Bumsted (Toronto: Oxford University Press 1986), 52–62. The immigrant groups of *filles du roi*, soldiers, and servants are discussed briefly in Conrad, Finkel, and Jaenen, *Canadian Peoples*, 133–6. Sources which provide more detail on each of these groups are: on *filles du roi*, Y Landry, *Orphelines en France, pionnières au Canada: Les filles du roi au XVI1 siècle* (Montreal: Lemeac, 1992); on soldiers, Y. Landry, 'Mortalité, nuptialité et canadianisation des troups francaises de la guerre de Sept Ans,' *Histoire sociale/Social History* 12/24 (November 1979): 298–315; on *engagés*, Peter Moogk, 'Reluctant Exiles: Emigrants from France in Canada before 1760,' *William and Mary Quarterly*, 3d ser., 46/3 (July 1989): 463–505. New France's low retention rate of immigrants is discussed in Mario Boleda, 'Trente milles Français a la conquete du Saint-Laurent,' *Histoire sociale/Social History* 23/45 (May 1990): 153–77. The role of the Canadian climate in discouraging immigration is examined by Leslie P. Choquette, 'Recruitment of French Emigrants to Canada, 1600–1760,' in *'To Make America': European Emigration in the Early Modern Period*, ed. Ida Altman and James Horn (Berkeley: University of California Press, 1991).

18 Harris and Warkentin, *Canada before Confederation*, 36–7.

19 Finlay and Sprague, *Structure of Canadian History*, 43. Royal measures to encourage population growth in New France are summarized in Hubert Charbonneau and Yves Landry, 'La politique démographique en Nouvelle-France,' *Annales de démographie historique* (1979): 29–57.

20 See G. Frégault, *Canada: The War of the Conquest* (Toronto: Oxford University Press, 1969), 65.

21 Norrie, Owram and Emery, *History of the Canadian Economy*, 65.

22 Ibid., 44.

23 Ibid., ch. 3; Bumsted, *Peoples of Canada*, 77; 86–90; Norrie, Owram and Emery, *History of the Canadian Economy*, 67.

24 Bruce G. Trigger, *The Children of Aataentsic* (Montreal: McGill-Queen's University Press, 1976), 3.

25 Francis, Jones, and Smith, *Origins*, 49.

26 See J.W. Grant, Moon of Wintertime: Missionaries and the Indians in Encounter since 1534 (Toronto: University of Toronto Press, 1984), 3–95.

27 Dickason, *Canada's First Nations*, 108–110; Bumsted, *Peoples of Canada*, 86–90.

28 These wars resulted from economic as well as tribal rivalries. By 1701, war and disease had exacted such a heavy toll on the Native people that they were forced to make peace, which marked the end of Iroquois resistance to French expansion: see Francis, Jones, and Smith, *Origins*, 74–6.

29 For an overview of the history of Native peoples, see Bruce G. Trigger and Wilcomb Washburn, eds., *The Cambridge History of the Native People of the Americas* (Cambridge: Cambridge University Press, 1996).

30 Cameron Nish, ed., *The French Canadians, 1759–1766* (Vancouver: Copp Clark, 1966).

31 Finlay and Sprague, Structure of Canadian History, 73; Dickason, Canada's First Nations, 160.

32 N. Griffiths, '1600–1650: Fish, Fur and Folk,' in *Atlantic Region*, ed. Buckner and Reid, 59; a recent history of the Acadians is the same author's *The Contexts of Acadian History, 1688–1784* (Montreal: McGill-Queen's University Press, 1992).

33 Harris and Warkentin, *Canada before Confederation*, 25.

34 Bumsted, *Peoples of Canada*, 118–119; maps and a chart illustrating the population of Acadia from 1671 to 1714 appear in *Historical Atlas*, vol. 1, ed. Harris, plate 29.

35 Francis, Jones, and Smith, *Origins*, 136.

36 Bumsted, Peoples of Canada, 141.

37 G. Rawlyk, '1720–1744: Cod, Louisbourg and the Acadians,' in *Atlantic Region*, ed. Buckner and Reid, 108.

38 The influx of immigrants to Nova Scotia from central Europe in the eighteenth century is explored in Winthrop Pickard Bell, *The Foreign Protestants and the Settlement of Nova Scotia* (Toronto: University of Toronto Press, 1961); Gertrud Waseem, 'German Settlement in Nova Scotia,' in *German Canadian Studies: Critical Approaches*, ed. Peter Liddell (Vancouver: Canadian Association of University Teachers of German, 1983).

39 Francis, Jones, and Smith, *Origins*, 142.

40 Fregault, *War of the Conquest*, 22; G. Plank, *An Unsettled Conquest: The British Campaign Against the Peoples of Acadia* (Philadelphia: University of Pennsylvania Press, 2001).

41 S. Patterson, '1744–1763: Colonial Wars and Aboriginal Peoples,' in *Atlantic Region*, ed. Buckner and Reid, 144; maps showing the paths of Acadian deportation and return appear in *Historical Atlas*, vol. 1, ed. Harris, plate 30.

42 N. Griffiths, ed., *The Acadian Deportation* (Toronto: Copp Clark, 1969); sources on Acadians after the deportation include C.A. Brasseaux, *The Founding of New Acadia: The Beginnings of Acadian Life in Louisiana*, 1765–1803 (Baton Rouge: Louisiana State University Press, 1987).

43 Bumsted, *Peoples of Canada*, 178–79. Black immigration to pre-Loyalist Nova Scotia is discussed in Gerry Harden, 'Bound for Nova Scotia: Slaves in the Planter Migration, 1759–1800,' in *Making Adjustments: Change and Continuity in Planter Nova Scotia, 1759–1800*, ed. Margaret Conrad (Fredericton: Acadiensis, 1991). The immigration of Scots is the subject of J.M. Bumsted, *The People's Clearance: Highland Emigration to British North America, 1770–1815* (Edinburgh: Edinburgh University Press; Winnipeg: University of Manitoba Press, 1982).

44 J.M. Bumsted, '1763–1783, Resettlement and Rebellion,' in *Atlantic Region*, ed. Buckner and Reid, 167.

45 Francis, Jones, and Smith, *Origins*, 149; maps illustrating the paths of major migrations to, and ethnic origin and religion of, the population of pre-Loyalist Nova Scotia appear in *Historical Atlas*, vol. 1, ed. Harris, plate 31. 46 Bumsted, *Peoples of Canada*, 197–98.

46 Dickason, *Canada's First Nations*, 206–208; Bumsted, *Peoples of Canada*, 129.

47 Dickason, *Canada's First Nations*, 162–163; Francis, Jones, and Smith, *Origins*, 341; British colonization of Newfoundland in the seventeenth century is described in Conrad, Finkel, and Jaenen, *Canadian Peoples*, 163–164.

48 Francis, Jones, and Smith, *Origins*, 341; British colonization of Newfoundland in the seventeenth century is described in Conrad, Finkel, and Jaenen, *Canadian Peoples*, 52–54.

49 W. Gordon Handcock, *Soe longe as there comes noe women: Origins of English Settlement in Newfoundland* (St. John's, NF: Breakwater, 1989), 45; D.W. Prowse, *A History of Newfoundland* (London: Macmillan, 1895), 217.

50 Rawlyk, '1720–1744,' 109; the population and ethnicity of eighteenth-century Newfoundland is displayed in *Historical Atlas*, vol. 1, ed. Harris, plate 25.

51 Francis, Jones, and Smith, *Origins*, 345–7.

52 Ibid., 201.

53 Norrie and Owram, *History of the Canadian Economy*, 92.

54 Ibid., 60.

55 Nova Scotian and Quebec neutrality during the American Revolution has been the subject of considerable research. See, for example, J.B. Brebner, *The Neutral Yankees of Nova Scotia: A Marginal Colony during the Revolutionary Years* (Toronto: McClelland & Stewart, 1969); George Rawlyk, ed., *Revolution Rejected: 1775–1776* (Scarborough, ON: Prentice-Hall, 1968); Gustave Lanctôt, *Canada and the American Revolution, 1774–1783* (Toronto: Clarke,

Irwin, 1967); and G.F.G. Stanley, *Canada Invaded, 1775–1776* (Toronto: Hakkert, 1973).

56 L.F.S. Upton, ed., *The United Empire Loyalists* (Toronto: Copp Clark, 1967); Wallace Brown and Hereward Senior, *Victorious in Defeat: The Loyalists in Canada* (Toronto: Methuen, 1984).

57 Christopher Moore, *The Loyalists: Revolution, Exile, Settlement* (Toronto: McClelland & Stewart, 1994); Conrad, Finkel, and Jaenen, *Canadian Peoples*, 290, put the total number of Loyalists who left the United States at 70,000. On the Loyalists in the Maritimes, see Esther Clark Wright, *The Loyalists of New Brunswick* (Moncton, NB: Moncton Publishing, 1955); Neil MacKinnon, This *Unfriendly Soil: The Loyalist Experience in Nova Scotia, 1783–1791* (Montreal: McGill-Queen's University Press, 1986); Robert J. Morgan, 'The Loyalists of Cape Breton,' in *Cape Breton Historical Essays*, ed. Don MacGillivray and Brian Tennyson (Sydney, NS: College of Cape Breton Press, 1980); J.M. Bumsted, *Land, Settlement, and Politics on Eighteenth Century Prince Edward Island* (Montreal: McGill-Queen's University Press, 1987). Maps showing the distribution of Loyalist immigrants in Quebec and New Brunswick appear in *Historical Atlas of Canada*, vol. 2, *The Land Transformed, 1800–1891*, ed. Louis Gentilcore (Toronto: University of Toronto Press, 1993), plate 7.

58 See W. Brown, 'The Black Loyalists in Canada,' *The Loyalist Gazette* 28 (1990): 11. On black Loyalists, see also James W. St.-G. Walker, *The Black Loyalists: The Search for a Promised Land in Nova Scotia and Sierra Leone, 1783–1870* (New York: Africana, 1976; reprinted Toronto: University of Toronto Press, 1992); Walker, 'The Establishment of a Free Black Community in Nova Scotia, 1783–1840,' in *The African Diaspora: Interpretive Essays*, ed. Martin L. Kilson and Robert I. Rotberg (Cambridge, MA: Harvard University Press, 1976); Harvey A. Whitfield, *From American Slaves to Nova Scotian Subjects: The Case of Black Refugees 1813–1840* (Toronto: Prentice Hall, 2005).

59 While many white Loyalist settlers from British North America received land grants and other forms of assistance and compensation for dislocation, many blacks never received any land grants at all, and those grants that were bestowed were much smaller and poorer in quality than those that had been promised. In addition, blacks were not entitled to trial by jury, and, in what later became New Brunswick, they were not entitled to vote in elections for the Legislative Assembly: Bumsted, *Peoples of Canada*, 171.

60 Ken Alexander and Avis Glaze, *Towards Freedom: The African-Canadian Experience* (Toronto: Umbrella Press, 1996), 41–2.

61 Robin Winks, *The Blacks in Canada: A History* (Montreal: McGill-Queen's University Press; New Haven, CT: Yale University Press, 1971), 9.

62 Ibid., ch. 3; Mavis C. Campbell, *The Maroons of Jamaica, 1655–1796* (Trenton, NJ: Africa World Press, 1990), 241–2; Simon Schama, *Rough Crossings: Britain, the Slaves and the American Revolution* (Toronto: Penguin Canada, 2008).

63 Dickason, *Canada's First Nations*, 197–200; Mohawk Loyalists are discussed briefly in Conrad, Finkel, and Jaenen, *Canadian Peoples*, 184–185.

64 Bumsted, *Peoples of Canada*, 319–20; Francis, Jones, and Smith, *Origins*, 202–3, 211–12; epidemics which devastated Native populations are discussed in Henry F. Dobyns, *Their Numbers Became Thinned: Native American Population Dynamics in Eastern North America* (Knoxville: University of Tennessee Press, 1983). Regional estimates of the effects of epidemics on Native populations appear in Douglas H. Ubelaker, 'North American Indian Population Size, A.D. 1500 to 1985,' *American Journal of Physical Anthropology* 77/3 (November 1988): 289–94.

65 Sir Guy Carleton was the first appointee to this position.

66 Land outside the seigneuries was to be granted in freehold. British criminal law was to be adopted, alongside French civil law, and an elected legislative assembly was to be established. Finlay and Sprague, *Structure of Canadian History*, 85.

67 Finlay and Sprague, *Structure of Canadian History*, 85.

68 Ibid. 101–111.

69 For descriptions of the Selkirk settlement at Red River, see Norrie, Owram, and Emery, *History of the Canadian Economy*, 128–129; Norman Macdonald, *Canada, 1763–1841: Immigration and Settlement: The Administration of the Imperial Land Regulations* (Toronto: Longmans, 1939), 161–74.

70 P.D. Dickson, 'We Prefer Trade to Dominion: Imperial Policy and the Settlement of the King's Royal Regiment,' *Ontario History* 82 (1990): 141–2.

71 Glenn J. Lockwood, 'The Pattern of Settlement in Eastern Ontario, 1784–1875,' *Families* 30 (November 1991): 235.

72 Norrie, Owram, and Emery, *History of the Canadian Economy*, 96; Macdonald, *Canada, 1763–1841*, chs. 2–5.

73 Werner Bausenhart, *German Immigration and Assimilation in Ontario, 1783–1918* (Toronto: Legas, 1989), 26–30.

74 Harris and Warkentin, *Canada before Confederation*, 177; the distribution of Loyalists in Atlantic Canada *ca* 1785 is presented in a map in *Historical Atlas*, vol. 1, ed. Harris, plate 32.

75 Moore, *Loyalists*, 162–3.

76 Ibid., 170.

77 Graeme Wynn, '1800–1810: Turning the Century,' in *Atlantic Region*, ed. Buckner and Reid, 216–17; Macdonald, *Canada, 1763–1841*, 153–5.

78 See Macdonald, *Canada, 1763–1841*, ch. 4; and Francis, Jones, and Smith, *Origins*, 161.

79 *PassengerAct (U.K.)*, 43 Geo. 3, c.56.

80 See Finlay and Sprague, *Structure of Canadian History*, 109.

81 Lower, *Colony to Nation*, 179. See Kenneth McNaught, *Manifest Destiny* (Toronto: Clarke Irwin, 1963), 83. See Gerald Craig, *Upper Canada: The Formative Years, 1784–1841* (Toronto: McClelland & Stewart, 1968), 124.

82 See Kenneth McNaught, *Manifest Destiny* (Toronto: Clarke Irwin, 1963).

83 See Gerald Craig, *Upper Canada: The Formative Years, 1784–1841* (Toronto: McClelland & Stewart, 1968), 124.

84 Cecil Houston and William Smyth, *Irish Immigration and Canadian Settlement* (Toronto: University of Toronto Press, 1990), 188–9; on Irish immigration, see also Kerby A. Miller, *Emigrants and Exiles: Ireland and the Irish Exodus to North America* (New York: Oxford University Press, 1985); Donald MacKay, *Flight from Famine: The Coming of the Irish to Canada* (Toronto: McClelland & Stewart, 1990). Maps showing the patterns of migrations in the 1830s and 1840s appear in *Historical Atlas*, vol. 2, ed. Gentilcore, plate 9.

85 See Stanley Johnson, A History of Emigration from the United Kingdom to North America, 1763–1912 (London: Frank Cass, 1913), ch. 3.

86 Lord Elgin to Lord Grey, Colonial Secretary, 15 June 1848; in *The Elgin-Grey Papers, 1846–1852*, vol. 1, ed. Arthur G. Doughty (Ottawa: King's Printer, 1937), 183. The population and governments of Atlantic Canada, however, were less favourable: see W.S. MacNutt, *The Atlantic Provinces: The Emergence of Colonial Society, 1712–1857* (Toronto: McClelland & Stewart, 1965), 155–9.

87 See Macdonald, *Canada, 1763–1841*, ch. 8; Johnson, *History of Emigration*, ch. 10.

88 *Lord Durham's Report*, 1839, 280, quoted in Johnson, *History of Emigration*, 160.

89 Johnson, *History of Emigration*, 86–95; British attempts to encourage emigration are discussed in Hugh J.M. Johnston, *British Emigration Policy, 1815–1830: 'Shovelling Out Paupers'* (Oxford: The Clarendon Press, 1972); Wendy Cameron and Maude M. McDougall, *Assisting Emigration to Upper Canada 1832–1837* (Montreal and Kingston: McGill-Queen's University Press, 2000).

90 Ibid., 72.

91 Ibid., 80–5.

92 Ibid., ch. 11.

93 Ibid., ch. 12.

94 Macdonald, *Canada, 1763–1841*, 20–1.

95 H.I. Cowan, *British Emigration to British North America: The First Hundred Years* (Toronto: University of Toronto Press, 1961), 150.

96 Macdonald, *Canada, 1763–1841*, 512. Upper Canadian land policies are the subject of Lillian F. Gates, *Land Policies of Upper Canada* (Toronto: University of Toronto Press. 1968); G.A. Wilson, *The Clergy Reserves in Upper Canada: A Canadian Martmain* (Toronto: University of Toronto Press, 1968); Leo A. Johnson, 'Land Policy, Population Growth and Social Structure in the Home District, 1793–1851,' in *Historical Essays on Upper Canada*, ed. J.K. Johnson (Ottawa: Carleton Library, 1975), 32–57.

97 Macdonald, *Canada, 1763–1841*, 330–5; Johnson, *History of Emigration*, 20–2.

98 Macdonald, *Canada, 1763–1841*, 329.

99 For a generalized account of the experiences of immigrants to Upper Canada between 1820 and 1850; see Frances Hoffman and Ryan Taylor, *Across the Waters: Ontario Immigrants' Experiences 1820–1850* (Milton, ON: Global Heritage Press, 1999).

100 Ibid., 155–61.

101 Ibid., 128–45; see also Frederick Coyne Hamil, *Lake Erie Baron: The Story of Colonel Thomas Talbot* (Toronto: Macmillan, 1955).

102 Norman Macdonald, *Canada: Immigration and Colonization, 1841–1903* (Aberdeen: Aberdeen University Press, 1966), 161. See also Clarence G. Karr, *The Canada Land Company: The Early Years* (Toronto: Ontario Historical Society, 1974).

103 For criticisms of land policies in the British North American colonies, see Macdonald, *Canada, 1763–1841*, and Johnson, *History of Emigration*, ch. 9.

104 Johnson, *History of Emigration*, 160; for the effects of the cholera epidemics, see Geoffrey Bilson, *A Darkened House: Cholera in Nineteenth-Century Canada* (Toronto: University of Toronto Press, 1980).

105 Johnson, *History of Emigration*, 124.

106 Macdonald, *Immigration and Colonization*, 161.

107 See Marcus Lee Hansen, *The Mingling of the Canadian and American Peoples* (New Haven, CT: Yale University Press, 1940), ch. 6. French-Canadian migration to the United States in the pre-Confederation period is the subject of several studies, including Bruno Ramirez, 'Emigration et Franco-Américanie: Bilan des recherches historiques,' in *Le Québec et les francophones de la Nouvelle-Angleterre*, ed. Dean Loder (Quebec: Presses de l'université Laval, 1991); Y. Roby, *Les Franco-Americains de la Nouvelle-Angleterre (1776–1930)* (Sillery, PQ: Septentrion, 1990); Claire Quintal, ed., *L'émigrant québécois vers les États-Unis, 1850–1920* (Quebec: Vie Française, 1982).

108 Paul W. Gates, 'Official Encouragement to Immigration to the Province of Canada,' *Canadian Historical Review* 15 (1934): 24.

109 See Macdonald, *Canada: Immigration and Colonization*, ch. 3; Houston and Smyth, *Irish Immigration*, 95–107.

110 See Norrie, Owram and Emery, *History of the Canadian Economy*, 96, 118, 174.

111 Harris and Warkentin, *Canada before Confederation*, 66.

112 Norrie, Owram and Emery, *History of the Canadian Economy*, 77.

113 Harris and Warkentin, *Canada before Confederation*, 66–7.

114 Ibid., 186. Black immigration to other Atlantic colonies is the subject of W.A. Spray, *The Blacks in New Brunswick* (Fredericton: Brunswick Press, 1972); Spray, 'The Settlement of Black Refugees in New Brunswick, 1815–1836,' *Acadiensis* 6/2 (Spring 1977): 64–79; Jim Hornby, *Black Islanders: Prince Edward Island's Historical Black Community* (Charlottetown: Institute of Island Studies, 1991).

115 Philip Buckner, 'The 1860s: An End and a Beginning,' in *Atlantic Region*, ed. Buckner and Reid, 365.

116 Rosemary Ommer, 'The 1830s: Adapting Their Institutions to Their Desires,' in *Atlantic Region*, ed. Buckner and Reid, 285.

117 Ian Robertson, 'The 1850s: Maturity and Reform,' in *Atlantic Region*, ed. Buckner and Reid, 333; Buckner, 'The 1860s,' 363.

118 Buckner, 'The 1860s,' 363.

119 Alexander and Glaze, *Towards Freedom*, 56.

120 See Winks, *Blacks in Canada*, chs. 6–7; Jacqueline Tobin, *From Midnight to Dawn: The Last Tracks of the Underground Railway*, (NY: Doubleday, 2007); Donald G. Simpson, *Under the North Star: Black Communities in Upper Canada* (Trenton New Jersey: Africa World Press Inc., 2005); Karolyn Smardz Frost, *I've Got a Home in Glory Land: A Lost Tale of the Underground Railroad* (Toronto: Thomas Allen Publishers, 2008).

121 Bumsted, *Peoples of Canada*, 341, 347; according to Conrad, Finkel, and Jaenen, about 20,000 French Canadians had left Canadian territory by 1812, most of them settling in New England: *Canadian Peoples*, 371–2.

122 Douglas Owram, *Promise of Eden: The Canadian Expansionist Movement and the Idea of the West, 1856–1900* (Toronto: University of Toronto Press, 1980).

123 Ibid., 8.

124 Ibid., 12.

125 Ibid., 13.

126 Macdonald, *Canada, 1763–1841*, 161–74; Harris and Warkentin, *Canada before Confederation*, 247–9; Conrad, Finkel, and Jaenen, *Canadian Peoples*, 213–15.

127 Macdonald, *Canada, 1763–1841*, 161–74; Harris and Warkentin, *Canada before Confederation*, 247–9; *Historical Atlas*, vol. 2, ed. Gentilcore, plate 18.

128 Harris and Warkentin, *Canada before Confederation*, 243.

129 Owram, *Promise of Eden*, 9.

130 Francis, Jones, and Smith, *Origins*, 372–3.
131 Ibid., 374–5.
132 Owram, *Promise of Eden*, 43; support for Western settlement is briefly described in Conrad, Finkel, and Jaenen, *Canadian Peoples*, 311–312.
133 Ibid., 311.
134 Ibid., 311 and 329.
135 Francis, Jones, and Smith, *Origins*, 386; early settlement in British Columbia is outlined in Conrad, Finkel, and Jaenen, *Canadian Peoples*, 467–9.
136 Francis, Jones, and Smith, *Origins*, 392; Harris and Warkentin, *Canada Before Confederation*, 294.
137 Francis, Jones, and Smith, *Origins*, 388–9.
138 Harris and Warkentin, *Canada before Confederation*, 290.
139 Alexander and Glaze, *Towards Freedom*, 61.
140 *Historical Atlas*, vol. 2, ed. Gentilcore, plate 36, demonstrates the impact of the gold rush on the B.C. population.
141 Dickason, *Canada's First Nations*, 218–19; Francis, Jones, and Smith, *Origins*, 393–4.
142 See Dickason, *Canada's First Nations*, 231.
143 Francis, Jones, and Smith, *Origins*, 6–7.

Chapter 3 Immigration and the Consolidation of the Dominion, 1867–1896: Fulfilling the Destiny

   1 On Confederation, monograph studies date from the 1960s, when the Centennial celebrations initiated a flurry of publications; see, for example, Peter B. Waite, *The Life and Times of Confederation, 1864–1867: Politics, Newspapers, and the Union of British North America* (Toronto: University of Toronto Press, 1962); William L. Morton, *The Critical Years: The Union of British North America, 1857–1873* (Toronto: McClelland & Stewart, 1964). On the repeal movement in Nova Scotia, see J.M. Beck, *Joseph Howe: Anti-Confederate* (Ottawa: Canadian Historical Association, 1965); Kenneth G. Pryke, *Nova Scotia and Confederation, 1864–1874* (Toronto: University of Toronto Press, 1979). For the rejection of Confederation by Newfoundland and Prince Edward Island, and the eventual joining of the latter, see, respectively, James K. Hiller, 'Confederation Defeated: The Newfoundland Election of 1869,' *Newfoundland in the Nineteenth and Twentieth Centuries: Essays in Interpretation*, ed. James K. Hiller and Peter Neary (Toronto: University of Toronto Press, 1980); and Frances W.P. Bolger, *Prince Edward Island and Confederation, 1863–1873* (Charlottetown: St. Dunstan's University Press, 1964).

2 See note see 6 below.

3 See William L. Morton, *The West and Confederation, 1857–1871* (Ottawa: Canadian Historical Association, 1958); W. George Shelton, ed., *British Columbia and Confederation* (Victoria: University of Victoria Press, 1967).

4 While historians have written a great deal on Macdonald's National Policy, they have tended to focus on the tariff issue. See, for example, Robert Craig Brown, *Canada's National Policy, 1883–1900: A Study in Canadian American Relations* (Princeton, N.J.: Princeton University Press, 1964); J.H. Dales, *The Protective Tariff in Canada's Development: Eight Essays on Trade and Tariff* (Toronto: University of Toronto Press, 1966); Ben Forster, *A Conjunction of Interests: Business, Politics, and Tariffs, 1823–1879* (Toronto: University of Toronto Press, 1986). The immigration component of the National Policy is neglected in these accounts. On the railway, see W.K. Lamb, *A History of the Canadian Pacific Railway* (Toronto: Macmillan, 1977); Hugh A. Dempsey, ed., *The CPR West: The Iron Road and the Making of a Nation* (Vancouver: Douglas & McIntyre, 1984).

5 One of the foremost proponents of expansion into the West was George Brown; his ideas are discussed in J.M.S. Careless, *Brown of the Globe*, vol. 2, *Statesman of Confederation* (Toronto: Macmillan, 1963).

6 At the conclusion of the American Civil War, American Secretary of State William Seward boasted: 'Nature designs that this whole continent ... shall be, sooner or later, within the magic circle of the American Union': quoted in Robert Bothwell, *Canada and the United States: The Politics of Partnership* (Toronto: University of Toronto Press, 1992), 5. For a detailed account of American designs on Canadian territory in the second half of the nineteenth century, see D.F. Warner, *The Idea of Continental Union: Agitation for the Annexation of Canada to the United States, 1849–1893* (Lexington: University of Kentucky Press, 1960); Alvin C. Glueck, *Minnesota and the Manifest Destiny of the Canadian Northwest: A Study in Canadian American Relations* (Toronto: University of Toronto Press, 1965); David Orchard, *The Fight for Canada: Four Centuries of Resistance to American Expansionism* (Don Mills, ON: Stoddart, 1993).

7 Douglas Owram, *Promise of Eden: The Canadian Expansionist Movement and the Idea of the West, 1856–1900* (Toronto: University of Toronto Press, 1980), 103. See also Carl Berger, *The Sense of Power: Studies in the Ideas of Canadian Imperialism, 1867–1914* (Toronto: University of Toronto Press, 1970), ch. 2.

8 Owram, *Promise of Eden*, 27.

9 Discussed more fully in this volume, 84–5.

10 So unreliable were the figures collected by the Department of Agriculture, which was responsible for immigration until 1892, that, when this

responsibility was transferred to the Department of the Interior in that year, the practice of collecting immigration statistics was discontinued. It was felt at that time that more reliable estimates could be obtained by reference to the number of people who acquired homesteads and through the use of decennial provincial censuses: 'Report of the Deputy Minister of the Interior,' Annual Report of the Department of the Interior for 1892, *Sessional Papers, 1893*, no. 13, xiii.

11 Department of Citizenship and Immigration, Immigration and Demographic Policy Group, *Immigration Statistics* (Ottawa: Queen's Printer, 1991).

12 Roderic P. Beaujot, *Growth and Dualism: The Demographic Development of Canadian Society* (Toronto: Gage, 1982), 83. Kenneth Norrie and Douglas Owram estimate that between 1870 and 1900 net emigration from Canada was approximately 485,000: *A History of the Canadian Economy* (Toronto: Harcourt Brace Jovanovich, 1991), 296.

13 This is not to suggest that this was the only reason for the enormous rise in Canadian wheat exports at the turn of the century. As Norrie and Owram explain, falling transportation rates were also a factor. The costs of overseas transportation fell as steel replaced iron in ships, transatlantic vessels were built larger, marine engines became more efficient, and port costs fell. As well, the cost of inland carriage also decreased with the introduction of steel rails and the improvement of train engines and rolling stock. In addition to falling transportation costs, the demand for wheat in Britain rose as a result of increases in population and incomes. Canada's ability to take advantage of these developments was, however, made possible through the introduction of new cultivation techniques suitable for prairie conditions: *A History of the Canadian Economy*, 4th ed. (Toronto: Thomson Nelson, 2008), 200–5.

14 See discussion in chapter 2, this volume, 56.

15 Department of the Secretary of State, Multiculturalism Directorate, *The Canadian Family Tree: Canada's Peoples* (Don Mills, ON: Corpus Information Services, 1977), 162.

16 John L. Finlay and Douglas N. Sprague, *The Structure of Canadian History*, 5th ed. (Toronto: Prentice-Hall, 1997), 230.

17 R. Douglas Francis, Richard Jones, and Donald B. Smith, *Destinies: Canadian History since Confederation*, 6th ed. (Toronto: Nelson, 2008), 38.

18 General accounts of the Metis resistance can be found in ibid., 28–35, 79–86; Finlay and Sprague, *Structure of Canadian History*, 187, 209, 227–8; and Arthur S. Morton, *History of Prairie Settlement* (Toronto: Macmillan, 1938), 41–9. Other more specific readings include: Douglas N. Sprague, *Canada and the Metis, 1869–1885* (Waterloo, ON: Wilfrid Laurier University Press, 1988); Bob Beal and Rob Macleod, *Prairie Fire: The 1885 North-West Rebellion* (Edmonton:

Hurtig, 1984); Thomas Flanagan, *Riel and the Rebellion: 1885 Reconsidered* (Saskatoon: Western Producer Prairie Books, 1983); Hartwell Bowsfield, *Louis Riel; The Rebel and the Hero* (Toronto: Oxford University Press, 1971); George F.G. Stanley, *Louis Reel* (Toronto: Ryerson, 1963); Maggie Siggins, *Riel: A Life of Revolution* (Toronto: HarperCollins, 1994).

19 'Report of the Minister of Agriculture,' Annual Report of the Department of Agriculture for 1885, *Sessional Papers, 1886*, no. 10, xxvii. [Annual Reports of the Department of Agriculture henceforth cited as ARDA.]

20 Finlay and Sprague, *Structure of Canadian History*, 213.

21 For overviews of the Canadian government's treaties with the Indians, see Francis, Jones, and Smith, *Destinies*, 63–7; and Finlay and Sprague, *Structure of Canadian History*, 210–13. Other sources include: Jean Friesen, 'Magnificent Gifts: The Treaties of the Indians of the Northwest, 1869–70,' *Transactions of the Royal Society of Canada*, ser. 5, vol. 1 (1986): 41–51; James R. Miller, *Skyscrapers Hide the Heavens: A History of Indian-White Relations in Canada*, rev. ed. (Toronto: University of Toronto Press, 1991); Richard Price, ed., *The Spirit of the Alberta Indian Treaties* (Montreal: Institute for Research on Public Policy, 1980); Olive Patricia Dickason, *Canada's First Nations: A History of Founding Peoples from Earliest Times*, 3rd ed. (Toronto: Oxford University Press, 2002).

22 See chapter 2, this volume, 48–51.

23 The federal government administered the lands policies of the Western provinces, while the provincial governments in central and eastern Canada controlled the lands within their respective provinces. The Ontario land system was much the same as that of the federal government, whereas in Quebec no free homesteading lands were offered, although lands were set aside for sale, the price of which could be paid in instalments. New Brunswick offered grants of land upon payment of $20 cash or upon an undertaking to do $10 worth of work on the public highways for three years. In Nova Scotia, arable land was not plentiful, and that which was available for sale was priced at $40 per acre. British Columbia offered lands along the same lines as the Dominion government, although larger tracts were available in remoter regions. Residence requirements and cultivation conditions which had to be fulfilled before title would pass to the homesteader were similar throughout the country: Stanley C. Johnson: *A History of Emigration from the United Kingdom to North America, 1763–1912* (London: G. Routledge, 1913), 223.

24 *Dominion Lands Act*, S.C. 1872, c.23, s.33.

25 *An Act to Amend the Dominion Lands Act*, S.C. 1874, c.19, s.8(2). Section 5.8 of this amendment also lowered the age requirement to eighteen years.

26 *Dominion Lands Act*, R.S.C. 1886, c.54, s.46.

27 For example, while any male over eighteen years could apply for a free grant, women applicants were restricted to those who were the 'sole head of a family namely: widows, divorcees or deserted wives with dependent children under 18 years of age': ibid.

28 Georgina Binnie-Clark, *Wheat and Women* (Toronto: University of Toronto Press, 1979), 229–300.

29 See Susan Jackal's introduction to ibid., xx–xxxi.

30 For more on this debate see Norrie and Owram, *History of the Canadian Economy*, 304. For whatever reason, throughout the period homestead entries remained below the number anticipated, averaging about 3,000 per year. In some years entries barely exceeded cancellations: Valerie Knowles, *Strangers at Our Gates: Canadian Immigration and Immigration Policy, 1540–1990* (Toronto: Dundurn, 2007), 74.

31 Norrie and Owram, *History of the Canadian Economy*, 306.

32 For example, the CPR tried to avoid purchase by speculators by attaching improvement and settlement conditions to the sale of its lands. If the purchaser failed to meet these settlement conditions within the specified time, the company reserved the right to cancel the agreement, with resulting forfeiture of the land to the company. Faced with disappointing land sales, the CPR eventually decided to sell large blocks of its land to colonization companies approved by the government. Again to encourage use of settlement, the company offered rebates to those purchasers or their assigns who actually colonized the land. By the 1890s, it had abandoned the rebate scheme in favour of giving preferential treatment to settlers by offering lower prices on lands with settlement conditions and extended payment periods. For a detailed discussion of the CPR's land policies of this period, see James B. Hedges, *Building the Canadian West: The Land and Colonization Policies of the Canadian Pacific Railway* (New York: Macmillan, 1939), 67–93.

33 Gulbrand Loken, *From Fjord to Frontier: A History of the Norwegians in Canada* (Toronto: McClelland & Stewart, 1980), 40; Morton, *History of Prairie Settlement*, 73, Hedges, *Building the Canadian West*, 71, and Norman Macdonald, *Canada: Immigration and Colonization, 1841–1903* (Toronto: Macmillan, 1966), 240–1.

34 Macdonald, *Canada: Immigration and Colonization*, 240–1.

35 For more on these schemes, see Johnson, *Emigration from the United Kingdom to North America*, 238.

36 For a map illustrating patterns of homesteading in the West during this period, see *Historical Atlas of Canada*, vol. 2, *The Land Transformed, 1800–1891*, ed. R. Louis Gentilcore (Toronto: University of Toronto Press, 1993), plate 42.

37 'Report of the Deputy Minister of the Interior,' Annual Report of the Department of the Interior for 1877, *Sessional Papers, 1878*, no. 9, xxiv. A general history of the Mennonite settlements in Canada during this period is Frank H. Epp, *Mennonites in Canada, 1786–1920: The History of a Separate People* (Toronto: Macmillan, 1974). See also William Janzen, *Limits on Liberty: The Experience of Mennonite, Hutterite, and Doukhobor Communities in Canada* (Toronto: University of Toronto Press, 1990), chs. 1 and 2; Royden K. Loewen, '"The Children, the Cows, My Dear Man and My Sister": The Transplanted Lives of Mennonite Farm Women, 1874–1900,' *Canadian Historical Review* 73/3 (September 1992): 344–73; Loewen, *Family, Church and Market: A Mennonite Community in the Old and the New Worlds, 1850–1930* (Toronto: University of Toronto Press, 1993).

38 Quoted in C. Henry Smith, *The Coming of the Russian Mennonites: An Episode in the Settling of the Last Frontier* (Berne, IN: Mennonite Book Concern, 1927), 189.

39 Ibid., 190.

40 Macdonald, *Canada: Immigration and Colonization*, 201.

41 'Report of the Special Immigration Agent, J.E. Klotz,' ARDA for 1877, *Sessional Papers, 1878*, no. 9, 166.

42 James Trow, *Manitoba and the Northwest Territories* (Ottawa: Department of Agriculture, 1878), 17.

43 Macdonald, *Canada: Immigration and Colonization*, 204.

44 See discussion in chapter 5, this volume, 187.

45 Regarding Canada's response to the pogroms in Russia following Tsar Alexander's assassination in 1881 see H. Troper, 'New Horizons in a New Land: Jewish Immigration to Canada,' in *From Immigration to Integration: The Canadian Jewish Experience: A Millennium Edition,* ed. Ruth Klein and Frank Diman (Toronto: Institute for International Affairs, B'nai Brith Canada, 2001), in particular pp. 6–9. For a more detailed account of Jewish immigration to Canada at this time, see Irving Abella, *A Coat of Many Colours: Two Centuries of Jewish Life in Canada* (Toronto: Lester & Orpen Dennys, 1990), in which the Macdonald quotation is found on p. 78. See also Joseph Kage, *With Faith and Thanksgiving: The Story of Two Hundred Years of Jewish Immigration and Immigrant Aid Effort in Canada (1760 to 1960)* (Montreal: Eagle, 1962), chs. 2 and 3; Henry Trachtenberg, 'Opportunism, Humanitarianism, and Revulsion: "The Old Clo" Move Comes to Manitoba, 1882–83,' *Canadian Ethnic Studies* 22/2 (1990): 1–18; Gerald Tulchinsky, *Taking Root: The Origins of the Canadian Jewish Community* (Toronto: Lester Publishing, 1992), part 3.

46 Abella, *A Coat of Many Colours*, 79–82.

47 Ibid.

48　At this time nativist sentiment in the United States was growing and, with it, there were calls for greater immigration restrictions. Reformers viewed foreigners as the cause of urban ills and corruption. Many workers regarded immigrants as harmful competitors. Several vocal Protestant groups saw Catholics, Jews, and others of foreign faiths as a source of moral degradation. In 1891, amid this groundswell of anti-immigrant sentiment, the U.S. government passed legislation which widened the list of inadmissible immigrants and broadened the scope of its contract-labour law to exclude those immigrants who had been encouraged to come to the United States through employer advertisements: John Higham, *Strangers in the Land: Patterns of American Nativism, 1860–1925* (New York: Atheneum, 1963), 68–105.

49　Multiculturalism Directorate, *The Canadian Family Tree*, 142.

50　For more on Hungarian immigration, see Paul Bödy, 'Emigration from Hungary, 1880–1956,' in *Struggle and Hope: The Hungarian-Canadian Experience*, ed. N.Y. Dreiszinger et al. (Toronto: McClelland & Stewart, 1982), 27.

51　'Joint Report on the Hungarian Colonies by G. Dory and R.S. Park,' ARDA for 1891, *Sessional Papers, 1892*, no. 7, 200.

52　'Report of Special Immigration Agent in Scandinavia, by H. Mattson,' ARDA for 1874, *Sessional Papers, 1875*, no. 40, 135. For a description of 'New Iceland,' see J. Thor, *Icelanders to North America: The First Settlers* (Winnipeg: University of Manitoba Press, 2002), 78–162.

53　Simon Simonarson, quoted in W.J. Lindal, *The Icelanders in Canada* (Ottawa: National Publishers, 1967), 123.

54　Ibid., 134; and see 'Report of the Icelandic Agent, by John Taylor,' ARDA for 1877, *Sessional Papers, 1878*, no. 9.

55　See 'Annual Report of the Winnipeg Immigration Agent,' 'Report on Icelandic Immigration,' and 'Report on Scandinavian Immigration,' ARDA for 1888, *Sessional Papers, 1889*, no. 5, 48, 99, and 105.

56　'Report of the Commissioner of Dominion Lands, by H.H. Smith,' ARDA for 1893, *Sessional Papers, 1894*, no. 13, 8. For maps showing pockets of settlement by various ethnic groups in Western Canada, see Morton, *History of Prairie Settlement*, 62–3; Donald Gurden Grady, Kerr, ed., *A Historical Atlas of Canada*, 2nd ed. (Don Mills, ON: Nelson, 1966), 66.

57　According to department reports throughout the period, agriculturalists, and farm and domestic labourers were in constant demand. The demand for industrial workers varied according to their skill and the level of industrial activity within the country. Thus when sawmills and other factories increased their productive capacities, the demand for foundrymen, machinists, turners, and fitters also expanded. Similarly, in the early and mid-1880s, there was an increased demand for railway workers to meet the needs of railway construction, as well as for masons and stonecutters to work on canal construction.

58 The act gives the provinces and the federal government joint responsibility over immigration. In particular, each provincial legislature is entitled to make laws in relation to immigration into its province as long such laws are not 'repugnant to any Act of the Parliament of Canada.': U.K. 30 & 31 Victoria c.3, s.95.

59 'Report of the Proceedings of a Conference on the Subject of Immigration Held in the Rooms of the Department of Agriculture on the 4th and 5th of November 1874,' *Sessional Reports, 1875*, no. 40, appendix no. 1.

60 H. Gordon Skilling, *Canadian Representation Abroad: From Agency to Embassy* (Toronto: Ryerson, 1945), 6.

61 These figures are taken from calculations made by Duncan M. McDougal in 'Immigration to Canada, 1851–1920,' *Canadian Journal of Economics and Political Science* 27 (1961): 170.

62 'Report on French-Canadian Repatriation,' ARDA for 1885, *Sessional Papers, 1886*, no. 10, 139.

63 Marcus Lee Hansen, *The Mingling of the Canadian and American Peoples* (New Haven, CT: Yale University Press, 1940), 217.

64 Ibid., 199.

65 Karel Denis Bicha, *The American Farmer and the Canadian West, 1896–1914* (Lawrence, KA: Colorado Press, 1968), 101; Carl Addington Dawson, *Group Settlement: Ethnic Communities in Western Canada* (Toronto: Macmillan, 1936), 189; and see Hansen, *Mingling of the Canadian and American Peoples*, 200. See also Brigham Y. Card, 'Charles Ora Card and the Founding of the Mormon Settlements in Southwestern Alberta, North-West Territories,' and Anthony W. Rasporich, 'Early Mormon Settlement in Western Canada: A Comparative Communitarian Perspective,' in Brigham Y. Card, Herbert C. Northcott, John E. Foster, Howard Palmer, and George K. Jarvis, eds., *The Mormon Presence in Canada* (Edmonton: University of Alberta Press, 1990), 77–107 and 136–49, respectively.

66 Skilling, *Canadian Representation Abroad*, 21.

67 Macdonald, *Canada: Immigration and Colonization*, 43.

68 Section 16 of the Immigration Act, 1869, authorized the Cabinet to prohibit the entry of paupers and destitute immigrants unless the master of the ship transporting them provided sufficient money to cover the cost of their temporary support and transportation within Canada: S.C. 1869, c.10. It was pursuant to this section that the 1879 order was passed. Similarly, in 1872 an amendment to the Immigration Act also empowered the Cabinet to prohibit

the landing of criminals or other vicious classes of immigrants: *Immigration Act*, 1872, s.10.

69 'Annual Report of Hamilton Immigration Agent,' ARDA for 1881, *Sessional Papers, 1882*, no. 11, 83.

70 W.H. Hingston, *The Climate of Canada and Its Relation to Life and Health* (Montreal: Dawson Brothers, 1884), 266. See also F. Clement Brown, 'Canadians Abroad,' *The Canadian Magazine 3* (January 1897), 254.

71 Berger, *The Sense of Power*, 130.

72 F.A. Wightman, *Our Canadian Heritage: Its Resources and Possibilities* (Toronto: William Briggs, 1905), 43–4.

73 George R. Parkin, *The Great Dominion: Studies of Canada* (London: Macmillan, 1895), 213–14.

74 James Trow, *A Trip to Manitoba* (Quebec: Marcotte, 1875), 61, and Charles Mair, 'The New Canada, Part 1,' *Canadian Monthly and National Review*, 8 (July 1875): 5, both quoted in Owram, *Promise of Eden*, 117.

75 George Grant, *Ocean to Ocean. Sandford Fleming's Expedition through Canada in 1872* (Toronto: J. Campbell, 1873), quoted in Owram, *Promise of Eden*, 109–10, and see 150–60.

76 Owram, *Promise of Eden*, 104–17.

77 Johnson, *History of Emigration from the United Kingdom to North America*, 116–17; and see discussion in chapter 2, this volume, 43, 45–6.

78 'Final Report of the Civil Service Commissioner,' ARDA for 1869, *Sessional Papers, 1870*, no. 64, 40.

79 S.C. 1869, c.10.

80 Ibid., ss.3, 2, 4, 11.

81 S.C., 1872, c.27.

82 See, for example, the annual reports of the medical doctor at Grosse Isle for the years 1875–82, in the annual reports of the Department of Agriculture, *Sessional Papers, 1876–1883*.

83 'Regulation Relating to Quarantine,' 18 July 1887.

84 *Immigration Act*, 1869, S.C. 1869, c.10, ss.17–23.

85 For a description of these organizations see chapter 2, this volume, 47. For a discussion of the 'culture' of domestic help see L. Chilton, *Agents of Empire: British Female Migration to Canada and Australia, 1860s–1930*, University of Toronto Press, Toronto, 2007, in particular Chapter 4, pp 82–94.

86 *An Act to Amend the Immigration Act of 1869, S.C.* 1872, ss.11–13.

87 ARDA for 1882, *Sessional Papers, 1883*, no. 14, 106–7.

88 ARDA for 1884, *Sessional Papers, 1885*, no. 8, 155.

89 ARDA for 1887, *Sessional Papers, 1888*, no. 4, 123–5. For a history of domestic workers in Canada see: Marilyn Barber, 'The Women Ontario Welcomed:

Immigrant Domestics from Ontario Homes, 1870–1930,' in *The Neglected Majority: Essays in Canadian Women's History*, vol. 2, ed. Alison Prentice and Susan Trofimenkoff (Toronto: McClelland & Stewart, 1985), 102; Genevieve Leslie, 'Domestic Service in Canada, 1880–1920,' in *Women at Work, Ontario, 1850–1930*, ed. Janice Acton et al. (Toronto: Canadian Women's Educational Press, 1980), 71; Barbara Roberts, '"A Work of Empire": Canadian Reformers and British Female Immigration,' in *A Not Unreasonable Claim: Women and Reform in Canada, 1880s-1920s*, ed. Linda Kealey (Toronto: The Women's Press, 1979), 185–201; Claudette Lacelle, *Urban Domestic Servants in Nineteenth-Century Canada* (Ottawa: Canadian Communications Group, 1987).

90 ARDA for 1884, *Sessional Papers, 1885*, no. 8, 155.

91 'Report of the Agent General, London, England,' ARDA for 1875, *Sessional Papers, 1876*, no. 8, 120.

92 ARDA for 1872, *Sessional Papers, 1873*, no. 26, 8.

93 Johnson, *History of Emigration from the United Kingdom to North America*, 98–9.

94 See, for example, ARDA for 1870, *Sessional Papers*, 1871, no. 64, 63.

95 Some municipalities endorsed the abolition of overseas transportation assistance but argued for the retention of inland assistance, concerned that otherwise they would have to assume the costs of the indigent that congregated in their cities.

96 John Duncan Cameron, 'Legislation Relating to Immigration to Canada,' PhD thesis, vol. 1, University of Toronto, 1942, 292.

97 For a discussion of the broad range of views within the labour movement see D. Goutor, *Guarding the Gates: The Canadian Labour Movement and Immigration 1872–1934* (Vancouver: UBC Press, 2007), 103–6 and ch. 6.

98 Eugene Forsey, *Trade Unions in Canada, 1812–1902* (Toronto: University of Toronto Press, 1982), 123, 422, and 437. For a broad discussion of labour's attitude towards Canadian immigration policy during this period see D.J. Goutor, *The Walls of Solidarity: The Mainstream Canadian Labour Movement and Immigration Policy, 1872 to the Early 1930s* (PhD thesis, University of Toronto, 2003), ch. 5, 173–243.

99 Discussed on 82, this volume.

100 'Minister's Report,' ARDA for 1888, *Sessional Papers, 1889*, no. 5, xxviii.

101 Cameron, 'Legislation Relating to Immigration to Canada,' 291–2.

102 These figures were compiled in 1897 by J.J. Kelso, superintendent of neglected and dependent children of Ontario. They are quoted in Kenneth Bagnell, *The Little Immigrants: The Orphans Who Came to Canada* (Toronto: Macmillan, 1980), 178.

103 Joy Parr, *Labouring Children: British Immigrant Apprentices to Canada, 1869–1924* (Montreal: McGill-Queen's University Press, 1980), 33.

104 Bagnell, *The Little Immigrants*, Parr, *Labouring Children*, Marjory Harper, 'The Juvenile Immigrant: Halfway to Heaven or Hell on Earth,' in *The Immigrant Experience: Proceedings of a Conference held at the University of Guelph, 8–11 June 1989*, ed. Catherine Kerrigan (Guelph, ON: University of Guelph Press, 1992), 179. Accounts of the experiences of child immigrants can be found in and P. Harrison, ed., *The Home Children: Their Personal Stories* (Winnipeg: J. Gordon Shillingford Publishing, 2003), chs. 1 and 2. It should not be forgotten, however, that child labour was the norm in nineteenth-century Canada; see, for example, John Bullen, 'Hidden Workers: Child Labour and the Family Economy in Late Nineteenth Century Urban Ontario,' *Labour/Le Travail* (Fall 1986): 163–88.

105 For a thorough description of the Doyle report see M. Kohili, *The Golden Bridge: Young Immigrants to Canada, 1833–1939* (Toronto: Natural Heritage Books, 2003), 21–3. See also R. Parker, *Uprooted: The Shipment of Poor Children to Canada, 1867–1917* (Vancouver: UBC Press, 2008), 49–52.

106 For a discussion of the hearings held by the Select Committee on Immigration and Colonization see Kohili, *Golden Bridge*, 21–8.

107 For a more detailed discussion on the Canadian reaction to Doyle's report see Bagnell, *The Little Immigrants*, 37–62.

108 For a discussion of Labour's attitudes towards impoverished British children being sent to Canada see D. J. Goutor, *The Walls of Solidarity*, 97.

109 See for example the comments by J.D. Moylan, Inspector of Penitentiaries, June 1891, quoted in Bagnell, *The Little Immigrants*, 72–3.

110 Quoted in ibid., 78–9; and see 206.

111 'Report of A.M. Burgess, Deputy Minister of the Interior,' Annual Report of the Department of the Interior for 1893, *Sessional Papers, 1894*, no. 13, xxviii. It is interesting that he goes on to write that, while he was in favour of child emigration, 'if not conducted upon too large a scale,' he felt that there was also room in philanthropy for emigration assistance to adult British males from the working class in rural areas, many of whom were educated and familiar with agriculture, and would make good workers in Canada.

112 'Report of the Clerk of Immigration,' Annual Report of the Department of the Interior for 1893, *Sessional Papers, 1894*, no. 13, 8.

113 60 Vic. (1897), c.53, ss. 3, 5.

114 Parr, *Labouring Children*, 57.

115 *An Act Respecting the Canadian Pacific Railway*, S.C. 44 Victoria, c. 1.

116 Francis, Jones, and Smith, *Destinies*, 62.

117 For an account of a particularly brutal incident and the subsequent trial see Patricia E. Roy, 'A Choice between Evils: The Chinese and the Construction of the Canadian Pacific Railway in British Columbia,' in *The CPR West: The Iron Road and the Making of a Nation*, ed. Hugh A. Dempsey (Vancouver: Douglas & McIntyre, 1984), 21.

118 In 1878 the Workingmen's Protective Association (WPA) was formed in Victoria; its professed platform was the improvement of working conditions, but its *raison d'être* the eradication of Chinese immigration. The association required its members to boycott all Chinese establishments, as well as all businesses which employed Chinese workers. It also demanded that its members refrain from engaging the services provided by Chinese immigrants, and to use all legitimate means to ensure their expulsion from the province. In 1879, the former chairperson of the WPA, Noah Shakespeare, formed a new organization, the Anti-Chinese Association, which sent petitions to the federal and provincial governments condemning the continued employment and immigration of Chinese workers. It, too, was short-lived, for it did not have the active support of the public at that time: Joseph F. Krauter and Morris Davis, *Minority Canadians: Ethnic Groups* (Toronto: Methuen, 1978), 61.

119 House of Commons *Debates*, 12 May 1882, 1477.

120 Wallace Clement, *The Canadian Corporate Elite: An Analysis of Economic Power* (Toronto: McClelland & Stewart, 1975), 65.

121 For a discussion of anti-Chinese sentiment in Vancouver at the end of the 1880s, see Patricia E. Roy, 'The Preservation of the Peace in Vancouver: The Aftermath of the Anti-Chinese Riot of 1887,' *B.C. Studies* 31 (Autumn 1976): 44–59.

122 The two commissioners of the inquiry were J.A. Chapleau, federal secretary of state, and Mr. Justice Gray of the Supreme Court of British Columbia. Chapleau let his position be known early in the proceedings by stating that the purpose of the investigation was to 'obtain proof that the principle of restricting Chinese immigration is proper and in the best interests of the Province and of the Dominion' 'Report of the Royal Commission on Chinese Immigration,' *Sessional Papers, 1885*, no. 54, viii–ix.

123 Ibid., 133.

124 At first the objections were confined to B.C. unions. By the mid-1880s, however, they had succeeded in enlisting the support of other unions across the country. Trade unions in Toronto, Hamilton, Montreal, and Quebec sent resolutions to Ottawa protesting Chinese immigration and calling upon the government to 'send back all the Chinese now in Canada or enforce such a poll tax as will drive them hence': House of Commons *Debates*, 2 July

1885, 3013. The National Trades and Labour Council of Canada also joined in this demand: Forsey, *Trade Unions in Canada*, 430–5.

125 W. Peter Ward, *White Canada Forever. Popular Attitudes and Public Opinion toward Orientals in British Columbia* (Montreal: McGill-Queen's University Press, 1978), 18; see also Roy, *White Man's Country*, ch. 3.

126 House of Commons *Debates, 2 July* 1885, 3006, per J.A. Chapleau.

127 S.C. 1885, c.71, s.5.

128 Speech delivered in Ottawa on 8 October 1886, quoted in Berger, *The Sense of Power*, 57.

129 House of Commons *Debates*, 4 May 1885, 1582.

130 (1878) 1 B.C.R. (Pt. 1) 101 (B.C.S.C.). The Court reasoned that the Dominion power over aliens included the power to define the rights and privileges of aliens. The Court characterized the law as not being for the purpose of collecting revenue but designed to 'drive the Chinese from the country.' Noting the severity of the law on all those affected, including employers who faced substantial fines if found employing Chinese workers without a lawful licence, the Court concluded that the law encroached upon the federal government's powers over aliens and over 'trade and commerce:' 111–12.

131 S.B.C., 1884, c.3.

132 The Constitution Act of 1897 preserved British authority to invalidate Canadian statutes through the powers of disallowance and reservation. Federal legislation could be disallowed by an Imperial order-in-council within two years of enactment, and the governor general was empowered to withhold or reserve Royal assent on any federal bill. Similarly, the governor general was also empowered to disallow any provincial act within one year from the receipt of an authentic copy from the secretary of state. The lieutenant-governors were also given the power of withholding Royal assent to provincial bills or reserving them for consideration of the governor general: see Bruce Ryder, 'Racism and the Constitution: The Constitutional Fate of British Columbia Anti-Asian Immigration Legislation, 1884–1909,' *Osgoode Hall Law Journal* 29 (1991). 619, 627.

133 *R. v Wing Chong* (1885), 1 B.C.R. (Pt. II) 150 (B.C.S.C.).

134 *An Act to Prevent the Immigration of Chinese*, S.B.C. 1885, c.13.

135 An additional act aimed at excluding Asian immigrants was reserved by Lieutenant-Governor Dunsmuir in 1907: see Ryder, 'Racism and the Constitution,' 641.

136 Ibid., 619.

137 See discussion in chapter 4, this volume, 143–4, 154–6.

138 Kenneth H. Norrie, 'The Rate of Settlement on the Canadian Prairies, 1870–1911,' in *Perspectives on Canadian Economic History*, ed. Douglas McCalla (Toronto: Copp Clark Pitman, 1987), 168.

139 See for example John Dyke's comments in 'Annual Report of the Liverpool (Eng.) Agent,' ARDA for 1884, *Sessional Papers, 1885*, no, 8, 167.

140 Macdonald, *Canada: Immigration and Colonization*, 217.

141 Norrie and Owram, *History of the Canadian Economy*, 296.

142 'Report of Mr. Buchanan, Chief Immigration Agent, Government Immigration Office, Quebec,' ARDA for 1866, *Sessional Papers*, 1867, no. 3, 13. See also Hansen, *The Mingling of the Canadian and American Peoples*, 193–5.

143 ARDA for 1872, *Sessional Papers, 1873*, no. 26, 150.

144 For a good review of the many complaints and suggestions made throughout the 1880s and 1890s, see 'Report by the Honourable T. Mayne Daly on his visit to Great Britain,' Annual Report of the Ministry of the Interior for 1896, *Sessional Papers, 1897*, no. 13, 174–83.

145 'Annual Report of the Duluth Agent,' by J.M. McGovern, ARDA for 1883, *Sessional Papers, 1884*, no. 14, 118.

146 ARDA for 1870, *Sessional Papers, 1871*, no. 64, 41.

147 Macdonald, *Canada: Immigration and Colonization*, 182.

148 For a thorough study of Anglo-Canadian emigration to the US between 1880–1920 see R.W. Widdis, *With Scarcely a Ripple: Anglo-Canadian Migration into the United States and Western Canada* (Montreal: McGill-Queen's University Press, 1998).

149 The population of Prince Edward Island dropped from 109,000 in 1881 to 103,000 in 1901 as a result of out-migration. While the rest of the Atlantic provinces still experienced population growth, the rate of growth dropped considerably: see Alvin Finkel, Margaret Conrad, and Veronica Strong-Boag, *History of the Canadian Peoples, vol. 2, 1867 to the Present* (Toronto: Copp Clark Pitman, 1993), 115–16. See also Patricia A. Thornton, 'The Problem of Out-Migration from Atlantic Canada, 1867–1921: A New Look, "in *Acadiensis Reader*, vol. 2, ed. P.A. Buckner and David Frank (Fredericton: Acadiensis, 1988), 34–65.

150 For a more thorough account of the migration south from the Maritimes, see Hansen, *The Mingling of the Canadian and American Peoples*, 160–4 and 207–10.

151 David C. Corbett, 'A Study of Factors Governing Canada's Absorption of Immigrants from 1867–1914, with Suggestions towards a Definition of Absorptive Capacity' (Masters thesis, University of Toronto, 1949), 96. On

the forces which were drawing some groups into the country, and others, particularly French Canadians, out, see Bruno Ramirez, *On the Move: French-Canadian and Italian Migrants in the North Atlantic Economy, 1860–1914* (Toronto: McClelland & Stewart, 1990).

152 'Report of P.E. Gendran, Special Agent,' ARDA for 1873, *Sessional Papers, 1874*, no. 9, 68–9.

153 Hansen, *The Mingling of the Canadian and American Peoples*, 173.

154 Ibid., 184–7.

155 According to Hansen, another contributing factor to the exodus was that, in the early 1880s, many pioneering settlers in Manitoba, after having broken the soil and cultivated the land, found that there were willing buyers for it. Once the land was sold, however, the settler was prohibited from acquiring another free homestead from the Canadian government. Although the capital from the sale of the first farm would have made the improvement of the second an easier undertaking, being prevented from doing so provided an incentive to emigrate to the United States. There, after declaring an intention to become an American citizen, the settler was free to homestead again. Since the American government also allowed a citizen to exercise a homestead right only once, many American farmers, after selling their homesteads, went to Canada to start again. The volume of this flow did not compare, however, with that in the opposite direction: ibid., 195.

156 ARDA for 1874, *Sessional Papers, 1875*, no. 40, v.

157 ARDA for 1885, *Sessional Papers, 1886*, no. 10, xlv.

158 An order-in-council dated 13 March 1874 set aside lands for repatriating French Canadians who began to arrive in 1875. In the next two years approximately 1,000 came from the United States; however, the numbers were far below the expectations of those promoting the scheme: see Morton, *History of Prairie Settlement*, 55.

159 For a discussion of dry farming and its application in Canada, see Norrie, 'Rate of Settlement on the Canadian Prairies,' 172–8.

160 Ibid.

161 Shin Imai, 'Canadian Immigration Law and Policy: 1867–1935' (LLM thesis, York University, Toronto, 1983), 27, 29.

162 The Immigration Act, 1869, section 12, did provide for the sending back of those who were considered to be mentally or physically impaired; however, when deportations under this act are compared with those in other periods, it appears the act was sufficiently limited so as not to have wide application.

163 *An Act Respecting Aliens and Naturalization, S.C.* 1868, c.66 ss.3, 4, 5, and *Naturalization Act, 1881,* S.C. 1881, c.13, s.17, both discussed by Imai in 'Canadian Immigration Law and Policy,' 28–9.

164 Peter H. Schuck, 'The Transformation of Immigration Law,' *Columbia Law Review* 84 (1984): 2. Schuck acknowledges that, in practice, 'a considerable portion even of American society – most notably slaves and, to some, extent, females – were denied this liberty.'

165 Imai, 'Canadian Immigration Law and Policy,' 16–17.

166 Ibid., 30.

167 Quoted in James W. Morton, *In the Sea of Sterile Mountains: The Chinese in British Columbia* (Vancouver: J. J. Douglas, 1974), 67.

168 House of Commons *Debates,* 12 May 1882, 1477, and 4 May 1885, 1582. For the values which predominated in the debates surrounding the emerging Canadian identity see J. Ajzenat, ed. *Canada's Founding Debates* (Toronto: University of Toronto Press, 2003), ch. 8, "What Is a Canadian,' 229–58.

169 According to T.W. Acheson, at the turn of the century one-third of the Canadian industrial elite held political office at some time in their careers: 'The Changing Social Origins of the Canadian Industrial Elite,' in *Enterprise and National Development: Essays in Canadian Business and Economic History,* ed. B. Porter and R. Cuff (Toronto: Hakkert, 1973), cited in Leo Panitch, 'The Role and Nature of the Canadian State,' in *The Canadian State: Political Economy and Political Power,* ed. Leo Panitch (Toronto: University of Toronto Press, 1977), 12.

170 Clement, *The Canadian Corporate Elite,* 69.

171 Loken, *From Fjord to Frontier,* 40–1. For more on the close relationships between companies and the government, see R.T. Naylor, *The History of Canadian Business: 1867–1916* (Toronto: Lorimer, 1975) and for organized labour's perspective see For a discussion of labour's understanding of the role of big business in Canadian immigration policy, see D.J. Gonter, *The Walls of Solidarity,* 207–10.

172 For a thorough discussion of Labour's attitude towards Chinese immigrants see ibid., 182–8.

173 *Empire,* 2 October 1890, quoted in Berger, *Sense of Power,* 164.

174 F. Clement Brown, 'Canadians Abroad,' *The Canadian Magazine* 3 (January 1897), 253.

175 Annual Report of the Department of the Interior for 1893, *Sessional Papers, 1894,* no. 13, xxxv. In his report of 1938–9, Charles Blair wrote that it 'would have been possible at any time during recent years to have obtained tens of

thousands of immigrants by the simple expedient of letting down the bars erected in 1930 to protect the Dominion against an influx of surplus labour. If quantity rather than quality was the objective sought, its attainment was simplicity itself,': 'Report of the Department of Mines and Resources including Report of the Soldier Settlement of Canada,' in *Annual Departmental Reports, 1938–39*, 268.

Chapter 4 Industrialization, Immigration, and the Foundation of Twentieth-Century Immigration Policy, 1896–1914

1 The economic context for this period is well covered in Robert Craig Brown and Ramsay Cook, *Canada, 1896–1921. A Nation Transformed* (Toronto: McClelland & Stewart, 1974).
2 'Report of the Department of Immigration and Colonization,' *Annual Departmental Reports, 1929–30*, 8–9.
3 Alvin Finkel, Margaret Conrad, and Veronica Strong-Boag, *History of the Canadian Peoples*, vol. 2, *1867 to the Present*, 4th ed. (Toronto: Pearson Longman, 2006), 112.
4 J.L. Finlay and D.N. Sprague, *The Structure of Canadian History*, 4th ed. (Toronto: Prentice-Hall, 1997), 287.
5 *The Canadian Annual Review of Public Affairs: 1913* (Toronto: Annual Review Publishing, 1914), 99.
6 In his book, *The Bunkhouse Man: A Study of Work and Pay in the Camps of Canada, 1903–1914* (Toronto: University of Toronto Press, *1972* [originally published 1928]), 7, Edmund W. Bradwin estimated that, between 1903 and 1914, 200,000 men were engaged in such work at different periods of the year.
7 The extent to which immigrants left Canada was the subject of heated debate in the House and in the press. The Conservative Opposition calculated that, given the government's immigration figures for this period, and accounting for natural increase, the population in 1911 should have been closer to 8 million. They questioned the government on the whereabouts of the missing 1 million, speculating that this represented the number who had emigrated to the United States or returned home. See House of Commons *Debates*, 1 May 1911, 8112–30, and *The Canadian Annual Review of Public Affairs 1911* (Toronto: Annual Review Publishing, 1912), 394–7.
8 Finlay and Sprague, *The Structure of Canadian History*, 287.
9 These percentage increases are approximate and are derived from *The Canada Year Book, 1932* (Ottawa: Dominion Bureau of Statistics, 1933), 103.

10 Censuses of Canada, as reproduced in *Report of the Royal Commission on Bilingualism and Biculturalism*, vol. 4, *The Cultural Contribution of the Other Ethnic Groups* (Ottawa: Queen's Printer, 1969), 22, 238–40 [henceforth cited as RRC 1969]. The most spectacular growth was in Saskatchewan and Alberta, both territories experiencing a population increase of over 400 per cent in the decade.

11 See chapter 3, this volume, 79.

12 Report of the Department of Immigration and Colonization, *Annual Departmental Reports, 1929–30*, 8–9.

13 RRC 1969, 248, 22. This shift in the ethnic composition of the population was most marked on the Prairies, which experienced a 'deepening cultural diversity that would remain unknown to much of the rest of Canada until well after the Second World War': Finkel, Conrad, and Strong-Boag, *History of the Canadian Peoples*, 112. A table showing the gains in population in the Prairie provinces according to racial origin appears in Arthur S. Morton, *History of Prairie Settlement* (Toronto: Macmillan, 1938), 127.

14 Discussed more fully this volume, 138–41.

15 For a fuller discussion of the urban social problems which accompanied industrialization, see Michael Bliss, *A Living Profit: Studies in the Social History of Canadian Business, 1883–1911* (Toronto: McClelland & Stewart, 1974), 55–73; T.J. *Copp, The Anatomy of Poverty: The Condition of the Working Class in Montreal* (Toronto: McClelland & Stewart, 1974); Michael Piva, *The Conditions of the Working Class in Toronto, 1900–1921* (Ottawa: University of Ottawa Press, 1979).

16 Finlay and Sprague, *The Structure of Canadian History*, 288.

17 For public hostility towards immigrant groups because of poor living conditions and their potential threat to public health, see, for example, Kay J. Anderson, *Vancouver's Chinatown: Racial Discourse in Canada, 1875–1980* (Montreal: McGill-Queen's University Press, 1991), ch. 3; Patricia Roy, *A White Man's Province: British Columbia Politicians and Japanese Immigrants, 1858–1914* (Vancouver: University of British Columbia Press, 1989), ch. 2.

18 For a vivid description of the life of the worker in such areas, see Bradwin, *The Bunkhouse Man*, which describes in detail the conditions of the railway construction camps at the turn of the century. See also Ian Radforth, *Bushworkers and Bosses: Logging in Northern Ontario, 1900–1980* (Toronto: University of Toronto Press, 1987).

19 Shin Imai, 'Canadian Immigration Law and Policy: 1867–1935' (LLM thesis, York University, Toronto, 1983), 86; Donald Avery, *Reluctant Host: Canada's Response to Immigrant Workers, 1896–1994* (Toronto: McClelland & Stewart, 1995), 29–40. For a comparison of the treatment of foreign workers in

Canada to that experienced by foreign labourers in the industrialized nations of Western Europe, see Avery, 'Continental European Immigrant Workers in Canada, 1896–1919: From "Stalwart Peasants" to "Radical Proletariat," ' *Canadian Review of Sociology and Anthropology* 12/1 (1988): 53, 54–5.

20 Avery, 'Continental European Immigrant Workers,' 56–7.

21 For a more detailed exploration of the eugenics movement, see Angus McLaren, *Our Own Master Race: Eugenics in Canada, 1885–1945* (Toronto: McClelland & Stewart, 1990).

22 Armand Lavergne, in House of Commons *Debates*, 9 April 1907, 6151.

23 One union official told Sifton, 'all the hundreds of thousands of dollars to aid immigration have been extorted principally out of the laboring classes in order to make the price of labour cheap, to inundate and slaughter the labor market': J.T. Mortimer to Sifton, 22 June 1899, quoted in D.J. Hall, *Clifford Sifton*, vol. 1, *The Young Napoleon, 1861–1900* (Vancouver: University of British Columbia Press, 1981), 268. For the use of immigrant workers as strike breakers, see Donald Avery, *'Dangerous Foreigners' European Immigrant Workers and Labour Radicalism in Canada* (Toronto: McClelland & Stewart, 1979), 32–3. For a discussion of Labour's attitudes towards immigrants throughout this period see D.J. Goutor, *The Walls of Solidarity: The Mainstream Canadian Labour Movement and Immigration Policy, 1872 to the Early 1930s* (PhD thesis, University of Toronto), chs. 5 and 6, 173–329.

24 See, for example, Donald Avery, 'Canadian Immigration Policy and the Alien Question, 1896–1919: The Anglo-Canadian Perspective' (PhD thesis, University of Western Ontario, 1973), 216; Brown and Cook, *Canada, 1896–1921*, 108.

25 William Lyon Mackenzie King, *The Mackenzie King Diaries (1893–1931)* (Toronto: University of Toronto Press, 1973), 10 January 1911, 10.

26 Quoted in *The Canadian Annual Review of Public Affairs, 1902* (Toronto: Annual Review Publishing, 1903), 329.

27 *The Canadian Annual Review of Public Affairs: 1906* (Toronto: Annual Review Publishing, 1907), 279. For further discussion on Sifton's changes to land policies, see Hall, *Sifton*, vol. 1, 129–33, 253–5.

28 In 1896, his department distributed 65,000 pamphlets. Within four years, it had sent out one million: R. Douglas Francis, Richard Jones, and Donald B, Smith, *Destinies: Canadian History since Confederation*, 6th ed. (Toronto: Nelson, 2008), 71–2; Hall, *Sifton*, vol. 1, 258–60.

29 Patrick A. Dunae, 'Promoting the Dominion: Records and the Canadian Immigration Campaign, 1872–1915,' *Archivaria* 19 (1984–5): 90.

30 Karel Denis Bicha, *The American Farmer and the Canadian West, 1896–1914* (Lawrence, KS: Colorado Press, 1968), 63.

31 Between 1898 and 1908, the government spent $2 million on propaganda activity in the United States, representing close to one-third of its total expenditure on immigration work: ibid., 80.

32 'Operations in the United States: Report of W.J. White,' Annual Report of the Department of the Interior for 1899, *Sessional Papers, 1900*, no. 13, 177.

33 Sir Clifford Sifton, 'The Immigrants Canada Wants,' *Maclean's*, 1 April 1922.

34 P.C. 902 (31 May 1902); and P.C. 1697 (20 September 1904); see also Hall, *Sifton*, vol. 1, 260.

35 Note, however, that bonuses continued to be paid to agents of the North Atlantic Trading Company and other booking agents approved by the minister for immigrants from Britain and Scandinavia.

36 It was also alleged that bonuses were paid to the company for immigrants procured by other organizations. Moreover, some MPs argued that the European bonus system should be discontinued and the money directed towards securing British immigrants: see House of Commons *Debates*, 20 April 1906,1795–818; 1 May 1906, 2357–74; 4 June 1906, 4451–73; D.J. Hall, *Clifford Sifton*, vol. 2: *A Lonely Eminence, 1901–1929* (Vancouver: University of British Columbia Press, 1985),184–5.

37 The *Canadian Annual Review: 1906*, 283; F.D. Monk, in House of Commons *Debates*, 4 June 1906, 4467. Note that, according to Donald Avery, statistics provided in later departmental reports suggest that, for the entire seven-year period of its existence, the scheme brought in close to 71,000 immigrants at a total cost of more than $350,000: Avery, 'Canadian Immigration Policy and the Alien Question,' 14, note 46.

38 House of Commons *Debates*, 17 April 1902, 2991; see also *Debates*, 26 July 1899, 8501.

39 See chapter 3, this volume, 99, and discussion in this chapter, 145–6.

40 See discussion this volume, 142, 149. The Alien Labour Acts of 1897 and 1906 made it unlawful to assist or encourage the importation of immigrants under contract to labour in Canada. The acts were of limited application and rarely enforced, reflecting the government's unwillingness to restrict the supply of foreign workers to Canadian enterprises: R.S.C. 1906, c.97. See Imai, 'Canadian Immigration Law and Policy,' 42–4; Paul Craven, '*An Impartial Umpire': Industrial Relations and the Canadian State, 1900–1911* (Toronto: University of Toronto Press, 1980), 120. For a discussion on why the Chinese head tax did not stem the tide of Chinese workers, see discussion this volume, 152–3.

41 Mabel F. Timlin, 'Canada's Immigration Policy, 1896–1910,' *Canadian Journal of Economics and Political Science* 24 (1960): 520.

42 House of Commons *Debates*, 26 July 1899, 8514.

43 Ibid., 14 June 1897, 4071.

44 Ibid., 26 July 1899, 8567–88.

45 *The Canada Year Book, 1914* (Ottawa: Dominion Bureau of Statistics, 1915), 91. Sifton had seriously considered resigning for a few years previous to his actually doing so. He felt beleaguered by criticism from the West about his immigration and settlement policies. However, the issue which precipitated his resignation was the controversy over the schools question in the Northwest; see Hall, *Sifton*, vol. 2, ch. 8.

46 'Report of the Department of Mines and Resources,' *Annual Departmental Reports*, 1944–5, 200.

47 For more literature on this, see Dunae, 'Promoting the Dominion,' 91 and accompanying notes.

48 Evelyn Eager, 'Our Pioneers Say,' *Saskatchewan History* 6/1 (1953): 2, quoted in Brown and Cook, *Canada, 1896–1921*, 80.

49 The Canadian Annual Review of Public Affairs: 1907 (Toronto: Annual Review Publishing, 1908), 357.

50 *The Canadian Annual Review: 1913*, 99.

51 Penman's company was one firm that was successful in its British recruitment practices. For a description of the immigration of 700 British hosiery workers assisted by Penman's, see Joy Parr, *The Gender of Breadwinners: Women, Men, and Change in Two Industrial Towns, 1880–1950* (Toronto: University of Toronto Press, 1990); Parr, 'The Skilled Emigrant and Her Kin: Gender, Culture, and Labour Recruitment,' *Canadian Historical Review* 68/4 (1987): 529–51.

52 Stanley Johnson, *A History of Emigration from the United Kingdom to North America, 1763–1912* (London: Routledge & Sons, 1913), 266–70. See also Julia Bush, '"The Right Sort of Woman": Female Emigrators and Emigration to the British Empire, 1890–1910,' *Women's History Review* 3/3 (1994): 385–410; Barbara Roberts, 'Ladies, Women and the State: Managing Female Immigration, 1880–1920,' in *Community Organization and the Canadian State*, ed. Roxana Ng, Gillian Walker, and Jacob Muller (Toronto: Garamond, 1990). For a discussion of some of the issues particular to British women who emigrated from Britain see L. Chilton, *Agents of Empire: British Female Migration to Canada and Australia, 1860s–1930* (Toronto: University of Toronto Press, 2007) and in regard to Finnish domestics, see V. Lindstrom, 'I Won't Be a Slave: Finnish Domestics in Canada 1911–1930,' in *A Nation of Immigrants: Women, Workers and Communities in Canadian History, 1840s–1960s*.

ed. Franca Iacovetta (Toronto: University of Toronto Press, 1998), 166–86.

53 Johnson, *A History of Emigration from the United Kingdom to North America, 1763–1912*, 260–4.

54 *The Canada Year Book, 1914*, 88.

55 Johnson, *History of Emigration from the United Kingdom*, 284. For more on how child immigration schemes operated and the dangers to which children were exposed, see chapter 3, this volume, 91–4. For a thorough discussion of Dr. Barnardo's homes see R. Parker, *Uprooted: The Shipment of Poor Children to Canada, 1867–1917* (Vancouver: UBC Press, 2008), 67–73, 166–7, 181–4. See also M. Kohili, *The Golden Bridge: Young Immigrants to Canada, 1833–1917* (Toronto: Natural Heritage Books, 2006), 148–56.

56 See for example *The Canadian Annual Review of Public Affairs: 1910* (Toronto: Annual Review Publishing, 1911), 386, which reported an incident in Ontario involving a farmer in Hallam, in Grey County, under whose charge a young girl suffering from gangrene caused by frostbite had to have her feet amputated. See more generally the first-hand accounts of the children in P. Harrison, ed., *The Home Children: Their Personal Stories* (Winnipeg: J. Gordon Shillingford Publishing, 2003), chs. 3–8.

57 It is interesting to note that many British boards of guardians refused to participate in child-emigration schemes. It was their conviction that a child under their care was their responsibility until able to look after him- or herself. Emigration before that time was thus inappropriate because it entailed the Guardians relinquishing their control to some agency over which they had no authority: Johnson, *History of Emigration from the United Kingdom*, 293.

58 It will be recalled that, in the West, the land had been divided into townships with alternating even- and odd-numbered sections of 640 acres each. The odd numbered sections had been reserved for railways, while the government retained even-numbered sections for homestead grants. See chapter 3, this volume, 69–70.

59 Bicha, *The American Farmer and the Canadian West*, 109–12.

60 Francis, Jones, and Smith, *Destinies*, 132.

61 'Report of the Department of Immigration and Colonization,' *Annual Departmental Reports*, 1929–30, 9–10. According to Karel Bicha, these numbers are unreliable, given that many Americans came across the border undetected and others slipped back unnoticed. Judging from census figures, nearly two-thirds of American immigrants returned home, many worn down by the harshness of life on the prairies, the relatively high prices of consumer goods, and, later, Canada's participation in the war,

which many Americans wanted to avoid. Thus, while immigration figures place the increase in the American-born population in Alberta and Saskatchewan between 1901 and 1916 at more than 500,000, census data place it much lower, at 179,000: Bicha, *The American Farmer and the Canadian West*, 138.

62　This concern was voiced by both English-Canadian and French-Canadian nationalists; see *The Canadian Annual Review of Public Affairs: 1908* (Toronto: Annual Review of Publishing, 1909), 119.

63　*The Canadian Annual Review: 1902*, 331.

64　Ibid.

65　Bicha, *The American Farmer and the Canadian West*, 101; see also Brigham Y. Card, Herbert C. Northcott, John E. Foster, Howard Palmer, and George K. Jarvis, eds., *The Mormon Presence in Canada* (Edmonton: University of Alberta Press, 1990).

66　*The Canadian Annual Review: 1907*, 296.

67　Carl Addington Dawson, *Group Settlement: Ethnic Communities in Western Canada* (Toronto: Macmillan, 1936), 275–6.

68　See Victor Peters, *All Things Common: The Hutterian Way of Life* (Minneapolis: University of Minnesota Press, 1965); William Janzen, *Limits on Liberty: The Experience of Mennonite, Hutterite, and Doukhobor Communities in Canada* (Toronto: University of Toronto Press, 1990).

69　Although the Department of the Interior's summary statistics placed the number of Scandinavian immigrants at close to 58,000 between 1901 and 1911, other reports suggest that this number was inflated. For example, between 1903 and 1911, J. Obed Smith estimated that fewer than 500 immigrants from Denmark and Sweden emigrated to Canada annually. The discrepancy may be explained in part by the fact that American immigrants of Scandinavian origin may have been included in the overall statistics, making the number from abroad difficult to determine. Donald Avery claims that this later group made up the bulk of the increase in the Canadian Scandinavian population from 31,000 in 1901 to approximately 108,000 in 1911: Avery, 'Canadian Immigration Policy and the Alien Question,' 127.

70　Heinz Lehmann, *The German Canadians, 1750–1937: Immigration, Settlement and Culture*, trans. Gerhard P. Bassler (St John's, NF: Jesperson, 1986), 128.

71　It will be recalled that one of the impediments facing would-be German immigrants to North America was the German prohibition on travelling on anything other than German-owned ships proceeding directly to North America. Such direct routes existed only to the United States: see chapter 3, this volume, 100.

72 For a discussion on the difficulties in ascertaining the exact number of
    German immigrants from Germany at this time, see Lehmann, *The German
    Canadians*, 127–31, 138–40. K.M. McLaughlin places the number of German
    immigrants from Germany for the entire forty-three-year period between
    1871 and 1914 at 39,900: see *The Germans in Canada* (Ottawa: Canadian
    Historical Association, 1985), 5.

73 Lehmann, *The German Canadians*, 129.

74 For more on the ethnic-German emigration, see ibid., 108–19. Sources that
    discuss Mennonites include Emerich K. Francis, *In Search of Utopia: The
    Mennonites in Manitoba* (Altona, MN: D.W. Friesen, 1955); Frank H. Epp,
    Mennonites in Canada, 1786–1920: The History of a Separate People (Toronto:
    Macmillan, 1974); Janzen, *Limits on Liberty;* Royden K. Loewen, '"The
    Children, the Cows, My Dear Man and My Sister": The Transplanted Lives of
    Mennonite Farm Women, 1874–1900,' *Canadian Historical Review 73/3*
    (September 1992): 344–73; Loewen, *Family, Church, and Market: A Mennonite
    Community in the Old and the New Worlds, 1850–1930* (Toronto: University of
    Toronto Press, 1993).

75 Lehman, *The German Canadians*, 118–25.

76 Censuses of Canada, in *RRC* 1969, 247.

77 In Saskatchewan and Alberta, the population of German origin was 14 and
    11 per cent, respectively: censuses of Canada, in ibid., 262, 264.

78 Much has been written about the Ukrainian settlements in Canada. Books on
    the subject include: Charles H. Young, *The Ukrainian Canadians: A Study in
    Assimilation* (Toronto: Nelson, 1931); Helen Potrebenko, *No Streets of Gold: A
    Social History of Ukrainians in Alberta* (Vancouver: New Star, 1977); Michael H.
    Marunchak, *The Ukrainian Canadians: A History* (Winnipeg: Ukrainian Free
    Academy of Sciences, 1970); Vladimir Kaye, *Early Ukrainian Settlements in
    Canada, 1895–1900* (Toronto: University of Toronto Press, 1964); Jaroslav
    Rozumnyj, ed., *New Soil, Old Roots: The Ukrainian Experience in Canada*
    (Winnipeg: Ukrainian Academy of Arts and Sciences in Canada, 1983); Orest
    T. Martynowych, *Ukrainians in Canada: The Formative Period, 1891–1924*
    (Edmonton: Canadian Institute of Ukrainian Studies 1991); Jaroslav
    Petrysbyn, with Luba Dzubak, *Peasants in the Promised Land: Canada and the
    Ukrainians, 1891–1914* (Toronto: Lorimer, 1985); Manoly R. Lupul, *A Heritage
    in Transition: Essays in the History of Ukrainians in Canada* (Toronto:
    McClelland & Stewart: Ottawa: Department of Secretary of State,
    Multiculturalism Directorate, 1982); Lubomyr Y. Luciuk and Iroida L.
    Wynnyckyj, eds., *Ukrainians in Ontario* (Toronto: Multicultural History Society
    of Ontario, 1986); Lubomyr Y. Luciuk and Stella Hryniuk, eds., *Canada's*

Ukrainians: Negotiating an Identity (Toronto: University of Toronto Press and Ukrainian Canadian Centennial Committee, 1991); Frances Swyripa, *Wedded to the Cause: Ukrainian-Canadian Women and Ethnic Identity, 1891–1991* (Toronto: University of Toronto Press, 1993).

79 O.W. Gerus and J.E. Rea, *The Ukrainians in Canada* (Ottawa: Canadian Historical Association, 1985), 3–4.

80 John C. Lehr, 'Peopling the Prairies with Ukrainians,' in *Immigration in Canada: Historical Perspectives*, ed. Gerald Tulchinsky (Toronto: Copp Clark Longman, 1994), 179.

81 Avery, 'Canadian Immigration Policy and the Alien Question,' 148.

82 Quoted in Howard Palmer, *Immigration and the Rise of Multiculturalism* (Toronto: Copp Clark, 1975), 45.

83 There is some controversy over whether the Ukrainians were forced by government officials to accept these lands or whether they chose them themselves and, in doing so, made a grave mistake. John Lehr argues that their land was not a product of governmental discrimination. Rather, it was the result of 'complicated relations between the immigrants, the officers of the Department of the Interior responsible for the settlement of the West, the Ottawa politicians, and the largely Anglophile Canadian public,': see Lehr, 'Peopling the Prairies with Ukrainians,' 178–82.

84 House of Commons *Debates*, 2 June 1898, 6829.

85 Gerus and Rea, *The Ukrainians in Canada*, 7, 9. For an in-depth study of the development and growth of one settlement bloc in the area north of Dauphin Manitoba from 1896 to the 1980s see J. Darlington, 'The Ukrainian Impress on the Canadian West,' in *A Nation of Immigrants: Women, Workers and Communities in Canadian History, 1840s–1960s*, ed. Franca Iacovetta (Toronto: University of Toronto Press, 1998), 128–53.

86 Most of the following account of Polish immigration is derived from D.H. Avery and J.K. Fedorowicz, *The Poles in Canada* (Ottawa: Canadian Historical Association, 1982). Other books on the subject include: Benedykt Heydenkorn, ed., *Memoirs of Polish Immigrants in Canada* (Toronto: Canadian-Polish Research Institute, 1979); Henry Radecki, *Ethnic Organizational Dynamics: The Polish Group in Canada* (Waterloo: Wilfrid Laurier University Press, 1979); Victor Turek, *The Poles in Manitoba* (Toronto: Polish Research Institute in Canada, 1967); Henry Radecki and Benedykt Heydenkorn, *A Member of a Distinguished Family: The Polish Group in Canada* (Toronto: McClelland & Stewart, 1976).

87 Thomas Sproule, in House of Commons *Debates*, 14 July 1903, 6594.

88 Ibid., 6591.

89 See, for example, ibid., 26 July 1899, 8506–26.

90 *Winnipeg Telegram*, 3 February 1899, quoted in Lehr, 'Peopling the Prairies with Ukrainians,' 185. Hall notes that the block settlement of groups such as Galicians and Doukhobors was met with 'an unprecedented groundswell of nativist hostility': Hall, *Sifton*, vol. 1, 262.

91 House of Commons *Debates*, 2 June 1898, 6829; 26 July 1899, 8568.

92 Lehr, 'Peopling the Prairies with Ukrainians,' 186.

93 House of Commons *Debates*, 26 July 1899, 8525.

94 Ibid., 8522–4.

95 Ibid., 12 April 1901, 2934.

96 Ibid., 26 July 1899, 8535–6.

97 Ibid., 12 April 1901, 2938.

98 Ibid., F.D. Monk, 13 April 1907, 6669–90.

99 Ibid., 6726. In 1908, Lavergne left the Liberal party and became a Nationaliste MP.

100 *The Canadian Annual Review: 1908*, 105.

101 Palmer, *Immigration and the Rise of Multiculturalism*, 29–30.

102 William H.P. Jarvis, *Trails and Tales in Cobalt* (Toronto: W. Briggs, 1908), 110, 115; quoted in Avery, 'Canadian Immigration and the Alien Question,' 263.

103 See Eleoussa Polyzoi, 'Psychologists' Perceptions of the Canadian Immigrant before World War II,' *Canadian Ethnic Studies* 18/1 (1986): 52–65.

104 As the Methodist Missionary Society stated in 1910, 'our greatest objective on behalf of European foreigners should be to assist in making them English-speaking Christian citizens who are clean, educated, and loyal to the Dominion and to Great Britain': quoted in Francis, Jones, and Smith, *Destinies*, 141.

105 For a description of the work that Woodsworth and other social reformers did to facilitate the assimilation of immigrants, see Avery, 'Canadian Immigration Policy and the Alien Question,' 327–9.

106 J.S. Woodsworth, *Strangers within Our Gates; or Coming Canadians* (Toronto: F.C. Stephenson, 1909; reprinted Toronto: University of Toronto Press, 1972).

107 Ibid., 84, 101, 110, 115, 137. For a critical discussion of Woodsworth's views on immigration, which attempts to place them in historical context, see Allen Mills, *Fool for Christ: The Political Thought of J.S. Woodsworth* (Toronto: University of Toronto Press, 1991), 42–56, 224–37.

108 Avery, 'Canadian Immigration Policy and the Alien Question,' 319–27.

109 House of Commons *Debates*, 13 June 1906, 5198.

110 Compare, for example, *An Act Respecting Immigration and Immigrants*, S.C. 1869, c.10, ss.17–23, with *Immigration Act*, S.C. 1906, c.19, s.93. See also discussion in chapter 3, this volume, 85–6.

111 House of Commons *Debates,* 13 June 1906, 5196, 5202, See also K. Tony Hollihan, '"A Brake Upon the Wheel": Frank Oliver and the Creation of the Immigration Act of 1906,' *Past Imperfect* 1 (1992); 93–112.

112 The act did provide that, in the case of an immigrant who was deaf, dumb, blind, or infirm, admission to Canada might be permissible if the person was accompanied by family members or had relatives in Canada who were willing and capable of providing permanent support: S.C. 1906, c.19, s.26. The increasing influence of psychiatric evaluations on admissions to the country is the subject of Ian Dowbiggin, '"Keeping This Young Country Sane": C.K. Clarke, Immigration Restriction, and Canadian Psychiatry, 1890–1925,' *Canadian Historical Review* 76/4 (December 1995): 598–627.

113 *Immigration Act, 1906,* ss.26–30. Some of these prohibitions had been passed in earlier orders-in-council. In 1900, Cabinet passed a regulation prohibiting the admission of paupers and destitute persons unless the captain of the vessel that brought them to Canada provided money sufficient to cover initial settlement costs: P.C. 1851 (23 July 1900). Criminal and vicious persons were prohibiting from entering Canada by P.C. 2062 (23 August 1900). Two years later, the act was amended to authorize the Cabinet to prohibit the landing in Canada of any immigrants suffering from a 'dangerous, loathsome or infectious disease': S.C. 1902, c.14: P.C. 1293 (15 August 1902).

114 *Immigration Act, 1906,* ss.31, 32. For the growing influence of medical inspections, see Alan Sears, 'Immigration Controls as Social Policy: The Case of Canadian Medical Inspection, 1900–1920,' *Studies in Political Economy* 33 (Autumn 1990): 91–112; see also Barbara Roberts, 'Doctors and Deports: The Role of the Medical Profession in Deportation Policy and Practice, 1900–1936,' *Canadian Ethnic Studies* 18/3 (December 1986): 17–36.

115 *Immigration Act, 1906, ss.30,* 20.

116 *The Canadian Annual Review. 1907,* 289.

117 P.C. 28 (8 January 1908).

118 *The Canadian Annual Review: 1908,* 116.

119 Johnson, *History of Emigration from the United Kingdom,* 332.

120 *Immigration Act, 1910, S.C.* 1910, c.27, s.38. The continuous journey provision was enacted primarily to keep Japanese and East Asian immigrants from landing in Canada: see discussion 149–54, this volume.

121 *Immigration Act, 1910,* ss.3, 40, 41.

122 Ibid., ss.13–24.

123 Ibid., s.23.

124 In fact, the 1906 act defined an immigrant as one arriving by sea, whereas the 1910 act had a broader definition, covering those entering by land as well: see S.C. 1906, c.19, s.2(a), and S.C. 1909–10, c.27, s.2(g) and ss.28, 32 regarding medical examinations.

125 Ibid., ss.39, 44–5. This was also the case where the person was found, within three years of arrival, to be a member of a prohibited and undesirable class.

126 'Report of the Chief Medical Officer,' Annual Report of the Department of the Interior for 1914, *Sessional Papers, 1915*, no. 25, 173–5.

127 *The Canadian Annual Review: 1906*, 281.

128 Quoted in Avery, 'Canadian Immigration and the Alien Question,' 248.

129 Censuses of Canada, *RRC* 1969, 247.

130 Bruno Ramirez, *The Italians in Canada* (Ottawa: Canadian Historical Association, 1989), 4–8; see also Roberto Perin, ed., *'Arrangiarsi': The Italian Immigration Experience in Canada* (Montreal: Guernica, 1989).

131 Ramirez, *The Italians in Canada*, 7.

132 Avery, 'Canadian Immigration Policy and the Alien Question,' 251.

133 For more on the *padroni* system see D. Goutor, *Guarding the Gates: The Canadian Labour Movement and Immigration 1872–1934* (Vancouver: UBC Press, 2007), 116–17.

134 See, for example, Robert F. Harney, 'The Padrone System and the Sojourner in the Canadian North, 1885–1920,' in *Immigration in Canada: Historical Perspectives*, ed. Gerald Tulchinsky (Toronto: Copp Clark Longman, 1994), 249. For more information on Italian immigration, including its impact on villages and families in Italy see R. Harney, 'Men without Women: Italian Migrants in Canada, 1885–1930,' in *A Nation of Immigrants: Women, Workers, and Communities in Canadian History, 1840s–1960s*, ed. Franca Iacovetta (Toronto: University of Toronto Press, 1998), 206–30.

135 Ramirez, *The Italians in Canada*, 11–16; John E. Zucchi, 'Italian Hometown Settlements and the Development of an Italian Community in Toronto, 1875–1935,' in *Gathering Places: Peoples and Neighbourhoods of Toronto, 1834–1945*, ed. Robert F. Harney (Toronto: Multicultural History Society of Ontario, 1985); Zucchi, *Italians in Toronto: Development of a National Identity* (Montreal: McGill-Queen's University Press, 1988).

136 S.C. 1897, 60–61 c.11. For a discussion of labour's views on the Alien Labour Act see D.J. Goutor, *The Walls of Solidarity*, 229–36.

137 For more on the recruitment practices and conditions of work of European immigrant labourers throughout this period, see Avery, *Reluctant Host*, 20–42.

138 For example, *Tai Sing v Maguire* (1878), 1 B.C.R. (Pt. 1) 101; *R v Wing Chong* (1885), 1 B.C.R. (Pt. II) 150; *Union Colliery v Bryden* [1899] A.C. 58; *Re Gold*

Commissioners of Victoria (1886), 1 B.C.R. (Pt. II); *Re Kanamura* (1904), 10
B.C.R. 354; *Re The Coal Mines Regulation Act, 1903* (1904), 10 B.C.R. 408
(B.C.S.C). See also chapter 3, this volume, 98–9.

139 See for example *Cunningham v Tomey Homma*, [1903] A.C. 151, discussed
this volume, 143–4.

140 *Quong Wing v The King* (1914), 49 S.C.R. 440. See also Constance Backhouse,
'White Female Help and Chinese-Canadian Employers: Race, Class, Gender
and Law in the Case of Yee Clun, 1924,' *Canadian Ethnic Studies* 26/3 (1994):
34–52; James W. St.-G. Walker, *Race, Rights and the Law in the Supreme Court of
Canada: Historical Case Studies* (Toronto and Waterloo: Osgoode Society and
Wilfrid Laurier University Press, 1997), ch. 2.

141 [1899] A.C. 580.

142 [1903] A.C. 151.

143 [1899] A.C. 580, 586–7. For a fuller discussion of the implications of this
case, see Ross Lambertson, 'After *Union Colliery:* Law, Race, and Class in
the Coalmines of British Columbia,' in *Essays in the History of Canadian Law,*
vol. 6, British Columbia and the Yukon, ed. Hamar Foster and John
McLaren (Toronto: Osgoode Society, 1995), 386–423.

144 R.S.C. 1886, c.113, s.15.

145 *Cunningham v Tomey Homma*, 156.

146 *Re The Coal Mines Regulation Act, 1903* (1904) 10 B.C.R. 408.

147 Shin Imai observes that the reluctance of the courts to prejudice employer
interests was also evident in cases involving prosecutions under the 1897
Alien Labour Act. He points in particular to prosecutions brought under a
section of the Act which prohibited the encouragement of immigrants from
the United States by the 'promise of employment through advertisements.'
The Court interpreted this section narrowly to encompass only advertisements that strictly bound the employer to hire the foreign applicants and
not ones which could be construed 'merely as an invitation to apply': *Downie
v Vancouver Engineering Works* (1904) 10 B.C.R. 367, 8 C.C.C. 66, 68.
According to Imai, the readings of other cases under the act 'expose a
general reluctance to construe facts in such away so that a conviction would
ensue': Imai, 'Canadian Immigration Law and Policy,' 50.

148 Laurier's refusal to relax Asian admission restrictions, at the request of
railway contractors, on the grounds that to do so would provoke riots in
British Columbia is discussed in Donald Avery, 'Canadian Immigration
Policy and the "Foreign" Navvy, 1896–1914,' Canadian Historical
Association, *Historical Papers* (1972), 140–1.

149 'Report of the Department of Immigration and Colonization,' *Annual
Departmental Reports*, 1929–30, 8–10.

150 'Report of the Royal Commission to Investigate Chinese and Japanese Immigration into British Columbia,' in *Sessional Papers, 1902*, no. 54 [hereinafter cited as RRC 1902], 327.

151 Under Japanese law, all persons had to be registered in their Native prefectures, from which they could not leave without a passport. The Japanese government demanded perpetual allegiance of its subjects and regarded emigration as a short-term educational or money-making investment. Accordingly, emigrants were issued passports limited to three years, and as most returned to Japan within this period: John D. Cameron, 'Law Relating to Immigration to Canada, Volume II' (PhD thesis, University of Toronto, 1942), 174–6. Additionally, the fact that the majority of Japanese immigrants were men who came without their families and faced open hostility to their permanent residence in Canada also helps to explain why so many repatriated within a relatively short period of time.

152 *Chinese Immigration Act*, S.C. 1900, c.32, s.6; S.C. 1903, c.8, s.6. For a fuller discussion of immigration restrictions on Orientals during this period, see Roy, *White Man's Country*, ch. 5.

153 *The Canada Year Book, 1936* (Ottawa: Dominion Bureau of Statistics, 1937), 196.

154 Discussed more fully in chapter 3, this volume. See Ward, *White Canada Forever*, ch. 6, for a fuller discussion of anti-Japanese sentiment during this period.

155 See, for example, testimonies before the 1902 Royal Commission, RRC 1902, 218, 380.

156 Avery, 'Canadian Immigration Policy and the Alien Question,' 55–7. Conscious that the principal opposition to Japanese immigration had arisen among labour, Laurier received a deputation of working men from British Columbia in April 1899. He explained to them the injurious effects on Imperial relations, and commercial interests generally, that legislation against Japan might have: Minto to Chamberlain, 29 April 1899, in *Lord Minto's Canadian Papers, 1898–1904*, ed. Paul Stevens and John T. Saywell (Toronto: Champlain Society, 1981), 61. For labour attitudes towards Oriental immigration, see Gillian Creese, 'Exclusion of Solidarity? Vancouver Workers Confront the Oriental Problem,' *B. C. Studies* 80 (Winter 1988–9): 24–51; Creese, 'Class, Ethnicity and Conflict: The Case of Chinese and Japanese Immigrants, 1880–1923,' in *Workers, Capital, and the State in British Columbia: Selected Papers*, ed. Rennie Warburton and David Coburn (Vancouver: University of British Columbia Press, 1988); Roy, *White Man's Province*, ch. 4.

157 *An Act relating to an Act to make better provision for the Qualification and Registration of Voters*, S.B.C. 1875, c.2, s.2.

158 British Columbia, *Statutes*, 35 Vic., c.37; Patricia E. Roy, 'Citizens without Votes: East Asians in British Columbia,' in *Ethnicity, Power and Politics in Canada*, ed. Jorgen Dahlie and Tissa Fernando (Toronto:Methuen, 1981), 152. The prohibition was extended to include East Indians in 1920: *Provincial Elections Act*, S.B.C. 1920, c.27, s.5 (1) (a).

159 See chapter 3, this volume, 98–9.

160 For example, the *Chinese Regulation Act*, 48 Vic. 1884 c.3 (B.C.) (imposing a $100 licensing fee for every Chinese person over fourteen years of age wishing to remain in British Columbia); *An Act to Prevent the Immigration of Chinese*, 47 Vic. 1884 c.3 (B.C.) (an absolute prohibition on the entry of any Chinese into the province); and the *Coal Mines Regulation Act*, R.S.B.C. 1897, c.138 (a ban on the employment of Chinese in the mines).

161 For a detailed examination of the fate of B.C. anti-Asian legislation, see B. Ryder, 'Racism and the Constitution' and B. Ryder, 'Racism and the Constitution: The Constitutional Fate of British Columbia Anti-Asian Legislation, 1872–1922,' ch. 3 [unpublished; a copy is on file in the library of Osgoode Hall Law School]. See chapter 3, this volume, note 132. In 1899, Laurier expressed reluctance to use disallowance: Minto to Chamberlain, 18 April 1899, in *Lord Minto's Canadian Papers*, ed. Stevens and Saywell, 55–6.

162 James W. Morton, *In the Sea of Sterile Mountains* (Vancouver: J.J. Douglas, 1974), 193. As Bruce Ryder explained, because the period between enactment and disallowance was often longer than the period that followed disallowance and reenactment, anti-Asian legislation was in force more often than not between 1900 and 1908: Ryder, 'Racism and the Constitution.' It should be noted that the British supported the Canadian government's disallowance of the B.C. acts; for example, when informed that such action had been taken against the B.C. Immigration Act of 1908, the colonial secretary reported to the governor general: 'His Majesty's Government have learnt with satisfaction of the disallowance of this Act. … I shall be glad to receive if possible reports of any cases in the courts by which the invalidity of this Act was established': Despatch 229, 31 March 1909, in *Documents on Canadian External Relations*, vol. 1, 1908–1918 (Ottawa: Department of External Affairs, 1967), 593.

163 According to Donald Avery, between 1903 and 1907 the daily wage of white navvies in British Columbia had increased from $1.50 to as high as $3.00: 'Canadian Immigration Policy and the "Foreign" Navvy,' 140.

164 Timlin, 'Canada's Immigration Policy,' 524.

165 *Vancouver Province,* 1 February 1907; see also Victoria *Colonist,* 2 February 1907, quoted in House of Commons *Debates,* 23 January 1908, 1748–52.

166 'Report of the Royal Commission Appointed to Investigate Losses Sustained by the Chinese Population of Vancouver, British Columbia on the Occasion of the Riots in that City in September, 1907,' *Sessional Papers, 1908,* no. 74f [hereinafter cited as *RRC,* 1907]; 'Report of the Royal Commission Appointed to Investigate Losses Sustained by the Japanese Population of Vancouver, British Columbia on the Occasion of the Riots in that City in September, 1907,' *Sessional Papers, 1908,* no. 74g, 14. For a general account of the Vancouver Riot, see Ward, *White Canada Forever,* ch. 4; Roy, *White Man's Province,* ch. 8; H.H. Sugimoto, 'The Vancouver Riots of 1907: A Canadian Episode,' *East Across the Pacific,* ed. F. Hilary Conroy and T. Scott Miyakawa (Santa Barbara, CA: Clio, 1972), 92–126.

167 'Report of the Royal Commission Appointed to Inquire into the Methods by which Oriental Labourers Have Been Induced to Come to Canada, 1908' [henceforth cited as *RRC* 1908] (Ottawa: Government Printing Bureau, 1908).

168 Note that King found that the Japanese government was not to blame for having issued exit permits contrary to its earlier agreement, since it had been given assurances that the labourers were needed on the federally funded Grand Trunk Railway and in the mines of the provincial lieutenant-governor: ibid., 18–19 and, re; conclusions, see 54.

169 For a general discussion of the mood of the Japanese people at this time, which followed the cessation of war with China and the defeat of the Russian navy, see Timlin, 'Canada's Immigration Policy,' 526. Patricia Roy discusses the Lemieux agreement in *White Man's Province,* 207–13.

170 In particular the Japanese offered to restrict emigration to the following persons: prior residents of Canada and their families; domestic servants and agricultural labourers employed by Japanese residents; *bona fide* students, merchants, tourists, and travellers in transit; and contract labourers whose employer destination and terms of employment had been approved by the Canadian government: R. Lemieux, in House of Commons *Debates,* 21 January 1908, 1611.

171 Ibid., 28 January 1908, 2055, 2110.

172 Ibid., 21 January 1908, 1613.

173 'RRC' 1908. For immigrants of Hawaiian origin, see Roy, *White Man's Province,* 187–9, 206–7; Janice M. Duncan, *Minority without a Champion: Kanakas on the Pacific Coast, 1788–1850* (Portland: Oregon Historical Society, 1972).

174 It will be recalled that Immigration Act, 1906, provided that the minister of the Interior could prohibit the landing in Canada of immigrants who did

not arrived directly from their country of birth or citizenship. This was subsequently done on 8 January 1908, P.C. 27. Since most Japanese in Hawaii retained their Japanese citizenship, they were thus barred from coming to Canada. The landing-money regulation empowered the Superintendent of Immigration to require that immigrants possess a minimum of $50 before landing in winter and $25 for those landing in the summer: P.C. 28 (8 January 1908).

175 Quoted in Ramdeo Sampat-Mehta, *International Barriers* (Ottawa: Harpell's, 1973), 217.

176 *The Canada Year Book, 1936,* 196. See also chapter 5, this volume, 204–5.

177 'Report by W.L. Mackenzie King, C.M.G., Deputy Minister of Labour, on Mission to England to Confer with British Authorities on the Subject of Immigration to Canada from the Orient and Immigration from India in Particular,' *Sessional Papers, 1908,* no. 36a.

178 P.C. 1255 (3 June 1908). The order applied to all Asians 'other than those whose countries the Government of Canada has special arrangements' [i.e., Japanese immigrants], or those 'for whom special statutory regulations exist' [i.e., Chinese immigrants].

179 *The Canadian Annual Review: 1908,* 121.

180 Imai, 'Canadian Immigration Law and Policy,' 96.

181 (1908) 13 B.C.R. 415.

182 (1908) 7 W.L.R. 781; (1906–8) 13 B.C.R. 477.

183 P.C. 662 (27 March 1908).

184 Quoted in Sampat-Mehta, *International Barriers,* 140.

185 *An Act to Amend the Immigration Act,* S.C. 1907–8, .33, s.1.

186 Sampat Mehta, *International Barriers,* 141–2.

187 Ibid., 141.

188 *The Canada Year Book, 1930* (Ottawa: Dominion Bureau of Statistics, 1931), 174.

189 P.C. 920 (9 May 1910) renewed the continuous-journey requirement, and P.C. 926 (9 May 1910) renewed the landing-money requirement.

190 See *In Re Rahim* (no. 2) (1911), 16 B.C.R. 471; and *Re. Thirty-Nine Hindus* (1913), 15 D.L.R 189. For a discussion of the continuous-journey provision and its impact on East Indian immigration see A. Verma, *The Making of Little Punjab in Canada. Patterns of Immigration* (Thousand Oaks: Sage Publications, 2002), 102–3.

191 Stanislaw Andracki, *Immigration of Orientals into Canada, with Special Reference to the Chinese* (New York: Arno, 1978), 110–12; Sampat-Mehta, *International Barriers,* 148–50.

192 P.C. 2662 (8 December 1913).

193 Quoted in Sampat-Mehta, *International Barriers*, 230.

194 This incident is recounted in detail in Hugh Johnson, *The Voyage of the 'Komagata Maru': The Sikh Challenge to Canada's Colour Bar* (Delhi: Oxford University Press, 1970). See also Norman Buchignani and Doreen M. Indra, *Continuous Journey: A Social History of South Asians in Canada* (Toronto: McClelland & Stewart; Ottawa: Department of the Secretary of State, Multiculturalism Directorate, 1985), 53–60; Narindar Singh, *Canadian Sikhs: History, Religion, and Culture of Sikhs in North America* (Nepean, ON: Canadian Sikhs' Studies Institute, 1994), 46–52; Ward, *White Canada Forever*, ch. 5.

195 *Vancouver Sun*, 23 May 1914, 1; 5 June 1914, 3; 22 May 1914, 1.

196 Ibid., 1 June 1914, 1. British and Canadian officials were informed that the expedition had sinister motives. Knowing that the ship would be denied permission to land, 'political agitators or secret revolutionary societies' financed the trip so that the incident could be used to 'foment prejudice and hatred among the people of India against the Empire': Governor General Arthur to Colonial Secretary, 3 August 1914, and R.L. Borden to Acting High Commissioner in United Kingdom, 17 July 1914, in *Documents on Canadian External Relations*, vol. 1, 649, 654. One newspaper report stated that the Canadian government has 'definite evidence Komagata Maru enterprise was arranged by German Government': telegram from Viceroy of India to Governor General, 4 December 1914, in ibid., 655.

197 *The Canadian Annual Review of Public Affairs: 1914* (Toronto: Annual Review Publishing, 1915), 119.

198 House of Commons *Debates*, 1 June 1914, 4863.

199 *Re Munshi Singh* (1914) 20 B.C.R. 243.

200 Ibid., 290, 292.

201 'Report of the Department of Immigration and Colonization,' *Annual Departmental Reports, 1945–46*. The *Komagata Maru* did not leave quietly. When ordered to leave the harbour, the passengers seized control of the ship. The captain was unable to reassert his authority and called for civilian assistance; when local authorities tried to board the ship, 'strenuous fight raised, firebricks, pieces of machinery, hatchets, coal, iron bars, clubs all being used which were showered down on tug from all parts of ship smashing windows of tug, injuring Captain also breaking two of his ribs. Chief of Police struck. Shots fired by Hindus but no fire returned. Twenty men now in hospital. …': telegram of Borden to Martin Burrell, Minister of Agriculture, 19 July 1914, in *Documents on Canadian External Relations*, vol. 1, 650. To ensure the ship's departure, the government then sent a navy cruiser, which at the time constituted one half of the Canada's naval forces,

to accompany the *Komagata Maru* out of Canadian waters: Singh, *Canadian Sikhs*, 51.

202 This was provided for in section 80 of the *Immigration Act, 1910*, R.S.C. 1927, c.93. For a full discussion of immigration restrictions, see Roy, *White Man's Country*, ch. 9.

203 S.C. 1908, c.14, ss.2, 3.

204 'Report of the Chief Controller of Chinese Immigration,' Annual Report of the Department of the Interior for 1915, *Sessional Papers, 1916*, no. 25, 80.

205 *The Canada Year Book, 1936*, 196.

206 *RRC* 1908, 95.

207 House of Commons *Debates*, 30 April 1923, 2316.

208 According to the report of the 1911 Royal Commission to Investigate Alleged Chinese Frauds and Opium Smuggling on the West Coast, many Chinese immigrants, with the complicity of a Chinese interpreter in Vancouver, avoided the tax by misrepresenting themselves as merchants. The commission also discovered that others would evade the tax by hiding in the coal bunkers of steamships, and sneaking to shore when the guards were in the ships' saloons. Another method of tax evasion was to land in Union Bay on Vancouver Island which the commissioner, Mr. Justice Murphy, described as 'practically a free port for the entrance of Chinese and for the smuggling of opium.' The report also revealed that, according to one Ottawa bureaucrat, the prime minister had mentioned that he would like to see the tax abolished completely in the interests of trade: *Report of Mr. Justice Murphy Royal Commissioner Appointed to Investigate Alleged Chinese Frauds and Opium Smuggling on the Pacific Coast, 1910–11* (Ottawa: Government Printing Bureau, 1913) [henceforth cited as *RRC* 1910–11]. The revelations of the Royal inquiry were particularly damaging for the Laurier government and undoubtedly contributed to its defeat in the general election three months later. Certainly the impact of the report was felt in British Columbia, where not one Liberal won a seat in the federal Parliament.

209 For a discussion of King's efforts in this regard, see Timlin, 'Canada's Immigration Policy,' 530.

210 William George Smith, *A Study in Canadian Immigration* (Toronto: Ryerson, 1920), 167.

211 *The Canada Year Book 1914* (Ottawa: Dominion Bureau of Statistics, 1915), 85.

212 Ward, *White Canada Forever*, 63.

213 S.C. 1908, c.50. For fuller discussions of the Opium Act, see J.A. Munro, 'British Columbia and the Chinese Evil: Canada's First Anti-Asiatic Immigration Law,' *Journal of Canadian Studies* 6 (1971): 42–51; N. Boyd, 'The

Origins of Canadian Narcotics Legislation: The Process of Criminalization in Historical Context,' *Dalhousie Law Journal* 8/1 (1984): 102–36.

214 Harold Troper, *Only Farmers Need Apply* (Toronto: Griffin House, 1972), 121–2. Troper's book provides an illuminating look into Canadian promotional activities in the United States from 1896 to 1911.

215 Woodsworth, *Strangers within Our Gates*, 158, Allen Mills characterizes Woodsworth's views as culturally imperialist rather than racist; for a discussion of Woodsworth's contradictory thinking on issues related to race, see Mills, *Fool for Christ*, 42–56, 224–37.

216 James W. St.-G. Walker, *A History of Blacks in Canada: A Study Guide for Teachers and Students* (Ottawa: Department of the Secretary State, Multiculturalism Directorate, 1980), 68.

217 Letter of L.M. Fortier, Ottawa to Rev. W.A. Lamb-Campbell, Galveston, Texas, 20 September 1906, quoted in Troper, *Only Farmers Need Apply*, 127. See also Robin W. Winks, *The Blacks in Canada: A History* 2nd ed. (Montreal: McGill-Queen's University Press; New Haven: Yale University Press, 1997), 296–7.

218 Troper, *Only Farmers Need Apply*, 127.

219 Report, W.J. White, to F. Oliver, 13 September 1910, quoted in ibid., 135–6.

220 Walker, *History of Blacks in Canada*, 68–9; Winks, *Blacks in Canada*, 301–13; Harold Troper, 'The Creek-Negroes of Oklahoma and Canadian Immigration, 1909–11,' *Canadian Historical Review* 53 (1972): 272–88; Stewart Grow, 'The Blacks of Amber Valley – Negro Pioneering in Northern Alberta,' *Canadian Ethnic Studies* 6 (1974): 17–38.

221 *Globe*, 4 April 1911; House of Commons *Debates*, 23 March 1911, 5943; and 3 April 1911, 6524, where various inflammatory press reports were quoted.

222 Made pursuant to section *38* of the *Immigration Act*, S.C. 1910, c.27.

223 House of Commons *Debates, 23* March 1911, 5943–7, where a number of MPs with black constituents complained about immigration restrictions facing blacks. See also Winks, *Blacks in Canada*, 307–9.

224 House of Commons *Debates*, 22 March 1911, 5912.

225 Troper, *Only Farmers Need Apply*, 144.

226 Agnes Calliste, 'Race, Gender and Canadian Immigration Policy: Blacks from the Caribbean, 1900–1932,' *Journal of Canadian Studies* 28/4 (Winter 1993–4): 134–5, 140.

227 House of Commons, *Journals XI* (1877), Appendix 6, 16, quoted in Henry Drystek, '"The Simplest and Cheapest Mode of Dealing with Them": Deportation from Canada before World War II,' *Histoire sociale/Social History* 30 (November 1982): 409.

228 *An Act to Amend the Immigration Act*, S.C. 1902, c.14. ss.1 and 2.

229 *The Canada Year Book, 1914,* 87.

230 See, for example, the case of *Ikezoya et al, v Canadian Pacific Railway Company* (1907), 12 B.C.R. 454 (B.C.C.A.), where it was held that the examination of the immigration officer was not final and conclusive but reviewable by the court on a *habeas corpus* application.

231 See discussion this volume, 137–8.

232 *Immigration Act, 1910,* S.C. 1910, c.27, ss.3, 40, 41, 42(5).

233 These statistics are derived from *The Canada Year Book, 1914,* 87.

234 Barbara Roberts, *Whence They Came. Deportation from Canada, 1900–1935* (Ottawa: University of Ottawa Press, 1988), 49; Drystek, 'The Simplest and Cheapest Mode of Dealing with Them,' 419.

235 See chapter 5, this volume.

236 S.C. 1910, c.27, s.24.

237 *Naturalization Act,* R.S.C. 1906, c.77. ss.14, 15, 19. It is of note that the act was paternalistic concerning women. Women and minors were deemed to be citizens of the state of their husbands and fathers, respectively: ss.82–4.

238 *Re Webster* (1870), 7 C.L.J. 39.

239 *Re Malsufuro* (1908), 13 B.C.R. 417.

240 *Re Fukuichi Aho* (1909), 9 W.L.R. 652 (Vancouver Co. Ct.), 655.

241 R.S.C. 1906, c.77 s.15. Also see discussion of these cases in Imai, 'Canadian Immigration Law and Policy,' 152–60.

242 (1911), 19 W.L.R. 171, 175.

243 *Naturalization Act,* S.C. 1914, c.44 ss.2, 7. For a discussion on Imperial conferences and on naturalization in general, see George Takakazu Tamaki, 'The Law Relating to Nationality in Canada' (LLM thesis, University of Toronto, 1944).

244 Since the Immigration Act did not authorize the removal of Canadian citizens who were defined as being: persons born in Canada; British subjects with Canadian domicile; or persons naturalized under the laws of Canada who had not subsequently become aliens (had their status revoked) or lost Canadian domicile: S.C. 1910, c.27, s.2(f).

245 *The Canada Year Book, 1914,* 91.

246 P.C. 2642 (8 December 1913); for instructions to immigration officers, see Sampat-Mehta, *International Barriers,* 230.

247 House of Commons *Debates,* 12 March 1914, 1612.

248 'Report of the Chief Medical Officer,' Annual Report of the Department of the Interior for 1907, *Sessional Papers, 1908,* no. 25, 136.

249 Annual Report of the Department of the Interior for 1914, *Sessional Papers, 1915,* no. 25, 181.

250 [1906] A.C. 542, 546. This case involved the right of the attorney-general to order the deportation of a person in Canada in violation of the Alien Labour Act.

251 House of Commons *Debates*, 1 June 1914, 4562.

Chapter 5 The War and the Recovery, 1914–1929: The Dominance of Economic Interests

1 Kenneth Norrie and Douglas Owram, *A History of the Canadian Economy* (Toronto: Thomson Nelson, 2008), 262–72.

2 Desmond Morton, *Canada and War* (Toronto: Butterworths, 1981), 82.

3 'Report of the Department of Mines and Resources,' *Annual Departmental Reports, 1944–45*, 200–20 [*Annual Departmental Reports* henceforth cited as *ADR*]; *Canada Year Book, 1930* (Ottawa: Dominion Bureau of Statistics, 1931), 164.

4 See discussions, in this volume on 167–8, 170 re: internment; on 188–9, 203–4 re: Asians and Africans; and on 178 re: foreign radicals.

5 'Report of the Department of Immigration and Colonization,' *ADR, 1929–30, 20*, table 3, and 15, table 10.

6 In 1913, 107,530 immigrants from the United States arrived in Canada, as compared with 59,779 the following year; ibid.

7 'Report of the Department of Immigration and Colonization,' *ADR, 1918–1919*, 35.

8 Robert Craig Brown and Ramsay Cook, *Canada, 1896–1921: A Nation Transformed* (Toronto: McClelland & Stewart, 1974), 224–7. For a discussion of the dilemma facing the Canadian government about enemy aliens in the early stages of the war, see *The Canadian Annual Review of Public Affairs: 1914* (Toronto: Annual Review Publishing, 1915), 275–86.

9 C.J. Doherty; Minister of Justice, in House of Commons *Debates*, 22 April 1918, 1018.

10 *Proclamation of the 15th of August 1914*, s.1, 48 Canada Gazette, 617; Public Notice (2 September 1914) reprinted in *Canada Law Journal* 54 (1918): 511. Borden was reluctant to implement a policy of mass internment early in the war because of the expense, and he suspected that municipalities advocated such action in an effort to rid themselves of the burden of paying for relief for the unemployed: Donald H. Avery, *Reluctant Host: Canada's Response to Immigrant Workers, 1896–1994* (Toronto: McClelland & Stewart, 1995), 72.

11 S.C. 1914, c.2, s.6.

12 *The Canadian Annual Review of Public Affairs: 1915* (Toronto: Annual Review
   Publishing, 1916), 353, cited in Donald Avery, *Dangerous Foreigners': European
   Immigrant Workers and Labour Radicalism in Canada, 1896–1932* (Toronto:
   McClelland & Stewart, 1979), 66. According to Lubomyr Luciuk, 88,000
   Ukrainians were registered as enemy aliens: *Time for Atonement: Canada's First
   National Internment Operation and the Ukrainian Canadians* (Kingston, ON:
   Limestone, 1988).

13 See chapter 4, this volume.

14 Desmond Morton, 'Sir William Otter and Internment Operations in Canada
   during the First World War,' *Canadian Historical Review* 55 (1974): 33–4.
   Historians of this era point to the dilemma faced by enemy-alien groups.
   According to Vera Lysenko, Canadians 'mistakenly regarded most Ukrain-
   ians as Austrians,' and subjected them to violence and property damage, to
   which the Ukrainians responded by publishing an appeal noting their
   substantial contributions to the war effort: *Men in Sheepskin Coats: A Study in
   Assimilation* (Toronto: Ryerson, 1947), 113–16; see also Frances Swyripa, 'The
   Ukrainian Image: Loyal Citizen or Disloyal Alien,' in *Loyalties in Conflict:
   Ukrainians in Canada during the Great War*, ed. Frances Swyripa and John Herd
   Thompson (Edmonton: Canadian Institute of Ukrainian Studies, University
   of Alberta, 1983), 47–68. Croatians were 'caught on the wrong side': Anthony
   W. Rasporich, *For a Better Life: A History of the Croatians in Canada* (Toronto:
   McClelland & Stewart; Ottawa: Department of Secretary of State, Multiculturalism Directorate, 1982), 75. John Herd Thompson contends that Ukrainians
   were more loyal than French Canadians, and Poles were also very loyal: *The
   Harvests of War: The Prairie West, 1914–1918* (Toronto: McClelland & Stewart,
   1978), 77–9, 82. The Canadian government does not appear to have
   regarded Poles as enemy aliens, but rather as potentially valuable allies in the
   war effort; in the early stages of the war, when the United States remained
   neutral, the Canadian government established a Polish army training ground
   at Niagara-on-the-Lake, so that American Poles could cross the border to
   train. Eventually, 22,000 Poles, of whom only 221 were Canadian, were
   trained there, and were assisted by the community; many Canadian Poles
   joined the Canadian contingent: see William Boleslaus Makowski, *History and
   Integration of Poles in Canada* (Lindsay, ON: Canadian Polish Congress, 1967),
   181–2.

15 Desmond Morton, 'Sir William Otter and Internment Operations in Canada,'
   33–4; see also *The Canadian Annual Review. 1914*, 275–8.

16 For more details on such rumours, see Brown and Cook, *Canada, 1896–
   1921*, 224; Donald Avery, 'Canadian Immigration Policy and the Alien

Question' (PhD thesis, University of Western Ontario, London, 1973), 373–45. According to John Herd Thompson, newspaper reports of German atrocities in Belgium, and about the sinking of the *Lusitania,* started the transition in public opinion by which Germans went from ideal immigrants to subhuman devils: *Harvests of War,* 74–5. See also Brenda Lee-Whiting, 'Enemy Aliens,' *The Beaver* 69/5 (October-November 1989): 53–9; Art Grenke, 'The German Community of Winnipeg and the English-Canadian Response to World War I,' *Canadian Ethnic Studies* 20/1 (1988): 77–97; Gerhard P. Bassler, 'The Enemy Alien Experience in Newfoundland, 1914–1918,' *Canadian Ethnic Studies* 20/3 (1988): 42–62. For descriptions of German attempts at subversion and invasion, see, respectively, Graeme S. Mount, *Canada's Enemies: Spies and Spying in the Peaceable Kingdom* (Toronto: Dundurn, 1993), ch. 3, and Michael L. Hadley and Roger Sarty, *Tin-Pots and Pirate Ships: Canadian Naval Forces and German Sea-Raiders, 1880–1918* (Montreal: McGill-Queen's University Press, 1991). *The Canadian Annual Review of Public Affairs: 1916* (Toronto: Annual Review Publishing, 1917), 432, lists several incidents of incendiarism which were widely attributed to German activities; nothing, however, was proven in any of these cases.

17 *Canada Law Journal* 51 (1915): 1.

18 See discussion this volume, 178.

19 Major General W.D. Otter, *Internment Operations, 1914–20* (Ottawa: King's Printer, 1921), 6; David J. Carter, *Behind Canadian Barbed Wire: Alien, Refugee and Prisoner of War Camps in Canada, 1914–1916* (Calgary: Tumbleweed, 1980). *The Canadian Annual Review: 1916* (p. 431) estimated that the total number of enemy aliens interned was as high as 10,000. According to Lubomyr Luciuk, of the approximately 8,500 enemy aliens interned, nearly 2,000 were German-Austrian POWs and the rest were civilians, of whom an estimated 5,000 were of Ukrainian origin: Luciuk, *Time for Atonement.* See also Peter Melnycky 'The Internment of Ukrainians in Canada,' in *Loyalties in Conflict: Ukrainians in Canada during the Great War,* ed. Swripya and Herd Thompson, 1–24. For an anecdotal account of the internment experience, see Bohdan S. Kordan and Peter Melnycky, eds., *In the Shadow of the Rockies: Diary of the Castle Mountain Internment Camp, 1915–1917* (Edmonton: Canadian Institute of Ukrainian Studies Press, 1991).

20 See, for example, *Re Gottesman* (1918), 41 O.L.R. 547 (Ont. H.C.); *Re Beranek* (1915), 42 C.C.C. 252 (Ont. S.C.); *Re Chamryk* (1914), 7 W.W.R. 548 (Man. KB.); *Re Guestu* (1915), 17 Que. P.R. 95 (Que. S.C.).

21 S.C. 1914, 15 Geo. V. c.2, s.11.

22 *Re Beranek* (1915), 42 C.C.C. 252 (Ont. S.C.), at 254.

23 *Topay v Crows Nest Pass Coal Co.* (1914), 18 D.L.R. 784 (B.C.S.C.)*; Viola v Mackenzie, Mann & Co.* (1915), 24 Que. KB. 31 (Que. C.A.); *Ragusz v Harbour Commrs. of Montreal* (1916), 18 Que. P.R. 98 (Que. C.A.); *Peskovitch v Western Canadian Flour Mills Co.* (1914), 18 D.L.R. (Man. KB.).

24 *Krusuz v Crows Nest Past Coal Co.* [1912] A.C. 590; *Johansdotter v Canadian Pacific Railway Co.* (1914), 47 Que. S.C. 76 (Que. S.C.); *Harasymczuk v Montreal Light Heat and Power Co.* (1916), 25 Que. K.B. 252 (Que. C.A.); *Oskey v Kingston (*1914), 20 D.L.R. 959 (Ont. H.C.).

25 *Kristo v Hollinger Consolidated Gold Mines* (1917), 41 O.L.R. 51 (Ont. H.C.).

26 *Latha v Halycznk* (1918), 14 O.W.N. 219 (Ont. G.A.); *Lampell v Berger* (1917), 40 O.L.R. 165 (Ont. H.C.); *Fabry v Finlay* (1916), 32 D.L.R. 673 (Que. C.A.); *White Ltd. v T. Eaton Co.* (1916), 30 D.L.R. 459 (Ont. C.A.).

27 For a more detailed description of labour shortages during the war and the influence of labour-intensive corporations, see Avery, *Reluctant Host,* 74–5. The demand for harvest labour on the prairies was an additional factor: ibid., 73.

28 Morton, 'Sir William Otter,' 49. The Vancouver council, for example, complained about the release of internees: *The Canadian Annual Review: 1916,* 432. Due to the acute labour shortage, Austrians and Germans were increasingly employed in businesses which were crucial to the war effort, and this situation undoubtedly caused some of the concern. According to *The Canadian Annual Review of Public Affairs: 1917* (Toronto: Annual Review Publishing, 1918), 438, aliens were employed at the Imperial Munitions Board, the Lindsay Arsenal, and many other munitions and industrial plants.

29 James Arthur, in House of Commons *Debates,* 22 April 1918, 986; see also *The Canadian Annual Review: 1917,* 439.

30 Letter to Borden, 26 March 1918, read in the House by Cooper, in House of Commons *Debates,* 22 April 1918, 987. Returning veterans were responsible for escalating levels of hostility towards enemy aliens, particularly those belonging to pacifist groups, to such a degree that vigilante action was feared. Veterans particularly objected to the prosperity which came to pacifist farmers because of the war: see Thompson, *Harvests of War,* 80–5.

31 Letter to Borden, 26 March 1918.

32 Avery, *'Dangerous Foreigners,'* 76. For Ukrainian attempts to obtain redress for their incarceration during the war, see Lubomyr Luciuk, ed., *Righting an Injustice: The Debate over Redress for Canada's First National Internment Operations* (Toronto: Justinian, 1994).

33 House of Commons *Debates, 22* April 1918, 1021.
34 In 1918, the Anti-Loafing Law was proclaimed; it provided that 'every male person residing in the Dominion of Canada should be regularly engaged in some useful occupation': P.C. 815 (4 April 1918).
35 House of Commons *Debates,* 22 April 1918, 1018. For an analysis of international law vis-à-vis the interned prisoner, see James R. Carruthers, 'The Great War and Canada's Enemy Alien Policy,' *Queen's Law Journal* 4 (1978): 43.
36 Borden attended the Imperial War Cabinet in the spring of 1917, where he was apprised of the overwhelming number of mutinies in the French army, the imminent collapse of Russia, the growing strength of the German offensive, and the need for massive recruitment to avert Allied defeat. Given that Canadian recruitment efforts had failed to replace even half the number of men lost in action, Borden regarded conscription as the only alternative: Morton, *Canada and War,* 71; Roger Graham, 'Through the First World War,' in *The Canadians, 1867–1967,* ed. J.M.S. Careless and Robert Craig Brown (Toronto: Macmillan, 1967), 187.
37 Moreover, it was asked why French Canadians should offer their lives in a war that did not jeopardize their security when there was a more important one to be fought at home. The abolition of bilingual education in Ontario, Manitoba, and the Northwest were cases in point: *Le Droit,* 7 May. For a full discussion of the controversy surrounding conscription in the First World War, see Ramsay Cook, R. Craig Brown, and Carl Berger, eds., *Conscription 1917* (Toronto: University of Toronto Press, 1969).
38 *Wartime Elections Act,* 1917, S.C. 7–8 George V, c.39.
39 House of Commons *Debates,* 10 September 1917, 5582, 5591, 5600, 5632, and 5807.
40 Ibid., 5577. For an analysis of this issue, see John Herd Thompson, 'The Enemy Alien and the Canadian General Election of 1917,' in *Loyalties in Conflict: Ukrainians in Canada during the Great War,* ed. Swyripa and Herd Thompson, 25–46.
41 House of Commons *Debates,* 10 September 1917, 5617.
42 Ibid., 5578.
43 Ibid., 5573.
44 Ibid., 5610; see also Graham, 5591.
45 Ibid., 5554; see also Edmond Proulx, 5625; Bovin, 5628.
46 Ibid., 5586.
47 The conscription crisis is discussed in J.L. Granatstein and J.M. Hitsman, *Broken Promises: A History of Conscription in Canada* (Toronto: Oxford University Press, 1977). The Union government and the 1917 election

campaign are explored fully in R. Craig Brown, *Robert Laird Borden: A Biography*, vol. 1, *1854–1914* (Toronto: Macmillan, 1975).

48 S.C. 1920, c.59, s.7.

49 See the reports of the Department of the Interior in the *Annual Departmental Reports* for these years.

50 Letter of W.D. Scott to Inspector of Prisons and Public Charities for Ontario, 5 November 1915; quoted in Barbara Roberts, *Whence They Came: Deportation from Canada, 1900–1935* (Ottawa: University of Ottawa Press, 1988), 766.

51 'Report of the Commissioner of Immigration for Canada, London, England,' Annual Report of the Department of Immigration and Colonization for 1918, *Sessional Papers, 1919*, no. 18, 22; Henry Drystek, 'The Simplest and Cheapest Mode of Dealing with Them: Deportation from Canada before World War II,' *Histoire sociale/Social History* 30 (November 1982): 421.

52 For more on left-wing ethnic parties, see Howard Palmer, *Ethnicity and Politics in Canada since Confederation* (Ottawa: Canadian Historical Association, 1991), 7–16.

53 'Report of the Royal Commission on Industrial Relations, 1919,' printed as a supplement to the *Labour Gazette*, July 1919, 6.

54 Ibid.

55 W.A. Wood, President of the Vallance Coal Company, Alta., to Borden, 16 May 1917, quoted in Avery, *'Dangerous Foreigners,'* 74.

56 *Vancouver Sun*, 3 August 1917, quoted in *The Canadian Annual Review: 1917*, 423.

57 House of Commons *Debates*, 22 April 1918, 975.

58 See, for example, the speech given by W.J. Bulman, President of the Canadian Manufacturers' Association, in *Industrial Canada* 20 (July 1991): 166.

59 For example, see an article in *Maclean's*, August 1919, entitled 'Planning Soviet Rule in Canada,' 33 ff.

60 Letters from C.H. Cahan to J. Doherty, 20 July 1918 and 11 September 1918: National Archives of Canada, no. O.C. 519.

61 These were as follows: the Industrial Workers of the World (IWW), the Russian Social Democratic Party, the Russian Revolutionary Group, the Russian Workers' Union, the Ukrainian Revolutionary Group, the Ukrainian Social Democratic Party, the Social Democratic Party, the Social Labour Party, the Group of Social Democrats of Bolsheviki, the Workers' International Industrial Union, the Chinese Nationalist League, the Chinese Labour Association, the Finnish Social Democratic Party, and the Revolutionary Party of North America.

62 P.C. 2384 (25 September 1918) and P.C. 2381 (25 September 1918).

63 Letter of W.D. Scott to Minister of Labour, 17 July 1917, quoted in Roberts, *Whence They Came*, 76. Regarding political deportations more generally, see B. Roberts, 'Shovelling Out the "Mutinous": Political Deportations from Canada before 1936,' *Labour/Le Travail* 18 (Fall, 1986): 77–110.

64 Avery, *Reluctant Host*, 75.

65 Letter of W.D. Scott to Winnipeg Commissioner of Immigration, 19 August 1917, quoted in Roberts, *Whence They Came*, 78. In the Immigration Act of 1919, the length of time a person had to be resident in Canada before acquiring domicile was extended from three to five years.

66 The Alien Labour Act made it unlawful to assist or encourage the importation of immigrants under contract to labour in Canada: R.S.C. 1906 c.97. See discussion, this volume, chapter 4, 123, 142, 149.

67 P.C. 815 (4 April 1918).

68 P.C. 1743 (11 July 1918).

69 For accounts of the Canadian labour movement at this time, see H.A. Logan, *Trade Unions in Canada: Their Development and Functioning* (Toronto: Macmillan, 1948); Jack Williams, *The Story of Unions in Canada* (Don Mills, ON: J.M. Dent & Sons, 1975); Craig Heron, *The Canadian Labour Movement* (Toronto: Lorimer, 1989); Bryan Palmer, *Working-Class Experience: Rethinking the History of Canadian Labour, 1800–1991*, 2d ed. (Toronto: McClelland & Stewart, 1992), Craig Heron, ed., *The Workers' Revolt in Canada, 1917–1925* (Toronto: University of Toronto Press, 1998).

70 Avery, *'Dangerous Foreigners'*, 80–1. See also Martin Robin, *Radical Politics and Canadian Labour 1890–1930* (Kingston: Industrial Relations Centre, Queen's University, 1968); David Bercuson, *Fools and Wise Men: The Rise and Fall of the One Big Union* (Scarborough, ON: McGraw-Hill Ryerson, 1978).

71 Letter of R.L. Borden to T. White, 29 April 1919, quoted in Brown and Cook, *Canada, 1896–1921*, 311.

72 For various descriptions and interpretations of the strike, see Avery, *'Dangerous Foreigners'*, 82; J.M. Bumsted, '1919: The Winnipeg General Strike Reconsidered,' *The Beaver* (June/July 1994): 27–44; and Bumsted, *The Winnipeg General Strike of 1919: An Illustrated History* (Winnipeg: Watson & Dwyer, 1994); David J. Bercuson, *Confrontation at Winnipeg: Labour, Industrial Relations, and the General Strike* (Montreal: McGill-Queen's University Press, 1974); A. Ross McCormack, *Reformers, Rebels, and Revolutionaries: The Western Canadian Radical Movement, 1899–1919* (Toronto: University of Toronto Press, 1977). An account by one of the strike's leaders can be found in William Beeching and Phyllis Clarke, eds., *Yours in the Struggle: Reminiscences of Tim Buck* (Toronto: NC Press, 1977), 73–86.

73 W.R. Pleuman, *Toronto Star*, 23 May 1919.

74 *Manitoba Free Press*, 22 May 1919.

75 House of Commons *Debates*, 2 June 1919, 3008.

76 See, for example, Kenneth McNaught, 'Political Trials and the Canadian Political Tradition,' *University of Toronto Law Journal* 24 (1974): 158.

77 See, for example, Peter R. Lederman, 'Sedition in Winnipeg: An Examination of the Trials for Seditious Conspiracy Arising from the General Strike of 1919,' *Queen's Law Journal* 3 (1973): 9–10; D.C. Masters, *The Winnipeg General Strike* (Toronto: University of Toronto Press, 1973), 65–6.

78 Note, however, that, while Bumsted acknowledges that most members of the Strike Committee had no intention of taking over the government by violent means, many did believe 'in the need for extreme social and economic change' and the general strike was one way of achieving 'great transformations outside the normal political channels': '1919: The Winnipeg General Strike Reconsidered,' 31–2.

79 *Western Labour News*, Special Strike Edition no. 19 (7 June 1919), quoted in Avery, *'Dangerous Foreigners'*, 84.

80 As J.A. Calder, the minister of Immigration and Colonization, explained: 'I am sure the House will agree that the extension is proper ... because we think it is necessary that there should be a longer period than three years in which to ascertain whether or not many of these people who get into the country are desirable': House of Commons *Debates*, 29 April 1919, 1872. For more on domicile and inadmissible classes see discussion in chapter 4, this volume.

81 *An Act to Amend the Immigration Act*, S.C. 1919, c.25 s.15.

82 'Canadian citizen' was defined in the act as including: (i) a person born in Canada; (ii) a British subject who has domicile; (iii) a person naturalized under the laws of Canada: ss.2(f). Section 41 exempted only categories (i) and (iii), thereby leaving British subjects open to removal if found to engage in the activities outlined in section 41.

83 S.C. 1919 c.38 s.7(1) and 2(c), respectively. Cabinet was also empowered to revoke the citizenship status of the wife (unless a British subject) and minor children of such a person. They, too, could be deported on the same basis.

84 Arthur Meighen, was in favour of instituting deportation proceedings against the British strike leaders. Nevertheless, in light of the wave of protests that had been registered across the country by labour organizations following the arrest of the strike leaders, it was considered unwise to follow such a course of action. In the end, the Anglo-Saxon detainees were released on bail and subsequently charged with seditious conspiracy. All but one were convicted.

85 Avery, *'Dangerous Foreigners,'* 86.

86 *An Act to Amend the Criminal Code*, S.C. 1919, c. 46, 0. For a discussion of laws and court cases arising from seditious language in the First World War, see Jonathan Swainger, 'Wagging Tongues and Empty Heads: Seditious Utterances and the Patriotism of Wartime in Central Alberta, 1914–1918,' in *Law, Society and the State: Essays in Modern Legal History*, ed. Louis A. Knafla and Susan W.S. Binnie (Toronto: University of Toronto Press, 1995), 263–89. See also *The Canadian Annual Review 1916*, 433–4, which claims that sedition was gently treated by the press and the courts; in one case cited, Charles Clansen of Red Deer, Alberta, was fined $500 for saying that, if King George were here, he would kill him. Further cases are cited in *The Canadian Annual Review: 1917*, 438.

87 Avery, '*Dangerous Foreigners*,' 87.

88 Roberts, *Whence They Came*, 90–1.

89 John Herd Thompson, with Allen Seager, *Canada, 1922–1939: Decades of Discord* (Toronto: McClelland & Stewart, 1979), 141.

90 Employer blacklists, vicious competition, intimidation by the TLC and its international union affiliates, and factionalism under the OBU itself contributed towards its collapse: see Stuart Jamieson, *Times of Trouble: Labour Unrest and Industrial Conflict in Canada, 1900–66* (Ottawa: Minister of Supply and Services 1968), 187–8; Bercuson, *Fools and Wise Men*.

91 Norrie and Owram, *A History of the Canadian Economy*, 1st ed. 436.

92 *Labour Gazette*, December 1920, 1630–4, cited in Avery, '*Dangerous Foreigners*', 94.

93 Thompson, *Canada, 1922–1939*, 76.

94 House of Commons *Debates*, 29 April 1919, 1873.

95 *An Act to Amend the Immigration Act*, S.C. 1919, c.25, s.3.

96 Ibid. s.13.

97 P.C. 1203 (9 June 1919).

98 P.C. 923 (1 May 1919) and P.C. 1204 (9 June 1919). These restrictions were undoubtedly attributable to residual resentment against many of the members of these sects for refusing to fight in the war. Most of the members of these groups in Canada were agriculturalists, that prospered because of the inflated grain prices created by wartime demand. Thus, pacifist farmers were resented, particularly by veterans of the war, not only because they refused to fight, but because their refusal to fight enriched them financially. They were seen to have benefited from the war while others made all the sacrifices: see Thompson, *Harvests of War*, 80–5. For a detailed discussion of these groups' exemptions from military service, see Thomas P. Socknat, *Witness against War: Pacifism in Canada, 1900–1945* (Toronto: University of Toronto Press, 1987), ch. 3; William Janzen, *Limits on Liberty: The Experience of Mennonite, Hutterite, and Doukhobor Communities in Canada* (Toronto: University of Toronto Press, 1990), ch. 8.

99 P.C. 1202 (9 June 1919).

100 P.C. 2668 (26 July 1921). In the case of farm families, the head of the family was required to have $250, other members over eighteen years of age had to have $125, and $50 was required for each child between five and eighteen years of age.

101 See, for example, Edwards, in House of Commons *Debates*, 30 April 1919, 1932.

102 *Industrial Canada*, July 1919, 120–2.

103 'Report of Department of Immigration and Colonization,' *ADR, 1929–1930*, 10, table 1, and 14, table 8.

104 'Report of W.J. White, Superintendent of United States Agencies,' Report of the Department of Immigration and Colonization for 1922, *Sessional Papers, 1923*, no. 13, 28.

105 'Report of the Inspector of United States Agencies, W.J. White,' Report of the Department of Immigration and Colonization for 1923, *Sessional Papers, 1924*, no. 13, 23.

106 For example, between 1920 and 1925, on average more than 25,000 people emigrated to Canada from the Continent: see 'Report of the Department of Immigration and Colonization', *ADR, 1929–30*, 3, table 4, and 15, table 11.

107 'Report of the Department of Immigration and Colonization for 1922, *Sessional Papers, 1923*, no. 13, 22–3.

108 Ibid., 21.

109 Avery, '*Dangerous Foreigners*', 93; Avery, *Reluctant Host*, 85.

110 Thompson, *Canada, 1922–1939*, 78. This spectacular rise represented a sixfold increase since 1914, and was due primarily to the increase in size and readership of American newspapers: see Norrie and Owram, *A History of the Canadian Economy*, 1st ed. 449.

111 Thompson, *Canada, 1922–1939*, 83; Norrie and Owram, *A History of the Canadian Economy* 4th ed., 285–286.

112 As expressed by Edward Beatty, 'The gates of Canada should be opened once more, not only to the British, French and American immigrant, but also to the Scandinavian and the more desirable type of Continental:' Edward Beatty, 'Position of the Canadian Pacific Railway on Immigration,' *The Canadian Annual Review of Public Affairs: 1921* (Toronto: Annual Review Publishing, 1922), 407.

113 David C. Corbett, *Canada's Immigration Policy: A Critique* (Toronto: University of Toronto Press, 1957), 14.

114 P.C. 1181 (2 June 1922). In 1926 the ban on Doukhobor immigration was also lifted: P.C. 418 (17 March 1926).

115 P.C. 717 (9 May 1922). Immediate relatives were initially defined as 'the wife and family of any person legally admitted and resident in Canada who is in a

position to receive and care for his dependents.' The following year, admissible relatives were restricted to 'a wife or child under 18 years of age': P.C. 183 (31 January 1923).

116 P.C. 642 (11 April 1923) and P.C. 183 (31 January 1923).

117 South Africa was included, since blacks there did not have British-subject status.

118 P.C. 616 (7 April 1923).

119 Again this was limited to only those persons born or naturalized in Great Britain, Ireland, Newfoundland, New Zealand, Australia, or the Union of South Africa: P.C. 185 (31 January 1923).

120 Ibid.

121 Preferred countries included Germany, France, Belgium, The Netherlands, Luxembourg, Switzerland, and the Scandinavian countries: see Robert England, *The Colonization of Western Canada: A Study of Contemporary Land Settlement (1896–1934)* (London: P.S. King, 1936), 83.

122 Discussed on 194–9, this volume.

123 'Report of the Department of Immigration and Colonization,' *ADR, 1929–30*, 10–12.

124 *The Empire Settlement Act*, 1922 (Imp.), 12 and 13 Geo. 5, c.13. See also P.C. 826 (9 May 1923); P.C. 213 (27 February 1924); P.C. 1741 (26 September 1925); P.C. 939 (17 June 1926); P.C. 204 (23 February 1927); P.C. 1216 (19 July 1929); and P.C. 129 (4 February 1930).

125 See discussion in chapter 3, this volume.

126 Avery, *'Dangerous Foreigners,'* 97. These schemes were heavily, and some said misleadingly, advertised. David Jones, a telephone wire man from Wales, emigrated to Saskatchewan in 1928 as an assisted agriculturalist, despite the fact that he had 'never seen a farm before I came here.' He and his family suffered great hardship as a result of inexperience and ill health. When asked to what extent the situation in this country met the expectations which he had formed in England, Jones replied, 'Right opposite. All they showed on the movies was in the summer time, in the nice summer weather. All you could see were men running about in motor cars. If you went to your next door neighbours, you had a car to take you.' Similarly, Alex Robertson said, 'I think the country has been grossly [misrepresented] to people in Europe. Time and again I have met people, Britishers who came out here, and who told me that what they found when they came out was entirely different to the picture that was painted by those who had sent them out, railway companies and so on:' Royal Commission on Immigration and Settlement (Saskatchewan) 1930, Archives of Saskatchewan, RGM6, vol. 1: 126–31; vol. 5: 9–19; reprinted in Kevin H. Burley, ed., *The Development*

of Canada's Staples, 1867–1939. A Documentary Collection (Toronto: McClelland & Stewart, n.d.), 73–6, 82–3.

127 England, *The Colonization of Western Canada*, 94–5; Simon Belkin, *Through Narrow Gates: A Review of Jewish Immigration, Colonization and Immigrant Aid Work* (1840–1940) (Montreal: Eagle, 1967), 158.

128 Avery, *'Dangerous Foreigners,'* 97.

129 'Report of the Department of Immigration and Colonization,' *ADR, 1929–30*, 65; see also Avery, *Reluctant Host*, 102–3.

130 Cited in Avery, *'Dangerous Foreigners'*, 107.

131 'Report of the Department of Immigration and Colonization,' *ADR, 1929–30*, 65.

132 P.C. 2359 (13 October 1920); 'Report of the Supervisor of Women's Branch, Miss M.V. Burnham,' in 'Report of the Department of Immigration and Colonization,' *ADR, 1927–28*, 78.

133 'Report of the Supervisor of the Women's Division, Miss M.V. Burnham,' Report of the Department of Immigration and Colonization for 1923, *Sessional Papers, 1924*, no. 13, 54.

134 Ibid.

135 Approved in P.C. 1850 and 1851 (9 August 1920).

136 Roberts, *Whence They Came*, 117–18.

137 Ibid., 117–23.

138 Ibid., 120.

139 Report of the Department of Immigration and Colonization for 1918, *Sessional Papers, 1919*, no. 18, 88. For details on how this movement operated, see chapter 3, this volume.

140 For first-hand accounts see P. Harrison, ed., *The Home Children: Their Personal Stories* (Winnipeg: J. Gordon Shillingford Publishing, 2003), chs. 9–12.

141 See, for example, 'Report of G. Rogue Smart, Supervisor of Juvenile Immigration,' Report of the Department of Immigration and Colonization for 1921. *Sessional Papers, 1922*, no. 18, 53.

142 See, for example, the 1924 comments of Charlotte Whitton, director of the Canadian Welfare Council, quoted in Kenneth Bagnell, *The Little Immigrants: The Orphans Who Came to Canada* (Toronto: Macmillan, 1980), 224.

143 'Report of G. Bogue Smart,' 53.

144 Daisy Peacock, quoted in Gail H. Corbett, *Barnardo Children in Canada* (Peterborough, ON: Woodland, 1981), 95.

145 *Report of the British Overseas Settlement Delegation to Canada 1924* (Parliamentary Papers 1924), quoted in Bagnell, *The Little Immigrants*, 225.

146 'Report on juvenile Immigration by G. Rogue Smart,' in 'Report of the Department of Immigration and Colonization,' *ADR, 1927–28*, 89; for

further details on these schemes, see R.L. Schnell, 'The Right Class of Boy: Youth Training Schemes and Assisted Emigration to Canada under the Empire Settlement Act, 1922–39,' *History of Education* 24/1 (March 1995): 73–90.

147 *The Canada Year Book, 1942* (Ottawa: Dominion Bureau of Statistics, 1943), 164, table 13.

148 Donald Avery, *'Dangerous Foreigners'*, 97.

149 According to Robert England, farmers and new settlers were estimated as having a customer value of between $200 and $400, depending on where they settled. This estimate was based on the freight charges a farmer paid for consumer goods, farm machinery, and travel, and for shipping livestock and produce: England, *The Colonization of Western Canada*, 110–15. Pressures to open up immigration policy came not only from the railway interests, but from mining companies and farmers. Organized labour and war veterans favoured the continuation of restrictive policies; see Avery, *'Reluctant Host'*, 85–6, 95–8.

150 Criticism of the agreement is discussed this volume, 210–12.

151 Avery, *'Dangerous Foreigners'*, 99–101.

152 P.C. 534 (8 April 1926).

153 K.M. McLaughlin, *The Germans in Canada* (Ottawa: Canadian Historical Association 1985), 13.

154 Heinz Lehmann, *The German Canadians: 1750–1937: Immigration, Settlement and Culture* (St. John's, NF: Jesperson, 1986), 154–61.

155 McLaughlin, *The Germans in Canada*, 12.

156 Ibid., 14.

157 'Report of the Department of Immigration and Colonization,' *ADR, 1929–30*, 10–12; see also Myron Gulka-Tiechko, 'Ukrainian Immigration to Canada under the Railways Agreement, 1925–30,' *Journal of Ukrainian Studies* 16/1–2 (Summer-Winter 1991): 29–60.

158 According to O.W. Gerus and J.E. Rea, the Ukrainian population in Czechoslovakia of approximately 450,000 was well treated there: *The Ukrainians in Canada* (Ottawa: Canadian Historical Association, 1985), 12.

159 'Report of the Department of Immigration and Colonization,' *ADR, 1929–30*, 10–12.

160 Donald Avery and J.K. Fedrowicz, *The Poles in Canada* (Ottawa: Canadian Historical Association, 1982), 10: See also Anna Reczynska, *For Bread and a Better Future: Emigration from Poland to Canada, 1918–1939* (Toronto: Multicultural History Society of Toronto, 1966); Thomas M. Prymak, 'Recent Scholarship on Polyethnic Emigration from the Republic of Poland to Canada between the Wars,' *Canadian Ethnic Studies* 23/1 (1991): 58–70.

161 'Report of the Department of Immigration and Colonization,' *ADR*, *1929–30*, 10–12.

162 See discussion in Bennett Kovrig, 'The Magyars and Their Homeland,' in *Struggle and Hope: The Hungarian-Canadian Experience*, ed. N.T. Dreisziger, with M.L. Kovacs, Paul Bödy, Bennet Kovrig (Toronto: McClelland & Stewart, 1982).

163 N.F. Dreisziger, 'The Years of Growth and Change, 1918–1929,' in *Struggle and Hope: The Hungarian-Canadian Experience*, ed. Dreisziger et al., 99.

164 Ibid., 102, 119, and 130. See also Avery, *Reluctant Host*, 99–100; Carmela Patrias, *Patriots and Proletarians: Politicizing Hungarian Immigrants in Interwar Canada* (Montreal: McGill-Queen's University Press, 1994).

165 'Report of the Department of Immigration and Colonization,' *ADR*, *1929–30*, 10–12.

166 P.C. 183 (31 January 1923). Chinese and Japanese immigrants were governed by specific legislation and agreements: see discussion this volume, 206–09.

167 See discussion in chapter 7, this volume.

168 Belkin, *Through Narrow Gates*, Bernard L. Vigod, *The Jews in Canada* (Ottawa: Canadian Historical Association, 1984); Joseph Kage, *With Faith and Thanksgiving: The Story of Two Hundred Years of Jewish Immigration and Immigrant Aid Effort in Canada (1760–1960)* (Montreal: Eagle, 1962), chs. 2–3; H. Troper, 'New Horizons in a New Land: Jewish Immigration to Canada,' in *From Immigration to Integration: The Canadian Jewish Experience: A Millennium Edition*, ed. Ruth Klein and Frank Dimant (Toronto: Institute for International Affairs, B'nai Brith Canada, 2001), in particular regarding the the impact of the 1923 'administrative refinements' making it more difficult for Jewish immigrants to enter.

169 Belkin, *Through Narrow Gates*, 139, and, more generally, 109–39.

170 Families had to first sell their farms, and then travel to Danzig for a visa. Frequently visas were refused on a technicality, leaving the family to travel to Warsaw, where they had to wait for the results of an appeal to the Canadian immigration commissioner in London: ibid., 160–5.

171 Ibid., 151.

172 Isabel Kaprielian-Churchill, 'Armenian Refugees and Their Entry into Canada, 1919–30,' *Canadian Historical Review* 71 (1990): 80–108. This discussion draws heavily from this article. See also her 'Armenian Refugee Women: The Picture Brides, 1920–30,' *Journal of American Ethnic History* 12/3 (Spring 1993): 3–29; and '"Rejecting Misfits": Canada and the Nansen Passport,' *International Migration Review* 28/2 (Summer 1994): 281–306; Avery, *Reluctant Host*, 90; and International Crisis Group, 'Turkey and Armenia: Opening Minds, Opening Borders,' Europe Report No. 199,

14 April 2009, for a brief summary of different historical accounts and recent efforts towards rapprochement.

173 Kaprielian-Churchill, 'Armenian Refugees and Their Entry into Canada,' 90.

174 They may also have avoided the continuous-journey regulation since, although it was not expressly targeted against 'Asians,' in practice immigration officers were instructed to give it that effect while not using it as a bar against other immigrants: see discussions, this volume, in chapter 4, 151–2.

175 In September 1930, immigration officers were notified that Armenians were to be considered under P.C. 183 governing the admission of Europeans and Americans. Within a month, however, they were reclassified again as Asians: PC. 2115 (28 October 1930). Kaprielian-Churchill, 'Armenian Refugees and Their Entry into Canada,' 101–2.

176 For discussion on the McQuarie Resolution and its reception in BC see P. Roy, *The Oriental Question: Consolidating A White Man's Province, 1914–1941* (Vancouver: UBC Press, 2003), 78–80.

177 House of Commons *Debates*, 8 May 1922, 1555–6 and 1575.

178 S.C. 1923, c.38, s.5.

179 The minister's definition was as follows: 'Merchants, as used in the Act, shall not include any person who does not devote his undivided attention to mercantile pursuits and who has less than $2,500 invested in a business dealing exclusively in goods grown, produced or manufactured in China or the exporting to China goods grown produced and manufactured in Canada, and who has not conducted such business for a period of at least three years, any merchant's clerk or any other employee, tailor, mechanic, huckster, peddler or person engaged in taking drying or otherwise conserving fish for home consumption or exportation, or having any connection whatever with a restaurant, laundry, or rooming house': quoted in H.F. Angus, 'Canadian Immigration: The Law and its Administration,' in *The Legal Status of Aliens in Pacific Countries*, ed. N. MacKenzie (Toronto: Oxford University Press, 1937), 63–4. For further discussion see Ward, *White Canada Forever*, ch. 7.

180 S.C. 1923, c.38, ss.10, 11, 13, 27(l).

181 P.C. 1272 (10 July 1923).

182 S.C. 1923, c.38, s.19, as compared with provisions in the *Immigration Act*, S.C. 1910, c.27, s.59.

183 S.C. 1923, c.38, s. 27.

184 *The Canada Year Book, 1946* (Ottawa: Dominion Bureau of Statistics, 1947), 185. On the effects of Chinese Immigration Act in British Columbia see P. Roy, *The Oriental Question*, 73–7.

185 Shin Imai, 'Canadian Immigration Law and Policy: 1867–1935' (LLM thesis, York University, Toronto, 1983), 208.

186 Those permitted to immigrate under the agreement were domestic servants, labourers and their dependents: Ramdeo Sampat-Mehta, *International Barriers* (Ottawa: Harpell's, 1973), 237. the effects of the restrictions in British Columbia are canvassed in P. Roy, *The Oriental Question*, 82–5.

187 S.B.C. c.49.

188 [1923] A.C. 450.

189 Ibid., 192.

190 Implemented in Canadian legislation by the *Japanese Treaty Act* of 1913, S.C. 1913, c.27.

191 [1924] A.C. 203.

192 Ibid., 212–13.

193 See discussion in chapter 4, this volume.

194 Bruce Ryder, 'Racism and the Constitution: British Columbia Anti-Asian Legislation, 1872–1923' (unpublished paper 1990).

195 'Report of the Department of Immigration and Colonization,' *ADR, 1935–36*, 77, table 63.

196 *Immigration Act 1910*, S.C.C. 27, ss.2 (d) and 33, as amended in 1919 S.C.C. 25, s.2(1) (d) (i).

197 Letter of Blair to Amyot, 7 May 1921; Amyot to Blair, 10 May 1921, quoted in Roberts, *Whence They Came*, 104.

198 Dennis Guest, *The Emergence of Social Security in Canada* (Vancouver: University of British Columbia Press, 1980), 65–70, cited in Drystek, 'The Simplest and Cheapest Mode of Dealing with Them,' 426.

199 Drystek, 'The Simplest and Cheapest Mode of Dealing with Them,' 426.

200 They went from approximately 40 per cent of the total between 1920 and 925 to 22 per cent of the total from 1925 to 1930. Medical causes, in contrast, rose from approximately 20 to 30 per cent of the total in that same period: 'Report of the Department of Immigration and Colonization,' *ADR, 1935–36*, 77.

201 For a thorough examination of the department's greater attention to case building and record keeping, and how it often concealed the real reasons for removal under statutory changes, see Roberts, *Whence They Came*, 99–123.

202 Ibid., 90–1.

203 S.C. 1910, c.27, s.23.

204 *R v Lantalum; ex parte Offman* (1921), 48 N.B.R. (N.B.C.A.).

205 *R v Barnstead; Hianson, ex parte; Moller, ex parte* (1920), 55 D.L.R. 287 (N.S.S.C) but note as well *Re Pappas*, [1921] 1 W.W.R. 949 (B.C.S.C.), and *R v Jungo Lee*, [1926] S.C.R. 652.

206 *Lancet v O'Connell* (1921), 61 Que. S.C. 9 (Que. S.C.), per Gibson J.; see also *Yershemsky v Moquin* (1928), 45 Que. KB. 166 (Que. C.A.); *Re Immigration Act*

and Wong Shee, [1922] 2 W.W.R. 156 (B.C.S.C.). The reluctance of the courts to interfere with deportation orders, even where they may have been based on improper considerations or illegal evidence, was clearly evident in cases involving deportations under the Opium and Narcotic Drug Act. See, for example, *R v Chow Tong*, [1924] 34 B.C.R. 12 (B.C.S.C.); *R v Gee Dew* [1924] 2 W.W.R. 793 (B.C.S.C.); note that in *R v Woo FongToy* [1926] 3 W.W.R. 703 (B.C.S.C.) 1; *R v Chang Song* [1924] 1 W.W.R. 778 (B.C.C.A.); but also see *R v Soo Gong* [1927] 1 W.W.R. 669, (B.C.S.C.); *Re Joe Fong* (1923), 53 O.L.R. 493 (Ont. H.C.); *R v Lee Park* [1924] 3 W.W.R. 490 (B.C.C.A).

207 *The Canada Year Book, 1930* (Ottawa: Dominion Bureau of Statistics, 1931), 165–6.

208 'Report of the Department of Immigration and Colonization,' *ADR, 1929–30*, 8, table 1.

209 Memorandum of F.C. Blair, 7 June 1927, cited in Avery, 'Dangerous Foreigners', 103.

210 For examples see ibid., 105–10; see also Donald H. Avery, 'Ethnic and Class Tensions in Canada, 1918–20: Anglo-Canadians and the Alien Worker,' in Loyalties in Conflict: Ukrainians in Canada during the Great War, eds. Frances Swyripa and Herd Thompson, 79–98; For a discussion of labour's views on the Railway agreement see D. J. Goutor, *The Walls of Solidarity: The Mainstream Canadian Labour Movement and Immigration Policy, 1872 to the Early 1930s* (PhD thesis, University of Toronto, 2003), 368–72. See also D.J. Goutor, *Guarding the Gates: The Canadian Labour Movement and Immigration 1872–1934* (Vancouver: UBC Press, 2007), 102.

211 Letter from F.C. Blair to Egan, 15 June 1927, cited in Avery, 'Dangerous Foreigners,' 105.

212 'The Great Immigration Myth,' *The Country Guide*, 1 June 1928, 33.

213 W.A. Carrothers, 'The Immigration Problem in Canada,' *Queen's Quarterly*, 36 (1929): 517. While not advocating the complete exclusion of Continental Europeans, Carrothers did support the exclusion of Orientals, arguing that racially 'we cannot assimilate the yellow, brown or black races,' nor can we economically 'without seriously affecting the standard of living of the white workmen already in the country': ibid., 520. A similar view was expressed by George Exton Lloyd: 'The question for Canada is this: Can we build up a great nation while racial groups with different traditions, instincts, and ideals are being poured into this country? The answer surely must be: We dare not run the risk of such an experiment...': 'Immigration and Nation Building,' *Empire Review*, February 1929, 105–6.

214 *Saskatoon Star* (5 June 1928), quoted in Avery, *'Dangerous Foreigners'*, 108. According to Robin Winks, in the late 1920s and early 1930s, the Ku Klux

Klan had a membership of more than 22,000 persons: see James W. St.-G. Walker's review of Winks's book in *The Black I: A Canadian Journal of Black Expression* 50/1 (March 1977): 6.

215 See Daniel J. Kelves, *In the Name of Eugenics: Genetics and the Use of Human Heredity* (Berkeley: University of California Press, 1983).

216 Cited in C.P. Blacker, *Eugenics: Galton and After* (London: Duckworth, 1952), 65, and Angus McLaren, *Our Own Master Race: Eugenics in Canada, 1885– 1945* (Toronto: McClelland & Stewart, 1990), 15.

217 Eleoussa Polyzoi, 'Psychologists' Perceptions of the Canadian Immigrant before World War II,' *Canadian Ethnic Studies* 7 (1986): 610. 506 Notes to pages 213–17.

218 W. Burton Hurd, 'Is There a Canadian Race?' *Queen's Quarterly* 35 (1928): 61527, cited in McLaren *Our Own Master Race*, 124–5.

219 See W.S. Wallace, 'The Canadian Immigration Policy,' *Canadian Magazine* 30 (1907–8), 358. According to Wallace, 'nearly all immigration is, in the nature of things, inferior.'

220 McLaren, *Our Own Master Race*, 55.

221 C.K. Clarke, 'The Defective Immigrant,' *The Public Health Journal* 7 (November 1916): 462–5. For further discussion of Clarke's views and their implications, see Ian Dowbiggin, '"Keeping This Young Country Sane": C.K. Clarke, Immigration Restriction, and Canadian Psychiatry, 1890–1925,' *Canadian Historical Review* 76/4 (December 1995): 598–627.

222 McLaren, *Our Own Master Race*, 27.

223 Ibid., 7–9, 95, 167.

224 Two of the more progressive voices in the immigration debate were Robert England and Watson Kirkconnell. England, who taught in rural Saskatchewan and later became continental superintendent for the CPR's Colonization Department, wrote a book in 1929 in which he made an impassioned plea for tolerance and appreciation for the strengths of Canada's ethnic groups. His prescription for future immigration policy included improved selection according to skills and Canadian require- ments, and not based on racial exclusions grounded on crude stereotypes: *The Central European Immigrant in Canada* (Toronto: Macmillan, 1929). Similarly, in a 1928 article, Kirkconnell criticized the 'insolent and un-Christian fulminations against European immigrants' as being both intolerant and ignorant, and argued that the greatness in civilization 'has almost invariably come from a blending of races and cultures': see 'Western Immigration,' *Canadian Forum*, July 1928, 706–7, reprinted in Howard Palmer, *Immigration and the Rise of Multiculturalism* (Toronto: Copp Clark, 1975), 56–7.

225 Select Standing Committee on Agriculture and Colonization, *Minutes of Proceedings and Evidence and Report* (Ottawa: King's Printer, 1928), x–xi; see also Avery, *Reluctant Host*, 106.

226 'Annual Review by President R.J. Hutchings,' 9, cited in Avery, *'Dangerous Foreigners'*, 112.

Chapter 6 The Depression Years, 1930–1937: Exclusion and Expulsion

1 P.C. 695 (21 March 1931).

2 *The Canadian Annual Review: 1930–31* (Toronto: Annual Review Publishing, 1931), 574.

3 'Report of the Department of Mines and Resources, Immigration Branch, *Annual Departmental Reports, 1944–45*, 200 *[Annual Departmental Reports* henceforth cited as ADR].

4 Ibid.

5 Ibid., 220.

6 Michiel Horn, 'The Great Depression Past and Present,' *Journal of Canadian Studies* 11/1 (February 1976): 42, 45. For a general account of the Depression era in Canada, see Robert Bothwell, Ian Drummond, and John English, *Canada, 1900–1945* (Toronto: University of Toronto Press, 1987), chs. 15 and 16.

7 For more on the causes and the effects of the Great Depression, see A.E. Safarian, *The Canadian Economy in the Great Depression* (Ottawa: Carleton University Press, 1970); L.M. Grayson and Michael Bliss, eds., *The Wretched of Canada: Letters to R.B. Bennett, 1930–1935* (Toronto: University of Toronto Press, 1971); Michiel Horn, ed., *The Dirty Thirties: Canada in the Great Depression* (Toronto: Copp Clark, 1972); Horn, 'The Great Depression Past and Present'; Alvin Finkel, *Business and Social Reform in the Thirties* (Toronto: Lorimer, 1979); Michiel Horn, *The Great Depression in Canada* (Ottawa: Canadian Historical Association 1984); John Herd Thompson, *Canada, 1922–1939: Decades of Discord* (Toronto: McClelland & Stewart, 1985); Douglas Owram, 'Economic Thought in the 1930s: The Prelude to Keynesianism,' *Canadian Historical Review* 66/3 (September 1985): 344–77; Desmond Morton, *Working People*, 3d ed. (Toronto: Summerhill, 1990); Kenneth Norrie and Douglas Owram, *A History of the Canadian Economy* (Toronto: Harcourt Brace Jovanovich, 1991); Larry A. Glassford, *Reaction and Reform: The Politics of the Conservative Party under R.B. Bennett, 1927–1938* (Toronto: University of Toronto Press, 1992).

8 James Gray, *The Winter Years: The Depression on the Prairies* (Toronto: Macmillan, 1966); Horn, ed., *The Dirty Thirties*, Donald H. Avery, *Reluctant*

Host: Canada's Response to Immigrant Workers, 1896–1994 (Toronto: McClelland & Stewart, 1995), 109–11.

9 Horn, ed., *The Dirty Thirties*, 533.

10 'Unemployment and Relief in Western Canada, June-August 1932, Report for the Prime Minister's Office,' U.N.B. Library, Bennett Papers, vol. 781, reprinted in *The Dirty Thirties*, ed. Horn, 263–4.

11 Gray, *The Winter Years*, 126. According to Keith Walden, unfavourable views of aliens permeated contemporary popular culture. Novels dealing with the RCMP contained an 'astounding' number of foreign villains, and that anxiety was fused with concern about the disruptive influence of labour unions: *Visions of Order: The Canadian Mounties in Symbol and Myth* (Toronto: Butterworths, 1982), 129–36.

12 Avery, *Reluctant Host*, 110–11. For the burdens under which municipalities suffered, see John Taylor, '"Relief from Relief": The Cities' Answer to Depression Dependency,' *Journal of Canadian Studies* 14/1 (Spring 1979): 16–23; Terry Copp, 'Montreal's Municipal Government and the Crisis of the 1930s,' in *The Usable Urban Past*, ed. Alan J. Artibise and Gilbert Stelter (Ottawa: Carleton University Press, 1979), 112–29.

13 During the 1930 election campaign, Mackenzie King stated that responsibility for immigration should fall more heavily on the provinces, a view which ran counter to public opinion, particularly in the West. For King's policies, see D. Owen Carrigan, *Canadian Party Platforms, 1867–1968* (Toronto: Copp Clark, 1968), 111–12.

14 For more on the League and its prescriptions for political and economic change, see League for Social Reconstruction, Research Committee, *Social Planning for Canada* (Toronto: Thomas Nelson & Sons, 1935); Michiel Horn, *League far Social Reconstruction: Intellectual Origins of the Democratic Left in Canada, 1930–1942* (Toronto: University of Toronto Press, 1980). The history of the CCF is the subject of Walter D. Young, *Anatomy of a Party: The National C.C.F., 1932–1961* (Toronto: University of Toronto Press, 1969); H. Blair Neatby, *The Politics of Chaos: Canada in the Thirties* (Toronto: Macmillan, 1972), ch. 6. The first leader of the CCF, J.S. Woodsworth, is the subject of two monographs: Kenneth McNaught, *A Prophet in Politics: A Biography of J.S. Woodsworth* (Toronto: University of Toronto Press, 1959); and Allen Mills, *Fool for Christ: The Political Thought of J.S. Woodsworth* (Toronto: University of Toronto Press, 1991). Others that also voiced concern for the treatment of South Asians were protestant foreign ministries canvassed in R.C. Brouwer, 'A Disgrace to "Christian Canada": Protestant Foreign Missionary Concerns about the Treatment of South Asians in Canada, 1907–1940,' in *A Nation of Immigrants: Women, Workers, and*

Communities in Canadian History, 1840s–1960s, ed. Franca Iacovetta
(Toronto: University of Toronto Press, 1998), 361–84.

15 See discussion this volume, 233–8.

16 See Martin Robin, *Shades of Right: Nativist and Fascist Politics in Canada,
1920–1940* (Toronto: University of Toronto Press, 1992); Jonathan Wagner,
Brothers Beyond the Sea: National Socialism in Canada (Waterloo, ON: Wilfrid
Laurier University Press, 1982).

17 Claiming fewer members but more closely committed to the aspirations
of the Nationalist Socialist Party were two other Nazi organizations open
to German citizens – The National Socialist Workers Party in Canada
(NSDAP) and the German Labour Front (DAF). Both reported to
Germany, and as with the Bund, received support from the German consul
in Winnipeg: Robert H. Keyserlingk, ' "Agents within the Gates": The
Search for Nazi Subversives in Canada during World War II,' *Canadian
Historical Review* 66/2 (1985): 221; Rudolf A. Helling, *A Socio-Economic
History of German Canadians: They, Too, Founded Canada* (Weisbaden: Franz
Steiner, 1984), 63.

18 Lita-Rose Betcherman, *The Swastika and the Maple Leaf.- Fascist Movements in
Canada in the Thirties* (Don Mills, ON: Fitzhenry & Whiteside, 1975), 65–6.

19 Frederick Edwards, 'Fascism in Canada,' *Maclean's Magazine*, 15 April and
1 May 1938. For other descriptions of Arcand and his popularity in Quebec,
see Betcherman, *The Swastika and the Maple Leaf* and David Rome, 'Clouds in
the Thirties: On Anti-Semitism in Canada, 1929–39,' *Canadian Jewish Archives*
(Montreal: Canadian Jewish Congress, 1977); and Jacques Langlais and David
Rome, *Jews and French Canadians: Two Hundred Years of Shared History*
(Waterloo, ON: Wilfrid Laurier University Press, 1991), 89–93.

20 The degree to which Arcand was tolerated by the Union Nationale is
illustrated by the fact that, in 1936, a time when his views were well known, he
edited its semi-official daily tabloid L'Illustration Nouvelle: see Betcherman,
The Swastika and the Maple Leaf, 85.

21 In addition to the texts mentioned above, Esther Delisle chronicles anti-
Semitism expressed in *L'Action Nationale* and *Le Devoir*, and by the political
movement Jeune-Canada, and the prominent historian and cleric Lionel
Groulx: see *The Traitor and the Jew: Anti-Semitism and the Delirium of Extremist
Right-Wing Nationalism in French Canada from 1929–39* (Montreal: Robert
Davies, 1993). See also Pierre Anctil, *Le rendez-vous manqué: Les Juifs de
Montréal face au Québec de l'entre-deux guerres* (Quebec City: Institut Québécois
de Recherche sur la Culture, 1988); Andrée Lévesque, *Virage à gauche interdit:
Les communistes, les socialistes et leurs ennemies au Québec, 1929–1939* (Montreal:
Boreal Express, 1984). Evelyn Dumas emphasizes the importance of Jews and

Eastern Europeans in Quebec strikes during the 1930s in *The Bitter Thirties in Quebec* (Montreal: Black Rose, 1975), 11.

22 See A.V. Spada, *The Italians in Canada* (Montreal: Riviera, 1969), 125.

23 It has been estimated that Communist Party in 1939 had a membership of 16,000: R. Douglas Francis, Richard Jones, and Donald B. Smith, *Destinies: Canadian History since Confederation* 6th ed. (Toronto: Nelson, 2008), 297. In contrast, Nazi sympathizers among the German community in Canada are estimated to have represented about 1 per cent of the German population, or 5,000 people: Helling, *History of German Canadians*, 64; and Keyserlingk, '"Agents within the Gates,"' 214. According to Betcherman there were at most a few thousand members of the Nationalist Social Christian Party: *The Swastika and the Maple Leaf*, 89, 120. In his study, *Brothers Beyond the Sea*, Jonathan Wagner emphasizes that the appeal of National Socialism lay outside the mainstream.

24 Gray, *The Winter Years*, 132.

25 See discussion in chapter 7, this volume.

26 See, for example, statistics provided in the reports of the Department of Immigration and Colonization in *ADR* for the years 1934–5 and in the reports of the Immigration Branch, Department of Mines and Resources, for the years 1956–8.

27 P.C. 1413, 7 August 1929.

28 See, for example, the 1933–4 annual report of the director of emigration in Europe, W.R. Little, in which he notes that a 'considerable number of key-men have been admitted for branch factories and skilled men have also been admitted temporarily to erect new machinery. These applications are submitted to the department and instructions are received in each case': 'Report of the Director of Emigration for Canada, W.R. Little,' in 'Report of the Department of Immigration and Colonization,' *ADR, 1933–34*, 81.

29 S.C. 1923, c.38, s.5. See discussion in chapter 5, this volume, 206–7.

30 Canada, Department of Trade and Commerce, Dominion Bureau of Statistics, *The Canada Year Book, 1946* (Ottawa: King's Printer 1946), 188.

31 P.C. 3173, 29 December 1931.

32 P.C. 2115, 16 September 1930.

33 See discussion in chapter 4, this volume, 161–3.

34 For example, in 1930 more than 4,000 British children arrived in Canada. The following year, the number dropped by 50 per cent, and fell still further in the next two years, when slightly more than 600 children were admitted. Fewer than 100 British juveniles emigrated to Canada between 1934 and 1938. Although their numbers started to rise by 1939, the

movement would soon be terminated altogether when the war made transatlantic crossings perilous: Canada, Department of Trade and Commerce, Dominion Bureau of Statistics, *Canada Year Book, 1942*, 164. For an account of the child-immigration schemes during this period, see R.L. Schnell, '"The Right Class of Boy": Youth Training Schemes and Assisted Emigration to Canada under the Empire Settlement Act, 1922–39,' *History of Education* 24/1 (March 1995): 73–90.

35 'Report of the Commissioner of Immigration, A.L. Jolliffe,' in 'Report of the Department of Immigration and Colonization,' *ADR, 1934–35*, 80.

36 Ibid.

37 'Report of the Supervisor of Juvenile Immigration, G. Bogue Smart,' in 'Report of the Department of Immigration and Colonization, *ADR, 1930–31*, 91.

38 See, for example, discussions of child immigration in chapter 3.

39 'Report of the Supervisor of Juvenile Immigration, G. Bogue Smart,' in 'Report of the Department of Immigration and Colonization,' *ADR 1931–32, 81.*

40 'Report of the Commissioner of Immigration, A.L. Jolliffe,' in 'Report of the Department of Immigration and Colonization,' *ADR 1934–35*, 81.

41 See summary of naturalization law in chapter 4, 161–3.

42 *Naturalization Act*, R.S.C. 1927, c.138, ss.4, 22–6.

43 Since the Naturalization Act was a federal statute, it could confer only entitlements that were within federal jurisdiction. Rights within provincial jurisdiction, such as the right to vote in provincial elections, were thus not guaranteed upon naturalization.

44 *Immigration Act*, R.S.C. 1927 (vol. II) c.93, s.40.

45 This followed from the fact that domicile could be acquired only by those who had entered Canada lawfully, which by definition meant that they were not inadmissible at the time of entry: see sections 2 and 3 of ibid.

46 See discussion in chapter 5, this volume, 184–5.

47 H.F. Angus, 'The Legal Status in British Columbia of Oriental Races and Their Descendants,' *Canadian Bar Review* 9/1 (January1931):10.

48 P .C. 1378, June 1931. P. Roy, *The Oriental Question: Consolidating A White Man's Province, 1914–1941* (Vancouver: UBC Press, 2003), 149–50.

49 H.F. Angus, 'The Status of Aliens in Canada,' in Canadian Political Science Association, *Papers and Proceedings of the Sixth Annual Meeting* (Kingston: Jackson, 1934), 85–6.

50 Shin Imai, 'Deportation in the Depression,' *Queen's Law Journal* 7/1 (1981): 70.

51 *Naturalization Act*, R.S.C. 1927, c.138, s.9.
52 Unless the wife was British subject by birth, there were special provisions in the Naturalization Act dealing with the citizenship status of wives and minors. Married women were deemed to have the citizenship of their spouses, and children were deemed to have the citizenship status of their fathers: R.S.C. 1927, c.138, ss.13–15.
53 Angus, 'The Status of Aliens in Canada,' 91–2.
54 In 1931, a commissioner was appointed to consider the revocation of naturalization certificates of those referred to him by the secretary of state. According to the secretary of state's annual report, this appointment 'cleared the way for the disposal of a large number of revocation cases': see 'Report of the Secretary of State, Naturalization Branch,' *ADR, 1931–32*, 363.
55 'Report of the Department of Mines and Resources, Immigration Branch,' *ADR, 1944–45*, 220, table 14.
56 See discussion in chapter 4, this volume, 138.
57 *Immigration Act*, R.S.C. 1927 (Vol. 11) c.93 ss.40, 41(d).
58 Ibid., ss.13–19.
59 Ibid., s.23.
60 *Samejima v R.*, [1932] 4 D.L.R. 246 (S.C.C.); *Vaaro [sic] v R.*, [1933] S.C.R. 36; *Re Naumiec*, [1932] 3 W.W.R. 693 (Man. K.–B.).
61 *Re Low Hong Hing* (1926), 37 B.C.R. 295.
62 Deportations for political reasons during this and previous periods are canvassed in B. Roberts, 'Shovelling Out the "Mutinous": Political Deportations from Canada before 1936,' *Labour/Le Travail* 18 (Fall, 1986): 77–110.
63 Francis, Jones, and Smith, eds., *Destinies*, 1st ed. 276–7.
64 Barbara Roberts, *Whence They Came; Deportation from Canada, 1900–35* (Ottawa: University of Ottawa Press, 1988), 162.
65 James Struthers, *No Fault of Their Own: Unemployment and the Canadian Welfare State, 1914–1941* (Toronto: University of Toronto Press, 1983), 75.
66 Ibid., 6.
67 In 1930 the relief burden assumed by all the provinces was close to $17 million. By 1934, it had climbed above $152 million: Norrie and Owram, *History of the Canadian Economy*, 494–5.
68 J.L. Granatstein, Irving Abella, T.W. Acheson, David Bercuson, R. Craig Brown, and H. Blair Neatby, *Nation: Canada since Confederation*, 3rd ed. (Toronto: McGraw-Hill Ryerson, 1990), 313.
69 Grayson and Bliss, eds., *The Wretched of Canada*, xii; Roberts, *Whence They Came*, 182.
70 House of Commons *Debates*, 11 May 1931, 1433.

71 Roberts, *Whence They Came*, 164–5.
72 House of Commons *Debates*, 31 March 1931, 470.
73 From a statement issued by the minister of immigration, W.A. Gordon, on 4 February 1931 and reported in the *Montreal Gazette*, 5 February 1931.
74 House of Commons *Debates*, 21 April 1932, 2258.
75 Ibid., 13 October 1932, 203.
76 Roberts, *Whence They Came*, 172; Avery, *Reluctant Host*, 112.
77 Roberts, *Whence They Came*, 183.
78 Ibid. According to the *Winnipeg Free Press*, there was 'unqualified confirmation by the Department' that no municipality in the country was reporting regularly immigrants who had been less than five years in Canada and who had claimed relief: 23 February 1934.
79 House of Commons *Debates*, 20 February 1934, 768–9.
80 Ibid.
81 'Report of the Commissioner of Immigration, A.L. Jolliffe,' in 'Report of the Department of Immigration and Colonization,' *ADR, 1932–33*, 82.
82 Ibid., 85.
83 Ibid.
84 'Report of the Commissioner of Immigration,' in 'Report of the Department of Mines and Resources, Immigration Branch,' *ADR, 1936–37*, 306.
85 Roberts, *Whence They Came*, 182.
86 Ibid., 189.
87 Department statistics show public charge deportations falling from close to 3,000 in 1932–3 to 464 in 1934–5, and further to 125 the following year: 'Report of the Department of Immigration and Colonization,' *ADR, 1935–36*, 77, table 63.
88 See, for example, 'Statistics on Cases Handled by the Canadian Labour Defence League, (CLDL) 1929–February 1930,' and 'Material on Section 98 and the Imprisonment of Communists,' in the Robert Kenny Collection (University of Toronto Library); and also discussions in Roberts, *Whence They Came*, 130–6; and Donald Avery, *Dangerous Foreigners: European Immigrant Workers and Labour Radicalism in Canada, 1896–1932* (Toronto: McClelland & Stewart, 1979), 136–7.
89 Avery, '*Dangerous Foreigners*', 118. General accounts of Canadian Communist movements and the Communist Party of Canada include Irving Martin Abella, *Nationalism, Communism, and Canadian Labour: The CIO, the Communist Party, and the Canadian Congress of Labour, 1935–1956* (Toronto: University of Toronto Press, 1973); Ivan Avakumovic, *The Communist Party in Canada: A History* (Toronto: McClelland & Stewart, 1975); William Beeching and Phyllis Clarke, eds., *Yours in the Struggle: Reminiscences of Tim Buck* (Toronto: NC Press,

1977); and Ian Angus, *Canadian Bolsheviks: An Early History of the Communist Party of Canada* (Montreal: Vanguard, 1981).

90 Avery, *'Dangerous Foreigners'*, 128. For a case study of union organization among Alberta sugar-beet workers, most of whom were Europeans, see John Herd Thompson and Allen Seager, 'Workers, Growers and Monopolists: The "Labour Problem" in the Alberta Sugar Beet Industry during the 1930s,' in *The Depression in Canada: Responses to Economic Crisis*, ed. Michiel Horn (Toronto: Copp Clark Pitman, 1985), 30–50. The president of the Beet Workers Industrial Union was Peter Meronik, a Ukrainian Communist who had previously worked to organize the Mine Workers' Union.

91 Morton, *Working People*, 143.

92 Stuart Jamieson, *Times of Trouble: Labour Unrest and Industrial Conflict in Canada, 1900–1966* (Ottawa: Ministry of Supply and Services, 1976), 216. See also Lorne Brown, *When Freedom Was Lost: The Unemployed, the Agitator and the State* (Montreal: Black Rose, 1987).

93 Ferguson to King, 11 August 1929, and Ferguson to Tolchard, 10 May 1930, quoted in Avery, *'Dangerous Foreigners'*, 135.

94 *Mail and Empire*, 5 February 1931, 1.

95 Lorne Brown and Caroline Brown, *An Unauthorized History of the RCMP* (Toronto: Lorimer, 1973), 63.

96 Ibid., 82.

97 23 January 1929. The *Evening Telegram* and the *Globe* were supportive of the Toronto police's actions, while the *Star* was more critical. For more on the Toronto press reaction and the public's acquiescence to the anti-Communist campaign, see Michiel Horn, 'Keeping Canada "Canadian": Anti-Communism and Canadianism in Toronto, 1928–29,' *Canada* 3/1 (September 1975): 34. The anti-Communist campaign is also recalled in the memoirs of Tom McEwen, one of the leaders of the CPC: see *The Forge Glows Red: From Blacksmith to Revolutionary* (Toronto: Progress, 1974).

98 House of Commons *Debates*, 8 May 1929, 2367.

99 Ibid., 2371–2. These views were also supported by Agnes Macphail, United Farmers of Ontario MP, and Liberal MP Joseph Bradette.

100 See, for example, House of Commons *Debates*, 1 May 1931, 1200–3; 5 May 1931, 1274–83; 26 May 1931, 1983–93; 7 July 1931, 3477–87; and 14 July 1933, 3748–51.

101 Buck's experiences are recounted in his reminiscences, *Yours in the Struggle*, 162–202.

102 S.C. 1919 c.46, ss.4, 5.

103 It would appear that this was not that unusual. For example, in 1929 Judge Emerson Coatsworth presided at the trial of an individual arrested for

participating in a Toronto street meeting. Judge Coatsworth was an advisory member of the Canadian Christian Crusade, organized to thwart the 'ever-increasing menace of communism, bolshevism and atheism': see House of Commons *Debates*, 8 May 1929, 2356–7.

104 *R v Buck et al.,* [1932] 3 D.L.R. 97 (O.C.A.).

105 Roberts, *Whence They Came*, 134.

106 Avery, *'Dangerous Foreigners'*, 137, 139.

107 House of Commons *Debates*, 6 May 1932, 2683.

108 In dismissing the *habeas corpus* application brought on behalf of Dan Holmes, the judge held that the provisions of the Immigration Act had been adhered to and the fact that Holmes was being detained in Halifax, where his immigration hearing would be held, was not a breach of justice. The judge reasoned that, in Halifax, Holmes would 'receive a due measure of British fair play and justice': *Rex v Holmes (or Chomicki)*, [1932] 3 W.W.R. 76.

109 House of Commons *Debates*, 23 May 1932, 3249.

110 Ibid.; and 'Report of the Commissioner of Immigration, A.L. Jolliffe,' in 'Report of the Department of Immigration and Colonization,' *ADR, 1930–31*, 77.

111 *Ottawa Citizen*, 5 May 1932, quoted by Woodsworth in House of Commons *Debates*, 6 May 1932, 2686.

112 House of Commons *Debates*, 23 May 1932, 3249.

113 Ibid., 6 May 1932, 2683–4.

114 Ibid., 2688.

115 Roberts, *Whence They Came*, 142–5.

116 *Vaaro [sic] et al. v The King*, [1933] 1 D.L.R. (S.C.C.), 364.

117 Ibid., 365–6.

118 *Canadian Forum*, February 1934, 165.

119 Roberts, *Whence They Came*, 149–54.

120 See, for example, *Canadian Forum*, February 1934, in which the government is censored for its efforts to remove Tom Cacic to his native Yugoslavia, where he had been previously imprisoned for his political activities.

121 For a description of the strike, see Morton, *Working People*, 144.

122 In January 1931, sixty-eight professors at the University of Toronto signed a letter protesting the actions of the Toronto police and warning that the 'right of free speech and free assembly is in danger of suppression in this city.' The letter was widely publicized and provoked much controversy. For a more detailed account of the reaction, see Michiel Horn, 'Free Speech within the Law: The Letter of the Sixty-Eight Toronto Professors, 1931,' *Ontario History* 1 (March 1980): 27. Illustrative of the different positions

taken were editorials in the *Toronto Globe*, 15 and 16 January 1931, and *Saturday Night*, 31 January 1931.

123 Monsignor A.J. Janssen, Vicar General, to Bennett, 1 October 1931, quoted in Avery, *'Dangerous Foreigners'*, 139.

124 House of Commons, *Debates*, 14 February 1933, 2102.

125 15 February 1934, cited in J. Petryshyn, 'R.B. Bennett and the Communists: 1930–1935,' *Journal of Canadian Studies* 9 (1974): 49.

126 Cited in Petryshyn, 'R.B. Bennett and the Communists,' 49; see also *Canadian Forum*, December 1933, 84.

127 Petryshyn, 'R.B. Bennett and the Communists,' 50–2.

128 For a description of the 'On to Ottawa Trek,' see Jamieson, *Times of Trouble*, 243–6; Morton, *Working People*, 147; and Horn, ed., *The Dirty Thirties*, 308–11.

129 2 July 1935.

130 Ibid.

131 Horn, ed., *The Dirty Thirties*, 388.

132 See, for example, the *Montreal Gazette*, 5 July 1935, 10; and the *Mail and Empire*, 2 July 1935, 6.

133 3 July 1935.

134 25 June 1935; quoted in Petryshyn, 'R.B. Bennett and the Communists,' 53.

135 4 July 1935.

136 'Report of the Department of Mines and Resources, Immigration Branch,' *ADR, 1944–45*, 200.

137 Ibid.

138 The Bennett and King governments were preoccupied with domestic economic conditions during the 1930s, and their immigration policies reflected these concerns. Some historians have suggested that the isolationist policies of Western democracies, including Canada, during the 1930s contributed to the international instability which erupted in war at the end of the decade. For Canada's isolationism in external relations during this period, see James Eayrs, *In Defence of Canada*, vol. 1, *From the Great War to the Great Depression* (Toronto: University of Toronto Press, 1964); Eayrs, *In Defence of Canada*, vol. 2, *Appeasement and Rearmament* (Toronto: University of Toronto Press, 1965); Robert Bothwell and Norman Hillmer, eds., *The In-Between Time: Canadian External Policy in the 1930s* (Toronto: Copp Clark, 1975); and C.P. Stacey, *Canada and the Age of Conflict*, vol. 2, *1921–1940, The Mackenzie King Era* (Toronto: University of Toronto Press, 1981).

139 The CCF won less than 10 per cent of the vote, electing only seven members of Parliament.

Chapter 7 The Recovery and the Second World War, 1938–1945:
Closure and Internment

1 Robert Bothwell, Ian Drummond, and John English, *Canada: 1900–1945* (Toronto: University of Toronto Press, 1987), 352–3.
2 Ibid., 112. For a more detailed discussion of the Canadian economy during the war, see Kenneth Norrie and Douglas Owram, *A History of the Canadian Economy* 4th ed. (Toronto: Thomson Nelson, 2008), 342–60.
3 R. Douglas Francis, Richard Jones, and Donald B. Smith, *Destinies: Canadian History since Confederation* (Toronto: Holt, Rinehart & Winston, 1988), 284.
4 P.C. 885 (23 April 1937); P.C. 7318 (21 September 1944). These regulations applied only to male residents of Canada or male members of the Canadian armed forces wishing to bring their spouses and dependants to Canada. The orders-in-council did not extend the same right to women residents and female members of the armed forces.
5 'Report of the Commissioner of Immigration,' in 'Report of the Department of Mines and Resources, Immigration Branch,' *Annual Departmental Reports, 1938–39*, 272 *[Annual Departmental Reports* henceforth cited as *ADR]*.
6 'Report of the Department of Mines and Resources, Immigration Branch,' *ADR, 1944–45*, 200, table 1.
7 'Report of the Department of Mines and Resources, Immigration Branch,' *ADR, 1940–41*, 193.
8 Among the new restrictions imposed on Jews was the revocation of citizenship and denial of the right to vote.
9 Gerald Dirks, *Canada's Refugee Policy: Indifference or Opportunism?* (Montreal: McGill-Queen's University Press, 1977), 45; German anti-Jewish propaganda is discussed in David Welch, *The Third Reich: Politics and Propaganda* (London: Routledge, 1993), 72–82. Events in Europe are summarized in William R. Keylor, *The Twentieth-Century World and Beyond: An International History Since 1900*, 5th ed. (New York: Oxford University Press, 2006), chs. 4–5; Gordon A. Craig, *Germany, 1866–1945* (New York: Oxford University Press, 1978), ch. 19. More detailed studies of the major events include Gordon Brook-Shepherd, *Anschluss: The Rape of Austria* (London: Macmillan, 1963); Ronald M. Smelser, *The Sudeten Problem, 1933–1938* (Middletown, CT: Wesleyan University Press, 1975); and James Thomas Emmerson, *The Rhineland Crisis* (London: Maurice Temple Smith, 1977). The impact of these events on European Jewry is discussed more explicitly in Paul Johnson, *A History of the Jews* (London: Weidenfeld & Nicolson, 1987), part 6; see also Irving Abella and Harold Troper, *None Is Too Many: Canada and the Jews of Europe, 1933–1948* (Toronto: Lester & Orpen Dennys, 1982), 3–4.

10 For a detailed account of the conference and of Mackenzie King's reluctance to send a Canadian representative, see Abella and Troper, *None Is Too Many*, 16–32 and the same authors in '"The line must be drawn somewhere": Canada and Jewish Refugees, 1933–1939,' in *A Nation of Immigrants: Women, Workers, and Communities in Canadian History, 1840s–1960s*, ed. Franca Iacovetta (Toronto: University of Toronto Press, 1998), 412–45, in particular 420–8

11 Eric Koch, *Deemed Suspect: A Wartime Blunder* (Agincourt, ON: Methuen, 1980), xiii.

12 See, for example, 'Canada Immigration,' a radio address given by Joseph Jenkins under the auspices of the (Montreal) City Improvement League, printed in *The Municipal Review of Canada*, December 1936, 20–4; James Colley, Department of Immigration and Colonization, and Development of the Canadian Pacific Railway, 'Immigration and Colonization,' an address to the Chartered Institute of Secretaries (Quebec Branch), printed in *Agriculture and Industrial Progress in Canada* (April 1945), 50–6; see also the views on immigration expressed to the Royal Commission on Dominion-Provincial Relations, 1940, CA1 21 37A21, Altu 2/Report of Hearings by J.C. Wilson, Board of Trade for the City of St George, 5494; and H.W. Morgan, Canadian Chamber of Commerce, 9556.

13 See discussion this volume, 264–76.

14 See, for example, the submissions made throughout the years by Liberals Samuel Jacobs and Sam Factor, as well as the submissions made by A.A. Heaps and other CCF colleagues such as M.J. Coldwell and Clarie Gillis.

15 The CNCR was formed by the League of Nations Society; one of its most vocal proponents was the first woman senator of Canada, Cairine Wilson.

16 Among the public displays of support it was able to marshal were petitions and mass meetings in several cities across the country in November 1938 to protest government policy: Erna Paris, *Jews: An Account of Their Experience in Canada* (Toronto: Macmillan, 1980), 88.

17 For a description of the events of Kristallnacht, see Johnson, *A History of the Jews*, 485–6; Craig, *Germany, 1866–1945*, 631–7; and, for the ensuing Canadian reaction, Abella and Troper, *None Is Too Many*, 38–47. Lita-Rose Betcherman notes that one of the leading columnists in the *Globe and Mail*, Judith Robinson, was very critical of Canada's closed-door approach: see Betcherman, *The Swastika and the Maple Leaf. Fascist Movements in Canada in the Thirties* (Don Mills, ON: Fitzhenry & Whiteside, 1975), 7. Note, however, that this columnist's condemnation did not necessarily represent the views of the editorial board.

18 Regarding the position of the *Winnipeg Free Press*, see 19 July 1939, and of *Saturday Night*, see 24 December 1938 and 20 March 1943.

19 As discussed more fully later in this chapter, Frederick Blair, the director of the Immigration Branch, was a staunch opponent of admitting Jewish refugees, as was Vincent Massey, the Canadian high commissioner in London, and Ernest Lapointe, the minister of Justice. For more on the opponents of Jewish immigration within the public service, see Abella and Troper, *None Is Too Many*.

20 See discussion this volume, 292–5.

21 For a discussion of anti-Japanese propaganda see P. Roy, *Triumph of Citizenship: The Japanese and Chinese in Canada 1941–1967* (Vancouver: UBC Press, 2007), ch. 1.

22 Abella and Troper, *None Is Too Many*, x.

23 In 1988, the Japanese community was compensated for the losses it sustained during the Second World War (see discussion this volume, 306–7). Several other communities, however, most notably the Ukrainian and Italian communities, are still seeking federal acknowledgment and redress for the unnecessary hardship many of their members endured in internment camps during the First and Second World War, respectively. While the federal government issued a formal apology to the Italian community in November 1990, it made no commitment to financial compensation: see *Globe and Mail*, 5 November 1990. At that time Prime Minister Mulroney hinted that a formal apology to the Ukrainian community would be forthcoming, but as yet no apology has been issued: see *Montreal Gazette*, 14 November 1990; *Vancouver Sun*, 30 March 1993.

24 Although the Liberal party was elected to leadership in a landslide in 1940, within a few years many of its supporters, weary of wartime controls and regulations, and worried about their futures in a postwar economy, switched their support to the CCF, attracted largely to its social-welfare platform. By 1944, the CCF had a strong following in British Columbia; it was the official Opposition in Ontario; and, in Saskatchewan, Tommy Douglas had been elected the first CCF premier in Canadian history. Federally, a 1943 public-opinion poll showed the CCF leading in popularity over both the other two major parties, and a number of federal by-election victories seemed to foreshadow electoral victory.

25 House of Commons *Debates*, 24 January 1939, 305.

26 Ibid., 9 July 1943, 4558–61.

27 Canadian Institute of Public Opinion, News release, 27 January 1943, *Winnipeg Tribune*, 27 January 1943; War Information Board Survey, no. 30, 12 February 1944, discussed in Abella and Troper, *None Is Too Many*, 129, 161–2.

28 See Betcherman, *The Swastika and the Maple Leaf*; Jacques Langlais and David Rome, *Jews and French Quebecers: Two Hundred Years of Shared History* (Waterloo,

ON: Wilfrid Laurier University Press, 1991), 86; Paula Jean Draper,
'Fragmented Loyalties: Canadian Jewry, the King Government and the
Refugee Dilemma,' in *On Guard for Thee: War, Ethnicity and the Canadian State*,
ed. Norman Hillmer, Bohdan Kordan, and Lubomyr Luciuk (Ottawa:
Canadian Committee for the History of the Second World War, 1988), 152.

29 For a more detailed analysis of anti-Semitism in Quebec, see: David Rome,
'Clouds in the Thirties: On Anti-Semitism in Canada, 1929–1939,' *Canadian
Jewish Archives* (Montreal: Canadian Jewish Congress, 1977); Langlais and
Rome, *Jews and French Quebecers;* Esther Delisle, *The Traitor and the Jew:
Anti-Semitism and the Delirium of Extremist Right-Wing Nationalism in French
Canada from 1929–1939* (Montreal: Robert Davies, 1992), and the accompany-
ing bibliographies to these publications.

30 Langlais and Rome, *Jews and French Quebecers*, 88.

31 Quoted in Betcherman, *The Swastika and the Maple Leaf*, 34. Quebec anti-
semitism was linked to strong anti-communist sentiment in that province;
most Jews were strong opponents of fascism, and were therefore suspected
of being communists: see Paris, *Jews*, 53; Draper, 'Fragmented Loyalties,'
152; Conrad Black, *Duplessis* (Toronto: McClelland & Stewart, 1977),
161–2, 175 and Abella and Troper, '"The line must be drawn somewhere",'
432–40.

32 Escott Reid, a Department of External Affairs second secretary posted in
Washington, noted: 'within the Canadian government humanitarian considerations were not strong enough to overcome the pressure on the government from anti-semites, especially those in Quebec': *Radical Mandarin: The
Memoirs of Escott Reid* (Toronto: University of Toronto Press, 1989), 127–8.

33 Abella and Troper, *None Is Too Many*, 41–2. While King was not unsympa-
thetic to the Jews, he was unable to persuade Cabinet to alter the government's exclusionary policy. At the November 1938 meeting of Cabinet, King
told his colleagues: 'The time has come when, as a Government, we would
have to perform acts that were expressive of what we believed to be the
conscience of the nation, and not what might be, at the moment, politically
most expedient,' but 'Lapointe had only to "look glum"... and the entire
subject was dropped': H. Blair Neatby, *William Lyon Mackenzie King, 1932–
1939: The Prism of Unity* (Toronto: University of Toronto Press, 1976);
see also Paris, *Jews*, 96.

34 Blair first joined the Immigration and Colonization department as an
immigration officer in 1905. In 1924 he became deputy minister.

35 'Report of the Department of Mines and Resources,' *ADR, 1938–39*, 268.

36 See Paris, *Jews*, 63; Draper, 'Fragmented Loyalties,' 163–6. For a thorough
analysis of Blair, his views on immigration, and on Jews in particular, and

the role he played in restricting their admission, see Abella and Troper, *None Is Too Many*, 7–10.

37 These statistics are derived from data in the 'Report of the Department of Mines and Resources, Immigration Branch,' *ADR, 1944–45*, 200.

38 See 'Racial Origins of Immigrants into Canada 1939–1942' (table), *The Canada Year Book, 1943–1944* (Ottawa: Statistics Canada, 1944), 180; and 'Racial Origins of Immigrants into Canada 1941–45,' *The Canada Year Book, 1946* (Ottawa: Statistics Canada, 1946), 185.

39 'Report of the Department of Mines and Resources, Immigration Branch,' *ADR, 1944–1945*, 192.

40 Abella and Troper, *None Is Too Many*, 54–5, 72–6.

41 P.C. 2653 (14 September 1939).

42 Letter of Blair to Van Scoy, 25 June 1939, quoted in Abella and Troper, *None Is Too Many*, 74. Note that Blair had used this as a reason for rejection before the regulation was passed.

43 Letter of Blair to Skelton, 22 August 1940, quoted in ibid., 71. These comments were made in relation to a situation which arose in 1940, whereby two Lithuanian Jews arrived in Vancouver with expired visas from the Canadian embassy in Tokyo. Blair wanted the practice of issuing visas stopped immediately, and he refused to make an exception for Jews in transit to other countries. For other examples of the hardship this policy caused, see Abella and Troper, *None Is Too Many*, 79, 81, 96. Blair's intransigence exasperated Escott Reid, then at the Canadian legation in Washington, who got an endless stream of requests for help from American Jews trying to get their relatives out of Europe via Canada. Reid wrote to his wife: 'If I could find a loop-hole I'd feel I'd justified my existence before I became a machine-like cold-blooded bureaucrat.' He believed Cuba was more humane than Canada: quoted in Reid, *Radical Mandarin*, 127. According to Reid, 'This was the first of two problems I had to deal with as a diplomat that aroused my contempt for the policy of my government. The other was the internment of Japanese Canadians after Japan entered the war': ibid., 128.

44 Abella and Troper, *None Is Too Many*. See also Joseph Kage, *With Faith and Thanksgiving: The Story of Two Hundred Years of Jewish Immigration and Immigrant Aid Effort in Canada (1760–1960)* (Montreal: Eagle, 1962), ch. 7, 'Years of Pain and Embarrassment.'

45 See, for example, Maurice Mitchell, '*A Man of Big Heart': The Memoirs of Maurice Mitchell* (Ottawa: Canadian Immigration Historical Society, 1988); Escott Reid, 'The Conscience of a Diplomat: A Personal Testament,' *Queen's Quarterly* 74 (1967): 574; and the reflections of Mark Sorenson, an

immigration agent for the Canadian Pacific Railway, in Abella and Troper, *None Is Too Many*, 72–6.

46 Rudolf A. Helling, *A Socio-Economic History of German-Canadians: They, Too, Founded Canada* (Weisbaden: Franz Steiner, 1984), 66–72.

47 Letter from V. Massey to W.L.M. King, 29 November 1938, quoted in Abella and Troper, *None Is Too Many*, 48.

48 Dirks, *Canada's Refugee Policy*, 81.

49 'Report of the Department of Mines and Resources, Immigration Branch,' *ADR, 1939–40*, 212.

50 For more detailed accounts of this voyage, see Gordon Thomas and Max Morgan Witts, *Voyage of the Damned* (New York: Stein & Day, 1974), 135–217; and Abella and Troper, *None Is Too Many*, 63–6.

51 'Report of the Department of Mines and Resources, Immigration Branch,' *ADR, 1940–1*, 198. See also Geoffrey Bilson, *The Guest Children: The Story of the British Child Evacuees Sent to Canada During World War II* (Saskatoon: Fifth House, 1989).

52 'Report of the Department of Mines and Resources, Immigration Branch,' *ADR, 1940–41*, 198.

53 Abella and Troper, *None Is Too Many*, 102.

54 'Report of the Department of Mines and Resources, Immigration Branch,' *ADR, 1941–42*, 172. Regarding Blair's refusal to admit Continental refugee children in the movement, see Abella and Troper, *None Is Too Many*, 103–5.

55 24 February 1943, in *Documents on Canadian External Relations*, vol. 9 (Ottawa: 1980), 539.

56 Abella and Troper, *None Is Too Many*, 125.

57 Attempts to secure the release of these refugees is the subject of Draper, 'Fragmented Loyalties.' Alexander Paterson insisted that the transfer of refugees along with internees was a 'gigantic and appalling mistake': quoted in ibid., 161.

58 Koch, *Deemed Suspect*. It is from Koch's detailed account that much of the following description of the British internee movement is drawn.

59 Ibid., 123.

60 Ibid., 189.

61 C.D. Howe's influence was instrumental in gaining the release of skilled labourers: Draper, 'Fragmented Loyalties,' 167–9.

62 Koch, *Deemed Suspect*, 230.

63 P.C. 9440 (10 December 1943).

64 Abella and Troper, *None Is Too Many*, 80.

65 Ibid., 84.

66 For a more thorough discussion, ibid., 81–8.

67 Dirks, *Canada's Refugee Policy*, 91.
68 *Debates*, 9 July 1943, 4650.
69 Abella and Troper, *None Is Too Many*, 157.
70 Ibid., 162.
71 Donald H. Avery, *Reluctant Host: Canada's Response to Immigrant Workers, 1896–1994* (Toronto: McClelland & Stewart, 1995), 139–40.
72 Abella and Troper document the many obstacles Cormier placed in the way of admissibility in *None Is Too Many*, 165–7.
73 'Report of the Department of Mines and Resources, Immigration Branch,' *ADR 1943–44*, 184.
74 R.S.C. 1927, c.206.
75 N.F. Dreisziger, 'The Rise of a Bureaucracy for Multiculturalism: The Origins of the Nationalities Branch, 1939–1941,' in *On Guard for Thee. War, Ethnicity and the Canadian State, 1939–1945*, ed. Hillmer et al., 5; see also Donald Avery, 'Divided Loyalties: The Ukrainian Left and the Canadian State,' in *Canada's Ukrainians: Negotiating an Identity*, ed. Lubomyr Luciuk and Stella Hryniuk (Toronto: University of Toronto Press and Ukrainian-Canadian Centennial Committee, 1991), 281–2.
76 William R. Young, 'Chauvinism and Canadianism: Canadian Ethnic Groups and the Failure of the Wartime Information,' in *On Guard for Thee: War, Ethnicity and the Canadian State, 1939–1945*, ed. Norman Hillmer et al. 33–4; Dreisziger, 'The Rise of a Bureaucracy for Multiculturalism,' 5–6.
77 Dreisziger, 'The Rise of a Bureaucracy for Multiculturalism,' 22.
78 Ibid., 23.
79 Young, 'Chauvinism and Canadianism,' 33, 38.
80 Ibid., 34, 36–7.
81 Ibid., 45, 53.
82 Ibid., 41.
83 *Winnipeg Tribune*, 27 January 1943; Young, 'Chauvinism and Canadianism,' 41.
84 According to Ramsay Cook, the regulations represented the 'most serious restriction on the civil liberties of Canadians since Confederation': see Ramsay Cook, 'Canadian Freedom in Wartime, 1939–1945,' in *His Own Man: Essays in Honour of Arthur Reginald Marsen Lower*, ed. W.H. Heick and Roger Graham (Montreal: McGill-Queen's University Press, 1974), 38. Lower went even further, saying that the regulations 'take us back to a period of autocracy not matched since the days of the early Stuarts': *My First Seventy-Five Years* (Toronto: Macmillan, 1967), 233. It should be noted that some government officials shared these concerns; for example, Pickersgill 'was worried about the sweeping powers ... which limited freedom of expression and repressed dissent': *My Years with Louis St Laurent: A Political Memoir* (Toronto: University

of Toronto Press, 1975), 10. See also Daniel Robinson, 'Planning for the "Most Serious Contingency": Alien Internment, Arbitrary Detention, and the Canadian State, 1938–39,' *Journal of Canadian Studies* 28/2 (Summer 1993): 5–20, in which the author discusses the opposing forces within the government on this issue.

85 According to Robert H. Keyserlingk, this regulation was not included in the original draft DOCR but was subsequently added to facilitate the internment of foreigners and Canadian citizens who were suspected of supporting potentially dangerous associations but for whom there was no proof of disloyal activity: 'Breaking the Nazi Plot: Canadian Government Attitudes towards German Canadians, 1939–1945,' in *On Guard for Thee. War Ethnicity and the Canadian State, 1939–1945*, ed. Hillmer et al., 58–9.

86 *Defence of Canada Regulations* (Ottawa: King's Printer, 1939), 47; and P.C. 3751 (13 August 1940).

87 For example, in 1940 a new regulation was promulgated which declared sixteen organizations illegal for the duration of the war. The following year the list of prohibited associations was doubled. According to the regulations, attendance at meetings, the distribution of literature, or advocacy for a prohibited organization was evidence of membership 'in the absence of proof to the contrary' and grounds for internment: P.C. 2363 (4 June 1940).

88 Regulations 39 and 39A.

89 Note that the regulations provided that, while detained under a minister's order, the person shall be deemed to be in lawful custody. As a result, *habeas corpus* relief was not possible: see comment on this by B.K. Sandwell, 'The Growing Sense of Insecurity,' *Saturday Night*, 9 November 1940.

90 A.R.M. Lower, 'Wartime Democracy in Canada,' *New Republic*, 15 April 1940, 503.

91 *War Measures Act*, S.C. 1914,15 George V, c.2.; and later in the R.S.C. 1927 c.206.

92 R.S.C. 1927, c.206, s.6.

93 Dreisziger, 'The Rise of a Bureaucracy for Multiculturalism,' 2.

94 Reg Whitaker, 'Official Repression of Communism during World War II,' *Labour/Le Travail* 17 (Spring 1986): 145–6.

95 Robert H. Keyserlingk, '"Agents within the Gates": The Search for Nazi Subversives in Canada during World War II,' *Canadian Historical Review* 66/2 (June 1985): 214.

96 House of Commons *Debates*, 11 June 1940, 670.

97 For more on Nazi links to Canadian-German organizations, *History of German-Canadians*, 63; and Keyserlingk, '"Agents within the Gates",' 221.

Norman Robertson acknowledged that membership lists were not a reliable indicator of treasonable activity: 'Too many naturalized Canadians of German origin,' he wrote, 'have put themselves in an awkward and embarrassing position by their active participation, in peacetime, in Nazi and Nazi-controlled political and social organizations. I quite realize that a good many persons of German origin or birth may have joined … in good faith without appreciating the strain which other people might think such membership put on their loyalty to Canada': quoted in J.L. Granatstein, *A Man of Influence: Norman A. Robertson and Canadian Statecraft, 1929–68* (Toronto: Deneau, 1981), 85. For official views of Germans, see Lois Foster and Anne Seitz, 'Official Attitudes to Germans during World War II: Some Australian and Canadian Comparisons,' *Ethnic and Racial Studies* 14/4 (October 1991): 474–92; R. Keyserlingk, 'Allies or Subversives? The Canadian Government's Attitude towards German Canadians in the Second World War,' in *Minorities in Wartime: National and Racial Groupings in Europe, North America and Australia during the Two World Wars,* ed. Panikos Panalyi (Providence, RI: Berg, 1993).

 98 Keyserlingk, '"Agents within the Gates",' 229.
 99 *Saturday Night,* 9 November 1940.
100 See Minister of Justice Ernest Lapointe's explanation for the exclusion in House of Commons *Debates,* 11 June 1940.
101 Keyserlingk, '"Agents within the Gates'," 231.
102 Keyserlingk, 'Breaking the Nazi Plot,' 59.
103 Regulation 21 is described on 279, this volume.
104 Cook, 'Canadian Freedom in Wartime,' 48–9.
105 *Winnipeg Free Press,* 24 January 1940; *Vancouver Sun,* 15 January 1940; *Le Devoir,* 16 February 1940.
106 Cook, 'Canadian Freedom in Wartime,' 45–6.
107 Keyserlingk, 'Breaking the Nazi Plot,' 59–60.
108 House of Commons *Debates,* 11 June 1940, 663.
109 Ibid., 664.
110 Ibid., 665.
111 Ibid., 666.
112 Ibid., 670.
113 Ibid., 670–4, per M.J. Coldwell.
114 King Diaries, 22 October 1940, referred to in Keyserlingk, '"Agents within the Gates",' 234. On ethnic relations in Alberta 1939–45 with respect to Germans, Italians, Ukrainians, Hutterites, Mennonites, and Doukhobors see H. Palmer, 'Ethnic Relations in Wartime: Nationalism and European Minorities in Alberta during the Second World War,' in *A Nation of*

Immigrants: Women, Workers and Communities in Canadian History,
1840s–1960s, ed Franca Iacovetta (Toronto: University of Toronto Press,
1998), 451–81.

115 According to Robert Keyserlingk, of this number half were Germans
and German Canadians, while the rest were Italian and Canadian
Fascists and left-wing radicals and unionists: '"Agents within the Gates",'
235. For a contrast of the German internments of the Second World War
with the more extensive internments of the First World War, see ibid.,
215–16; Helling, *History of German Canadians,* 81–2; and K.M.
McLaughlin, *The Germans in Canada* (Ottawa: Canadian Historical
Association, 1986), 16.

116 *Globe and Mail,* 9 June 1990.

117 Bruno Ramirez, 'Ethnicity on Trial: The Italians of Montreal and the Second
World War', in *On Guard for Thee. War Ethnicity and the Canadian State,*
1939–1945, ed. Hillmer et al., 73.

118 Kenneth Bagnell, *Canadese: A Portrait of the Italian Canadians*
(Toronto: Macmillan of Canada, 1989), 77.

119 Norman Robertson himself recognized this and urged authorities to
exercise restraint and arrest only the leaders of Italian organizations: see
Granatstein, *A Man of Influence,* 85.

120 Ramirez, 'Ethnicity on Trial,' 77.

121 Ibid., 73.

122 *Globe and Mail,* 9 June 1990.

123 Ibid., 11 June 1940.

124 Bagnell, *Canadese,* 76–81.

125 Whitaker, 'Official Repression of Communism,' 139.

126 Ibid.; Keyserlingk, '"Agents within the Gates"'; Lorne Brown and Caroline
Brown, *An Unauthorized History of the RCMP* (Toronto: Lorimer, 1973).

127 See letters from Pickersgill and from J.A. Gibson in the Department of
External Affairs to King, as discussed in Young, 'Chauvinism and Canadianism,' 38–9, 48 note 19; and Pickersgill, *My Years with Louis St Laurent,*
20.

128 Whitaker, 'Official Repression of Communism,' 140–52.

129 Ibid.

130 Ibid., 154.

131 William Repka and Kathleen M. Repka, *Dangerous Patriots: Canada's Unknown
Prisoners of War* (Vancouver: New Star, 1982), 24.

132 Peter Krawchuk, *Interned Without Cause: Internment of Canadian Anti-Fascists
During World War II,* trans. Pat Prokup (Toronto: Kobzar, 1985), 43.

Krawchuk was interned in 1940 on the grounds that he was a Communist organizer and formerly associated with the Youth Section of the ULFTA. He recalls his experiences in this book.

133 See Repka and Repka, *Dangerous Patriots*, 53; and Krawchuk, *Interned without Cause*, 97.

134 Adrian Arcand was the leader of the National Socialist Christian Party: see discussion in chapter 6, this volume.

135 Krawchuk, *Interned without Cause*, 97.

136 Ibid., 76. Typically the indictment facing the reviewing judge charges that the person was being detained to prevent the person from doing something detrimental to the state. The conclusion was often supported by the allegation that the person was a member of an unlawful organization. (e.g., Communist Party) despite the fact that the organization may have been lawful at the time of membership, or that the person had not made statements thought to be prejudicial to the state.

137 See affidavit submitted to the House and read by Angus MacInnis in House of Commons *Debates*, 9 February 1942, 443–4.

138 His recommendations included: specifying the offences for which one could be interned; informing the public of the reasons why individuals were interned; expanding the number of review tribunals which would be privy to RCMP secret classified information and which would be presided over by the highest judicial officers. He also recommended that the right of review be extended to non-citizens and that the minister be obliged to follow tribunal decisions except in extraordinary circumstances: House of Commons *Debates*, 9 May 1942, 2083–5.

139 Cook, 'Canadian Freedom in Wartime,' 41.

140 *Saturday Night*, 9 November 1940.

141 *Toronto Daily Star*, 2 August 1941; Repka and Repka, *Dangerous Patriots*, 217. See also *Toronto Daily Star*, 13 September 1941.

142 House of Commons *Debates*, 4 May 1942, 2080.

143 Pearson to Robertson, 12 October 1941, quoted in Whitaker, 'Official Repression of Communism,' 149. According to Pearson, 'It seemed silly ... to keep them locked up, let alone to continue adding to their number. But security authorities do not adapt easily to sudden changes': *Mike: The Memoirs of the Right Honourable Lester B. Pearson*, vol. 1, *1897–1948* (Toronto: University of Toronto Press, 1972), 198.

144 Turnbull to King, 6 July 1942, quoted in Young, 'Chauvinism and Canadianism,' 39.

145 Whitaker, 'Official Repression of Communism,' 151.

146 Quoted in J.W. Pickersgill, *The Mackenzie King Record*, vol. 1, *1939–1944* (Toronto: University of Toronto Press, 1960), 354–5.

147 Whitaker, 'Official Repression of Communism,' 152.

148 As revealed in the annual reports of the Royal Canadian Mounted Police for the years 1940–6.

149 Jonathan F. Wagner, *Brothers beyond the Sea: National Socialism in Canada* (Waterloo, in Wilfrid Laurier University Press, 1981), 131–2; John Sawatsky, *Men in the Shadows: The RCMP Security Service* (Toronto: Doubleday, 1980), 67 ff; and Nora Kelly and W.H. Kelly, *The Royal Canadian Mounted Police: A Century of History* (Edmonton: Hurtig, 1973), 190; Keyserlingk, ' "Agents within the Gates," ' 212; Keyserlingk, 'Breaking the Nazi Plot,' 54.

150 *Globe and Mail*, 9 June 1990.

151 Bagnell, *Canadese*, 96.

152 Ramirez, 'Ethnicity on Trial,' 74.

153 Ibid., 81.

154 Ibid.

155 Bohdan S. Kordan and Lubomyr Y. Luciuk, 'A Prescription for Nation Building: Ukrainian Canadians and the Canadian State, 1939–1945,' in *On Guard for Thee: War, Ethnicity and the Canadian State*, ed. Hillmer et. al., 89. See also Thomas M. Prymak, *Maple Leaf and Trident: The Ukrainian Canadians during the Second World War* (Toronto: Multicultural History Society of Ontario, 1988); Anna Reczynska, 'Ukrainians and the "Ukrainian Question" as Seen by Poles in Canada during the Second World War,' *Journal of Ukrainian Studies* 16/1–2 (Summer-Winter 1991): 195–210.

156 Whitaker, 'Official Repression of Communism,' 157.

157 Ibid., 158; Kordan and Luciuk, 'A Prescription for Nation-building,' 93; Avery, 'Divided Loyalties,' 280–5.

158 Ann Comer Sunahara, *The Politics of Racism: The Uprooting of Japanese Canadians During the Second World War* (Toronto: Lorimer, 1981), 7, 38.

159 Canada, House of Commons, Special Committee on Elections and Franchise Acts, *Minutes of Proceedings of Evidence* (Ottawa: 1936), 200–9, 254, cited in Patricia Roy, 'Citizens Without Votes: East Asians in British Columbia,' in *Ethnicity, Power and Politics in Canada*, ed. Jorden Dahlie and Tissa Fernando (Toronto: Methuen, 1981), 160. Anti-Japanese sentiment during this period is traced in detail in W. Peter Ward, *White Canada Forever: Popular Attitudes and Public Policy Toward Orientals in British Columbia*, 2d ed. (Montreal: McGill-Queen's University Press, 1990), ch. 8.

160 For more on A.W. Neill's desire to halt all Japanese immigration to Canada see, Patricia E. Roy, *Triumph of Citizenship*, 59–60.

161 House of Commons *Debates*, 17 February 1938, 557.

162 Ibid., 509.

163 Ibid., 552, per Neill. For more on the Bill and support for it in B.C. see
     Patricia E. Roy, *The Oriental Question: Consolidating A White Man's Province,
     1914–1941* (Vancouver: UBC Press, 2003), 194–7. The agreement reached
     with Japan in 1928 limited the number of Japanese emigrants to Canada at
     150 per year: see chapter 5, this volume.

164 House of Commons *Debates*, 17 February 1938, 564–7.

165 Ibid., 568.

166 Ibid., 30 January 1939, 430.

167 This certainly was the view held by MacGregor Macintosh, an MLA in British
     Columbia; see *Vancouver Sun*, 23 March 1938. On the proceedings of the
     board and the position of Duff Patullo, see Ramdeo Sampat-Mehta,
     International Barriers (Ottawa: Harpell's, 1973), 240–1; and W. Peter Ward,
     'British Columbia and the Japanese Evacuation,' in *Readings in Canadian
     History*, 2d ed., ed. R. Douglas Francis and D.B. Smith (Toronto: Holt,
     Rinehart &Winston, 1986).

168 Board of Review [Immigration], *Final Report*, 29 September 1938, 38, quoted
     in Sampat-Mehta, *International Barriers*, 244–6.

169 Sunahara, *The Politics of Racism*, 18.

170 Department of National Defence Records, 'Memorandum of the Joint
     Service Committee, Pacific Coast, on the matter of the Defences of the
     Pacific Coast of Canada,' 12 July 1940, cited in J.L. Granatstein and Gregory
     A. Johnson, 'The Evacuation of the Japanese Canadians, 1942: A Realist
     Critique of the Received Version,' in *On Guard for Thee, War, Ethnicity and the
     Canadian State, 1939–1945*, ed. Hillmer et al., 113.

171 Granatstein and Johnson, 'Evacuation of the Japanese Canadians,' 115.

172 King Diary, 27 February 1942, cited in Sunahara, *The Politics of Racism*, 44–5.

173 P.C. 9591 (7 December 1941); P.C. 9760 (16 December 1941); and see Ken
     Adachi, *The Enemy That Never Was: A History of the Japanese Canadians*
     (Toronto: McClelland & Stewart, 1976), 231.

174 P.C. 251 (13 January 1942); and P.C. 288 (13 January 1942). According to
     Escott Reid, an RCMP operative had reported on a secret meeting of
     Japanese fishermen in Vancouver, at which the fishermen stated that 'they
     realized that the seizure of the Japanese fishing fleet was inevitable under
     war conditions': *Radical Mandarin*, 162.

175 For a discussion of the seizure of the 1.200 boats see Patricia E. Roy, *Triumph
     of Citizenship*, 24–6.

176 Reid, *Radical Mandarin*, 162. The RCMP representative told the meeting
     that 'the police had received excellent co-operation from the leaders of the
     Japanese population in British Columbia. They had pointed out to the RCMP,

Japanese who should be interned as dangerous ... The RCMP considered that no further action needed to be taken': ibid. Previously an RCMP representative had said that, of the 20,000 or more Japanese in B.C., 'there were only some thirty or so who the police thought would bear watching in the event of war.' The Army spokesman at the meeting echoed the views of the RCMP: 'I cannot see that they constitute the slightest menace to national security': Maurice Pope, *Soldiers and Politicians: The Memoirs of Lt.-Gen. Maurice A. Pope* (Toronto: University of Toronto Press, 1962), 177.

177 Reid, 'Conscience of a Diplomat,' 587–8; Reid, *Radical Mandarin*, 163–4; Pope, *Soldiers and Politicians*, 177.

178 P.C. 385 (16 January 1942).

179 Sunahara, *The Politics of Racism*, 38.

180 Ibid., 39–40.

181 On 19 February, King recorded in his diary: 'Public prejudice is so strong in B.C. that it is going to be difficult to control the situation': quoted in Pickersgill, *Mackenzie King Record*, vol. 1, 354. About the events which were rapidly developing in B.C., Muriel Kitigawa wrote: 'We are Israelites on the move. The public is getting bloodthirsty and will have our blood Nazi-fashion. Okay we move. But where? Signs up on all the highways ... JAPS KEEP OUT': Muriel Kitigawa to her brother, 3 March 1942; reprinted in Muriel Kitigawa, *This Is My Own: Letters to Wes and Other Writings on Japanese Canadians, 1941–1948*, ed. Roy Miki (Vancouver: Talonbooks, 1985), 92.

182 P.C. 1486 (24 February 1942).

183 'And so the Japanese were expelled from their homes at a time when Canadians were priding themselves that they were fighting for freedom': Pope, *Soldiers and Politicians*, 178.

184 P.C. 1665 (4 March 1942).

185 Adachi, *The Enemy That Never Was*, 233.

186 Ibid., 246.

187 Maryka Omatsu, *Bittersweet Passage: Redress and the Japanese-Canadian Experience* (Toronto: Between the Lines, 1992), 73.

188 Ibid., 74. Other accounts of internment can be found in Kitigawa, *This Is My Own;* Takeo Ujo Nakano, with Leatrice Nakano, *Within the Barbed Wire Fence: A Japanese Man's Account of His Internment in Canada* (Toronto: University of Toronto Press, 1980); Keibo Oiwa, ed., *Stone Voices: Wartime Writings of Japanese-Canadian Issei* (Montreal: Véhicule, 1991).

189 For a more detailed discussion of these interests, see Sunahara, *The Politics of Racism*, 101.

190 Ibid., 105.

191 H.F. Angus to W.L.M. King, 15 March 1943, quoted in ibid., 106.

192 Sunahara, *The Politics of Racism*, 109–10; *Nakashima et al. v R.* [1947] 4 D.L.R. 487; *Vancouver Sun*, 29 May 1944; Adachi, *The Enemy That Never Was*, 322–3.

193 In 1988, Price Waterhouse estimated that the Canadian Japanese community's wartime losses in income and property amounted to approximately $450 million in 1986 dollars: *Economic Losses of Japanese Canadians after 1941* (Winnipeg: National Association of Japanese Canadians, 1985), 1–2.

194 P.C. 946 (5 February 1943): see Adachi, *The Enemy That Never Was*, 261.

195 Sunahara, *The Politics of Racism*, 110–11.

196 The people, events, and ideas which informed the government's Japanese removal policies is extensively canvassed in Ann Gomer Sunahara, 'Deportation: The Final Solution to Canada's "Japanese Problem,"' in *Ethnicity, Power and Politics in Canada*, ed. Dahlie and Fernando. The subsequent discussion is largely based on this article.

197 Ibid., 257.

198 House of Commons, *Debates*, 4 August 1944, 5915.

199 Sunahara, 'Deportation: The Final Solution.'

200 Ibid., 259–60. The reason for the latter uncertainty was that, during the war, the government had understandings with Saskatchewan, Alberta, Ontario, and Quebec that Japanese persons who had resettled in those provinces would be removed after the war. At the time of the survey, only the CCF government in Saskatchewan had agreed to accept Japanese Canadians permanently.

201 Ibid.

202 Ibid., 261.

203 Ward, *White Canada Forever*, 163–6.

204 Sunahara, 'Deportation: The Final Solution,' 263; *The New Canadian*, 19 July, 8 August, 18 and 19 September 1945.

205 Sunahara, 'Deportation: The Final Solution,' 263.

206 P.C. 7355, 7356, 7357 (15 December 1945).

207 For the CCJC's reaction to the proposed repatriation see Patricia E. Roy, *Triumph of Citizenship*, 145–6, 202–3.

208 *Reference Re Deportation of Japanese*, [1946] 3 D.L.R. 321 (S.C.C.).

209 Ibid., 357.

210 For more on the Court's decision see Patricia E. Roy, *Triumph of Citizenship*, 200–2.

211 Ibid., 336. For discussion of this case, see chapter 4, this volume, 162.

212 Ibid., 377. Justices Rand and Kellock, however, disagreed with the majority on this point. As reasoned by Justice Rand, the revocation of naturalization was a 'penal provision of a drastic nature' and one could not simply imply that persons signing repatriation requests were necessarily disaffected or

disloyal. While he agreed that it was within the power of Cabinet to deport naturalized Canadians pursuant to the orders in question, he nevertheless concluded that Cabinet was not authorized under the Naturalization Act to revoke their naturalized status on this ground alone (347). For justice Kellock's reasoning, see 367–8.

213 Ibid., 342, per Hudson J., and 379, per Estey J.

214 Ibid., 343. In dissenting opinions, justices Rand and Kellock held that the deportation of natural-born Canadians was invalid. Referring to the agreement existing between Canada and General McArthur, Justice Rand notes that reference was made to 'repatriation' which by definition infers the return of a person to his or her country of origin and not the expulsion of a citizen to a foreign territory. The latter he claimed was a violation of the foreign state's sovereignty and outside the powers of the Canadian government: see 350 and 361–4, per Kellock J. Moreover, the fact that Canadian-born citizens could revoke their removal requests up until the time an order for their deportation was issued, suggests that their removal was not deemed to be necessary otherwise it would be non-revocable: see 352.

215 Three of the justices held that the orders were valid in so far as the deportation of the dependants was concerned. They were of the view that it could be assumed that the Cabinet deemed their removal necessary for the security and welfare of the country without there being expressed words to this effect contained within the order itself: see 338, where justice Rinfret writes for the minority on this point.

216 R.S.C. 1927 c.138, s.9; and see discussions in chapters 5 and 6, this volume.

217 Sunahara, 'Deportation: The Final Solution,' 272.

218 *Co-operative Committee on Japanese Canadians et al. v Attorney General of Canada et al.,* [1947] 1 D.L.R. 577 (Imp. P.C.).

219 Peter Ward, *The Japanese in Canada,* Ethic Groups Booklet no. 3 (Ottawa: Canadian Historical Association, 1982), 15; Roy Miki and Cassandra Kobayashi, *Justice in Our Time: The Japanese-Canadian Redress Settlement* (Vancouver: Talonbooks, 1991), 55.

220 Sunahara, 'Deportation: The Final Solution,' 271.

221 Omatsu, *Bittersweet Passage,* 94.

222 Expressed in an interview with Sunahara: see *The Politics of Racism,* 47. This is certainly the view of Peter Ward, who outlines the stages of anti-Japanese hysteria in B.C. in detail in *White Canada Forever,* ch. 8.

223 According to Norman Robertson, Canadian policy 'has been largely influenced by what we understood the policy of the United States to be': Robertson to King, 20 August 1943, in *Documents on Canadian External Relations,* vol. 9, 552.

224 Sunahara, *The Politics of Racism*, 31.
225 Granatstein and Johnson, 'The Evacuation of the Japanese Canadians,' 119.
226 Massey to Prime Minister, February 28, 1941, quoted in ibid., 107.
227 Ibid., 120. Similar views are expressed in Patricia Roy, J.L. Granatstein, Masako Iino, and Hiroko Takamura, *Mutual Hostages: Canadians and Japanese during the Second World War* (Toronto: University of Toronto Press, 1990), ch. 4. For Reginald Whitaker's critical review of that book, see *Canadian Historical Review* 72/2 (June 1991): 224–8.
228 Referred to in Mary Halloran, 'Ethnicity the State and War: Canada and Its Ethnic Minorities, 1939–45,' *International Migration Review*, 21/1: 159–67.
229 Miki and Kobayashi, *Justice in Our Time*, Omatsu, *Bittersweet Passage*, 19–20; R. Daniels, 'From Relocation to Redress: Japanese Americans and Canadians, 1941–1988,' in *Minorities in Wartime: National and Racial Groupings in Europe, North America and Australia during the Two World Wars*, ed. Panayi.
230 House of Commons *Debates*, 22 September 1988, per Prime Minister Brian Mulroney, 19499.
231 For the reversal of King's Second World War conscription policy, see J.L. Granatstein and J.M. Hitsman, *Broken Promises: A History of Conscription in Canada* (Toronto: Oxford University Press, 1977).
232 Donald Avery, 'Canada's Response to European Refugees, 1939–1945: The Security Dimension,' in *On Guard for Thee: War, Ethnicity and the Canadian State, 1939–1945*, ed. Hillmer et al., 179–216.
233 Ibid., 181.
234 Avery, 'Canada's Response to European Refugees,' 188–90. Note, however, that, according to Reg Whitaker, Canada's internment measures compared unfavourably with those in Britain: 'Britain, which had four times the population of Canada and was but a few miles from Nazi-occupied Europe and feared an imminent invasion, interned about 1,800 people. By the war's end, Canada had interned 2,423 of its own citizens or residents (excluding the forcible relocation of the entire Japanese population of British Columbia)': 'Official Repression of Communism,' 145.
235 In May 1993, Minister of Multiculturalism Gerry Weiner offered to have the prime minister make an 'omnibus apology' for past discriminatory actions by Canadian governments. Among those groups Prime Minister Mulroney had previously cited as having been unfairly treated were: Ukrainian Canadians interned during the First World War; Chinese immigrants obliged to pay a head tax and those excluded entirely on the basis of their race; Jewish refugees denied entry to Canada in the 1930s and 1940s; and Sikhs who were also excluded from Canada in the first several decades of the century. Although no compensation would be paid under the proposed

offer, the government proposed building a 'National Builders Hall of Record' in Ottawa to commemorate the contributions of ethnic groups to Canada. Several groups felt that this proposal was inadequate: see *Globe and Mail*, 29 May 1993.

236 In 1941, Canadians of Japanese descent were prohibited from joining the Canadian armed forces. In January 1945, however, Nisei were permitted to enlist as translators and interpreters to help British forces in Asia. Despite their fear of racism within the army and the possibility of their not being allowed to return to Canada, more than 100 Nisei volunteered to serve: see Roy et al., *Mutual Hostages*, 156.

Chapter 8 The Postwar Boom, 1946–1962: Reopening the Doors Selectively

 1 For useful historical reviews of the period, see Ramsay Cook, *Canada: A Modern Study* (Toronto: Irwin, 1977), ch. 18; Kenneth McNaught, *The Penguin History of Canada*, new ed. (Harmondsworth: Penguin, 1988); J.M.S. Careless, *Canada: A Story of Challenge* (Toronto: Macmillan, 1970), ch. 20; Robert Bothwell, Ian Drummond, and John English, *Canada Since 1945: Power Politics, and Provincialism*, 2d ed. (Toronto: University of Toronto Press, 1989); J.L. Granatstein, Irving Abella, T.W. Acheson, David Bercuson, R. Craig Brown, and H. Blair Neatby, *Nation: Canada Since Confederation*, 3rd ed. (Toronto: McGraw-Hill Ryerson, 1990), chs. 8–10; R. Douglas Francis, Richard Jones, and Donald B. Smith, *Destinies: Canadian History since Confederation*, 6th ed. (Toronto: Nelson, 2008), chs. 14–15; J.M. Bumsted, *The Peoples of Canada: A Post-Confederation History*, 2d ed. (Toronto: Oxford University Press, 2004), chs. 14–19; J.L. Finlay and D.N. Sprague, *The Structure of Canadian History*, 5th ed. (Toronto: Prentice-Hall Allyn and Bacon Canada, 1997), chs. 26 and 27; Kenneth Norrie, Douglas Owram and JC Herbert Emery, *A History of the Canadian Economy*, 4th ed. (Toronto: Thomson Nelson, 2008), chs. 19 and 20; Alvin Finkel, Margaret Conrad, and Veronica Strong-Boag, *A History of the Canadian Peoples*, vol. 2, *1867 to the Present*, 4th ed. (Toronto: Pearson Longman, 2006), chs. 15–19.

 2 Harry Cunliffe, 'The Liberalization of Immigration Policy from 1945 to 1956: An Insider's View,' in *Breaking Ground: The 1956 Hungarian Refugee Movement to Canada*, ed. Robert H. Keyserlingk (Toronto: York Lanes, 1993), 13–23.

 3 Prime Minister Mackenzie King, in House of Commons *Debates*, 1 May 1947, 2644–7.

 4 For information on these groups, see, in addition to works cited elsewhere, Joseph M. Kirschbaum, *Slovaks in Canada* (Toronto: Canadian Ethnic Press

Association of Ontario, 1967); Anthony W. Rasporich, *For a Better Life: A History of the Croatians in Canada* (Toronto; McClelland & Stewart; Ottawa: Department of the Secretary of State, Multiculturalism Directorate, 1982), 167–91; Herman Ganzevoort, A *Bittersweet Land: The Dutch Experience in Canada, 1890–1980* (Toronto: McClelland & Stewart; Ottawa: Department of the Secretary of State, Multiculturalism Directorate, 1988), 61–73; Lubomyr Luciuk, " 'Trouble All Around": Ukrainian Canadians and Their Encounter with the Ukrainian Refugees of Europe, 19431951,' *Canadian Ethnic Studies* 23/3 (1989): 37–54.

5 See Reports of the Department of Citizenship and Immigration in *Annual Departmental Reports* [henceforth cited as *ADR*] for these years.

6 Franca Iacovetta, *Gatekeepers: Reshaping Immigrant Lives in Cold War Canada* (Toronto: Between the Lines, 2006).

7 See Franca Iacovetta, *Gatekeepers: Reshaping Immigrant Lives in Cold War Canada,* ibid.

8 Reg Whitaker, *Double Standard: The Secret History of Canadian Immigration* (Toronto: Lester & Orpen Dennys, 1987), 62.

9 George Davidson, 'Canadian Immigration and Citizenship Policies,' address to the annual American Immigration and Citizenship Conference, 24 March 1961, 33–4; Robert Craig Brown, 'Full Partnership in the Fortunes and in the Future of the Nation,' in *Ethnicity and Citizenship: The Canadian Case,* ed. Jean Laponce and William Safran (London: Frank Cass, 1996), 11. Prior to this time, the highest status that could be obtained by immigrants was British-subject status, which was conferred by naturalization: see chapters 4 and 6, this volume.

10 The TLC was not affiliated politically, whereas the CCL was allied to the CCF but could not deliver its members votes: Nathaniel Constantine Allyn, *European Immigration into Canada, 1946–1951* (Toronto: McClelland & Stewart, 1977), 140.

11 David Corbett, *Canada's Immigration Policy: A Critique* (Toronto: University of Toronto Press, 1957), 4–8; Whitaker, *Double Standard,* 155.

12 *Proceedings* of *the Senate Standing Committee on Immigration and Labour* [henceforth cited as *Senate Standing Committee*], 215.

13 Ibid., 222.

14 Allyn, *European Immigration into Canada,* 140. This explanation came from the Quebec division of the union after the national board produced a statement opposing immigration. The CCCL claimed 70,367 members at the end of 1946: ibid., 136, 140.

15 *Senate Standing Committee* (1946), 310.

16 Ibid., (1946) 309.

17 Ibid., (1946) 313.
18 Ibid., (1946) 311.
19 Ibid., *Senate Standing Committee* (1947), 394–8. For example, if a father was able to sponsor his whole family with the exception of one son because the son was married, there was no administrative procedure for the immigration officer to follow to make an exception in such a case. The committee called on the officer, on behalf of the applicant, to apply for a special order-in-council.
20 Allyn, *European Immigration into Canada*, 135. The 1946 report was adopted on 19 August 1946, the 1947 report on 15 July 1947, and the 1948 report on 26 June 1948.
21 W. Burton Hurd, 'Some Implications of Prospective Population Changes in Canada,' *Canadian Journal of Economics and Political Sciences* (1939): 492.
22 Arthur Lower, 'The Myth of Mass Immigration,' *Maclean's*, 15 May 1949, 16. For the views on wartime immigration held by Lower, Angus, and Sandwell, see chapter 7, this volume.
23 H.F. Angus, 'The Future of Immigration in Canada,' *Canadian Journal of Economics and Political Science* 12 (1946): 379.
24 The United States imposed restrictions in the Immigration Act of 1924 on each ethnic group who wished to emigrate to America. The quota limited the number of immigrants in each ethnic group, in a given year, to a number not to exceed two per cent of that group's 1890 population of the United States. An amendment in 1929 further limited total immigration to the United States to 150,000 annually, and restricted each national group to the same ratio of the 150,000 as it had to the 1929 American population: ibid., 383–4.
25 H.F. Angus, 'Immigration,' *International Journal* 1 (1946): 65.
26 B.K Sandwell, 'Our Immigration Problem: Some Facts and Fallacies,' *Queen's Quarterly* 53 (1946): 509.
27 Mabel Timlin, *Does Canada Need More People?* (Toronto: Oxford University Press, 1953).
28 Ibid., 19.
29 Ibid., 78.
30 Ibid., 16.
31 Letter from Mr. H. Luke Robinson to Timlin, cited in ibid., 79.
32 Ibid., 123.
33 See this volume, 329–30.
34 Under such schemes, immigrants were brought to Canada under contracts to meet the labour needs of Canadian industries: see this chapter, 334–6.
35 Regarding Canada's changing role in the world, see, for example, James Eayrs, *In Defence of Canada*, vol. 2, *Peacemaking and Deterrence* (Toronto:

University of Toronto Press, 1972), and vol. 3, *Growing Up Allied* (Toronto: University of Toronto Press, 1980); John W. Holmes, *The Shaping of Peace: Canada and the Search for World Order 1943–1957,* 2 vols. (Toronto: University of Toronto Press, 1979 and 1982); David Dewitt and John Kirton, *Canada as a Principal Power: A Study in Foreign Policy and International Relations* (Toronto: John Wiley & Sons, 1983).

36 See this volume, 321.

37 See this volume, 326–7.

38 See this volume, 331.

39 P.C. 183 (31 January 1923).

40 P.C. 695 (31 March 1931).

41 P.C. 2115 (16 September 1930). The word 'Asiatic' was interpreted to include Africans and West Indians of African or Asian race.

42 Freda Hawkins, *Canada and Immigration: Public Policy and Public Concern,* 2d ed. (Montreal: McGill-Queen's University Press, 1988), 94–5.

43 42 P.C. 2071 (28 May 1946).

44 However, it was not until 1947 that the Immigration Branch sent officers to Europe to process their applications: 'Department of Citizenship and Immigration, Canada's Refugee Programmes – 1945–1961,' in *Studies and Documents on Immigration and Integration in Canada,* ed. Joseph Kage (Montreal: JIAS, 1963). See also Whitaker, *Double Standard,* 26, who notes that the first two officers to arrive in Europe were sent by the RCMP to carry out security screening.

45 P.C. 371 (30 January 1945).

46 P.C. 1734 (1 May 1947).

47 This act was the only immigration statute that was overtly racist. All other policies regarding race were reflected in orders-in-council. The following exchange between the CCF's Stewart and the minister responsible for Immigration, James Glen, illustrates why this is important:

MR GLEN: The hon. gentleman's statement was that the regulations under the Immigration Act characterized Ukrainians as inferior people, and I should like to know the evidence for that.

MR STEWART: I say that they are regarded by this government as inferior when they are put in the non-preferred class.

MR GLEN: That is not what the hon. gentleman stated. He said that the regulations under the Immigration Act considered and treated Ukrainians as inferior people, and I want his evidence.

MR STEWART: Obviously, when the government characterizes by regulation a group of people as non-preferred I can only accept the premise that these people are regarded by the same government as inferior.

MR GLEN: Will the hon. gentleman tell me the section of the act says so.

MR STEWART: Good gracious! You do not need the act for that. Do you not know your own regulations? (House of Commons *Debates*, 4 February 1947, 114).

48 Mosher had advocated the removal of racial categories from immigration regulations. His views are described further below.

49 Mr Reid, in House of Commons *Debates*, 11 February 1947, 317.

50 Mr Green, in ibid., 311.

51 John Gibson, independent member from B.C., in ibid., 323.

52 In 1948, the Senate committee unanimously endorsed the call of the Committee for the Repeal of the Chinese Immigration Act for the repeal of P.C. 1930–2115.

53 Senate *Debates*, 29 January 1948, 97.

54 P.C. 4186 (16 September 1948). P.C. 5593 (10 December 1948) defines citizens of France as 'citizens of France born in France.' This was probably intended to keep out Asians and Africans who had acquired French citizenship.

55 Hawkins, *Canada and Immigration*, 225–6.

56 Francis, Jones, and Smith, *Destinies*, 450–1; Whitaker, *Double Standard*, 56–8. For further information on French collaborators with the Nazis who entered Canada in the postwar period, see Yves Lavertu, *The Bernonville Affair: French War Criminals in Canada after World War II*, trans. George Tombs (Westmount, PQ: Robert Davies, 1995).

57 Whitaker, *Double Standard*, 125–7.

58 Ibid., 159.

59 Note that the term 'suitable' in the regulation would allow for rejection on the basis of race.

60 P.C. 4364 (14 September 1950). This order indicated that Germans were considered equivalent to other Europeans in every respect. For further details, see Angelika E. Sauer, 'A Matter of Domestic Policy? Canadian Immigration Policy and the Admission of Germans, 1945–50,' *Canadian Historical Review* 74/2 (June 1993): 226–63. Enemy nationals other than Germans were still prohibited from entering Canada, unless an applicant could satisfy the minister that he was opposed to the enemy government ('Report of the Department of Immigration,' *ADR, 1950–1*, 19). Italians were removed from the enemy alien list by P.C. 2908 in January 1947. Japanese were considered enemy aliens until July 1952; see Ken Adachi, *The Enemy That Never Was: A History of the Japanese Canadians* (Toronto: McClelland & Stewart, 1977), 351.

61 Whitaker, *Double Standard*, 62. For postwar immigration of Italians, see, for example, Franca Iacovetta, *Such Hardworking People: Italian Immigrants in*

Postwar Toronto (Montreal: McGill-Queen's University Press, 1992); Susan Gabori, *In Search of Paradise: The Odyssey of an Italian Family* (Montreal: McGill-Queen's University Press, 1993).

62 *The Canada Year Book, 1952–53* (Ottawa: King's Printer, 1953), 164. This inducement was a relic from earlier times; see chapters 3 and 4, this volume.

63 P.C. 1954–1352, s.5.

64 Louis Parai, *Immigration and Emigration of Professional and Skilled Manpower during the Post-War Period* (Ottawa: Queen's Printer, 1965), 86.

65 Corbett, *Canada's Immigration Policy*, 49.

66 Report of the Department of Citizenship and Immigration,' *ADR, 1955–56*, 23.

67 The 1970 report of the Department of Citizenship and Immigration *(ADR, 1969 70)* merely says that the loans were made available on a worldwide basis as of that year. Caribbean immigrants were made eligible in 1966.

68 W.E. Greening, 'Is the French-Canadian Attitude towards Immigration Changing?' *Dalhousie Review* 31 (1951): 43–7.

69 The act was introduced on 2 June 1952 and passed third reading on 23 June 1952. The Senate approved the bill three days later. The act was proclaimed into law on 1 June 1953: Corbett, *Canada's Immigration Policy*, 101–2.

70 Subsection 20(1). Canadian citizens could enter the country as a matter of right, but were still subject to an examination: s.3 (1) of the 1952 Immigration Act.

71 Noseworthy reading letter from Harris, in House of Commons Debates, 1953, 4351–2. When Noseworthy asked the department to supply him with the empirical data that verified these conclusions, he consistently received a response of 'statistics not available' from departmental authorities. Therefore, he did not accept that these assumptions were a 'matter of record': ibid., 4352.

72 However, subsection 5(d) relaxed this restriction. Whereas in 1910 these people were banned outright from Canada, now they could be admitted if five years had elapsed (two if they committed the crime under the age of twenty-one) from when their sentence had been served, and if they had been rehabilitated. If they were never convicted but still admitted to the crime, the law required the five-year period to commence from when the crime was committed.

73 Subsections 5(a)–(t).

74 *Immigration Act*, 1910, ss. 3(a), (e), and (t); *Immigration Act*, 1952, ss.5 (e), (j), and (k).

75 Section 17 of the Immigration Regulations, P.C. 1953–859.

76 The executive could not choose among the three members the SIO whose decision was being appealed. The SIO who made the initial decision was

precluded by subsection 12(3) of the Immigration Act from sitting on the appeal. This reflects the fact that the IAB was intended to be an arm of the Department of Citizenship and Immigration.

77 The exceptions to this rule were anyone being deported because of a previous drug offence or because a medical certificate had been produced finding the applicant to be insane, epileptic, mentally or physically abnormal, or suffering from tuberculosis.

78 *Immigration Act*, 1952, ss.30 and 31(1).

79 Ibid., ss.31(2), 31(3), and 31(4).

80 Ibid., s. 29.

81 This provision was upheld by the Supreme Court in *Narine Singh v Canada*, [1955] S.C.R. 395.

82 Report of Civil Liberties Section of the Canadian Bar Association, *Proceedings of the Canadian Bar Association* (1952): 203.

83 John A. Stevenson, 'A New Target for the Opposition,' *Saturday Night*, 5 March 1955, 12.

84 Fulton, in House of Commons *Debates*, 1955, 1158.

85 Ibid., 1161.

86 As discussed above, under subsection 20(4) of these regulations, SIOs were given complete discretion to apply subsection 61(g) of the Immigration Act. The SIOs were allowed to make decisions based on, among other criteria, their customs, habits, mode of life, suitability, and assimilation potential. Subsection 20(4) of the immigration regulations would later be found invalid in the *Brent* decision, discussed below.

87 Fulton, in House of Commons *Debates*, 1955, 1164.

88 Ibid., 1170.

89 Diefenbaker, in ibid., 1256.

90 Ibid., 1257.

91 *Globe and Mail*, 21 February 1955.

92 Ibid., 21 February 1956.

93 *A.G. for Canada v Brent*, [1956] S.C.R. 318,2 D.L.R. (2d) 503.

94 Corbett, *Canada's Immigration Policy*, 39.

95 Ibid., 39–40.

96 Ibid., 40.

97 Ibid.

98 Ibid., 41.

99 P.C. 1956–785, s.21.

100 J.W. Pickersgill, in *Minutes of Proceedings and Evidence of the House of Commons Special Committee on Estimates*, no. 11, 14 March 1955, 301.

101 Corbett, *Canada's Immigration Policy*, 29.

102 Hawkins, *Canada and Immigration*, 72.
103 Ibid., 74–5.
104 Ibid., 114.
105 Ibid., 112, 137.
106 Dave Archer, 'Labour's Concern with Immigration,' *Canadian Labour 5* (July-August 1960): 22.
107 *Montreal Gazette*, 3 June 1952. In 1951, Canada admitted 194,391 immigrants, a number that had not been reached since 1913. The quota for 1952 was set between 100,000 and 150,000 new immigrants. In fact, Canada admitted 164,498 new immigrants in that year.
108 Hugh Keenleyside, *Canadian Immigration Policy* (Vancouver; University of British Columbia Press, 1948), 8.
109 'Report of the Department of Citizenship and Immigration,' *ADR*, 1958–59, 23–4.
110 Alan G. Green, *Immigration and the Postwar Canadian Economy* (Toronto: Macmillan, 1976), 35.
111 'Report of the Department of Citizenship and Immigration,' *ADR 1958–59*, 23.
112 *Financial Post*, 31 May 1958.
113 That order, passed on 24 May 1956, had listed the countries whose emigration to Canada was controlled following the *Brent* decision (see below). For a detailed explanation of P.C. 56–785, see this chapter, 328–9.
114 Corbett, *Canada's Immigration Policy*, 43.
115 Diefenbaker, in House of Commons Debates, 1959, 2295. The order also barred any applicant from Egypt regardless of whether or not he or she had a sponsor.
116 P.C. 507 (23 April 1959); House of Commons *Debates*, 15 April 1959, 2711–12; and 22 April 1959, 2933–9.
117 Hawkins, *Canada and Immigration*, 131–2.
118 David Chuenyan Lai, *Chinatowns: Towns within Cities in Canada* (Vancouver: University of British Columbia Press, 1988), 104.
119 These people were in Canada illegally because they had falsely misrepresented themselves as being dependants of Canadian citizens on their applications for landed-immigrant status.
120 Hawkins, *Canada and Immigration*, 132–4.
121 Fred Bodsworth, 'What's Behind the Immigration Wrangle,' *Maclean's*, 14 May 1955, 12. By limiting all immigration (including white immigration) from predominantly black countries or colonies, even if they were members of the Commonwealth, Canada effectively prohibited black immigration.

122 The Negro Citizenship Association, formed in 1952 to promote the equal treatment of blacks in the human-rights field, was a small Quebec-based organization with 500 members in 1967: *Minutes of Proceedings and Evidence of the Special Point Committee of the Senate and the House of Commons on Immigration* (1967), 609.

123 Donald Gordon, 'Britain Puts the Pressure on Canada,' *Saturday Night*, 13 May 1961, 37.

124 P.C. 1962–86 (18 January 1962). Tabled in Parliament in House of Commons, 19 January 1962, 9–11; and 27 February 1962, 1326–36.

125 Subsection 31 (a) of P.C. 1962–86.

126 Hawkins, *Canada and Immigration*, 131.

127 The qualification 'in any case where an appeal lies against a deportation order under the Act' meant that those who were denied appeals under the act – namely, those convicted of a drug offence or those faced with a medical certificate which gave grounds for their being banned, could still not appeal: see Pickersgill's comments in House of Commons *Debates*, 19 January 1962, 11.

128 Hawkins, *Canada and Immigration*, 126. The 'Report of the Department of Citizenship and Immigration,' *ADR, 1962–63*, 15, claims that the IAB is 'completely independent of the Immigration Branch,' but this was not really true until 1967.

129 House of Commons *Debates*, 19 January 1962, 10.

130 Ibid. It appears that these quotas were not eliminated until 1967. For a full discussion of this group of immigrants, see Norman Buchignani and Doreen M. Indra, with Ram Srivastiva, *Continuous Journey: A Social History of South Asians in Canada* (Toronto: McClelland & Stewart; Ottawa: Department of the Secretary of State, Multiculturalism Directorate, 1985).

131 Department of External Affairs file 5475–EA-140, internal memorandum, 14 February 1962, cited in Gerald Dirks, *Canada's Refugee Policy. Indifference or Opportunism?* (Montreal: McGill-Queen's University Press, 1977), 225.

132 P.C. 4561 (26 June 1945) and P.C. 7254 (7 December 1945).

133 P.C. 6687 (25 October 1945); see chapter 7, this volume.

134 Irving Abella and Harold Troper, *None Is Too Many: Canada and the Jews of Europe, 1933–1948* (Toronto: Lester and Orpen Dennys, 1982), 201–2.

135 See chapter 7, this volume.

136 'Report of the Department of Citizenship and Immigration,' *ADR* 194 7–48, 244.

137 Ibid.; additional groups of Maltese were also authorized, so that, by 1955, more than 6,000 had emigrated to Canada: see *Canadian Immigration Aims and Objectives, 1946–1955* (Ottawa: Department of Citizenship and Immigration, 8 March 1956), 4.

138 P.C. 3112 (23 July 1946); Dirks, *Canada's Refugee Policy*, 141–2.

139 Dirks, *Canada's Refugee Policy*, 141–2; Whitaker *Double Standard*, 28j. Calbert Best, 'Canadian Immigration Patterns and Policies,' *Labour Gazette 50* (1950): 1517–19; Benedykt Heydenkorn, ed., A *Community in Transition: The Polish Group in Canada* (Toronto: Canadian Polish Research Institute, n.d.).

140 Suitability entailed that the employer was honest and would not abuse the workers.

141 For example, Bengough described an incident in which a textile owner had applied to the Department of Labour for contract labour during a textile strike.

142 Jean Tweed, 'D.P.'s Answer to Domestic Help Problem?' *Saturday Night*, 31 January 1948.

143 *Globe and Mail*, 29 July 1946; Avery, *Reluctant Host*, 150.

144 Dirks, *Canada's Refugee Policy*, 152. See also Franca Iacovetta, 'Ordering in Bulk: Canada's Postwar Immigration Policy and the Recruitment of Contract Workers from Italy,' *Journal of American Ethnic History* 11/1 (Fall 1991): 50–80.

145 'Report of the Department of Citizenship and Immigration,' *ADR 1956–57*, 27.

146 Agnes Calliste, 'Canada's Immigration Policy and Domestics from the Caribbean: The Second Domestic Scheme,' in *Race*, Class, *Gender: Bonds and Barriers. Socialist Studies: A Canadian Annual*, vol. 5, ed. Jesse Vorst (Toronto: Between the Lines, 1989), 141. See also Robin Winks, *The Blacks in Canada: A History* (Montreal: McGill-Queen's University Press, 1971), 439; James W. St.-G. Walker, *The West Indians in Canada* (Ottawa: Canadian Historical Association, 1984), 10; Linda Carry, 'African Canadian Women and the State: "Labour Only, Please,"' in *We're Rooted Here and They Can't Pull Us Up: Essays in African Canadian Women's History*, ed. Peggy Bristow, Dionne Brand, Linda Carty, Afua P. Cooper, Sylvia Hamilton, and Adrienne Shadd (Toronto: University of Toronto Press, 1994), 217–20. See also Agnes Calliste, 'Women of "Exceptional Merit": Immigration of Caribbean Nurses to Canada,' *Canadian Journal of Women and the Law* 6 (1993): 85–99.

147 See Reports of the Department of Citizenship and Immigration in *ADR* for 1955–67.

148 Health tests included rigorous gynecological examinations to test for venereal diseases. Macklin attributes this policy to the racist preconceptions about the promiscuous nature of black women: Audrey Macklin, 'Foreign Domestic Workers: Surrogate Housewife or Mail Order Servants?' *McGill Law Journal* 37 (1992): 689.

149 Calliste, 'Second Domestic Scheme,' 144.

150 Ibid., 150.

151 Ibid., 149.

152 Senator Wilson was also a member of the Senate committee and became its chair in 1948. For more on the CNCR, see chapter 7, this volume.

153 Senator Wilson, quoting from J. Cameron, European colonization manager of CPR, letter dated 25 June 1946: *Senate Standing Committee* (1946), 228. For international attempts to assist displaced persons, and Canada's involvement in those schemes, see Gerald E. Dirks, 'Canada and Immigration: International and Domestic Considerations in the Decade Preceding the 1956 Hungarian Exodus,' in *Breaking Ground: The 1956 Hungarian Refugee Movement to Canada*, ed. Robert H. Keyserlingk (Toronto: York Lanes, 1993), 3–11.

154 Dirks, *Canada's Refugee Policy*, 124. Until that year, these camps were known as UNHRA camps.

155 Although they did not all take the same position, all called for a more active immigration program. Hlynka stated that Canada could not wait for its economy to rebound because European refugees would die in the interim. Strum and Zaplitny called for Canada to bring in 10,000 orphans because they would not pose a threat to labour: House of Commons *Debates*, 1945, 3529; 1946, 352.

156 'Report of the Department of Citizenship and Immigration,' *ADR 1946–47*, 241–2. 538 Notes to pages 338–40.

157 Abella and Troper, *None Is Too Many*, 244.

158 These included P.C. 2180 (6 June 1947) and P.C. 2856 (18 July 1947), which authorized 5,000 DPs each; P.C. 3926 (1 October 1947) permitted 10,000; P.C. 1628 (22 April 1948) admitted 10,000; P.C. 3721 (5 October 1948) authorized 10,000.

159 Dirks, *Canada's Refugee Policy*, 167.

160 'Report of the Department of Citizenship and Immigration,' *ADR, 1948–49*, 222; Dirks, *Canada's Refugee Policy*, 166. The figure of 1,000 is from the Department of Citizenship and Immigration's 'Canada's Refugee Programmes – 1945–1961,' 2.

161 Department of Citizenship and Immigration, 'Canada's Refugee Programmes – 1945–1961.' These were accepted without examination.

162 Dirks, *Canada's Refugee Policy*, 134.

163 These religious and welfare groups included the Catholic Immigration Aid Services (CLAS), the Canadian Mennonite Board of Colonization, the German Baptist Board of Immigration and Colonization Society, the Canadian Lutheran World Relief, the Sudetan Committee, and the Latvian Relief Committee.

164 Allyn, European Immigration into Canada, 122–3; Corbett, Canada's Immigration Policy, 15.

165 Hawkins, *Canada and Immigration*, 304–6.

166 This organization represented the Anglican, United, Baptish, Presbyterian, and Disciple Churches, in addition to other bodies such as the Salvation Army and the Bible Society.

167 Hawkins, *Canada and Immigration*, 304–6.

168 House of Commons *Debates*, 26 January 1948, 573.

169 Holmes, *The Shaping of Peace*, vol. 1, 101.

170 For example, after Cabinet approved the admission of 1,000 women as domestics on 18 July 1947, a consultant to the labour minister advised that 'Jews aren't willing to be domestics. It is not their forte'. This view was given effect to in selecting domestics in the DP camps: Abella and Troper, *None Is Too Many*, 24950.

171 Ibid., 258–71.

172 Canadian Institute of Public Opinion, Public Opinion News Service Release, 30 October 1946.

173 P.C. 1647 (29 April 1947). Described by Abella and Troper in *None Is Too Many*, 271–4, and discussed in chapter 7, this volume.

174 Whitaker, *Double Standard*, 53. See also Dirks, *Canada's Refugee Policy*, 179–82.

175 Whitaker, *Double Standard*, 31–2. Whitaker notes that the IRO was run by Western governments and boycotted by the Soviet bloc.

176 'Report of the Department of Citizenship and Immigration,' *ADR, 1958–59*, 26.

177 This scheme, adopted in February 1951, is discussed in this chapter, 323. For further details, see Robert H. Keyserlingk, ed., *Breaking Ground: The 1956 Hungarian Refugee Movement to Canada* (Toronto: York Lanes, 1993).

178 Dirks, *Canada's Refugee Policy*, 190–4.

179 Ibid., 199.

180 Pickersgill in House of Commons *Debates*, 25 January 1957, 666.

181 *Globe and Mail*, 28 November 1956. Those that had already come to Canada would not have to pay back the loan. Only 1,029 Hungarians had arrived in Canada at this point.

182 *Montreal Gazette*, 29 November 1956.

183 Dirks, *Canada's Refugee Policy*, 200.

184 Whitaker, *Double Standard*, 85.

185 Dirks, *Canada's Refugee Policy*, 210–11.

186 Hawkins, *Canada and Immigration*, 116.

187 *Financial Post*, 15 December 1956. Ontario Hydro promised jobs to twenty students, Polymer to fifteen, Abitibi Power to ten, and IBM to five.

188 *Globe and Mail*, 14 December 1956.

189 Dirks, *Canada's Refugee Policy*, 192.

190 *Winnipeg Free Press*, 29 November 1956.

191 Dirks, *Canada's Refugee Policy*, 204. As the Hungarian refugees were being admitted into the country, hundreds of 'hard core' refugees still remained in European reception centres. The Canadian government was criticized by some for accepting Hungarian refugees while there were still war refugees who had yet to find adequate asylum. The government's response expressly disclaimed that it had acted exclusively for humanitarian reasons: see ibid., 210.

192 Whitaker, *Double Standard*, 67.

193 Ibid., 68. Hawkins, *Canada and Immigration*, 137, reports that the JIAS was also involved in the rescue of 800 Romanian Jews during the Fairclough ministry (1958 to 1962).

194 Anne Francis, 'Open the Door to Refugees,' *Canadian Welfare*, 15 September 1959, 227; *Canadian Commentator* 4 (February 1960): 23.

195 'Report of the Department of Citizenship and Immigration,' *ADR, 1959–60*, 26–7. A detailed review is included in the Department of Citizenship and Immigration's 'Canada's Refugee Programmes – 1945–1961.'

196 'Report of the Department of Citizenship and Immigration,' *ADR, 1961–62*, 19.

197 Dirks, *Canada's Refugee Policy*, 218–19.

198 Whitaker, *Double Standard*, 19–20.

199 Ibid., 29–30.

200 Ibid., 159.

201 Ibid., 61–3.

202 Ibid., 62.

203 Ibid., 211.

204 Ibid., 169–70.

205 Ibid., 166.

206 Ibid., 80. Interestingly, immigrants from Israel and North Africa were also subject to the two-year rule, which may simply have been another way of maintaining a racially biased immigration policy.

207 Ibid., 89–93.

208 House of Commons *Debates*, 21 February 1967, 13280.

209 A Cabinet decision not to give reasons in security-related denials was upheld by the Ontario Court of Appeal in 1959: *Re Iantoro* (1959), 124 C.C.C. 397.

210 House of Commons *Debates*, 21 February 1967, 13283.

211 Ibid., 13294.

212 However, between 1959 and 1961, 13,000 people were admitted under special orders-in-council: *Immigration and Population Statistics* (Ottawa: Department of Manpower and Immigration, 1974), 47.

213 This qualification, 'in any case where an appeal lies against a deportation order under the Act,' meant that those who were denied appeals under the Act – namely, those convicted of a drug offence or those faced with a medical certificate which gave grounds for their being banned – could still not appeal. See Pickersgill's comments in House of Commons *Debates*, 19 January 1962, 11.

214 S.C. 1952, c.42, s.31(2).

215 *The Canada Year Book*, 1946 to 1961 editions.

Chapter 9 Immigration Policy, 1963–1976: Democracy and Due Process

1 See Kenneth Norrie, Douglas Owram, and J.C. Herbert Emery, *A History of the Canadian Economy*, 4th ed. (Toronto: Thomson Nelson, 2008), chs. 19–21.

2 For a general analysis of changing ideals in immigration policy, see K.W. Taylor, 'Racism in Canadian Immigration Policy,' *Canadian Ethnic Studies* 23/1 (1991): 1–20.

3 'Report of the Department of Manpower and Immigration,' *Annual Departmental Reports, 1969–70*, 8 [*Annual Departmental Reports* henceforth cited as *ADR*]. In absolute terms, the change was still more remarkable: almost a tenfold increase in immigration from Asia and the West Indies, from 2,800 and 1,300 in 1961 to 25,301 and 11,202 in 1971, respectively.

4 Freda Hawkins, *Canada and Immigration. Public Policy and Public Concerns*, 2nd ed. (Montreal: McGill-Queen's University Press, 1988), 167–73.

5 Freda Hawkins, *Critical Years in Immigration: Canada and Australia Compared* (Montreal: McGill-Queen's University Press, 1989), 40.

6 John Wood, a political scientist at University of British Columbia, cited the growing concern with ethnic voters as the reason why the Liberals reduced the number of years it took for a landed immigrant to be eligible for citizenship from five to three: Wood, 'East Indians and Canada's New Immigration Policy,' *Canadian Public Policy* 4 (1978): 561.

7 The Department of Citizenship and Immigration was commissioned to complete the review and issue the report. However, by the time the paper was ready to be tabled, the new Department of Manpower and Immigration had been created.

8 Donald H. Avery, *Reluctant Host: Canada's Response to Immigrant Workers, 1896–1994* (Toronto: McClelland & Stewart, 1995), 179.

9 Department of Manpower and Immigration, *White Paper on Immigration* (Ottawa: 1966), 7 [henceforth cited as *White Paper*].

10 Ibid., 12.

11 *Globe and Mail*, 17 October 1966.

12 *Montreal Gazette*, 17 October 1966.
13 *Vancouver Sun*, 15 October 1966.
14 *White Paper*, 8.
15 Hawkins, *Canada and Immigration*, 160.
16 Hawkins, *Canada and Immigration*, 161.
17 P.C. 86 (18 January 1962), s.31 (a).
18 Minutes of Proceedings and Evidence of the Special Joint Committee of Senate and the House of Commons on Immigration [hereinafter cited as Joint Committee (1967)] (Ottawa: Queen's Printer, 1966–7), 168.
19 *Joint Committee* (1967), 933.
20 Taken from Economic Council of Canada, *Economic and Social Impacts of Immigration* (Ottawa: Ministry of Supply and Services, 1991), 15.
21 'Report of the Department of Manpower and Immigration,' *ADR, 1967–68*, 21–4. The regulations came into effect on 1 October 1967 under P.C. 1616 (16 August 1967).
22 Hawkins, *Canada and Immigration*, 162.
23 Ibid., 404–5. The nominated category was treated as separate from that of independent immigrants. In 1967, independent applicants had to obtain 50 points out of 100 to be accepted, whereas nominated applicants had to obtain either 20 or 25 points, depending on whether their sponsor was a Canadian citizen or landed immigrant, respectively. As described below, the Immigration Department could control immigration levels by adjusting these pass marks.
24 According to subsection 33(4) (a) of P.C. 1967–1616 (part of the 1967 revision to Part I of the Immigration Regulations), the nominating Canadian had to undertake to provide the necessary care and maintenance for the new immigrant and his or her family for a period of five years. A Canadian citizen or landed immigrant was eligible to nominate an immigrant only if the nominator had previously carried out his or her other sponsorship obligations: s.33(4) (b).
25 P.C. 1967–1616, schedules A and B.
26 Louis Parai, 'Canada's Immigration Policy, 1962–74,' *International Migration Review* (1975): 459.
27 *Montreal Gazette*, 15 September 1967; *Winnipeg Free Press* and the *Globe and Mail*, 14 September 1967.
28 'Report of the Department of Manpower and Immigration,' *ADR, 1969–70*, 9. The scheme is described in the previous chapter. See also Vic Satzewich, 'Racism and Canadian Immigration Policy: The Government's View of Caribbean Migration, 1962–1966,' *Canadian Ethnic Studies* 21/1 (1989): 77–97.

29 'Report of the Department of Manpower and Immigration,' *ADR, 1969–70,* 9.
30 'Report of the Department of Manpower and Immigration,' *ADR, 1966–7,* 23. The figure is for the fiscal year, which ran to 31 March 1967.
31 'Report of the Department of Manpower and Immigration,' *ADR, 1970–1,* 15. The figure is for 1 April 1970 to 31 March 1971.
32 'Report of the Department of Manpower and Immigration,' *ADR, 1969–70,* 8. Although the requirement that all recipients have occupations in strong demand is not mentioned explicitly in the report, it can be inferred that it was introduced between 1967 and 1970.
33 P.C. 3073 (21 December 1972), which came into effect on 1 January 1973: see 'Report of the Department of Manpower and Immigration,' *ADR, 1972–73,* 13–14.
34 Avery, *Reluctant Host,* 187.
35 Shirley B. Seward and Kathryn McDode, *Immigrant Women in Canada: A Policy Perspective* (Ottawa: Canadian Advisory Council on the Status of Women, 1988), 40.
36 P.C. 318 (21 February 1974).
37 P.C. 2351 (22 October 1974). See 'Report of the Department of Manpower and Immigration,' *ADR, 1974–5,* 18.
38 According to Freda Hawkins, the program was hampered by difficulties in enforcement and investigation. As well, 'the program itself did not get at the heart of the problem which was organized crime on a large scale, high profits, and very flexible operations:' Hawkins, *Canada and Immigration,* 133.
39 'Report of the Department of Manpower and Immigration,' *ADR, 1963–64,* 19.
40 Hawkins, *Canada and Immigration,* 133.
41 'Report of the Department of Manpower and Immigration,' *ADR, 1966–67,* 19. The agricultural workers were imported to deal with a labour shortage in Southern Ontario. See also Vic Satzewich, 'The Canadian State and the Radicalization of Caribbean Migrant Farm Labour, 1947–1966,' *Ethnic and Racial Studies 11/3* (July 1988): 282–304; Brian Douglas Tennyson, ed., *Canada and the Commonwealth Caribbean* (Lanham, MD: University Press of America, 1988); R.G. Cecil and G.E. Banks, 'The Human Condition of West Indian Migrant Farm Labour in Southwestern Ontario,' *International Migration* 29/3 (September 1991): 389–406.
42 'Report of the Department of Manpower and Immigration,' *ADR, 1966–67,* 24.
43 Hawkins, *Canada and Immigration,* 413.
44 Robert Harney, '"So Great a Heritage as Ours": Immigration and the Survival of the Canadian Polity,' *Daedalus* 117 (Fall 1988): 61–2.

45 J.D. Gagnon, 'Immigrants and French-Canadian Nationalism,' in *Immigration and the Rise of Multiculturalism,* ed. Howard Palmer (Toronto: Copp Clark, 1975), 154. On the other hand, the Canadian Jewish Congress testified before the joint committee in 1975 that the 10,000 francophone Jews from Morocco who moved to Montreal were forced to seek employment in the English-speaking sector because they could not get jobs in the Quebec francophone sector: *Minutes of Proceedings and Evidence of the Special Joint Committee of the Senate and the House of Commons on Immigration Policy* [henceforth cited as *Joint Committee* (1975)] (Ottawa: Ministry of Supply and Services, 1975), 43.

46 See Rosaire Horin, *L'immigration au Canada* (Montreal: Editions de l'Action Nationale, 1966).

47 The Quebec Immigration department, the first Canadian government department concerned solely with immigration, was established by Bill 75, Quebec's Immigration Department Act, on 5 November 1968: Hawkins, *Canada and Immigration,* 227.

48 Ibid., 229.

49 'Report of the Department of Manpower and Immigration,' *ADR, 1975–6,* 21. The agreement gave Quebec's overseas immigration officers greater, though not complete, control over the selection process for independent immigrants willing to locate in the province. In addition, the Quebec Immigration department and Immigration Canada agreed to exchange information they possessed about potential immigrants. Despite this enhanced role for Quebec in immigration policy (or perhaps because of it), a low proportion of immigrants continued to choose Quebec as their new home. In 1962, 26 per cent of all immigrants settled in Quebec, a figure that fell almost every year in the following decade, reaching 14 per cent in 1972. In 1976, the proportion increased substantially, to 19 per cent. Figures based on *Immigration Statistics* (Ottawa: Department of Citizenship and Immigration, Immigration Branch, 1957).

50 'Report of the Department of Manpower and Immigration,' *ADR, 1962–63,* 18.

51 'Report of the Department of Manpower and Immigration,' *ADR, 1963–64,* 18.

52 Gerald Dirks, *Canada's Refugee Policy: Indifference or Opportunism?* (Montreal: McGill-Queen's University Press, 1977), 231; 'Report of the Department of Manpower and Immigration,' *ADR, 1965–66,* 5.

53 Reginald Whitaker, *Double Standard: The Secret History of Canadian Immigration* (Toronto: Lester & Orpen Dennys, 1987), 290.

54 Ibid., 57–8.

55 In addition to immigration officials, the team included members of the Canada Council and National Research Council, and representatives of universities: Dirks, *Canada's Refugee Policy*, 233–5; 'Report of the Department of Manpower and Immigration,' *ADR, 1968–69*, 11.

56 Dirks, Canada's Refugee Policy, 235; and Hawkins, Canada and Immigration, 384.

57 John Brewin, 'Deserter Dodging,' *Canadian Forum* 49 (May 1969), 30–1.

58 Dirks, *Canada's Refugee Policy*, 238.

59 House of Commons Debates, 22 May 1969, 8930.

60 Roger Neville Williams, *The New Exiles* (New York: Liveright, 1971), 84.

61 Department of Manpower and Immigration annual reports for 1965 to 1969.

62 Dirks, *Canada's Refugee Policy*, 235–6; 'Report of the Department of Manpower and Immigration,' *ADR, 1971–72*, 12, and ibid., *ADR, 1972–73*, 13, mention these refugees, but are typically optimistic about their establishment in Canada: 'All reports indicate that the Tibetans are progressing well in their new Canadian environment and seem to be settling happily.'

63 Dirks, *Canada's Refugee Policy*, 238–40.

64 'Report of the Department of Manpower and Immigration,' *ADR, 1972–3* 13.

65 Hawkins, *Critical Years in Immigration*, 167–8.

66 House of Commons *Debates*, 22 June 1973, 5026.

67 Hawkins, *Critical Years in Immigration*, 166–9.

68 Dirks, *Canada's Refugee Policy*, 245–9.

69 Ibid., 254–8. Harold Troper points out the significance of the episode, indicating there was more to Canadian policy than humanitarianism concern. 'And if humanitarian concerns might sometimes take second place to economic selfinterest, economic self-interest often had an ideological spin': 'Canada's Immigration Policy since 1945,' *International Journal* 48 (Spring 1993): 273. For a general discussion, see Alan B. Simmons, 'Latin American Migration to Canada: New Linkages in the Hemispheric Migration and Refugee Flow Systems,' *International Journal* 48 (Spring 1993): 282–309.

70 Dirks, *Canada's Refugee Policy*, 247; Whitaker, *Double Standard*, 258.

71 For example, when the Canadian ambassador to Chile was confronted with the fact that some 70,000 civilians had been killed in the aftermath of the coup, he told a *Globe and Mail* reporter, 'The story has been exaggerated out of all proportion ... you have to remember this is South America.' This reporter found the staff at the Canadian embassy generally supportive of the new junta: Ian Adams, 'From Chile, Canada's Hurdles Look Formidable,' *Globe and Mail*, 28 November 1973, 7.

72 Hawkins, Critical Years in Immigration, 169.

73 Dirks, *Canada's Refugee Policy*, 258.

74 Brewin, in House of Commons *Debates*, 30 November 1973, 8299.

75 Eppin, ibid., 8964.

76 John Rodriguez, in ibid., 8 January 1974, 9178.

77 Ibid., 29 October 1973, 7303.

78 Arrol, ibid., 7912.

79 Caouette, in ibid., 8387.

80 *Joint Committee* (1975), 33: 9–13.

81 Clive Cocking, 'How Did the Canadian Mounties Develop Their Unfortunate Habit of Deporting People They Don't Happen to Like?' *Saturday Night*, June 1970, 28–30.

82 Hawkins, *Canada and Immigration*, 147.

83 Ibid., 145.

84 Joseph Sedgwick, *Report on Immigration*, Part I (Ottawa: Department of Citizenship and Immigration, 1965).

85 *Globe and Mail*, 3 April 1965, 9.

86 Joseph Sedgwick, *Report on Immigration*, Part II (Ottawa: Department of Citizenship and Immigration, January 1966).

87 Hawkins, *Canada and Immigration*, 148.

88 House of Commons *Debates*, 21 February 1967, 13312.

89 *Immigration Appeal Board Act*, S.C. 1967, c.13, ss.3, 4, 5, and 6. Subsection 7(1) of the act states that 'the Board is a Court of Record and shall have an official seal, which shall be judicially noticed.'

90 S.C. 1952, c.42, s.12.

91 *Immigration Appeal Board Act*, s.11.

92 Bell, in House of Commons *Debates*, 21 February 1967, 13282.

93 P.C. 1967–1956, ss.2(a) and (b), respectively.

94 Judicial review of IAB decisions was in the Federal Court after its establishment in 1971. *Federal Court Act*, R.S.C. 1985, F-7.

95 S.15(1) (a).

96 Bell, House of Commons *Debates*, 1967, 13282. Liberal Joe Macaluso agreed with Bell. Macaluso believed that this type of discretion should reside only with a department or a minister, and not with a quasi judicial tribunal: ibid., 13300.

97 S.21(1)(a).

98 S.21(2).

99 Lewis, in House of Commons *Debates*, 21 February 1967, 13286.

100 [1970] S.C.R. 699.

101 'Report of the Department of Manpower and Immigration,' *ADR 1966–67*, 19. The new policy was announced on 8 July 1966.

102 (1972), 23 D.L.R. (3d) 331 (S.C.C.).

103 Christopher Wydrzynski, 'Civil Liberties of Aliens in the Canadian
     Immigration Process,' (LLM thesis, Osgoode Hall Law School, York
     University, Toronto, 197), 181.
104 (1972), 23 D.L.R. (3d) 476 (S.C.C.).
105 Hawkins, *Canada and Immigration*, 166–7. From 1967 to 1970, 10 per cent of
     all immigrants received their landed-immigrant status in Canada. In 1971,
     the figure rose to 28 per cent. There is some evidence that applicants in
     Canada were considered more favourably than those abroad: L.W. St. John
     Jones, 'Canadian Immigration: Policy and Trends in the 1960's,' *International
     Migration Review* 11/4 (1973): 162.
106 Law Reform Commission, *The Immigration Appeal Board* (Ottawa: Ministry of
     Supply and Services, 1976, 77.
107 P.C. 2502 (3 November 1972). See 'Report of the Department of Manpower
     and Immigration,' *ADR 1972–73*, 13; and Hawkins, *Critical Years in
     Immigration*, 47.
108 *An Act to Amend the Immigration Appeal Board Act, S.C.* 1973, c.27, s.11(1).
109 Because a deportation order was the sole mechanism for excluding a person
     from Canada, if a special inquiry officer decided to deny an American entry
     into Canada, it was necessary to issue a deportation order. Although the
     SIO's decision may have been based on technical non-compliance with the
     act, a deportation order barred the deportee from ever entering Canada
     again without the minister's permission. Knowing the severe consequences
     of being turned down by an SIO, the incentive for many visitors to Canada
     who were turned down by an immigration official was to return voluntarily:
     see John Hucker, 'Immigration, Natural Justice and the Bill of Rights,'
     Osgoode Hall Law Journal 13 (1975): 659–60.
110 House of Commons *Debates*, 20 June 1973, 4954, 4959.
111 Hawkins, *Critical Years in Immigration*, 48–9. About half of the successful
     applicants came from the United States and Hong Kong, which – according
     to Hawkins – attested to the continuing vigor of the illegal Chinese migra-
     tion industry in Hong Kong.
112 See, for example, *Re Gooliah and Minister of Citizenship and Immigration*
     (1967), 63 D.L.R. (2d) 224 (Man. C.A.), where the court quashed a deporta-
     tion order because the SIO was biased.
113 Hawkins, *Critical Years in Immigration*, 44–5.
114 House of Commons *Debates*, 17 September 1973, 6611–12.
115 There were four principal volumes: (1) 'Immigration Policy Perspectives';
     (2) 'The Immigration Program' (a history of Canadian immigration and
     description of current practice); (3) 'Immigration and Population
     Statistics'; and (4) 'Three Years in Canada,' a three-year long longitudinal

study of how a group of immigrants fared in Canada [hereinafter, each volume is cited as *Green Paper*, with volume number]. Nine supplemental studies were also published, including: Warren E. Kalbach, *The Effect of Immigration on Population*; Nancy Tienharra, *Canadian Views on Immigration and Populations An Analysis* of *Post War Gallup Polls*; Anthony Richmond, *Aspects of the Absorption and Adaptation of Immigrants*; Raymond Breton, Jill Armstrong, and Les Kennedy, *The Social Impact of Changes in Population Size and Composition*; Louis Parai, *The Economic Impact of Immigration;* and Larry Epstein, *Immigration and Inflation*. All were published by the Department of Manpower and Immigration (Ottawa: Information Canada, 1974).

116 Anthony Richmond, 'Canadian Immigration: Recent Developments and Future Prospects,' *International Migration* 13 (1975): 174.
117 Martin Loney and Allan Moscovitch, 'The Immigration Green Paper in Black and White,' *Canadian Dimension* 100 (1975): 4.
118 *Green Paper I*, 3.
119 John Vandercamp, 'Introduction,' *Canadian Public Policy 1* (1975): 279.
120 *Green Paper* 119–28.
121 Warren Kalbach, 'The National Conference on Canadian Immigration and the Green Paper in Retrospect,' *Canadian Ethnic Studies* 7 (1975): 71–3.
122 Hawkins, *Canada and Immigration;* Dirks, *Canada's Refugee Policy*.
123 All of the articles discussed below critiquing the Green Paper can be found in one of these two journals' special editions published in 1975.
124 Freda Hawkins, 'Immigration and Population: The Canadian Approach,' *Canadian Public Policy* 1 (1975): 286.
125 Anthony Richmond, 'The Green Paper: Reflections on the Canadian Immigration and Population Study,' *Canadian Ethnic Studies* 7 (1975): 10, 20.
126 *Green Paper I*, 66–7, 71.
127 Gerald Dirks, 'The Green Paper and Canadian Refugee Policy,' *Canadian Ethnic Studies* 7 (1975): 63.
128 Hawkins, *Critical Years in Immigration*, 57.
129 It must be noted that this comparison is based upon editorials published the day after the Green Paper was tabled. All other commentators had months to prepare their briefs.
130 *Monteal Gazette*, 4 February 1975.
131 *Vancouver Sun*, 4 February 1975; *Globe and Mail*, 5 February 1975.
132 Wood, 'East Indians and Canada's New Immigration Policy,' 555.
133 Both chairmen were Liberals.
134 The one other area of agreement was a call for the government to expand the sponsorship class.

135 See, for example, the testimony of the Vancouver Chinese community's Immigration Policy Action Committee (created in response to the Green Paper): *Joint Committee* (1975), 27: 69.

136 At this time, if an applicant already in Canada was denied admission as a landed immigrant he or she was entitled to an inquiry conducted by an SIO. As one former officer explained: 'An immigration inquiry is defined as an administrative tribunal. Its presiding SIO presents the government's case and then allows the person concerned to tell his story, with the aid of counsel and witnesses if desired. At the end of the inquiry the presiding officer decides, on the basis of whatever evidence he considers credible, whether to admit or deport. The onus is on a newly arrived person to prove he is not prohibited. An inquiry is not a court, but it operates much like one except that judge, jury and prosecutor are the same person ... In a sense, the presiding officer's duty is to weigh his own arguments against those of another person. It is not a system likely to deal out impartial justice. Even with the best intentions, it is nearly impossible to be fair': Roy Blake, 'Saying "No" to the Alien Hordes,' *Saturday Night,* July-August 1976), 35–6.

137 For a detailed description of the Department of Manpower and Immigration's deportation procedures, see ibid., where Blake describes his experiences as both a regular immigration officer and a special inquiry officer.

138 John Hucker, 'Immigration, Natural Justice and the Bill of Rights,' *Osgoode Hall Law Journal* 13 (1975): 660; see also *Morris v Minister of Manpower and Immigration* (1974), 50 D.L.R. (3d), 459.

139 *Report*, 46; Canadian Bar Association, *Joint Committee* (1975), 48: 77–9.

140 *Report*, 8.

141 Ibid., 18–20.

142 Ibid., 21–3.

143 Refugees were to be exempted from the quota.

144 The special inquiry officers were members of the Manpower and Immigration Department.

145 *Report*, 35, 37, 43, and 40.

146 Hawkins, *Critical Years in Immigration*, 61–2. This statement indicated that, for the most part, these members were satisfied with the committee's report.

Chapter 10 Regulating the Refugee Influx, 1977–1994: The Fraying of the Consensus

1 See Kenneth Norrie, Douglas Owram, and J.C. Herbert Emery, *A History of the Canadian Economy*, 4th ed. (Toronto: Thomson Nelson, 2008), chs. 21–2.

2 Jane Badets and Tina Chui, *Canada's Changing Immigrant Population* (Ottawa: Statistics Canada, 1994), 12–13.

3 Ibid., 10. These two cities proved a particular magnet for immigrants from Hong Kong seeking greater personal and business security in the face of the Chinese takeover of Hong Kong in 1997. See Margaret Cannon, *China Tide: The Revealing Story of the Hong Kong Exodus to Canada* (Toronto: HarperCollins, 1989); John DeMont, *Hong Kong Money: How Chinese Families and Fortunes Are Changing Canadian Business* (Toronto: Key Porter, 1989).

4 *The Economist*, 13 November 1993, 45.

5 Economic Council of Canada, *Economic and Social Impacts of Immigration*, ed. Neil Swan, et al. (Ottawa: The Council, 1991).

6 Letter signed by R. Hougen, QC (chairman of the board) and T. Reid (president), 22 June 1990.

7 Ibid.

8 R. White, *Minutes of Proceedings and Evidence of Legislative Committee on Bill C-86, An Act to amend the Immigration Act and other Acts in consequence thereof*, 12–8–1992, 8: 7.

9 Ibid., 8: 10–1.

10 Michael Valpy, 'Mr. Marchi's Immigration Mess,' *Globe and Mail*, 13 July 1994, A2; Valpy, 'Let's Take Another Look at the Immigration Data,' *Globe and Mail*, 14 July 1994, A2.

11 Daniel Stoffman, *Toward a More Realistic Immigration Policy for Canada* (Toronto: C.D. Howe Institute, 1993).

12 Andrew Coyne, 'No Limits, No Quotas: All Who Want to Immigrate Should Be Admitted,' *Globe and Mail*, 18 July 1994, A10; Coyne, 'How Do We Know Canada Couldn't Take in a Million People a Year?' *Globe and Mail*, 1 August 1994, A8; Coyne, 'The Case for Open Immigration,' *The Next City* 1/2 (1995): 34.

13 In J. Whalley, ed., *Domestic Policies and the International Economic Environment* (Toronto; University of Toronto Press, 1985), 57. This research was commissioned by the Royal Commission on the Economic Union and Development Prospects for Canada (Ottawa: Ministry of Supply and Services, 1985).

14 Don J. DeVoretz, 'Immigration and Employment Effects' (Discussion Paper, Institute for Research on Public Policy, November 1989).

15 Prepared by Neil Swan, Ludwig Auer, Denis Chénard, Angélique dePlaa, Arnold de Silva, Douglas Palmer, and John Serjak (Ottawa: The Council, 1991).

16 Don DeVoretz, ed., *Diminishing Returns: The Economics of Canada's Recent Immigration Policy* (Toronto: C.D. Howe Institute, 1995).

17 Freda Hawkins, *Canada and Immigration: Public Policy and Public Concern*, 2nd ed. (Montreal: McGill-Queen's University Press, 1988), 378.

18 S.C. 1992, c.49, s.3, introducing s.7.(1), (2) to the act.
19 *Annual Report to Parliament: Immigration Plan for 1991–1995* (Ottawa: Ministry of Supply and Services, 1990), 1.
20 These numbers were merely targets and were subject to revision from year to year at the federal government's discretion.
21 These numbers were merely targets and were subject to revision from year to year at the federal government's discretion.
22 *Annual Report to Parliament: Immigration Plan for 1991–1995*, 11–12.
23 *Annual Report to Parliament: Immigration for 1991–1995, Year Two* (Ottawa: Ministry of Supply and Services, 1991), 13.
24 S. O'Malley, 'Immigrants' Education Ontario's Responsibility,' *Globe and Mail*, 29 October 1990, A1, A2.
25 Shirley Seward, 'Now Is a Bad Time to Raise Number of Immigrants Coming to Canada,' *Financial Post*, 20–2, October 1990, 8.
26 David K. Foot, 'A Move That Doesn't Make Sense,' *Globe and Mail*, 26 October 1990, A13.
27 See V. Matthews Lemieux, 'Immigration: A Provincial Concern,' *Manitoba Law Journal* 13/1 (1983): 111–40.
28 'Cullen Says Ottawa Willing to Cooperate on Immigration,' *Vancouver Sun*, 15 April 1977, 9.
29 *Montreal Star*, 19 February 1977, A6.
30 'Complete Quebec Immigration Control Urged,' *Montreal Star*, 23 November 1977, A6.
31 Laurier Bonhomme, in ibid.
32 'Agreement on Immigration,' *Globe and Mail*, 27 January 1978.
33 'Immigration: Quebec Signs,' *Winnipeg Free Press*, 21 February 1978.
34 J. Ruimy, 'Law Puts Non-French Speaking at a Disadvantage,' *Halifax Chronicle Herald*, 9 June 1979, 9.
35 Ibid.
36 'Immigration Deal Due as Bourassa Keeps Ottawa Line Open,' *Vancouver Sun*, 25 June 1990, B4.
37 P. Mooney, 'New Deal Gives Quebec Right to Pick Immigrants,' *Winnipeg Free Press*, 28 December 1990, 9; 'Quebec's Powers Enhanced with Deal,' *Globe and Mail*, 28 December 1990, A1.
38 G.E. Dirks, *Controversy and Complexity: Canadian Immigration Policy during the 1980s* (Montreal: McGill-Queen's University Press, 1995), 110–11.
39 'Report of the Department of Manpower and Immigration,' *Annual Departmental Reports, 1990–91*, 15. [*Annual Departmental Reports* henceforth cited as *ADR*].
40 Dirks, *Controversy and Complexity*, 109.

41 F. Shalom, 'Ottawa's Tardiness on Refugee Influx Assailed in Quebec,' *Globe and Mail*, 24 February 1987, A9.
42 *Immigration Regulations, 1978*, SOR/78–172.
43 Section 37 (2) and s. 114 (2) of the act. Orders-in-Council are made by Cabinet under section 114 of the act and are used to overcome the requirement for a visa in order to allow people who have already landed in Canada, and otherwise qualify, to remain. Minister's permits, governed by section 37, grant temporary (short-term or long-term) permission to visitors to come into Canada and override all other grounds for refusal. Christopher Wydrzynski, *Canadian Immigration Law and Procedure* (Aurora, ON: Canada Law Book, 1883), 345.
44 Ibid., 346.
45 These ministerial permits are often used to allow spouses of Canadians to stay while their claims are processed, in cases of individual hardship (including compassionate and humanitarian reasons) and for certain situations involving refugee claimants: J.H. Grey, *Immigration Law in Canada* (Toronto: Butterworths, 1984), 131–3.
46 Ibid., 138. For a further discussion of family class and exceptions to these rules, see ibid., 138–41.
47 Wydrzynski, *Canadian Immigration Law and Procedure*, 98.
48 David C. Corbett, *Canada's Immigration Policy: A Critique* (Toronto: University of Toronto Press, 1957), 43–4.
49 Stoffman, *Toward a More Realistic Immigration Policy for Canada*, 13.
50 See *Canada Year Book, 1994*, 116.
51 *Annual Report to Parliament: Immigration Plan for 1991–1995, Year Two*, 3.
52 *Globe and Mail*, 6 November 1991.
53 SOR/93–4, 0(1).
54 SOR/94–242, s.1(1), 1(2).
55 Grey, *Immigration Law in Canada*, 147–8.
56 Ibid., 114.
57 Employment and Immigration Canada, 'Helping a Relative Immigrate to Canada,' Immigration Fact Sheet no. 2, January 1993.
58 Ibid.
59 'Report of the Department of Employment and Immigration,' *ADR, 1982–83*, 40.
60 *Immigration Statistics, 1982* (Ottawa: Employment and Immigration Canada, 1982) and *Immigration Statistics, 1984* (Ottawa: Employment and Immigration Canada, 1984).
61 *Annual Report to Parliament on Future Immigration Levels, 1985* (Ottawa: Ministry of Supply and Services, 1985), 3.

62 'Report of the Department of Employment and Immigration,' *ADR 1983–84,* 31.

63 Shirley B. Seward and Kathryn McDade, *Immigrant Women in Canada: A Policy Perspective* (Ottawa: Canadian Advisory Council on the Status of Women, 1988).

64 *Pinto v Minister of Employment and Immigration* 12 *Imm. L.R.* (2d) 194 (F.C.T.D.).

65 E. Oziewicz, 'Ottawa Ending Nanny Program,' *Globe and Mail,* 20 December 1991, Al–2.

66 Frank Marrocco and Henry Goslett, *The Annotated Immigration Act of Canada, 1993* (Scarborough, ON: Thomson, 1993), 40–1.

67 Immigration officials interpreted the ruling to mean that they could no longer assess domestics applying for temporary work permits on the basis of their ability to settle permanently in Canada. Consequently, they recommended to the minister in 1991 the termination of the provision in the Foreign Domestic Worker Program that allowed domestic workers to apply for permanent status. Minutes of Proceedings and Evidence of the House of Commons Standing Committee on Labour Employment and Immigration, Issue no. 8, 26 February 1992.

68 Department of Employment and Immigration, *The Live-In Caregiver Program* (Ottawa: Ministry of Supply and Services, 1992), 9.

69 Employment and Immigration Canada, 'The Live-in Caregiver Program,' Immigration Fact Sheet no. 1, January 1993.

70 See Audrey Macklin, "Foreign Domestic Workers: Surrogate Housewife or Mail-Order Servant?" *McGill Law Journal* 37 (1992): 691.

71 'Racist in Deed, If Not in Thought,' *Montreal Gazette,* 5 May 1992, B2; E. Oziewicz, 'Immigrant Nannies Must Have Grade 12 Under New Rules,' *Globe and Mail,* 31 January 1992, Al, A4.

72 Letters to the Editor, *Globe and Mail,* 15 February 1992, Carmencita Hernandez, Chair, Women's Committee, Canadian Ethnocultural Council.

73 'Ottawa Set to Ease Rules on Foreign Nannies,' *Toronto Star,* 3 September 1994, Al0; *A Broader Vision: Immigration and Citizenship Plan 1995–2000: Annual Report to Parliament* (Ottawa: Ministry of Citizenship and Immigration, 1994), 11.

74 Dirks, *Controversy and Complexity,* 28.

75 *Annual Report on Future Immigration Levels, 1990,* 3.

76 Wydrzynski, *Canadian Immigration Law and Procedure,* 115–17.

77 Ibid.

78 'Report of the Department of Employment and Immigration,' *ADR, 1979–80,* 14. 82

79 'Report of the Department of Employment and Immigration,' *ADR 1985–86*, 40.
80 Ibid.
81 In an attempt to encourage investment in certain provinces, the government introduced a two-tier designation for the provinces. The $250,000 investment minimum was for those provinces designated as 'Tier II,' or more popular, provinces. These included Ontario, British Columbia, Quebec, and Alberta. Tier I designation was reserved for the remaining provinces, less likely to be the choice of business immigrants, and the minimum investment in these provinces was only $150,000.
82 These requirements were subsequently revised, and new regulations were introduced that increased the duration of the investment from three to five years, and the minimum investment from $250,000 to $350,000 and $150,000 to $250,000 for Tier I and Tier II provinces, respectively: 'Report of the Department of Employment and Immigration,' *ADR, 1990–91*, 39.
83 Keith Martin, 'What Hong Kong Immigrants Can Do for Canada,' *Business Insight* (November-December 1990): 12–13. Martin, the director of international policy at the Canadian Chamber of Commerce, argued that the business class program increased the tax base of federal and provincial governments, thus allowing the cost of other areas of immigration (e.g., refugees and family class) to be more easily absorbed. Martin also argued that this class increased jobs and labour productivity, and could assist in deficit reduction. He called for an expansionary program, particularly with regard to Hong Kong immigrants.
84 See, for example, 'Alta. Seeks Immigrant Capital,' *Winnipeg Free Press*, 17 December 1986, 43.
85 B. Critchley, 'Immigrant Investors: If They've Got Money, Our Door Swings Open Wide,' *Financial Post*, 17 November 1986, 1–2; B. Tierney, 'Wealthy Hong Kong Residents Jumping Immigration Queues,' *Vancouver Sun*, 31 January 1991, A3; P. Watson, 'Rich Buy Their Way into Canada While Poorer Immigrants Wait,' *Toronto Star*, 5 August 1989, A1 and A15.
86 'Immigration for Investors,' *Globe and Mail*, 22 June 1989, A6.
87 'Report of the Department of Employment and Immigration,' *ADR, 1990–91*, 39; see also 'Report of the Department of Employment and Immigration,' *ADR, 1983–84*, 57–8, for a description of the monitoring plans.
88 *Into the 21st Century: A Strategy for Immigration and Citizenship* (Ottawa: Ministry of Citizenship and Immigration, 1994), 32.
89 *Immigration Act 1967.* s. 6(3).
90 *Immigration Regulations, 1978*, s.7(2).
91 Freda Hawkins, *Critical Years in Immigration: Canada and Australia Compared* (Montreal: McGill-Queen's University Press, 1989), 75.

92 Departmental Annual Reports for 1989 to 1993.

93 *Indochinese Designated Class Regulations,* SOR/78–931; *Self-Exiled Persons Designated Class Regulations,* SOR/78–933; and *Political Prisoners and Oppressed Persons Designated Class Regulations,* SOR/82–977.

94 'Political Prisoners and Oppressed Persons Class and the Soviet Union,' *Refuge* 10 (1990): 3/6.

95 *Indochinese Designated Class Regulations,* s.2.

96 SOR/78–932, s.2 (a). In November 1982, following the imposition of martial law, Poland was added to the list of countries, which then included Argentina, Chile, and Uruguay, in the 'political prisoners and oppressed persons' category; 'Report of the Department of Employment and Immigration,' *ADR, 1982–83,* 40. For further information on Latin American immigrants, see Alan B. Simmons, 'Latin American Migration to Canada: New Linkages in the Hemispheric Migration and Refugee Flow Systems,' *International Journal* 48 (Spring 1993): 282–309.

97 Between 1980 and 1989 the refugee population in the Central American region skyrocketed from 100,000 to more than 1 million persons. UNHCR, *The State of the World's Refugees 2000: Fifty Years of Humanitarian Action* (Oxford: Oxford University Press, 2000), 124.

98 Howard Adelman, 'Canadian Policy on Indochinese Refugees,' in *Southeast Asian Exodus: From Tradition to Resettlement,* ed. Elliot L. Tepper (Ottawa: The Canadian Asian Studies Association, Carleton University, 1980), 135.

99 'At Our Own Door,' *Globe and Mail,* 6 December 1978, 6.

100 *Globe and Mail,* 23 December 1978, 2.

101 *Globe and Mail,* 23 June 1979, 8.

102 Howard Adelman, 'Canadian Refugee Policy in the Postwar Period: An Analysis,' in *Refugee Policy: Canada and the United States,* ed. H. Adelman (Toronto: York Lanes, 1991), 211.

103 *Globe and Mail,* 19 September 1979, 1.

104 *Annual Report to Parliament on Future Immigration Levels, 1982* (Ottawa: Ministry of Supply and Services, 1982), 19.

105 Howard Adelman, 'The Policy Maker and the Advocate: Case Studies in Refugee Policy,' in *Making Knowledge Count: Advocacy and Social Science,* ed. Peter Harries-Jones (Montreal: McGill-Queen's University Press, 1991), 61.

106 See Morton Beiser, *Strangers at the Gate: The 'Boat People's' First Ten Years in Canada* (Toronto: University of Toronto Press, 1999).

107 See Barbara McDougall, 'Notes on Canadian Refugee Policy,' in *Refugee Policy,* ed. Adelman, 2; 'Regulatory Impact Analysis Statement,' in the Schedule to the *Indochinese Designated Class (Transitional) Regulations,* SOR/90–627.

108 Hawkins, *Critical Years in Immigration,* 172.

109 'Report of the Department of Employment and Immigration,' *ADR, 1982–83*, 46.

110 'Report of the Department of Employment and Immigration,' *ADR, 1989–90*, 45.

111 'Report of the Department of Employment and Immigration,' *ADR, 1982–83*, 45. See also Richard P. Baker, 'The Adaptation and Ethnicity of Polish Immigrants in Toronto: The Solidarity Wave,' *Canadian Ethnic Studies* 21/3 (1989): 74–90.

112 'Report of the Department of Employment and Immigration,' *ADR, 1981–82*, 34.

113 'Report of the Department of Employment and Immigration,' *ADR, 1982–83*, 40; Dirks, *Controversy and Complexity*, 74.

114 'Report of the Department of Employment and Immigration,' *ADR, 1989–90*, 39.

115 Approximately 3.3 million Afghan refugees were residing in Pakistan and 3 million in Iran. UNHCR, *State of the World's Refugees 2000*, 117.

116 *Annual Report to Parliament on Future Immigration Levels, 1985*, 5.

117 J. Thomas, 'The Canadian Response to Afghanistan,' *Refuge 9* (October 1989): 4–7.

118 'Report of the Department of Employment and Immigration,' *ADR, 1983–84*, 39.

119 Ibid., 69.

120 UNHCR, *State of the World's Refugees 2000*, 106–15.

121 *Canadian Annual Review, 1981* (Toronto: University of Toronto Press, 1981), 317.

122 Based on statistics in the *Annual Report on Future Immigration Levels* for the years 1980 to 1989.

123 'Report of the Department of Employment and Immigration,' *ADR, 1986–87*, 50.

124 *Refuge* 9/2 (December 1989): 14.

125 S.C. 1976–7, c.52, s.45(1).

126 Ibid., ss.70(1) and 71(1).

127 Ibid., s.47(1).

128 Ibid., s.72(2).

129 This news was transmitted by what Freda Hawkins calls 'the migration grapevine,' which includes immigration and travel agents around the world: see Hawkins, 'The Asylum-Seekers,' *Behind the Headlines* 52/2 (Winter 1994–5): 1.

130 *Refugee Perspectives, 1985–86* (Ottawa: Employment and Immigration Canada, 1985), 39.

131 W.G. Robinson (Chair), *The Refugee Status Determination Process: A Report of the Task Force on Immigration Practices and Procedures*, Final Report to the Minister of Employment and Immigration (Ottawa: Minister of Supply and Services, 1981). This task force, established as an advisory committee by Lloyd Axworthy, included individuals who would go on to play important roles in the immigration debate during this period, such as Carter Hoppe (Chair, CBA Immigration Law Section), David Matas (author and refugee advocate), and Edward Ratushny (later author of the 'Ratushny Report,' discussed below).

132 Ibid., x, xxl, xvi, xxii, 2–5, 194. The recommendation concerning visas was used with some success in stemming the flow of bogus refugee claimants from Turkey and Portugal in 1986.

133 Ed Ratushny (Special Adviser), *A New Refugee Status Determination Process for Canada* (Ottawa: Minister of Supply and Services, 1984).

134 W.G. Plaut, *Refugee Determination in Canada* (Ottawa: Minister of Supply and Services, 1985).

135 See, generally, the Plaut Report, 99–117. With reference to appeals to the Federal Court, Plaut argued that two of his models possessed an internal appeal process, and thus appeals to the Federal Court with a leave requirement could be justified. However, the third model did not provide for an internal review within the process itself, and thus an appeal to the Federal Court should be as of right.

136 (1985) 1 S.C.R. 177.

137 *Singh*, 202, per Wilson J.

138 *Singh*, 207, per Wilson J.

139 Minister McLean, in House of Commons *Debates*, 26 September 1985, 152. Note that C-55, enacted in 1985, should not be confused with Bill C-55, the Refugee Reform Act, introduced in 1987 as a major overhaul of the previous refugee determination system.

140 Ibid.

141 'Report of the Department of Employment and Immigration,' *ADR, 1987–88*, 78; SOR/86–701.

142 V. Malarek, *Haven's Gate: Canada's Immigration Fiasco* (Toronto: Macmillan, 1987), 150–70.

143 Ibid., 167–8.

144 Political considerations aside, the Immigration Department considers the withholding of visa exemptions a valuable tool to regulate the flow of migrants from a particular country, the advantage being that applicants can be screened in their own country, with no access to the Canadian appeal system: see Dirks, *Controversy and Complexity*, 48–50.

145 'Report of the Department of Employment and Immigration,' *ADR, 1981–82*, 37.
146 'Report of the Department of Employment and Immigration,' *ADR, 1983–84*, 59. This trend was continued when the government imposed a visa requirement on eight additional countries in May 1992: see *Globe and Mail*, 6 May 1992, A6.
147 *Maclean's*, 9 March 1987, 8–10. Note that return to the United States was an exception to Canada's general policy, also observed by the United States, of voluntary departure or adjudication in the country. Canada and the United States were rare in not having policies of forcible exclusion: see H. Patrick Glenn, *Refugee Claims, the Canadian State and North American Regionalism in Hemispheric Integration, Migration and Human Rights* (Toronto: York University Centre for Refugee Studies, 1994), 11.
148 SOR/87–115, 19 February 1987. See Regulatory Impact Analysis Statement.
149 *Immigration Act*, R.S.C. 1985, c.1–2.
150 Subsequent amendments created a third adjudication division, which made deportation decisions that could then be appealed to the IAD: Bill C-86, S.C. 1992, c.49, s.47(1).
151 *Immigration Act*, s. 46(1) (b), as enacted by R.S.C. 1985 (4th Supp.), c.28
152 Ibid., s.46.01(1).
153 Ibid. ss.30(1)–(2) 46(3) and SOR 78–172, ss. 27(2), 28.
154 Ibid., s.46(1)(c).
155 Ibid., s.49 (1)(b). It should be noted that recent cases – e.g., *Toth v Canada (Minister of Employment and Immigration)* (1988), 6 *Imm. L.R.* (2d) 123 (Fed. C.A.); *Bhattia v Minister of Employment and Immigration* (1989), 7 *Imm. L.R.* (2d) 63 – have suggested that the judiciary has the inherent authority to grant a stay beyond the seventy-two-hour period, when a 'serious issue is presented and irreparable harm would be caused by removal.'
156 Ibid., s.82.1(1).
157 Ibid., s.46.02(2).
158 *Convention Refugee Determination Division Rules*, SOR/88–1026, ss.2, 13. Such information might normally include advice about conditions in the claimant's country.
159 Sam Laredo, Elaine Pollock, and Jan Marshall, 'The Evolution in Perception of the Role of the RHO,' *Refuge* 9/2 (December 1989): 4–5.
160 *Immigration Act*, s.69.1(10).
161 S.C. 1992, c.49, s.73, amending s.82.1 (1) of the act.
162 Ibid., amending s.83(1) of the act.
163 Bouchard, in House of Commons *Debates*, 11 August 1987, 7910.
164 Dirks, *Controversy and Complexity*, 92.

165 'The East Asian Threat: Canada's Attempt to Create a Restrictive Refugee Policy,' *Georgetown Immigration Law Journal 2* (1988): 605–15.
166 House Speaker, in House of Commons *Debates*, 18 September 1987, 9098.
167 Ibid., 26 January 1988, 12308.
168 'Report of the Department of Employment and Immigration,' *ADR, 1990–91*, 17.
169 'Report of the Department of Employment and Immigration,' *ADR, 1989–90*, 17–18. See also 'Initiatives to Expedite Refugee Determination before the Refugee Division of the Immigration and Refugee Board' (Immigration and Refugee Board, 1991).
170 In 1989, the percentage was as high as 45 per cent: see 'Refugee Determination,' *Refuge* 11/2 (1991): 13.
171 *Ken Yhap v Minister of Employment and Immigration* (1990), 9 *Imm. L.R.* (2d) 243 (Fed. TD.).
172 Ss. 114.
173 Law Reform Commission of Canada, 'The Determination of Refugee Status in Canada: A Review of the Procedure' (Draft Final Report), March 1992; see also Glenn, *Strangers at the Gate*.
174 Law Reform Commission, 'Refugee Status,' 52.
175 Ibid., 68–9.
176 Ibid., 79–81.
177 Ibid., 146–9, 150–2, and 153–8, respectively. Other roles examined included immigration consultants and interpreters.
178 *Immigration Regulation* 19(4) (j).
179 House of Commons *Debates*, 18 November 1992, 13561.
180 Government of Canada, 'New Immigration Legislation Comes into Force' (News release), 1 February 1993.
181 *Immigration Act*, S.C. 1952, c.42, s.5.
182 Hawkins, *Canada and Immigration*, 378–9.
183 *Immigration Act*, s.46.01(1) (b), as enacted by R.S.C. 1985 (4th Supp.), c.28.
184 'An interview with Gordon Fairweather [IRB Chairman],' *Refuge* 9/4 (May 1990): 3.
185 See Jonas Widgren, 'The Asylum Crisis in Europe and North America' (paper commissioned by the Program on International and U.S. Refugee Policy, The Fletcher School of Law and Diplomacy, Tufts University, November 1990).
186 The reasons included strong opposition from refugee interest organizations and the potential for political embarrassment arising from designating countries like the United States 'unsafe' for their treatment of Latin American refugees.

187 S.C. 1992, c.49, s.36(l), amending s.46.01(1) (b) of the act.

188 S.C. 1992, c.49, s. 102(11), introducing s. 114(8) to the act.

189 Ibid., s.36, amending s.46.01(1), (1.1) of the act.

190 S.C. 1976–7, c.52, s.19(1) (a).

191 See Kenneth Post, 'Excessive Demands on Health and Social Services: s.19(1) (a) (ii) of the Immigration Act,' *Journal of Law and Social Policy* 8 (1992): 142.

192 Frank Marrocco and Henry Goslett, *Transition Guide: Bill C-86* (Scarborough, ON: Thomson, 1993).

193 S.C. 1992, c.49, s.11(1).

194 Ibid., s. 19.1 (c) as amended by Bill C-86.

195 Bill C-86, s.99(1), introducing s.110(2) (a.1), (a.2) to the act.

196 Bill C-86, s.84, amending s.94.1 of the act. On indictment, fines were raised from a maximum of $10,000 to a maximum of $100,000, while, for a summary conviction, fines were raised from a maximum of $2,000 to a maximum of $10,000, and terms of imprisonment were raised from a maximum of six months to a maximum of one year.

197 Prior to 1914, the domicile period had been only three years.

198 Wydrzynski, *Canadian Immigration Law and Practice*, 74.

199 An example of a 'serious ground' for removal would be the commission of a major criminal offence.

200 [1992] 1 S.C.R. 711.

201 *Kindler v. Canada (Minister of Justice)* [1991] 2 SCR 779.

202 For a more thorough analysis of this case and other post-Charter SCC decisions affecting immigrants, see Ninette Kelley 'Rights in the Balance: Non-Citizens and State Sovereignty under the Charter,' in *The Unity of Public Law*, ed. David Dyzenhaus (Oxford: Hart Publishing, 2004), 253.

203 *Canada Minister of Employment and Immigration v Chiarelli* [1992] 1 SCR 711.

204 Ninette Kelley 'Rights in the Balance.'

205 UNHCR, *State of the World's Refugees 2000,* 117 .

206 R. White, *Legislative Committee on Bill C-86,* 1208–1992, 8: 7.

Chapter 11 Retrenchment, 1995–2008: A Return to Executive Discretion

1 Citizenship and Immigration Canada (hereafter CIC), *Facts and Figures, 2008,* 'Immigration Overview: Permanent Residents and Temporary Foreign Workers and Students': http://www.cic.gc.ca/english/pdf/research-stats/facts2008.pdf.

2 Statistics Canada, 'Immigration in Canada: A Portrait of the Foreign-born Population,' *2006 Census*: http://www12.statcan.ca/english/census06.

3 Ibid.
4 Susan Davis, Roslyn Kunin, and Robert Trempe, *Not Just Numbers: A Canadian Framework for Future Immigration* (Ottawa: Minister of Public Works and Government Services Canada, 1997).
5 'Overhaul of Immigration System Recommended,' *Globe and Mail*, 7 January 1998.
6 David Bercuson and Barry Cooper, 'Language Was Never an Issue,' *Globe and Mail*, 17 January 1998.
7 'Minister Agrees with Critics: Robillard Seeks to Cool Immigrant Tempers over Language Proposal,' *Globe and Mail*, 28 February 1998.
8 Polls throughout the summer in areas where the boats landed showed that more than 90 per cent of respondents favoured deportation. 'Third Ship Spotted off B.C. Coast,' *Globe and Mail*, 31 August 1999.
9 'Minister Rejects Call to Get Tough on Illegal Aliens,' *Globe and Mail*, 29 July 1999.
10 'Police Assailed for Strip Search of Children,' *Globe and Mail*, 25 August 1999; 'Handcuffed Children Ask Canada for Asylum, Smuggled Chinese Youths Fight Backlash,' *Globe and Mail*, 20 August 1999; and 'Go Back to China Migrant Children Told,' *Globe and Mail*, 27 August 1999. In total more than 100 children, many of them unaccompanied, arrived on the boats in 1999. The subsequent decision of the provincial government to accommodate all the children in group homes where they would receive specialized care has been characterized as 'exceptionally courageous' given the strain that the decision placed on the ministry's budget. Interview with Peter Showler, former chair, Immigration and Refugee Board, October 2008.
11 'RCMP "Dropped the Ball" on Migrants, Critics Say,' *Globe and Mail*, 15 September 1999.
12 For further description and analysis of the events surrounding these arrivals, see: Joanne van Selm and Betsy Cooper, 'The New Boat People: Ensuring Safety and Determining Status,' Migration Policy Institute (MPI), January 2006: http://www.migrationpolicy.org/pubs/Boat_People_Report.pdf; Victor Wong, 'Globalization and Migration: Canada's Response to the Chinese Boat Refugees,' Economic Commission for Latin America and the Caribbean (ECLAC) and International Organization for Migration, November 2002: http://www.eclac.org/celade/noticias/paginas/2/11302/VWong.pdf; and Alison Mountz, et al., 'The Challenges to Responding to Human Smuggling in Canada: Practitioners Reflect on the 1999 Boat Arrivals in British Columbia,' Research on Immigration and Integration in the Metropolis, Working Paper Series No. 02–23, December 2002.
13 'Ottawa Reconsiders Refugee Process,' *Globe and Mail*, 6 November 1999.

14 Auditor General of Canada, *Annual Report 2000*, 'Chapter 3: Citizenship and Immigration Canada: The Economic Component of the Canadian Immigration Program': http://www.oag-bvg.gc.ca/domino/reports.nsf/html/0003ce.html. See also Benjamin Dolin and Margaret Young, 'Canada's Immigration Program,' Background Paper, Parliamentary Information and Research Service, Library of Parliament, October 2004.

15 Anti-terrorism Act (Bill C-36), 'An Act to Amend the Criminal Code, the Official Secrets Act, the Canada Evidence Act, the Proceeds of Crime (Money Laundering) Act and other Acts, and to Enact Measures Respecting the Registration of Charities in Order to Combat Terrorism,' came into force 24 December 2001. Ronald Daniels, Patrick Macklem, and Kent Roach, eds, *The Security of Freedom: Essays on Canada's Anti-Terrorism Bill* (Toronto: University of Toronto Press, 2001).

16 Michael Holden, 'Not Just the FTA: Factors Affecting Growth in Canada–United States Trade since 1988,' 4 March 2003: http://dsp-psd.tpsgc.gc.ca/Collection-R/LoPBdP/BP/prb0251-e.htm.

17 Migration Policy Institute, 'U.S.–Canada–Mexico Fact Sheet on Trade and Migration,' November 2003.

18 Department of Foreign Affairs and International Trade, 'Canada–U.S. Smart Border Declaration': www.dfait.maeci.gc.ca/anti-terrorism/actionplan-en.asp.

19 'Ottawa Proposes Immigration Overhaul,' *Globe and Mail*, 7 April 2000; 'Caplan Tables New Immigration and Refugee Protection Act,' *Immigration News*, 6 April 2000. The bill died with the election but was revised and reintroduced the following year.

20 Catherine Dauvergne, 'Evaluating Canada's New Immigration and Refugee Protection Act in Its Global Context,' *Alberta Law Review* 4/13 (2003): 741.

21 François Crépeau and Delphine Nakache, 'Controlling Irregular Migration: Reconciling Security Concerns with Human Rights Protection,' *IRPP Choices* 12/1 (February 2006) 1–42: http://www.irpp.org/choices/archive/vol12no1.pdf.

22 Non-governmental organizations expressed alarm at this provision, fearing that its broad wording could be used against those assisting refugees to make claims in Canada. Their fears were borne out in 2007 when an American church worker was so charged in Quebec: 'Rights Worker Charged for Helping Asylum Seekers in Quebec,' Canadian Broadcasting Corporation (CBC), 28 September 2007: http://www.cbc.ca/canada/montreal/story/2007/09/28/rights-worker.html.

23 LEXBASE, 'Immigration Policy and Operations – 2008,' June 2008. The Department of Citizenship and Immigration explained that targets were determined based on processing capacity and case inventories and that they

were not quotas. Nevertheless, officers were expected to meet yet not exceed the targets, leading Richard Kurland to observe that 'if you deliver exactly the target and you can't exceed it and you can't underachieve it, it's a quota,' and that the government was simply playing politics in not acknowledging this: 'Waiting at the Back of Canada's Line,' *Asian Pacific Post*, 19 June 2008.

24 CIC, *Facts and Figures 2008*.

25 Peter Rekai, *US and Canadian Immigration Policies: Marching Together to Different Tunes* (Toronto: C.D. Howe Institute, The Border Papers No. 171, November 2002), 5. Some argued that the ineffectiveness of the previous system was in part a result of the pressure exerted by protectionist professional and labour bodies.

26 CIC, *Six Selection Factors and Pass Mark*: http://www.cic.gc.ca/english/skilled/ qual-5.html.

27 Immigration and Refugee Protection Regulations, SOR/2002–227, s.76 (hereafter IRPA Regulations).

28 Lorne Waldman, *Canadian Immigration and Refugee Law Practice* (Toronto: Butterworths, 2008), 45–67. See also Emily Carasco, Sharryn Aiken, Donald Galloway, and Audrey Macklin, *Immigration and Refugee Law: Cases, Materials and Commentary* (Toronto: Emond Montgomery Publications, 2007). For a case that involved negative discretion – that is, the immigration officer rejected the application notwithstanding that the applicant's point total was sufficient – see *Chen v. Canada (Minister of Employment and Immigration)*, [1995] 1 S.C.R. 725. The Supreme Court rejected the visa officer's use of discretion. The Supreme Court adopted the dissenting reasoning of the Federal Court of Appeal, which argued that a visa officer's discretion in deciding a person's ability to successfully establish him or herself in Canada should be limited to 'matters relating to their ability to make a living' and that such a 'determination cannot and should not be influenced by conduct which suggests moral turpitude.' *Chen v. Canada (Minister of Employment and Immigration)* (C.A.), [1994] 1 FC 639.

29 CIC, *Facts and Figures, 2008*.

30 IRPA Regulations, s.88(1). See also CIC, *Annual Report to Parliament on Immigration, 2007*: http://www.cic.gc.ca/ENGLISH/RESOURCES/ PUBLICATIONS/annual-report2007/index.asp.

31 Waldman, *Canadian Immigration and Refugee Law Practice*, 13–167–13–169 (para. 13.312).

32 Auditor General of Canada, *Annual Report 2000*.

33 David Ley, 'Seeking Homo Economicus: The Strange Story of Canada's Business Immigration Program,' *Annals of the Association of American Geographers*, 93/2 (2004) 426.

34 CIC, *Facts and Figures, 2008*. In 2008, the Auditor General of Nova Scotia called for a police investigation into irregular practices found in the Provincial Nominee Program. Among the reported deficiencies with the program were objectives that were not met or could not be evaluated; inappropriate approval mechanisms for participating businesses; awarding of an untendered contract to a company that engaged in irregular practices; inadequate oversight and irregular fees charged to immigrants; and services not appropriately rendered. Nova Scotia Office of the Auditor General: http://www.oag-ns.ca/Special%20 Report.pdf; and Canadian Press, 'N.S.Auditor General Sends Tough Report on Immigration to RCMP,' 2 October 2008.

35 House of Commons Standing Committee on Citizenship and Immigration, *The Provincial Nominee Program: A Partnership to Attract Immigrants to All Parts of Canada: Report and Recommendations*, May 2003: http://www.parl.gc.ca.

36 Louise Langevin and Marie-Claire Belleau, 'Trafficking in Women in Canada: A Critical Analysis of the Legal Framework Governing Immigrant Live-In Caregivers and Mail-Order Brides,' 28–31: http://www.swc-cfc.gc.ca/pubs/ pubspr/066231252X/200010_066231252X_8_e.html.

37 IRPA Regulations, s.2 and 113.

38 CIC, *Facts and Figures, 2008*.

39 Audrey Macklin, 'On the Inside Looking In: Foreign Domestic Workers in Canada,' in *Maid in the Market: Women's Paid Domestic Labour*, ed. Wenona Giles and Sedef Arat-Koc (Halifax: Fernwood Publishing, 1994), 13–15. Langevin and Belleau, 'Trafficking in Women,' 31.

40 Currently the Ministry of Human Resources and Skills Development.

41 CIC, *Facts and Figures, 2008*. In 2007 employers hired more than 165,000 temporary workers, an increase of 60 per cent in four years.See also Douglas Watt, Tim Krywulak, and Kurtis Kitagawa, *Renewing Immigration: Towards a Convergence and Consolidation of Canada's Immigration Policies and Systems* (Ottawa: Conference Board of Canada, October 2008). These authors examined how the permanent and temporary programs were meeting the needs of employers and immigrants.

42 Veena Verma, 'The Mexican and Caribbean Seasonal Agricultural Workers Program, Regulatory and Policy Framework, Farm Industry Level Employment Practices and the Future of the Program under Unionization,' paper prepared for the North-South Institute, 7–9: http://www.nsi-ins.ca/ english/pdf/exec_sum_verma.pdf; Tanya Basok, *Tortillas and Tomatoes: Transmigrant Mexican Harvesters in Canada* (Montreal and Kingston: McGill-Queen's University Press, 2002); Audrey Macklin, 'Dancing across Borders: "Exotic Dancers," Trafficking, and Canadian Immigration Policy,' *The International Migration Review* 37/2 (Summer 2003): 466.

43 Karl Flecker, 'Building the World's Most Flexible Workforce: The Harper Government's "Double-Doubling" of the Foreign Worker Program,' 31 October 2007: http://canadianlabour.ca/index.php/antiracism_publicati/1266.

44 For examples of this and some local union efforts to assist temporary workers, see ibid.

45 Verda Cook, 'Workers of Colour within a Global Economy,' Canadian Labour Congress (CLC) research paper, December 2004; and see CLC, 'Statement on International Temporary Workers,' 31 October 2005: http://www.mfl. mb.ca/pdfs/int-wrkrs.pdf.

46 Verma, 'Mexican and Caribbean Seasonal Agricultural Workers Program,' 19–20.

47 See for example, Martin Ruhs, 'Designing Viable and Ethical Labour Immigration Policies,' in *Immigration and Refugee Law*, ed. Carasco, et al., 250.

48 CIC, *Annual Report to Parliament, 2006*, 7: http://www.cic.gc.ca/ENGLISH/ pdf/pub/immigration2006_e.pdf.

49 CIC, 'Canada Experience Class Now Open for Business,' 8 September 2008. According to Douglas Watt, Tim Krywulak, and Kurtis Kitagawa, in *Renewing Immigration*, this sets Canada's program apart from policies in most other places in the world.

50 Canadian Chamber of Commerce, 'Social Policy: Canada's Permanent Immigration System,' 2005: http://www.chamber.ca/cmslib/general/S051.pdf.

51 Canadian Federation of Independent Business (CFIB), 'Immigration and Small Business: Ideas to Better Respond to Canada's Skills and Labour Shortage,' 2007: www.cfib.ca.

52 'Business Applauds Proposed New Immigration Law,' *Globe and Mail*, 28 March 2008.

53 'Opposition, Lawyers, Advocacy Groups Overwhelmingly Oppose Bill and the Broad Powers It Grants to Immigration Minister,' *Globe and Mail*, 28 March 2008.

54 See, for example, Colin R. Singer, 'The New Immigration Law: A Dangerous Piece of Work,' *National Post*, 8 May 2008. For a more recent critique of recommendations on policies related to the economic class, see Naomi Alboim and Maytree, 'Fixing Canada's Economic Immigration Policies,' 2009: http://www.maytree.com/policy.

55 According to the *Toronto Star*, 610 such visas were approved overseas in 2005 and 339 in the first four months of 2006, the latest figure available. Nicholas Keung, 'Mother Gains Last Hope Appeal: Kids' Case One of Many Threatened by Changes,' *Toronto Star*, 22 April 2008.

56 Canadian Council for Refugees (hereafter CCR), 'Legislative Amendments Will Hurt Family Reunification for Children,' news release, 17 March 2008: http://www.ccrweb.ca/eng/media/pressreleases/17march08.htm.

57 IRPA s.3(d).

58 Martin Collacott, *Canada's Immigration Policy: The Need for Major Reform* (Vancouver: Fraser Institute, Public Policy Sources No. 64, 2003): www.fraserinstitute.ca/admin/books/files/immigration-2ndEdition.pdf.

59 Herbert Grubel, 'Immigration and the Welfare State,' Fraser Institute, 1 October 2005: 51–2: http://www.fraserinstitute.org/Commerce.Web/publication_details.aspx?pubID=3096.

60 Michael Trebilcock, 'The Law and Economics of Immigration Policy,' *American Law and Economics Review* 5/2 (2003):271–317, at 298–303, 306–9.

61 Audrey Macklin, 'Public Entrance/Private Member,' in *Privatisation, Feminism and Law*, ed. J. Fudge and Brenda Cossman (Toronto: University of Toronto Press, 2002) ; Colleen Sheppard, 'Women as Wives: Immigration Law and Domestic Violence,' *Queen's Law Journal* 26 (2000): 1.

62 For persons who are stateless, they must be outside their country of habitual residence.

63 CIC, *Facts and Figures, 2008.*

64 IRPA s.97.

65 IRPA s.105; CCR, 'Refugee Appeal Division Backgrounder,' December 2006: . http://www.ccrweb.ca/RADbackgrounder.pdf.

66 Andrew Brouwer, 'Permanent Protection: Why Canada Should Grant Permanent Resident Status Automatically to Recognized Refugees,' *Refuge* 22/2 (Winter 2005); Michael Kingsley Nyinah, 'Exclusion under Article 1F: Some Reflections on Context, Principles and Practice,' *International Journal of Refugee Law* 12 (Special Supplementary Issue) (2000): 305. See, for example, the Inter-American Commission on Human Rights, 'Report on the Situation of Human Rights Asylum Seekers within the Canadian Refugee Determination System': www.cidh.oas.org/countryrep/Canada2000en/canada.htm#11.%20INTRODUCTION. See also CCR, 'First Annual Report Card on Canada's Refugee and Immigration Programs,' November 2003: www.ccrweb.ca/reportcard2003.htm; and U.S.Committee for Refugees and Immigrants, *Country Report*, 2003: www.refugees.org.

67 Article 1E of the Convention Relating to the Status of Refugees and the 1967 Protocol.

68 Ibid., Article 1F.

69 UNHCR, 'Guidelines on International Protection: Application of the Exclusion Clauses: Article 1F of the 1951 Convention relating to the Status of Refugees,' HCR/GIP, 4 September 2003: http://www.unhcr.org/publ/PUBL/3f7d48514.pdf.

70 CCR, 'Comments on Canada's Compliance with Article 3 of the Convention Against Torture,' 28 April 2005: www.ccrweb.ca/catcompliance.html.

71 An exception being for exclusion on the basis of crimes against peace, crimes against humanity, and acts falling under Article 1F(c), as the acts covered are so heinous.UNHCR, 'Guidelines.'

72 Such as where the person has remained a member of a government or group clearly engaged in activities that fall within Article 1F. Ibid., para. 19.

73 For example there was a recognition rate of just 1.5 per cent in 2004. According to the May 2007 Report of the Standing Committee on Citizenship and Immigration, 'Safeguarding Asylum – Sustaining Canada's Commitments to Refugees,' the acceptance rate has remained low, between 1 and 3 per cent.

74 Pursuant to s.101 (1) of IRPA and s.159 of the Regulations, which provide that the United States was a safe third country because it conformed with Article 33 of the Convention relating to the Status of Refugees (the right of non-*refoulement*) and Article 2 of the Convention Against Torture (the right of non-*refoulement* to face torture).

75 CIC, 'Minister Coderre Seeks Government Approval of Safe Third Country Agreement,' press release, 10 September 2002: www.cic.gc.ca/english/press/02/0226–pre.html.

76 See for example Harvard Law Student Advocates for Human Rights, the International Human Rights Clinic, Human Rights Program, and Harvard Immigration and Refugee Clinical Program, 'Bordering on Failure: The U.S.–Canada Safe Third Country Agreement Fifteen Months after Implementation,' March 2006: http://www.law.harvard.edu/academics/clinical/asylum_law/Harvard_STCA_Report.pdf. See also CCR 'Less Safe Than Ever: Challenging the Designation of the US as a Safe Third Country for Refugees,' November 2006: http://www.ccrweb.ca/releaselesssafedec06.html.

77 Alexander Moens and Martin Collacott, eds, *Immigration Policy and the Terrorist Threat in Canada and the United States* (Vancouver: Fraser Institute, May 2008), 59: http://www.fraserinstitute.org/COMMERCE.WEB/product_files/ImmigrationPolicyTerroristThreatCanadaUS.pdf.

78 CCR, 'Closing the Front Door on Refugees: Report on the First Year of the Safe Third Country Agreement,' 29 December 2005: www.web.ca/ccr/closingdoordec05.pdf; Harvard Law Student Advocates for Human Rights, et al., 'Bordering on Failure.' The impact of this has been felt disproportionately by Colombian refugee applicants.

79 Immigration and Refugee Board of Canada, 'Information Sheets: Refugee Claims': http://www.irb-cisr.gc.ca/en/media/infosheets/rpdfacts_e.htm.

80 CCR, 'Less Safe Than Ever,' discusses the return to torture from Guantanamo and renditions to secret detention facilities as two examples.Harvard Law Student Advocates for Human Rights, et al., 'Bordering on Failure.'

81 This, they claim, was also true of other groups of refugees, noting in particular Colombian refugee claims. Between 2003 and 2005, approximately 80 per cent of all Colombian refugee applicants received protected status in Canada as compared to between 28 and 45 per cent of Colombian applicants who were determined in the United States.Sonia Akibo-Bets, 'The Canada–U.S.Safe Third Country Agreement: Why the U.S. Is Not a Safe Haven for Refugee Women Asserting Gender-Based Asylum Claims,' *Windsor Review of Legal and Social Issues* 105 (2005).

82 *Canadian Council for Refugees, Canadian Council of Churches, Amnesty International and John Doe v The Queen*, Federal Court of Canada, (Justice Phelen), 29 November 2007, NO. IMM-7818–05: http://decisions.fct-cf.gc.ca/en/2007/2007fc1262/2007fc1262.html; and *The Queen v Canadian Council for Refugees, Canadian Council of Churches, Amnesty International and John Doe*, Federal Court of Appeal, 27 June 2008, 2008 FCA 229: http://decisions.fca-caf.gc.ca/en/2008/2008fca229/2008fca229.html. Leave to appeal to the Supreme Court of Canada was denied by the court in February 2009.

83 The petition was found at http://www.ccrweb.ca/IACHRpet.PDF.

84 UNHCR, 'UNHCR Expresses Deep Concern over Canada's Continued Policy of Direct Backs,' 10 October 2007: http://www.newswire.ca/en/releases/archive/October2007/10/c2460.html.

85 See CCR, 'Refugee Appeal Division Backgrounder': http://www.ccrweb.ca/RADpage/PAGE0001.HTM; see also CCR, 'The Refugee Appeal: Is No One Listening?' 31March 2005: www.ccrweb.ca/refugeeappeal.pdf.

86 Ibid. For the critique by the Inter-American Commission on Human Rights, see 'Report on the Situation of Human Rights of Asylum Seekers within the Canadian Refugee Determination System,' February 2000: http://www.cidh.org/countryrep/Canada2000en/table-of-contents.htm.

87 Parliamentary Standing Committee on Citizenship and Immigration, 'Committee Calls for the Implementation of the Refugee Appeal Division of the Immigration and Refugee Board,' 17 December 2004: http://cmte.parl.gc.ca/cmte/CommitteePublication.aspx?COM=8975&SourceId=96506.

88 Peter Showler, 'A Primer for the Immigration Minister: Refugee Laws Are Not the Problem,' *Globe and Mail*, 27 April 2005: A21.

89 For the government perspective, see 'The Selection Process for Governor in Council Appointments to the Immigration and Refugee Board of Canada': www.irb-cisr.gc.ca/en/about/employment/members/process_e.htm. For critiques, see Joan Bryden, 'Critics Slam New Selection Process for Refugee Adjudicators,' *Toronto Star*, 9 July 2007; Ontario Council of Agencies Serving Immigrants (OCASI), 'Groups Dismayed over Politicization of the

Appointments to the Immigration and Refugee Board,' 27 February 2007: http://www.ocasi.org/index.php?qid=922.

90 'Tories Act on Refugee Board Vacancies,' *Toronto Star*, 25 June 2008.

91 IPRA Regulations, s.223–6. As previously, however, the legislation provided for different types of removal orders.These included the relatively milder departure order, under which a person could still be admitted to Canada once removed; the more stringent exclusion order, where written permission to return was necessary within a one-to-two-year period after the order was made; and the most severe, a deportation order after which a person must have written authorization to return to Canada at any time after the enforcement of the order.

92 IRPA, ss.33–42.

93 Ibid., s.36(1).

94 Ibid., s.36(2).

95 *Medovarski v Canada (Minister of Citizenship and Immigration); Esteban v Canada (Minister of Citizenship and Immigration)*, [2005] 2 S.C.R. 539, 2005 SCC 51 at para. 10.

96 Those who were prevented from appealing a removal order to the Immigration and Refugee Board still had a right to seek a reversal of the order by the minister on the basis of humanitarian and compassionate grounds. Unlike the review by the IRB, however, no oral hearing before the minister or designate was required.

97 Bill C-44, see above, chapter 10.

98 IRPA, ss.77–82. For a complete discussion of this process see Barbara Jackman, 'National Security under the Immigration and Refugee Protection Act,' unpublished paper (March 2005): 10–17. See also Barbara Jackman, 'One Measure of Justice in Canada: Judicial Protection for Non-Citizens,' speech presented to the Canadian Bar Association, Banff (April 2005): 7. According to the Federal Court of Canada the 'reasonable' test requires a 'bona fide belief in a serious possibility based on credible evidence.' See *Chiau v. Canada (Minister of Citizenship and Immigration)*, [1998] 2 F.C. 642.

99 IRPA, s.84 (2). Kent Roach and Michael Code, 'The Role of the Independent Lawyer and Security Certificates,' *Criminal Law Quarterly* 52 (2006): 94, 96–7. For a similar argument see Hamish Stewart, 'Is Indefinite Detention of Terrorist Suspects Really Constitutional?' *University of New Brunswick Law Journal* 54 (Fall 2005): 242.

100 IRPA s.84(2). See also Jackman, 'National Security under the Immigration and Refugee Protection Act,' 15, and Jackman, 'One Measure of Justice in Canada.' In 2006 and 2007 a number of persons detained for more than six years on security certificates went on a prolonged hunger strike,

prompting an Amnesty International appeal, 16 February, 2007: http://www
.amnesty.ca/take_action/actions/canada_certificate_detainees.php.

101 Kent Roach, 'Canada's Response to Terrorism,' in *Global Anti-Terrorism Law
and Policy*, ed. Kent Roach et al. (Cambridge: Cambridge University Press,
2005), 521.

102 Barbara Jackman, 'Charter Rights to Privacy and Security: The Impact of
International Terrorism and Globalization, Impact on Charter Rights in
Immigration Law,' paper presented to the Ontario Bar Association Fourth
Annual Charter Conference, 30 September 2005. Section 83.01(1)(b)(ii)
(A) removes acts that are the result of advocacy, protest, dissent or stoppage
of work not intended to result in the intimidation of the public or a
segment of the public or compelling a person, a government, or a domestic
or international organization to do or refrain from doing any act.

103 *Suresh v Canada (Minister of Citizenship and Immigration)*, [2002] 1 S.C.R. 3.

104 Ibid., para. 88.

105 Lorne Waldman, 'National Security: Have We Gone Too Far? Part I,'
Canada's Immigration and Citizenship Bulletin (July 2004): 1–2. Two of the
cases he refers to are *Henrie v Canada (Security Intelligence Review Committee)*
(1988), 53 D.L.R. (4th) 568 (F.C.T.D.), affd 88 D.L.R. (4th) 575 (F.C.A.) and
Chiarelli v Canada (Minister of Employment and Immigration), [1992] 1 S.C.R.
711. This perspective is also endorsed in Craig Forcese, 'Through a Glass
Darkly: The Role and Review of National Security Concepts in Canadian
Law,' *Alberta Law Review* 43/4 (May 2006): 990; Nicholas Daube, 'Charkaoui:
The Impact of Structure on Judicial Activism in Times of Crisis, *Journal of
Law and Equality* 4/2 (Fall 2005): 105, 111–15.

106 The Commission of Inquiry into the Actions of Canadian Officials in
Relation to Maher Arar, *Report of the Events Relating to Maher Arar: Analysis
and Recommendations (2006)* ('Arar Inquiry'), at 30.

107 The Honourable Frank Iacobucci, Q.C., Commissioner, *Internal Inquiry
into the Actions of Canadian Officials in Relation to Abdullah Almalki, Ahmed
Abou-Elmaati and Muayyed Nureddin*: http://www.iacobucciinquiry.ca/en/
documents/final-report.htm; 'Iacobucci Releases Report on Canadian
Citizens Detained Abroad,' *Globe and Mail*, 21 October 2008; see also Kerry
Pither, *Dark Days: The Story of Four Canadians Tortured in the Name of Fighting
Terror* (Toronto: Viking Canada, 2008), which provides an analysis and
timelines of the experiences of the men with the Canadian Security
Intelligence Service, the RCMP, and Syrian military intelligence.

108 See *Re Charkaoui* [2007] SCC 9.

109 Ron Gillies, 'Canada's Lower House Passes Anti-terror Law Allowing
Indefinite Detention of Suspects,' Associated Press, 6 February 2008.

110 This change was introduced following a highly publicized case of adoptive parents who returned their nine-year-old adopted child to Romania five months after having adopted her. The Romanian authorities did not recognize the child as a citizen (because the official adoption papers indicated she was born in Canada), and because the child had not yet been naturalized in Canada, she became a stateless person. As stateless, she was denied the right to an education and health care. Consequently, according to a lawsuit she later brought against her Canadian parents, the Ontario and Canadian governments, and the airlines that flew her back fourteen years later, she was confined to a life of poverty: 'Romanian Suing Canadian Couple over Adoption,' Canadian Press, 17 February 2005. The amendments to the Citizenship Act (Bill C-14) that came into force in December 2007 facilitate the granting of citizenship for children adopted overseas by Canadian parents by not requiring the adoptees to establish permanent residence first.

111 One line of reasoning maintained that actual physical presence in the country was necessary to meet the residency requirement, while another line recognized exceptions for those who were not in the country for reasons of employment yet who retained a substantial connection to Canada: *Pourghasemi Re* (1993), 62 FTR 122, 19 *Imm. L.R.* (2d) 259; *Papadogiorgakis Re* [1978] 2 FC 208; and *Koo Re*, [1993] 1 FC 286.

112 Bill C-63 was introduced in December 1998. Bill C-16 was introduced less than one year later, in November 1999, and passed its third reading in the House of Commons in May 2000 before dying as the result of an election call and the dissolution of Parliament. Bill C-18 was introduced during the second session of the 37th Parliament (September 2002) and also died when Parliament was prorogued in late 2003.

113 Bill C-18, section 7(1)(b), to deal with sojourners or 'astronaut' immigrants who maintain Canadian citizenship without any substantial physical connection to the country. Critics claimed, however, that it was too restrictive, for it would also unjustly exclude individuals with valid reasons for being outside Canada, such as to accompany a citizen spouse or partner employed overseas in the public government or military service. Canadian Bar Association, National Citizenship and Immigration Law Section, 'Submission on Bill C-18 Citizenship of Canada Act,' November 2002, 13: www.cba.org/CBA/pdf/c18submission.pdf. Refugee advocates complained that the proposals unfairly discriminated against protected persons by not fully counting time spent in Canada from the moment they received their protected status. Mosaic, 'Submissions on Bill C-18 The Citizenship of Canada Act,' submitted to the House of Commons Select

Standing Committee on Citizenship and Immigration, 14 February 2003: www.mosaicbc.com/Bill%20C-18%20submissionsI.pdf.

114 Bill C-18, sections 21 and 22. These provisions were criticized for being too vague, for not sufficiently defining the extent of ministerial power, and for not providing a standard to review the exercise of ministerial discretion. Mosaic, 'Submissions on Bill C-18'; CCR, 'Comments to the Standing Committee on Citizenship and Immigration on Bill C- 18,' 21 November 2002: www.web.net/%7Eccr/c-18.htm.

115 Bill C-18, section 28(c) and (d). Refugee advocates pointed out that this could have an unjust effect on refugees who might well have fled from false accusations of serious crimes, while the Canadian Bar Association similarly noted that an unsolved criminal charge against a person abroad could stem from 'dubious circumstances in a jurisdiction of dubious fairness.' CCR, 'Comments to the Standing Committee'; Canadian Bar Association, 'Submission on Bill C-18,' 27.

116 Such as for being inadmissible at the time of entry and/or for posing a threat to national security, having violated human or international rights, or being engaged in organized crime. CCR, 'Comments to the Standing Committee,' 23.

117 House of Commons Standing Committee on Citizenship and Immigration, 10th Report, *Citizenship Revocation: A Question of Due Process and Respecting Charter Rights*, June 2005: http://cmte.parl.gc.ca/Content/HOC/committee/381/cimm/reports/rp1901753/cimmrp10/03-cov2-e.htm; House of Commons Standing Committee on Citizenship and Immigration, 12th Report, *Updating Canada's Citizenship Laws: It's Time*, October 2005: http://cmte.parl.gc.ca/Content/HOC/committee/381/cimm/reports/rp2014194/cimmrp12/05-hon-e.htm.

118 House of Commons Standing Committee on Citizenship and Immigration, 10th Report, *Citizenship Revocation*.

119 A partial move was taken in 2005 with Bill S-2, which amended some aspects of the Citizenship Act in a way that restored citizenship to those who had lost it because their parent had taken up citizenship in another country or renounced Canadian citizenship. CIC, *Amendment to Section 11 of the Citizenship Act*, 28 March 2006: www.cic.gc.ca/english/resources/manuals/bulletins/ob020.asp.

120 For more detail on the 'lost Canadians,' see Don Chapman, 'Lost Canadians: Nine Categories of Citizens,' 1 February 2007: www.lostcanadian.com/main.asp.

121 CBC, 'In Depth: Lost Canadians,' March 2007: www.cbc.ca/news/background/lostcanadians/index.html.

122 For more information on the categories of lost Canadians see Don
    Chapman, 'Lost Canadians'.

123 *Benner v Canada (Secretary of State)*, [1997] 1 S.C.R. 358

124 For a comprehensive review of the legislation, including background, its
    coverage, and commentary, see Penny Becklumb, 'Bill C-37: An Act to
    Amend the Citizenship Act,' Legislative Summaries, Library of Parliament:
    http:/www.parl.gc.ca.

125 Particularly contentious was the provision that would deny Canadian
    citizenship to children born outside the country to Canadian parents who
    were also born abroad. CCR, 'Comments to the Standing Committee on
    Citizenship and Immigration on Bill C-37 (An Act to Amend the Citizenship
    Act),' 11 February 2008; 'Critics Denounce Citizenship Bill,' *The Gazette*
    (Montreal), 11 April 2008.

126 For example, the Global Commission on International Migration was
    launched by the United Nations secretary general and a number of govern-
    ments, on 9 December 2003, to provide the framework for the formulation
    of a comprehensive and coherent global response to the issue of inter-
    national migration. See its report, summarizing a number of independent
    studies, 'Migration in an Interconnected World: New Directions for Action,'
    October 2005, at http://www.gcim.org/attachements/GCIM%20Report%20
    Annex%20II.pdf.

127 See, for example, Philippe Legrain, *Immigrants: Your Country Needs Them*
    (London: Little, Brown, 2006), for a thorough discussion of the economic
    benefits of immigration. See also, Michael Trebilcock and Matthew Sudak,
    'The Political Economy of Emigration and Immigration,' *New York University
    Law Review* 81/1 (April 2006): 234–93; Howard Chang, 'The Economic
    Impact of International Labor Migration: Recent Estimates and Policy
    Implications,' *Temple Political and Civil Rights Law Review* 16 (2007): 321.

128 Legrain, *Immigrants*, 65, and Chang, 'Economic Impact,' 4. See also Bob
    Hamilton and John Whalley, 'Efficiency and Distributional Implications of
    Global Restrictions on Labour Mobility: Calculations and Policy
    Implications,' *Journal of Development Economics* 14/1–2 (1984): 61–75; and
    Jonathon Moses and Bjørn Letnes, 'The Economic Costs to International
    Labor Restrictions: Revisiting the Empirical Discussion,' *World Development*
    32/10 (2004): 1610.

129 See chapters 3, 4, 6, and 7 in Legrain, *Immigrants*.

130 Chang, 'Economic Impact,' 10.

131 Ibid., and Legrain, *Immigrants*, 66–79.

132 Trebilcock and Sudak, 'Political Economy of Emigration and Immigration,'
    269–71.

133 See for example, Abdurrahman Aydemir and Mikal Skuterod. 'Explaining the Deteriorating Entry Earnings of Canada's Immigrant Cohorts: 1966–2000,' research paper series, catalogue no. 11F0019MIE – No. 225 (Ottawa: Statistics Canada, Analytical Studies Branch, 2004). Other studies with similar results include Collacott, 'Canada's Immigration Policy: The Need for Major Reform'; Diane Francis, *Immigration: The Economic Case* (Toronto: Key Porter Books, 2002); Marc Frenette and Rene Morisette, 'Will They Ever Converge? Earnings of Immigrant and Canadian-born Workers over the Last Two Decades,' research paper series, catalogue no. 11F0019Mie-No. 215 (Ottawa: Statistics Canada, Analytical Studies Branch, 2003); Derek Hum and Wayne Simpson, 'Economic Integration of Immigrants to Canada: A Short Survey,' *Canadian Journal of Urban Research* 13/1 (Summer 2004): 46–61; Jeffrey G. Reitz, 'Immigrant Skill Utilization in the Canadian Labour Market: Implications of Human Capital Research,' *Journal of International Migration and Integration* 2/3 (2001): 347–78 and, also by Reitz, 'Immigrant Success in the Knowledge Economy: Institutional Change and the Immigrant Experience in Canada, 1970–1995,' *Journal of Social Issues* 57/3 (2001): 579–613; Daniel Stoffman, *Who Gets In: What's Wrong with Canada's Immigration Program and How to Fix It* (Toronto: McFarlane, Walter and Ross, 2002); Herbert Grubel, ed., *The Effects of Mass Immigration on Canadian Living Standards and Society* (Vancouver: Fraser Institute, 2009).

134 CIC, *Annual Report to Parliament, 2006,* and *2007.*

135 This represented a 3 per cent increase from the previous year, largely due to the 19 per cent increase in the number of temporary foreign workers admitted. CIC, *Facts and Figures,* 2007, Foreword.

136 Peter Li, *Destination Canada: Immigration Debates and Issues* (Toronto: Oxford University Press, 2003), 69. Therefore, whereas there were potentially 5.8 working people to share the tax burden of one elderly person in 1991, Li argues that number could be reduced to 3.7 in 2021 and 2.7 in 2041 if current demographic trends continue.

137 Ibid., 77; and see Watt, Krywulak, and Kitagawa, *Renewing Immigration.*

138 Legrain, *Immigrants,* 112.

139 Grubel, 'Immigration and the Welfare State in Canada.' This argument was disputed by Peter Li, *Destination Canada,* 95, where he argued that 'immigrants contribute taxes that exceed the costs of social assistance and social benefits they receive.'

140 Yvan Guillemette and William B.P. Robson, 'No Elixir of Youth: Immigration Cannot Keep Canada Young,' C.D. Howe Institute Backgrounder (Toronto: C.D. Howe Institute, September 2006). See also Alan G. Green, 'What Is the Role of Immigration in Canada's Future?' in *Canadian Immigration Policy for*

the 21st Century, ed. C. Beach, et al. (Kingston: John Deutsch Institute for the Study of Economic Policy, Queen's University, published in cooperation with McGill-Queen's University Press, 2003), 42–4.

141 The undesirability and infeasibility of large increases in annual admissions was further argued in Grubel, ed., *The Effects of Mass Immigration on Canadian Living Standards and Society.*

142 David K. Foot, *Boom, Bust and Echo: How to Profit from the Coming Demographic Shift* (Toronto: Macfarlane, Walter and Ross, 1996).

143 Martin Collacott, 'Is There Really a Looming Labour Shortage in Canada, and If There Is Can Increased Immigration Fill the Gap?' in *Immigration and Refugee Law*, ed. Carasco, et al., 328–33. Full text available at: http://www.fraserinstitute.ca/admin/books/files/lbrshortage.pdf. See also Collacott, 'Canada's Immigration Policy: The Need For Major Reform.

144 Joseph Schaafsma and Arthur Sweetman, 'Immigrant Earnings: Age at Immigration Matters,' *Canadian Journal of Economics* 34/4 (November 2001): 1066–99.

145 'Immigrant Skills "Squandered", Volpe Urges Businesses to Hire More Newcomers to Canada,' *Toronto Star*, 9 February 2005.

146 Canadian Chamber of Commerce, 'Social Policy: Settlement and Integration Programs for Immigrants: Capitalizing on Canada's Skilled Immigrants,' 2005: http://www.chamber.ca/cmslib/general/S054.pdf.

147 Christopher Worswick, 'Immigrants' Declining Earnings: Reasons and Remedies,' C.D. Howe Institute Backgrounder 81 (Toronto: C.D. Howe Institute, 2004).

148 Ibid.

149 Beginning in the 1990s, the court has often emphasized the right of the legislature to confer discretionary powers on the minister and has accorded deference to those decisions where the minister has comparative expertise, such as on the criteria for admission and removal of non-citizens and the assessment of risks to national security or threats to life upon removal. Ninette Kelley, 'Rights in the Balance: Non-Citizens and State Sovereignty under the Charter,' in *The Unity of Public Law*, ed. David Dyzenhaus (Oxford and Portland, OR: Hart Publishing, 2004), 277.

150 Above note 133, and Daniel Stoffman, 'Truths and Myths about Immigration,' in *Immigration Policy and the Terrorist Threat in Canada*, ed. Moens and Collacott, 3. Studies by Miles Corak, however, showed that the degree of educational mobility for second-generation Canadian children who grew up in the 1980s and attained young adulthood in the new millennium was no different from that of those raised in the 1950s to 1970s. In addition, he found that adult earnings were not strongly tied to parental

earnings, whether among immigrants or the population at large. At the same time, he observed that challenges remain, particularly with respect to sons of immigrants from the Caribbean, West Africa, and some Latin American countries. Miles Corak, 'Immigration in the Long Run: The Education and Earnings Mobility of Second Generation Canadians,' *IRPP Choices* 14/13 (October 2008) 4–26: http://www.irpp.org/choices/archive/vol12no1.pdf.

151 *Mack v Canada (Attorney General)*, (2001), 55 O.R. (3d) 113, upheld on appeal, 2002 CanLII 45062 (ON C.A.). For an analysis of these decisions as well as the window they provide on the larger legal, political, and philosophical issues related to such claims of racism, see *Calling Power to Account: Law, Reparations and the Chinese Canadian Head Tax Case*, ed. David Dyzenhaus and Mayo Moran (Toronto : University of Toronto Press, 2005).

152 Canadian Chinese National Council, 'Chinese Head Tax and Exclusion Act: CCNC Redress Campaign': http://www.ccnc.ca/sectionEntry.php?entryID=10&type=Advocacy; Canadian Broadcasting Corporation, 'Pay Blacks and Chinese for Past Racism UN Suggests,' 12 March 2004: http://www.cbc.ca/canada/story/2004/03/12/un_pay040312.html.

153 James Bissett, 'Security Threats in Immigration and Refugee Policies,' in *Immigration Policy and the Terrorist Threat in Canada*, ed. Moens and Collacott, 82.

154 Ninette Kelley, 'International Refugee Protection Challenges and Opportunities,' *International Journal of Refugee Law* 19 (October 2007); 401–39.

155 UN Convention Against Transnational Organized Crime, 154: (1) The Protocol to Prevent, Suppress and Punish Trafficking in Persons, Especially Women and Children, Supplementing the United Nations Convention Against Transnational Organized Crime, and (2) The Protocol Against Smuggling of Migrants by Land Sea and Air, Supplementing the United Nations Convention Against Transnational Organized Crime: http://untreaty.un.org/English/TreatyEvent2003/index.htm. For a full discussion of the origins and development of the convention and accompanying protocols see Anne Gallagher, 'Human Rights and the New UN Protocols on Trafficking and Migrant Smuggling: A Preliminary Analysis,' *Human Rights Quarterly* 23/4 (2001): 975.

156 Crépeau and Nakache, 'Controlling Irregular Migration in Canada.'

157 For articles on Canada–U.S. cooperation, see Connie Smith, 'Closing the Door on Immigrants,' *Capital News Online* 1/10 (18 January 2002): www.carleton.ca/jmc/cnews/18012002/connections/c1.shtml. See also Tanya

Chute, 'Globalization, Security and Exclusion,' CRS Working Paper Series No. 3 (Toronto: Centre for Refugee Studies, York University, 2005): www .yorku.ca/crs; Peter Andreas, 'A Tale of Two Borders: The U.S.–Canada and the U.S.–Mexico Lines after 9–11'; and Stephen Clarkson, 'The View from the Attic: Toward a Gated Community?' in *The Re-Bordering of North America: Integration and Exclusion in a New Security Context*, ed. Peter Andreas and Thomas Biersteker (New York: Routledge, 2003), 9–10, 81–2.

Chapter 12 Conclusion

1 Joel P. Trachtman, *The International Law of Economic Migration: Toward the Fourth Freedom* (Kalamazoo, MI: W.E. Upjohn Institute of Employment Research, 2009).
2 *Singh v Minister of Employment and Immigration*, [1985] 1 S.C.R. 177.
3 Jane Badets and Tina Chui, *Canada's Changing Immigrant Population* (Ottawa: Statistics Canada, 1994), 6; Michael Trebilcock and Mathew Sudak, 'The Political Economy of Emigration and Immigration,' *New York University Law Review* 81 (2006): at 240.
4 See Economic Council of Canada, *Economic and Social Impacts of Immigration* (Ottawa: The Council, 1991), 9.
5 Many of the historical accounts of specific immigration movements cited throughout this book, as well as those which focus on specific interest groups, make this very clear. See also more generally, J.L. Granatstein, Irving Abella, T.W. Acheson, David Bercuson, R. Craig Brown, and H. Blair Neatby, *Nation: Canada since Confederation*, 3rd ed. (Toronto: McGraw-Hill Ryerson, 1990), 337.
6 *Canada Year Book, 1930* (Ottawa: King's Printer), 165, 166.
7 Badets and Chui, *Canada's Changing Immigrant Population*, 13; Statistics Canada, 'Immigration in Canada: A Portrait of the Foreign-born Population,' *2006 Census*: www12.statcan.ca/english/census06/analysis/ immcit/index.cfm.
8 Statistics Canada, 'Canada's Ethnocultural Portrait: The Changing Mosaic," catalogue no. 96F0030XIE2001008, 6. Online: http://www12.statcan.ca/ english/census01/products/analytic/companion/etoimm/contents.cfm; Michael Adams, *Unlikely Utopia: The Surprising Triumph of Canadian Pluralism* (Toronto: Viking Canada, 2007), 57.
9 Granatstein et al., *Nation*, 338.
10 See Trebilcock and Sudak, 'Political Economy of Emigration and Immigration,'; Howard Chang, 'The Economic Impact of International Labor Migration: Recent Estimates and Policy Implications,' *Temple Political*

and Civil Rights Law Review 16 (2007): 321; Philippe Legrain, *Immigrants: Your Country Needs Them* (London: Little, Brown, 2006), chs 3, 4, 5, 6, 7.

11 See e.g., Robert Putnam, 'E. Pluribus Unum: Diversity and Community in the Twenty-first Century,' The 2006 Johan Skytte Prize Lecture, *Scandinavian Political Studies* 30/2 (2007); Legrain, *Immigrants*, chs 5, 11, 13, 14.

12 Adams, *Unlikely Utopia*, 13, 14.

13 Ibid., 17.

14 See Jeffrey Reitz, 'Immigrant Success in the Knowledge Economy: Institutional Change and the Immigrant Experience in Canada, 1970–1995,' *Journal of Social Issues* 57 (2001): 579–613; Reitz, 'Immigrant Employment Success in Canada Part I: Individual and Contextual Causes,' *International Migration and Integration* 8 (2007): 11–36; Reitz, "Immigrant Employment Success Canada Part II: Understanding the Decline,' *International Migration and Integration* 8 (2007): 37–62; Reitz, 'Tapping Immigrants' Skills: New Directions for Canadian Immigration Policy in the Knowledge Economy,' *Immigration and Refugee Policy Choices* (February 2005) (Institute for Research on Public Policy, Montreal); Christopher Worswick, 'Immigrants' Declining Earnings: Reasons and Remedies,' C.D. Howe Institute Backgrounder No. 81 (Toronto: C.D. Howe Institute, April 2004). For a more optimistic view of the empirical evidence on the economic performance of recent immigrants, particularly second-generation immigrants, see Miles Corak, 'Immigration in the Long Run: The Education and Earnings Mobility of Second-Generation Canadians,' *Immigration and Refugee Policy Choices* 14/13 (October 2008) (Institute for Research on Public Policy, Montreal); and see more generally, Charles Beach, Alan Green, and Jeffrey Reitz, eds, *Canadian Immigration Policy for the 21st Century* (Montreal and Kingston: McGill-Queen's University Press, 2003).

15 For a defence of a restrictive communitarian approach to immigration, see Peter Brimelow, *Alien Nation: Commonsense about America's Immigration Disaster* (New York: Random House, 1995).

16 See Will Kymlicka, *Multicultural Citizenship* (Oxford: The Clarendon Press, 1995).

Select Bibliography

Abella, Irving. A *Coat of Many Colours: Two Centuries of Jewish Life in Canada*. Toronto: Lester & Orpen Dennys, 1990.

– *Nationalism, Communism, and Canadian Labour: The CIO, the Communist Party, and the Canadian Congress of Labour, 1935–1956*. Toronto: University of Toronto Press, 1973.

Abella, Irving, and Harold Troper. *None Is Too Many: Canada and the Jews of Europe, 1933–1948*. Toronto: Lester & Orpen Dennys, 1982.

– '"The line must be drawn somewhere": Canada and Jewish Refugees, 1933–1939,' in *A Nation of Immigrants: Women, Workers and Communities in Canadian History, 1840s–1960s*, edited by Franca Iacovetta. Toronto: University of Toronto Press, 1998.

Acheson, T.W. 'The Changing Social Origins of the Canadian Industrial Elite.' In *Enterprise and National Development: Essays in Canadian Business and Economic History*, edited by B. Porter and R. Cuff. Toronto: Hakkert, 1973.

Adachi, Ken. *The Enemy That Never Was: A History of the Japanese Canadians*. Toronto: McClelland & Stewart, 1976.

Adams, Michael. *Unlikely Utopia: The Surprising Triumph of Canadian Pluralism*. Toronto: Viking Canada, 2007.

Adelman, Howard. *Canada and the Indochinese Refugees*. Regina, SA: L.A. Weigl Educational Associates, 1982.

– 'Canadian Policy on Indochinese Refugees.' In *Southeast Asian Exodus: From Tradition to Resettlement*, edited by Elliot L. Tepper. Ottawa: Canadian Asian Studies Association, Carleton University, 1980.

– 'Canadian Refugee Policy in the Postwar Period: An Analysis.' In *Refugee Policy: Canada and the United States*, edited by H. Adelman. Toronto: York Lanes, 1991.

- 'The Policy Maker and the Advocate: Case Studies in Refugee Policy.' In *Making Knowledge Count: Advocacy and Social Science*, edited by Peter Harries-Jones. Montreal: McGill-Queen's University Press, 1991.
- ed. *Refugee Policy: Canada and the United States*. Toronto: York Lanes, 1991.

Agricultural Workers Program, Regulatory and Policy Framework, Farm Industry Level Employment Practices and the Future of the Program Under Unionization." Prepared for the North-South Institute. Online: http://www.nsi-ins.ca/english/pdf/exec_sum_verma.pdf.

Ahenakew, Edward. *Voices of the Plains Cree*. Toronto: McClelland & Stewart, 1973.

Ajzenat, J., ed. *Canada's Founding Debates*. Toronto: University of Toronto Press, 2003.

Akbari, Ather, and Don DeVoretz. 'The Sustainability of Foreign Born Labour and Canadian Production circa 1980.' *Canadian Journal of Economics* 25 (1992): 604–14.

Akibo-Bets, S. 'The Canada-U.S Safe Third Country Agreement: Why The U.S. Is Not a Safe Haven for Refugee Women Asserting Gender-Based Asylum Claims.' *Windsor Review of Legal and Social Issues* 105 (2005).

Alboim, Naomi, and Maytree. 'Fixing Canada's Economic Immigration Policies.' Maytree Foundation. July 2009. Online: http.//www.maytree.com/policy.

Alexander, Ken, and Avis Glaze. *Towards Freedom: The African-Canadian Experience*. Toronto: Umbrella Press, 1996.

Allyn, Nathaniel Constantine. *European Immigration into Canada, 1946–1951*. Toronto: McClelland & Stewart, 1977.

Anctil, Pierre. *Le Rendez-vous manqué: Les Juifs de Montréal face au Québec de l'entre-deux-guerres*. Quebec: Institut Québécois de Recherche sur la Culture, 1988.

Anderson, Kay J. *Vancouver's Chinatown: Racial Discourse in Canada, 1875–1980*. Montreal: McGill-Queen's University Press, 1991.

Andracki, Stanislaw. *Immigration of Orientals into Canada, with Special Reference to the Chinese*. New York: Arno Press, 1978.

Andreas, P. 'A Tale of Two Borders: The U.S.–Canada and the U.S.–Mexico Lines After 9-11.' Working paper 77, The Center for Comparative Immigration Studies, University of California, San Diego, May 2003. Online: http://www.ccis-ucsd.org/publications/wrkg77.pdf.

Angus, H.F. 'Canadian Immigration: The Law and Its Administration.' In *The Legal Status of Aliens in Pacific Countries*, edited by N. MacKenzie. Toronto: Oxford University Press, 1937.
- 'The Future of Immigration in Canada.' *Canadian Journal of Economics and Political Science* 12 (1946): 379–86.
- 'Immigration.' *International Journal* 1 (1946): 65–7.
- 'The Legal Status in British Columbia of Oriental Races and Their Descendants.' *Canadian Bar Review* 9/1 (January 1931): 1–12.

- 'The Status of Aliens in Canada.' In Canadian Political Science Association, *Papers and Proceedings of the Sixth Annual Meeting*, vol. 6. Kingston: Jackson, 1934.
Angus, Ian. *Canadian Bolsheviks*. Montreal: Vanguard, 1981.
Anonymous. 'The Boat People: A Left Perspective.' *Canadian Dimension* 14 (1979): 3–5.
Archer, Dave. 'Labour's Concern with Immigration.' *Canadian Labour* 5/7–8 (July/August 1960): 20–2.
Atkinson, Michael M., ed. *Governing Canada: Institutions and Public Policy*. Toronto: Harcourt Brace, 1983.
Auditor General of Canada. *Annual Report 2000*. Chapter 3 'Citizenship and Immigration Canada: The Economic Component of the Canadian Immigration Program.' http://www.oag-bvg.gc.ca/domino/reports.nsf/html/0003ce.html.
Avakumovic, Ivan. *The Communist Party in Canada: A History*. Toronto: McClelland & Stewart, 1975.
Avery, Donald H. 'Canada's Response to European Refugees, 1939–1945: The Security Dimension.' In *On Guard for Thee: War, Ethnicity and the Canadian State*, edited by Norman Hillmer, Bohdan Kordan, and Lubomyr Luciuk. Ottawa: Canadian Committee for the History of the Second World War, 1988.
- 'Canadian Immigration Policy and the Alien Question.' PhD thesis, University of Western Ontario, London, 1973.
- 'Canadian Immigration Policy and the "Foreign" Navvy, 1896–1914.' Canadian Historical Association *Historical Papers* (1972): 140–1.
- 'Continental European Immigrant Workers in Canada, 1896–1919: From "Stalwart Peasants" to "Radical Proletariat".' *Canadian Review of Sociology and Anthropology* 12/ 1 (1988): 53–64.
- *'Dangerous Foreigners': European Immigrant Workers and Labour Radicalism in Canada, 1896–1932*. Toronto: McClelland & Stewart, 1979.
- 'Divided Loyalties: The Ukrainian Left and the Canadian State.' In *Canada's Ukrainians: Negotiating an Identity*, edited by Lubomyr Luciuk and Stella Hryniuk. Toronto: University of Toronto Press and Ukrainian Canadian Centennial Committee, 1991.
- 'Ethnic and Class Tensions in Canada, 1918–20: Anglo-Canadians and the Alien Worker.' In *Loyalties in Conflict: Ukrainians in Canada During the Great War*, edited by Frances Swyripa and John Herd Thompson. Edmonton: Canadian Institute of Ukrainian Studies, University of Alberta, 1983.
- *Reluctant Host: Canada's Response to Immigrant Workers, 1896–1994*. Toronto: McClelland & Stewart, 1995.
Avery, Donald H., and J.K. Fedorowicz. *The Poles in Canada*. Ottawa: Canadian Historical Association, 1982.

Aydemir, M., and Mikal Skuterod. 'Explaining the Deteriorating Entry Earnings of Canada's Immigrant Cohorts: 1966–2000.' Research paper series. Catalogue no. 11F0019MIE – No. 225. Ottawa: Statistics Canada, Analytical Studies Branch, 2004.

Backhouse, Constance. 'White Female Help and Chinese-Canadian Employers: Race, Class, Gender and Law in the Case of Yee Clun, 1924.' *Canadian Ethnic Studies* 26/3 (1994): 34–52.

Badets, Janet, and Tina Chui. *Canada's Changing Immigration Population.* Ottawa: Statistics Canada, 1994.

Bagnell, Kenneth. *Canadese: A Portrait of the Italian Canadians.* Toronto: Macmillan, 1989.

– *The Little Immigrants: The Orphans Who Came to Canada.* Toronto: Macmillan, 1980.

Baker, Richard P. 'The Adaptation and Ethnicity of Polish Immigrants in Toronto: The Solidarity Wave.' *Canadian Ethnic Studies* 21/3 (1989): 74–90.

Barber, Marilyn. 'The Women Ontario Welcomed: Immigrant Domestics from Ontario Homes, 1870–1930.' In *The Neglected Majority: Essays in Canadian Women's History, vol. 2,* edited by Alison Prentice and Susan Trofimenkoff. Toronto: McClelland & Stewart, 1985.

Basok, Tanya. *Tortillas and Tomatoes: Transmigrant Mexican Harversters in Canada.* McGill-Queen's University Press, Montreal & Kingston, 2002.

Bassler, Gerhard P. 'The Enemy Alien Experience in Newfoundland, 1914–1918.' *Canadian Ethnic Studies* 20/3 (1988):42–62.

Bausenhart, Werner. *German Immigration and Assimilation in Ontario, 1783–1918.* Toronto: Legas, 1989.

Beach, Charles M., Alan Green, and Jeffrey G. Reitz, eds. *Canadian Immigration Policy for the 21st Century.* Kingston: John Deutsch Institute for the Study of Economic Policy, Queen's University, 2003.

Beach, Charles M., Alan G. Green, and Christopher Worswicki. 'Improving Canada's Immigration Policy.' C.D. Howe Institute, e-brief, 23 September 2009. http://www.cdhowe.org/pdf/ebrief_87.pdf.

Beal, Bob, and Rob Macleod. *Prairie Fire: The 1885 North-West Rebellion.* Edmonton: Hurtig, 1984.

Bean, Charles M., and Alan C. Green. *Policy Forum on the Role of Immigration in Canada's Future.* Kingston, ON: John Deutche Institute for the Study of Economic Policy, 1988.

Beaujot, Roderic P. *Growth and Dualism: The Demographic Development of Canadian Society.* Toronto: Gage, 1982.

Beck, J.M. *Joseph Howe: Anti-Confederate.* Ottawa: Canadian Historical Association, 1965.

Becklumb, Penny. 'Bill C-37: An Act to amend the Citizenship Act.' Legislative Summaries, Library of Parliament. http://www.parl.gc.ca.

Begg, Alexander. *History of the North-West.* Toronto: Hunter, Rose, 1894.

Beiser, Morton, Phyllis Johnson, and Daniel Roshi. The Mental Health of Southeast Asian Refugees Resettling in Canada. *Final Report to Canada Health and Welfare.* Toronto: Clarke Institute of Psychiatry, 1994.

Beitz, Charles. *Political Theory and International Relations.* Princeton, NJ: Princeton University Press, 1979.

Belkin, Simon. *Through Narrow Gates: A Review of Jewish Immigration, Colonization and Immigrant Aid Work (1840–1940).* Montreal: Eagle, 1967.

Bell, Winthrop Pickard. *The 'Foreign Protestants' and the Settlement of Nova Scotia.* Toronto: University of Toronto Press, 1961.

Bercuson, David J. *Confrontation at Winnipeg: Labour, Industrial Relations, and the General Strike.* Montreal: McGill-Queen's University Press, 1974.

– *Fools and Wise Men: The Rise and Fall of the One Big Union.* Scarborough, ON: McGraw-Hill Ryerson, 1978.

Berger, Carl. *The Sense of Power: Studies in the Ideas of Canadian Imperialism, 1867–1914.* Toronto. University of Toronto Press, 1970.

– *The Writing of Canadian History: Aspects of English-Canadian Historical Writing since 1900,* 2nd ed. Toronto: University of Toronto Press, 1986.

Berton, Pierre. *The Last Spike: The Great Railway, 1881–1885.* Toronto: McClelland & Stewart, 1971.

– *The National Dream: The Great Railway, 1871–1881.* Toronto: McClelland & Stewart, 1970.

Best, J.C. 'Canada's Immigration Patterns and Policies.' *Labour Gazette* 50 (1950): 1512–22.

Betcherman, Lita-Rose. *The Swastika and the Maple Leaf: Fascist Movements in Canada in the Thirties.* Don Mills, ON: Fitzhenry & Whiteside, 1975.

Bicha, Karel Denis. *The American Farmer and the Canadian West, 1896–1914.* Lawrence, KA: Colorado Press, 1968.

Bilson, Geoffrey. *A Darkened House: Cholera in Nineteenth-Century Canada.* Toronto: University of Toronto Press, 1980.

– *The Guest Children: The Story of the British Child Evacuees Sent to Canada during World War II.* Saskatoon: Fifth House, 1989.

Binnie-Clark, Georgina. *Wheat and Women.* Toronto: University of Toronto Press, 1979.

Bissett, J. 'Security Threats in Immigration and Refugee Policies.' In *Immigration Policy and the Terrorist Threat in Canada,* edited by A. Moens and Martin Collacott. Vancouver: Fraser Institute, May 2008. Online: http://www.fraserinstitute.org/COMMERCE.WEB/product_files/ImmigrationPolicyTerroristThreatCanadaUS.pdf.

Black, Conrad. *Duplessis*. Toronto: McClelland & Stewart, 1977.

Blacker, C.P. *Eugenics: Galton and After*. London: Duckworth, 1952.

Bliss, Michael. *A Living Profit: Studies in the Social History of Canadian Business, 1883–1911*. Toronto: McClelland & Stewart, 1974.

Bödy, Paul. 'Emigration from Hungary, 1880–1956.' In *Struggle and Hope: The Hungarian-Canadian Experience*, edited by N.F. Dreisziger, M.L. Kovacs, Paul Bödy, and Bennett Kovrig. Toronto: McClelland & Stewart, 1982.

Boleda, Mario. 'Trente mille français à la conquête du Saint-Laurent.' *Histoire sociale/Social History* 23/45 (May 1990): 153–78.

Bolger, Francis W.P. *Prince Edward Island and Confederation, 1863–1873*. Charlottetown: St Dunstan's University Press, 1964.

Borjas, George J. *Friends or Strangers: The Impact of Immigrants on the U. S. Economy*. New York: Basic Books, 1990.

– 'The Economic Benefits of Immigration.' *Journal of Economic Perspectives* 9 (1995): 3–22.

– 'The Economics of Immigration.' *Journal of Economic Literature* 32 (1994): 1667–1717.

– 'Immigration and Welfare 1970–1990,' Working Paper no. 4872, National Bureau of Economic Research, Washington, D.C., 1994.

Bothwell, Robert. *Canada and the United States: The Politics of Partnership*. Toronto: University of Toronto Press, 1992.

Bothwell, Robert, Ian Drummond, and John English. *Canada: 1900–1945*. Toronto: University of Toronto Press, 1987.

– *Canada since 1945: Power, Politics, and Provincialism*, 2d ed. Toronto: University of Toronto Press, 1989.

Bothwell, Robert, and Norman Hillmer, eds. *The In-Between Time: Canadian External Policy in the 1930s*. Toronto: Copp Clark, 1975.

Bowsfield, Hartwell. *Louis Riel. The Rebel and the Hero*. Toronto: Oxford University Press, 1971.

Boyd, N. 'The Origins of Canadian Narcotics Legislation: The Process of Criminalization in Historical Context.' *Dalhousie Law Journal* 8/1 (1984): 102–36.

Bradwin, Edmund W. *The Bunkhouse Man: A Study of Work and Pay in the Camps in Canada, 1903–1914*. Toronto: University of Toronto Press, 1972; originally published in 1928.

Brasseaux, C.A. *The Founding of New Acadia. The Beginnings of Acadian Life in Louisiana, 1765–1803*. Baton Rouge: Louisiana State University Press, 1987.

Brebner, J.B. *The Neutral Yankees of Nova Scotia: A Marginal Colony during the Revolutionary Years*. Toronto: McClelland & Stewart, 1969.

Breton, Raymond, Jill Armstrong, and Les Kennedy. *The Social Impact of Changes in Populational Size and Composition: Reactions to Patterns of Immigration.* Ottawa: Information Canada, Department of Manpower and Immigration, 1974.

Brimelow, Peter. *Alien Nation: Common Sense about America's Immigration Disaster.* New York: Random House, 1995.

Bristow, Peggy, Dionne Brand, Linda Carty, Afua P. Cooper, Sylvia Hamilton, and Adrienne Shadd, eds. *'We're Rooted Here and They Can't Pull Us Up': Essays in African-Canadian Women's History.* Toronto: University of Toronto Press, 1994.

Brook-Shepherd, Gordon. *Anschluss: The Rape of Austria.* London: Macmillan, 1963.

Brouwer, A. 'Permanent Protection: Why Canada Should Grant Permanent Resident Status Automatically to Recognized Refugees,' Refuge, 22: 2 Winter 2005.

Brouwer, R.C. 'A Disgrace to "Christian Canada": Protestant Foreign Missionary Concerns about the Treatment of South Asians in Canada, 1907–1940.' In *A Nation of Immigrants: Women, Workers and Communities in Canadian History, 1840s–1960s,* edited by Franca Iacovetta. Toronto: University of Toronto Press, 1998.

Brown, Lorne. *When Freedom Was Lost: The Unemployed, the Agitator and the State.* Montreal: Black Rose, 1987.

Brown, Lorne, and Caroline Brown. *An Unauthorized History of the RCMP.* Toronto: Lorimer, 1973.

Brown, Robert Craig. *Canada's National Policy, 1883–1900: A Study in Canadian-American Relations.* Princeton, NJ: Princeton University Press, 1964.

– 'Full Partnership in the Fortunes and in the Future of the Nation.' In *Ethnicity and Citizenship: The Canadian Case,* edited by Jean Laponce and William Safran. London: Frank Cass, 1996.

– *Robert Laird Borden: A Biography,* vol. 1, 1854–1914. Toronto: Macmillan, 1975.

Brown, Robert Craig, and Ramsay Cook. *Canada, 1896–1921: A Nation Transformed.* Toronto: McClelland & Stewart, 1974.

Brown, W. 'The Black Loyalists in Canada.' *The Loyalist Gazette* 28 (1990): 11–14.

Brown, Wallace, and Hereward Senior. *Victorious in Defeat: The Loyalists in Canada.* Toronto: Methuen, 1984.

Bryce, George. *Manitoba: Its Infancy, Growth and Present Condition.* London: 1882.

Buchignani, Norman, and Doreen M. Indra, with Ram Srivastiva. *Continuous Journey: A Social History of South Asians in Canada.* Toronto: McClelland & Stewart; Ottawa: Department of the Secretary of State, Multiculturalism Directorate, 1985.

Buck, Tim. *Yours in the Struggle: Reminiscences of Tim Buck*, edited by William Beeching and Phyllis Clarke. Toronto: NC Press, 1977.

Buckner, Philip. 'The 1860s: And End and a Beginning.' In *The Atlantic Region to Confederation*, edited by P. Buckner and J. Reid. Toronto: University of Toronto Press, 1994.

Buckner, Philip, and J. Reid, eds. *The Atlantic Region to Confederation*. Toronto: University of Toronto Press, 1994.

Bullen, John. 'Hidden Workers: Child Labour and the Family Economy in Late Nineteenth Century Urban Ontario.' *Labour/Le Travail* 18 (Fall 1986): 163–88.

Bumsted, J.M. *Land, Settlement, and Politics on Eighteenth-Century Prince Edward Island*. Montreal: McGill-Queen's University Press, 1987.

– *The People's Clearance: Highland Emigration to British North America, 1770–1815*. Edinburgh: Edinburgh University Press; Winnipeg: University of Manitoba Press, 1982.

– *The Peoples of Canada: A Pre-Confederation History*. 2nd ed. Toronto: Oxford University Press, 2003.

– *The Peoples of Canada: A Post-Confederation History*. 2nd ed. Toronto: Oxford University Press, 2004.

– *The Scots in Canada*. Ottawa: Canadian Historical Association, 1982.

– '1763–1783, Resettlement and Rebellion.' In *The Atlantic Region to Confederation*, edited by P. Buckner and J. Reid. Toronto: University of Toronto Press, 1994.

– *The Winnipeg General Strike of 1919: An Illustrated History*. Winnipeg: Watson & Dwyer, 1994.

Burley, Kevin H., ed. *The Development of Canada's Staples, 1867–1939. A Documentary Collection*. Toronto: McClelland & Stewart, n.d.

Bush, Julia. '"The Right Sort of Woman": Female Emigrators and Emigration to the British Empire, 1890–1910.' *Women's History Review* 3/3 (1994): 385–409.

Calliste, Agnes. 'Canada's Immigration Policy and Domestics from the Caribbean: The Second Domestic Scheme.' In *Race, Class, Gender: Bonds and Barriers. Socialist Studies: A Canadian Annual*, vol. 5, edited by Jesse Vorst. Toronto: Between the Lines, 1989.

– 'Race, Gender and Canadian Immigration Policy: Blacks from the Caribbean, 1900–1932.' *Journal of Canadian Studies* 28/4 (Winter 1993–4): 131–48.

– 'Women of "Exceptional Merit": Immigration of Caribbean Nurses to Canada.' *Canadian Journal of Women and the Law* 6/1 (1993): 85–102.

Cameron, Ruth. 'The Wheat from the Chaff.' MA thesis, Concordia University, Montreal, 1976.

Cameron, Wendy and Maude M. McDougall, *Assisting Emigration to Upper Canada 1832–1837* (Montreal and Kingston: McGill-Queen's University Press, 2000).

Campbell, Mavis C. *The Maroons of Jamaica, 1655–1796*. Trenton, NJ: Africa World Press, 1990.

Canada. Department of the Secretary of State. Multiculturalism Directorate. *The Canadian Family Tree: Canada's Peoples*. Toronto: Corpus Information Services, 1979.

Canadian Bar Association, National Citizenship and Immigration Law Section. *Submission on Bill C-18 Citizenship of Canada Act*. November 2002. Online: www .cba.org/CBA/pdf/c18submission.pdf.

Canadian Chamber of Commerce. 'Social Policy: Settlement and Integration Programs for Immigrants: Capitalising on Canada's skilled Immigrants.' 2005. http://www.chamber.ca/cmslib/general/S054.pdf.

– 'Social Policy: Canada's Permanent Immigration System.' 2005. http://www .chamber.ca/cmslib/general/S051.pdf.

Canadian Council for Refugees, articles and press releases, Online: www.ccrweb .ca/reportcard2003.htm.

Canadian Federation of Independent Business (CFIB). 'Immigration and Small Business: Ideas to Better Respond to Canada's Skills and Labour Shortage, 2007.' www.cfib.ca.

Canadian Labour Congress. *Workers of Colour Within a Global Economy*. 2005. http://canadianlabour.ca/node/1083.

Cannon, Margaret. *China Tide: The Revealing Story of the Hong Kong Exodus to Canada*. Toronto: Harper Collins, 1989.

Carasco, E., et al. *Immigration and Refugee Law*. Toronto: Emond Montgomery Publications Ltd, 2007.

Card, Brigham Y. 'Charles Ora Card and the Founding of the Mormon Settlements in Southwestern Alberta, North-West Territories.' In *The Mormon Presence in Canada*, edited by Brigham Y. Card, Herbert C. Northcott, John E. Foster, Howard Palmer, and George K. Jarvis. Edmonton: University of Alberta Press, 1990.

Card, Brigham Y., Herbert C. Northcott, John E. Foster, Howard Palmer, and George K. Jarvis, eds. *The Mormon Presence in Canada*. Edmonton: University of Alberta Press, 1990.

Careless, J.M.S. *Brown of the Globe*, vol. 2, Statesman of Confederation. Toronto: Macmillan, 1963.

– *Canada: A Story of Challenge*. Toronto: Macmillan, 1970.

Careless, J.M.S., and R. Craig Brown, eds. *The Canadians, 1867–1967*. Toronto: Macmillan, 1967.

Carens, Joseph. 'Aliens and Citizens: The Case for Open Borders.' *The Review of Politics* 49/2 (1987): 251–73.
– 'Membership and Morality: Admission to Membership in Liberal Democratic States.' In *Immigration and the Politics of Citizenship in Europe and North America*, edited by William Rogers. New York: University Press of America, 1989.
Carrigan, D. Owen. *Canadian Party Platforms, 1867–1968*. Toronto: Copp Clark, 1968.
Carrothers, W.A. 'The Immigration Problem in Canada.' *Queen's Quarterly* 36 (1929): 517–31.
Carruthers, James R. 'The Great War and Canada's Enemy Alien Policy.' *Queen's Law Journal* 4 (1978): 43–110.
Carter, David J. *Behind Canadian Barbed Wire: Alien Refugee and Prisoner of War Camps in Canada, 1914–1946*. Calgary: Tumbleweed, 1980.
Carter, Sarah. *Lost Harvests: Prairie Indian Reserve Farmers and Government Policy*. Montreal: McGill-Queen's University Press, 1990.
Carty, Linda. 'African Canadian Women and the State: "Labour Only, Please".' In *'We're Rooted Here and They Can't Pull Us Up': Essays in African-Canadian Women's History*, edited by Peggy Bristow, Dionne Brand, Linda Carty, Afua P. Cooper, Sylvia Hamilton, and Adrienne Shadd. Toronto: University of Toronto Press, 1994.
Cecil, R.G., and G.E. Banks. 'The Human Condition of West Indian Migrant Farm Labour in Southwestern Ontario.' *International Migration* 29/3 (September 1991): 389–405.
Chang, H. 'The Economic Impact of International Labor Migration: Recent Estimates and Policy Implications.' *Temple Political and Civil Rights Law Review* 16 (2007).
Chapman, D. *Lost Canadians: Nine Categories of Citizens*. 1 February 2007. Online: www.lostcanadian.com/main.asp.
Charbonneau, Hubert, and Yves Landry. 'La Politique démographique en Nouvelle-France.' *Annales de démographie historique* (1979): 29–57.
Charlton, Alexandra, Suzanne Duff, Dan Grant, et al. 'The Challenges to Responding to Human Smuggling in Canada: Practitioners Reflect on the 1999 Boat Arrivals in British Columbia.' Research on Immigration and Integration in the Metropolis, Working Paper Series No. 02–23, December 2002.
Chilton, L. *Agents of Empire: British Female Migration to Canada and Australia, 1860s–1930s*. Toronto: University of Toronto Press, 2007.
Chiswick, Barry R. 'The Effect of Americanization on the Earnings of Foreign-Born Men.' *Journal of Political Economy* 86 (1978): 897–921.

Choquette, Leslie P. 'Recruitment of French Emigrants to Canada, 1600–1760.' In '*To Make America': European Emigration in the Early Modern Period*, edited by Ida Altman and James Horn. Berkeley: University of California Press, 1991.

Chute, T. 'Globalization, Security and Exclusion.' CRS Working Paper Series No. 3. Toronto: Centre for Refugee Studies, York University, 2005. Online: www.yorku.ca/crs.

Citizenship and Immigration Canada. *Annual Report to Parliament on Immigration, 2007.* http://www.cic.gc.ca/ENGLISH/RESOURCES/PUBLICATIONS/annual-report2007/index.asp.

– *Annual Report to Parliament on Immigration, 2006.* http://www.cic.gc.ca/EnGLIsh/_pdf/pub/immigration2006_e.pdf.

– *Facts and Figures 2007.* 'Immigration Overview: Permanent Residents and Temporary Foreign Workers and Students.' http://www.cic.gc.ca/english/resources/statistics/facts2007/foreword.asp.

– *Facts and Figures 2008.* 'Immigration Overview: Permanent Residents and Temporary Foreign Workers and Students.' http://www.cic.gc.ca/english/pdf/research-stats/facts2008.pdf.

Clarke, C.K. 'The Defective Immigrant.' *The Public Health Journal* 7 (November 1916): 462–5.

Clarkson, S. 'The View from the Attic: Toward a Gated Community?' In *The Re-Bordering of North America: Integration and Exclusion in a New Security Context*, edited by P. Andreas and T. Biersteker. New York: Routledge, 2003.

Clement, Wallace. *The Canadian Corporate Elite: An Analysis of Economic Power.* Toronto: McClelland & Stewart, 1975.

Code M., and Kent Roach. 'The Role of the Independent Lawyer and Security Certificates.' *Criminal Law Quarterly* 52 (2006): 94.

Collacott, M. 'Canada's Immigration Policy: The Need for Major Reform.' Public Policy Sources No. 64. Vancouver: Fraser Institute, 2003. www.fraserinstitute.ca/admin/books/files/immigration-2nd Edition.pdf.

– 'Is There Really a Looming Labour Shortage in Canada, and, If There Is Can Increased Immigration Fill the Gap?' In *Immigration and Refugee Law: Cases, Materials and Commentary*. Toronto: Emond Montgomery Publications Limited, 2007.

Commission of Inquiry into the Actions of Canadian Officials in Relation to Maher Arar. *Report of the Events Relating to Maher Arar: Analysis and Recommendations*. Ottawa: Author, 2006.

Conrad, Margaret, ed. *Making Adjustments: Change and Continuity in Planter Nova Scotia, 1759–1800*. Fredericton: Acadiensis, 1991.

Conrad, Margaret, Alvin Finkel, and Cornelius Jaenen. *History of the Canadian Peoples*, vol. 1: *Beginnings to 1867*. 4th ed. Toronto: Pearson Longman, 2006.

Cook, Ramsay. *Canada, 1896–1921: A Nation Transformed.* Toronto: McClelland & Stewart, 1974.

– *Canada: A Modern Study.* Toronto: Irwin Publishing, 1977.

– 'Canadian Freedom in Wartime, 1939–1945.' In *His Own Man: Essays in Honour of Arthur Reginald Marsen Lower,* edited by W.H. Heick and Roger Graham. Montreal: McGill-Queen's University Press, 1974.

Cook, Ramsay, R., Craig Brown, and Carl Berger, eds. *Conscription 1917.* Toronto: University of Toronto Press, 1969.

Copp, Terry. *The Anatomy of Poverty: The Condition of the Working Class in Montreal, 1897–1929.* Toronto: McClelland & Stewart, 1974.

– 'Montreal's Municipal Government and the Crisis of the 1930s.' In *The Usable Urban Past,* edited by Alan J. Artibise and Gilbert Stelter. Ottawa: Carleton University Press, 1979.

Corak, Miles. 'Immigration in the Long Run: The Education and Earnings Mobility of Second Generation Canadians.' Institute for Research on Public Policy, *Immigration and Refugee Policy Choices* 14/13 (October 2008): 4–26.

Corbett, David C. *Canada's Immigration Policy: A Critique.* Toronto: University of Toronto Press, 1957.

– 'A Study of Factors Governing Canada's Absorption of Immigrants from 1867–1914, with Suggestions towards a Definition of Absorptive Capacity.' MA thesis, University of Toronto, 1949.

Corbett, Gail H. *Barnardo Children in Canada.* Peterborough, ON: Woodland, 1981.

Cowan, H.I. *British Emigration to British North America: The First Hundred Years.* Toronto: University of Toronto Press, 1961.

Craig, Gerald. *Upper Canada: The Formative Years, 1784–1841.* Toronto: McClelland & Stewart, 1968.

Craig, Gordon A. *Germany, 1866–1945.* New York: Oxford University Press, 1978.

Craven, Paul. *'An Impartial Umpire': Industrial Relations and the Canadian State, 1900–1911.* Toronto: University of Toronto Press, 1980.

Creese, Gillian. 'Class, Ethnicity and Conflict: The Case of Chinese and Japanese Immigrants, 1880–1923.' In *Workers, Capital, and the State in British Columbia: Selected Papers,* edited by Rennie Warburton and David Coburn. Vancouver: University of British Columbia Press, 1988.

– 'Exclusion or Solidarity? Vancouver Workers Confront the "Oriental Problem."' *B.C. Studies* (1988): 24–51.

– 'The Politics of Refugees in Canada.' In *Deconstructing a Nation,* edited by V.C. Satzewich. Halifax: Fernwood, 1992.

Crepeau, F., and D. Nakache. 'Controlling Irregular Migration in Canada: Reconciling Security Concerns with Human Rights Protection.' Institute for

Research on Public Policy, *Immigration and Refugee Policy Choices* 12/1 (February 2006): 1–42.

Culliton, J.T. *Assisted Emigration and Land Settlement.* Montreal: McGill University, Economic Studies no. 9, 1928.

Cunliffe, Harry. 'The Liberalization of Immigration Policy from 1945 to 1956: An Insider's View.' In *Breaking Ground: The 1956 Hungarian Refugee Movement to Canada,* edited by Robert H. Keyserlingk. Toronto: York Lanes, 1993.

Dahlie, Jorden, and Tissa Fernando, eds. *Ethnicity, Power and Politics in Canada.* Toronto: Methuen, 1981.

Dales, J.H. *The Protective Tariff in Canada's Development: Eight Essays on Trade and Tariff.* Toronto: University of Toronto Press, 1966.

Daniels, R. 'From Relocation to Redress: Japanese Americans and Canadians, 1941–1988.' In *Minorities in Wartime: National and Racial Groupings in Europe, North America and Australia during the Two World Wars,* edited by Panikos Panayi. Providence, RI: Berg, 1993.

Daniels, Ronald, Patrick Macklem, and Kent Roach, eds. *The Security of Freedom: Essays on Canada's Anti Terrorism Bill.* Toronto; University of Toronto Press, 2001.

Darlington, J. 'The Ukrainian Impress on the Canadian West.' In *A Nation of Immigrants: Women, Workers and Communities in Canadian History, 1840s–1960s,* edited by Franca Iacovetta, 128–53. Toronto: University of Toronto Press, 1998.

Daube, N. 'Charkaoui: The Impact of Structure on Judicial Activism in Times of Crisis.' *Journal of Law and Equality* 4/2 (Fall 2005): 105.

Dauvergne, C. 'Evaluating Canada's New Immigration and Refugee Protection Act in Its Global Context.' *Alberta Law Review* 4/13 (2003): 741.

Davidson, George. 'Canadian Immigration and Citizenship Policies.' Address to the annual American Immigration and Citizenship Conference, 24 March 1961.

Davis, Susan, and Lorne Waldman. 'The Quality of Mercy: A Study of the Processes Available to Persons Who Are Determined Not to Be Refugees and Who Seek Humanitarian and Compassionate Treatment.' Report commissioned by the Minister of Citizenship and Immigration Canada, March 1994.

Davis, Susan, Roslyn Kunin, and Robert Trempe. *Not Just Numbers, A Canadian Framework for Future Immigration.* Ottawa: Minister of Public Works and Government Services Canada, 1997.

Dawson, Carl Addington. *Group Settlement: Ethnic Communities in Western Canada.* Toronto: Macmillan, 1936.

Delisle, Esther. *The Traitor and the Jew: Anti-semitism and the Delirium of Extremist Right-Wing Nationalism in French Canada from 1929–1939.* Montreal: Robert Davies, 1992.

DeMont, John. *Hong Kong Money: How Chinese Families and Fortunes Are Changing Canadian Business.* Toronto: Key Porter, 1989.

Dempsey, Hugh A., ed. *The CPR West: The Iron Road and the Making of a Nation.* Vancouver: Douglas & McIntyre, 1984.

DeVoretz, Don J. 'Immigration and Employment Effects.' Discussion paper, Institute for Research on Public Policy, November 1989.

DeVoretz, Don J., ed. *Diminishing Returns: The Economics of Canada's Recent Immigration Policy.* Toronto: C.D. Howe Institute, 1995.

Dewitt, David, and John Kirton. *Canada as a Principal Power: A Study in Foreign Policy and International Relations.* Toronto: Wiley, 1983.

Dickason, Olive Patricia. *Canada's First Nations: A History of Founding Peoples from Earliest Times* 3rd ed. Toronto: Oxford University Press, 2002.

Dickson, Paul Douglas. 'We Prefer Trade to Dominion: Imperial Policy and the Settlement of the Kings Royal Regiment.' *Ontario History* 82 (1990): 129–48.

Dirks, Gerald E. 'Canada and Immigration: International and Domestic Considerations in the Decade Preceding the 1956 Hungarian Exodus.' In *Breaking Ground: The 1956 Hungarian Refugee Movement to Canada,* edited by Robert H. Keyserlingk. Toronto: York Lanes, 1993.

– *Canada's Refugee Policy: Indifference or Opportunism?* Montreal: McGill-Queen's University Press, 1977.

– *Controversy and Complexity: Canadian Immigration Policy during the 1980s.* Montreal: McGill-Queen's University Press, 1995.

– 'The Green Paper and Canadian Refugee Policy.' *Canadian Ethnic Studies* 7/1 (1975): 61–4.

Dobuzinskis, Laurent, Michael Howlett, and David Laycock, eds. *Policy Studies in Canada: The State of the Art.* Toronto: University of Toronto Press, 1996.

Dobyns, Henry F. *Their Numbers Became Thinned: Native American Population Dynamics in Eastern North America.* Knoxville: University of Tennessee Press, 1983.

Dolin, B., and M. Young. 'Canada's Immigration Program.' Background Paper, Parliamentary Information and Research Service. Ottawa: Library of Parliament, October 2004.

Doughty, Arthur G., ed. *The Elgin-Grey Papers, 1846–1852,* vol. 1. Ottawa: King's Printer, 1937.

Dowbiggin, Ian. 'Keeping This Young Country Sane: C.K. Clarke, Immigration Restriction, and Canadian Psychiatry, 1890–1925.' *Canadian Historical Review* 76/4 (December 1995): 598–627.

Draper, Paula Jean. 'Fragmented Loyalties: Canadian Jewry, the King Government and the Refugee Dilemma.' In *On Guard for Thee: War Ethnicity and the Canadian State,* edited by Norman Hillmer, Bohdan Kordan, and

Lubomyr Luciuk. Ottawa: Canadian Committee for the History of the Second World War, 1988.

Dreisziger, N.F. 'The Rise of a Bureaucracy for Multiculturalism: The Origins of the Nationalities Branch, 1939–1941.' In *On Guard for Thee: War Ethnicity and the Canadian State, 1939–1945*, edited by Norman Hillmer, Bohdan Kordan, and Lubomyr Luciuk. Ottawa: Canadian Committee for the History of the Second World War, 1988.

– 'The Years of Growth and Change, 1918–1929.' In *Struggle and Hope: The Hungarian-Canadian Experience*, edited by N.F. Dreisziger, M.L. Kovacs, Paul Bödy, and Bennett Kovrig. Toronto: McClelland & Stewart, 1982.

Dreisziger, N.F., M.L. Kovacs, Paul Bödy, and Bennett Kovrig, eds. *Struggle and Hope: The Hungarian-Canadian Experience*. Toronto: McClelland & Stewart, 1982.

Drystek, Henry. '"The Simplest and Cheapest Mode of Dealing with Them": Deportation from Canada before World War II.' *Histoire sociale/Social History* 25/30 (November 1982): 407–41.

Dumas, Evelyn. *The Bitter Thirties in Quebec*. Montreal: Black Rose, 1975.

Dunae, Patrick A. 'Promoting the Dominion: Records and the Canadian Immigration Campaign, 1872–1915.' *Archivaria* 19 (1984–5): 73–93.

Duncan, Janice M. *Minority without a Champion: Kanakas on the Pacific Coast, 1788–1850*. Portland: Oregon Historical Society, 1972.

Duncan, K.J. 'Patterns of Settlement in the East.' In *Scottish Tradition in Canada*, edited by W. Stanford Reid. Toronto: McClelland & Stewart, 1976.

Dyzenhaus, D., and Mayo Moran, ed. *Calling Power to Account: Law, Reparations and the Chinese Canadian Head Tax Case*. Toronto: University of Toronto Press, 2005.

Eager, Evelyn. 'Our Pioneers Say.' *Saskatchewan History* 6/1 (1953): 1–12.

Eagle, John A. *The Canadian Pacific Railway and the Development of Western Canada, 1896–1914*. Kingston: McGill-Queen's University Press, 1989.

'The East Asian Threat: Canada's Attempt to Create a Restrictive Refugee Policy.' *Georgetown. Immigration Law Journal* 2 (1988): 605–15.

Easterbrook, W.T., and H.G.J. Aitken. *Canadian Economic History*. Toronto: Macmillan, 1965.

Eayrs, James. *In Defence of Canada*, 5 vols. Toronto: University of Toronto Press, 1964–83.

Eccles, W.J. *Canada under Louis XIV, 1663–1701*. Toronto: McClelland & Stewart, 1968.

Economic Council of Canada. *Economic and Social Impacts of Immigration: A Research Report*. ed. Neil Swan et al. Ottawa: The Council, 1991.

Emmerson, James Thomas. *The Rhineland Crisis*. London: Maurice Temple Smith, 1977.

England, Robert. *The Central European Immigrant in Canada*. Toronto: Macmillan, 1929.
– *The Colonization of Western Canada: A Study of Contemporary Land Settlement (1896–1934)*. London: P.S. King, 1936.
Epp, Frank H. *Mennonites in Canada, 1786–1920: The History of a Separate People*. Toronto: Macmillan, 1974.
Epstein, Larry. *Immigration and Inflation*. Ottawa: Information Canada, Department of Manpower and Immigration, 1974.
Farber, Daniel. 'Democracy and Disgust: Reflections on Public Choice.' *Chicago-Kent Law Review* 65 (1989): 161–76.
Farber, Daniel, and Philip Frickey. *Law and Public Choice: A Critical Introduction*, Chicago: University of Chicago Press, 1991.
Finkel, Alvin. *Business and Social Reform in the Thirties*. Toronto: Lorimer, 1979.
Finkel, A., Margaret Conrad, and Veronica Strong-Boag. *History of the Canadian Peoples, vol. 2, 1867 to the Present*. 4th ed. Toronto: Pearson Longman, 2006.
Finlay John L., and Douglas N. Sprague, *The Structure of Canadian History*, 5th ed. Toronto: Prentice-Hall, 1997.
Flanagan, Thomas. *Riel and the Rebellion: 1885 Reconsidered*. Saskatoon: Western Producer Prairie Books, 1983.
Flecker, Karl. 'Building "The World's Most Flexible Workforce": The Harper Government's "double-doubling" of the Foreign Worker Program.' *Briar Patch Magazine*, 31 October 2007. Online: http://briarpatchmagazine.com/2007/10/.
Foot, D. *Boom, Bust and Echo: How to Profit from the Coming Demographic Shift*. Toronto: Macfarlane, Walter and Ross, 1996.
Forcese, D. 'Through a Glass Darkly: The Role and Review of National Security Concepts in Canadian Law.' *Alberta Law Review* 43/4 (May 2006): 990.
Forsey, Eugene. *Trade Unions in Canada, 1812–1902*. Toronto: University of Toronto Press, 1982.
Forster, Ben. *A Conjunction of Interests: Business, Politics, and Tariffs, 1823–1879*. Toronto: University of Toronto Press, 1986.
Foster, Hamar, and John McLaren, eds. *Essays in the History of Canadian Law*. Vol. 6: *British Columbia and the Yukon*. Toronto: Osgoode Society, 1995.
Foster, Lois, and Anne Seitz. 'Official Attitudes to Germans During World War II: Some Australian and Canadian Comparisons.' *Ethnic and Racial Studies* 14/4 (October 1991): 474–92.
Francis, D. *Immigration: The Economic Case*. Toronto: Key Porter Books, 2002.
Francis, Emerich K. *In Search of Utopia: The Mennonites in Manitoba*. Altona, MA: Friesen, 1955.
Francis, R. Douglas, Richard Jones, and Donald B. Smith, *Destinies: Canadian History since Confederation*, 6th ed. Toronto: Nelson, 2008.

– *Origins: Canadian History to Confederation.* Toronto: Holt, Rinehart & Winston, 1988.

Frégault, G. *Canada: The War of the Conquest.* Toronto: Oxford University Press, 1969.

Frenette, M., and Rene Morisette. 'Will They Ever Converge? Earnings of Immigrant and Canadian-born Workers Over the Last Two Decades.' Research paper series. Catalogue no. 11F0019Mie-No. 215. Ottawa: Statistics Canada, Analytical Studies Branch, 2003.

Friedberg, Rachel M., and Jennifer Hunt. 'The Impact of Immigrants on Host Country Wages, Employment and Growth.' *Journal of Economic Perspectives* 9 (1995): 23–44.

Friedman, Wolfgang. *German Immigration into Canada.* Toronto: Ryerson, 1952.

Friesen, Gerald. *The Canadian Prairies: A History.* Toronto: University of Toronto Press, 1984.

Friesen, Jean. 'Magnificent Gifts: The Treaties of the Indians of the Northwest, 1869–70.' In *Transactions of the Royal Society of Canada,* ser. 5, vol. 1 (1986): 41–51.

Frost, Karolyn Smardz. *I've Got a Home in Glory Land: A Lost Tale of the Underground Railroad.* Toronto: Thomas Allen Publishers, 2008.

Gabori, Susan. *In Search of Paradise: The Odyssey of an Italian Family.* Montreal: McGill-Queen's University Press, 1993.

Gagnon, J.D. 'Immigrants and French-Canadian Nationalism.' In *Immigration and the Rise of Multiculturalism,* edited by Howard Palmer. Toronto: Copp Clark, 1975.

Gallagher, A. 'Human Rights and the New UN Protocols on Trafficking and Migrant Smuggling: A Preliminary Analysis.' *Human Rights Quarterly* 23/4 (2001): 975.

Gallagher, S. 'Canada's Broken Refugee Policy System.' In *Immigration Policy and the Terrorist Threat in Canada and the United States,* edited by A. Moens and M. Collacott. Vancouver: Fraser Institute, May 2008.

Ganzevoort, Herman. *A Bittersweet Land: The Dutch Experience in Canada, 1890–1980.* Toronto: McClelland & Stewart; Ottawa: Department of the Secretary of State, Multiculturalism Directorate, 1988.

Gates, Lillian F. *Land Policies of Upper Canada.* Toronto: University of Toronto Press, 1968.

Gates, Paul W. 'Official Encouragement to Immigration to the Province of Canada.' *Canadian Historical Review* 15 (1934): 24–38.

Gentilcore, R. Louis, ed. *Historical Atlas of Canada,* vol. 2, *The Land Transformed, 1800–1891.* Toronto: University of Toronto Press, 1993.

Gerus, O.W., and J.E. Rea. *The Ukrainians in Canada.* Ottawa: Canadian Historical Association, 1985.

Glassford, Larry A. *Reaction and Reform: The Politics of the Conservative Party under R.B. Bennett, 1927–1938.* Toronto: University of Toronto Press, 1992.

Glenn, H. Patrick. *Refugee Claims, the Canadian State and North American Regionalism in Hemispheric Integration, Migration and Human Rights.* Toronto: York University Centre for Refugee Studies, 1994.

– *Strangers at the Gate: Refugees, Illegal Entrants and Procedural Justice.* Cowansville, PQ: Les Éditions Yvon Blais, 1992.

Global Commission on International Migration. *Migration in an Interconnected World: New Directions for Action.* October 2005.

Glueck, Alvin C. *Minnesota and the Manifest Destiny of the Canadian Northwest. A Study in Canadian American Relations.* Toronto: University of Toronto Press, 1965.

Goutor, D. J. *The Walls of Solidarity: The Mainstream Canadian Labour Movement and Immigration Policy, 1872 to the Early 1930s.* PhD Thesis, University of Toronto, 2003.

– *Guarding the Gates: The Canadian Labour Movement and Immigration, 1872–1934.* Vancouver: UBC Press, 2007.

Graham, Roger. 'Through the First World War.' In *The Canadians, 1867–1967,* edited by J.M.S. Careless and R. Craig Brown. Toronto: Macmillan, 1967.

Granatstein, J.L. *A Man of Influence: Norman A. Robertson and Canadian Statecraft, 1929–68.* Toronto: Deneau, 1981.

Granatstein, J.L., Irving Abella, T.W. Acheson, David Bercuson, R. Craig Brown, and H. Blair Neatby. *Nation: Canada since Confederation,* 3d ed. Toronto: McGraw-Hill Ryerson, 1990.

Granatstein, J.L., and J.M. Hitsman. *Broken Promises: A History of Conscription in Canada.* Toronto: Oxford University Press, 1977.

Granatstein, J.L., and Gregory A. Johnson. 'The Evacuation of the Japanese Canadians, 1942: A Realist Critique of the Received Version.' In *On Guard for Thee: War, Ethnicity and the Canadian State, 1939–1945,* edited by Norman Hillmer, Bohdan Kordan, and Lubomyr Luciuk. Ottawa: Canadian Committee for the History of the Second World War, 1988.

Grant, George. *Ocean to Ocean: Sanford Fleming's Expedition through Canada in 1872.* Toronto: J. Campbell, 1873.

Grant, John W. *Moon of Wintertime: Missionaries and the Indians in Encounter since 1534.* Toronto: University of Toronto Press, 1984.

Gray, James. *The Winter Years: The Depression on the Prairies.* Toronto: Macmillan, 1966.

Grayson, L.M., and Michael Bliss, eds. *The Wretched of Canada: Letters to R.B. Bennett, 1930–1935.* Toronto: University of Toronto Press, 1971.

Green, Alan G. *Immigration and the Postwar Canadian Economy.* Toronto: Macmillan, 1976.

– 'What Is the Role of Immigration in Canada's Future?' In Charles M. Beach, et al., eds, *Canadian Immigration Policy for the 21st Century*. Kingston: John Deutsch Institute for the Study of Economic Policy, Queen's University (published in cooperation with McGill-Queen's University Press), 2003.

Greening, W.E. 'Is the French-Canadian Attitude towards Immigration Changing?' *Dalhousie Review* 31 (1951): 43–7.

Grenke, Art. 'The German Community of Winnipeg and the English-Canadian Response to World War I.' *Canadian Ethnic Studies* 20/1 (1988): 21–44.

Grey, J.H. *Immigration Law in Canada*. Toronto: Butterworths, 1984.

Griffiths, N. *The Contexts of Acadian History, 1688–1784*. Montreal: McGill-Queen's University Press, 1992.

– '1600–1650: Fish, Fur and Folk.' In *The Atlantic Region to Confederation*, edited by P. Buckner and J. Reid. Toronto: University of Toronto Press, 1994.

– ed. *The Acadian Deportation*. Toronto: Copp Clark, 1969.

Grow, Stewart. 'The Blacks of Amber Valley – Negro Pioneering in Northern Alberta.' *Canadian Ethnic Studies* 6/1–2 (1974): 17–38.

Grubel, H. 'Immigration and the Welfare State,' Fraser Institute, October 1, 2005.

Grubel, Herbert, ed. *The Effects of Mass Immigration on Canadian Living Standards and Society.* Vancouver: Fraser Institute, 2009.

Guest, Dennis. *The Emergence of Social Security in Canada*. Vancouver: University of British Columbia Press, 1980.

Guillemette, Yvan, and William B.P. Robson. 'No Elixir of Youth: Immigration Cannot Keep Canada Young.' C.D. Howe Institute Backgrounder. Toronto: C.D. Howe Institute, September 2006.

Gulka-Tiechko, Myron. 'Ukrainian Immigration to Canada under the Railways Agreement, 1925–30.' *Journal of Ukrainian Studies* 16/1–2 (Summer/Winter 1991): 29–59.

Hadley, Michael L., and Roger Sarty. *Tin-Pots and Pirate Ships: Canadian Naval Forces and German Sea-Raiders, 1880–1918*. Montreal: McGill-Queen's University Press, 1991.

Hall, D.J. *Clifford Sifton, The Young Napoleon, 1861–1900*, vol. 1. Vancouver: University of British Columbia Press, 1981.

– *Clifford Sifton, A Lonely Eminence, 1901–1929*, vol. 2. Vancouver: University of British Columbia Press, 1985.

Halloran, Mary. 'Ethnicity, the State and War: Canada and Its Ethnic Minorities, 1939–45.' *International Migration Review* 21/1 (1987): 159–67.

Hamil, Frederick Coyne. *Lake Erie Baron: The Story of Colonel Thomas Talbot*. Toronto: Macmillan, 1955.

Hamilton, Bob, and John Whalley. 'Efficiency and Distributional Implications of Global Restrictions on Labour Mobility: Calculations and Policy Implications.' *Journal of Development Economics* 14 (1984): 61–75.

Handcock, W. Gordon. *Soe longe as there comes noe women: Origins of English Settlement in Newfoundland.* St John's, NF: Breakwater, 1989.

Hansen, Marcus Lee. *The Mingling of the Canadian and American Peoples.* New Haven, CT: Yale University Press, 1940.

Harney, Robert F. 'The Padrone System and the Sojourner in the Canadian North, 1885–1920.' In *Immigration in Canada: Historical Perspectives,* edited by Gerald Tulchinsky. Toronto: Copp Clark Longman, 1994.

– '"So Great a Heritage as Ours": Immigration and the Survival of the Canadian Polity.' *Daedalus* 117/4 (Fall 1988): 51–97.

– ed. *Gathering Places: Peoples and Neighbourhoods of Toronto, 1834–1945.* Toronto: Multicultural History Society of Ontario, 1985.

– 'Men Without Women: Italian Migrants in Canada, 1885 – 1930.' In *A Nation of Immigrants: Women, Workers and Communities in Canadian History, 1840 –1960s,* edited by Franca Iacovetta. Toronto: University of Toronto Press, 1998.

Harper, Marjory. 'The Juvenile Immigrant: Halfway to Heaven or Hell on Earth.' In *The Immigrant Experience: Proceedings of a Conference held at the University of Guelph,* 8–11 June 1989, edited by Catherine Kerrigan. Guelph, ON: University of Guelph Press, 1992.

Harris, R. Cole. 'The French Background of Immigrants to Canada before 1700.' In *Interpreting Canada's Past,* vol. 1, *Before Confederation,* edited by J.M. Bumsted. Toronto: Oxford University Press, 1986.

– ed. *Historical Atlas of Canada, vol. 1, From the Beginning to 1800.* Toronto: University of Toronto Press, 1987.

Harris, R. Cole, and John Warkentin. *Canada before Confederation.* Toronto: Oxford University Press, 1974.

Harrison, Phyllis, ed. *The Home Children: Their Personal Stories,* J Gordon Shillingford Publications, 2003.

Harden, Gerry. 'Bound for Nova Scotia: Slaves in the Planter Migration, 1759–1800.' In *Making Adjustments: Change and Continuity* in *Planter Nova Scotia, 1759–1800,* edited by Margaret Conrad. Fredericton: Acadiensis, 1991.

Harvard Law Student Advocates for Human Rights, The International Human Rights Clinic, Human Rights Program and Harvard Immigration and Refugee Clinical Program. 'Bordering on Failure: The U.S.–Canada Safe Third Country Agreement Fifteen Months After Implementation.' March 2006. Online: http://www.law.harvard.edu/academics/clinical/asylum_law/Harvard_STCA_Report.pdf.

Hathaway, James C. *Rebuilding Trust: Report of the Review of Fundamental Justice in Information Gathering and Dissemination of the Immigration and Refugee Board of Canada.* Toronto: York University Centre for Refugee Studies, 1993.

Hathaway, James C., and R. Alexander Neve. 'Fundamental Justice and the Deflection of Refugees from Canada.' *Osgoode Hall Law Journal* 34 (1996): 213–70.

Hawkins, Freda. *The Asylum-Seekers.* Toronto: Canadian Institute of International Affairs, 1994.

– *Canada and Immigration: Public Policy and Public Concern*, 2nd ed. Montreal: McGill-Queen's University Press, 1988.

– *Critical Years in Immigration: Canada and Australia Compared.* Montreal: McGill-Queen's University Press, 1989.

– 'Immigration and Population: The Canadian Approach.' *Canadian Public Policy* 1 (1975):285–95.

Hedges, James B. *Building the Canadian West: The Land and Colonization Policies of the Canadian Pacific Railway.* New York: Macmillan, 1939.

Heick, W.H., and Roger Graham, eds. *His Own Man: Essays in Honour of Arthur Reginald Marsen Lower.* Montreal: McGill-Queen's University Press, 1974.

Helling, Rudolf A. A *Socio-Economic History of German Canadians: They, Too, Founded Canada.* Weisbaden: Franz Steiner, 1984.

Heron, Craig. *The Canadian Labour Movement.* Toronto: Lorimer, 1989.

– ed. *The Workers' Revolt in Canada, 1917–1925.* Toronto: University of Toronto Press, 1998.

Heydenkorn, Benedykt, ed. *A Community in Transition: The Polish Group in Canada.* Toronto: Canadian-Polish Research Institute, n.d.

– *Memoirs of Polish Immigrants in Canada.* Toronto: Canadian-Polish Research Institute, 1979.

Higham, John. *Strangers in the Land: Patterns of American Nativism, 1860–1925.* New York: Atheneum, 1963.

Hill, Douglas. *The Opening of the Canadian West*, Don Mills, ON: Academic Press, 1973.

Hiller, James K. 'Confederation Defeated: The Newfoundland Election of 1869.' In *Newfoundland in the Nineteenth and Twentieth Centuries: Essays in Interpretation*, edited by James K. Hiller and Peter Neary. Toronto: University of Toronto Press, 1980.

Hillmer, Norman, Bohdan Kordan, and Lubomyr Luciuk, eds. *On Guard for Thee: War, Ethnicity and the Canadian State, 1939–1945.* Ottawa: Canadian Committee for the History of the Second World War, 1988.

Hingston, W.H. *The Climate of Canada and Its Relation to Life and Health.* Montreal: Dawson Brothers, 1884.

Hoffman, Frances, and Ryan Taylor. *Across the Waters: Ontario Immigrants'
Experiences 1820–1850*. Milton, ON: Global Heritage Press, 1999.

Holden, Michael. 'Not Just the FTA: Factors Affecting Growth in Canada-United
States Trade since 1988.' 4 March 2003. http://dsp-psd.tpsgc.gc.ca/
Collection-R/LoPBdP/BP/prb0251–e.htm.

Hollihan, K. Tony. '"A Brake Upon the Wheel": Frank Oliver and the Creation of
the Immigration Act of 1906.' *Past Imperfect* 1 (1992): 93–112.

Holmes, John W. *The Shaping of Peace: Canada and the Search for World Order,
1943–1957*, 2 vols. Toronto: University of Toronto Press, 1979 and 1982.

Horn, Michiel. 'Free Speech within the Law: The Letter of the Sixty-Eight
Toronto Professors, 1931.' *Ontario History* 72 (1980): 27–48.

– *The Great Depression in Canada*. Ottawa: Canadian Historical Association, 1984.

– 'The Great Depression: Past and Present.' *Journal of Canadian Studies* 11/1
(February 1976): 41–50.

– 'Keeping Canada "Canadian": Anti-Communism and Canadianism in Toronto,
1928–29.' *Canada: An Historical Magazine* 3/1 (September 1975): 34–47.

– *League for Social Reconstruction: Intellectual Origins of the Democratic Left in Canada,
1930–1942*. Toronto: University of Toronto Press, 1980.

– ed. *The Depression in Canada: Responses to Economic Crisis*. Toronto: Copp Clark
Pitman, 1985.

– ed. *The Dirty Thirties: Canada in the Great Depression*. Toronto: Copp Clark, 1972.

Hornby, Jim. *Black Islanders: Prince Edward Island's Historical Black Community*.
Charlottetown: Institute of Island Studies, 1991.

House of Commons Standing Committee on Citizenship and Immigration. 'The
Provincial Nominee Program: A Partnership to Attract Immigrants to All Parts
of Canada.' Report and Recommendations, May 2003. http://www.parl.gc.ca.

– *Citizenship Revocation: A Question of Due Process and Respecting Charter Rights*.
10th Report. June 2005. Online: http://cmte.parl.gc.ca/Content/HOC/
committee/381/cimm/reports/rp1901753/cimmrp10/03–cov2–e.htm.

– *Updating Canada's Citizenship Laws: It's Time*. 12th Report. October 2005.
Online: http://cmte.parl.gc.ca/Content/HOC/committee/381/cimm/
reports/rp2014194/cimmrp12/05–hon-e.htm. http://canadianlabour.ca/
index.php/antiracism_publicati/1266. http://www.cic.gc.ca/ENGLISH/pdf/
pub/immigration2006_e.pdf.

Houston, Cecil, and William Smyth. 'Irish Emigrants to Canada: Whence They
Came.' In *Untold Story: The Irish in Canada*, edited by Robert O'Driscoll and
Lorna Reynolds. Toronto: Celtic Arts of Canada, 1988.

– *Irish Immigration and Canadian Settlement*. Toronto: University of Toronto Press,
1990.

Howe, C.D. Institute Backgrounder, No. 81, Toronto, April 2004.

Howell, A. *Naturalization and Nationality in Canada, Expatriation and Repatriation of British Subjects.* Toronto: Carswell, 1884.

Hucker, J. 'Immigration, Natural Justice and the Bill of Rights.' *Osgoode Hall Law Journal* 13 (1975): 649–92.

Huddle, Donald. 'The Costs of Immigration.' Department of Economics, Rice University (4 June 1993).

Hum, D., and Wayne Simpson. 'Economic Integration of Immigrants to Canada: A Short Survey.' *Canadian Journal of Urban Research* (Summer 2004): 13.

Hurd, W. Burton. 'Is There a Canadian Race?' *Queen's Quarterly* 35 (1928): 615–27.

– 'Some Implications of Prospective Population Changes in Canada.' *Canadian Journal of Economics and Political Science* 5 (1939): 492–503.

Iacobucci, Frank. *Internal Inquiry into the Actions of Canadian Officials in Relation to Abdullah Almalki, Ahmed Abou-Elmaati and Muayyed Nureddin.* http://www.iacobucciinquiry.ca/en/documents/final-report.htm.

Iacovetta, Franca. *Gatekeepers: Reshaping Immigrant Lives in Cold War Canada.* Toronto: Between the Lines, 2006.

– 'Ordering in Bulk: Canada's Postwar Immigration Policy and the Recruitment of Contract Workers from Italy.' *Journal of American Ethnic History* 11/1 (Fall 1991): 50–80.

– *Such Hardworking People: Italian Immigrants in Postwar Toronto.* Montreal: McGill-Queen's University Press, 1992.

– ed. *A Nation of Immigrants: Women, Workers and Communities in Canadian History, 1840s–1960s.* Toronto: University of Toronto Press, 1998.

Ignatieff, Michael. *Blood and Belonging: Journeys into the New Nationalism.* Toronto: Viking, 1993.

Imai, Shin. 'Canadian Immigration Law and Policy: 1867–1935.' LLM thesis, York University, Toronto, 1983.

– 'Deportation in the Depression.' *Queen's Law Journal* 7/1 (1981): 66–94.

Inter-American Commission on Human Rights. 'Report on the Situation of Human Rights Asylum Seekers within the Canadian Refugee Determination System.' Online: www.cidh.oas.org/countryrep/Canada2000en/canada.htm#11.%20INTRODUCTION.

Jackman, B. 'Charter Rights to Privacy and Security: The Impact of International Terrorism and Globalization, Impact on Charter Rights in Immigration Law.' Ontario Bar Association, 4th Annual Charter Conference, 30 September 2005.

– 'National Security under the Immigration and Refugee Protection Act.' Unpublished paper. March 2005.

– 'One Measure of Justice in Canada: Judicial Protection for Non-Citizens.' Canadian Bar Association Conference, Banff, April 2005.

Jamieson, Stuart. *Times of Trouble: Labour Unrest and Industrial Conflict in Canada, 1900–1966.* Ottawa: Minister of Supply and Services, 1976.

Janzen, William. *Limits on Liberty: The Experience of Mennonite, Hutterite, and Doukhobor Communities in Canada.* Toronto: University of Toronto Press, 1990.

Jarvis, William H.P. *Traits and Tales in Cobalt.* Toronto: W. Briggs, 1908.

Johnson, J.K., ed. *Historical Essays on Upper Canada.* Ottawa: Carleton Library, 1975.

Johnson, Leo A. 'Land Policy, Population Growth and Social Structure in the Home District, 1793–1851.' In *Historical Essays on Upper Canada,* edited by J.K. Johnson. Ottawa: Carleton Library, 1975.

Johnson, Paul. *A History of the Jews.* London: Weidenfeld & Nicolson, 1987.

Johnson, Stanley C. *A History of Emigration from the United Kingdom to North America, 1763–1912.* London: G. Routledge, 1913.

Johnston, Hugh J.M. *British Emigration Policy, 1815–1830: 'Shovelling Out Paupers.'* Oxford: Clarendon Press, 1972.

– *The Voyage of the Komagata Maru: The Sikh Challenge to Canada's Colour Bar.* Delhi: Oxford University Press, 1970.

Kage, Joseph. *With Faith and Thanksgiving: The Story of Two Hundred Years of Jewish Immigration and Immigrant Aid Effort in Canada (1760–1960).* Montreal: Eagle, 1962.

– ed. *Studies and Documents on Immigration and Integration in Canada.* Montreal: JIAS, 1963.

Kalbach, Warren E. *The Effect of Immigration on Population.* Ottawa: Information Canada, Department of Manpower and Immigration, 1974.

– 'The National Conference on Canadian Immigration and the Green Paper in Retrospect.' *Canadian Ethnic Studies* 7/1 (1975): 71–9.

Kaprielian-Churchill, Isabel. 'Armenian Refugee Women: The Picture Brides, 1920–30.' *Journal of American Ethnic History* 12/3 (1993): 3–29.

– 'Armenian Refugees and Their Entry into Canada, 1919–30.' *Canadian Historical Review* 71 (1990): 80–108.

– 'Rejecting "Misfits": Canada and the Nansen Passport.' *International Migration Review* 28/2 (1994): 281–306.

Karr, Clarence G. *The Canada Land Company: The Early Years.* Toronto: Ontario Historical Society, 1974.

Kaye, Vladimir. *Early Ukrainian Settlements in Canada, 1895–1900.* Toronto: University of Toronto Press, 1964.

Keenleyside, Hugh. *Canadian Immigration Policy.* Vancouver: University of British Columbia Press, 1948.

Kelly, Nora, and W.H. Kelly. *The Royal Canadian Mounted Police: A Century of History.* Edmonton: Hurtig, 1973.

Kelley, N. 'International Refugee Protection Challenges and Opportunities.' *International Journal of Refugee Law* 19 (October 2007): 401.

– 'Rights in the Balance: Non-Citizens and State Sovereignty under the Charter.' In *The Unity of Public Law,* edited by David Dyzenhaus. Oxford and Portland, OR: Hart Publishing, 2004.

– ed. *Immigration in Canada: Historical Perspectives.* Toronto: Copp Clark Longman, 1994.

Kelman, Steven. *Making Public Policy: A Hopeful View of American Government.* New York: Basic Books, 1987.

Kelves, Daniel J. *In the Name of Eugenics: Genetics and the Use of Human Heredity.* Berkeley: University of California Press, 1985.

Kerr, Donald Gordon Grady, ed. *A Historical Atlas of Canada,* 2nd ed. Don Mills, ON: Nelson, 1966.

Kerrigan, Catherine, ed. *The Immigrant Experience: Proceedings of a Conference Held at the University of Guelph,* 8–11 June 1989. Guelph, ON: University of Guelph Press, 1992.

Keylor, William R. *The Twentieth Century World: An International History,* 2nd ed. New York: Oxford University Press, 1992.

– *The Twentieth-Century World and Beyond: An International History since 1900.* 5th ed. New York: Oxford University Press, 2006.

Keynes, John Maynard. *The General Theory of Employment, Interest and Money.* London: Macmillan, 1936.

Keyserlingk, Robert H. '"Agents within the Gates": The Search for Nazi Subversives in Canada during World War II.' *Canadian Historical Review* 66 (1985): 211–39.

– 'Allies or Subversives? The Canadian Government's Attitude towards German Canadians in the Second World War.' In *Minorities in Wartime: National and Racial Groupings in Europe, North America and Australia during the Two World Wars,* edited by Panikos Panalyi. Providence, RI: Berg, 1993.

– 'Breaking the Nazi Plot: Canadian Government Attitudes towards German Canadians, 1939–1945.' In *On Guard for Thee: War, Ethnicity and the Canadian State,* edited by Norman Hillmer, Bohdan Kordan, and Lubomyr Luciuk. Ottawa: Canadian Committee for the History of the Second World War, 1988.

– ed. *Breaking Ground: The 1956 Hungarian Refugee Movement to Canada.* Toronto: York Lanes, 1993.

King, William Lyon Mackenzie. *The Mackenzie King Diaries, 1893–1931.* Toronto: University of Toronto Press, 1973.

Kirkconnell, Watson. 'Western Immigration.' *The Canadian Forum* 8/94 (July 1928): 706–7.

Kirschbaum, Joseph M. *Slovaks in Canada*. Toronto: Canadian Ethnic Press Association of Ontario, 1967.

Kitigawa, Muriel. *This Is My Own: Letters to Wes and Other Writings on Japanese Canadians, 1941–1948*. Edited by Roy Miki. Vancouver: Talonbooks, 1985.

Knafla, Louis A., and Susan W.S. Binnie, eds. *Law, Society and the State: Essays in Modern Legal History*. Toronto: University of Toronto Press, 1995.

Knowles, Valerie. *Strangers at Our Gates: Canadian Immigration and Immigration Policy, 1540–1990*. Toronto: Dundurn, 2007.

Knowles, Virginia. *Forging Our Legacy: Canadian Citizenship and Immigration 1900–1997*. Ottawa: Public Works and Government Services Canada (in conjunction with Citizenship and Immigration Canada, 2000.

Koch, Eric. *Deemed Suspect: A Wartime Blunder*. Agincourt, ON: Methuen, 1980.

Kohli, M. *The Golden Bridge: Young Immigrants to Canada 1833–1939*. Toronto: Natural Heritage Books, 2003.

Kordan, Bohdan S., and Lubomyr Y. Luciuk. 'A Prescription for Nationbuilding: Ukrainian Canadians and the Canadian State, 1939–1945.' In *On Guard for Thee: War, Ethnicity and the Canadian State*, edited by Norman Hillmer, Bohdan Kordan, and Lubomyr Luciuk. Ottawa: Canadian Committee for the History of the Second World War, 1988.

Kordan, Bohdan S., and Peter Melnycky, eds. *In the Shadow of the Rockies: Diary of the Castle Mountain Internment Camp, 1915–1917*. Edmonton: Canadian Institute of Ukrainian Studies Press, 1991.

Kovrig, Bennett. 'The Magyars and Their Homeland.' In *Struggle and Hope: The Hungarian-Canadian Experience*, edited by N.F. Dreisziger, M.L. Kovacs, Paul Body, and Bennett Kovrig. Toronto: McClelland & Stewart, 1982.

Krauter Joseph F., and Morris Davis. *Minority Canadians: Ethnic Groups*. Toronto: Methuen, 1978.

Krawchuk, Peter. *Interned without Cause, Internment of Canadian Anti-Fascists during World War II*. Translated by Pat Prokop. Toronto: Kobzar, 1985.

Kymlicka, Will. *Multicultural Citizenship*. Oxford: The Clarendon Press, 1995.

Lacelle, Claudette. *Urban Domestic Servants in Nineteenth-Century Canada*. Ottawa: Canadian Communications Group, 1987.

Lai, David Chuenyan. *Chinatown: Towns within Cities in Canada*. Vancouver: University of British Columbia Press, 1988.

Lamb, W.K. *A History of the Canadian Pacific Railway*. Toronto: Macmillan, 1977.

Lambertson, Ross. 'After *Union Colliery:* Law, Race, and Class in the Coalmines of British Columbia.' In *Essays in the History of Canadian Law*, vol. 6, *British Columbia and the Yukon*, edited by Hamar Foster and John McLaren. Toronto: Osgoode Society, 1995.

Lanctôt, Gustave. *Canada and the American Revolution, 1774–1783.* Toronto: Clarke, Irwin, 1967.

Landry, Y. 'Mortalité, nuptialité et canadianisation des troups françaises de la guerre de Sept Ans.' *Histoire sociale/Social History* 12/24 (November 1979): 298–315.

– *Orphelines en France, pionnières au Canada: Les Filles du roi au XVIIe siècle.* Montreal: Leméac, 1992.

Langevin, L., and Marie-Claire Belleau. *Trafficking in Women in Canada: A Critical Analysis of the Legal Framework Governing Immigrant Live-In Caregivers and Mail-Order Brides.* Online:<http://www.swc-cfc.gc.ca/pubs/pubspr/066231252 X/200010_066231252X_8_e.html.

Langlais, Jacques, and David Rome. *Jews and French Quebecers: Two Hundred Years of Shared History.* Waterloo, ON: Wilfrid Laurier University Press, 1991.

Lavertu, Yves. *The Bernonville Affair: French War Criminals in Canada after World War II.* Trans. George Tombs. Westmount, PQ: Robert Davies, 1995.

Law Reform Commission of Canada. 'The Determination of Refugee Status in Canada: A Review of the Procedure.' Draft Final Report, March 1992.

– *The Immigration Appeal Board.* Ottawa: Ministry of Supplies and Services, 1976.

League for Social Reconstruction, Research Committee. *Social Planning for Canada.* Toronto: Nelson, 1935.

Lederman, Peter R. 'Sedition in Winnipeg: An Examination of the Trials for Seditious Conspiracy Arising from the General Strike of 1919.' *Queen's Law Journal* 3 (1976–7): 3–24.

Legrain, P. *Immigrants: Your Country Needs Them.* London: Little, Brown, 2006.

Lehmann, Heinz. *The German Canadians, 1750–1937: Immigration, Settlement and Culture.* Trans. Gerhard P. Bassler, St John's, Newfoundland: Jesperson, 1986.

Lehr, John C. 'Peopling the Prairies with Ukrainians.' In *Immigration in Canada: Historical Perspectives*, edited by Gerald Tulchinsky. Toronto: Copp Clark Longman, 1994.

Lemieux, V. Matthews. 'Immigration: A Provincial Concern.' *Manitoba Law Journal* 13/1 (1983): 111–40.

Leslie, Genevieve. 'Domestic Service in Canada, 1880–1920.' In *Women at Work, Ontario 1850–1930*, edited by Janice Acton, Penny Goldsmith, and Bonnie Shepard. Toronto: Canadian Women's Educational Press, 1980.

Lévesque, Andrée. *Virage à gauche interdit: Les Communistes, les socialistes et leurs enemies au Quebec, 1929–1939.* Montreal: Boréal Express, 1984.

Ley, D. 'Seeking Homo Economicus: The Strange Story of Canada's Business Immigration Program.' *Annals of the Association of American Geographers* 93/2 (2004): 426.

Li, P. *Destination Canada: Immigration Debates and Issues.* Toronto: Oxford University Press, 2003.

Lindal, W.J. *The Icelanders in Canada.* Ottawa: National Publishers, 1967.

Lindstrom, V. 'I Won't Be a Slave: Finnish Domestics in Canada, 1911–1930.' In *A Nation of Immigrants: Women, Workers and Communities in Canadian History, 1840s–1960s,* edited by Franca Iacovetta. Toronto: University of Toronto Press, 1998.

Lockwood, Glenn J. 'The Pattern of Settlement in Eastern Ontario 1784–1875.' *Families* 30/4 (November 1991): 235–57.

Loewen, Royden K. '"The Children, the Cows, My Dear Man and My Sister": The Transplanted Lives of Mennonite Farm Women, 1874–1900.' *Canadian Historical Review* 73/3 (September 1992): 344–73.

– *Family, Church, and Market: A Mennonite Community in the Old and the New Worlds, 1850–1930.* Toronto: University of Toronto Press, 1993.

Logan, H.A. *Trade Unions in Canada: Their Development and Functioning,* Toronto: Macmillan, 1948.

Loken, Gulbrand. *From Fjord to Frontier: A History of the Norwegians in Canada.* Toronto: McClelland & Stewart, 1980.

Loney, Martin, and Allan Moscovitch. 'The Immigration Green Paper in Black and White.' *Canadian Dimension* 10 (1975): 4–8.

Louder, Dean R., ed. *Le Québec et les francophones de la Nouvelle-Angleterre.* Quebec: Presses de l'Université Laval, 1991.

Lower, Arthur Reginald Marsden. *Colony to Nation: A History of Canada,* 5th ed. Toronto: McClelland & Stewart, 1977.

– *My First Seventy-Five Years.* Toronto: Macmillan, 1967.

Luciuk, Lubomyr. *Time for Atonement: Canada's First National Internment Operation and the Ukrainian Canadians.* Kingston, ON: Limestone, 1988.

– '"Trouble All Around": Ukrainian Canadians and Their Encounter with the Ukrainian Refugees of Europe, 1943–1951.' *Canadian Ethnic Studies* 21/3 (1989): 37–54.

– ed. *Righting an Injustice: The Debate over Redress for Canada's First National Internment Operations.* Toronto: Justinian Press, 1994.

Luciuk, Lubomyr Y., and Stella Hryniuk, eds. *Canada's Ukrainians: Negotiating an Identity.* Toronto: University of Toronto Press and Ukrainian Canadian Centennial Committee, 1991.

Luciuk, Lubomyr Y., and Iroida L. Wynnyckyj, eds. *Ukrainians in Ontario.* Toronto: Multicultural History Society of Ontario, 1986.

Lupul, Manoly R., ed. *A Heritage in Transition: Essays in the History of Ukrainians in Canada.* Toronto: McClelland & Stewart; Ottawa: Department of the Secretary of State, Multiculturalism Directorate, 1982.

Lysenko, Vera. *Men in Sheepskin Coats: A Study in Assimilation.* Toronto: Ryerson, 1947.

Macdonald, Norman. *Canada: Immigration and Colonization, 1841–1903.* Toronto: Macmillan; Aberdeen: Aberdeen University Press, 1966.

– *Canada, 1763–1841: Immigration and Settlement: The Administration of the Imperial Land Regulations.* Toronto: Longmans, 1939.

MacKay, Donald. *Flight from Famine: The Coming of the Irish to Canada.* Toronto: McClelland & Stewart, 1990.

MacKinnon, Neil. *This Unfriendly Soil: The Loyalist Experience in Nova Scotia, 1783–1791.* Montreal: McGill-Queen's University Press, 1986.

Macklin, Audrey. 'Foreign Domestic Workers: Surrogate Housewife or Mail Order Servants?' *McGill Law Journal* 37 (1992): 681–760.

– 'Public Entrance/Private Member.' In J. Fudge and B. Cossman, eds, *Privatization, Feminism, and Law.* Toronto: University of Toronto Press, 2002.

– 'Dancing Across Borders: 'Exotic Dancers,' Trafficking, and Canadian Immigration Policy.' *International Migration Review* 37 (Summer 2003): 466.

– 'On the Inside Looking In: Foreign Domestic Workers in Canada.' In *Maid in the Market: Women's Paid Domestic Labour,* edited by W. Giles and S. Arat-Koc. Halifax: Fernwood Publishing, 1994.

MacNutt, W.S. *The Atlantic Provinces: The Emergence of Colonial Society, 1712–1857.* Toronto: McClelland & Stewart, 1965.

Makowski, William Boleslaus. *History and Integration of Poles in Canada.* Lindsay, ON: The Canadian Polish Congress, 1967.

Malarek, Victor. *Haven's Gate. Canada's Immigration Fiasco.* Toronto: Macmillan, 1987.

Marrocco, Frank, and Henry Goslett. *The Annotated Immigration Act of Canada, 1993.* Scarborough, ON: Thomson, 1993.

– *Transition Guide: Bill C-86.* Scarborough, ON: Thomson, 1993.

Martynowych, Orest T. *Ukrainians in Canada: The Formative Period, 1891–1924.* Edmonton: Canadian Institute of Ukrainian Studies, 1991.

Marunchak, Michael H. *The Ukrainian Canadians: A History.* Winnipeg: Ukrainian Free Academy of Sciences, 1970.

Mashaw, Jerry. 'The Economics of Politics and the Understanding of Public Law.' *Chicago-Kent Law Review* 65 (1989): 3–191.

Masters, D.C. *The Winnipeg General Strike.* Toronto: University of Toronto Press, 1973.

McCormack, A. Ross. *Reformers, Rebels, and Revolutionaries: The Western Canadian Radical Movement, 1899–1919.* Toronto: University of Toronto Press, 1977.

McDougal, Duncan M. 'Immigration into Canada, 1851–1920.' *Canadian Journal of Economics and Political Science* 27 (1961): 162–75.

McDougall, Barbara. 'Notes on Canadian Refugee Policy.' In *Refugee Policy: Canada and the United States*, edited by H. Adelman. Toronto: York Lanes, 1991.

McEwen, Tom. *The Forge Glows Red: From Blacksmith to Revolutionary*. Toronto: Progress Books, 1974.

McLaren, Angus. *Our Own Master Race: Eugenics in Canada, 1885–1945*. Toronto: McClelland & Stewart, 1990.

McLaughlin, Kenneth M. *The Germans in Canada*. Ottawa: Canadian Historical Association, 1985.

McNaught, Kenneth. *Manifest Destiny*. Toronto: Clarke Irwin, 1963.

– *The Penguin History of Canada*. New ed. Harmondsworth: Penguin, 1988.

– 'Political Trials and the Canadian Political Tradition.' *University of 'Toronto Law Journal* 24 (1974):149–69.

– *A Prophet in Politics: A Biography of J. S. Woodsworth*. Toronto: University of Toronto Press, 1959.

Melnycky, Peter. 'The Internment of Ukrainians in Canada.' In *Loyalties in Conflict: Ukrainians in Canada during the Great War*, edited by Frances Swyripa and John Herd Thompson. Edmonton: Canadian Institute of Ukrainian Studies, University of Alberta, 1983.

Miki, Roy, and Cassandra Kobayashi, *Justice in Our Time: The Japanese-Canadian Redress Settlement*. Vancouver: Talonbooks, 1991.

Miller, Kerby A. *Emigrants and Exiles: Ireland and the Irish Exodus to North America*. New York: Oxford University Press, 1985.

Miller, James R. *Skyscrapers Hide the Heavens: A History of Indian-White Relations in Canada*, Rev. ed. Toronto: University of Toronto Press, 1991.

Mills, Allen. *Fool for Christ: The Political Thought of J.S. Woodsworth*. Toronto: University of Toronto Press, 1991.

Mitchell, Maurice. *'A Man of Big Heart' The Memoirs of Maurice Mitchell*. Ottawa: Canadian Immigration Historical Society, 1988.

Moens, Alexander, and Martin Collacott, eds. *Immigration Policy and the Terrorist Threat in Canada and the United States*. Vancouver: Fraser Institute, May 2008. http://www.fraserinstitute.org/COMMERCE.WEB/product_files/ImmigrationPolicyTerroristThreatCanadaUS.pdf (Gallagher).

Moogk, Peter. 'Reluctant Exiles: Emigrants from France in Canada before 1760.' *William and Mary Quarterly*, 46/3 (July 1989): 463–505.

Moore, Christopher. *The Loyalists: Revolution, Exile, Settlement*. Toronto: McClelland & Stewart, 1994.

Morgan, Robert J. 'The Loyalists of Cape Breton.' In *Cape Breton Historical Essays*, edited by Don MacGillivray and Brian Tennyson. Sydney, NS: College of Cape Breton Press, 1980.

Morin, Rosaire. *L'Immigration au Canada*. Montreal: Éditions de faction nationale, 1966.

Morton, Arthur S. *History of Prairie Settlement*. Toronto: Macmillan, 1938.

Morton, Desmond. *Canada and War*. Toronto: Butterworths, 1981.

– 'Sir William Otter and Internment Operations in Canada during the First World War.' *Canadian Historical Review* 55 (1974): 32–58.

– *Working People*, 3d ed. Toronto: Summerhill, 1990.

Morton, James W. *In the Sea of Sterile Mountains: The Chinese in British Columbia*. Vancouver: J.J. Douglas, 1974.

Morton, William L. *The Critical Years: The Union of British North America, 1857–1873*. Toronto: McClelland & Stewart, 1964.

– *The West and Confederation, 1857–1871*. Ottawa: Canadian Historical Association, 1958.

Mosaic. *Submissions on Bill C-18 The Citizenship of Canada Act*. Submitted to the House of Commons Select Standing Committee on Citizenship and Immigration, 14 February 2003. Online: www.mosaicbc.com/Bill%20C-18%20 submissionsI.pdf.

Moses, J., and B. Letnes. 'The Economic Costs to International Labor Restrictions: Revisiting the Empirical Discussion.' *World Development* 32/10 (2004): 1610.

Mount, Graeme S. *Canada's Enemies: Spies and Spying in the Peaceable Kingdom*. Toronto: Dundurn, 1993.

Mueller, Dennis. *Public Choice II*. Cambridge: Cambridge University Press, 1989.

Muller, Thomas. *Immigrants and the American City*. New York: New York University Press, 1993.

Munro, J.A. 'British Columbia and the Chinese Evil: Canada's First Anti-Asiatic Immigration Law.' *Journal of Canadian Studies* 6 (1971): 42–51.

Murray, W. 'Continental Europeans in Western Canada.' *Queen's Quarterly* 38 (Winter 1931): 63–75.

Nakano, Takeo Ujo. *Within the Barbed Wire Fence: A Japanese Man's Account of His Internment in Canada*. With Leatrice Nakano. Toronto: University of Toronto Press, 1980.

Naylor, RT. *The History of Canadian Business, 1867–1916*. Toronto: Lorimer, 1975.

Neatby, H. Blair. *The Politics of Chaos: Canada in the Thirties*. Toronto: Macmillan, 1972.

– *William Lyon Mackenzie King, 1932–1939: The Prism of Unity*. Toronto: University of Toronto Press, 1976.

Ng, Roxana, Gillian Walker, and Jacob Muller, eds. *Community Organization and the Canadian State*. Toronto: Garamond, 1990.

Nish, Cameron, ed. *The French Canadians, 1759–1766.* Vancouver: Copp Clark, 1966.

Norrie, Kenneth H. 'The Rate of Settlement on the Canadian Prairies, 1870–1911.' In *Perspectives on Canadian Economic History,* 2nd ed., edited by Douglas McCalla. Toronto: Copp Clark Pitman, 1994.

Norrie, Kenneth, Douglas Owram, and J.C. Herbert Emery. *A History of the Canadian Economy.* 4th ed. Toronto: Thomson Nelson, 2008.

Nova Scotia Office of the Auditor General. http://www.oag-ns.ca/Special%20 Report.pdf.

Nozick, Robert. *Anarchy, State and Utopia.* Oxford: Basil Blackwell, 1974.

Nyinah, M.K. 'Exclusion under Article 1F: Some Reflections on Context, Principles and Practice.' *International Journal of Refugee Law,* Special Supplementary Issue, 12 (2000).

Oiwa, Keibo, ed. *Stone Voices: Wartime Writings of Japanese-Canadian Issei.* Montreal: Véhicule, 1991.

Omatsu, Maryka. *Bittersweet Passage: Redress and the Japanese-Canadian Experience.* Toronto: Between the Lines, 1992.

Ommer, Rosemary. 'The 1830s: Adapting Their Institutions to Their Desires.' In *The Atlantic Region to Confederation,* edited by P. Buckner and J. Reid. Toronto: University of Toronto Press, 1994.

Orchard, David, *The Fight for Canada: Four Centuries of Resistance to American Expansionism.* Don Mills, ON: Stoddart, 1993.

Owram, Douglas. 'Economic Thought in the 1930s: The Prelude to Keynesianism.' *Canadian Historical Review* 66/3 (September 1985): 344–77.

– *Promise of Eden: The Canadian Expansionist Movement and the Idea of the West, 1856–1900.* Toronto: University of Toronto Press, 1980.

Palmer, Bryan. *Working-Class Experience: Rethinking the History of Canadian Labour, 1800–1991,* 2nd ed. Toronto: McClelland & Stewart, 1992.

Palmer, Howard. *Ethnicity and Politics in Canada since Confederation.* Ottawa: Canadian Historical Association, 1991.

– *Immigration and the Rise of Multiculturalism.* Toronto: Copp Clark, 1975.

– 'Ethnic Relations in Wartime: Nationalism and European Minorities in Alberta during the Second World War.' In *A Nation of Immigrants: Women, Workers and Communities in Canadian History, 1840–1960s,* edited by Franca Iacovetta. Toronto: University of Toronto Press, 1998.

Panitch, Leo. 'The Role and Nature of the Canadian State.' In *The Canadian State: Political Economy and Political Power,* edited by Leo Panitch. Toronto: University of Toronto Press, 1977.

– ed. *The Canadian State: Political Economy and Political Power.* Toronto: University of Toronto Press, 1977.

Pastore, R. 'The 16th Century: Aboriginal People and European Contact.' In *The Atlantic Region to Confederation*, edited by P. Buckner and J. Reid. Toronto: University of Toronto Press, 1994.

Parai, Louis. 'Canada's Immigration Policy, 1962–74.' *International Migration Review* 9/4 (1975): 449–77.

– *The Economic Impact of Immigration*. Ottawa: Information Canada, Department of Manpower and Immigration, 1974.

– *Immigration and Emigration of Professional and Skilled Manpower during the Post-War Period*. Ottawa: Queen's Printer, 1965.

Paris, Erna. *Jews: An Account of Their Experience in Canada*. Toronto: Macmillan, 1980.

Parker, R. *Uprooted: The Shipment of Poor Children to Canada, 1867–1917*. Vancouver: University of British Columbia Press, 2008.

Parkin, George R. *The Great Dominion: Studies of Canada*. London: Macmillan, 1895.

Parr, Joy. *The Gender of Breadwinners: Women, Men, and Change in Industrial Towns, 1880–1950*. Toronto: University of Toronto Press, 1990.

– *Labouring Children: British Immigrant Apprentices to Canada, 1869–1924*. Montreal: McGill-Queen's University Press, 1980.

– 'The Skilled Emigrant and Her Kin: Gender, Culture, and Labour Recruitment.' *Canadian Historical Review* 68 (December 1987): 529–51.

Patrias, Carmela. *Patriots and Proletarians: Politicizing Hungarian Immigrants in Interwar Canada*. Montreal: McGill-Queen's University Press, 1994.

Patterson, P. '1744–1763: Colonial Wars and Aboriginal People.' In *The Atlantic Region to Confederation*, edited by P. Buckner and J. Reid. Toronto: University of Toronto Press, 1994.

Pearson, Lester B. *Mike: The Memoirs of the Right Honourable Lester B. Pearson*, vol. 1, *1897–1948*. Toronto: University of Toronto Press, 1972.

Perin, Roberto, ed. *Arrangiarsi: The Italian Immigration Experience in Canada*. Montreal: Guernica, 1989.

Peters, Victor. *All Things Common: The Hutterian Way of Life*. Minneapolis: University of Minnesota Press, 1965.

Peterson, William. *Planned Migration: The Social Determinants of the Dutch Canadian Movement*. Berkeley: University of California Press, 1955.

Petryshyn, Jaroslav, with Luba Dzubak. *Peasants in the Promised Land: Canada and the Ukrainians, 1891–1914*. Toronto: Lorimer, 1985.

– 'R.B. Bennett and the Communists: 1930–1935.' *Journal of Canadian Studies* 9 (1974): 43–55.

Pickersgill, J.W. *The Mackenzie King Record*, vol. 1, *1939–1944*. Toronto: University of Toronto Press, 1960.

– *My Years with Louis St Laurent: A Political Memoir.* Toronto: University of Toronto Press, 1975.

Pither, Kerry. *Dark Days: The Story of Four Canadians Tortured in the Name of Fighting Terror.* Toronto: Viking Canada, 2008.

Piva, Michael. *The Conditions of the Working Class in Toronto, 1900–1921.* Ottawa: University of Ottawa Press, 1979.

Plank, G. *An Unsettled Conquest: The British Campaign against the Peoples of Acadia.* Philadelphia: University of Pennsylvania Press, 2001.

Plaut, W.G. *Refugee Determination in Canada.* Ottawa: Minister of Supply and Services, 1985.

Polyzoi, Eleoussa. 'Psychologists Perceptions of the Canadian Immigrant before World War II.' *Canadian Ethnic Studies* 18 (1986): 52–65.

Pogge, Thomas. *Realizing Rawls.* Ithaca, NY: Cornell University Press, 1989.

Pope, Maurice. *Soldiers and Politicians: The Memoirs of Lt.-Gen. Maurice A. Pope.* Toronto: University of Toronto Press 1962), 177.

Post, Kenneth. 'Excessive Demands on Health and Social Services: s.19 (1) (a) (ii) of the Immigration Act.' *Journal of Law and Social Policy* 8 (1992): 142–77.

Potrebenko, Helen. *No Streets of Gold: A Social History of Ukrainians in Alberta.* Vancouver: New Star, 1977.

Prentice, Alison, Paula Bourne, Gail Cuthbert Brandt, Beth Light, Wendy Mitchinson, and Naomi Black, eds. *Canadian Women: A History*, 2nd ed. Toronto: Harcourt Brace, 1996.

Prentice, Alison, and Susan Trofimenkoff, eds. *The Neglected Majority: Essays in Canadian Women's History*, vol. 2. Toronto: McClelland and Stewart, 1985.

Price, Richard, ed. *The Spirit of the Alberta Indian Treaties.* Montreal: Institute for Research on Public Policy, 1980.

Price Waterhouse, *Economic Losses of Japanese Canadians after 1941.* Winnipeg: National Association of Japanese Canadians, 1985.

Prowse, D.W. *A History of Newfoundland from the English, Colonial and Foreign Records.* London: Macmillan, 1895; reprinted Belleville, ON: Mika Studio, 1972.

Pryke, Kenneth G. *Nova Scotia and Confederation, 1864–1867*, Toronto: University of Toronto Press, 1979.

Prymak, Thomas M. *Maple Leaf and Trident: The Ukrainian Canadians during the Second World War.* Toronto: Multicultural History Society of Ontario, 1988.

– 'Recent Scholarship on Polyethnic Emigration from the Republic of Poland to Canada between the Wars.' *Canadian Ethnic Studies* 23/1 (1991): 58–70.

Putnam, Robert. 'E Pluribus Unum: Diversity and Community in the Twenty-first Century.' The 2006 Johan Skytte Prize Lecture. *Scandinavian Political Studies* 30/2 (2007).

Quintal, Claire, ed. *L'Émigrant québécois vers les États-Unis, 1850–1920*. Quebec: Vie Française, 1982.

Radecki, Henry. *Ethnic Organizational Dynamics: The Polish Group in Canada*. Waterloo, ON: Wilfrid Laurier University Press, 1979.

Radecki, Henry, and Benedykt Heydenkorn. *A Member of a Distinguished Family: The Polish Group in Canada*. Toronto: McClelland & Stewart, 1976.

Radforth, Ian. *Bushworkers and Bosses: Logging in Northern Ontario, 1900–1980*. Toronto: University of Toronto Press, 1987.

Ramirez, Bruno. 'Emigration et Franco-Américanie: Bilan des recherches historiques.' In *Le Québec et les francophones de la Nouvelle-Angleterre*, edited by Dean R Louder. Quebec: Presses de l'Université Laval, 1991.

– 'Ethnicity on Trial: The Italians of Montreal and the Second World War.' In *On Guard for Thee: War, Ethnicity and the Canadian State*, edited by Norman Hillmer, Bohdan Kordan, and Lubomyr Luciuk. Ottawa: Canadian Committee for the History of the Second World War, 1988.

– *The Italians in Canada*. Ottawa: Canadian Historical Association, 1989.

– *On the Move: French-Canadian and Italian Migrants in the North Atlantic Economy, 1860–1914*. Toronto: McClelland & Stewart, 1990.

Ramirez, Judith. *The Immigration and Refugee Board of Canada*. Toronto: Centre for Refugee Studies, York University, n.d.

Rasporich, Anthony W. 'Early Mormon Settlement in Western Canada: A Comparative Communitarian Perspective.' In *The Mormon Presence in Canada*, edited by Brigham Y Card, Herbert C. Northcott, John E. Foster, Howard Palmer, and George K Jarvis. Edmonton: University of Alberta Press, 1990.

– *For a Better Life: A History of the Croatians in Canada*. Toronto: McClelland & Stewart; Ottawa: Department of the Secretary of State, Multiculturalism Directorate, 1982.

Ratushny, Edward. *A New Refugee Status Determination Process for Canada*. Ottawa: Minister of Supply and Services, 1984.

Rawls, John. *A Theory of Justice*. Cambridge, MA: Harvard University Press, 1971.

– *The Law of Peoples*. Cambridge, MA: Harvard University Press, 1999.

Rawlyk, George. '1720–1744: Cod, Louisburg, and the Acadians.' In *The Atlantic Region to Confederation*, edited by P. Buckner and J. Reid. Toronto: University of Toronto Press, 1994.

– ed. *Revolution Rejected: 1775–1776*. Scarborough, ON: Prentice-Hall, 1968.

Ray, Arthur J. *I Have Lived Here Since the World Began: An Illustrated History of Canada's Native People*. Toronto: Lester Publishing, 1996.

Reczynska, Anna. *For Bread and a Better Future: Emigration from Poland to Canada, 1918–1939*. Toronto: Multicultural History Society of Toronto, 1966.

– 'Ukrainians and the "Ukrainian Question" as Seen by Poles in Canada during the Second World War.' *Journal of Ukrainian Studies* 16/1–2 (Summer/Winter 1991): 195–210.

Reid, Escott. 'The Conscience of a Diplomat: A Personal Testament,' *Queen's Quarterly* 74 (1967): 574–92.

– *Radical Mandarin: The Memoirs of Escott Reid.* Toronto: University of Toronto Press, 1989.

Reitz, Jeffrey G. 'Immigrant Employment Success in Canada Part I: Individual and Contextual Causes.' *Journal of International Migration and Integration* 8 (2007): 11–36.

– 'Immigrant Employment Success in Canada Part II: Understanding the Decline.' *Journal of International Migration and Integration* 8 (2007): 37–62.

– 'Immigrant Skill Utilization in the Canadian Labour Market: Implications of Human Capital Research.' *Journal of International Migration and Integration* 2/3 (2001).

– 'Immigrant Success in the Knowledge Economy: Institutional Change and the Immigrant Experience in Canada, 1970–1995.' *Journal of Social Issues* 57/3 (2001): 579–613.

– 'Tapping Immigrants' Skills: New Directions for Canadian Immigration Policy in the Knowledge Economy.' Institute for Research on Public Policy. Institute for Research on Public Policy, *Immigration and Refugee Policy Choices* (February 2005).

– *Warmth of the Welcome.* Boulder, CO: Westview Press, 1998.

Rekai, Peter. 'US and Canadian Immigration Policies: Marching Together to Different Tunes.' C.D. Howe Institute, The Border Papers No. 171 (November 2002): 5.

Repka, William, and Kathleen M. Repka. *Dangerous Patriots: Canada's Unknown Prisoners of War.* Vancouver: New Star, 1982.

Reynolds, L.G. *The British Immigrant: His Social and Economic Adjustment in Canada.* Toronto: Oxford University Press, 1935.

Richmond, Anthony. *Aspects of the Absorption and Adaptation of Immigrants.* Ottawa: Information Canada, Department of Manpower and Immigration, 1974.

– 'Canadian Immigration: Recent Developments and Future Prospects.' *International Migration* 13 (1975): 163–82.

– 'The Green Paper: Reflections on the Canadian Immigration and Population Study.' *Canadian Ethnic Studies* 7/1 (1975): 5–21.

Roach, K. 'Canada's Response to Terrorism.' In *Global Anti-Terrorism Law and Policy,* edited by Roach et al. Cambridge: Cambridge University Press, 2005.

Roach, K., and M. Code. 'The Role of the Independent Lawyer and Security Certificates.' *Criminal Law Quarterly* 52 (2006), 94.

Roberts, Barbara. 'Doctors and Deports: The Role of the Medical Profession in Deportation Policy and Practice, 1900–1936.' *Canadian Ethnic Studies* 18/3 (1986): 17–36.

– 'Ladies, Women and the State: Managing Female Immigration, 1880–1920.' In *Community Organization and the Canadian State*, edited by Roxana Ng, Gillian Walker, and Jacob Muller. Toronto: Garamond, 1990.

– 'Shovelling out the "Mutinous" Political Deportations from Canada before 1936.' *Labour/Le Travail* 18 (Fall 1986): 77–110.

– *Whence They Came: Deportation from Canada, 1900–1935*. Ottawa: University of Ottawa Press, 1988.

– '"A Work of Empire": Canadian Reformers and British Female Immigration.' In *A Not Unreasonable Claim: Women and Reform in Canada, 1880s-1920s*, edited by Linda Kealey. Toronto: The Women's Press, 1979.

Robin, Martin. *Radical Politics and Canadian Labour 1890–1930*. Kingston: Industrial Relations Centre, Queen's University, 1968.

– *Shades of Right: Nativist and Fascist Politics in Canada, 1920–1940*. Toronto; University of Toronto Press, 1992.

Robinson, Daniel. 'Planning for the "Most Serious Contingency": Alien Internment, Arbitrary Detention, and the Canadian State, 1938–39.' *Journal of Canadian Studies* 28/2 (Summer 1993): 5–20.

Robinson, W.G. *The Refugee Status Determination Process: A Report of the Task Force on Immigration Practices and Procedures*. Final report to the Minister of Employment and Immigration. Ottawa: Minister of Supply and Services, 1981.

Roby, Y. *Les Franco-Americains de la Nouvelle-Angleterre (1776–1930)*. Sillery, PQ: Septentrion, 1990.

Rogers, William, ed. *Immigration and the Politics of Citizenship in Europe and North America*. New York: University Press of America, 1989.

Rome, David. 'Clouds in the Thirties: On Anti-Semitism in Canada, 1929–39.' *Canadian Jewish Archives*. Montreal: Canadian Jewish Congress, 1977.

Roy, Patricia E. 'A Choice between Evils: The Chinese and the Construction of the Canadian Pacific Railway in British Columbia.' In *The CPR West: The Iron Road and the Making of a Nation*, edited by Hugh A. Dempsey. Vancouver: Douglas & McIntyre, 1984.

– 'Citizens without Votes: East Asians in British Columbia.' In *Ethnicity, Power and Politics in Canada*, edited by Jorden Dahlie and Tissa Fernando. Toronto: Methuen, 1981.

– *The Oriental Question: Consolidating A White Man's Province, 1914–1941*. Vancouver: University of British Columbia Press, 2003.

– 'The Preservation of the Peace in Vancouver: The Aftermath of the Anti-Chinese Riot of 1887.' *B.C. Studies* 31 (Autumn 1976): 44–59.

–   *The Triumph of Citizenship: The Japanese and Chinese in Canada 1941–1967.*
    Vancouver: University of British Columbia Press, 2007.
–   *A White Man's Province. British Columbia Politicians and Japanese Immigrants,
    1858–1914.* Vancouver: University of British Columbia Press, 1989.
Roy, Patricia, J.L. Granatstein, Masako Iino, and Hiroko Takamura, *Mutual
    Hostages: Canadians and Japanese during the Second World War.* Toronto:
    University of Toronto Press, 1990.
Rozumnyj, Jaroslav, ed. *New Soil, Old Roots: The Ukrainian Experience in Canada.*
    Winnipeg: Ukrainian Academy of Arts and Sciences in Canada, 1983.
Ruhs, M. *Designing Viable and Ethical Labour Immigration Polices* in *Immigration and
    Refugee Law: Cases, Materials and Commentary.* Toronto: Emond Montgomery
    Publications Limited, 2007.
Russell, Sharon Stanton, and Michael Teitelbaum. *International Migration and
    International Trade.* Washington, DC: World Bank, 1992.
Ryder, Bruce. 'Racism and the Constitution: British Columbia Anti-Asian
    Legislation, 1872–1923.' Unpublished paper, 1990.
–   'Racism and the Constitution: The Constitutional Fate of British Columbia
    Anti-Asian Immigration Legislation, 1884–1909.' *Osgoode Hall Law Journal* 29
    (1991): 619–76.
Safarian, A.E. *The Canadian Economy in the Great Depression.* Ottawa: Carleton
    University Press, 1970.
St. John Jones, L.W. 'Canadian Immigration: Policy and Trends in the 1960's.'
    International Migration 11/4 (1973): 141–70.
Sampat-Mehta, Ramdeo. *International Barriers.* Ottawa: Harpell's, 1973.
Sandwell, B.K. 'Our Immigration Problem: Some Facts and Fallacies.' *Queen's
    Quarterly* 53 (1946): 502–10.
Satzewich, Vic. 'The Canadian State and the Radicalization of Caribbean Migrant
    Farm Labour, 1947–1966.' *Ethnic and Racial Studies* 11/3 (July 1988): 282–304.
–   'Racism and Canadian Immigration Policy: The Government's View of
    Carribean Migration, 1962–1966.' *Canadian Ethnic Studies* 21/1 (1989): 77–97.
–   ed. *Deconstructing a Nation.* Halifax: Fernwood, 1992.
Sauer, Angelika E. 'A Matter of Domestic Policy? Canadian Immigration Policy
    and the Admission of Germans, 1945–50.' *Canadian Historical Review* 74/2
    (June 1993): 227–63.
Sawatsky, John. *Men in the Shadows: The RCMP Security Service.* Toronto:
    Doubleday, 1980.
Saywell, John T., ed. *Canadian Annual Review of Politics and Public Affairs.* Toronto:
    University of Toronto Press, 1981.
Schaafsma, J., and A. Sweetman. 'Immigrant Earnings: Age at Immigration
    Matters.' *Canadian Journal of Economics* 34/4 (November 2001): 1066–99.

Schama, Simon. *Rough Crossings: Britain, the Slaves and the American Revolution.* Toronto: Penguin Canada, 2008.

Schlesinger, Arthur. *The Disuniting of America.* New York: Norton, 1992.

Schnell, R.L. 'The Right Class of Boy: Youth Training Schemes and Assisted Emigration to Canada Under the Empire Settlement Act, 1922–39.' *History of Education* 24/1 (March 1995): 73–90.

Schuck, Peter H. 'The Transformation of Immigration Law.' *Columbia Law Review* 84 (1984): 1–90.

Schwartz, Warren F., ed. *Justice in Immigration.* Cambridge: Cambridge University Press, 1995.

Scott, William, 'Immigration and Population.' In *Canada and Its Provinces*, edited by Adam Shortt and Arthur Doughty. Toronto: Publishers' Association of Canada, 1913.

Sears, Alan. 'Immigration Controls as Social Policy: The Case of Canadian Medical Inspection, 1900–1920.' *Studies in Political Economy* 33 (Autumn 1990): 91–112.

Sedgwick, Joseph. *Report on Immigration.* Ottawa: Department of Citizenship and Immigration, 1965–6.

Seward, Shirley B., and Kathryn McDade. *Immigrant Women in Canada; A Policy Perspective.* Ottawa: Canadian Advisory Council on the Status of Women, 1988.

Shelton, W. George, ed. *British Columbia and Confederation.* Victoria: University of Victoria Press, 1967.

Sheppard, C. 'Women as Wives: Immigration Law and Domestic Violence.' *Queen's Law Journal* 26 (2000): 1.

Siggins, Maggie. *Riel. A Life of Revolution.* Toronto: HarperCollins, 1994.

Simmons, Alan B. 'Latin American Migration to Canada: New Linkages in the Hemispheric Migration and Refugee Flow Systems.' *International Journal* 48/2 (Spring 1993): 282–309.

Simon, Julian L. *The Economic Consequences of Immigration.* Cambridge, MA: Basil Blackwell, 1989.

Simpson, Donald G. *Under the North Star: Black Communities in Upper Canada.* Trenton, NJ: Africa World Press Inc., 2005.

Singh, Narindar. *Canadian Sikhs: History, Religion, and Culture of Sikhs in North America.* Nepean, ON: Canadian Sikhs' Studies Institute, 1994.

Skilling, H. Gordon. *Canadian Representation Abroad: From Agency to Embassy.* Toronto: Ryerson, 1945.

Smelser, Ronald M. *The Sudeten Problem, 1933–1938.* Middletown, CT: Wesleyan University Press, 1975.

Smith, C. 'Closing the Door on Immigrants.' *Capital News Online* 1/10 (18 January 2002): www.carleton.ca/jmc/cnews/18012002/connections/c1.shtml.

Smith, C. Henry. *The Coming of the Russian Mennonites: An Episode in the Settling of the Last Frontier.* Berne, IN: Mennonite Book Concern, 1927.

Smith, William George. *A Study in Canadian Immigration.* Toronto: Ryerson, 1920.

Socknat, Thomas P. *Witness against War: Pacifism in Canada, 1900–1945.* Toronto: University of Toronto Press, 1987.

Spada, A.V. *The Italians in Canada.* Montreal: Riviera, 1969.

Sprague, D.N. *Canada and the Metis, 1869–1885.* Waterloo, ON: Wilfrid Laurier University Press, 1988.

Spray, W.A. *The Blacks in New Brunswick.* Fredericton: Brunswick Press, 1972.

– 'The Settlement of Black Refugees in New Brunswick, 1815–1836.' *Acadiensis* 6/2 (Spring 1977): 64–79.

Stacey, C.P. *Canada and the Age of Conflict,* vol. 2, *1921–1940, The Mackenzie King Era.* Toronto: University of Toronto Press, 1981.

Stanley, George F.G. *Canada Invaded, 1775–1776.* Toronto: Hakkert, 1973.

– *Louis Riel.* Toronto: Ryerson, 1963.

Statistics Canada. 'Immigration in Canada: A Portrait of the Foreign-born Population.' *2006 Census:* Findings at www12.statcan.ca/english/census06/ analysis/immcit/index.cfm.

Stevens, Paul, and John T. Saywell, eds. *Lord Minto's Canadian Papers, 1898–1904.* Toronto: Champlain Society, 1981.

Stewart, H. 'Is Indefinite Detention of Terrorist Suspects Really Constitutional?' *University of New Brunswick Law Journal* 54 (Fall 2005).

Stoffman, Daniel. *Toward a More Realistic Immigration Policy for Canada.* Toronto: C.D. Howe Institute, 1993.

– 'Truths and Myths about Immigration.' In *Immigration Policy and the Terrorist threat in Canada,* edited by A. Moens and M. Collacott. Vancouver: Fraser Institute, 2008.

– *Who Gets In: What's Wrong with Canada's Immigration Program and How to Fix It.* Toronto: McFarlane, Walter and Ross, 2002.

Struthers, James. *No Fault of Their Own: Unemployment and the Canadian Welfare State, 1914–1941.* Toronto: University of Toronto Press, 1983.

Sugimoto, H.H. 'The Vancouver Riots of 1907: A Canadian Episode.' In *East Across the Pacific. Historical and Sociological Studies of Japanese Immigration and Assimilation,* edited by F. Hilary Conroy and T. Scott Miyakawa. Santa Barbara, CA: Clio, 1972.

Sunahara, Ann Gomer. 'Deportation: The Final Solution to Canada's "Japanese Problem".' In *Ethnicity, Power and Politics in Canada,* edited by Jorden Dahlie and Tissa Fernando. Toronto: Methuen 1981.

– *The Politics of Racism: The Uprooting of Japanese Canadians during the Second World War.* Toronto: Lorimer, 1981.

Swainger, Jonathan. 'Wagging Tongues and Empty Heads: Seditious Utterances and the Patriotism of Wartime in Central Alberta, 1914–1918.' In *Law, Society and the State: Essays in Modern Legal History*, edited by Louis A. Knafla and Susan W.S. Binnie. Toronto: University of Toronto Press, 1995.

Swyripa, Frances. 'The Ukrainian Image: Loyal Citizen or Disloyal Alien.' In *Loyalties in Conflict: Ukrainians in Canada during the Great War*, edited by Frances Swyripa and John Herd Thompson. Edmonton: Canadian Institute of Ukrainian Studies, University of Alberta, 1983.

– *Wedded to the Cause: Ukrainian-Canadian Women and Ethnic Identity, 1891–1991.* Toronto: University of Toronto Press, 1993.

Swyripa, Frances, and John Herd Thompson, eds. *Loyalties in Conflict: Ukrainians in Canada during the Great War.* Edmonton: Canadian Institute of Ukrainian Studies, University of Alberta, 1983.

Sykes, Alan O. 'The Welfare Economics of Immigration Law: A Theoretical Survey with an Analysis of U.S. Policy.' In *Justice in Immigration*, edited by Warren Schwartz. Cambridge: Cambridge University Press, 1995.

Tamaki, George Takakazu. 'The Law Relating to Nationality in Canada.' LLM thesis, University of Toronto, 1944.

Tassé, Roger. 'Removals: Processes and People in Transition.' Report commissioned by Citizenship and Immigration Canada, February 1996.

Taylor, K.W. 'Racism in Canadian Immigration Policy.' *Canadian Ethnic Studies* 23/1 (1991): 1–20.

Taylor, John. '"Relief from Relief": The Cities' Answer to Depression Dependency.' *Journal of Canadian Studies* 14/1 (Spring 1979): 16–23.

Tennyson, Brian Douglas, ed. *Canada and the Commonwealth Caribbean.* Lanham, MD: University Press of America, 1988.

Tepper, Elliot L., ed. *Southeast Asian Exodus: From Tradition to Resettlement.* Ottawa: The Canadian Asian Studies Association, Carleton University, 1980.

Thomas, Gordon, and Max Morgan Witts. *Voyage of the Damned.* New York: Stein & Day, 1974.

Thompson, John Herd. 'The Enemy Alien and the Canadian General Election of 1917.' In *Loyalties in Conflict: Ukrainians in Canada during the Great War*, edited by Frances Swyripa and John Herd Thompson. Edmonton: Canadian Institute of Ukrainian Studies, University of Alberta, 1983.

– *The Harvests of War: The Prairie West, 1914–1918.* Toronto: McClelland & Stewart, 1978.

Thompson, John Herd, and Allen Seager. *Canada, 1922–1939: Decades of Discord.* Toronto: McClelland & Stewart, 1985.

– 'Workers, Growers and Monopolists: The "Labour Problem" in the Alberta Sugar Beet Industry during the 1930s.' In *The Depression in Canada: Responses to Economic Crisis*, edited by Michiel Horn. Toronto: Copp Clark Pitman, 1985.

Thor, J. *Icelanders to North America: The First Settlers.* Winnipeg: University of
    Manitoba Press, 2002.
Thornton, Patricia A. 'The Problem of Out-Migration from Atlantic Canada,
    1867–1921: A New Look.' In *Acadiensis Reader,* vol. 2, edited by P.A. Buckner
    and David Frank. Fredericton: Acadiensis, 1988.
Tienharra, Nancy. *Canadian Views on Immigration and Population: An Analysis of
    Post War Gallup Polls.* Ottawa: Information Canada, Department of Manpower
    and Immigration, 1974.
Timlin, Mabel F. 'Canada's Immigration Policy, 1896–1910.' *Canadian Journal of
    Economics and Political Science* 26 (1960): 517–32.
– *Does Canada Need More People?* Toronto: Oxford University Press, 1953.
Tobin, Jacqueline. *From Midnight to Dawn: The Last Tracks of the Underground
    Railway.* New York: Doubleday, 2007.
Trachtenberg, Henry. 'Opportunism, Humanitarianism, and Revulsion: "The
    Old Clo' Move" Comes to Manitoba, 1882–83.' *Canadian Ethnic Studies* 22/2
    (1990):1–18.
Trachtman, Joel P. *The International Law of Economic Migration: Towards the Fourth
    Freedom.* Kalamazoo, MI: W.E. Upjohn Institute for Employment Research,
    2009,
Trail, C.P. *The Canadian Settler's Guide.* Toronto: 1855.
– *The Female Emigrants' Guide.* Toronto: 1850.
Trebilcock, Michael J. 'The Case for a Liberal Immigration Policy.' In *Justice in
    Immigration,* edited by Warren Schwartz. Cambridge: Cambridge University
    Press, 1995.
– 'The Law and Economics of Immigration Policy.' *American Law and Economics
    Review* 5 (2003): 271.
Trebilcock, Michael J., Douglas Hartle, Robert Prichard, and Donald Dewees. *The
    Choice of Governing Instrument.* Ottawa: Economic Council of Canada, 1982.
Trebilcock, Michael J., and M. Sudak. 'The Political Economy of Emigration and
    Immigration.' *New York University Law Review* 81/1 (April 2006).
Trigger, Bruce G. *The Children of Aataentsic.* Montreal: McGill-Queen's University
    Press, 1976.
Trigger, Bruce G., and Wilcomb Washburn, eds. *The Cambridge History of the Native
    People of the Americas.* Cambridge: Cambridge University Press, 1996.
Troper, Harold. 'Canada's Immigration Policy since 1945.' *International Journal*
    48/2 (Spring 1993): 255–81.
– 'The Creek-Negroes of Oklahoma and Canadian Immigration, 1909–11.'
    Canadian Historical Review 53 (1972): 272–88.
– 'New Horizons in a New Land: Jewish Immigration to Canada.' In *From
    Immigration to Integration: The Canadian Jewish Experience A Millennium Edition,*

edited by Ruth Klein and Frank Dimant. Ottawa: Institute for International Affairs, B'nai Brith Canada, 2001.

– *Only Farmers Need Apply.* Toronto: Griffin House, 1972.

Trow, James. *Manitoba and the Northwest Territories.* Ottawa: Department of Agriculture, 1878.

– *A Trip to Manitoba.* Quebec: Marcotte, 1875.

Tulchinsky, Gerald. *Taking Root: The Origins of the Canadian Jewish Community.* Toronto: Lester Publishing, 1992.

Turek, Victor, *The Poles in Manitoba.* Toronto: Polish Research Institute in Canada, 1967.

Ubelaker, Douglas H. 'North American Indian Population Size, A.D. 1500 to 1985.' *American Journal of Physical Anthropology* 77/3 (November 1988): 289–94.

UNHCR. 'Guidelines on International Protection: Application of the Exclusion Clauses: Article 1F of the 1951 Convention relating to the Status of Refugees.' September 2003. Online: www.unhcr.org.

– *The State of the World's Refugees 2000: Fifty Years of Humanitarian Action.* Oxford: Oxford University Press, 2000.

Upton, L.F.S., ed. *The United Empire Loyalists.* Toronto: Copp Clark Publishing, 1967.

U.S. Committee for Refugees and Immigrants. *Country Report 2003.* Online: www.refugees.org.

Van Selm, Joanne, and Besty Cooper. 'The New Boat People: Ensuring Safety and Determining Status.' Migration Policy Institute. January 2006. Online: http://www.migrationpolicy.org/pubs/Boat_People_Report.pdf.

Vandercamp, John. 'Introduction.' *Canadian Public Policy* 1 (1975): 449–51.

Vedder, Richard, Lowell Gallaway, and Stephen Moore. *Immigration and Unemployment.* Arlington, VA: Alexis de Tocqueville Institution, March 1994.

Veena, Verma. 'The Mexican and Caribbean Seasonal Agricultural Workers Program, 'Regulatory and Policy Framework, Farm Industry Level Employment Practices and the Future of the Program under Unionization.' Report to the North-South Institute. Ottawa: North-South Institute, 2003.

Verma, A. *The Making of Little Punjab in Canada. Patterns of Immigration.* New Delhi; Thousand Oaks, CA: Sage Publications, 2002.

Vigod, Bernard L. *The Jews in Canada.* Ottawa: Canadian Historical Association, 1984.

Wagner, Jonathan F. *Brothers beyond the Sea: National Socialism in Canada.* Waterloo, ON: Wilfrid Laurier University Press, 1981.

Waldman, L. *Canadian Immigration Law and Practice 2008.* Markham: LexisNexis, 2007.

Waite, Peter B. *Canada, 1874–1896: Arduous Destiny*. Toronto: McClelland & Stewart, 1971.
– *The Life and Times of Confederation, 1864–1867: Politics, Newspapers and the Union of British North America*. Toronto: University of Toronto Press, 1962.
Walden, Keith. *Visions of Order: The Canadian Mounties in Symbol and Myth*. Toronto: Butterworths, 1982.
Walker, James W. St. G. *The Black Loyalists: The Search for a Promised Land in Nova Scotia and Sierra Leone, 1783–1870*. New York: Africana, 1976; reprinted Toronto: University of Toronto Press, 1992.
– 'The Establishment of a Free Black Community in Nova Scotia, 1783–1840.' In *The African Diaspora: Interpretive Essays*, edited by Martin L. Kilson and Robert I. Rotberg. Cambridge: Harvard University Press, 1976.
– *A History of Blacks in Canada: A Study Guide for Teachers and Students*. Ottawa: Department of the Secretary of State, Multiculturalism Directorate, 1980.
– *Race, Rights and the Law in the Supreme Court of Canada: Historical Case Studies*. Toronto and Waterloo: Osgoode Society and Wilfrid Laurier University Press, 1997.
– *The West Indians in Canada*. Ottawa: Canadian Historical Association, 1984.
Walzer, Michael. *Spheres of Justice: A Defense of Pluralism and Equality*. New York: Basic Books, 1983.
Warburton, Rennie, and David Coburn, eds. *Workers, Capital, and the State in British Columbia: Selected Papers*. Vancouver: University of British Columbia Press, 1988.
Ward, W. Peter. 'British Columbia and the Japanese Evacuation.' In *Readings in Canadian History*, 2d ed., edited by R. Douglas Francis and D.B. Smith. Toronto: Holt Reinhart & Winston, 1986.
– *The Japanese in Canada*. Ethnic Groups Booklet no. 3. Ottawa: Canadian Historical Association, 1982.
– *White Canada Forever: Popular Attitudes and Public Policy toward Orientals in British Columbia*, 2d ed. Montreal: McGill-Queen's University Press, 1990.
Warner, D.F. *The Idea of Continental Union: Agitation for the Annexation of Canada to the United States, 1849–1893*. Lexington: University of Kentucky Press, 1960.
Waseem, Gertrud. 'German Settlement in Nova Scotia.' In *German Canadian Studies: Critical Approaches*, edited by Peter Liddell. Vancouver: Canadian Association of University Teachers of German, 1983.
Watt, Douglas, Tim Krywulak, and Kurtis Kitagawa, 'Renewing Immigration: Towards a Convergence and Consolidation of Canada's Immigration Policies and Systems.' Toronto: Conference Board of Canada, October 2008.
Weaver, R. Kent, and Bert A. Rockman, eds. *Do Institutions Matter?* Washington, DC: The Brookings Institution, 1993.

Welch, David. *The Third Reich: Politics and Propaganda.* London: Routledge, 1993.

Whalley, J., ed. *Domestic Policies and the International Economic Environment.* Toronto: University of Toronto Press, 1985.

Whitaker, Reg. *Double Standard: The Secret History of Canadian Immigration.* Toronto: Lester & Orpen Dennys, 1987.

– 'Official Repression of Communism During World War II.' *Labour/Le Travail* 7 (Spring 1986): 135–66.

Whitfield, Harvey A. *From American Slaves to Nova Scotian Subjects: The Case of Black Refugees 1813–1840.* Toronto: Prentice Hall, 2005.

Widdis, R.W. *With Scarcely a Ripple: Anglo-Canadian Migration into the United States and Western Canada.* Montreal: McGill-Queen's University Press, 1998.

Widgren, Jonas. 'The Asylum Crisis in Europe and North America.' Paper commissioned for the Program on International and U.S. Refugee Policy, The Fletcher School of Law and Diplomacy, Tufts University, November 1990.

Wightman, F.A. *Our Canadian Heritage: Its Resources and Possibilities.* Toronto: William Briggs, 1905.

Williams, Jack. *The Story of Unions in Canada.* Don Mills, ON: Dent, 1975.

Williams, Roger Neville. *The New Exiles.* New York: Liveright, 1971.

Wilson, G.A. *The Clergy Reserves in Upper Canada: A Canadian Mortmain.* Toronto: University of Toronto Press, 1968.

Winks, Robin W. *The Blacks in Canada: A History* 2nd ed. Montreal: McGill-Queen's University Press; New Haven: Yale University Press, 1997.

Wong, Victor, 'Globalization and Migration: Canada's Response to the Chinese Boat Refugees.' Economic Commission for Latin America and the Caribbean (ECLAC) and International Organization for Migration. November 2002. Online: http://www.eclac.org/celade/noticias/paginas/2/11302/VWong.pdf

Wood, John. 'East Indians and Canada's New Immigration Policy.' *Canadian Public Policy* 4 (1978): 547–67.

Woodsworth, J.S. *Strangers within Our Gates; or, Coming Canadians.* Toronto: F.C. Stephenson, 1909. Reprinted, Toronto: University of Toronto Press, 1972.

Worswick, C. 'Immigrants' Declining Earnings: Reasons and Remedies.' C.D. Howe Institute Backgrounder 81. Toronto: C.D. Howe Institute, 2004.

Wright, Esther Clark. *The Loyalists of New Brunswick.* Moncton, NB: Moncton Publishing, 1955.

Wydrzynski, Christopher. *Canadian Immigration Law and Procedure.* Aurora, ON: Canada Law Book, 1983.

– 'Civil Liberties of Aliens in the Canadian Immigration Process.' LLM thesis, York University, Toronto, 1976.

Wynn, Graeme. '1800–1810; Turning the Century.' In *The Atlantic Region to Confederation*, edited by P. Buckner and J. Reid. Toronto: University of Toronto Press, 1994.

Young, Charles H. *The Ukrainian Canadians: A Study in Assimilation*. Toronto: Nelson, 1931.

Young, Walter D. *Anatomy of a Party: The National C.C.F., 1932–1961*. Toronto: University of Toronto Press, 1969.

Young, William R. 'Chauvinism and Canadianism: Canadian Ethnic Groups and the Failure of the Wartime Information.' In *On Guard for Thee: War, Ethnicity and the Canadian State* edited by Norman Hillmer, Bohdan Kordan, and Lubomyr Luciuk. Ottawa: Canadian Committee for the History of the Second World War, 1988.

Zimmerman, Klaus. 'Tackling the European Migration Problem.' *Journal of Economic Perspectives* 9 (1995): 45–62.

Zowall, H., et al. 'HIV Antibody Screening among Immigrants: A Cost Benefit Analysis.' *Canadian Medical Association Journal* 143/2 (1990): 101–7.

Zucchi, John E. 'Italian Hometown Settlements and the Development of an Italian Community in Toronto, 1875–1935.' In *Gathering Places: Peoples and Neighbourhoods of Toronto, 1834–1945*, edited by Robert F. Harney. Toronto. Multicultural History Society of Ontario, 1985.

– *Italians in Toronto: Development of a National Identity*. Montreal: McGill-Queen's University Press, 1988.

Index

Ceylon, 317, 339; immigration from, 320, 334

Champlain, Samuel de, 27–8, 30, 31, 32

Charkaoui, Adil, 450–1

Chiarelli v Canada (Ministry of Employment and Immigration) (re constitutionality of the Immigration Act), 411, 412–13

Chicago, 102

child emigration schemes, 91–2, 505n57

child immigration, 91–4, 126, 196–8, 227–8; regulation of, 93–4

child refugees, 268–70, 437

Chile, 354, 367, 583n71

Chilean immigration, 354, 367–9

Chinese: anti-Chinese sentiment, 95–9, 111, 146, 147–8, 156, 459, 495nn118, 122, 124, 496n130; and the CPR, 95–6, 98, 110; head taxes, 15, 98, 123, 145, 154, 155, 156, 207, 393, 459–60, 503n40, 518n208, 565n235; illegal-immigration movement (1959), 336–7; immigration, 23, 58, 110, 111, 319–20, 327, 399, 418 (*see also* Asian immigration); —, 1900–15, 155; —, 1952–5, 319; —, exclusion of Chinese nationals, 294; migrants' arrival off the coast of British Columbia (1999), 20, 421–2, 458, 599n10; —, refugees, 365, 399–400; —, restrictions on, 99, 147, 154–6, 203, 207–8, 226–7, 293, 314, 495n122, 514n160; labour(ers), 95–6, 97, 98, 110, 155–6, 458; naturalization refusals (1930–7), 230; protests against, 96, 148; Tax Act (British Columbia), 99

Chinese Adjustment Statement Program (1960), 337, 363–4

Chinese Canadian National Council (CCNC), 459

Chinese Immigration Act, 98, 108, 111, 154–5, 156, 226, 459; 1923 revisions, 207, 325, 459; repeal of, 319, 325, 326, 570n52

Chinese Immigration Act (British Columbia), 99

cholera, 47, 51, 85, 97

Church of England, 49

Citizenship Act, 319, 324, 452, 453, 609n110, 610n119

Clarke, C.K., 93, 111, 217, 213–14

Clement, Wallace, 110

Clements, H.S., 175, 180

Clergy Reserves, 49

coal production, 104

Cobalt (Ontario), 136

Colbert, Jean-Baptiste, 29

Coldwell, M.J., 288, 327

Colombian refugees, 606n81

Colonial Office, 41, 48

colonization companies, 71–2, 488n32

Committee on Cooperation in Canadian Citizenship (CCCC), 277

communism (communist): activity in Canada (Depression years), 225, 239–40, 241, 242; characterizations of Jews as, 224, 263, 552n31; deportation of communists, 169, 179, 220, 224, 238, 239, 240, 247, 319; fear of (1930s), 16; internments of sympathizers, 259, 260, 280, 284, 285–8, 289, 290, 291, 313, 558–9n132; as Jewish conspiracy, 241; and naturalization revocations, 230, 231; perceived sympathies (1940s), 17; Red Scare, 348;

propaganda, 81; restrictions on emigration, 101; Seven Years' War, 31; Treaty of Aix-la-Chapelle (1748), 34; Treaty of Breda (1667), 33; Treaty of Paris (1763), 31, 35, 37, 40; Treaty of Ryswick (1697), 33; Treaty of Saint-Germain-en-Laye (1632), 28, 33; Treaty of Utrecht (1713), 30, 33, 36; War of Austrian Succession, 34; war with England, 28; war with Spain, 27

Francis I (king of France), 27

Fraser River, 58

French: Catholics, 28; fishermen, 26, 34, 36; immigration, 23, 101, 118, 133, 327–8, 331, 333, 530n112, 570n54

French Canadian(s), 21, 53, 68, 312, 381, 525n37; anti-immigrant sentiments, 118, 262, 327; emigration to United States, 79, 104–5, 106, 483n121; nationalists, 118; post-Confederation, 13–14; pro-fascist sentiments, 225, 287

Front de Libération du Québec (FLQ), 353

Fulton, Davie, 332

fur trading, 27–8, 30, 31, 41, 54–5, 55

Galicia, 130–4, 137, 200, 509n90

Galton, Francis, 215

Gana v MMI (IAB powers), 371–2

Garland, Edward J., 247

Gendreau, P.E., 106

General Agreement on Tariffs and Trade (GATT), 317

George I (king of England), 35–6, 529n86

German (*see also* Germany): agitators in Canada, 180; applications of nationals, 265–6; communist characterizations of Jews, 263; dissatisfaction in Hungary, 130; German immigration (immigrants), 23, 34, 35, 42, 100–1, 128, 129, 328, 506n71; —, grants of landed immigrant status (post-Second World War), 339; —, hostility towards, 200, 278, 522–3n16, 531n121; —, internments, 271–2, 278–84, 287–90, 313; —, interwar years, 199–200; —, permission to serve in armed forces, 290; —, post-Second World War, 328; —, promotional activities, 52, 81; —, refugees, 318; —, support for, 133, 137; —, suspicions of, 172–3; invasion of Holland and Belgium, 276; mercenaries, 38–9, 42; move into France, 269; settlements in Ontario, 100; spies and secret agents, 172–3, 262, 278

German American Land Company, 128

German National Socialist Party, 224. *See also* Nazis

Germany (*see also* German): acquisition of Sudeten Czechoslovakia, 266; activists in, 248; anti-Jewish sentiment in, 256; attitudes towards immigrants (2006 poll), 469; concern over deportation of nationals (1932), 236; emigration controls, 100–1, 129; Kristallnacht, 258; Nuremberg Laws, 256, 300; prohibition of emigration propaganda, 81

Glen, James, 569–70n47

global migration trends, 3–4, 415, 454

Manitoba Free Press, 74, 183
Manitoba Gypsum Company, 180
Marchand, Jean, 359
Marchi, Sergio, 399–400
Maritimes: emigration from, 104
Marr, W.L., 384
Marxism. *See* communism
Massey, Vincent, 267, 551n19
measles, 40, 56, 85, 140
Meighen, Arthur, 177–8, 190,
   528n84
Mennonite immigration, 42, 73–5,
   134, 187, 188, 191, 192, 199–200;
   group settlement schemes, 73
Mennonites: anti-Jewish sentiments,
   76; exodus from Russia, 129
Metal Trades Council, 183
Methodist Missionary Society,
   509n104
Miami, 419
Middle Eastern immigration, 381,
   418, 419, 467
Military Service Act, 176
Minister of the Interior, 15, 151,
   515–16n174. *See also* Department of
   the Interior
Mongolian immigration, 96
Montreal, 27, 31, 38, 51, 53, 86, 87,
   102–3, 281, 302, 356, 364, 419, 423,
   495n124, 582n45; deportee
   accommodations in, 246; Italian
   immigration to, 142; Polish
   settlement in, 132; population
   growth (1901–10), 114; urban
   conditions (1896–1914), 117
Montreal Gazette, 250, 359, 362, 376,
   401
Montreal Jewish Labour Committee,
   275
Montreal Star, 153

Mormon immigration, 80–1; to
   Western Canada, 127–8
*Morris v Minister of Manpower and
   Immigration* (re SIOs and IAB), 377
Mosher, A.R., 321, 327, 570n48
Mountain Lumber Manufacturers'
   Association, 212
Mulock, Sir William, 240–1, 243
Mulroney, Brian, 551n23, 565n235
Murray, James, 31

Napoleonic War, 12, 24, 44, 45, 46, 59
National Council of Women of
   Canada, 126, 304, 342
National Defence Act, 424
National Emergency Transitional
   Powers Act (NETPA), 305, 307
National Employment Service (NES),
   335, 340
National Social Christian Party, 224,
   542n23, 559n134
Native peoples, 21, 23, 25–6, 27,
   30, 32, 37, 55, 58, 59–60, 66–9;
   Abenaki, 35; Algonquians, 30–1, 38;
   Assiniboine, 56; Beothuk, 37;
   Blackfoot, 56; in British Columbia,
   58; Huron, 30–1, 38; Indian Act
   (1876), 69; Iroquois, 31, 38, 39, 40,
   477n28; Malecite, 35; Management
   of Indian Lands and Properties Act
   (1860), 60; Métis, 41, 55–6, 66–8,
   95; Mi'kmaq, 33, 35–6; Mississauga
   (Ojibwa), 39–40
naturalization: restrictions, 161–3,
   165–6; —, during Depression years
   (1930–7), 229–31; revocations,
   230–1
Naturalization Act, 144, 162–3, 165,
   178, 184–5, 229, 231, 307, 308,
   543n43, 544n52, 563–4n212